ACCOUNTING FOR NON-ACCOUNTING STUDENTS

Sixth Edition

J. R. DYSON

 Prentice Hall
FINANCIAL TIMES

An imprint of **Pearson Education**

Harlow, England • London • New York • Boston • San Francisco • Toronto
Sydney • Tokyo • Singapore • Hong Kong • Seoul • Taipei • New Delhi
Cape Town • Madrid • Mexico City • Amsterdam • Munich • Paris • Milan

Pearson Education Limited

Edinburgh Gate
Harlow
Essex CM20 2JE
England

and Associated Companies around the world

Visit us on the World Wide Web at:
www.pearsoned.co.uk

First edition published in Great Britain under the Pitman Publishing imprint in 1987
Second edition 1991
Third edition 1994
Fourth edition published under the Financial Times Pitman Publishing imprint in 1997
Fifth edition 2001
Sixth edition 2004

ISBN 0 273 68385 3

British Library Cataloguing-in-Publication Data
A CIP catalogue record for this book can be obtained from the British Library.

10 9 8 7 6 5 4 3 2 1
09 08 07 06 05 04

Typeset by 30.
Printed and bound in Great Britain by Ashford Colour Press Ltd., Gosport.

Contents

Preface	xi
Guided tour of the book	xvi
Acknowledgements	xviii
Publisher's acknowledgements	xix

Part 1
INTRODUCTION TO ACCOUNTING — 1

1 The accounting world — 2

About this chapter	2
Learning objectives	3
The nature of accounting	3
Why accounting is important for non-accountants	4
Why this chapter is important for non-accountants	6
The development of accounting	7
Branches of accounting	10
The accountancy profession	15
Public and private entities	17
Questions non-accountants should ask	22
Conclusion	22
Key points	23
Check your learning	23
News story quiz	24
Tutorial questions	25

2 Accounting rules — 26

About this chapter	26
Learning objectives	27
Why this chapter is important for non-accountants	27
Historical development	28
Boundary rules	30
Measurement rules	32
Ethical rules	36
A conceptual framework	38

Questions non-accountants should ask	40
Conclusion	41
Key points	41
Check your learning	41
News story quiz	42
Tutorial questions	43
Appendix: Summary of the accounting rules	45

Part 2
FINANCIAL ACCOUNTING — 47

3 Recording data — 48

About this chapter	48
Learning objectives	49
Why this chapter is important for non-accountants	49
The accounting equation	50
Double-entry book-keeping	52
Working with accounts	54
A ledger account example	60
Balancing the accounts	61
The trial balance	63
Trial balance errors	66
Questions non-accountants should ask	68
Conclusion	68
Key points	69
Check your learning	70
News story quiz	70
Tutorial questions	71

4 Sole trader accounts — 79

About this chapter	79
Learning objectives	80
Why this chapter is important for non-accountants	80
The basic accounts	80
Cash versus profit	81

Preparation	83
An illustrative example	84
Questions non-accountants should ask	87
Conclusion	88
Key points	88
Check your learning	88
News story quiz	89
Tutorial questions	89

5 Last minute adjustments — 93

About this chapter	93
Learning objectives	94
Why this chapter is important for non-accountants	94
Stock	95
Depreciation	97
Accruals and prepayments	100
Bad and doubtful debts	102
A comprehensive example	105
Accounting profit	108
Questions non-accountants should ask	109
Conclusion	109
Key points	110
Check your learning	110
News story quiz	111
Tutorial questions	112

6 Company accounts — 119

About this chapter	119
Learning objectives	120
Why this chapter is important for non-accountants	120
Limited liability	121
Structure and operation	122
The profit and loss account	127
The balance sheet	128
A comprehensive example	130
Questions non-accountants should ask	134
Conclusion	134
Key points	135
Check your learning	135
News story quiz	136
Tutorial questions	136

7 Other entity accounts — 143

About this chapter	143
Learning objectives	144
Why this chapter is important for non-accountants	144
Manufacturing accounts	145
Service entity accounts	150
Not-for-profit entity accounts	153
Government accounts	156
Questions non-accountants should ask	157
Conclusion	158
Key points	158
Check your learning	159
News story quiz	160
Tutorial questions	160

8 Cash flow statements — 163

About this chapter	163
Learning objectives	165
Why this chapter is important for non-accountants	165
Accounting profit and cash	165
Construction	167
FRS1 format	171
An illustrative example	174
Questions non-accountants should ask	176
Conclusion	177
Key points	177
Check your learning	177
News story quiz	178
Tutorial questions	178

Case studies

Preparation of financial statements	**185**
Accounting policies	**187**
Cash flow statements	**190**

**Part 3
FINANCIAL REPORTING** — 193

9 Information disclosure — 194

About this chapter	195
Learning objectives	195
Why this chapter is important for non-accountants	195
Disclosure	196
User groups	197
Sources of authority	199

Questions non-accountants should ask	205
Conclusion	205
Key points	206
Check your learning	206
News story quiz	207
Tutorial questions	207

10 The annual report — 208

About this chapter	208
Learning objectives	210
Why this chapter is important for non-accountants	210
Introductory material	210
Chairman's statement	212
Operating and financial review	214
Directors' report	215
Corporate governance	216
Remuneration report	218
Shareholder information	219
Questions non-accountants should ask	220
Conclusion	220
Key points	221
Check your learning	221
News story quiz	222
Tutorial questions	223

11 The annual accounts — 224

About this chapter	225
Learning objectives	226
Why this chapter is important for non-accountants	226
Setting the scene	227
Auditors' report	231
Group profit and loss account	231
Group statement of total recognized gains and losses	234
Group balance sheet	235
Group cash flow statement	237
Notes to the accounts	239
Periodic summary	240
Questions non-accountants should ask	242
Conclusion	242
Key points	243
Check your learning	243
News story quiz	244
Tutorial questions	245

12 Interpretation of accounts — 246

About this chapter	246
Learning objectives	247
Why this chapter is important for non-accountants	247
Nature and purpose of interpretation	248
Basic procedure	250
Ratio analysis	253
Profitability ratios	253
Liquidity ratios	256
Efficiency ratios	258
Investment ratios	260
An illustrative example	264
Interpretation guide	270
Drawing conclusions	272
Questions non-accountants should ask	274
Conclusion	274
Key points	275
Check your learning	276
News story quiz	277
Tutorial questions	277
Appendix: Summary of the main ratios	283

13 Contemporary issues — 285

About this chapter	286
Learning objectives	286
Why this chapter is important for non-accountants	286
Overview	287
Accounting scandals	288
Company law reform	295
Internationalization	297
Revenue recognition	301
Questions non-accountants should ask	304
Conclusion	304
Key points	305
Check your learning	305
News story quiz	306
Tutorial questions	307

Case studies

The communication of financial information	**308**
Interpretation of accounts	**312**

Part 4
MANAGEMENT ACCOUNTING 317

14 Foundations 318
About this chapter 318
Learning objectives 319
Why this chapter is important for
  non-accountants 319
Nature and purpose 319
Historical review 320
Main functions 322
Behavioural considerations 325
Questions non-accountants should ask 327
Conclusion 327
Key points 328
Check your learning 328
News story quiz 329
Tutorial questions 329

15 Direct costs 331
About this chapter 332
Learning objectives 332
Why this chapter is important for
  non-accountants 333
Responsibility accounting 334
Classification of costs 335
Direct materials 337
Direct labour 342
Other direct costs 343
Questions non-accountants should ask 344
Conclusion 344
Key points 345
Check your learning 345
News story quiz 346
Tutorial questions 346

16 Indirect costs 349
About this chapter 349
Learning objectives 350
Why this chapter is important for
  non-accountants 350
Production overhead 351
A comprehensive example 358
Non-production overhead 360
Predetermined absorption rates 362
Activity based costing 363

Questions non-accountants should ask 367
Conclusion 367
Key points 368
Check your learning 369
News story quiz 370
Tutorial questions 370

17 Budgeting 375
About this chapter 376
Learning objectives 376
Why this chapter is important for
  non-accountants 376
Budgeting and budgetary control 377
Procedure 378
Functional budgets 382
A comprehensive example 382
Fixed and flexible budgets 387
Behavioural consequences 390
Questions non-accountants should ask 391
Conclusion 391
Key points 392
Check your learning 392
News story quiz 393
Tutorial questions 393

18 Standard costing 399
About this chapter 399
Learning objectives 400
Why this chapter is important for
  non-accountants 400
Operation 401
Cost variances 407
A comprehensive example 410
Sales variances 415
Operating statements 416
Questions non-accountants should ask 418
Conclusion 419
Key points 419
Check your learning 420
News story quiz 420
Tutorial questions 421

19 Contribution analysis 426
About this chapter 427
Learning objectives 427
Why this chapter is important for
  non-accountants 427

Marginal costing   428
Contribution   429
Assumptions   430
Format   431
Application   432
Charts and graphs   434
Criticisms   439
Formulae   440
An illustrative example   442
Limiting factors   444
Questions non-accountants should ask   447
Conclusion   447
Key points   448
Check your learning   448
News story quiz   449
Tutorial questions   449

20 Specific decisions   453

About this chapter   453
Learning objectives   454
Why this chapter is important for
   non-accountants   454
Decision making   454
Cost classification   457
Closure and shutdown decisions   459
Make or buy decisions   461
Pricing decisions   463
Special orders   467
Questions non-accountants should ask   469
Conclusion   470
Key points   470
Check your learning   471
News story quiz   472
Tutorial questions   472

21 Capital investment   476

About this chapter   476
Learning objectives   477
Why this chapter is important for
   non-accountants   477
Background   477
Main methods   478
Selecting a method   491
Net cash flow   491

Sources of finance   493
Questions non-accountants should ask   496
Conclusion   497
Key points   497
Check your learning   497
News story quiz   498
Tutorial questions   499

22 Emerging issues   504

About this chapter   504
Learning objectives   505
Why this chapter is important for
   non-accountants   505
The business environment   505
Changes in management accounting   507
Activity based management   509
Better budgeting   510
Environmental accounting and reporting   511
Performance measurement   514
Product life cycle costing   517
Social accounting and reporting   518
Strategic management accounting   520
Target costing   521
Value chain analysis   522
Questions non-accountants should ask   524
Conclusion   524
Key points   525
Check your learning   526
News story quiz   527
Tutorial questions   527

Case studies

Fixed and flexible budgets   529
Standard cost operating statements   531
Pricing   533

Appendices

1 Further reading   535
2 Discount table   536
3 Answers to activities   537
4 Answers to tutorial questions   542

Index   572

In memory of my aunt
Miss Clarice Haigh
1903–2002
without whom this and previous
editions would not have been possible.

Preface

This is a book for non-accountants. It is intended primarily for students who are required to study accounting as part of a non-accounting degree or professional studies course. It should also be of value to those working in commerce, government or industry who find that their work involves them in dealing with accounting information. It is hoped that the book will help to explain why there is need for such information.

Non-accounting students (such as engineers, personnel managers, purchasing officers and sales managers) are sometimes unable to understand why they are required to study accounting. This is often found to be the case when they have to take an examination in the subject, especially when they are then presented with a paper of some considerable technical rigour.

Accounting books written specifically for the non-accountant are also often extremely demanding. The subject needs to be covered in such a way that non-accounting students do not become confused by too much technical information. They do not require the same detailed analysis that is only of relevance to the professional accountant. Some accounting books specially written for the non-accountant go to the opposite extreme. They outline the subject so superficially that they are of no real practical help either to examination candidates or to those non-specialists requiring some guidance on practical accounting problems.

The aim of this book is to serve as a good introduction to the study of accounting. The subject is not covered superficially. In certain areas the book goes into considerable detail, but only where it is necessary for a real understanding of the subject. It is appreciated that non-accountants are unlikely to be involved in the *detailed* preparation of accounting information, such as the compilation of a company's annual accounts. However, if such accounts are to provide the maximum possible benefit to their users, it is desirable that users should have a good knowledge of how they are prepared and how to extract the maximum possible information from them.

Accounting is now a compulsory subject for many non-accounting students on certificate, diploma and degree courses in colleges and universities. While the syllabuses for such courses have sometimes to be approved by external bodies, their detailed contents are often left to the individual lecturer to determine. This book was written with that type of course very much in mind.

The book is divided into four parts. Part 1 introduces the student to the subject of accounting and the profession of accountancy. Part 2 deals with financial accounting and Part 3 with financial reporting, while Part 4 is concerned with management accounting.

Many further and higher education institutions have now adopted a modular structure for the delivery of their courses. The book will be useful on those modules offered to non-accountants that include elements of both financial accounting and management accounting. It will also avoid students having to purchase two textbooks if financial accounting and management accounting are taken in separate modules. Equally, if some chapters in the various parts of the book are not relevant for some syllabuses, module leaders will find that it is quite easy to omit those chapters that do not relate to their particular modules.

The sixth edition

My thanks are due to those lecturers and students who once again have been kind enough to suggest improvements for the new edition. I have tried to take all their recommendations into account. Unfortunately, some of their ideas could not be accommodated because they were either too specialized for non-accounting students or they would add too much to the size of the book.

Changes

The fifth edition has been revised and brought up to date. A number of changes have been made. The most significant ones are as follows.

1 The fifth edition was divided into three parts. The sixth edition is in four parts, the previous Part 2 (Financial Accounting and Reporting) being divided into Financial Accounting (Part 2) and Financial Reporting (Part 3).

2 The number of chapters has been increased from 20 to 22. The material in the old Chapter 11 (The annual report) is now covered in a new Chapter 10 (The annual report) and a new Chapter 11 (The annual accounts). Similarly, the old Chapter 14 (Cost accounting) is now covered in a new Chapter 15 (Direct costs) and a new Chapter 16 (Indirect costs). This should make *cost accounting* more manageable as lecturers had found that the old Chapter 14 was too long.

3 The old Chapter 9 (Interpretation of accounts) has been moved towards the end of Part 3 (Financial Reporting) and it now becomes a new Chapter 12. This change means that it is possible to use company accounts in interpretation exercises.

4 Two new chapters and the move of one other has meant some changes to some other chapter numbers. An opportunity has also been taken to rename a few chapters. The details are shown in Table 1.

5 The chapter structure now follows a consistent pattern. A news story opens each chapter. This is followed by an explanation of what the chapter covers, the learning objectives and then a new section explaining why the chapter is important for non-accountants. The chapter contents follow and then, once the main material has been covered, there is a section dealing with questions that non-accountants might like to ask about the material covered in the chapter. A brief conclusion and a revision of the key points is then followed by some self-test questions called 'check your learning'. Students are then advised to go back to the beginning of the chapter and reread the news story printed before they answer some questions based on it. Finally, there are some 'tutorial questions' (in the fifth edition they were split into 'group discussion' and 'practice' questions) that students can attempt on their own. Some of them have answers in Appendix 4 while the answers to the other questions are in the *Lecturer's Guide*.

6 Each chapter now contains a number of 'activities'. These generally relate to a particular section in the chapter. The idea of the activities is to encourage students to stop and think about what they have just read. Many of the activities involve students in

having to do something for themselves, such as consulting a dictionary or deciding what they would do in certain circumstances. Others involve attempting the demonstration examples included in the chapters (without looking at the answers). Some activities have specific answers. The answers to such activities have been included in Appendix 3.

7 The 'check your learning' section has been redesigned. It now covers a list of questions that test students' knowledge of the entire contents of the chapter. The answers to these question may be found within the text.

8 The fifth edition contained four case studies. These have now been withdrawn and replaced with eight entirely new ones. Three may be found at the end of Part 2, two at the end of Part 3 and three at the end of Part 4.

9 Lecturers have requested that the examples and case studies used in the book should relate to actual events. Wherever possible this has been done.

Table 1 Changes to the text of the sixth edition

This edition	Amendments	Previous edition
1 The accounting world	Substantial rewrite	1 The accounting world
2 Accounting rules	Fairly minor	2 Accounting rules
3 Recording data	Minor	3 Recording data
4 Sole trader accounts	Minor	4 Trading entity accounts
5 Last minute adjustments	Minor	5 Accounting for adjustments
6 Company accounts	Minor	6 Company accounts
7 Other entity accounts	Minor	7 Other accounts
8 Cash flow statements	Fairly substantial	8 Cash flow statements
9 Information disclosure	Substantial rewrite	10 Disclosure of information
10 The annual report	Rewrite	11 The annual report
11 The annual accounts	Rewrite	11 The annual report
12 Interpretation of accounts	Fairly substantial	9 Interpretation of accounts
13 Contemporary issues	Mainly new	12 Contemporary issues in financial reporting
14 Management accounting foundations	Minor	13 The framework of management accounting
15 Direct costs	Re-arranged	14 Cost accounting
16 Indirect costs	Re-arranged plus some material from the old Chapter 20	14 Cost accounting
17 Budgeting	Minor	15 Planning and control: budgeting
18 Standard costing	Minor	16 Planning and control: standard costing
19 Contribution analysis	Minor	17 Decision-making: contribution analysis
20 Specific decisions	Minor	18 Decision-making: specific decisions
21 Capital investment	Minor	19 Decision-making: capital investment
22 Emerging issues	Mainly new	20 Contemporary issues in management accounting

Recent events in accounting

The use of actual examples has caused a problem. Some of the examples may appear to give a very negative impression of accountants and the accountancy profession. If this were to be the case, then it would be misleading.

During the last two years (2001/03) the accountancy profession has not had a particularly good press. This was mainly caused by the alleged Enron fraud case in the United States of America. This case has had two main effects:

1 *Loss of faith in accountants.* Accountants and the accountancy profession lost their reputation for absolute honesty and probity. There are rogues in every profession and their behaviour cannot be condoned no matter what the circumstances. There is no evidence, however, that there has been an increase in the number of unscrupulous individuals joining the accountancy profession in recent years or of long-standing members resorting to unacceptable professional behaviour.

2 *Suspicion of accounting practices.* The public became suspicious of what accountants did when it began to realize that accounting procedures involved a considerable amount of individual judgement. The second point is very interesting and it is particularly relevant as far as this book is concerned. We discuss it in more detail below.

A theme that has run constantly through the first and subsequent editions of this book has been that accounting involves a great deal more than following a series of mechanical steps. We have argued consistently that non-accountants should not be mesmerized by the apparent arithmetical accuracy and symmetry of accounting statements. Accounting information is not absolute. Various assumptions have to be made in preparing and presenting it. This means that a considerable amount of *judgement* is required in doing so. As different accountants are likely to come to different decisions about what to do, different outcomes are possible.

The public has not always understood this point but the Enron case certainly helped to highlight it. Despite the media hysteria, it is still possible to rely on accounting information and to have confidence in those that prepare it. There is one proviso: *you must question the assumptions upon which it is based and you must be willing to be critical of those assumptions.*

Notwithstanding the recent accounting 'scandals', the British Government appears to have faith in the UK accountancy profession. In the summer of 2002 the Government published its White Paper on company law reform. In broad terms, what it proposed to do was to lay down some general legal requirements for the preparation and disclosure of accounting information. The detailed application of the Government's policies was to be left to a number of private sector bodies. Accountants would be members of such bodies, although non-accountants would also be members. In essence, these proposals confirmed the existing arrangements.

It seems reasonable to assume, therefore, that if the Government had been worried about the probity of the accountancy profession it would not allow it to be so heavily involved in implementing its company legislation. This is very reassuring for all those members of the public who had lost faith in the accountancy profession following the Enron case.

More specialist texts are available if a particular syllabus requires students to go into more detail than is covered in this book, and some guidance on suitable reading is given in

Appendix 1: Further reading. Even so, unless particular modules are covered by national requirements, we would urge some caution. It is as well to consider whether most non-accountants really need to know much more about accounting than is covered in this book.

A word to students

If you are using this book as part of a formal course, your lecturer will provide you with a work scheme. The work scheme will outline just how much of the book you are expected to cover each week. In addition to the work done in your lecture, you will probably have to read each chapter two or three times. As you work your way through a chapter you will come across a number of 'activities'. Most of the them require you to do something or to find something out. The idea of these activities is to encourage you to stop your reading of the text at various points and to think about what you have just read. Remember that there are few right and wrong answers in accounting, so we want you to gain some experience in deciding for yourself what you would do if you were faced with a number of accounting related problems.

You are also recommended to attempt as many of the questions that follow each chapter as you can. Avoid looking at the answers until you are absolutely certain that you do not know how to answer the question. The more questions that you attempt, the more confident you will be that you really do understand the subject matter.

Many students study accounting without having the benefit of attending lectures. If you fall into this category, it is suggested that you adopt the following study plan:

1 Organise your private study so that you have covered every topic in your syllabus by the time of your examination.
2 Read each chapter slowly, being careful to do each activity and to work through each Example. Do not worry if you do not immediately understand each point. Read on to the end of the chapter.
3 Read the chapter again, this time making sure that you understand each point. Try doing each activity that relates to various examples without looking at the answer.
4 Attempt as many questions at the end of the chapter as you can, but do not look at the answers until you have finished or you are certain that you cannot do the question.
5 If you have time, reread the chapter.

One word of caution. Accounting is not simply a matter of elementary arithmetic. The solution to many accounting problems often calls for a considerable amount of personal judgement; hence there is bound to be some degree of subjectivity attached to each answer.

The problems demonstrated in this book are not readily solved in the real world and the suggested answers ought to be subject to a great deal of argument and discussion. It follows that non-accountants ought to be severely critical of any accounting information that is supplied to them. It is difficult to be constructive in your criticism unless you have some knowledge of the subject matter. This book aims to provide you with that knowledge.

Guided tour of the book

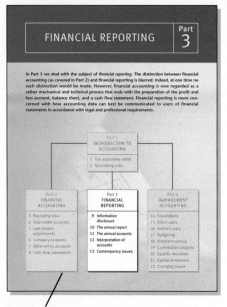

Part openers contain a diagram to help you find your way around the book

Chapter openers feature a topical news article relating chapter content to the real world

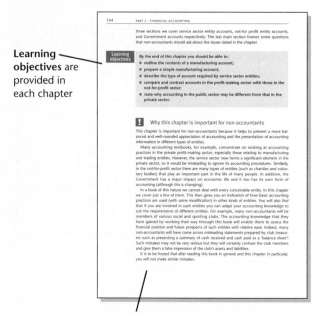

Learning objectives are provided in each chapter

Why this chapter is important for non-accountants explore the applications and benefits of chapter content for the non-accountant

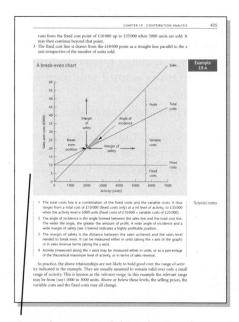

Examples are spread throughout the chapter

Activities test student understanding at regular intervals throughout the chapter

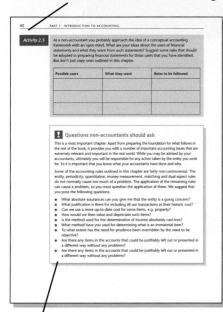

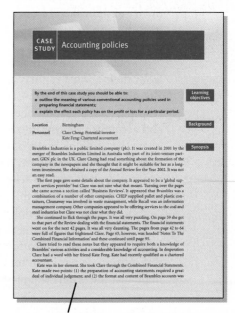

Key points recap the main concepts studied in the chapter

Check your learning test absorption of chapter content and offer a useful revision aid

Questions non-accountants should ask offer questions business managers might ask to assist in the decision-making process

News story quizes provide thought-provoking questions relating to topical news articles

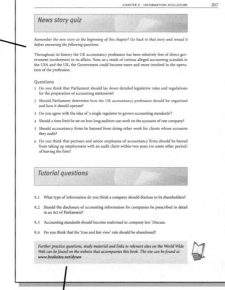

Tutorial questions offer ideas for assignments or class discussion

Case studies appear at the end of each part

Visit the Companion Website at **www.booksites.net/dyson** to find valuable teaching and learning material. See opposite the title page for full contents.

Acknowledgements

This book could not have been written and revised without the help of a considerable number of people. Many of them have contributed directly to the ideas that have gone into the writing of it, while in other cases I may have absorbed their views without always being fully conscious of doing so.

I am indebted to far too many people to name them all individually, but I would like to place on record my thanks to all of my former colleagues at both Heriot-Watt University and Napier University. Without their ready assistance and tolerant benevolence, this book would be all the poorer. I would also like to thank all those lecturers, reviewers and students who have made various suggestions for improving the sixth edition.

My thanks are also due to the editors of the following journals and newspapers for permission to reproduce copyright material: *Accountancy, Accountancy Age, CA, Daily Telegraph, Financial Management, Financial Times, The Guardian, The Herald, The Independent, The Times, The Scotsman,* and *The Yorkshire Post.* This material may not be reproduced or transmitted unless written permission is obtained from the original owner or publisher. I hope that the inclusion of some actual new stories will enliven the introduction to each chapter and encourage students to think about the various issues covered in the stories.

I would also like to thank the following companies for permission to extract material from their annual reports and accounts: Aggreko plc, A.G. Barr plc, Bett Brothers plc, Brambles Industries plc, Cairn Energy plc, Devro plc, HF Holidays Ltd, J. Smart & Co. (Contractors) plc, and Robert Wiseman Dairies plc. It is hoped that by using actual reports and accounts to illustrate various aspects of accounting practice, students will be able to relate the textbook material more easily with the real world. I am particularly grateful to these companies, therefore, for enabling me to introduce non-accounting students to the real world, and I wish to acknowledge the valuable contribution that such companies have made to the contents of this book. The companies are, of course, not responsible for any comments made in the book about their respective annual reports and accounts.

I would also like to thank my editors, Paula Harris and Paula Parish, and their colleagues at Pearson Education for all of the hard work that they have put into producing this edition. It has been tough going for everyone involved in the process. I can only hope that the results will prove that it was all worthwhile.

Publisher's acknowledgements

We are grateful to the following for permission to reproduce copyright material:

HF Holidays Limited for Figure 8.1 from HF Holidays Limited Annual Report and Accounts; Aggreko plc for Appendix to Chapter 8 from Aggreko plc Annual Report and Accounts; Devro plc for Figures 10.2, 10.5, 10.6 and 22.1 from Devro plc Annual Report and Accounts; J. Smart & Co. (Contractors) plc for Figures 10.3 and 10.4 and Example 11.1 from J. Smart & Co. plc Annual Report and Accounts; Cairn Energy plc for Figures 10.5 and 10.6 from Cairn Energy plc Annual Report and Accounts; A.G. Barr plc for Figure 11.3 and Examples 11.1–11.6 and 12.1 from A.G. Barr plc Annual Report and Accounts; Guardian News Service Ltd for Table 13.1 from "Uncle Sam's scandal" published in *The Guardian* 26th July 2002 © Guardian; Bett plc for Case Study after Chapter 13 from Bett plc Annual Report and Accounts; Robert Wiseman Dairies plc for Case Study after Chapter 13 from Robert Wiseman Dairies plc Annual Report and Accounts; Brambles Industries plc for Case Study after Chapter 24 from Brambles Industries plc Annual Report and Accounts.

VNU Business Publications for the articles "Revenue recognition lacks consistency published in *Accountancy Age* 4th April 2002, "PwC fried over caterer's books" by Philip Smith published in *Accountancy Age* 26th September 2002, "The truth about bad news" by Damian Wild published in *Accountancy Age* 24th October 2002, "Pushing for accruals" published in *Accountancy Age* 21st November 2002 and "The Ministry of Defence's accounts" published in *Accountancy Age* 28th November 2002 © Accountancy Age.com; Accountancy Magazine for the articles "Conservative accounting policies" published in *Accountancy* September 2002, "MyTravel losses catch market by surprise" and "Results posted for holding company only" published in *Accountancy* January 2003; Telegraph Group Limited for the articles "HIH collapse could result in charges" by Philip Aldrick published in *The Daily Telegraph* 14th January 2002 and "Charter dives after hole appears in US accounts" by Malcolm Moore published in *The Daily Telegraph* 29th January 2003 © Telegraph Group Limited; CA Magazine for the articles "Can't get to sleep? It's probably because of your cashflow" by Mark Sim published in *CA Magazine* December 2002 and "Company annual reports need to consider user's needs, report says" published in *CA Magazine* January 2003; The Scotsman Publications Ltd for the article "Hewitt unveils new rules for UK accountancy" by William Lyons published in *The Scotsman* 31st January 2003 © The Scotsman Publications Ltd; Independent Newspapers Ltd for the articles "BAE tops blue-chip list of slowest payers" by Michael Harrison published in the *Independent* 21st January 2003 and "Spade maker cuts 160 jobs and closes factory" published in the *Independent* 29th January 2003; CIMA Enterprises Ltd for the articles "Ministers plan to extend IAS" by Anita Howarth published in *Financial Management* November 2002, "Accountants make reporting improvements a priority" and "Uplifting growth for on-line underwear company" published in *Financial Management* March 2003; Times Newspapers Limited for the article "Tomkins boosted by cost-cutting campaign" by Angela Jameson published in *The Times* 15th January 2003; The Herald and Evening Times (Newsquest) Ltd for the article "Murgitroyd warns rising costs are taking their toll" published in *The Herald* 21st January 2003; Guardian News Service Ltd for the articles "Slug and Lettuce accounts holed" by Ian Griffiths published in *The Guardian* 13th November 2002 and "Eurotunnel breaks even in cash" by Andrew Clarke published in *The Guardian* 11th February 2003 © Guardian; and Yorkshire Press for the article "Hilton to cut back project spend" published in *Yorkshire Press* 15th December 2002.

INTRODUCTION TO ACCOUNTING

This book is divided into four main parts, as shown below. Part 1 contains two chapters. In Chapter 1 we provide some background about accounting, the accountancy profession, and the organizations that accountants work for. In Chapter 2 we outline the conventional rules that accountants normally follow when preparing accounting statements.

Part 1
INTRODUCTION TO ACCOUNTING

1 The accounting world
2 Accounting rules

Part 2
FINANCIAL ACCOUNTING

3 Recording data
4 Sole trader accounts
5 Last minute adjustments
6 Company accounts
7 Other entity accounts
8 Cash flow statements

Part 3
FINANCIAL REPORTING

9 Information disclosure
10 The annual report
11 The annual accounts
12 Interpretation of accounts
13 Contemporary issues

Part 4
MANAGEMENT ACCOUNTING

14 Foundations
15 Direct costs
16 Indirect costs
17 Budgeting
18 Standard costing
19 Contribution analysis
20 Specific decisions
21 Capital investment
22 Emerging issues

The accounting world

The accountancy profession takes a hammering . . .

The truth about bad news

By Damian Wild

If it feels like accountancy has taken a hammering in the national press like no other sector figures prepared for *Accountancy Age* this week confirm it

In terms of negative press coverage over the past 12 months, accountancy ranks a distant 45th out of the 45 leading UK business sectors. Accountants fared worse than banks, telecoms companies and estate agents, according to the PressWatch index, which measures the balance of positive and negative publicity.

Only Deloitte & Touche enjoyed more positive coverage than negative. PKF, Saffrey Champness and BDO Stoy Hayward all finished in negative territory – though only just.

But it was the rest of the then Big Five that really suffered. Ernst & Young,

which has endured a hard time over its handling of the Equitable Life audit, scored minus 105; KPMG (accused of violating auditor independence rules) scored minus 362; while PricewaterhouseCoopers (criticised for its audit of Russia's biggest company, Gazprom) scored minus 438.

Not surprisingly, Andersen's demise hurt accountancy the most. The firm scored minus 5,133 making it the worst performing of all UK companies assessed. It was run close by Marconi.

But there was some good news in the figures. Since Andersen's collapse, the sector has begun to recover. Recent figures show accountancy climbed back up to a comparatively respectable 36th place out of 43 in September.

Accountancy Age, 24 October 2002.

Questions relating to this news story may be found on page 24 ▸▸

About this chapter

This chapter sets the scene for the rest of the book.

The discipline of accounting is probably almost a complete mystery to most users of this book. We begin, therefore, by explaining what we mean by 'accounting'. We then consider why it is important for non-accountants to know something about the subject. This is followed by an explanation of why this particular chapter is an important one for non-accountants. A further section provides a brief review of the development of accounting as a major discipline and the following one with the structure of the accountancy profession in the United Kingdom. You will find that accounting practices vary in different types of organizations. So we then examine some of the main organizations that we will be coming across as you work your way through the book. The last main section in the chapter outlines some questions that non-accountants might like to ask about the issues raised in the chapter.

By the end of this chapter, you should be able to:
- summarize the nature and purpose of accounting;
- outline its history;
- explain why non-accountants need to know something about accounting;
- identify the main branches of accounting;
- list the major accountancy bodies that operate within the United Kingdom;
- outline the main types of public and private entities operating in the United Kingdom.

The nature of accounting

We assume that at the moment you know very little about accounting. It would be useful, therefore, if we tell you briefly what accounting *is* and what it *does*.

Accounting is a service provided for those who need information about an organization's financial performance, its assets and its liabilities.

We will break this description down for you in order to make it clearer what is involved in providing that service.

1 The information collected is restricted to quantifiable information that can be converted into monetary terms.
2 The financial performance of an organization is measured over a period of time by matching what sales and other incomes an organization has made against what it has cost to make them. This information is usually provided for users in the form of what is called a *profit and loss account*.
3 Assets relate to those possessions and property that the organization *owns*. This information is normally shown in a financial statement called a *balance sheet*.
4 Liabilities are what the organization *owes* to parties outside the organization. This information is also shown in a balance sheet.

You will see from the above description that the information collected for accounting purposes is restricted, and it is used (at least it was originally) for only a limited number of purposes. We may summarize these restrictions and limitations as follows:

- The information relates to the past, i.e. it is historical.
- Only quantifiable information is collected.
- It must be capable of being converted into monetary terms.
- It only relates to the organization's affairs.

Such restrictions and limitations have grown up through custom and practice. We shall be returning to them in Chapter 2.

Non-accountants often do not understand that accounting is constrained in the way described above. They expect it to do more than it can do and more that it does. This is known as the *expectations gap*.

Many of the so called accounting scandals that we feature in this book result from the expectations gap. The public's perception about accounting has caused enormous difficulty for the accountancy profession during the last two years. The profession is having to fight hard to counteract the criticisms levelled against it in the media and among the public. Fortunately, the views expressed are not shared by the Government. Its proposals on company law reform, for example, do not indicate any major change to either the organization of the accountancy profession or the way that accounting is practised.

Nevertheless, although the information with which accountants traditionally deal is restricted, there is still a great deal of it. Such information has to be collected, stored, extracted, summarized, prepared and communicated to those parties who want it. Basically, they want to be satisfied on three counts. They are as follows:

1 *Performance.* How did the organization perform over the period in question? For a profit-making organization, for example, we might want to know whether it had made a profit, and for a not-profit making one whether it received more cash than the cash it paid out.
2 *Debts owed.* How much money was owed to the organization at the end of a period and who owed it?
3 *Amounts owing.* Similarly, how much did the organization owe to other people at the end of the period and who were they?

An accounting system is designed to provide the information that satisfies the above questions. But who are the people who want such information and why do they want it?

There are two main parties connected with any organization: owners and managers. Owners want to know about their organization if they have left it to managers to run; for example, whether assets (i.e. its property) are being looked after and whether it is being run efficiently. This is what is called the *stewardship* function of management. Managers themselves want information so that they can be assured that they are safeguarding the assets and running the organization efficiently.

Now that we have provided you with an outline of what accounting is about and what it does, we can move on to explain why it is an important subject for non-accountants to study. We do so in the next section.

Activity 1.1   Look up the definition of accounting in three well-known dictionaries (such as the Oxford Dictionary). Copy the definitions into your notebook. Then try to frame your own definition of accounting.

! Why accounting is important for non-accountants

We assume that as a non-accountant student you aim to become a senior manager in some entity (accountants use the term *entity* to mean any type of organization). That entity might be profit-making, e.g. a company selling goods and services, or a not-for-profit entity, such as a charity or a government department.

At a more junior level your work might be fairly routine, it may not be very demanding and you might have little responsibility. As you become more experienced and competent you may be promoted to a more responsible post. Alternatively, you may already hold a senior post but one perhaps of a technical nature. For example, you might be in charge of a chemical laboratory or one of the company's engineering sections. Nevertheless, your present duties may be restricted to the technical aspects of the job and you may not be involved in the wider aspects of running the entity.

That position will change as you become more senior. You will become much more involved in the planning of the entity, the control of its resources, and in taking an active part in decision-making, i.e. in determining its future.

In performing such duties you will be supplied with a great deal of information relating to the administrative, production and sales functions of the entity. Such technical information will have been stored, extracted, summarized and translated into a language that all managers are expected to understand. That language is called *accounting* and hence accounting is often referred to as the language of business. By using a common language managers can understand each other without it being necessary for them to become an expert in the other functions of an entity.

But, as a manager, what accounting information will be given to you? What are you expected to do with it? Is it given to you just because it might be of interest?

We shall be answering these questions as we go through the book. As far as the last question is concerned, the simple answer is 'no'. You are given that information for a purpose. You are supposed to do something with it. But what?

In broad terms, there are three main functions that, as a senior manager, you will be expected to undertake. The accounting information that your receive should help you to carry out such functions more effectively and efficiently. In summary, they are as follows:

1 *Planning.* As a manager you will be a vital member of the management team responsible for both the long-term and the short-term planning of the entity.
2 *Control.* You will use the entity's agreed long- and short-term plans to help you control the day-to-day activities of the entity.
3 *Decision making.* You will use the information to make decisions about the entity's progress and its long-term future, e.g. whether to invest in a new factory or close down a loss-making unit.

In order to help you carry out these functions you will be supplied with and will come to depend upon the type of information prepared by your accounting team. The information will obviously not mean much to you if you do not understand it. It would be like receiving reports written in French if you did not know a word of French. So you need to be reasonably fluent in speaking accounting. Otherwise, you will not be able to communicate with your fellow managers and you might be taking decisions based on information that means nothing to you.

The relationship between accounting information and the use management makes of it is shown in Figure 1.1.

There is another reason why you need to know something about accounting. In most types of entities there is a legal obligation placed upon you as a senior manager to

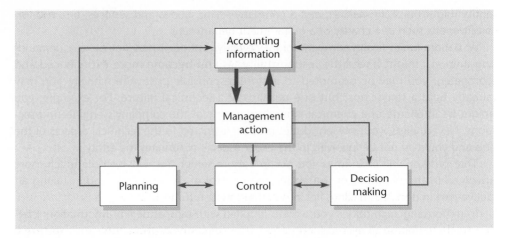

Figure 1.1 **The relationship between accounting information and management**

comply with various statutory accounting provisions. It would be very unwise, therefore, if you ignored your legal responsibilities and you did not take the necessary steps to ensure that you did as the law required. Ignorance of the law is no excuse for breaking it.

At this point you might be thinking along the following lines:

OK, I accept that accounting is an important subject but I still don't really see why I have to know much about it. The accountants can't tell me how to do my job and they will make sure that I follow the legal requirement. All that number crunching that accountants do is a waste of time as far as I am concerned.

You might have a point. It may not be *absolutely* essential for you to do much 'number crunching' but it does give you a better idea of where the information comes from and what it means. If you are familiar with its source then you will be able to judge much more keenly how much reliance to place on it.

In summary, therefore, we would argue that accounting is a vital subject for non-accountants to study because, as a manager:

1 it will help you to take more meaningful and effective decisions based on information that you have been able to check; and
2 you can ensure that the entity carries out its legal obligations.

❗ Why this chapter is important for non-accountants

Apart from laying the foundations for the rest of the book, this chapter will also help to make your job as a non-accountant just a little easier. This is because most employees in almost any type of organization will have to deal with *'the accountants'* from time to time. Indeed, in your job you may be constantly interrupted by accountants asking you questions and wanting certain types of information. If you know who those accountants are, what they want and why they want it, you are likely to waste less time in dealing with their requests. It also helps to make relations between you and the accountants much more cordial and less strained if you can talk to them with some knowledge about the organization and requirements of their respective professional bodies, and the business environment in which they operate.

By the end of the chapter you will have a sound basic knowledge of the discipline of accounting, the profession that governs it, and the business environment in which it operates.

The development of accounting

The word *account* in everyday language is often used as a substitute for an *explanation* or a *report* of certain actions or events. If you are an employee, for example, you may have to explain to your employer just how you have been spending your time, or if you are a manager, you may have to report to the owner on how the business is doing. In order to explain or to report, you will, of course, have to remember what you were doing or what happened. As it is not always easy to remember, you may need to keep some written record. In effect, such records can be said to provide the basis of a rudimentary account-ing (or reporting) system.

In a primitive sense, man has always been involved in some form of accounting. It may have gone no further than a farmer (say) measuring his worth simply by counting the number of cows or sheep that he owned. However, the growth of a monetary system enabled a more sophisticated method to be developed. It then became possible to calcu-late the increase or decrease in individual wealth over a period of time, and to assess whether (say) a farmer with ten cows and fifty sheep was wealthier than one who had sixty pigs. Table 1.1 illustrates just how difficult it would be to assess the wealth of a farmer in a non-monetary system.

Even with the growth of a monetary system, it took a very long time for formal docu-mentary systems to become commonplace, although it is possible to trace the origins of modern book-keeping at least as far back as the twelfth century. We know that from about that time, traders began to adopt a system of recording information that we now refer to as *double-entry book-keeping*. By the end of the fifteenth century, double-entry book-keeping was widely used in Venice and the surrounding areas; indeed, the first-known book on the subject was published in 1494 by an Italian mathematician called

Table 1.1 Accounting for a farmer's wealth

His possessions	A year ago	Now	Change
Cows	●●●●●●●●●●	●●●●●●●●●●●●●●●	+5
Hens [● = 10]	●●●●●●●●●●●	●●●●●●●●	−30
Pigs	●●●●●●	●●●●	−2
Sheep [● = 10]	●●●●●	●●●●●●●	+20
Land [● = 1 acre]	●●●●	●●●●	no change
Cottage	●	●	no change
Carts	●●●	●	−2
Ploughs	●	●●	+1

Pacioli. Modern book-keeping systems are still based on principles established in the fifteenth century, although they have had to be adapted to suit modern conditions.

Why has a recording system devised in medieval times lasted for so long? There are two main reasons:

1 it provides an accurate record of what has happened to a business over a specified period of time;
2 information extracted from the system can help the owner or the manager operate the business much more effectively.

In essence, the system provides the answers to the three basic questions that we outlined earlier and that owners (and managers) want to know. These questions are depicted in Figure 1.2, and they can be summarized as follows:

1 What profit has the business made?
2 How much does the business owe?
3 How much is owed to it?

The medieval system dealt largely with simple agricultural and trading *entities*. In the eighteenth century, however, the UK underwent what was called the *Industrial Revolution*. Economic activity gradually moved away from growing things to making or manufacturing them. In the early days of the Industrial Revolution managers had to

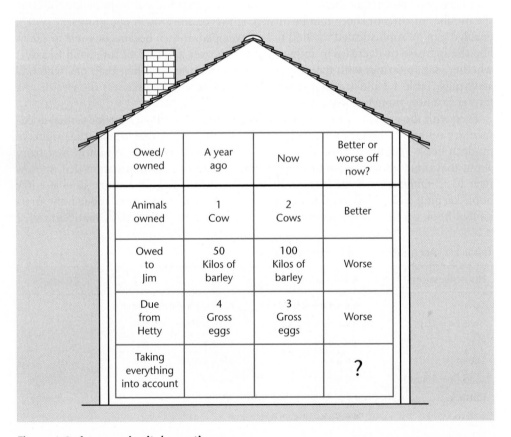

Owed/ owned	A year ago	Now	Better or worse off now?
Animals owned	1 Cow	2 Cows	Better
Owed to Jim	50 Kilos of barley	100 Kilos of barley	Worse
Due from Hetty	4 Gross eggs	3 Gross eggs	Worse
Taking everything into account			?

Figure 1.2 **An owner's vital questions**

depend upon the type of information supplied to the owners. The owners' need was for *financial* purposes, i.e. to calculate how much profit they had made. Financial information was prepared infrequently (perhaps only once a year) and then not in any great detail. Managers needed information largely for *costing* purposes, i.e. to work out the cost of making individual products. Such information was required more than once a year and in some considerable detail.

As a result of the different information needs of owners and managers, separate accounting systems were developed. However, as much of the basic data were common to both systems, they were gradually brought together. It would be rare now find any entity that had a separate financial accounting system and a separate costing system.

Another change in more recent years is that it is possible to identify more than two user groups. As Figure 1.3 shows, besides owners and managers, information may also be required by a wide range of other parties, for example, creditors, customers, employees, governments, investors, lenders, the public.

Accounting is now a major activity in both the profit-making and not-for-profit sectors of the economy and accountants hold some very senior positions in all types of entities. However, it is a service industry and accountants have to satisfy their clients.

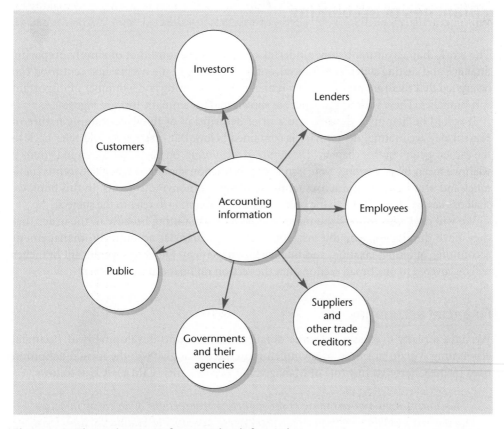

Figure 1.3 The main users of accounting information

Source: ASB (1999) *Statement of Principles for Financial Reporting.*

Activity 1.2

Insert the missing words in each of the following sentences:

(a) The word _____ in everyday language means an explanation or a report.

(b) Traders in the fifteenth century began to adopt a system of _____ to record information.

(c) The owners of a business want to know how much _____ a business has made.

(d) An _____ is a term used to describe any type of organisation.

(e) In the eighteenth century the United Kingdom underwent an _____ _____.

While accounting gradually evolved in two main branches in the nineteenth century (financial accounting and cost accounting), there were additional developments in the twentieth century. Furthermore, while new terminology has been introduced some old terms are still in common use. It would be helpful, therefore, if we explore with you some of the main branches of accounting. We do so in the next section.

Branches of accounting

The work that accountants now undertake ranges far beyond that of simply preparing financial and costing statements. Indeed, at the beginning of the twenty-first century it can be argued that there are now five main branches of accounting and a number of important sub-branches. These various branches are shown in diagrammatic form in Figure 1.4.

It would be helpful if we gave you a brief description of the wide-ranging nature of present-day accounting. A summary is contained below. But first you should refer back to the earlier section in this chapter, 'The nature of accounting', on pages 3–4 to remind yourself what we mean by *accounting*. Note also that a distinction should be made between *accountancy* and *accounting*. Some accountants use them as synonymous terms. In this book we shall use *accountancy* to refer to the profession, and *accounting* to refer to the subject.

We will deal with each of the main branches of accounting broadly in the order that they have developed over the last 100 years, i.e. financial accounting, management accounting, auditing, taxation, and financial management. Other less significant branches will be covered in one broad section after the section on financial management.

Financial accounting

We have already discussed in some detail the nature and development of financial accounting. We do not need to say much more except to give you the formal definition used by the Chartered Institute of Management Accountants (CIMA). It is as follows:

> *The classification and recording of the monetary transactions of an entity in accordance with established concepts, principles, accounting standards and legal requirements and their presentation, by means of profit and loss accounts, balance sheets and cash flow statements, during and at the end of an accounting period. (CIMA, 2000)*

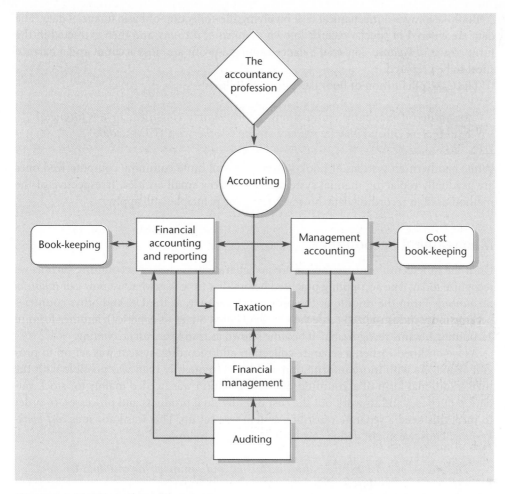

Figure 1.4 **The branches of accounting**

Note that we shall be covering 'concepts, principles, accounting standards and legal requirements' in the next chapter.

A distinction can be made between *financial accounting* and *financial reporting*. We do so in this book mainly for practical reasons in order to break down the information into manageable parts. However, in accounting circles such a distinction is sometimes made, although it remains somewhat blurred. We suggest that you regard *financial accounting* as being the accounting process that ends with the preparation of the profit and loss account, the balance sheet and the cash flow statement (these topics are dealt with later in the book). *Financial reporting* is the process of communicating financial accounting to users of such information; it may involve supplying additional information and a detailed quantitative and qualitative analysis of the underlying data.

Book-keeping

An important sub-branch of financial accounting is book-keeping. Indeed, book-keeping may be regarded as the foundation upon which the entire discipline of accounting is built.

Book-keeping is a mechanical task involving the collection of basic financial data. The data are entered in special records known as *books of account*, and then extracted in the form of a *trial balance*. The trial balance enables a profit and loss account and a balance sheet to be prepared.

The CIMA definition of book-keeping is as follows:

> *Recording of monetary transactions, appropriately classified, in the financial records of an entity, either by manual means, or otherwise. (CIMA, 2000)*

While handwritten systems of book-keeping are still quite common, computerized ones are gradually replacing manual systems even in very small entities. Irrespective of the method used in recording data, however, the same principles still apply.

Management accounting

Until the nineteenth century there were no separate branches of accounting such as we recognize today. The accounting practised before that time was what we now call *financial accounting*. From the middle of the nineteenth century, as the UK and other countries became more industrialized (especially in the United States of America), another form of accounting became recognizable. It became known as *costing* or *cost accounting*.

As we outlined earlier, a separate collection and recording system was set up to provide managers with more information and more frequently than was possible with the then traditional form of accounting. Such information was needed mainly for stock valuation purposes and to work out the cost of individual products and processes. In order to meet this need a separate recording system was set up. This was known as *cost book-keeping*. Thus, we might define cost book-keeping as follows:

> *The process of collecting, recording, extracting and summarizing cost data for stock valuation and product costing purposes.*

While cost accounting may be defined as:

> *The compilation, adaptation and reporting of cost data and information for managerial decision-making purposes.*

The distinction between cost book-keeping and cost accounting is similar to that between book-keeping and financial accounting/reporting.

During the twentieth century separate book-keeping and cost book-keeping systems were gradually abandoned, but stock valuation and product costing continued to be the two main functions of a cost accounting system. However, as the century developed accountants were called upon to supply managers with accounting and cost information for some additional purposes. These included information for planning and control, and information for decision-making. Such functions meant that cost accounting had increased its boundaries and it was no longer confined to dealing with historical data. Planning and decision-making, for example, primarily looks towards the future while cost accounting is based very much on the past.

The term 'cost accounting' was, therefore, no longer appropriate to describe a much wider range of functions and the much broader description of 'management accounting' has taken its place. Hence, cost accounting is now regarded as being merely a branch of *management accounting*.

The formal definition of management accounting given by CIMA is as follows:

> *The application of the principles of accounting and financial management to create, protect, preserve and increase value so as to deliver that value to stakeholders of profit and not-for-profit enterprises, both public and private. (CIMA, 2000)*

The definition is all-embracing and somewhat worthy but it will be useful to keep it in mind until you reach Part 4 of the book.

Auditing

We may define auditing as:

> *An examination and assessment of the activities, controls, records and systems that underpin accounting information.*

Not all entities have their accounts audited but for some organizations (such as large limited liability companies) it is a legal requirement.

Auditors are often trained accountants who specialize in ascertaining whether the accounts are credible, i.e. whether they can be believed. There are two main types of auditors. They are as follows.

1 *External auditors.* External auditors are appointed by the owners of an entity. They are independent of the entity and they are not employed by it. They report to the owners and not to the managers of the entity. Large limited liability companies are required to have an external audit. External auditors are responsible for ensuring that the financial accounts represent what is called 'a true and fair view' of the entity's affairs for a certain period of time. They may do some detailed checking of its records in order to be able to come to such a view but normally they would be selective. If they are then satisfied, they will be able to report their findings to the owners. The public often believe that the job of an auditor is to discover whether any fraud has taken place. This is not so. This misconceived perception forms part of the expectations gap that we discussed earlier in the chapter.

2 *Internal auditors.* Some entities employ internal auditors. Internal auditors are appointed by the managers of the entity; they are employees of the entity and they answer to its management. Internal auditors perform routine tasks and undertake some detailed checking of the entity's accounting procedures. Their task may also go beyond the financial accounts; for example, they may do some checking of the planning and control procedures and conduct 'value-for-money' tests.

External auditors and internal auditors usually work very closely together. Nevertheless, they do have separate roles and responsibilities. External auditors have always to remember that internal auditors are employees of the entity; they may be strongly influenced by the management of the entity and they may be subject to the pressures of other employees, e.g. job security, pay, and promotion prospects.

External auditors also do not enjoy complete independence. In the case of a large company, for example, the directors (i.e. the managers) will appoint them and, in practice, dismiss them. It is possible for the auditors to appeal directly to the shareholders but the shareholders usually accept the directors' recommendations.

Taxation

Taxation is a highly complex and technical branch of accounting. Those accountants who are involved in tax work are responsible for computing the amount of tax payable by both business entities and individuals. It is not necessary for anybody or any entity to pay more tax than is required by the law. It is, therefore, perfectly legitimate to search out all legal means of minimizing the amount of tax that might be demanded by the Government. This is known as *tax avoidance*. The non-declaration sources of income on which tax might be payable is known as *tax evasion*. Tax evasion is a very serious offence and it can lead to a long prison sentence. In practice, the borderline between tax avoidance and tax evasion is a narrow one and tax accountants have to steer a fine line between what is lawful and what might not be acceptable.

Financial management

Financial management is a relatively new branch of accounting. It has grown rapidly over the last 30 years. Financial managers are responsible for setting financial objectives, making plans based on those objectives, obtaining the finance needed to achieve the plans, and generally safeguarding all the financial resources of the entity.

Financial managers are much more likely to be heavily involved in the *management* of an entity than is generally the case with other management accountants (although that is changing). It should also be noted that financial managers draw on a much wider range of disciplines (e.g. economics and mathematics) than does the more traditional accountant, and they also rely more heavily on non-financial and more qualitative data.

Other branches

The main branches of accounting described above cannot always be put into such neat categories. Accountants in practice (that is, those who work from an office and offer their services to the public, like a solicitor) usually specialize in auditing, financial accounting or taxation. Most accountants working in commerce, industry or the public sector will be employed as management accountants, although some may deal specifically with auditing, financial accounting or taxation matters.

One other highly specialist branch of accounting that you may sometimes read about is that connected with *insolvency*, i.e. with bankruptcy or liquidation. *Bankruptcy* is a formal legal procedure. The term is applied to individuals when their financial affairs are so serious that they have to be given some form of legal protection from their creditors. The term *liquidation* is usually applied to a company when it also gets into serious financial difficulties and its affairs have to be 'wound up' (that is, arranged for it to go out of existence in an orderly fashion).

Companies do not necessarily go immediately into liquidation if they get into financial difficulties. An attempt will usually be made either to rescue them or to protect certain types of creditors. In these situations, accountants sometimes act as *administrators*. Their appointment freezes creditors' rights. This prevents the company from being put into liquidation during a period when the administrators are attempting to manage the company. By contrast, *receivers* may be appointed on behalf of loan creditors. The creditors' loans may be secured on certain property, and the receivers will try to obtain the income from that property, or they may even attempt to sell it.

We hope that you never come into contact with insolvency practitioners, and so we will move on to have a look at another topic, namely the structure of the accountancy profession.

Activity 1.3

State whether each of the following statements is true or false:

(a) An auditor' job is to find out whether a fraud has taken place.   *True/False*

(b) Management accounts are required by law.   *True/False*

(c) Tax avoidance is lawful.   *True/False*

(d) A balance sheet is a list of assets and liabilities.   *True/False*

(e) Companies have to go into liquidation if they get into
financial difficulties.   *True/False*

The accountancy profession

There is nothing to stop anyone in the United Kingdom calling himself or herself an accountant, and setting up in business as an accountant. However, some accounting work is restricted (such as the auditing of large limited liability companies) unless the accountant holds a recognized qualification. Indeed, accountants are sometimes described as being *qualified accountants*. This term is usually applied to someone who is a member of one of the major accountancy bodies (although many 'non-qualified' accountants would strongly dispute that they were not equally 'qualified'). There are six major accountancy bodies operating in the United Kingdom and they are as follows:

1 Institute of Chartered Accountants in England and Wales (ICAEW);
2 Institute of Chartered Accountants in Ireland (ICAI);
3 Institute of Chartered Accountants of Scotland (ICAS);
4 Association of Chartered Certified Accountants (ACCA);
5 Chartered Institute of Management Accountants (CIMA);
6 Chartered Institute of Public Finance and Accountancy (CIPFA).

The Irish Institute (ICAI) is included in the above list because it has a strong influence in Northern Ireland.

The organization of the accountancy profession is also shown in Figure 1.5.

Although all of the six major professional accountancy bodies now have a Royal Charter, it is still customary to refer only to members of ICAEW, ICAI, and ICAS as *chartered accountants*. Such chartered accountants have usually had to undergo a period

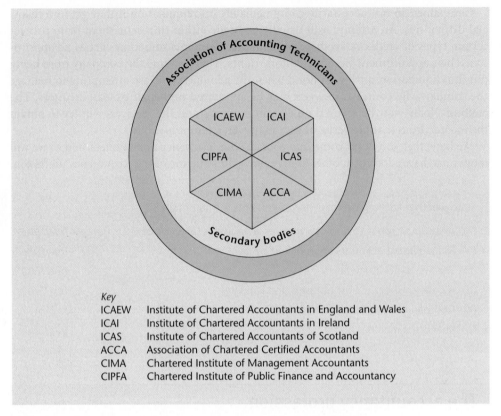

Figure 1.5 Organization of the accountancy profession in the UK

of training in a practising office, i.e. one that offers accounting services directly to the public. This distinguishes them from members of the other three accountancy bodies. Much practice work is involved in auditing and taxation but, after qualifying, many chartered accountants go to work in commerce or industry. ACCA members may also obtain their training in practice, but relevant experience elsewhere counts towards their qualification. CIMA members usually train and work in industry, while CIPFA members specialize almost exclusively in central and local government.

Apart from the six major bodies, there are a number of important (although far less well-known) smaller accountancy associations and societies, e.g. the Association of Authorised Public Accountants, the Institute of Company Accountants, and the Institute of Cost and Executive Accountants. Such bodies offer some form of accountancy qualification but they have not yet managed to achieve the status or prestige attached to being a member of one of the six major bodies. Hence, they are referred to as *secondary bodies*.

There is also another very important accountancy body, known as the Association of Accounting Technicians. The Association was formed in 1980 as a professional organization especially for those accountants who *assist* qualified accountants in preparing accounting information. In order to become an accounting technician, it is necessary to take (or be exempt from) the Association's examinations. These are not easy, although they tend to be less technically demanding and more practical than those of the six major bodies.

You can see that the accountancy profession is extremely diverse, and if you meet people who call themselves accountants, you may not be able to tell exactly what that means. Nevertheless, whatever their qualifications, all accountants will have one thing in common: their job is to help *you* do your job more effectively. Accountants offer a service. They can do a lot to help you but you do not necessarily have to do what they say. You should listen to their advice but, as accountants are largely specialists in financial matters, you also should obtain advice from other sources. You can then make up your own mind what you should do. If things go wrong, never ever blame the accountant (or the computer!). As a manager, it is *your* responsibility if things go wrong, even if you did receive bad advice.

You may be thinking, 'This is all very well, but I am not really in a position to disregard the accountant's advice.' Exactly! That is what this book is about. By the end of it you will be in an excellent position to judge the quality of the advice given. We shall be examining in later chapters what you need, but before we end this chapter it will be useful if we outline the basic structure of the UK economy and the main types of entities with which we shall be dealing.

Which is the odd one out among the following professional accountancy bodies. State your reasons for the one that you select.

(a) AAT
(b) CIMA
(c) CIPFA
(d) ICAEW

Activity 1.4

Public and private entities

The main aim of this section is to introduce you to the two main types of entities with which we shall be primarily concerned in this book: *sole traders* and *companies*. Before we can do this we need to explain a little bit about the structure of the national economy of the United Kingdom.

In order to simplify our analysis, we will assume that the UK economy can be classified into two broad groupings: the *profit-making sector* and the *not-for-profit sector*. Within each of these sectors it is then possible to distinguish a number of different types of organizations (or entities, as we have referred to them earlier). The basic structure that we shall be following in this section is illustrated in Figure 1.6. We begin by examining the profit-making sector.

The profit-making sector

The profit-making sector is extremely diverse, but it is possible to recognize three major subdivisions. These are (a) the manufacturing sector; (b) the trading sector; and (c) the service sector.

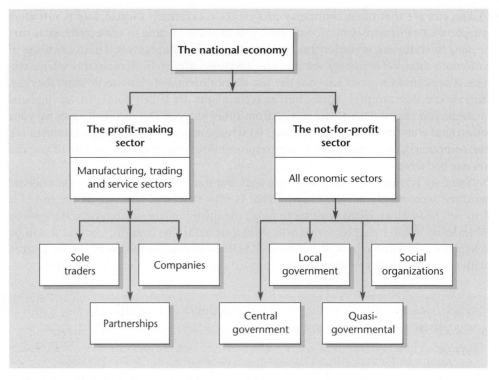

Figure 1.6 **Public and private entities**

The manufacturing sector is involved in purchasing raw materials and component parts, converting (or incorporating) them into finished goods, and then selling them to customers. Examples of manufacturing enterprises include the chemicals, glass, iron and steel, and textile industries.

The trading sector purchases finished goods and then sells them to their customers without any further major conversion work normally being done on them. Trading enterprises are found in the retailing and wholesaling sectors, such as shops, supermarkets and builders' merchants.

The service sector provides advice or assistance to customers or clients, such as hairdressing, legal, and travel services. Unlike the manufacturing and trading sectors, the service sector does not usually deal in physical or tangible goods. However, there are some exceptions: the hotel and restaurant trade, for example, is normally classed as part of the service sector even though it provides major tangible services such as the provision of accommodation, food and drink.

The accounting systems required of manufacturing, trading and service sector entities are all slightly different, although they are based on similar principles and procedures. Manufacturing entity accounts are the most complex, trading entity are fairly straightforward, while service entity accounts are usually fairly simple.

Until about 15 years ago, accounting texts tended to concentrate on the manufacturing and trading sectors. This emphasis reflected the origins of nineteenth-century accounting requirements, when the manufacturing and trading sectors were of major significance. More recently, the manufacturing sector has declined in importance and the service sector has become much more significant.

In this text we shall still be spending a great deal of time examining manufacturing and trading entity accounts. We do so for three main reasons: (1) the manufacturing sector still forms an important part of the national economy; (2) the manufacturing and trading sectors enable us to demonstrate a wide range of accounting techniques and procedures; and (3) you may need the knowledge if you move around the various sectors during your career.

Although there are differences in the nature of the product or the service that they offer, entities within the manufacturing, trading and service sectors may be organized on similar lines. Three main types of entities can be recognized; these are (1) *sole trader* entities; (2) *partnership* entities; and (3) *companies*. The basic distinction between such entities reflects who owns them, how they are financed, and what the law requires of them.

Sole traders

The term 'sole trader' is rather misleading for two reasons: (1) 'sole' does not necessarily mean that only one person is involved in the entity; and (2) 'trader' may also encompass manufacturing and service entities.

The term really reflects the *ownership* of the entity; the main requirement is that only one individual should own the entity. The owner would normally also be the main source of finance and he would be expected to play a reasonably active part in its management.

Sole traders usually work on a very informal basis and some private matters relating to the owner are often indistinguishable from those of the business. Sole trader accounts are fairly straightforward and there is no specific legislation that covers the accounting arrangements. We shall be using sole trader accounts in Chapters 3, 4 and 5 in order to demonstrate some basic accounting techniques.

Partnerships

A partnership entity is very similar to a sole trader entity except that there must be at least *two owners* of the business. Partnerships sometimes grow out of a sole trader entity, perhaps because more money needs to be put into the business or because the sole trader needs some help in managing it. It is also quite common for a new business to start out as partnerships, for example when some friends get together to start a home-decorating service or to form a car-repair business.

The partners should agree among themselves how much money they will each put into the business, what jobs they will do, how many hours they will work, and how the profits and losses will be shared. In the absence of any agreement (whether formal or informal), partnerships in the United Kingdom are covered by the Partnership Act 1890.

There is also a new type of partnership. This was introduced in 2001. It is known as a *Limited Liability Partnership* (LLP). An LLP has a separate legal personality from that of its owners (like a company), and it protects the partners from personal bankruptcy.

As partnership accounts are very similar in principle to those of sole traders, we shall not be dealing with them in any detail in this book.

Companies

A company is another different type of business organization. There are many different forms of companies but generally the law regards all companies as having a separate existence from that of their owners. In this book, we are going to be primarily concerned with *limited liability companies*. The term 'limited liability' means that the owners of such companies are only required to finance the business up to an agreed amount; once they have contributed that amount, they cannot be called upon to contribute any more, even if the company gets into financial difficulties.

As there is a risk that limited liability companies may not be able to pay off their debts, Parliament has had to give some legal protection to those parties who may become involved with them. The details are contained within the Companies Act 1985. For the moment, we will not say anything more about such entities because we shall be dealing with them in some detail in Chapters 6, 9, 10 and 11.

Activity 1.5	Insert in the following table one advantage and one disadvantage of operating a business as (a) a sole trader; (b) a partnership; and (c) as a limited liability company.

Type of entity	Advantage	Disadvantage
(a) Sole trader		
(b) Partnership		
(c) Limited liability company		

The not-for-profit sector

By 'not-for-profit' we mean those entities whose primary purpose is to provide a service to the public rather than to make a profit from their operations. We will consider this sector under four main headings: (1) central government; (2) local government; (3) quasi-governmental bodies; and (4) social organizations.

Within the three governmental groups, there is a wide variety of different types of entities. We do not need to consider them in any detail since governmental accounting is extremely specialized and it would require a book of its own. We shall also not be dealing with the accounts of social organizations in any great depth because their accounting procedures are similar to profit-making entities.

Central government

Central government is responsible for services such as macro-economic policy, education, defence, foreign affairs, health, and social security. These responsibilities are directly controlled by Cabinet ministers who answer to Parliament at Westminster for their actions. In 1999, some of these central government responsibilities were 'devolved', i.e. they became the direct responsibility of elected bodies in Northern Ireland, Scotland, and Wales.

Local government

For well over a century, central government has also devolved many of its responsibilities to 'local' authorities, i.e. smaller units of authority that have some geographical and community coherence. Councillors are elected by the local community. They have responsibility for those services that central government has delegated, for example, the local administration of education, housing, the police and social services.

Quasi-governmental bodies

Central government also operates indirectly through quasi-governmental bodies, such as the British Broadcasting Corporation (BBC), the Post Office, colleges and universities. Such bodies are nominally independent of central government, although their main funds are normally provided by central government and their senior managers may be appointed by government ministers.

Social organizations

The social organizations category covers a wide range of cultural, educational, recreational and social bodies. Some are formally constituted and professionally managed, such as national and international charities, while others are local organizations run by volunteers on a part-time basis, e.g. bridge and rugby clubs.

Into which category may the following functions/services best be placed? Tick the appropriate column.

Activity 1.6

Function/service	Central government	Local government	Quasi-governmental	Social organization
1 Broadcasting				
2 Famine relief				
3 Postal deliveries				
4 Social services				
5 Work and pensions				

Questions non-accountants should ask

This is an introductory chapter, so at this stage there are not many technical questions that you might be able to put to your accountants. Your questions, therefore, are more likely to revolve round the accountants themselves, the organization of the accounting function within the entity, and the role that the accountants see themselves playing within the entity. The following is a sample of the types of general questions that as a non-accountant you might like to put to the accountants employed within your entity.

- How many accountants are employed by the entity?
- How many of them are 'qualified' and what are their respective professional accountancy bodies?
- How is the accounting function organized?
- What can the accountants do to help me do my job more effectively and efficiently?
- What information do the accountants want me to give to them, when is it wanted, and in what form?
- What is it to be used for?
- What information are they going to give back to me?
- What am I supposed to do with it?
- How can all of the managers and all of the accountants in the entity work together as a team?

Conclusion

The main aim of this chapter has been to introduce the non-accountant to the world of accounting. We have emphasized that the main purpose of accounting is to provide financial information to those parties that need it.

Of course, information must be useful if it is to have any purpose but, as a non-accountant, you may feel reluctant to question any accounting information that lands on your desk. You may also not understand why the accountant is always asking you what you might think are irrelevant questions, and so you respond with any old nonsense. You then perhaps feel a bit guilty and a little frustrated; you would like to know more, but you dare not ask. We hope that by the time you have worked your way through this book, you will have the confidence to ask and, furthermore, that you will understand the answer. Good luck!

Now that the world of accounting has been outlined, we can turn to more detailed subject matter. The first task is to learn the basic rules of accounting. These are covered in the next chapter, but it might be as well if you first read through this chapter again before you move on to Chapter 2. We suggest that you might then attempt some of the questions that end this chapter.

1 To account for something means to explain about it, or report on it.

2 Owners of an entity want to know (a) how well it is doing; (b) what it owes; and (c) how much it is owed to it.

3 Accounting is important for non-accountants because (a) they must make sure their own entity complies with any legal requirements; and (b) an accounting system can provide them with information that will help them do their jobs more effectively and efficiently.

4 The five main branches of accounting are: auditing, financial accounting/reporting financial management, management accounting, and taxation.

5 Sub-branches of accounting include book-keeping (a function of financial accounting), and cost book-keeping, a function of management accounting).

6 There are six major professional accountancy bodies in the UK: the Institute of Chartered Accountants in England and Wales, the Institute of Chartered Accountants in Ireland, the Institute of Chartered Accountants of Scotland, the Association of Chartered Certified Accountants, the Chartered Institute of Management Accountants and the Chartered Institute of Public Finance and Accountancy.

7 There are two economic sectors within the UK economy: the profit-making sector and the not-for-profit sector. Within the profit-making sector, business operations can be classified as being either manufacturing, trading or servicing, and they may be organized as sole trader entities, as partnerships, or as companies.

8 The not-for-profit sector includes central government and local government operations, quasi-governmental bodies, and social organizations. Governmental operations are extremely complex and the accounting requirements are highly specialized. Social organizations are also diverse and they include various associations, charities, clubs, societies and sundry voluntary organizations. Their accounting requirements are usually similar to those found in the profit-making sector.

Check your learning

The answers to these questions may be found within the text.

1 What is accounting?

2 What is an *entity*?

3 Give three reasons why accounting is an important subject for non-accountants to study.

4 Name three main functions that managers undertake.

5 What is meant by the word 'account'?

6 What name is given to the system of recording information that evolved in medieval times?

7 What are the three basic questions that the owner of a business needs to know?

8 What economic event happened in the United Kingdom during the eighteenth century?

9 What happened to the ownership and management of businesses during the nineteenth century in the UK?

10 For what purpose did managers in nineteenth-century industrial entities require more detailed information than had previously been the case?

11 List seven user groups of accounting information.

12 What are the five main branches of accounting?

13 Of which main branch of accounting does cost accounting form a part?

14 What is the difference between *book-keeping* and *cost book-keeping*?

15 Explain what is the difference between 'bankruptcy' and 'liquidation'.

16 List the six major UK professional accountancy bodies.

17 What function does the *Association of Accounting Technicians* fill?

18 Name three types of entities that fall within the profit-making sector of the UK economy.

19 What is meant by the concept of 'limited liability'?

20 What role do local authorities play in the not-for-profit sector of the economy?

21 Name one quasi-governmental body.

News story quiz

Remember the news story at the beginning of this chapter? Go back to that story and reread it before answering the following questions.

From mid-2001 onwards the mass media has been full of stories about alleged accounting 'scandals'. So it is not surprising that the accountancy profession has taken some hard knocks during this period. However, it will perhaps surprise many accountants that their profession appears to be less highly regarded than estate agents and telecom companies.

Questions

1 Looking back over the last couple of years or so, are you aware that there has been a great deal of adverse coverage of the accountancy profession?

2 Can you think of a specific example of a well-publicized accounting scandal? [If you cannot think of an example, log on to the web and type in the search words UK company accounting scandals.]

3 Did the scandal appear to be caused by fraud, human error or a genuine difference of opinion? [If you are not sure, log on to the web.]

4 Who was most to blame for the scandal: (a) company's external auditors; (b) the company's directors; (c) the company's accountants; or (d) the mass media for stirring the whole thing up? Or was it none of these parties?

Tutorial questions

The answers to questions marked with an asterisk may be found in Appendix 4.

1.1 'Accountants stifle managerial initiative and enterprise.' Discuss.

1.2 Do you think that auditors should be responsible for detecting fraud?

1.3 The following statement was made by a student: 'I cannot understand why accountants have such a high status and why they yield such power.' How would you respond to such an assertion?

1.4* Why should a non-accountant study accounting?

1.5* Describe two main purposes of accounting.

1.6* What statutory obligations require the preparation of management accounts in any kind of entity?

1.7 State briefly the main reasons why a company may employ a team of accountants.

1.8* What statutory obligations support the publication of financial accounts in respect of limited liability companies?

1.9 Why does a limited liability company have to engage a firm of external auditors, and for what purpose?

1.10 Assume that you are a personnel officer in a manufacturing company, and that one of your employees is a young engineering manager called Joseph Sykes. Joseph has been chosen to attend the local university's Business School to study for a diploma in management. Joseph is reluctant to attend the course because he will have to study accounting; as an engineer, he thinks that it will be a waste of time for him to study such a subject.

Required:
Draft an internal memorandum addressed to Joseph explaining why it would be of benefit to him to study accounting.

1.11 Clare Wong spends a lot of her time working for a large local charity. The charity has grown enormously in recent years, and the trustees have been advised to overhaul their accounting procedures. This would involve its workers (most of whom are voluntary) in more book-keeping, and there is a great deal of resistance to this move. The staff have said that they are there to help the needy and not to get involved in book-keeping.

Required:
As the financial consultant to the charity, prepare some notes that you could use in speaking to the voluntary workers in order to try to persuade them to accept the new proposals.

Further practice questions, study material and links to relevant sites on the World Wide Web can be found on the website that accompanies this book. The site can be found at **www.booksites.net/dyson**

Contracting companies particularly need to be prudent...

Conservative accounting policies

Following much discussion about the accounting policies used by support services groups, especially those involved with the public sector, Capita went out of its way in its six month results to 30 June 2002 to stress how conservative its accounting policies are.

Executive chairman Rod Aldridge pointed out that Capita consistently applied more conservative accounting than required by the relevant accounting standards, had a simple corporate structure, no special purpose financing vehicles, no associated companies and no long term Private Finance Initiative (PFI) contracts.

The directors of Capita have noted the recent comments regarding accounting policies adopted by companies in the support services sector, particularly with regard to accounting for contract costs.

The relevant accounting standards for contract costs are SSAP 9 Stocks and Long-Term Contracts; FRS 15 Tangible Fixed Assets; and UITF 34 Pre-contract Costs. Capita claims that it has consistently exceeded the requirements of these accounting standards.

The directors consider that Capita's policies are robust, appropriate and consistently more conservative than those required by the relevant accounting standards. The directors have always adopted this approach and they are committed to continuing to follow this prudent policy in the future.

The effect of complying with UITF 34 is, because only of deferral of success fees, to reduce previously reported net, assets at 31 March 2001 by a cumulative £1.8m and net assets at 31 March 2002 by £0.9m.

Profit before tax cumulative to 31 March 2001 is lower by £2.9m and profit before tax for year ended 31 March 2002 by £1.3m.

The results of W S Atkins for the year ended 31 March 2002 were after charging £8.9m (v £6.1m) on PFI bidding, including the Metronet bid for London Underground and the bid for the Colchester Garrison.

The group capitalises its PFI bidding costs in compliance with UITF 34 from the point at which its consortium is appointed sole preferred bidder and when such costs may be foreseen with virtual certainty as recoverable at financial close. W S Atkins capitalised no costs at 31 March 2002 (v £0.1m).

Accountancy, September 2002.

Questions relating to this news story may be found on page 42 ▸▸

About this chapter

Before you can begin to play any card or board game you normally have to learn the rules laid down by the inventor. You could devise your own rules. It might take some time and the game that you play might not be as enjoyable as it would be if you adopted the inventor's rules. Similarly, with accounting. You could adopt your own rules but no one else would understand the accounting information prepared on that basis and it would not be very useful.

Unlike a card or a board game, however, no one sat down and devised a set of rules for preparing accounting information. What happened over a long period of time was that a common procedure gradually evolved. So much so that it is now possible to identify a number of accounting practices that appear to be generally accepted.

In this book we will refer to such practices as *accounting rules*, although some accountants use a number of other terms, e.g. assumptions, axioms, concepts, conventions, postulates, principles and procedures.

This chapter outlines those conventional accounting rules that are widely accepted. The chapter is divided into seven main sections. In the first main section we explain why this chapter is particularly important and relevant for non-accountants. This is followed by a review of the background to the subject. The next three sections outline the main accounting rules. We have classified them under three main headings: *boundary rules, measurement rules* and *ethical rules*. These sections are followed by a section that considers the possibility of preparing accounting information on the basis of what is called a 'conceptual framework'. Before we conclude the chapter we pose some questions that non-accountants should ask about the accounting rules adopted by their own particular entity.

Learning objectives

By the end of this chapter you should be able to:

- **identify the main accounting rules used in preparing accounting information;**
- **classify them into three broad groupings;**
- **describe each accounting rule;**
- **explain why each one of them is important;**
- **outline the main features of a conceptual framework of accounting.**

! Why this chapter is important for non-accountants

As a non-accountant, do you need to question the information that accountants give you? Do you have to know what procedures they use in preparing accounting information? Does it matter if you do not? We think that the answer to all three questions is 'yes'. As a senior manager, you will be ultimately responsible for any decisions made by the entity and you cannot fall back on the excuse that '*it was the accountants that did it*'.

In order to satisfy yourself that the accountants have got it right, you need to be aware of what procedure or rules they have used in preparing any information given to you. In general, they will have used a number of conventional rules that have evolved over many centuries. However, the detailed application of them is subject to a considerable amount of individual interpretation. This means that if you interpret the circumstances differently you can quite easily change the results. For example, it is easy to change the profit or loss that an entity has made by altering the amount charged for the depreciation of fixed assets (such as machinery) or the provision set aside for bad debts (these topics are considered in Chapter 5). Similarly, the cost of making a particular product can be altered by changing the way that overheads are charged to products (see Chapter 16).

We are not suggesting that accountants deliberately act mischievously or even fraudulently in presenting information to management. The important point to grasp is that a considerable amount of individual judgement is required in preparing accounting information. Hence you, as a senior non-accounting manager, need to approve the assumptions and estimates adopted by your accountants. You cannot do that in a meaningful way if you have no idea how accountants go about preparing the information they present to you.

The first step in understanding what they have done is to know what rules they have adopted. The second step is to consider whether they are appropriate for that particular entity. And the third step (if need be) is to challenge the accountants' adoption or interpretation of the rules that they have adopted. It follows that this chapter is a vital one underpinning all that follows in the rest of the book.

We will turn to those rules shortly but first we want to give you more of the background to the subject. We do so in the next section.

Historical development

The practice of accounting has evolved slowly over many centuries. Accounts were prepared originally for stewardship purposes and it is only in more recent times that they have become more widely used. This has meant that some of the traditional practices have had to be adapted to suit more recent requirements. For example, the demand to produce accounts on an annual basis means that a number of arbitrary decisions have to be taken to deal with some events that last for more than one year, such as the building of a power plant.

Users of accounts are not always aware of such difficulties. They sometimes expect accounts to be prepared in a certain way and then they become upset when they find that this not the case. We referred to this phenomena in the last chapter as the 'expectations gap'. It follows that in order to bridge the expectations gap users should be aware of the basis upon which accounts have been prepared, i.e. they have to know the rules.

Until the middle of the nineteenth century accounting rules were largely conventions. They were the ones that had gradually become generally accepted by custom and practice. A number of laws were then introduced to regulate company accounting practices but it was not until 1948 that accounting become much more rule based. Nevertheless, accountants still had a great deal of discretion in how they prepared a set of financial accounts for companies. With other types of entities they had almost complete freedom to do as they wished.

A major change took place in 1971 when the various professional bodies began to issue a series of guides called *Statements of Standard Accounting Practice* (SSAPs). The responsibility for issuing accounting standards was taken over in 1991 by a body called the Accounting Standards Board (ASB). The ASB took responsibility for the existing SSAPs but it also began to issue its own guides called Financial Reporting Standards (FRSs). It is mandatory for professionally qualified accountants to follow the requirements of both SSAPs and FRSs.

SSAPs and FRSs lay down in much greater detail than any legal requirement the way that financial statements must be prepared and presented. They are not absolutely prescriptive but a professionally qualified accountant would have to have some good reasons for ignoring their requirements. We shall be returning briefly to the work of the ASB later in the chapter and then in more detail in Chapter 9.

In this chapter we are going to deal with the conventional rules of accounting that have been developed over a period of time. There are a considerable number that may be identified (perhaps over 100) but we are going to deal with only 14 of them. For convenience we are going to classify them as follows:

1 boundary rules;
2 measurement rules;
3 ethical rules.

A diagrammatic representation of them is shown in Figure 2.1. The way that we have chosen to classify these rules is largely arbitrary. It has been done this way to make it easier for you to understand them. For convenience we also show these accounting rules in an Appendix at the end of the chapter.

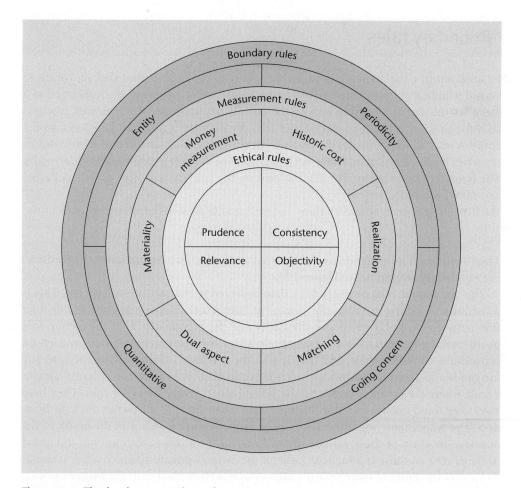

Figure 2.1 **The basic accounting rules**

Activity 2.1	Consult a reputable dictionary (such as the Oxford English) and write down the meaning of the following words. They may each have several meaning so extract the ones that relate more to fact or truths.

(a) assumptions
(b) axioms
(c) concepts
(d) conventions
(e) postulates
(f) principles
(g) procedures.

Consider the definitions that you have extracted carefully. Do they all have a similar meaning?

Boundary rules

In small entities, the owners can probably obtain all the information that they want to know by finding out for themselves. In larger entities this is often impracticable, and so a more formal way of reporting back to the owners has to be devised. However, it would be difficult to inform the owners about literally *everything* that had happened to the entity. A start has to be made, therefore, by determining what should and should not be reported. Hence, accountants have devised a number of what we will call *boundary rules*. The boundary rules attempt to place a limit on the amount and type of data collected and stored within the entity.

There are four main boundary rules, and we examine them in the following subsections.

Entity

There is so much information available about any entity that accountants start by drawing a boundary around it (see Figure 2.2).

The accountant tries to restrict the data collected to that of the entity itself. This is sometimes very difficult, especially in small entities where there is often no clear distinction between the public affairs of the entity and the private affairs of the owner. In a profit-making business, for example, the owners sometimes charge their household expenditure to the business, and they might also use their private bank account to pay for goods and services meant for the business. In such situations, accountants have to decide where the business ends and the private affairs of the owners begin. They have then to establish exactly what the business owes the owner and the owner owes the business. The accountants will, however, only be interested in recording in the books of the business the effect of these various transactions on the *business*; they are not interested in the effect that those transactions have on the owner's private affairs. Indeed, it would be an entirely different exercise if the accountants were to deal with the owner's private affairs. This would mean that they were accounting for different entities altogether, i.e. private entities instead of public ones, although there may be a great deal of overlap between the two types.

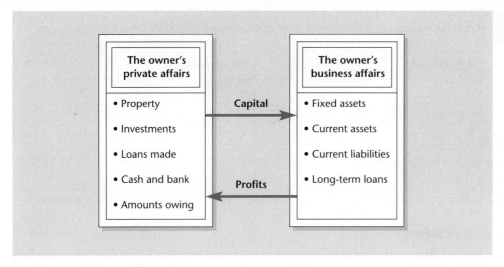

Figure 2.2 **The entity rule: the owner's business and private affairs are kept quite separate**

Periodicity

Most entities have an unlimited life. They are usually started in the expectation that they will operate for an indeterminate period of time, but it is clearly unhelpful for an owner to have to wait years before any report is prepared on how an entity is doing. The owner would almost certainly wish to receive regular reports at frequent short intervals.

If an entity has an unlimited life, any report must be prepared at the end of what must inevitably be an arbitrary period of time. In practice, financial accounting statements are usually prepared annually. Such a time period has developed largely as a matter of custom. It does, however, reflect the natural agricultural cycle in Western Europe, and there does seem to be a natural human tendency to compare what has happened this year with what happened last year. Nevertheless, where entities have an unlimited life (as is usually the case with manufacturing organizations), the preparation of annual accounts presents considerable problems in relating specific events to appropriate accounting periods. We shall be having a look at these problems in Chapter 5.

Apart from custom, there is no reason why an accounting period could not be shorter or longer than twelve months. Management accounts are usually prepared for very short periods, but sometimes this also applies to financial accounts. In the fashion industry, for example, where the product designs may change very quickly, managers may want (say) quarterly reports. By contrast, the construction industry, faced with very long-term contract work, may find it more appropriate to have (say) a five-year reporting period. In fact, irrespective of the length of the main accounting period (i.e. whether it is quarterly or five-yearly), managers usually need regular reports covering a very short period. Cash reports, for example, could be prepared on a weekly, or even on a daily basis.

It must also not be forgotten that some entities (e.g. limited liability companies) are required by law to produce annual accounts, and as tax demands are also based on a calendar year it would not be possible for most entities to ignore the conventional twelve-month period. In any case, given the unlimited life of most entities, you will appreciate that *any* period must be somewhat arbitrary, no matter how carefully a particular entity has tried to relate its accounting period to the nature of its business.

Activity 2.2   List three advantages and disadvantages of preparing financial accounts only once a year.

Advantages	Disadvantages
1	1
2	2
3	3

Going concern

The periodicity rule requires a regular period of account to be established, regardless either of the life of the entity or of the arbitrary nature of such a period. The going concern rule arises out of the periodicity rule. This rule requires an assumption that an entity will continue in existence for the foreseeable future unless some strong evidence exists to suggest that this is not going to be the case. It is important to make absolutely certain that this assumption is correct, because a different set of accounting rules need to be adopted if an entity's immediate future is altogether uncertain.

Quantitative

Accountants usually restrict the data that are collected to those that are easily quantifiable. For example, it is possible to count the number of people that an entity employs, but it is difficult to quantify the *skill* of the employees. Such a concept is almost impossible to put into numbers and it is, therefore, not included in a conventional accounting system.

Measurement rules

The boundary rules determine *what* data should be included in an accounting system, whereas the measurement rules explain *how* those data should be recorded. There are six main measurement rules, and we outline them briefly below.

Money measurement

It would be very cumbersome to record information simply in terms of quantifiable amounts. It would also be impossible to make any fair comparisons between various types of assets (such as livestock and farm machinery), or different types of transactions (such as the sale of eggs and the purchase of corn). In order to make meaningful comparison, we need to convert the data into a common recognizable measure.

As we suggested in Chapter 1, the monetary unit serves such a purpose. It is a useful way of converting accounting data into a common unit, and since most quantifiable information is capable of being translated into monetary terms, there is usually no difficulty in adopting the monetary measurement rule.

Historic cost

The historic cost rule is an extension of the money measurement rule. It requires transactions to be recorded at their *original* (i.e. their historic) cost. Subsequent changes in prices or values, therefore, are usually ignored. Increased costs may arise because of a combination of an improved product, or through changes in the purchasing power of the monetary unit, i.e. through inflation.

Inflation tends to overstate the level of accounting profit as it is traditionally calculated. Over the last 35 years, there have been several attempts in the United Kingdom to change the method of accounting in order to allow for the effects of inflation. There has been so much disagreement on what should replace what is called *historic cost accounting* (HCA) that no other method has been acceptable. Throughout most of this book, we shall be adopting the historic cost rule.

Realization

One of the problems of putting the periodicity rule into practice is that it is often difficult to relate a specific transaction to a particular period. For example, assume that a business arranges to sell some goods in 2004, it delivers them in 2005, and it is paid for them in 2006. In which year were the goods *sold*: 2004, 2005 or 2006? In conventional accounting it would be most unusual to include them in the sales for 2004, because the business has still got a legal title to them. They could be included in the accounts for 2006 when the goods have been paid for. Indeed, this method of accounting is not uncommon. It is known as *cash flow accounting* (CFA). In CFA, transactions are only entered in the books of account when a cash exchange has taken place. By contrast, in HCA it is customary to enter most transactions in the books of account when the legal title to the goods has been transferred from one party to another and when there is an *obligation* for the recipient to pay for them. This means that, in the above example, under HCA the goods would normally be considered to have been sold in 2005.

The realization rule covers this point. It requires transactions relating to the sale of goods to be entered in the accounts for that period in which the legal title for them has been transferred from one party to another. In the jargon of accounting, they are then said to be *realized*. It is important to appreciate that for goods and services to be treated as realized, they do not need to have been paid for: the cash for them may be received during a later period (or for that matter, may have been received in an earlier period).

The realization rule is normally regarded as applying to sales, but *purchases* (meaning goods that are intended for resale) may be treated similarly. Thus, they would not be included in an entity's accounts until it had a legal title to them (i.e. until in law it would be regarded as owning them).

The realization rule can produce some rather misleading results. For example, a company may treat goods as having been sold in 2004. In 2005 it finds that the purchaser cannot pay for them. What can it do? Its accounts for 2004 have already been approved and it is too late to change them, but obviously the sales for that year were overstated (and so too, almost certainly, was the profit). The customer defaults in 2005, and so how can the *bad debt* (as it is known) be dealt with in *that* year? We shall be explaining how in Chapter 5.

<table>
<tr><td>Activity 2.3</td><td>A contracting company divides each of its orders into five stages: (1) on order; (2) on despatch; (3) on installation; (4) on commissioning; and (5) on completion of a 12-month warranty period. Assume that an order for Contract A (worth £100,000) is signed on 1 January 2004 and the warranty period ends on 31 December 2006. In which accounting period or periods would you treat the £100,000 as revenue (i.e. sales)? Would it be appropriate to apportion it over the three years of the contract?</td></tr>
</table>

Matching

The realization rule relates mainly to the purchase and sale of goods, in other words to what are known as *trading items*. However, a similar rule known as the *matching rule* applies to other incomes (such as dividends and rents received) and expenditure (such as electricity and wages). The matching rule is illustrated in Figure 2.3.

A misleading impression would be given if the cash received during a particular period was simply compared with the cash paid out during the same period. The exact period in which the cash is either received or paid may bear no relationship to the period in which the business was transacted. Thus, accountants normally adjust cash received and cash paid on what is known as an *accruals and prepayments* basis. An accrual is an amount that is *owed* by the entity at the end of an accounting period in respect of services received during that period. A prepayment is an amount that is *owing* to the entity at the end of the accounting period as a result of it paying in advance for services to be rendered in respect of a future period.

The conversion of cash received and cash paid to an accruals and prepayments basis at the end of an accounting period often involves a considerable amount of arithmetical adjustment. Account has to be taken for accruals and prepayments at the end of the previous period (i.e *opening* accruals and prepayments), as well as for accruals and prepayments at the end of the current period (i.e. *closing* accruals and prepayments). Accruals and prepayments are covered in more detail in Chapter 5.

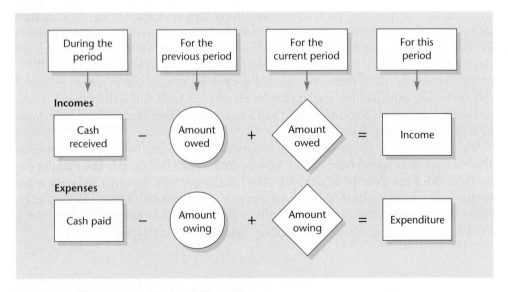

Figure 2.3 **Illustration of the matching rule**

An accruals and prepayments system of accounting enables the incomes of one period to be matched much more fairly against the costs of the same period. The comparison is not distorted by the accidental timing of cash receipts and cash payments. However, as the matching rule requires the accountant to estimate the level of both accruals and prepayments at the end of each accounting period, a degree of subjectivity is automatically built into the estimate.

Dual aspect

The dual aspect rule is a useful practical rule, although it really only reflects what is obvious. It is built round the fact that every time something is given, someone (or something) else receives it. In other words, every time a transaction take place, there is always a twofold effect. For example, if the amount of cash in a business goes up, someone must have given it; or if the business buys some goods, then someone else must be selling them.

We explained in Chapter 1 that this twofold effect was recognized many centuries ago. It gave rise to the system of recording information known as *double-entry book-keeping*. This system of book-keeping is still widely used. Although the concept is somewhat obvious, it has proved extremely useful, so much so that even modern computerized recording systems are based on it. From long experience, it has been found that the system is a most convenient way of recording all sorts of useful information about the entity, and of ensuring some form of control over its affairs.

There is no real need to adopt the dual aspect rule in recording information: it is entirely a practical rule that has proved itself over many centuries. Voluntary organizations (such as a drama club or a stamp collecting society) may not think that it is worthwhile to adopt the dual aspect rule, but you are strongly recommended to incorporate it into your book-keeping system in any entity with which you are concerned. If you do, you will find that it gives you more control over the entity's affairs besides providing you with a great deal more information.

Double-entry book-keeping will be examined in more detail in the next chapter.

Materiality

Strict application of the various accounting rules may not always be practical. It could involve a considerable amount of work that may be out of all proportion to the information that is eventually obtained. The materiality rule permits other rules to be ignored if the effects are not considered to be *material*, that is, if they are not significant.

Hence, the materiality rule avoids the necessity to follow other accounting rules to the point of absurdity. For example, it would normally be considered unnecessary to value the closing stock of small amounts of stationery, or to maintain detailed records of inexpensive items of office equipment. However, it should be borne in mind that what is immaterial for a large organization may not be so for a small one.

If you decide that a certain item is immaterial, then it does not matter how you deal with it in the accounts, because it cannot possibly have any significant effect on the results. When dealing with insignificant items, therefore, the materiality rule permits the other accounting rules to be ignored.

Ethical rules

There is an old story in accounting about the company chairman who asked his chief accountant how much profit the company had made. The chief accountant replied by asking how much profit the chairman would like to make. Accountants recognize that there is some truth in this story, since it is quite possible for different accountants to use the same basic data in preparing accounting statements yet still arrive at different levels of profit!

You might think that by faithfully following all of the accounting rules, *all* accountants should be able to calculate exactly the same amount of profit. Unfortunately this is not the case since, as we have seen, most of the main accounting rules are capable of wide interpretation. The matching rule, for example, requires an estimate to be made of amounts owing and owed at the end of an accounting period, while the materiality rule allows the accountant to decide just what is material. Both rules involve an element of subjective judgement, and so no two accountants are likely to agree precisely on how they should be applied.

In order to limit the room for individual manoeuvre, a number of other rules have evolved. These rules are somewhat ethical in nature and, indeed, some authors refer to them as accounting *principles* (thereby suggesting that there is a moral dimension to them). Other authors, however, refer to *all* of the basic accounting rules as principles, but it really does not matter what you call them as long as you are aware of them. Basically, the ethical rules require accountants to follow not just the letter but the spirit of the other rules.

There are four main ethical accounting rules. They are reviewed below.

Prudence

The prudence rule (which is sometimes known as *conservatism*) arises out of the need to make a number of estimates in preparing periodic accounts. Managers and owners are often naturally over-optimistic about future events. As a result, there is a tendency to be too confident about the future, and not to be altogether realistic about the entity's prospects. There may, for example, be undue optimism over the creditworthiness of a particular customer. Insufficient allowance may therefore be made for the possibility of a bad debt. This might have the effect of overstating profit in one period and understating it in a future period. We shall come across this problem again in Chapter 5.

The prudence rule is sometimes expressed in the form of a simple maxim:

> *If in doubt, overstate losses and understate profits.*

Activity 2.4

Supermarket companies sometimes receive a discount in advance from suppliers for meeting a specified sales target. Such discounts may be paid in advance. The accounting treatment of the discount could be dealt with in several ways: (1) it could be included in the profit and loss account for the period in which it was received; or (2) it could be amortized (apportioned) over the span of the contract; or (3) it could be included in the profit and loss account for the period in which the sales target is met.

To what extent is the accounting treatment of such discounts an ethical decision? Prepare some notes indicating how you think this problem should be dealt with.

Consistency

As we have seen, the preparation of traditional accounting statements requires a considerable amount of individual judgement to be made in the application of the basic accounting rules. To compensate for this flexibility, the consistency rule states that, once specific accounting policies have been adopted, they should be followed in all subsequent accounting periods.

It would be considered quite unethical to change rules just because they were unfashionable, or because alternative ones gave better results. Of course, if the circumstances of the entity change radically it may be necessary to adopt different policies, but this should only be done in exceptional circumstances. If different policies are adopted, then the effect of any change should be clearly highlighted and any comparative figure adjusted accordingly.

The application of this rule gives confidence to the users of accounting statements, because if the accounts have been prepared on a consistent basis they can be assured that they are comparable with previous sets of accounts.

Objectivity

Accounts should be prepared with the minimum amount of bias. This is not an easy task, since individual judgement is required in interpreting the rules and adapting them to suit particular circumstances. Owners may want, for example, to adopt policies which would result in higher profit figures, or in disguising poor results.

If optional policy decisions are possible within the existing rules, it is advisable to fall back on the prudence rule. Indeed, it tends to be an overriding one. If there is any doubt about which rule to adopt (or how it should be interpreted), the prudence rule tends to take precedence.

It must be recognized, however, that if the prudence rules is always adopted as the easy way out of a difficult problem, someone preparing a set of accounts could be accused of lacking objectivity. In other words, you must not use this rule to avoid making difficult decisions. Indeed, it is just as unfair to be as excessively cautious as it is to be wildly optimistic. Extremism of any kind suggests a lack of objectivity, so you should avoid being either over-cautious or over-optimistic.

Relevance

The amount of information that could be supplied to any interested party is practically unlimited. If too much information is disclosed, it becomes very difficult to absorb, and so it should only be included if it is it going to help the user.

The selection of relevant information requires much experience and judgement, as well as a great understanding of the user's requirements. The information needs to be designed in such a way that it meets the *objectives* of the specific user group. If too much information is given, the users might think that it is an attempt to mislead them and, as a result, all of the information may be totally rejected.

A conceptual framework

This chapter discusses the basic accounting rules, which have evolved over a period of time; nobody worked them out on paper before they were applied in practice. This means that when some new accounting problem arises, we do not always know how to deal with it. Some accountants (especially university lecturers) argue that what is needed is a *conceptual framework*. In other words, we ought to devise a theoretical model of accounting, and then any new accounting problem could be solved merely by running it through the model.

It sounds very sensible, but it is not easy to devise such a model. Several attempts have been made, and none of them has been particularly successful. Basically, there are two approaches that can be adopted:

1 We can list all the accounting rules that have ever been used, and then extract the ones that are the most widely used. There are two main problems in adopting this approach:
   (a) To be meaningful, we would have to conduct an extremely wide survey of existing practice. As yet, the sheer scale required by this exercise has defeated most researchers.
   (b) Such an exercise would simply freeze existing practice: it would not improve it.
2 Alternatively, we could determine:
   (a) who uses accounting statements;
   (b) what they want them for (i.e. we would need to establish *user objectives*); and
   (c) what rules we need to adopt to meet those objectives.

The Accounting Standards Board (ASB) referred to at the beginning of the chapter has attempted to construct a conceptual framework using the second approach. The details are contained in a document published in 1999 called *Statement of Principles for Financial Reporting*.

The Statement is not an accounting standard and it is not mandatory for professionally qualified accountants to adopt it. Nevertheless, it is highly influential. It sets out the basic principles that the ASB believes should underpin what it calls 'general purpose financial statements' such as annual financial statements, financial statements in interim reports, preliminary announcements and summary financial statements.

The Statement is 30 pages long and it is divided into eight chapters. A brief summary of its contents is outlined below.

Chapter 1 lays down the objectives of financial statements, i.e. 'to provide information that is useful to those for whom they are prepared'. However, consideration needs to be given to those parties who use the information, what information they need and what role financial statements play in that process.

Chapter 2 identifies those entities that ought to publish financial statements. These include those entities that are cohesive economic units and where there is a legitimate demand for the information contained within such statements.

Chapter 3 describes the qualitative characteristics of financial information. As it complements much of the material in *this* chapter, it would be useful if we outline its main contents in a little more detail. The Statement argues that in order to make financial information useful it should consist of the following qualities:

1 *Materiality.* Information should be provided to users if their economic decisions would be affected either by its omission or by misstating it.

2 *Relevance.* Information should be capable of (a) influencing the economic decisions of users; and (b) being provided in time to influence the decisions. You will recall that earlier we regarded 'relevance' as being an 'ethical' rule.

3 *Reliability.* Information should (a) reflect the substance of events and transactions; (b) be free from deliberate bias and material error; and (c) incorporate a degree of caution when containing uncertain circumstances.

4 *Comparability.* Information should be presented in such a way that it is possible to ascertain similarities and spot differences over time and between entities.

5 *Comprehensibility.* The ASB does not object to information being provided even if some users would not understand it. Generally, it expects users to have a 'reasonable knowledge of business and economic activities and accounting and a willingness to study with reasonable diligence the information provided'. Now you know why you are studying accounting.

Chapter 4 identifies the main elements that should go to make up the financial statements such as assets (what the entity owns) and liabilities (what the entity owes). It refers to these elements as 'building blocks'. In subsequent chapters of this book, we will be dealing with the 'building blocks' of accounting.

Chapter 5 considers when events and transactions should be recognized in financial statements. We dealt with this particular aspect in the earlier part of this chapter when outlining the 'measurement' rules. *Chapter 6* complements Chapter 5 and considers how assets and liabilities should be measured. Again, we have covered much of this topic in our 'measurement rule' section earlier in this chapter. *Chapter 7* considers the characteristics of 'good' presentation so that financial statements are communicated clearly and effectively.

Chapter 8 is a highly specialized chapter involving the inclusion of information in financial statements that reflects an entity's interest in other entities. We shall only be dealing briefly with this topic in Chapters 10 and 11 of this book.

You will appreciate from the above summary that the Statement is couched in very general terms. It does not provide a precise set of rules for the preparation of financial statements and it certainly is not prescriptive. Thus it is not like the instructions that you get if you purchase a board game such as *Cluedo* or *Monopoly*. Rather, the ASB has put forward some basic concepts underpinning the preparation of financial statements. You then need to know how to apply those concepts when you prepare a set of financial statements. Part 2 of this book aims to provide you with the guidance you need.

You may have found it disappointing (especially if you are an engineer or a scientist) that by the end of this section we have not been able to provide you with a precise conceptual framework equivalent to a laboratory or a physical model for the presentation of financial statements. Unfortunately, there are so many variable factors in the social sciences that this is almost an impossible task.

Thus to a non-accountant, the ASB's *Statement of Principles* may appear totally unsatisfactory. Nevertheless it is a considerable landmark in the history of accounting. There has been much opposition to the ideas being pursued by the ASB and the Board has not felt itself to be in a position to make its principles mandatory. It is likely to be very many years before that position is reached and it is even more doubtful whether a more detailed framework can ever be formulated.

Activity 2.5

As a non-accountant you probably approach the idea of a conceptual accounting framework with an open mind. What are your ideas about the users of financial statements and what they want from such statements? Suggest some rules that should be adopted in preparing financial statements for those users that you have identified. But don't just copy ones outlined in this chapter.

Possible users	What they want	Rules to be followed

❗ Questions non-accountants should ask

This is a most important chapter. Apart from preparing the foundation for what follows in the rest of the book, it provides you with a number of important accounting issues that are extremely relevant and important in the real world. While you may be advised by your accountants, ultimately you will be responsible for any action taken by the entity you work for. So it is important that you know what your accountants have done and why.

Some of the accounting rules outlined in this chapter are fairly non-controversial. The entity, periodicity, quantitative, money measurement, matching and dual aspect rules do not normally cause too much of a problem. The application of the remaining rules can cause a problem, so you must question the application of them. We suggest that you pose the following questions.

- What absolute assurances can you give me that the entity is a going concern?
- What justification is there for including all our transactions at their historic cost?
- Can we use a more up-to-date cost for some items, e.g. property?
- How would we then value and depreciate such items?
- Is the method used for the determination of income absolutely cast-iron?
- What method have you used for determining what is an immaterial item?
- To what extent has the need for prudence been overridden by the need to be objective?
- Are there any items in the accounts that could be justifiably left out or presented in a different way without any problems?

Conclusion

In this chapter we have identified 14 basic accounting rules that accountants usually adopt in the preparation of accounting statements. We have described four of these rules as boundary rules, six as measurement rules and four as ethical rules. We have argued that the boundary rules limit the amount and type of information that is traditionally collected and stored in an accounting system. The measurement rules provide some guidance on how that information should be recorded, and the ethical rules lay down a code of conduct on how all the other rules should be interpreted.

The exact number, classification and description of these various accounting rules is subject to much debate among accountants. Most entities can adopt what rules they like, although it would be most unusual if they did not accept the going concern, matching, prudence and consistency rules.

In the next chapter, we shall examine the dual aspect rule in a little more detail. This rule is at the heart of double-entry book-keeping and most modern accounting systems are based upon it.

Key points

1 In preparing accounting statements, accountants adopt a number of rules that have evolved over a number of centuries.

2 There are four main boundary rules: entity, periodicity, going concern, and quantitative.

3 Measurement rules include: money measurement, historic cost, realization, matching, dual aspect, and materiality.

4 Ethical rules include: prudence, consistency, objectivity, and relevance.

5 No satisfactory conceptual framework of accounting has yet been developed by the accountancy profession. The ASB has issued a *Statement of Principles for Financial Reporting*, but this Statement is neither highly prescriptive nor mandatory.

Check your learning

The answers to these questions may be found within the text.

1 Name three other terms that mean the same as accounting rules.

2 What do the following initials stand for: (a) SSAP; (b) FRS; and (c) ASB?

3 List three categories of accounting rules.

4 What is meant by an 'entity'?

5 What accounting rule is used to describe a defined period of time?

6 What is a 'going concern'?

7   What types of qualitative information is normally included in financial statements?

8   Name three non-monetary items included in most financial statements.

9   Name one type of asset that may not be included at its historic cost in financial statements?

10   What is another term for 'matching'?

11   What does 'dual aspect mean?

12   How do you decide whether or not a transaction is 'material'?

13   Are *prudence* and *objectivity* compatible?

14   Is the consistency rule ever disregarded?

15   What concept is used to determine whether any items included in financial statements is relevant?

16   What is a conceptual framework?

17   What two approaches may be adopted in framing a conceptual framework?

18   What is the ASB's approach to the adoption of a conceptual framework?

19   Name the five qualities that the ASB regard as being desirable in order to make financial statements useful.

News story quiz

Remember the news story at the beginning of this chapter? Go back to that story and reread it before answering the following questions.

This news story deals with two companies (Capita and W S Atkins) both of whom are involved in the construction industry. If a contract takes longer than one year to complete, at what point should the company take any expected profit? A prudent approach would be to wait until the contract has finished. A highly imprudent one would be to take all the expected profit when the contract was signed. The accountancy profession's answer is to take some profit on account provided certain conditions are met.

Questions

1   What do you think the directors of Capita mean when they state that they have exceeded the requirements of various accounting standards?

2   Do you think that W S Atkins is adopting a conservative (i.e. prudent) accounting approach when it capitalizes building costs 'from the point at which its consortium is appointed sole preferred bidder and when such costs may be seen with virtual certainty as recoverable at financial close'? Is there such a thing as 'virtual certainty'?

3   In which accounting period should a construction company take the profit on a contract: (a) when the contract is signed; (b) apportioned over the life of the contract; (c) when the contract is completed; (d) when the warranty period is over; (e) when it is clear a profit will be made?

4   What are the repercussions of taking profit before the contracting company's obligations have completely ended?

5   What can such a company do if it takes a profit and then the contract ultimately results in a loss?

Tutorial questions

The answers to questions marked with an asterisk may be found in Appendix 4.

2.1   Do you think that when a set of financial accounts is being prepared, the prudence rule should override the objectivity rule?

2.2   'The law should lay down precise formats, contents, and methods for the preparation of limited liability company accounts.' Discuss.

2.3   The Accounting Standards Board now bases its Financial Reporting Standards on what might be regarded as a 'conceptual framework'. How far do you think that this approach is likely to be successful?

In questions 2.4, 2.5 and 2.6 you are required to state which accounting rule the accountant would most probably adopt in dealing with the various problems.

2.4*   Electricity consumed in period 1 and paid for in period 2.
        Equipment originally purchased for £20 000 which would now cost £30 000.
        The company's good industrial relations record.
        A five-year construction contract.
        A customer who might go bankrupt owing the company £5000.
        The company's vehicles, which would only have a small scrap value if the company goes into liquidation.

2.5*   A demand by the company's chairman to include every detailed transaction in the presentation of the annual accounts.
        A sole-trader business which has paid the proprietor's income tax based on the business profits for the year.
        A proposed change in the methods of valuing stock.
        The valuation of a litre of petrol in one vehicle at the end of accounting period 1.
        A vehicle which could be sold for more than its purchase price.
        Goods which were sold to a customer in period 1, but for which the cash was only received in period 2.

2.6*   The proprietor who has supplied the business capital out of his own private bank account.
        The sales manager who is always very optimistic about the creditworthiness of prospective customers.
        The managing director who does not want annual accounts prepared as the company operates a continuous 24-hour-a-day, 365-days-a-year process.

At the end of period 1, it is difficult to be certain whether the company will have to pay legal fees of £1000 or £3000.

The proprietor who argues that the accountant has got a motor vehicle entered twice in the books of account.

Some goods were purchased and entered into stock at the end of period 1, but they were not paid for until period 2.

2.7 The following is a list of problems which an accountant may well meet in practice:

The transfer fee of a footballer.

Goods are sold in one period, but the cash for them is received in a later period.

The proprietor's personal dwelling house has been used as security for a loan which the bank has granted to the company.

What profit to take in the third year of a five-year construction contract.

Small stocks of stationery held at the accounting year end.

Expenditure incurred in working on the improvement of a new drug.

Required:
State:
(1) which accounting rule the accountant would most probably adopt in dealing with each of the above problems; and
(2) the reasons for your choice.

2.8 FRS 18 (Accounting Policies) states that profits shall be treated as realized and included in the profit and loss account only when the cash due 'can be assessed with reasonable certainty' (para. 28).

How far do you think that this requirement removes any difficulty in determining in which accounting period a sale has taken place?

2.9 The adoption of the realization and matching rules in preparing financial accounts requires a great deal of subjective judgement.

Required:
Write an essay examining whether it would be fairer, easier, and more meaningful to prepare financial accounts on a cash received/cash paid basis.

Further practice questions, study material and links to relevant sites on the World Wide Web can be found on the website that accompanies this book. The site can be found at **www.booksites.net/dyson**

Appendix   Summary of the accounting rules

It would be convenient at this stage if we summarized the basic accounting rules outlined in the chapter so that it will be easy for you to refer back when studying later chapters. In summary they are as follows.

Boundary rules

1 **Entity**. Accounting data must be restricted to the entity itself. The data should exclude the private affairs of those individuals who either own or manage the entity, except in so far as they impact directly on it.

2 **Periodicity**. Accounts should be prepared at the end of a defined period of time, and this period should be adopted as the regular period of account.

3 **Going concern**. The accounts should be prepared on the assumption that the entity will continue in existence for the foreseeable future.

4 **Quantitative**. Only data that are capable of being easily quantified should be included in an accounting system.

Measurement rules

1 **Money measurement**. Data must be translated into monetary terms before they are included in an accounting system.

2 **Historic cost**. Financial data should be recorded in the books of account at their historic cost, that is, at their original purchase cost or at their original selling price.

3 **Realization**. Transactions that reflect financial data should be entered in the books of account when the legal title to them has been transferred from one party to another party, irrespective of when a cash settlement takes place.

4 **Matching**. Cash received and cash paid during a particular accounting period should be adjusted in order to reflect the economic activity that has actually taken place during that period.

5 **Dual aspect**. All transactions should be recorded in such a way that they capture the giving and the receiving effect of each transaction.

6 **Materiality**. The basic accounting rules must not be rigidly applied to insignificant items.

Ethical rules

1 **Prudence**. If there is some doubt over the treatment of a particular transaction, income should be underestimated and expenditure overestimated, so that profits are more likely to be understated and losses overstated.

2 **Consistency**. Accounting rules and policies should not be amended unless there is a fundamental change in circumstances that necessitates a reconsideration of the original rules and policies.

3 **Objectivity**. Personal prejudice must be avoided in the interpretation of the basic accounting rules.

4 **Relevance**. Accounting statements should not include information that prevents users from obtaining a true and fair view of the information being communicated to them.

FINANCIAL ACCOUNTING

Part 2

In Part 2 we outline the principles of double-entry book-keeping and explain how to prepare financial accounts for sole traders, companies, and for some other types of entities in the not-for-profit sector. The relationship of Part 2 to the rest of the book is shown below.

Part 1
INTRODUCTION TO ACCOUNTING

1 The accounting world
2 Accounting rules

Part 2
FINANCIAL ACCOUNTING

3 Recording data
4 Sole trader accounts
5 Last minute adjustments
6 Company accounts
7 Other entity accounts
8 Cash flow statements

Part 3
FINANCIAL REPORTING

9 Information disclosure
10 The annual report
11 The annual accounts
12 Interpretation of accounts
13 Contemporary issues

Part 4
MANAGEMENT ACCOUNTING

14 Foundations
15 Direct costs
16 Indirect costs
17 Budgeting
18 Standard costing
19 Contribution analysis
20 Specific decisions
21 Capital investment
22 Emerging issues

Was a poor data recording system also to blame? . . .

HIH collapse could result in charges

BY PHILIP ALDRICK

CRIMINAL charges are likely to be brought against several former directors of HIH Insurance, which was Australia's biggest corporate collapse, after lawyers yesterday identified more than 1,000 possible breaches of the law.

Presenting its final submission after 201 sittings and testimony from 194 witnesses, the prosecution argued that the primary reason for HIH's collapse in March 2001 with debts estimated at A\$5.3 billion (£2 billion) was an inability to estimate its liabilities.

However, Wayne Martin, senior counsel for the royal commission – Australia's highest form of public inquiry – also attacked HIH's founder and former chief executive Ray Williams alongside other executives for their "dishonest" actions. Senior executives were said to have manipulated accounts to show non-existent profits and hide losses in Britain and the United States.

Among the policies written by HIH's British branch were personal injury for the Taiwan military and insurance on football results.

HIH's auditors, the now defunct Arthur Andersen, did not escape censure. "They were well aware of the aggressive accounting approach taken by management and of the risks, yet failed to respond with appropriate diligence and resolve," Mr Martin said.

False accounting, executive "self-indulgence" and faulty business decisions were said to have preceded HIH's meltdown. "The numbers of adverse findings [on] undesirable corporate governance, inappropriate discharge of regulatory obligation or possible breaches of civil or criminal law, are … well over 1,000," Mr Martin said. However, the "simplistic answer as to why HIH collapsed is its recurrent failure to adequately estimate the claims liabilities from the underwriting risks taken."

The submissions are expected to continue until Wednesday.

The Daily Telegraph, 14 January 2003.

Questions relating to this news story may be found on page 70 ▸▸

About this chapter

In the last chapter a number of basic accounting rules were outlined. You may recall that one of these rules was the *dual aspect* rule. In this chapter we are going to examine the dual aspect rule in much more detail.

This chapter explains how accountants use the dual aspect rule to record data and how periodically the records are checked to ensure that they are accurate. This is done by compiling what is known as a 'trial balance'. The trial balance is then used to prepare a profit and loss account and a balance sheet. We deal with such financial statements in Chapter 4.

The current chapter is divided into nine main sections. We start with an explanation of why the chapter is of importance to non-accountants. The following section introduces you to what is known as 'the accounting equation'. After that we go into some detail about the complex topic of double-entry book-keeping. This is followed by a section that illustrates how to work with various types of accounts. The material so far used in the chapter is then brought together in a comprehensive example. The next section after that shows you how to balance accounts and the one after that how to insert the various account balances in a trial balance. That section is followed by a discussion of the errors not disclosed in a trial balance. The last main section of the chapter poses some questions that are relevant for non-accountants to ask about the contents of the chapter.

Learning objectives

By the end of this chapter, you should be able to:
- **explain what is meant by the accounting equation;**
- **define the terms 'debit' and 'credit';**
- **write up some simple ledger accounts;**
- **extract a trial balance;**
- **identify six errors not revealed in a trial balance.**

! Why this chapter is important for non-accountants

This chapter is important for non-accountants for the following reasons.

1 *To learn the language accountants use.* The chapter will enable you to become familiar with the language and terminology used by accountants. Hence it will be much easier to discuss with them any issues arising from the reports that they prepare for you.
2 *To check the reliability of information presented to you.* The chapter gives you a basic knowledge of the fundamental recording systems used by all types of entities throughout the world. You will then be able to assess the reliability of any accounting information based on the data that has been included in the system. You will also be more aware of what information has *not* been recorded. This will enable you to take into account what is missing from the accounts when considering the usefulness of any information presented to you by your accountants.
3 *To debate with accountants on equal terms.* Accounting information is based on a considerable number of questionable assumptions. These may not be valid in particular circumstances. If you are familiar with the language and nuances of fundamental accounting procedures, you will be able to have a much more meaningful and relevant debate with your accountants about the type of information that is useful to you in your job.

We suggest that in studying this chapter you adopt the following procedure.

1 Read the descriptive material in each section very carefully.
2 Make sure that you understand the requirements of each example.
3 Examine the answer to each example, paying particular attention to the following points:
   (a) the way in which it has been presented;
   (b) how the data in the exhibit have been converted in response to the requirements of the example.

4 Once you have worked through the answer, try to do the example on your own without looking at the answer.

5 If you do go wrong or you find that you do not know how to do the example, reread the earlier parts of the chapter and then have another go at doing it.

6 Attempt each 'Activity' as you come across them (some of them remind you to try doing each example on your own).

We begin our study of the dual aspect rule by explaining what is meant by the 'accounting equation'.

The accounting equation

As we explained in Chapters 1 and 2, the system that accountants use to record financial data is known as *double-entry book-keeping*. Double-entry book-keeping is based on the dual aspect rule, i.e. a recognition that every transaction has a twofold effect. Thus if I loan you £100, a two-fold effect arises because (1) I give you some money; and (2) you receive it. The transaction, however, has also a twofold effect on *both of us*. This point may be a little clearer if we summarize the position as follows:

● *The effect on you*: (1) your cash goes up by £100; and (2) what you owe me also goes up by £100.
● *The effect on me*: (2) my cash goes down by £100; and (2) what I am owed by you goes up by £100.

In practice, an accountant would probably only deal with one or other of the entities, i.e. either 'you' or 'me'. This is what accountants mean about a 'twofold effect' and a double-entry book-keeping system captures this effect.

Before we describe how this system works in practice, it is necessary to introduce you to three essential accounting terms. These are as follows:

1 *Assets*: Assets are possessions or resources *owned* by an entity. They include physical or tangible possessions such as property, plant, machinery, stock, and cash and bank balances. They also include intangible assets, i.e. non-physical possessions such as copyright and patent rights, as well as debts owed to the entity, i.e. trade and other debtors.

2 *Capital*: 'Capital' is the term used to describe the amount which the owners have invested in an entity. In effect, their 'capital' is the amount owed by the entity to its owners.

3 *Liabilities*: Liabilities are the opposite of assets. They are the amounts owed *by* an entity to outside parties. They include loans, bank overdrafts, creditors, i.e. amounts owing to parties for the supply of goods and services to the entity that have not yet been settled in cash.

There is a close relationship between assets, capital and liabilities and it is frequently presented in the form of what is called the 'accounting equation'. It is as follows:

Assets = Capital and Liabilities

In other words, what the entity owns in terms of possessions has been financed by a combination of funds provided by the owners and amounts borrowed.

We will illustrate the use of the accounting equation with a simple example. Let us assume that you have decided to go into business. You do so by transferring £1000 in cash from your own private bank account. Invoking the entity rule, we are not interested in your private affairs, but we do want to keep track of how the business deals with your £1000.

You have invested £1000 in the business. This is its capital. However, it now possesses £1000 in cash. The cash is an asset. Hence the £1000 asset equals the £1000 of capital. In other words we can express the relationship between the assets and the capital in equation form as follows:

Assets		Capital	
Cash	£1000	Capital	£1000

The equation captures the twofold effect of the transaction: the assets of the business have been increased by the capital that has been contributed by the owner.

Now suppose that you then decide to transfer £500 of the cash to a business bank account. The effect on the equation is as follows:

Assets		Capital	
	£		£
Bank	500	Capital	1000
Cash	500		
	1000		1000

As you can see, there has simply been a change on the *assets* side of the equation.

Suppose now that you borrow £500 in cash from one of your friends to provide further financial help to the business. The assets will be increased by an inflow of £500 in cash, but £500 will be owed to your friend. The £500 owed is a liability and your friend has become a creditor of the business. The business has total assets of £1500 (£500 at the bank and £1000 in cash). Its capital is £1000 and it has a liability of £500. The equation then reads as follows:

Assets		Capital		Liabilities	
	£		£		£
Bank	500	Capital	1000	Creditor	500
Cash	1000				
	1500		1000		500

If £800 of goods are purchased in cash for subsequent resale to the entity's customers, the equation would read:

Assets				Capital				Liabilities	
	£				£				£
Stocks	800	=	Capital	1000	+	Creditor	500
Bank	500						
Cash	200			1000			500
	1500						

Again there has been a change on the assets side of the equation when £800 of the cash (an asset) was used to purchase £800 of goods for resale (i.e. stocks), another asset.

The equation is becoming somewhat complicated but it does enable us to see the effect that *any* transaction has on it. The vital point to remember about the accounting equation may be summarized as follows:

> If an adjustment is made to one side of the equation, you *must* make an identical adjustment *either* to the other side of the equation *or* to the same side.

This maxim reflects the basic rule of double-entry book-keeping:

> **Every transaction must be recorded twice.**

We will explain how this is done in the next section.

Activity 3.1

Fill in the missing blanks in the following statements:

(a) The accounting equation is represented by _____ = _____ + _____.

(b) Every transaction must be recorded _____.

Double-entry book-keeping

The accounting equation reflects the twofold effect of every transaction and a double-entry book-keeping system records that effect. This means that just as every transaction results in two adjustments being made to the accounting equation, two 'entries' are made in 'the books of account'.

All transactions are classified into appropriate groups and each group is stored separately in what is known as an *account*. An account is simply a history or a record of a particular type of transaction. The accounts are usually kept in bound books known as *ledgers*, although most entities now use a computerized system. Both computerized and non-computerized recording systems adopt the same basic accounting principles, so that a study of a manually based system of double-entry book-keeping is still relevant.

The effect of entering a particular transaction once in one ledger account and again in another ledger account is to cause the balance on each of the two accounts either to go up or to go down (in just the same way as happens to the accounting equation). So a particular transaction could either *increase* or *decrease* the total amount held in an account. In other words, an account either *receives* an additional amount or it *gives* (i.e. releases) an existing amount. It is this receiving and giving effect that has given rise to two terms from Latin that are commonly used in accounting. These terms are as follows:

> **Debit:** *meaning to receive, or value received.*
> **Credit:** *meaning to give, or value given.*

Accountants judge the twofold effect of all transactions on particular accounts from a receiving and giving point of view and each transaction is recorded on that basis. Thus when a transaction takes place, it is necessary to ask the following questions:

1 Which account should *receive* this transaction, i.e. which account should be debited?
2 Which account has *given* this amount, i.e. which account should be credited?

Accounts have been designed to keep the debit entries separate from the credit entries. This helps to emphasize the opposite, albeit equal, effect that each transaction has within the recording system. The separation is achieved by recording the debit entries on the left-hand side of the page, and the credit entries on the right-hand side. In a handwritten system, each account is normally kept on a separate page in a book of account (although if there are a lot of accounts, it may be necessary to keep several books of account). A book of account is also sometimes known as a ledger, and hence accounts are often referred to as *ledger accounts*. The format of a typical handwritten ledger account is illustrated in Figure 3.1.

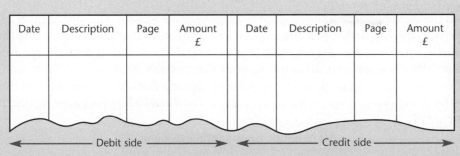

Date	Description	Page	Amount £	Date	Description	Page	Amount £

← ——— Debit side ——— → ← ——— Credit side ——— →

Notes

1 The columnar headings would normally be omitted.
2 The description of each entry is usually limited to the *title* of the corresponding account in which the equal entry and opposite entry may be found.
3 The page column is used to refer to the page number of the corresponding account.
4 This example of a ledger account may nowadays only be found in a fairly basic handwritten book-keeping system. Computerized systems of recording information usually necessitate an alternative format.

Figure 3.1 Example of a ledger account

There is no logical reason why debits should be entered on the left-hand side of an account and credits on the right-hand side. It is purely a matter of custom, like driving on either the left-hand or the right-hand side of the road.

In the next section we will show you how particular transactions are recorded in appropriate ledger accounts.

Activity 3.2	In once sentence describe what is meant by each of the following terms: (a) an account is _____ . (b) a ledger is _____ . (c) debit is _____ . (d) credit is _____ .

Working with accounts

It would not be helpful to the owners or the managers of a business if data were not recorded systematically. What has evolved is a practical method of capturing the twofold nature of all transactions in separate accounts. The book-keeper has then to decide in which two accounts to enter a particular transaction. The following subsections illustrate the procedure that the book-keeper will adopt.

Choice of accounts

Most transactions can be easily assigned to an appropriate account. The total number and type will depend partly upon the amount of information that the owner wants (for example, salaries and wages might be kept in separate accounts), and partly upon the nature of the business (a manufacturing entity will probably need more accounts than a service entity). In practice, there are a number of accounts that are common to most entities, but if you do not know which account to use, you should adopt the following rule:

> **If in doubt, open another account.**

If an account does eventually prove unnecessary, it can always be closed down. While some accounts are common to most entities, it will not always be clear what they should be used for. An idea of the overall system is shown in Figure 3.2, and we also list below a brief summary of the main types of accounts.

Capital

The *Capital Account* records what the owner has contributed (or given) to the entity out of his private resources in order to start the business and keep it going. In other words, it shows what the business owes him.

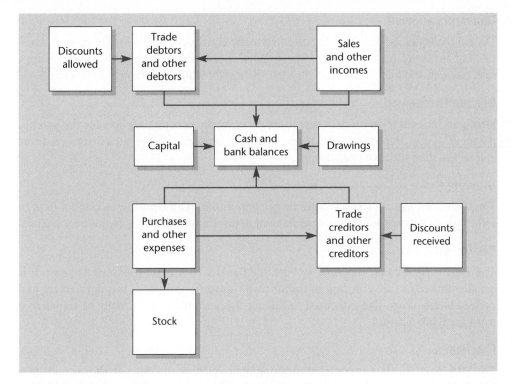

Figure 3.2 **The interlinking of different types of accounts**

Cash at bank

The *Bank Account* records what money the entity keeps at the bank. It shows what has been put in (usually in the form of cash and cheques) and what has been taken out (usually by cheque payments).

Cash in hand

The *Cash Account* works on similar lines to that of the Bank Account, except that it records the physical cash received (such as notes, coins and cheques) before they are paid into the bank. The cash received may be used to purchase goods and services, or it may be paid straight into the bank. From a control point of view, it is best not to pay for purchases directly out of cash receipts, but to draw an amount out of the bank specifically for sundry cash purchases. Any large amount should be paid by cheque.

Creditors

Creditor Accounts record what the entity owes its suppliers for goods or services purchased or supplied on credit (see also trade creditors).

Debtors

Debtor Accounts record what is owed to the entity by its customers for goods or services sold to them on credit (see also trade debtors).

Discounts allowed

Discounts allowed are cash discounts granted to the entity's customers for the prompt settlement of any debts due to the entity. The amount of cash received from debtors who claim a cash discount will then be less than the total amount for which they have been invoiced.

Discounts received

Discounts received relate to cash discounts given by the entity's suppliers for the prompt payment of any amounts due to them. Thus, the amount paid to the entity's creditors will be less than the invoiced amount.

Drawings

The term *drawings* has a special meaning in accounting. The *Drawings Account* is used to record what cash (or goods) the owner has withdrawn from the business for his personal use.

Petty cash

The *Petty Cash Account* is similar to both the Bank Account and the Cash Account. It is usually limited to the recording of minor cash transactions, such as bus fares, or tea and coffee for the office. The cash used to finance this account will normally be transferred from the Bank Account.

Purchases

The term *purchases* has a restricted meaning in accounting. It relates to those goods that are bought primarily with the intention of selling them (normally at a profit). The purchase of some motor cars, for example, would not usually be recorded in the *Purchases Account* unless they have been bought with the intention of selling them to customers. Goods not intended for resale are usually recorded in separate accounts. Some purchases may also require further work to be done on them before they are eventually sold.

Trade creditors

Trade Creditor Accounts are similar to Creditor Accounts except that they relate specifically to trading items, i.e. purchases.

Trade debtors

Trade Debtor Accounts are similar to Debtor Accounts except that they also relate specifically to trading items, i.e. sales.

Trade discounts

Trade discounts are a form of special discount. They may be given for placing a large order, for example, or for being a loyal customer. Trade discounts are deducted from the normal purchase or selling price. They are not recorded in the books of account and they will not appear on any invoice.

Sales

The *Sales Account* records the value of goods sold to customers during a particular accounting period. The account includes both cash and credit sales. It does not include receipts from (say) the sale of a motor car originally purchased for use within the business.

Stock

Stock includes goods which have not been sold at the end of an accounting period. In accounting terminology, this would be referred to as *closing stock*. The closing stock at the end of one period becomes the *opening stock* at the beginning of the next period.

Once the book-keeper has chosen the accounts in which to record all the transactions for a particular accounting period, it is then necessary to decide which account should be debited and which account should be credited. We examine this problem in the next subsection.

Activity 3.3

Which two ledger accounts would you use in recording each of the following transactions?

(a) cash sales

(b) rent paid by cheque

(c) wages paid in cash

(d) a supplier of goods paid by cheque

(e) goods sold on credit to Ford.

Entering transactions in accounts

There is one simple rule that should be followed when entering a transaction in an account.

Debit the account which receives

and

Credit the account which gives.

This rule is illustrated in Example 3.1, which contains some common ledger account entries.

Example 3.1

Example of some common ledger account entries

Entry 1

The proprietor contributes some cash to the business.

    Debit: Cash Account   *Credit*: Capital Account

Reason: The Cash Account receives some cash given to the business by the owner. His Capital Account is the giving account and the Cash Account is the receiving account.

Entry 2

Some cash in the till is paid into the business bank account.

    Debit: Bank Account   *Credit*: Cash Account

Reason: The Cash Account is the giving account because it is releasing some cash to the Bank Account.

▶

**Example 3.1
continued**

Entry 3

A van is purchased for use in the business; it is paid for by cheque.

    Debit: Van Account   *Credit*: Bank Account

Reason: The Bank Account is giving some money in order to pay for a van, so the Bank Account must be credited as it is the giving account.

Entry 4

Some goods are purchased for cash.

    Debit: Purchases Account   *Credit*: Cash Account

Reason: The Cash Account is giving up an amount of cash in order to pay for some purchases. The Cash Account is the giving account, and so it must be credited.

Entry 5

Some goods are purchased on credit terms from Fred.

    Debit: Purchases Account   *Credit*: Fred's Account

Reason: Fred is supplying the goods on credit terms to the business. As he is the giver, his account must be credited.

Entry 6

Some goods are sold for cash.

    Debit: Cash Account   *Credit*: Sales Account

Reason: The Cash Account receives the cash from the sale of goods, the Sales Account being the giving account.

Entry 7

Some goods are sold on credit terms to Sarah.

    Debit: Sarah's Account   *Credit*: Sales Account

Reason: Sarah's Account is debited because she is receiving the goods, and the Sales Account is credited because it is supplying (or giving) them.

Activity 3.4

Is there anything wrong with the following abbreviated bank account?

Debit			Credit		
		£000			£000
10.3.06	Wages paid	1000	6.6.06	Interest received	500

It is not easy for beginners to think of the receiving and of the giving effect of each transaction. You will find that it is very easy to get them mixed up and to then reverse the entries. If we look at Entries 6 and 7 in Example 3.1 for example, it is difficult to understand why the Sales Account should be credited. Why is the Sales Account the giving account? Surely it is *receiving* an amount and not giving anything? In one sense, it is receiving something, but that applies to any entry in any account. So, in the case of the sales account, regard it as a *supplying* account, because it gives (or releases) something to another account.

If you find this concept difficult to understand, think of the effect on the opposite account. A cash sale, for example, results in cash being increased (not decreased). The cash account must, therefore, be the receiving account, and it must be debited. Somebody (say Jones) must have given the cash, but as it is a cash sale, we credit it straight to the sales account. It is perhaps easier to think of the Sales Department having supplied, given or sold the goods to Jones.

Most students prefer to work out the double-entry effect of respective transactions by relating them to the movement of cash. You might find, therefore, the following procedure useful:

Either	**DEBIT**	the Cash (or Bank) Account and
	CREDIT	the corresponding account, if the entity *receives* some cash.
Or	**DEBIT**	the corresponding account and
	CREDIT	the Cash (or Bank) Account, if the entity *gives* some cash.

If a movement of cash is not involved in a particular transaction, work out the effect on the corresponding account on the assumption that one account is affected by a cash transaction. In the case of a credit sale, for example, the account that benefits from the receipt of the goods must be that of an individual, so that individual's account must be debited. The corresponding entry must, therefore, be credited to some account. In this case it will be to the sales account.

You might also find it useful to remember another general rule used in double-entry book-keeping:

> **For every debit there must be a credit
> and
> For every credit there must be a debit.**

There are no exceptions to this rule – think back to the accounting equation covered earlier in this chapter. As this chapter develops, more practice will be obtained in deciding which account to debit and which account to credit. After some time, it becomes largely a routine exercise, and you will find yourself making the correct entries automatically.

It would now be helpful to illustrate the entry of a number of transactions in specific ledger accounts. We do so in the next section.

Activity 3.5

State which account should be debited and which account should be credited in respect of each of the following terms:

(a) cash paid to a supplier

(b) office rent paid by cheque

(c) cash sales

(d) dividend received by cheque.

A ledger account example

This section illustrates the procedure adopted in entering various transactions in ledger accounts. The section brings together the basic material covered in the earlier part of this chapter. It demonstrates the use of various types, and the debiting and crediting effect of different types of transactions.

The example shown in Example 3.2 relates to a sole trader commencing business on his own account. As we explained in earlier chapters, while most non-accountants will not be involved in sole-trader entities, this type of entity is useful in illustrating the basic principles of double-entry book-keeping. Indeed, a more complex form of entity would only obscure those principles.

The example is also confined to a business that purchases and sells goods on cash terms. Businesses that buy and sell goods on credit terms will be a feature of later examples.

Example 3.2	Joe Simple: a sole trader

The following information relates to Joe Simple, who started a new business on 1 January 2004:

1 1.1.04 Joe started the business with £5000 in cash.
2 3.1.04 He paid £3000 of the cash into a business bank account.
3 5.1.04 Joe bought a van for £2000 paying by cheque.
4 7.1.04 He bought some goods, paying £1000 in cash.
5 9.1.04 Joe sold some of the goods, receiving £1500 in cash.

Required:
Enter the above transactions in Joe's ledger accounts.

Answer to Example 3.2

Joe Simple's books of account:

Cash Account

		£			£
1.1.04	Capital (1)	5 000	3.1.04	Bank (2)	3 000
9.1.04	Sales (5)	1 500	7.1.04	Purchases (4)	1 000

Capital Account

		£			£
			1.1.04	Cash (1)	5 000

Bank Account

		£			£
3.1.04	Cash (2)	3 000	5.1.04	Van (3)	2 000

Van Account

		£			£
5.1.04	Bank (3)	2 000			

Purchases Account

£		£
1 000		

Sales Account

£			£
	9.1.04	Cash (5)	1 500

...ch entry refer to the example notes; they have been

...ount in which the equal and opposite entry may be

...ons for a particular period in appropriate ledger ...cise is to calculate the balance on each account as at ...We show you how to do this in the next section.

...2 without looking at the answer.

Answer to Example 3.2 continued

Tutorial notes

Activity 3.6

Balancing the accounts

During a particular accounting period, some accounts (such as the bank and cash accounts) will contain a great many debit and credit entries. Some accounts may contain either mainly debit entries (e.g. the purchases account), or largely credit entries (e.g. the sales account). It would be somewhat inconvenient to allow the entries (whether mainly debits, credits, or a mixture of both) to build up without occasionally striking a balance. Indeed, the owner will almost certainly want to know not just what is in each account, but also what its overall or *net* balance is (i.e the total of all the debit entries less the total of all the credit entries). Thus on occasions it will be necessary to calculate the balance on each account.

Balancing an account requires the book-keeper to add up all the respective debit and credit entries, take one total away from the other, and arrive at the net balance.

Accounts may be balanced fairly frequently, e.g. once a week or once a month, but some entities may only do so when they prepare their annual accounts. However, in order to keep a tight control on the management of the business, it is advisable to balance the accounts at reasonably short intervals. The frequency will depend upon the nature and the size of the entity, but once a month is probably sufficient for most entities.

The balancing of the accounts is part of the double-entry procedure, and the method is quite formal. In Example 3.3 we show how to balance an account with a *debit* balance on it (i.e. when its total debit entries exceed its total credit entries).

Example 3.3

Balancing an account with a debit balance

Cash Account

		£			£
1.1.04	Sales (1)	2 000	10.1.04	Jones (1)	3 000
15.1.04	Rent received (1)	1 000	25.1.04	Davies (1)	5 000
20.1.04	Smith (1)	4 000			
31.1.04	Sales (1)	8 000	31.1.04	Balance c/d (2)	7 000
	(3)	15 000		(3)	15 000
1.2.04	Balance b/d (4)	7 000			

Note: The number shown after each narration relates to the tutorial notes below.

Tutorial notes

1. The total debit entries equal £15 000 (2000 + 1000 + 4000 + 8000). The total credit entries equal £8000 (3000 + 5000). The net balance on this account, therefore, at 31 January 2004 is a *debit balance* of £7000 (15 000 – 8000). Until both the debit entries and the credit entries have been totalled, of course, it will not usually be apparent whether the balance is a debit one or a credit one. However, it should be noted that there can never be a credit balance in a cash account, because it is impossible to pay out more cash than has been received.

2. The debit balance of £7000 is inserted on the *credit* side of the account at the time that the account is balanced (in the case of Example 3.3, at 31 January 2004). This then enables the total of the credit column to be balanced so that it agrees with the total of the debit column. The abbreviation 'c/d' means carried down. In this example the debit balance is carried down in the account in order to start the new period on 1 February 2004.

3. The £15 000 shown as a total in both the debit and the credit columns demonstrates that the columns balance (they do so, of course, because £7000 has been inserted in the credit column to make them balance). The totals are double-underlined in order to signify that they are a final total.

4. The balancing figure of £7000 is brought down ('b/d') in the account to start the new period on 1 February 2004. The double entry has been completed because £7000 has been debited below the line (i.e. below the £15 000 debit total), and the £7000 balancing figure credited above the line (i.e. above the £15 000 total).

Examples 3.3 demonstrates how an account with a debit entry is balanced. In Example 3.4, we illustrate a similar procedure, but this time the account has a *credit* balance.

Example 3.4

Balancing an account with a credit balance

Scott's Account

		£			£
31.1.04	Bank (1)	20 000	15.1.04	Purchases (1)	10 000
31.1.04	Balance c/d (2)	5 000	20.1.04	Purchases (1)	15 000
	(3)	25 000		(3)	25 000
			1.2.04	Balance b/d (4)	5 000

Note: The number shown after each narration relates to the tutorial notes below.

1 Apart from the balance, there is only one debit entry in Scott's account: the bank entry of £20 000. The total credit entries amount to £25 000 (10 000 + 15 000). Scott has a *credit balance*, therefore, in his account as at 31 January 2004 of £5000 (10 000 + 15 000 − 20 000). With many more entries in the account it would not always be possible to tell immediately whether the balance was a debit one or a credit one.

2 The credit balance of £5000 at 31 January 2004 is inserted on the *debit* side of the account in order to enable the account to be balanced. The balance is then carried down (c/d) to the next period.

3 The £25 000 shown as the total for both the debit and the credit columns identifies the balancing of the account. This has been made possible because of the insertion of the £5 000 balancing figure on the debit side of the account.

4 The balancing figure of £5000 is brought down (b/d) in the account in order to start the account in the new period beginning on 1 February 2004. The double-entry has been completed because the debit entry of £5000 above the £25 000 line on the debit side equals the credit entry below the £25 000 line on the credit side.

Write down in you notebook what is meant by

(a) an account having a debit balance

(b) an account having a credit balance.

Activity 3.7

Examples 3.3 and 3.4 demonstrate the importance of always obeying the cardinal rule of double-entry book-keeping:

> **For every debit there must be a credit**
> and
> **For every credit there must be a debit.**

This rule must still be followed even if the two entries are made in the same account (as is the case when an account is balanced). If this rule is not obeyed, the accounts will not balance. This could mean that a lot of time is spent looking for an apparent error or some incorrect information may be given to the owner or managers of the business as there is bound to be a mistake in at least one account.

The next stage after balancing each account is to check that the double entry has been completed throughout the entire system. This is done by compiling what is known as a *trial balance.*

The trial balance

A trial balance is a statement compiled at the end of a specific accounting period. It is a convenient method of checking that all the transactions and all the balances have been entered correctly in the ledger accounts. The trial balance is, however, a working paper, and it does not form part of the double-entry process.

A trial balance lists all of the debit balances and all of the credit balances extracted from each of the accounts throughout the ledger system. The total of all the debit balances is then compared with the total of all the credit balances. If the two totals agree, we can be reasonably confident that the book-keeping procedures have been carried out accurately.

We illustrate the preparation of a trial balance in Example 3.5. We also take the opportunity of giving some more examples of how transactions are entered in ledger accounts. You are recommended to work through part (a) of Example 3.5 before moving on to part (b).

Example 3.5

Edward – compilation of a trial balance

Edward started a new business on 1 January 2004. The following transactions took place during his first month in business:

2004

1.1	Edward commenced business with £10 000 in cash.
3.1	He paid £8000 of the cash into a business bank account.
6.1	He bought a van on credit from Perkin's garage for £3000.
9.1	Edward rented shop premises for £1000 per quarter; he paid for the first quarter immediately by cheque.
12.1	He bought goods on credit from Roy Limited for £4000.
15.1	He paid shop expenses amounting to £1500 by cheque.
18.1	Edward sold goods on credit to Scott and Company for £3000.
21.1	He settled Perkin's account by cheque.
24.1	Edward received a cheque from Scott and Company for £2000; this cheque was paid immediately into the bank.
27.1	Edward sent a cheque to Roy Limited for £500.
31.1	Goods costing £3000 were purchased from Roy Limited on credit.
31.1	Cash sales for the month amounted to £2000.

Required:

(a) Enter the above transactions in appropriate ledger accounts, balance off each account as at 34 January 2004, and bring down the balances as at that date; and

(b) extract a trial balance as at 31 January 2004.

Answer to Example 3.5(a)

Cash Account

		£			£
1.1.04	Capital (1)	10 000	3.1.04	Bank (2)	8 000
31.1.04	Sales (12)	2 000	31.1.04	Balance c/d	4 000
		12 000			12 000
1.2.04	Balance b/d	4 000			

Capital Account

		£			£
			1.1.04	Cash (1)	10 000

Answer to
Example 3.5(a)
continued

Bank Account

		£			£
3.1.04	Cash (2)	8 000	9.1.04	Rent payable (4)	1 000
24.1.04	Scott and		15.1.04	Shop expenses (6)	1 500
	Company (9)	2 000	21.1.04	Perkin's garage (8)	3 000
			27.1.04	Roy Limited (10)	500
			31.1.04	Balance c/d	4 000
		10 000			10 000
1.2.04	Balance b/d	4 000			

Van Account

		£		£
6.1.04	Perkin's Garage (3)	3 000		

Perkin's Garage Account

		£			£
21.1.04	Bank (8)	3 000	6.1.04	Van (3)	3 000

Rent Payable Account

		£		£
9.1.04	Bank (4)	1 000		

Purchases Account

		£			£
12.1.04	Roy Limited (5)	4 000			
31.1.04	Roy Limited (11)	3 000	31.1.04	Balance c/d	7 000
		7 000			7 000
1.2.04	Balance b/d	7 000			

Roy Limited Account

		£			£
27.1.04	Bank (10)	500	12.1.04	Purchases (5)	4 000
31.1.04	Balance c/d	6 500	31.1.04	Purchases (11)	3 000
		7 000			7 000
			1.2.04	Balance b/d	6 500

Shop Expenses Account

		£		£
15.1.04	Bank (6)	1 500		

Sales Account

		£			£
			18.1.04	Scott & Company (7)	3 000
31.1.04	Balance c/d	5 000	31.1.04	Cash (12)	2 000
		5 000			5 000
			1.2.04	Balance b/d	5 000

Scott and Company Account

		£			£
18.1.04	Sales (7)	3 000	24.1.04	Bank (9)	2 000
			31.1.04	Balance c/d	1 000
		3 000			3 000
1.2.04	Balance b/d	1 000			

1 The number shown after each narration has been inserted for tutorial guidance only in order to illustrate the insertion of each entry in the appropriate account.

2 There is no need to balance an account and carry down the balance when there is only a single entry in one account (for example, Edward's Capital Account).

3 Note that some accounts may have no balance in them at all as at 31 January 2004 (for example, Perkin's Garage Account).

Trial Balance at 31 January 2004

	Dr	Cr
	£	£
Cash	4 000	
Capital		10 000
Bank	4 000	
Van	3 000	
Rent payable	1 000	
Purchases	7 000	
Roy Limited		6 500
Shop expenses	1 500	
Sales		5 000
Scott and Company	1 000	
	21 500	21 500

1 The total debit balance agrees with the total credit balance, and therefore the trial balance balances. This confirms that the transactions appear to have been entered in the books of account correctly.

2 The total amount of £21 500 shown in both the debit and credit columns of the trial balance does not have any significance, except to prove that the trial balance balances.

Activity 3.8   Prepare the solution to Example 3.5 without looking at the solution.

Trial balance errors

A trial balance confirms that the books of account balance arithmetically. This means that the following procedures have all been carried out correctly:

(a) for every debit entry there appears to be a credit entry;

(b) the value for each debit and credit entry has been entered in appropriate accounts;

(c) the balance on each account has been calculated, extracted and entered correctly in the trial balance; and

(d) the debit and credit columns in the trial balance are the same.

There are, however, some errors that are not disclosed by the trial balance. In summary they are as follows.

1 *Omission:* a transaction could have been completely omitted from the books of account.
2 *Complete reversal of entry:* a transaction could have been entered in (say) Account A as a debit and in Account B as a credit, when it should have been entered as a credit in Account A and as a debit in Account B.
3 *Principle:* a transaction may have been entered in the wrong *type* of account, e.g. the purchase of a new delivery van may have been debited to the purchases account, instead of the delivery vans account.
4 *Commission:* a transaction may have been entered in the correct type of account, but in the wrong *personal* account, e.g. in Bill's Account instead of in Ben's Account.
5 *Compensating:* an error may have been made in (say) adding the debit side of one account, and an identical error made in adding the credit side of another account; the two errors would then cancel each other out.
6 *Original entry:* a transaction may be entered incorrectly in both accounts, e.g. as £291 instead of as £921.

Such errors may only be discovered if an audit is done of the double-entry book-keeping system. They may also become apparent when the financial statements are prepared and the results are compared with previous periods. Similarly, some errors may also come to light if they affect creditors' and debtors' balances and they complain about receiving incorrect invoices. Notwithstanding these possible errors, the compilation of a trial balance still serves the following three useful purposes.

1 The arithmetical accuracy of the entries made in the books of account can be confirmed.
2 The balance owed or owing on each account can easily be extracted.
3 The preparation of the financial statements is simplified.

State whether each of the following errors would be discovered as a result of preparing a trial balance.   **Activity 3.9**

(a) £342 has been entered in both ledger accounts instead of £432.   *Yes/No*

(b) The debit column in Prim's account has been overstated by £50.   *Yes/No*

(c) £910 has been put in Anne's account instead of Agnes'.   *Yes/No*

Questions non-accountants should ask

As a non-accountant it is unlikely that you will become involved in the detailed recording, extraction and summary of basic accounting information. As such information will be used to prepare the entity's financial statements, however, it is important that it is accurate, relevant and fairly presented.

Your particular responsibility as a senior manager in the entity will be to ensure that (1) adequate accounting records are kept; (2) they are accurate; and (3) an appropriate profit and loss account and a balance sheet (as required by any legislation) can be prepared from such records. At very least, the accounting records should be capable of dealing with all cash received and paid by the entity and that they contain details of all its assets and liabilities.

In order to satisfy yourself about these requirements you should ask the following questions.

● Do we use a double-entry book-keeping system?

● Is it a manual or a computerized one?

● Does the system include a cash book in which all cash and bank transactions are entered?

● Is the balance shown in the cash book checked regularly against the balance disclosed in the bank's pass sheets or statements of account?

● Is a separate account kept for each identifiable group of fixed assets, current assets and current liabilities?

● What is included in such groups?

● Is a balance calculated regularly for each of the accounts?

● How often is a trial balance prepared?

● What steps are taken to ensure that errors not disclosed in a trial balance are minimized?

● What is the system for the separation of duties affecting the recording of the accounting information and for preparing the trial balance?

● Does a senior manager (not involved with the accounting function) receive a copy of the trial balance?

Conclusion

As a non-accountant, you will probably not have to write up ledger accounts or enter transactions into a computerized accounting system. In this chapter, therefore, we have avoided going into too much detail about double-entry book-keeping that is irrelevant for your purposes. As part of your managerial role, you will almost certainly be supplied with information that has been extracted from a ledger system. In order to assess its real benefit to you, we believe that it is most important that you should know something about where it has come from, what it means, and what reliability can be placed on it.

We recommend that before leaving this chapter, you make absolutely sure that you are familiar with the following features of a double-entry book-keeping system:

- the accounting equation;
- the type of accounts generally used in practice;
- the meaning of the terms *debit* and *credit*;
- the definition of the terms *debtor* and *creditor*;
- the method of entering transactions in ledger accounts;
- the balancing of ledger accounts;
- the importance of the trial balance.

This chapter has provided you with the basic information necessary to become familiar with the seven features listed above. If you are reasonably confident that you now have a basic grasp of double-entry book-keeping, you can move on to an examination of how financial accounts are prepared. Before doing so, however, you are recommended to test your understanding of the contents of this chapter by attempting some of the questions at the end of the chapter.

The answers to these questions may be found in the text.

Key points

1   The accounting equation is represented by the formula: Assets = Capital + Liabilities. The equation underpins the dual aspect rule and it forms the basis of a conventional accounting recording system.

2   An account is an explanation, a record, or a history of a particular event.

3   A book of account is known as a ledger.

4   A transaction is the carrying out and the performance of any business.

5   All transactions have a twofold effect.

6   A double-entry system records that twofold effect.

7   A debit means a transaction is received into an account.

8   A credit means that a transaction is given by an account.

9   Debits are entered on the left-hand side of an account.

10   Credits are entered on the right-hand side of an account.

11   For every debit entry, there must be a credit entry.

12   Accounts are balanced periodically.

13   The accuracy of the book-keeping is tested by preparing a trial balance.

14   The trial balance does not reveal all possible book-keeping errors.

Check your learning

1   What is the accounting equation?

2   What is the basic rule of double-entry book-keeping?

3   What is an account?

4   What is a ledger?

5   What is meant by the terms 'debit' and 'credit'?

6   What factor would indicate whether or not a new account should be opened?

7   What distinguishes a cash account from a bank account?

8   What are the following accounts used for: (a) capital; (b) trade creditors; (c) trade debtors; (d) stock; (e) sales; (f) purchases; and (g) drawings?

9   What is the difference between a discounts allowed account and a discounts received account?

10 What must there be for (a) every debit; and (b) every credit?

11 What is (a) a debit balance; and (b) a credit balance?

12 What is a trial balance?

13 Name three main functions that it fulfils.

14 List six book-keeping errors that a trial balance does not detect.

News story quiz

Remember the news story at the beginning of this chapter? Go back to that story and reread it before answering the following questions.

This is the story of an Australian company that allegedly broke the law on an almost unimaginable scale. Among the many points covered in the story was 'an inability to estimate its liabilities'. According to Mr Wayn Martin, the senior counsel for the Royal Commission, the simplistic answer as to why HIH collapsed was a 'recurrent failure to adequately (sic) estimate the claims liabilities from the underwriting risks taken'.

Questions

1   How likely was it that the company operated a computerized double-entry book-keeping system?

2   What is a 'liability'?

3   How does a double-entry book-keeping system normally show the extent of an entity's liabilities?

4   Why then should the company have difficulty in estimating its 'claims liabilities from the underwriting risks'?

5   To what extent do you think that this difficulty had anything to do with the recording system adopted by the company?

Tutorial questions

The answers to questions marked with an asterisk may be found in Appendix 4.

3.1   Do you think that non-accounting managers need to know anything about double-entry book-keeping?

3.2   'My accountant has got it all wrong,' argued Freda. 'She's totally mixed up all her debits and credits.'
'But what makes you say that?' queried Dora.
'Oh! I've only to look at my bank statement to see that she's wrong,' responded Freda. 'I know I've got some money in the bank, and yet she tells me I'm in debit when she means I'm in credit.'
Is Freda right?

3.3   'Double-entry book-keeping is a waste of time and money because everything has to be recorded twice.' Discuss.

3.4*   Adam has just gone into business. The following is a list of his transactions for the month of January 2004:

(a) Cash paid into the business by Adam.
(b) Goods for resale purchased on cash terms.
(c) Van bought for cash.
(d) One quarter's rent for premises paid in cash.
(e) Some goods sold on cash terms.
(f) Adam buys some office machinery for cash.

Required:
State which account in Adam's books of account should be debited and which account should be credited for each transaction.

3.5*   The following is a list of Brown's transactions for February 2005:

Transfer of cash to a bank account.
Cash received from sale of goods.
Purchase of goods paid for by cheque.
Office expenses paid in cash.
Cheques received from customers from sale of goods on cash terms.
A motor car for use in the business paid for by cheque.

Required:
State which account in Brown's books of account should be debited and which account should be credited for each transaction.

3.6   Corby is in business as a retail distributor. The following is a list of his transactions for March 2006:

Goods purchased from Smith on credit.
Corby introduces further capital in cash into the business.
Goods sold for cash.
Goods purchased for cash.
Cash transferred to the bank.
Machinery purchased, paid for in cash.

Required:
State which account in Corby's books of account should be debited and which account should be credited for each transaction.

3.7   Davies buys and sells goods on cash and credit terms. The following is a list of her transactions for April 2004:

1   Capital introduced by Davies paid into the bank.
2   Goods purchased on credit terms from Swallow.
3   Goods sold to Hill for cash.
4   Cash paid for purchase of goods.
5   Dale buys goods from Davies on credit.
6   Motoring expenses paid by cheque.

Required:
State which account in Davies's books of account should be debited and which account should be credited for each transaction.

3.8   The following transactions relate to Gordon's business for the month of July 2007:

1   Bought goods on credit from Watson.
2   Sold some goods for cash.
3   Sold some goods on credit to Moon.
4   Sent a cheque for half the amount owing to Watson.
5   Watson grants Gordon a cash discount.
6   Moon settles most of his account in cash.
7   Gordon allows Moon a cash discount that covers the small amount owed by Moon.
8   Gordon purchases some goods for cash.

Required:
State which accounts in Gordon's books of accounts should be debited and which account should be credited for each transaction.

3.9   Harry started a new business on 1 January 2004. The following transactions cover his first three months in business:

1   Harry contributed an amount in cash to start the business.
2   He transferred some of the cash to a business bank account.
3   He paid an amount in advance by cheque for rental of business premises.
4   Bought goods on credit from Paul.

   5 Purchased a van paying by cheque.
   6 Sold some goods for cash to James.
   7 Bought goods on credit from Nancy.
   8 Paid motoring expenses in cash.
   9 Returned some goods to Nancy.
10 Sold goods on credit to Mavis.
11 Harry withdrew some cash for personal use.
12 Bought goods from David paying in cash.
13 Mavis returns some goods.
14 Sent a cheque to Nancy.
15 Cash received from Mavis.
16 Harry receives a cash discount from Nancy.
17 Harry allows Mavis a cash discount.
18 Cheque withdrawn at the bank in order to open a petty cash account.

Required:
State which accounts in Harry's books of account should be debited and which account should be credited for each transaction.

3.10* The following is a list of transactions which relate to Ivan for the first month that he is in business:

1.9.06	Started the business with £10 000 in cash.
2.9.06	Paid £8000 into a business bank account.
3.9.06	Purchased £1000 of goods in cash.
10.9.06	Bought goods costing £6000 on credit from Roy.
12.9.06	Cash sales of £3000.
15.9.06	Goods sold on credit terms to Norman for £4000.
20.9.06	Ivan settles Roy's account by cheque.
30.9.06	Cheque for £2000 received from Norman.

Required:
Enter the above transactions in Ivan's ledger accounts.

3.11* Jones has been in business since 1 October 2006. The following is a list of her transactions for October 2006:

1.10.06	Capital of £20 000 paid into a business bank account.
2.10.06	Van purchased on credit from Lang for £5000.
6.10.06	Goods purchased on credit from Green for £15 000.
10.10.06	Cheque drawn on the bank for £1000 in order to open a petty cash account.
14.10.06	Goods sold on credit for £6000 to Haddock.
18.10.06	Cash sales of £5000.
20.10.06	Cash purchases of £3000.
22.10.06	Miscellaneous expenses of £500 paid out of petty cash.
25.10.06	Lang's account settled by cheque.
28.10.06	Green allows Jones a cash discount of £500.
29.10.06	Green is sent a cheque for £10 000.
30.10.06	Haddock is allowed a cash discount of £600.
31.10.06	Haddock settles his account in cash.

Required:
Enter the above transactions in Jones's ledger accounts.

3.12   The transactions listed below relate to Ken's business for the month of November 2005:

1.11.05   Started the business with £150 000 in cash.

2.11.05   Transferred £14 000 of the cash to a business bank account.

3.11.05   Paid rent of £1000 by cheque.

4.11.05   Bought goods on credit from the following suppliers:

Ace	£5000
Mace	£6000
Pace	£7000

10.11.05   Sold goods on credit to the following customers:

Main	£2000
Pain	£3000
Vain	£4000

15.11.05   Returned goods costing £1000 to Pace.

22.11.05   Pain returned goods sold to him for £2000.

25.11.05   Additional goods purchased from the following suppliers:

Ace	£3000
Mace	£4000
Pace	£5000

26.11.05   Office expenses of £2000 paid by cheque.

27.11.05   Cash sales for the month amounted to £5000.

28.11.05   Purchases paid for in cash during the month amounted to £4000.

29.11.05   Cheques sent to the following suppliers:

Ace	£4000
Mace	£5000
Pace	£6000

30.11.05   Cheques received from the following customers:

Main	£1000
Pain	£2000
Vain	£3000

30.11.05   The following cash discounts were claimed by Ken:

Ace	£200
Mace	£250
Pace	£300

30.11.05   The following cash discounts were allowed by Ken:

Main	£100
Pain	£200
Vain	£400

30.11.05   Cash transfer to the bank of £1000.

Required:

Enter the above transactions in Ken's ledger accounts.

3.13*   The following transactions relate to Pat's business for the month of December 2007:

1.12.07   Started the business with £10 000 in cash.

2.12.07   Bought goods on credit from the following suppliers:

Grass	£6000
Seed	£7000

10.12.07   Sold goods on credit to the following customers:

Fog	£3000
Mist	£4000

12.12.07 Returned goods to the following suppliers:

        Grass   £1000

        Seed   £2000

15.12.07 Bought additional goods on credit from Grass for £3000 and from Seed for £4000.

20.12.07 Sold more goods on credit to Fog for £2000 and to Mist for £3000.

24.12.07 Paid office expenses of £5000 in cash.

29.12.07 Received £4000 in cash from Fog and £6000 in cash from Mist.

31.12.07 Pat paid Grass and Seed £6000 and £8000, respectively, in cash.

Required:

(a) Enter the above transactions in Pat's ledger accounts.

(b) Balance off the accounts as at 31 December 2007.

(c) Bring down the balances as at 1 January 2008.

(d) Compile a trial balance as at 31 December 2007.

3.14* Vale has been in business for some years. The following balances were brought forward in his books of account as at 31 December 2004:

	£ Dr	£ Cr
Bank	5000	
Capital		20000
Cash	1000	
Dodd		2000
Fish	6000	
Furniture	10000	
	22000	22000

During the year to 31 December 2005 the following transactions took place:

1 Goods bought from Dodd on credit for £30000.

2 Cash sales of £20000.

3 Cash purchases of £15000.

4 Goods sold to Fish on credit for £50000.

5 Cheques sent to Dodd totalling £29000.

6 Cheques received from Fish totalling £45000.

7 Cash received from Fish amounting to £7000.

8 Office expenses paid in cash totalling £9000.

9 Purchase of delivery van costing £12000 paid by cheque.

10 Cash transfers to bank totalling £3000.

Required:

(a) Compile Vale's ledger accounts for the year 31 December 2005, balance off the accounts and bring down the balances as at 1 January 2006.

(b) Extract a trial balance as at 31 December 2005.

3.15 Brian started in business on 1 January 2004. The following is a list of his transactions for his first month of trading:

1.1.04 Opened a business bank account with £25000 obtained from private resources.

2.1.04 Paid one month's rent of £2000 by cheque.

3.1.04	Bought goods costing £5000 on credit from Linda.
4.1.04	Purchased motor car from Savoy Motors for £4000 on credit.
5.1.04	Purchased goods costing £3000 on credit from Sydney.
10.1.04	Cash sales of £6000.
15.1.04	More goods costing £10 000 purchased from Linda on credit.
20.1.04	Sold goods on credit to Ann for £8000.
22.1.04	Returned £2000 of goods to Linda.
23.1.04	Paid £6000 in cash into the bank.
24.1.04	Ann returned £1000 of goods.
25.1.04	Withdrew £500 in cash from the bank to open a petty cash account.
26.1.04	Cheque received from Ann for £5500; Ann also claimed a cash discount of £500.
28.1.04	Office expenses of £250 paid out of petty cash.
29.1.04	Sent a cheque to Savoy Motors for £4000.
30.1.04	Cheques sent to Linda and Sydney for £8000 and £2000, respectively. Cash discounts were also claimed from Linda and Sydney of £700 and £100, respectively.
31.1.04	Paid by cheque another month's rent of £2000.
31.1.04	Brian introduced £5000 additional capital into the business by cheque.

Required:
(a) Enter the above transactions in Brian's ledger accounts for January 2004, balance off the accounts and bring down the balances as at 1 February 2004.
(b) Compile a trial balance as at 31 January 2004.

3.16 An accounts clerk has compiled Trent's trial balance as at 31 March 2006 as follows:

	Dr £	Cr £
Bank (overdrawn)	2 000	
Capital	50 000	
Discounts allowed		5 000
Discounts received	3 000	
Dividends received	2 000	
Drawings		23 000
Investments		14 000
Land and buildings	60 000	
Office expenses	18 000	
Purchases	75 000	
Sales		250 000
Suspense (unexplained balance)		6 000
Rates		7 000
Vans	20 000	
Van expenses		5 000
Wages and salaries	80 000	
	310 000	310 000

Required:
Compile Trent's corrected trial balance as at 31 March 2006.

3.17   Donald's transactions for the month of March 2009 are as follows:

Cash receipts	£
Capital contributed	6 000
Sales to customers	3 000
Cash payments	
Goods for sale	4 000
Stationery	500
Postage	300
Travelling	600
Wages	2 900
Transfers to bank	500
Bank receipts	£
Receipts from trade debtors:	
Smelt	3 000
Tait	9 000
Ure	5 000
Bank payments	£
Payments to trade creditors:	
Craig	2 800
Dobie	5 000
Elgin	6 400
Rent and rates	3 200
Electricity	200
Telephone	100
Salaries	2 000
Miscellaneous expenses	600
Other transactions	
Goods purchased from:	
Craig	3 500
Dobie	7 500
Elgin	7 500
Goods returned to Dobie	400
Goods sold to:	
Smelt	4 000
Tait	10 000
Ure	8 000
Goods returned by Ure	900
Discounts allowed:	
Smelt	200
Tait	500
Ure	400
Discounts received:	
Craig	50
Dobie	100
Elgin	200

Required:
(a) Enter the above transactions in appropriate ledger accounts;
(b) balance each account as at 31 March 2009; and
(c) extract a trial balance as at that date.

Further practice questions, study material and links to relevant sites on the World Wide Web can be found on the website that accompanies this book. The site can be found at **www.booksites.net/dyson**

Sole trader accounts

Revenue recognition: a major problem in accounting today . . .

Revenue recognition lacks consistency

More than 40% of companies ignore revenue recognition, says monitor

Revenue recognition is in a state of flux with a severe lack of consistency in accounting policies, according to monthly financial reporting monitor Company Reporting, writes Michelle Perry.

Of 600 companies analysed by the monthly publication, 43% do not even disclose a revenue recognition policy. Revenue recognition – or when a company books its sales – was a topic picked up by the Accounting Standards Board last year when it published a discussion paper intended as the first step in what is expected to be a protracted debate.

Until now, there has been no guidance in the UK on revenue recognition and accountants have been using their judgement as to what accounting policy should be applied, or turning to international or US standards.

According to the ASB: 'The recognition and measurement of revenue are of funda-mental importance to proper financial reporting.'

But, it is still unknown whether the ASB will recommend companies disclose revenue for each separate revenue stream or if it will follow the US model and stop at policy disclosure.

A Company Reporting analysis said: 'Disclosure of how revenue is recognised is beneficial to analysts however an even more useful disclosure, which would allow comparability between companies, is the level of revenue that flows from each separate stream.

'Thus far, it appears that company's [*sic*] seem oblivious to the demand for this additional disclosure or are unwilling to provide it.'

Accountancy Age, 4 April 2002.

Questions relating to this news story may be found on page 89 ▶▶

About the chapter

This chapter leads on from the last one. You will recall that at the end of that chapter we explained how to compile a trial balance. The trial balance is used to prepare the basic financial accounts. These normally consist of a trading account, a profit and loss account, and a balance sheet. In this chapter we explain how such financial statements are prepared.

The chapter is divided into six main sections. After the learning objectives in the first main section we explain why the chapter is important for non-accountants. The following section provides the foundation on which the chapter is based. A further section emphasizes why profit is not the same as cash. We then take you through the two main stages involved in the preparation of a basic trading, profit and loss account, and a balance sheet. The section after that contains a detailed example of how to prepare such accounts. The last main section before we conclude the chapter poses some questions that non-accountants ought to ask about the reliability and usefulness of trading, profit and loss accounts, and balance sheets.

Learning objectives

By the end of this chapter you should be able to:
- **describe what accountants mean by profit;**
- **prepare a basic set of accounts for a trading entity.**

! Why this chapter is important for non-accountants

This chapter is important for non-accountants for two main reasons:

1 *To distinguish between capital and revenue items.* The chapter explains that a distinction has to be made between items called capital and items called revenues. In practice, this distinction requires some judgement and there may be some disagreement about what is a capital item and what is a revenue item. This is important because the decision can affect the amount of profit earned during the year.
2 *To distinguish between cash and profit.* The chapter points out that the figure for profit shown in the profit and loss account does not necessarily result in an equivalent increase in cash and bank balances. This is a point not always appreciated by non-accountants.

The next section provides a foundation for the rest of the chapter.

The basic accounts

The last chapter finished with an explanation of how to prepare a trial balance. A trial balance has two important functions:

1 it enables the accuracy of book-keeping to be checked; and
2 it provides the basic data for the preparation of the financial accounts.

The composition of the financial accounts will depend upon whether the entity is in the profit-making sector or the not-for-profit sector, and whether it is a manufacturing, trading or service entity. Most profit-making entities usually prepare a *profit and loss account* and a *balance sheet*. The profit and loss account enables the question to be answered: '*What profit has the business made?*' A balance sheet answers the questions: '*How much does the business owe?*' and '*How much is owed to it?*'

In this chapter we are going to concentrate on *trading entities* because their accounts enable us to demonstrate a comprehensive range of procedures involved in preparing a set of basic financial accounts. In addition to the profit and loss account, a trading entity also prepares a *trading account*. A trading account shows the difference between what the

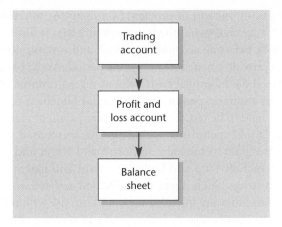

Figure 4.1 **Basic accounts of a trading entity**

entity paid for goods purchased from outside suppliers and what they were sold for to its own customers.

The relationship between the trading account, the profit and loss account and the balance sheet is shown in diagrammatic format in Figure 4.1.

Before we show you how to prepare a basic set of financial accounts for a trading entity, we need to examine why there is a difference between cash and profit. We do so in the next section.

Cash versus profit

The owners of a business often try to measure the profit that it has made (i.e. how well it has done) by deducting the cash held at the end of a period from cash held at the beginning (after allowing for capital introduced or withdrawn during the period). It is then assumed that the difference represents profit (if the cash has increased) or loss (if the cash has decreased). This is *not* what accountants mean by profit.

As was outlined in Chapter 2, accounts are normally prepared by adopting a certain number of accounting rules. You will remember that the realization rule requires us to match the sales revenue for a particular period against the cost of selling those goods during the same period. The matching rule requires a similar procedure to be adopted for other types of incomes and expenses. It is unlikely that the difference between cash received and cash paid will be the same as the difference between income and expenditure. Cash transactions may relate to earlier or later periods, whereas incomes and expenditure (as defined in accounting) measure the *actual* economic activity that has taken place during a clearly defined period of time. By *income* we mean something that the entity has gained during a particular period, and by *expenditure* we mean something the entity has lost during the same period.

There are a great many problems, of course, in trying to measure income and expenditure in this way, rather than on a cash receipts and cash payments basis. In calculating profit, expenditure is especially difficult to determine. If the entity purchases a machine, for example, that has an estimated life of 20 years, how much of the cost should be charged against the income for (say) Year 1 compared with Year 20?

Accountants deal with this sort of problem by attempting to classify expenditure into *capital* and *revenue*. *Capital expenditure* is expenditure that is likely to provide a benefit to the entity for more than one accounting period, and *revenue expenditure* is expenditure that is likely to provide a benefit for only one period. As the basic financial accounts are normally prepared on an annual basis, we can regard revenue expenditure as being virtually the same as annual expenditure. If a similar benefit is required the next year, then the service will have to be reordered and another payment made.

Examples of revenue expenditure include goods purchased for resale, electricity charges, business rates paid to the local authority, and wages and salaries. Examples of capital expenditure include land and buildings, plant and machinery, motor vehicles, and furniture and fittings. Such items are described as *fixed assets*, because they are owned by the entity and they are intended for long-term use within it.

It is also possible to classify income into *capital* and *revenue*, although the terms capital income and capital revenue are not normally adopted. *Income of a revenue nature* would include the revenue from the sale of goods to customers, dividends and rents received. *Income of a capital nature* would include the resources invested by the owner in the business, and long-term loans made to it (such as bank loans).

In practice, it is not always easy to distinguish between capital and revenue items, and the distinction is often an arbitrary one. Some items of expenditure are particularly difficult to determine, although most transactions fall into recognizable categories.

The distinction between capital and revenue items is very important because, essentially, accounting profit is the difference between revenue income and revenue expenditure (see Figure 4.2). If capital and revenue items are not classified accurately, the accounting profit will be incorrectly calculated. This could be extremely misleading, especially if the amount was overstated, because the owner might then draw too much out of the business, or have to pay more tax. Bearing in mind the prudence rule, it would be much less serious if the profit was understated, because it is likely that more cash would then have been retained within the business.

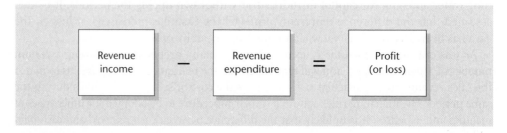

Figure 4.2 **Accounting profit**

<table>
<tr><td>**Activity 4.1**</td><td colspan="2">Are the following statements true or false?</td></tr>
<tr><td></td><td>(a) Accounting profit is normally the difference between cash received and cash paid.</td><td>*True/False*</td></tr>
<tr><td></td><td>(b) Capital expenditure only provides a short-term benefit.</td><td>*True/False*</td></tr>
<tr><td></td><td>(c) Fixed assets are normally written off to the trading account.</td><td>*True/False*</td></tr>
</table>

Preparation

We are now in a position to examine how a set of basic financial accounts for a trading entity is compiled, and hence how to calculate the amount of profit a business has made. We will assume that a trial balance has been prepared and that the books balance. There are then two main stages we have to go through in order to compile the accounts. We will deal with each stage separately.

The trading and profit and loss account stage

Once the trial balance has been compiled, the next step is to prepare a trading account and a profit and loss account. In order to do so, all the revenue income and expenditure items are extracted from the trial balance. These are then matched against each other in the form of a statement called (as you would expect) a *trading and profit and loss account*. By deducting the total of the revenue balances from the total of the revenue expenditure balances, we can determine the level of the profit (or loss) for the period. There are two important points to note. These are as follows.

1 The *trading account* comes before the profit and loss account. It matches the sales revenue for a certain period against the cost of goods sold (i.e. purchases) for the same period. The difference between the sales revenue and the cost of goods sold is known as *gross profit*. The gross profit is then transferred to the profit and loss account, where it is added to the other revenue incomes of the business. That total is then matched against the other expenses of the business (such as heat and light, and wages and salaries). The difference between the gross profit plus other non-trading incomes, less the other expenses is known as *net profit* (or net loss). This all sounds very complicated, but we can express it in the form of two equations:

$$Sales\ revenue - cost\ of\ goods\ sold = gross\ profit$$
$$(Gross\ profit + revenue\ income) - revenue\ expenditure =$$
$$net\ profit\ (or\ net\ loss)$$

2 Both the trading account and the profit and loss account are accounts in their own right. This means that any transfer to or from them forms part of the double-entry procedure, and so a corresponding and equal entry has to be made in some other account.

The balance sheet stage

Once the trading account and profit and loss account balances have been extracted, all the balances left in the trial balance are summarized in the form of a statement called a *balance sheet*. A balance sheet is simply a listing of all the remaining balances left in the ledger account system following the preparation of the trading account and the profit and loss account. Unlike trading and profit and loss accounts, a balance sheet does not form part of the double-entry system: it is merely a listing of the remaining balances in the ledger system at the end of an accounting period. We could also describe it another way, and suggest that it is a listing of all the capital revenue and capital expenditure balances.

Activity 4.2	Fill in the missing words in the following equations.
	(a) Sales revenue less ____ __ _____ ____ = gross profit
	(b) (___ profit plus revenue income) less revenue _____ = ___ profit/(loss)

We are now in a position to show you how to prepare a set of basic trading entity accounts.

An illustrative example

In this section, we explain how to compile a trading account, a profit and loss account, and a balance sheet. The procedure is illustrated in Example 4.1.

Example 4.1	Preparation of basic financial accounts

The following trial balance has been extracted from Bush's books of account as at 30 June 2004:

Name of account		Dr £	Cr £
Bank (1)		5 000	
Capital (at 1 July 2000) (2)			11 000
Cash (3)		1 000	
Drawings (4)		8 000	
Motor vehicle at cost (5)		6 000	
Motor vehicle expenses (6)	(R)	2 000	
Office expenses (7)	(R)	3 000	
Purchases (8)	(R)	30 000	
Trade creditors (9)			4 000
Trade debtors (10)		10 000	
Sales (11)	(R)		50 000
		65 000	65 000

Notes:
There were no opening or closing stocks.
R = revenue items.

Required:

(a) Prepare Bush's trading and profit and loss account for the year to 30 June 2004.
(b) Prepare a balance sheet as at that date.

The horizontal format

Bush
Trading and profit and loss account for the year to 30 June 2004

	£		£
Purchases (8)	30 000	Sales (11)	50 000
Gross profit c/d	20 000		
	50 000		50 000
Motor vehicle expenses (6)	2 000	Gross profit b/d	20 000
Office expenses (7)	3 000		
Net profit c/d	15 000		
	20 000		20 000
		Net profit b/d	15 000

Tutorial notes

1 The number shown in brackets after each narration refers to the account number of each balance extracted from the trial balance.

2 Both the trading account and the profit and loss account cover a period of time. In this example it is for the year to (or alternatively, *ending*) 30 June 2004.

3 It is not customary to keep the trading account totally separate from the profit and loss account. The usual format is the one shown above whereby the trading account balance (that is, the gross profit) is carried down straight into the profit and loss account.

4 Note that the proprietor's drawings (4), are not an expense of the business. They are treated as an *appropriation*, i.e. an amount withdrawn by the proprietor in advance of any profit that the business might have made.

The above trading and profit and loss account has been prepared in a ledger account format. This is known as the horizontal format because the debit entries (expenses) are shown on the left-hand side of the page, while the credit entries (incomes) are shown on the right-hand side. Trading and profit and loss accounts are ledger accounts in their own right, but they are also used to pass on information to parties who are not involved in the detailed recording procedures. Research evidence suggests that this format is not particularly helpful for those users who are not trained in double-entry book-keeping. A more acceptable presentation is when the information is presented on a line-by-line basis, starting from the top of the page and working downwards towards the bottom of the page. This is known as the vertical format. In accordance with modern practice, we will adopt this format for the presentation of financial statements throughout the rest of the book.

In the vertical account format Bush's trading and profit and loss account would appear as set out overleaf.

Answer to
Example 4.1(a)
continued

The vertical format

Bush
Trading and profit and loss account for the year to
30 June 2004

	£	£
Sales		50 000
Less: cost of goods sold:		
Purchases		30 000
Gross profit		20 000
Less: expenses		
Motor vehicle expenses	2 000	
Office expenses	3 000	5 000
Net profit for the year		15 000

Answer to
Example 4.1(b)

Bush's balance sheet, also prepared in the **vertical format**, would appear as follows.

Bush
Balance sheet at 30 June 2004

	£	£
Fixed assets		
Motor vehicles at cost (5)		6 000
Current assets		
Trade debtors (10)	10 000	
Bank (1)	5 000	
Cash (3)	1 000	
	16 000	
Current liabilities		
Trade creditors (9)	4 000	12 000
		18 000
Capital		
Balance at 1 July 2004 (2)		11 000
Add: Net profit for the year*	15 000	
Less: Drawings (4)	8 000	7 000
		18 000

* Obtained from the profit and loss account.

Tutorial notes

1 The balance sheet is prepared at a particular moment in time. It depicts the balances as they were at a specific date. In this example, the balances are shown as at 30 June 2004.

2 The balance sheet is divided into two main sections. The first section shows the net assets that the entity owned at 30 June 2004. The net assets include the fixed assets plus the current assets less the current liabilities. The net assets total of £18 000 shows how much was invested in the business as at the balance sheet date. The second section shows how the net assets have been financed, i.e. by a combination of capital and retained profits. The total amount of £18 000 is, of course, the same amount as the total of the net assets. In other words, as the net assets section equals the capital section, the balance sheet balances.

3 This arrangement of the balance sheet is a little different from the way that we presented the accounting equation in Chapter 3, i.e. Assets = Capital + Liabilities. Here, the balance sheet is presented in the format: Assets – Liabilities = Capital. This format is quite common and we shall follow it in all subsequent examples.

4 The fixed assets represent those assets that are intended for long-term use within the business. Fixed assets are usually shown at their original (i.e. their historic) cost, and this should be stated on the balance sheet

5 The current assets include those assets that are constantly being turned over, e.g. stock, debtors, and cash.

6 Both fixed assets and current assets should be listed in the order of the least liquid (or realizable) assets being placed first, e.g. property should come before machinery, and stock before trade debtors. The total of fixed assets and current assets is known as *total assets*.

7 The current liabilities section shows the amounts owed to various parties outside the entity due for payment within the next 12 months. They should be listed in the order of those that are going to be paid last being placed first, e.g. a short-term loan should come before trade creditors.

8 The capital section of the balance sheet shows the capital at the beginning of the year. This is then increased by the profit earned for the year (the balance is extracted from the profit and loss account). The profit and loss account balance has to be added to the capital balance (or deducted if there is a loss) because it is a summary balance, i.e. it is a net balance obtained after matching the revenue income and expenditure balances. However, the profit for the year is reduced by the total of the proprietor's 'drawings' for the year. It is then possible to see how much profit was left in the business out of the current year's profit. Proprietor's *drawings* represent the amounts of cash and the value of any goods withdrawn by the owner of the business during the year in anticipation of any profit that might be made (or was made in previous years).

Answer to
Example 4.1(b)
continued

Referring to Example 4.1, prepare Bush's trading and profit and loss account for the year to 30 June 2004 and a balance sheet at that date in the vertical format without looking at the solution.

Activity 4.3

 ## Questions non-accountants should ask

This has been a short chapter but it has shown you how a simple trading and profit and loss account and a balance sheet may be prepared using the information extracted from a trial balance. When faced with such financial statements you might put the following questions to your accountants.

● What criteria have you adopted for determining whether a transaction is a capital item or a revenue item?

● Are there any such items included in the accounts where the distinction is arguable?

● How have you determined whether revenue income should or should not be included in the current trading account?

These questions would also apply to the material included in Chapters 5, 6 and 7.

Conclusion

In this chapter we have examined the preparation and format of a basic set of financial accounts for a trading entity. In practice, once a trial balance has been agreed, a number of end-of-year adjustments would normally be made before the financial accounts are eventually finalized. These adjustments will be examined in the next chapter.

Key points

1 A trial balance provides the basic data for the preparation of the financial accounts.

2 The basic financial accounts for a trading entity normally consist of a trading account, a profit and loss account, and a balance sheet.

3 Revenue transactions are transferred to either the trading account or the profit and loss account, and capital items to the balance sheet.

4 The trading account and the profit and loss account form part of the double-entry system. The balance sheet is merely a listing of the balances that remain in the ledger system once the trading and profit and loss accounts have been prepared.

Check your learning

The answers to these questions may be found within the text.

1 Suggest two reasons why this chapter is important for non-accountants.

2 Name two important functions of a trial balance.

3 What are the three financial statements that make up a set of basic accounts?

4 What are the two broad groups into which all transactions may be classified?

5 Explain why accounting profit is not the same as an increase in cash.

6 Express accounting profit in the form of a simple equation.

7 Name the two stages involved in preparing the basic accounts.

8 What term is given to the difference between sales revenue and the cost of goods sold?

9 What term is given to the difference between the total of all revenue income and the total of all revenue expenditure?

10 What two formats may be used for the presentation of financial statements?

11 Which format is the one now commonly used in practice?

News story quiz

Remember the news story at the beginning of this chapter? Go back to that story and reread it before answering the following questions.

In order to compile an entity's trading and profit and loss account, it is necessary to distinguish between capital and revenue items. In practice, this is not always easy and a great deal of individual discretion may be required. Furthermore, even if a revenue item can be recognized fairly easily it is not always clear to which accounting period it relates. This article emphasizes the importance of disclosing what criteria have been used in determining the 'revenue' for a particular accounting period.

Questions

1 What is meant by the term 'revenue recognition'?

2 Why is there a problem in determining how much revenue has been earned in a particular accounting period?

3 How should revenue be determined or measured?

4 Do you think that entities should have to disclose their revenue recognition policies?

Tutorial questions

The answers to questions marked with an asterisk may be found in Appendix 4.

4.1 Explain why an increase in cash during a particular accounting period does not necessarily mean that an entity has made a profit.

4.2 'The differentiation between so-called capital and revenue expenditure is quite arbitrary and unnecessary.' Discuss.

4.3 How far does a balance sheet tell users how much an entity is worth?

4.4* The following trial balance has been extracted from Ethel's books of accounts as at 31 January 2004:

	Dr £	Cr £
Capital		10 000
Cash	c/f 3 000	

	Dr	Cr
	£	£
	b/f 3 000	10 000
Creditors		3 000
Debtors	6 000	
Office expenses	11 000	
Premises	8 000	
Purchases	20 000	
Sales		35 000
	48 000	48 000

Required:
Prepare Ethel's trading and profit and loss account for the year to 31 January 2004 and a balance sheet as at that date.

4.5* Marion has been in business for some years. The following trial balance has been extracted from her books of account as at 28 February 2005:

	Dr	Cr
	£000	£000
Bank	4	
Buildings	50	
Capital		50
Cash	2	
Creditors		24
Debtors	30	
Drawings	55	
Heat and light	10	
Miscellaneous expenses	25	
Purchases	200	
Sales		400
Wages and salaries	98	
	474	474

Required:
Prepare Marion's trading and profit and loss account for the year to 28 February 2005 and a balance sheet as at that date.

4.6 The following trial balance has been extracted from Jody's books of account as at 30 April 2004:

	Dr	Cr
	£000	£000
Capital (as at 1 May 2003)		30
Cash	1	
Electricity	2	
Maintenance	4	
Miscellaneous expenses	7	
	c/f 14	30

		Dr	Cr
		£000	£000
	b/f	14	30
Purchases		40	
Rent and rates		6	
Sales			85
Vehicle (at cost)		30	
Wages		25	
		115	115

Required:

Prepare Jody's trading and profit and loss account for the year to 30 April 2004 and a balance sheet as at that date.

4.7 The following trial balance has been extracted from the books of Garswood as at 31 March 2005:

	Dr	Cr
	£	£
Advertising	2 300	
Bank	300	
Capital		55 700
Cash	100	
Discounts allowed	100	
Discounts received		600
Drawings	17 000	
Electricity	1 300	
Investments	4 000	
Investment income received		400
Office equipment	10 000	
Other creditors		800
Other debtors	1 500	
Machinery	20 000	
Purchases	21 400	
Purchases returns		1 400
Sales		63 000
Sales returns	3 000	
Stationery	900	
Trade creditors		5 200
Trade debtors	6 500	
Wages	38 700	
	127 100	127 100

Required:

Prepare Garswood's trading and profit and loss account for the year to 31 March 2005 and a balance sheet as at that date.

4.8   Pete has extracted the following trial balance from his books of account as at 31 May 2005:

	Dr	Cr
	£000	£000
Bank		15
Building society account	100	
Capital (as at 1 June 2004)		200
Cash	2	
Heat, light and fuel	18	
Insurances	10	
Interest received		1
Land and property (at cost)	200	
Long-term loan		50
Long-term loan interest paid	8	
Motor vehicles (at cost)	90	
Motor vehicle expenses	12	
Plant and equipment (at cost)	100	
Property maintenance	7	
Purchases	300	
Repairs to machinery	4	
Rent and rates	65	
Sales		900
Wages and salaries	250	
	1166	1166

Required:
Prepare Pete's trading and profit and loss account for the year to 31 May 2005 and a balance sheet as at that date.

Further practice questions, study material and links to relevant sites on the World Wide Web can be found on the website that accompanies this book. The site can be found at **www.booksites.net/dyson**

Last minute adjustments

Provisions for doubtful sales affect profits . . .

PwC fried over caterer's books

By Philip Smith

French catering giant Sodexho Alliance has slammed its auditor over serious accounting errors found at a UK subsidiary.

PricewaterhouseCoopers, the company's UK auditor, had not been 'sufficiently vigilant', according to the company, which reported a rapid deterioration of profitability in its UK operations last week.

Following a management reshuffle earlier this year at Sodexho Land Technology, the company's UK grounds maintenance subsidiary, the company uncovered 'serious errors of management as well as accounting anomalies'.

'The impact of these management errors has been made more serious and sudden because they have occurred in a difficult economic environment,' the company said.

Although there was no indication of fraud, the company said it had called in an independent expert to strengthen its analysis and internal audit processes.

The anomalies were understood to include the recording of sales for which payment looked doubtful.

The troubles at the UK subsidiary forced Sodexho to restate its forecasts for the year – the group predicted it would achieve revenues of between €180m (£113m) and €190m instead of the €210m previously announced.

A spokesman for PwC declined to comment.

Accountancy Age, 26 September 2002.

Questions relating to this news story may be found on page 111 ▶▶

About this chapter

The last chapter explained how the trial balance is used to prepare the financial accounts, i.e. a trading account, a profit and loss account, and a balance sheet.

Even if the book-keeping system has been kept up to date there are always some outstanding matters at the end of the financial year. Such matters have to be included in the accounts, so it is usually necessary to make some last minute adjustments.

In this chapter we are going to deal with four such adjustments: (1) stock; (2) depreciation; (3) accruals and prepayments; and (4) bad and doubtful debts. These are shown in Figure 5.1.

If adjustments have to be made for such matters then they will have to be eventually entered into the books of account before all of the accounts can be balanced and closed off for the year. We shall not be involved in the tidying up process that takes place after the financial accounts have been prepared.

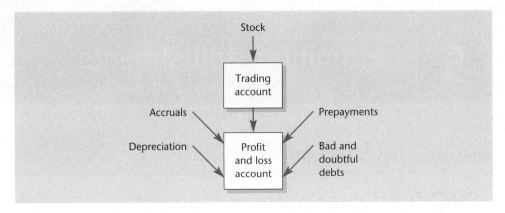

Figure 5.1 **Main adjustments**

We want to concentrate on the four last minute adjustments listed above. They are very important because all of them involve exercising a great deal of personal judgement. The decisions taken about how to treat them can have a significant effect on the profit or loss reported for the year, so it is necessary to give a great deal of thought to what should be done.

The chapter is divided into eight main sections. After the learning objectives the first main section explains why this chapter is particularly important for non-accountants. The following four sections then deal respectively with the last minute adjustments normally made before the financial accounts are finalized, *viz.* stocks, depreciation, accruals and prepayments, and bad and doubtful debts. We then bring them together in a comprehensive example. The penultimate main section provides a warning about relying too much on the absolute level of profit disclosed in a profit and loss account. The last main section poses some critical questions that non-accountants ought to ask of their accountants about the type of adjustments covered in this chapter.

But first we explain why this chapter is of particular interest to non-accountants.

Learning objectives

By the end of this chapter you should be able to:

● **make adjustments for stock, depreciation, accruals and prepayments, and bad and doubtful debts in a set of financial accounts;**

● **prepare a set of financial accounts incorporating such adjustments;**

● **list five main defects of conventional accounts.**

! Why this chapter is important for non-accountants

This chapter is particularly important for non-accountants.

The various last minute adjustments covered in the chapter are explained by using a number of arithmetical examples. In practice, of course, as a non-accountant you would not have to do the calculations yourself. Your accountants will do them for you.

Nevertheless, in our view you do need to know (a) what each adjustment means; (b) why it is made; (c) what methods can be used for making it; and (d) the impact that the adjustment has on the accounting profit for the year. Why?

Generally, there is little disagreement about what the adjustments mean and why there is a need to make them. Most accountants would accept that the conventional method of preparing accounting statements means that such adjustments are necessary. Otherwise the financial accounts would not include all the economic activity that has taken place during a particular period and the accounting profit would not be representative of what has happened. Different accountants, however, may use different assumptions and different estimates in making any necessary last minute adjustments because they generally require a great deal of personal judgement.

By using different assumptions and different estimates, accountants may produce different levels of profit. This is something that non-accounting managers cannot ignore. They must be involved in such decisions if they are responsible for approving the financial accounts. Thus they must review what assumptions their accountants have used and they must question the estimates that have been built into preparing the accounts.

Non-accountants cannot do so, of course, if they do not understand why various adjustments have been made. This chapter will enable you to become fully involved in a discussion with your accountants about how stock, depreciation, various accruals and prepayments, and bad and doubtful debts should be treated in the accounts.

It is in your own interest for you to grasp fully the various issues discussed in the chapter. Otherwise, you will be leaving it to the accountants to decide how much profit your company has made. That is surely something no non-accounting manager would want to do or feel safe in doing.

We now move on to discuss the first of the last minute adjustments that most manufacturing and trading entities have to make: stock adjustments.

Stock

It is most unlikely that all of the purchases that have been made during a particular period will have been sold by the end of it. There almost certainly will still be some purchases in the stores at the period end. In accounting terminology, purchases still on hand at the period end are referred to as *stock* (the Americans use the term *inventory*).

In calculating the gross profit for the period, therefore, it is necessary to make some allowance for closing stock, since we want to match the sales revenue earned for the period with the cost of goods sold, and not the cost of all of those goods actually purchased during the period. So we have to check the quantity of stock we have on hand at the end of the accounting period and then put some value on it. In practice, this is an extremely difficult exercise, and we shall be returning to it in a little more detail in Chapter 15. Most examples used in this part of the book assume that the value of the closing stock is readily available.

We also have another problem in dealing with stock. Closing stock at the end of one period becomes the opening stock at the beginning of the next period. In calculating the cost of goods sold, therefore, we have to allow for opening stock. The cost of goods sold can be quite easily calculated by adopting the following formula:

Cost of goods sold = (opening stock + purchases) – closing stock

The book-keeping entries are not quite as easy to understand, but they may be summarized as follows:

1. Enter the opening stock in the trading account. To do so, make the following entries: DEBIT the trading account; CREDIT the stock account; with the value of the opening stock as estimated at the end of the previous period. This should have been brought down as a debit balance in the stock account at the beginning of the current period.
2. Estimate the value of the closing stock (using one of the methods described in Chapter 15).
3. Enter the closing stock in the trading account. To do so, make the following entries: DEBIT the stock account; CREDIT the trading account; with the value of the closing stock as estimated in stage 2 above.

By making these adjustments the trading account should now appear as in Example 5.1

Example 5.1	**Example of a trading account with stock adjustments**

	£		£
Opening stock	1 000	Sales	4 000
Purchases	2 000	Closing stock	1 500
Gross profit c/d	2 500		
	5 500		5 500
		Gross profit b/d	2 500

This format does not show clearly the cost of goods sold, and so it is customary to *deduct the closing stock* from the total of opening stock and purchases. The information will then be presented as follows:

	£	£
Sales		4 000
Less: Cost of goods sold		
Opening stock	1 000	
Purchases	2 000	
	3 000	
Less: Closing stock	1 500	1 500
Gross profit		2 500

Study this format very carefully; it will be encountered frequently in subsequent examples.

Activity 5.1	Assume that Company A has a sales revenue of £10 000 for the year. The opening stock had a value of £2000 and during year the company made purchases of £6000.

What would be the gross profit if the closing stock was valued at

(a) £1500
(b) £2000
(c) £2500?

We now move on to the second of our last minute adjustments: depreciation.

As w   ore than one accounting period
is kno   s not normally included in either
the trad   but it would be misleading to exclude
it altogether

Expenditure on fixed assets (such as plant and machinery, motor vehicles, and furniture) is necessary in order to help provide a general service to the business. The benefit
received from the purchase of fixed assets must (by definition) extend beyond at least
one accounting period. The cost of the benefit provided by fixed assets ought, therefore,
to be charged to those accounting periods that benefit from such expenditure. The problem is in determining what charge to make. In accounting terminology, such a charge is
known as *depreciation*.

There is also another reason why fixed assets should be depreciated. By *not* charging
each accounting period with some of the cost of fixed assets, the level of profit will be
correspondingly higher. Thus the owner will be able to withdraw a higher level of profit
from the business. If this is the case, insufficient cash may be left in the business and the
owner may then find it difficult to buy new fixed assets.

In practice, it is not easy to measure the benefit provided to each accounting period by
some groups of fixed assets. Most depreciation methods tend to be somewhat simplistic.
The one method most commonly adopted is known as *straight-line depreciation*. This
method charges an equal amount of depreciation to each accounting period that benefits
from the purchase of a fixed asset. The annual depreciation charge is calculated as follows:

Annual depreciation charge =

$$\frac{Original\ cost\ of\ the\ asset - estimated\ residual\ value}{Estimated\ life\ of\ the\ asset}$$

You can see that in order to calculate the annual depreciation charge it is necessary to
work out (a) how long the asset is likely to last, and (b) what it can be sold for when its
useful life is ended.

Although it is customary to include fixed assets at their historic (i.e. original) cost in
the balance sheet, some fixed assets (such as property) may be revalued at regular intervals. If this is the case, the depreciation charge will be based on the revalued amount and
not on the historic cost. It should also be noted that even if the asset is depreciated on
the basis of its revalued amount there is still no guarantee that it can be replaced at that
amount. A combination of inflation and obsolescence may mean that the eventual
replacement cost is far in excess of either the historic cost or the revalued amount. It
follows that when the fixed asset eventually comes to be replaced, the entity may still not
have sufficient cash available to replace it.

The cost of a company's plant was £50 000. It was estimated that the plant would have
a life of 20 years and that it could then be sold for £5000.

Using the straight-line method of depreciation, how much depreciation would you
charge to the profit and loss account for Year 1?

Activity 5.2

Besides straight-line depr
that is sometimes used (altho   s
known as the *reducing balance*   m
in that it is based on the historic   ade
of the life of the asset and of its es   ually
expressed as a percentage and the   e of the
asset, i.e. after the depreciation charge in   The procedure is illustrated in Example 5.2.

Example 5.2	**Illustration of the reducing balance method of depreciating fixed assets**

Assume that an asset costs £1000, and that the depreciation rate is 50 per cent of the reduced balance. The depreciation charge per year would then be as follows:

Year		£
1. 1. 01	Historic cost	1 000
31.12.01	Depreciation charge for the year (50%)	500
	Reduced balance	500
31.12.02	Depreciation charge for the year (50%)	250
	Reduced balance	250
31.12.03	Depreciation charge for the year (50%)	125
	Reduced balance	125

. . . and so on, until the asset has been written down to its estimated residual value.

The reducing balance depreciation rate can be calculated by using the following formula:

$$r = 1 - \sqrt[n]{\frac{R}{C}}$$

where: r = the depreciation rate to be applied;
n = the estimated life of the asset;
R = its estimated (residual or scrap) value; and
C = its historic cost.

The reducing balance method results in a much higher level of depreciation in the first few years of the life of an asset and a much lower charge in later years. It is a suitable method to adopt when calculating the depreciation rate for such fixed assets as vehicles, because vehicles tend to have a high initial depreciation rate and a low rate as they become older. In addition, maintenance costs tend to be low to begin with and greater as the vehicles become older. So the combined depreciation charge plus maintenance costs produce a more even pattern of total vehicle costs than does the straight-line method.

There are other methods of depreciating fixed assets but since these are rarely used, we do not think that it is necessary for us to go into them in this book.

The ledger account entries for depreciation are quite straightforward. The annual charge for depreciation will be entered into the books of account as follows:

DEBIT Profit and loss account.
CREDIT Accumulated depreciation account with the depreciation charge for the year.

(*Note*: Each group of fixed assets will normally have its own accumulated depreciation account.)

As far as the balance sheet is concerned, it is customary to disclose the following details for each group of fixed assets:

1 historic cost (or revalued amount), i.e. the gross book value (GBV);
2 accumulated depreciation;
3 net book value (NBV).

(In other words, line 1 minus line 2 = line 3.)

We illustrate how this is normally shown in a balance sheet in Example 5.3. The example shows how the accumulated depreciation is deducted from the original cost for each group of assets, thereby arriving at the respective net book value for each group. The total net book value (£88 000 in Example 5.3) forms part of the balancing of the balance sheet. The total cost of the fixed assets and the total accumulated depreciation are shown purely for information. Such totals do not form part of the balancing process.

Balance sheet disclosure of fixed assets

Example 5.3

Fixed assets	Cost	Depreciation	Net book value
	£	£	£
Buildings	100 000	30 000	70 000
Equipment	40 000	25 000	15 000
Furniture	10 000	7 000	3 000
	150 000	62 000	88 000
Current assets			
Stocks		10 000	
Debtors		8 000	
Cash		2 000	
			20 000
			108 000

The third of our last minute adjustments relates to accruals and prepayments.

Accruals and prepayments

We explained in Chapter 2 why it is sometimes necessary to make an adjustment for accruals and prepayments. We will now examine this procedure in a little more detail.

Accruals

An accrual is an amount owing for a service provided during a particular accounting period and still unpaid for at the end of it. It is expected that the amount due will normally be settled in cash in a subsequent accounting period. The entity may, for example, have paid the last quarter's electricity bill one week before the year end. In its accounts for that year, therefore, it needs to allow for (or *accrue*) the amount that it will owe for the electricity consumed during the last week of the year.

The accrual will be based on an estimate of the likely cost of one week's supply of electricity, or as a proportion of the amount payable (if it has already received the invoice).

The ledger account entries are reasonably straightforward. It is not normal practice to open a separate account for accruals, the double entry being completed within the account that relates to that particular service. Example 5.4 illustrates the procedure.

Example 5.4	**Accounting for accruals**

Electricity Account

		£			£
1.4.04	Bank	400	1.4.04	Balance b/d*	400
1.7.04	Bank	300			
1.9.04	Bank	100			
1.1.05	Bank	500			
31.3.05	Balance c/d**	600	31.3.05	Profit and loss account	1 500
		1 900			1 900
			1.4.05	Balance b/d	600

* This balance is assumed to be an accrual made in the year to 31 March 2004.
** This amount is an accrual for the year to 31 March 2005.

You will note from Example 5.4 that the balance on the electricity account at 31 March 2005 is transferred to the profit and loss account. The ledger account entries are as follows:

> DEBIT   Profit and loss account.
> CREDIT   Electricity account with the electricity charge for the year.

The double entry has been completed for the accrual by debiting it in the accounts for the year to 31 March 2005 (i.e. above the line), and crediting it in the following year's account (i.e. below the line). The accrual of £600 will be shown on the balance sheet at 31 March 2005 in the current liabilities section under the subheading 'accruals'.

You owed £500 to the telephone company at 31 December 2003. During the year to 31 December 2004 you paid the company £4000. At 31 December 2004 you owed the company £1000.

What amount for telephone charges would you debit to the profit and loss account for the year to 31 December 2004?

Prepayments

A prepayment is an amount paid in cash during an accounting period for a service that will be provided in a subsequent period. For example, if a company's year end is 31 December and it buys a van halfway through 2004 and licences it for 12 months, half of the fee paid will relate to 2004 and half to 2005. It is necessary, therefore, to adjust 2004's accounts so that only half of the fee is charged in that year. The other half will eventually be charged to 2005's accounts. The book-keeping procedure is illustrated in Example 5.5.

Accounting for prepayments

Van tax account

		£			£
1.1.04	Balance b/d*	40	31.12.04	Profit and	
1.7.04	Bank	100		loss account	90
			31.12.04	Balance c/d**	50
		140			140
1.1.05	Balance b/d	50			

* This balance is assumed to be a prepayment arising in the previous year.
** This amount is assumed to be a prepayment as at 31 December 2004.

You will note from Example 5.5 that the balance on the van tax account is transferred to the profit and loss account. The double-entry procedure is as follows:

> **DEBIT** Profit and loss account.
> **CREDIT** Van tax account with the annual cost of the tax on the van.

The double entry has been completed by debiting the prepayment in next year's accounts (i.e. below the line) and crediting it to this year's accounts (i.e. above the line).

The prepayment of £50 made at 31 December 2004 will be shown in the balance sheet at that date in the current assets section under the subheading 'prepayments'.

Activity 5.4

Jill had paid £3000 in advance for insurance at 31 December 2004. During the year to 31 December 2005 she paid the insurance company £10 000. At 31 December 2004 she estimated that she had paid £2000 for insurance cover that related to the following year.

What amount for insurance charges should Jill debit to her profit and loss account for the year to 31 December 2005?

Our fourth last minute adjustment relates to bad and doubtful debts.

Bad and doubtful debts

The fourth main adjustment made in finalizing the annual accounts involves making adjustments for bad debts and provisions for bad and doubtful debts.

It was explained in Chapter 2 that the realization rule allows us to claim profit for any goods that have been sold, even if the cash for them is not received until a later accounting period. This means that we are taking a risk in claiming the profit on those goods in the earlier period, even if the legal title has been passed to the customer. If the goods are not eventually paid for, we will have overestimated the profit for that period. The owner might already have taken the profit out of the business (e.g. by increasing his cash drawings), and it then might be too late to do anything about it.

Fortunately, there is a technique whereby we can build in an allowance for any possible *bad debts* (as they are called). This is quite a tricky operation, and so we will need to explain it in two stages: (a) how to account for bad debts; and (b) how to allow for the possibility that some debts may be *doubtful*.

Bad debts

Once it is clear that a debt is bad (in other words, that it is highly unlikely it will ever be paid), then it must be written off immediately. This means that we have to charge it to the current year's profit and loss account, even though it may relate to an earlier period. It is usually impractical to change accounts once they have been finalized because the owner may have already drawn a share of the profits out of the business.

The double-entry procedure for writing off bad debts is quite straightforward. The entries are as follows:

DEBIT   Profit and loss account.
CREDIT   Trade debtor's account with the amount of the bad debt to be written off.

Trade debtors will be shown in the balance sheet *after* deducting any bad debts that have been written off to the profit and loss account.

Activity 5.5

Gibson's trade debtors at 31 December 2005 amount to £75 000. One of the trade debtors has owed Gibson £5000 since 1998. Gibson thinks that the debtor now lives abroad in exile.

Should Gibson write off the £5000 as a bad debt to the profit and loss account for the year to 31 December 2005? If so, which account should be debited and which account should be credited? And what amount for trade debtors should be shown in Gibson's balance sheet at 31 December 2005?

Provisions for bad and doubtful debts

The profit in future accounting periods would be severely distorted if the entity suffered a whole series of bad debts. It seems prudent, therefore, to allow for the possibility that some debts may become bad. We can do this by seting up a *provision* for bad and doubtful debts (a provision is simply an amount set aside for something that is highly likely to happen), and opening a special account for that purpose.

In order to do so, it is necessary to estimate the likely level of bad debts. The estimate will normally be based on the experience that the entity has had in dealing with specific bad debts. In simple book-keeping exercises, the provision is usually expressed as a percentage of the outstanding trade debtors. The double-entry procedure is as follows:

DEBIT   Profit and loss account.
CREDIT   Provision for bad and doubtful debts account with the amount of the
             provision needed to meet the expected level of bad and doubtful debts.

The procedure is illustrated in Example 5.6.

Example 5.6

Accounting for bad and doubtful debts

You are presented with the following information for the year to 31 March 2004:

	£
Trade debtors at 1 April 2003	20 000
Trade debtors at 31 March 2004 (including £3000 of specific bad debts)	33 000
Provision for bad and doubtful debts at 1 April 2003	1 000

Note: A provision for bad and doubtful debts is maintained equivalent to 5 per cent of the trade debtors as at the end of the year.

Required:
(a) Calculate the increase required in the bad and doubtful debts provision account for the year to 31 March 2004; and
(b) show how both the trade debtors and the provision for bad and doubtful debts account would be featured in the balance sheet at 31 March 2004.

Answer to Example 5.6(a)

	£
Trade debtors as at 31 March 2004	33 000
Less: Specific bad debts to be written off to the profit and loss account for the year to 31 March 2004	3 000
	30 000
Provision required: 5% thereof	1 500
Less: Provision at 1 April 2003	1 000
Increase in the bad and doubtful debts provision account*	500

* This will be charged to the profit and loss account for the year to 31 March 2004

Tutorial note

The balance on the provision for bad and doubtful debts account will be higher at 31 March 2004 than it was at 1 April 2003. This arises because the level of trade debtors is higher at the end of 2004 than it was at the end of 2003. The required increase in the provision of £500 will be *debited* to the profit and loss account. If it had been possible to reduce the provision (because of a lower level of trade debtors at the end of 2004 compared with 2003), the decrease would have been *credited* to the profit and loss account.

Answer to Example 5.6(b)

Balance sheet extract at 31 March 2004

	£	£
Current assets		
Trade debtors	30 000	
Less: Provision for bad and doubtful debts	1 500	
		28 500

The treatment of bad debts and doubtful debts in ledger accounts is a fairly complicated and technical exercise. However, as a non-accountant it is important for you to grasp just two essential points:

1 A debt should never be written off until it is absolutely certain that it is bad. Once it is written off, it is highly likely that no further attempt will probably ever be made to recover it.
2 It is prudent to allow for the possibility of some doubtful debts. Nevertheless it is perhaps rather a questionable decision to reduce profit by an arbitrary amount, e.g. by guessing whether it should be 3 per cent or 5 per cent of outstanding debtors. Obviously, the level that you choose can make a big difference to profit.

Activity 5.6

Watson keeps a provision for bad and doubtful debts account. It is maintained at a level of 3% of his total outstanding trade debtors as at the end of the year. The balance on the provision account at 1 January 2006 was £9000. His trade debtors at 31 December 2006 amounted to £250 000.

What balance on his provision for bad and doubtful debts does he need to carry forward as at 31 December 2006? What amount does he need to write off to the profit and loss account for that year? And will it increase or decrease his profit?

We have covered a great deal of technical matter in this chapter, and so it would now be helpful to bring all the material together in the form of a comprehensive example.

A comprehensive example

In this section, we use a comprehensive example to cover all the basic procedures that we have outlined in both this chapter and the preceding one. The example used in Example 5.7 is a fairly detailed one, so take your time in working through it.

Example of basic accounting procedures

Example 5.7

Wayne has been in business for many years. His accountant has extracted the following trial balance from his books of account as at 31 March 2005:

	£	£
Bank	1 200	
Capital		33 000
Cash	300	
Drawings	6 000	
Insurance	2 000	
Office expenses	15 000	
Office furniture at cost	5 000	
Office furniture: accumulated depreciation at 1 April 2004		2 000
Provision for bad and doubtful debts at 1 April 2004		500
Purchases	55 000	
Salaries	25 000	
Sales		100 000
Stock at 1 April 2004	10 000	
Trade creditors		4 000
Trade debtors	20 000	
	139 500	139 500

Notes: The following additional information is to be taken into account:

1 Stock at 31 March 2005 was valued at £15 000.
2 The insurance included £500 worth of cover which related to the year to 31 March 2006.
3 Depreciation is charged on office furniture at 10 per cent per annum of its original cost (it is assumed not to have any residual value).
4 A bad debt of £1000 included in the trade debtors balance of £20 000 is to be written off.
5 The provision for bad and doubtful debts is to be maintained at a level of 5 per cent of outstanding trade debtors as at 31 March 2005, i.e. after excluding the bad debt referred to in note 4 above.
6 At 31 March 2005, there was an amount owing for salaries of £1000.

Required:
(a) Prepare Wayne's trading and profit and loss account for the year to 31 March 2005; and
(b) prepare a balance sheet as at that date.

(a)

Wayne

Trading and profit and loss account for the year to 31 March 2005

	£	£	(Source of entry)
Sales		100 000	(TB)
Less: Cost of goods sold:			
Opening stock	10 000		(TB)
Purchases	55 000		(TB)
	65 000		
Less: Closing stock	15 000		(QN 1)
		50 000	
Gross profit		50 000	
Less: Expenses:			
Insurance (2000 – 500)	1 500		(Wkg 1)
Office expenses	15 000		(TB)
Depreciation: office furniture (10% × 5000)	500		(Wkg 2)
Bad debt	1 000		(QN 4)
Increase in provision for bad and doubtful debts	450		(Wkg 3)
Salaries (25 000 + 1000)	26 000		(Wkg 4)
		44 450	
Net profit for the year		5 550	

(b)

Wayne

Balance sheet at 31 March 2005

	£	£	£	(Source of entry)
Fixed assets	Cost	Accumulated depreciation	Net book value	
Office furniture	5 000	2 500	2 500	(TB and Wkg 5)
Current assets				
Stock		15 000		(QN 1)
Trade debtors (20 000 – 1000)	19 000			(Wkg3)
Less: Provision for bad and doubtful debts	950	18 050		(Wkg 3)
Prepayment		500		(QN2)
Cash at bank		1 200		(TB)
Cash in hand		300		(TB)
		35 050		
Less: Current liabilities				
Trade creditors	4 000			(TB)
Accrual	1 000			(QN 6)
		5 000	30 050	
			32 550	

	£	£	£	(Source of entry)
Financed by:				
Capital				
Balance at 31 March 2004			33 000	(TB)
Add: Net profit for the year		5 550		(P&L A/c)
Less: Drawings		6 000	(450)	
			32 550	

Answer to Example 5.7 continued

Key:
TB = from trial balance;
QN = extracted straight from the question and related notes;
Wkg = workings (see below);
P&L A/c = balance obtained from the profit and loss account.

Workings

		£
1	Insurance:	
	As per the trial balance	2 000
	Less: Prepayment (QN 2)	500
	Charge to the profit and loss account	1 500
2	Depreciation:	
	Office furniture at cost	5 000
	Depreciation: 10% of the original cost	500
3	Increase in provision for bad and doubtful debts:	
	Trade debtors at 31 March 2005	20 000
	Less: Bad debt (QN 4)	1 000
		19 000
	Provision required: 5% thereof	950
	Less: Provision at 1 April 2004	500
	Increase in provision: charge to profit and loss	450
4	Salaries:	
	As per the question	25 000
	Add: Accrual (QN 6)	1 000
		26 000
5	Accumulated depreciation:	
	Balance at 1 April 2004 (as per TB)	2 000
	Add: Depreciation for the year (Wkg 2)	500
	Accumulated depreciation at 31 March 2005	2 500

Attempt Example 5.7 without looking at the answer.

Activity 5.7

We are nearly at the end of a difficult chapter, but before we move on to other matters, we ought to examine somewhat critically what we have done in both this chapter and the preceding one.

Accounting profit

In previous sections of the book, we have emphasized that the calculation of accounting profit calls for a great deal of subjective judgement. Accounting involves much more than merely being very good at mastering some complicated arithmetical exercises. So we think that it would be helpful (indeed essential) if we summarized the major defects inherent in the traditional method of calculating accounting profit.

As a non-accountant, it is most important that you appreciate one vital fact: the method that we have outlined in calculating the profit for a period results in an *estimate* of what the accountant thinks the profit should be. You must not place too much reliance on the *absolute* level of accounting profit. It can only be as accurate and as reliable as the assumptions upon which it is based. If you accept the assumptions, then you can be fairly confident that the profit figure is reliable. You will then not go too far wrong in using the information for decision-making purposes. But you must know what the assumptions are and you must support them. The message can, therefore, be put as follows:

Always question accounting information before accepting it.

A summary of the main reasons why you should not place too much reliance on the actual level of accounting profit (especially if you are unsure about the assumptions upon which it is based) is outlined below:

1 Goods are treated as being sold when the legal title to them changes hands, and not when the customer has paid for them. In some cases, the cash for some sales may never be received.
2 Goods are regarded as having been purchased when the legal title to them is transferred to the purchaser, although there are occasions when they may not be received, e.g. if a supplier goes into receivership.
3 Goods that have not been sold at the period end have to be quantified and valued. This procedure involves a considerable amount of subjective judgement.
4 There is no clear distinction between so-called capital and revenue items.
5 Estimates have to be made to allow for accruals and prepayments.
6 The cost of fixed assets is apportioned between different accounting periods using methods that are fairly simplistic and highly questionable.
7 Arbitrary reductions in profit are made to allow for bad and doubtful debts.
8 Historic cost accounting makes no allowance for inflation. In a period of inflation, for example, the value of £100 at 1 January 2004 is not the same as £100 at 31 December 2004. Hence, profit tends to be overstated, partly because of low closing stock values and partly because depreciation charges will be based on the historic cost.

The above disadvantages of historic cost accounting are fairly severe but accountants have not yet been able to suggest anything better. If at this stage you are feeling somewhat disillusioned, therefore, then take comfort in the old adage that 'it is better to be vaguely right than precisely wrong'.

Activity 5.8

Are the following statements true or false?

(a) A provision for bad and doubtful debts results in cash leaving the business.   *True/False*
(b) An amount owing for rent at the end of the year is an accrual.   *True/False*
(c) There is no such thing as the correct level of accounting profit.   *True/False*

 Questions non-accountants should ask

It is important that as a non-accountant you should grasp the significance of this chapter. The decisions that your accountants will have taken in making a series of last minute adjustments to the financial accounts (particularly for stocks, depreciation, accruals and prepayment, and bad and doubtful debts) will have a significant effect on the amount of profit that the entity has earned during the year.

We suggest that perhaps you should ask the following questions.

● Was a physical stock check done at the year end?
● What method (such as historic cost, net realizable value, or current cost) was used to value the closing stock?
● What depreciation method has been used?
● Has historic cost been used to depreciate the fixed assets?
● If not, how has the current cost of fixed assets been determined?
● How has the expected life of the assets been assessed?
● How do such lives compare with those used by our competitors?
● How have any residual values for the fixed assets been estimated?
● How have estimated values been determined for any accruals and prepayments?
● Have any bad debts been written off?
● How can we be certain that they are indeed bad?
● What basis is used to determine an appropriate level of provision for bad and doubtful debts?

Conclusion

In this chapter, we have examined in some detail the main adjustments made to financial accounts at the end of an accounting period. You should now be in a far better position to assess the relevance and reliability of any accounting information that is presented to you.

The material that we have covered has provided a broad foundation for all the remaining chapters. It is essential that before moving on to them you satisfy yourself that you really do understand the mechanics behind the preparation of a set of basic financial accounts. To test your understanding of this subject, you are recommended to work through all of the examples contained in this chapter and the preceding one once again, and then to attempt some of the exercises that end this chapter.

Key points

1 Following the completion of the trial balance, some last minute adjustments have usually to be made to the financial accounts. The main adjustments are: stock, depreciation, accruals and prepayments, and bad and doubtful debts.

2 Accounting profit is merely an estimate. The method used to calculate it is highly questionable, and it is subject to very many criticisms. Undue reliance should not be placed on the actual level of profit shown in the accounts. The assumptions upon which profit is based should be carefully examined, and it should be viewed merely as a guide to decision making.

Check your learning

The answers to these questions may be found within the text.

1 What is stock?

2 What is the American term for it?

3 What is meant by 'opening stock' and 'closing stock'?

4 What three items make up the closing stock?

5 To which account are opening and closing stock transferred?

6 Is opening stock debited or credited to such account?

7 Similarly, is closing stock debited or credited to that account?

8 Is opening stock shown on the balance sheet at the end of an accounting period?

9 Is closing stock shown on the balance sheet at the end of an accounting period?

10 What is depreciation?

11 Name two methods of depreciating fixed assets.

12 How are each of those methods calculated?

13 Is depreciation debited or credited to the profit and loss account?

14 What is meant by the terms 'gross book value' and 'net book value'?

15 What amount for depreciation is shown on the balance sheet?

16 What is (a) an accrual; and (b) a prepayment?

17 Where are they normally disclosed in the profit and loss account?

18 Where are they to be found in the balance sheet?

19 What is (a) a bad debt; and (b) a doubtful debt?

20 What is a provision for bad and doubtful debts?

21 On what might the provision be based?

22 List eight reasons why the calculation of accounting profit is an arbitrary exercise.

News story quiz

Remember the news story at the beginning of this chapter? Go back to that story and reread it before answering the following questions.

Conventional accounting practice allows sales revenue to be included in an accounting period than the one in which cash relating to the sale is received. This is risky because debtors may not always pay what they owe. Hence the need to set up a provision for bad and doubtful debts.

This article shows that Sodexho Alliance got into some difficulties over doubtful sales.

Questions

1 Do you think that only the cash received from the sale of goods and services should be included in the financial accounts?

2 How might the risk be reduced of taking revenue to the trading account (or other income to the profit and loss account) before the cash for sales made has been received?

3 What factors would you take into account in deciding which of your outstanding trade debtors might be bad or doubtful?

4 What do you think the company meant when it stated that it had uncovered 'serious errors of management as well as accounting anomalies'?

Tutorial questions

The answers to questions marked with an asterisk may be found in Appendix 4.

5.1 'Depreciation methods and rates should be prescribed by law.' Discuss.

5.2 Explain why it is quite easy to manipulate the level of gross profit when preparing a trading account.

5.3 How far is it possible for an entity to build up hidden amounts of profit (known as *secret reserves*) by making some adjustments in the profit and loss account for bad and doubtful debts?

5.4* The following information has been extracted from Lathom's books of account for the year to 30 April 2004:

	£
Purchases	45 000
Sales	60 000
Stock (at 1 May 2003)	3 000
Stock (at 30 April 2004)	4 000

Required:
(a) Prepare Lathom's trading account for the year to 30 April 2004; and
(b) State where the stock at 30 April 2004 would be shown on the balance sheet as at that date.

5.5 Rufford presents you with the following information for the year to 31 March 2005:

	£
Purchases	48 000
Purchases returns	3 000
Sales	82 000
Sales returns	4 000
Stock at 1 April 2004	4 000

He is not sure how to value the stock as at 31 March 2005. Three methods have been suggested. They all result in different closing stock values, namely:

	£
Method 1	8 000
Method 2	16 000
Method 3	4 000

Required:
(a) Calculate the effect on gross profit for the year to 31 March 2005 by using each of the three methods of stock valuation; and
(b) state the effect on gross profit for the year to 31 March 2006 if method 1 is used instead of method 2.

5.6* Standish has been trading for some years. The following trial balance has been extracted from his books of account as at 31 May 2006:

	Dr £	Cr £
Capital		22 400
Cash	1 200	
Creditors		4 300
Debtors	6 000	
Drawings	5 500	
Furniture and fittings	8 000	
Heating and lighting	1 500	
Miscellaneous expenses	6 700	
Purchases	52 000	
Sales		79 000
Stock (at 1 June 2005)	7 000	
Wages and salaries	17 800	
	105 700	105 700

Note: Stock at 31 May 2006: £12 000.

Required:

Prepare Standish's trading and profit and loss account for the year to 31 May 2006 and a balance sheet as at that date.

5.7 Witton commenced business on 1 July 2006. The following trial balance was extracted from his books of account as at 30 June 2007:

	Dr £	Cr £
Capital		3 000
Cash	500	
Drawings	4 000	
Creditors		1 500
Debtors	3 000	
Motor car at cost	5 000	
Office expenses	8 000	
Purchases	14 000	
Sales		30 000
	34 500	34 500

Additional information:

1 Stock at 30 June 2007: £2000.

2 The motor car is to be depreciated at a rate of 20 per cent per annum on cost; it was purchased on 1 July 2006.

Required:

Prepare Witton's trading and profit and loss account for the year to 30 June 2007 and a balance sheet as at that date.

5.8   The following is an extract from Barrow's balance sheet at 31 August 2008:

Fixed assets	Cost	Accumulated depreciation	Net book value
	£	£	£
Land	200 000	–	200 000
Buildings	150 000	60 000	90 000
Plant	55 000	37 500	17 500
Vehicles	45 000	28 800	16 200
Furniture	20 000	12 600	7 400
	470 000	138 900	331 100

Barrow's depreciation policy is as follows:

1 a full year's depreciation is charged in the year of acquisition, but none in the year of disposal;
2 no depreciation is charged on land;
3 buildings are depreciated at an annual rate of 2 per cent on cost;
4 plant is depreciated at an annual rate of 5 per cent on cost after allowing for an estimated residual value of £5000;
5 vehicles are depreciated on a reduced balance basis at an annual rate of 40 per cent on the reduced balance;
6 furniture is depreciated on a straight-line basis at an annual rate of 10 per cent on cost after allowing for an estimated residual value of £2000.

Additional information:

1 During the year to 31 August 2009, new furniture was purchased for the office. It cost £3000 and it is to be depreciated on the same basis as the old furniture. Its estimated residual value is £300.
2 There were no additions to, or disposals of, any other fixed assets during the year to 31 August 2009.

Required:
(a) Calculate the depreciation charge for each of the fixed asset groupings for the year to 31 August 2009; and
(b) show how the fixed assets would appear in Barrow's balance sheet as at 31 August 2009.

5.9*   Pine started business on 1 October 2004. The following is his trial balance at 30 September 2005:

	£	£
Capital		6 000
Cash	400	
Creditors		5 900
Debtors	5 000	
Furniture at cost	8 000	
General expenses	14 000	
Insurance	2 000	
Purchases	21 000	
Sales		40 000
Telephone	1 500	
	51 900	51 900

The following information was obtained after the trial balance had been prepared:

1 Stock at 30 September 2005: £3000.
2 Furniture is to be depreciated at a rate of 15 per cent on cost.
3 At 30 September 2005, Pine owed £500 for telephone expenses and insurance had been prepaid by £200.

Required:
Prepare Pine's trading and profit and loss account for the year to 30 September 2005 and a balance sheet as at that date.

5.10 Dale has been in business for some years. The following is his trial balance at 31 October 2006:

	Dr	Cr
	£	£
Bank	700	
Capital		85 000
Depreciation (at 1 November 2005):		
Office equipment		14 000
Vehicles		4 000
Drawings	12 300	
Heating and lighting	3 000	
Office expenses	27 000	
Office equipment, at cost	35 000	
Rates	12 000	
Purchases	240 000	
Sales		350 000
Stock (at 1 November 2005)	20 000	
Trade creditors		21 000
Trade debtors	61 000	
Vehicles at cost	16 000	
Wages and salaries	47 000	
	474 000	474 000

Additional information (not taken into account when compiling the above trial balance):
1 Stock at 31 October 2006: £26 000.
2 Amount owing for electricity at 31 October 2006: £1500.
3 At 31 October 2006, £2000 had been paid in advance for rates.
4 Depreciation is to be charged on the office equipment for the year to 31 October 2006 at a rate of 20 per cent on cost and on the vehicles at a rate of 25 per cent on cost.

Required:
Prepare Dale's trading and profit and loss account for the year to 31 October 2006 and a balance sheet as at that date.

5.11 The following information relates to Astley for the year to 30 November 2004:

Item	Cash paid during the year to 30 November 2004	As at 1 December 2003 Accruals/ Prepayments		As at 30 November 2004 Accruals/ Prepayments	
	£	£	£	£	£
Electricity	26 400	5 200	–	8 300	–
Gas	40 100	–	–	–	4 900
Insurance	25 000	–	12 000	–	14 000
Rates	16 000	–	4 000	6 000	–
Telephone	3 000	1 500	–	–	200
Wages	66 800	1 800	–	–	–

Required:
(a) Calculate the charge to the profit and loss account for the year to 30 November 2004 for each of the above items.
(b) Demonstrate what amounts for accruals and prepayments would be shown in the balance sheet as at 30 November 2004.

5.12 Duxbury started in business on 1 January 2006. The following is his trial balance as at 31 December 2006:

	Dr £	Cr £
Capital		40 000
Cash	300	
Delivery van, at cost	20 000	
Drawings	10 600	
Office expenses	12 100	
Purchases	65 000	
Sales		95 000
Trade creditors		5 000
Trade debtors	32 000	
	140 000	140 000

Additional information:
1 Stock at 31 December 2006 was valued at £10 000.
2 At 31 December 2006 an amount of £400 was outstanding for telephone expenses, and the business rates had been prepaid by £500.
3 The delivery van is to be depreciated at a rate of 20 per cent per annum on cost.
4 Duxbury decides to set aside a provision for bad and doubtful debts equal to 5 per cent of trade debtors as at the end of the year.

Required:
Prepare Duxbury's trading and profit and loss account for the year to 31 December 2006 and a balance sheet as at that date.

5.13 Beech is a retailer. Most of his sales are made on credit terms. The following information relates to the first four years that he has been in business:

	2004	2005	2006	2007
Trade debtors as at 31 January:	£60 000	£55 000	£65 000	£70 000

The trade is one that experiences a high level of bad debts. Accordingly, Beech decides to set aside a provision for bad and doubtful debts equivalent to 10 per cent of trade debtors as at the end of the year.

Required:
(a) Show how the provision for bad and doubtful debts would be disclosed in the respective balance sheets as at 31 January 2004, 2005, 2006 and 2007; and
(b) calculate the increase/decrease in provision for bad and doubtful debts transferred to the respective profit and loss accounts for each of the four years.

5.14 The following is Ash's trial balance as at 31 March 2005:

	Dr	Cr
	£	£
Bank		4 000
Capital		20 500
Depreciation (at 1 April 2004): furniture		3 600
Drawings	10 000	
Electricity	2 000	
Furniture, at cost	9 000	
Insurance	1 500	
Miscellaneous expenses	65 800	
Provision for bad and doubtful debts (at 1 April 2004)		1 200
Purchases	80 000	
Sales		150 000
Stock (at 1 April 2004)	10 000	
Trade creditors		20 000
Trade debtors	21 000	
	199 300	199 300

Additional information:
1 Stock at 31 March 2005: £15 000.
2 At 31 March 2005 there was a specific bad debt of £6000. This was to be written off.
3 Furniture is to be depreciated at a rate of 10 per cent per annum on cost.
4 At 31 March 2005 Ash owes the electricity board £600, and £100 had been paid in advance for insurance.
5 The provision for bad and doubtful debts is to be set at 10 per cent of trade debtors as at the end of the year.

Required:
Prepare Ash's trading and profit and loss account for the year to 31 March 2005 and a balance sheet as at that date.

5.15 Lime's business has had liquidity problems for some months. The following trial balance was extracted from his books of account as at 30 September 2007:

	Dr £	Cr £
Bank		15 200
Capital		19 300
Cash from sale of office equipment		500
Depreciation (at 1 October 2006):		
office equipment		22 000
Drawings	16 000	
Insurance	1 800	
Loan (long-term from Cedar)		50 000
Loan interest	7 500	
Miscellaneous expenses	57 700	
Office equipment, at cost	44 000	
Provision for bad and doubtful debts		
(at 1 October 2006)		2 000
Purchases	320 000	
Rates	10 000	
Sales		372 000
Stock (at 1 October 2006)	36 000	
Trade creditors		105 000
Trade debtors	93 000	
	586 000	586 000

Additional information:
1 Stock at 30 September 2007: £68 000.
2 At 30 September 2007, accrual for rates of £2000 and insurance prepaid of £200.
3 Depreciation on office equipment is charged at a rate of 25 per cent on cost. During the year, office equipment costing £4000 had been sold for £500. Accumulated depreciation on this equipment amounted to £3000. Lime's depreciation policy is to charge a full year's depreciation in the year of acquisition and none in the year of disposal.
4 Specific bad debts of £13 000 are to be written off.
5 The provision for bad and doubtful debts is to be made equal to 10 per cent of outstanding trade debtors as at 30 September 2007.

Required:
Prepare Lime's trading, and profit and loss account for the year to 30 September 2007, and a balance sheet as at that date.

Further practice questions, study material and links to relevant sites on the World Wide Web can be found on the website that accompanies this book. The site can be found at **www.booksites.net/dyson**

Yet another company reports accounting irregularities . . .

MyTravel losses catch market by surprise

Troubled tour operator MyTravel has revealed a staggering overall loss of £72.8m for the year to September 2002 following three profit warnings in the last few months disclosing numerous accounting irregularities.

The revelation could have a dangerous impact on the UK accountancy profession which has insisted that the recent spate of US accounting scandals couldn't happen here. The losses were larger than predicted by analysts.

Accounting errors resulted in a £54.9m hit to the company's bottom line, and led to the sudden departure of finance director David Jardine and global development division

chief executive Richard Carrick. Non-executive director and audit committee member Kazia Kantor, who is credited with rescuing the Coats Viyella textiles group, has been brought in to take over from Jardine.

By moving its policies on revenue recognition to a more conservative basis, the company's 2001 accounts had to be adjusted by £20.3m, and the prior year by £19m. In addition, 'serious control failures' in MyTravel's new Rochdale accounting centre has resulted in a one-off £26m hit because of 'misallocations of costs between seasons and years and differences in intercompany accounts'. However, a change in

the treatment of costs on guaranteed accommodation and changes to its depreciation policy have apparently resulted in a beneficial impact of £10.4m.

The results – which were delayed when the company's bankers initially refused to renew a crucial £250m overdraft – have been described by chief executive Peter McHugh as 'extremely poor', adding that he is determined that 'we now draw a line in the sand'. Chairman David Crossland admitted the tour operator had gone through the worst year in its history, with an 'unacceptable' performance.

Accountancy, January 2003.

Questions relating to this news story may be found on page 136 ▶▶

About this chapter

In the two previous chapters we have shown you how to prepare a set of basic accounts for a sole trader entity. The management and organization of such entities are not normally very complex, so we have been able to cover the overall procedures without becoming too bogged down in the detail.

However, many non-accountants using this book are likely to work for a *company*. There are many different types of companies but the most common are private limited liability companies and public limited liability companies. By law, all companies have to prepare a set of annual accounts and supply a copy to their shareholders. They also have to file a copy (i.e. send one) with the Registrar of Companies. This means that it is then open to inspection by the public. The amount of detail disclosed or published in company accounts (i.e. included) depends upon their type and size.

We shall be dealing with the disclosure requirements of companies in Chapters 9, 10 and 11. In this chapter we explain how to prepare a company's financial accounts for internal management purposes. There are no legal requirements covering the presentation and contents of financial accounts for such purposes, so a company can do more or less as it wants. Nevertheless, in order to cut down on the amount of work involved most companies probably produce internal accounts that mirror the ones required for external purposes. Internal accounts are, however, likely to be much more detailed than the external ones and they may be compiled several times a year.

The chapter is divided into seven main sections. The next section explains why this chapter is important for non-accountants. The following section explores the concept of limited liability and the following one describes how companies are structured and organized. We then show in separate sections how a company's profit and loss account and balance sheet differ from those of a sole trader entity. All of the material covered in the chapter is then put together in a comprehensive example. The last main section frames some questions that non-accountants should ask about the issues raised in the chapter.

Learning objectives	By the end of this chapter you should be able to:

- explain what is meant by limited liability;
- distinguish between private and public companies;
- describe how companies are organized;
- prepare a basic set of accounts for a company.

❗ Why this chapter is important for non-accountants

This chapter is important for a non-accountant because it shows how the material covered in earlier chapters can be adapted for use in preparing company accounts. Many non-accountants work for a company while other non-accountants will have some contact with various types of companies in their professional and private life.

Non-accountants should be able to do their jobs more effectively if they know something about the origin, structure and operation of companies. They will be even better placed if they can use the available accounting information to assess the past performance and future prospects of particular companies.

In order to be in a position to do so, it is necessary to know where the accounting information comes from, what it includes, how it has been summarized, and any deficiencies that it may have. All of this can be best achieved by being able to prepare a simple set of financial accounts. This chapter provides non-accountants with that opportunity.

In practice, of course, non-accountants will not have to prepare their company's accounts. This will be done for them by the accountants. Similarly, published accounts will also be in the format that we will show in later chapters. Nevertheless, you will be able to get more out of them if you have some knowledge of how they have been prepared.

We start our study of company accounts with an explanation of what is meant by 'limited liability'.

Limited liability

There is a great personal risk in operating a business as a sole trader or as a partnership. If the business runs short of funds, the owners may be called upon to settle the business's debts out of their own private resources. This type of risk can have a damaging effect on the development of new businesses. Hence the need for a different type of entity that will neither make the owners bankrupt nor inhibit new developments. This need became apparent in the nineteenth century as a result of the Industrial Revolution when, in order to finance new and rapidly expanding industries (such as the railways, and iron and steel), enormous amounts of capital were required.

These sorts of ventures were undertaken at great personal risk. By agreeing to become involved in them, investors often faced bankruptcy if the ventures were unsuccessful (as they often were). It became apparent that the development of industry would be hindered unless some means could be devised of restricting the personal liability of prospective investors.

Hence the need for a form of *limited liability*. In fact, the concept of limited liability was not entirely an innovation of the nineteenth century but it did not receive legal recognition until the Limited Liability Act was passed in 1855. The Act only remained in force for a few months before it was repealed and incorporated into the Joint Stock Companies Act 1856.

By accepting the principle of limited liability, the 1855 Act also recognized the *entity* concept. By distinguishing between the private and public affairs of business proprietors, it effectively created a new form of entity. Since the 1850s, Parliament has passed a number of other Companies Acts, all of which have continued to give legal recognition to the concept of limited liability.

The important point about a limited liability company is that no matter what financial difficulties it may get into, its members cannot be required to contribute more than an agreed amount of capital. Thus there is no risk of members being forced into bankruptcy.

The concept of limited liability is often very difficult for business owners to understand, especially if they have formed a limited liability company out of what was originally a sole trader or a partnership entity. Unlike such entities, companies are bound by some fairly severe legal restrictions that affect their operations.

The legal restrictions can be somewhat burdensome but they are necessary for the protection of all those parties who might have dealings with the company (such as creditors and employees). This is because if a limited liability company runs short of funds the creditors and employees might not get paid. It is only fair, therefore, to warn all those people who might have dealings with it that they run a risk in doing business with it. So, companies have to be more open about their affairs than do sole traders and partnerships.

Activity 6.1

Limited liability companies have to disclose some information about their operations. They also have to put 'limited' (abbreviation 'ltd') or public limited company (abbreviation 'plc') after their name to warn the public that their liability is limited.

Do you think that such safeguards are adequate? What more can be done? How far do you think that it is fair for individuals to set up businesses under the protection of limited liability, as the business may then go into liquidation and the creditors are left without any means of getting their money back from the owners of the company? Is this acceptable if the concept of limited liability encourages new businesses to be formed?

Write down your responses in your notebook.

Structure and operation

In this section, we examine the structure and operation of limited liability companies. In order to make it easier to follow, we have broken down our examination into a number of subsections. In order to make it clearer, a summary of the section is presented in diagrammatic format in Figure 6.1.

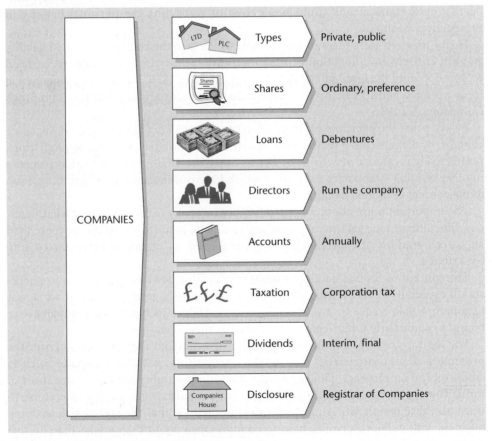

Figure 6.1 **Structure and operation of companies**

Share capital

Although the law recognizes that limited liability companies are separate beings with a life of their own (i.e. separate from those individuals who collectively own and manage them), it also accepts that someone has to take responsibility for promoting the company, i.e. bringing it into being. Only one person is now required to form a private company (two for a public company), and that person (or persons, if there are more than one), agrees to make a capital contribution by buying a number of shares. The capital of a company is known as its *share capital*. The share capital will be made up of a number of shares of a certain denomination, such as 10p, 50p and £1. Members may hold only one share, or many hundreds or thousands, depending upon the total share capital of the company, the denomination of the shares, and the amount that they wish to contribute.

The maximum amount of capital that the company envisages ever raising has to be stated. This is known as its *authorized share capital*, although this does not necessarily mean that it will issue shares up to that amount. In practice, it will probably only issue sufficient capital to meet its immediate and foreseeable requirements. The amount of share capital that it has actually issued is known as the *issued share capital*. Sometimes when shares are issued, prospective shareholders are only required to pay for them in instalments. Once all of the issued share capital has been received in cash, it is described as being *fully paid*.

There are two main types of shares: *ordinary shares* and *preference shares*. Ordinary shares do not usually entitle the shareholder to any specific level of dividend (see definition below), and the rights of other types of shareholders always take precedence over the rights of the ordinary shareholders, e.g. if the company goes into liquidation. Preference shareholders are normally entitled to a fixed level of dividend, and they usually have priority over the ordinary shareholders if the company is liquidated. Sometimes the preference shares are classed as *cumulative*; this means that if the company cannot pay its preference dividend in one year, the amount due accrues until such time as the company has the profits to pay all of the accumulated dividends.

The main types of shares and their structure are shown in outline form in Figure 6.2.

There are many other different types of shares, but in this book we need only concern ourselves with ordinary shares and preference shares.

Types

A prospective shareholder may invest in either a public company or a private company. A *public company* must have an authorized share capital of at least £50 000, and it becomes a public company merely by stating that it is a public company. In fact, most public limited companies in the United Kingdom have their shares listed on the London Stock Exchange, and hence they are often referred to as *listed* companies.

As a warning to those parties who might have dealings with them, public companies have to include the term 'public limited liability company' after their name (or its abbreviation 'plc').

Any company that does not make its shares available to the public is regarded as being a *private company*. Like public companies, private companies must also have an authorized share capital, although no minimum amount is prescribed. Otherwise, they are very similar to public companies in respect of their share capital requirements.

Private companies also have to warn the public that their liability is limited. They must do so by describing themselves as 'limited liability companies', and attaching the term 'limited' after their name (or the abbreviation 'ltd').

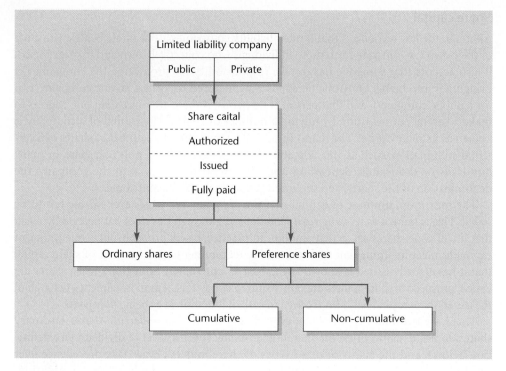

Figure 6.2 **Types of shares**

Loans

Besides obtaining the necessary capital from their shareholders, companies often borrow money in the form of *debentures*. A company may invite the public to loan it some money for a certain period of time (although the period can be unspecified) at a certain rate of interest. A debenture loan may be secured on specific assets of the company, on its assets generally, or it might not be secured at all. If it is secured and the company cannot repay it on its due repayment date, the debenture holders may sell the secured assets and use the amount to settle the amount owing to them.

Debentures, like shares, may be bought and sold freely on the Stock Exchange. The nearer the redemption date for the repayment for the debentures, the closer the market price will be to their nominal (i.e. their face, or stated paper) value, but sometimes if they are to be redeemed at a premium (i.e. in excess of their nominal value), the market price may exceed the nominal value.

Debenture holders are not shareholders of the company, and they do not have voting rights. From the company's point of view, one further advantage of raising capital in the form of debenture loans is that for taxation purposes the interest can be charged as a business expense against the profit for the year (unlike dividends paid to shareholders).

Disclosure of information

It is necessary for both public and private companies to supply a minimum amount of information to their members. The detailed requirements will be examined in later chapters. You might find it surprising to learn that shareholders have neither a right of access to the company's premises, nor a right to receive any information that they demand. This might not seem fair, but it would clearly be difficult for a company's managers to cope with thousands of shareholders, all of who suddenly turned up one day demanding to be let into the buildings in order to inspect the company's books of account.

Instead, shareholders in both private and public companies have to be supplied with an annual report containing at least the minimum amount of information required by the Companies Act 1985. The company also has to file (as it is called) a copy of the report with the Registrar of Companies. This means that, on payment of a small fee, the report is open for inspection by any member of the public who wants to consult it. Some companies (defined as small or medium-sized) are permitted to file an abbreviated version of their annual report with the Registrar, although the full report must still be sent to their shareholders.

The disclosure requirements are shown for quick reference purposes in Figure 6.3.

Accounts

Company accounts are very similar to those of sole traders. They do, however, tend to be more detailed, and some modifications have to be made in order to comply with various legal requirements. We shall be looking at company accounts later on in the chapter.

Directors

A limited liability company must always be regarded as a separate entity, i.e. separate from those shareholders who own it collectively, and separate from anyone who works for it. This

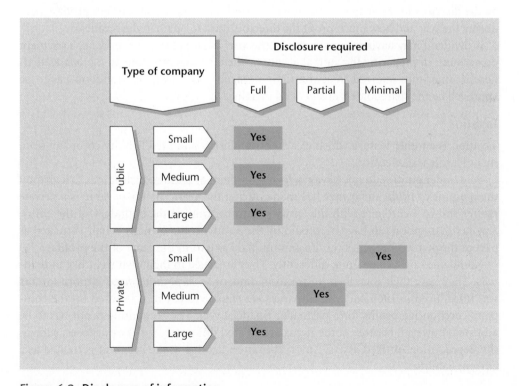

Figure 6.3 Disclosure of information

means that all those who are employed by it are its employees, no matter how senior they are Nevertheless someone has to take responsibility for the management of the company and so the shareholders usually delegate that responsibility to *directors*.

Directors are the most senior level of management. They are responsible for the day-to-day running of the company and they answer to the shareholders. Directors are officers of the company, and any remuneration paid to them as directors is charged as an expense of the business. They may also be shareholders but any payment that they receive as such is regarded as being a private matter. It must not be confused with any income that they receive as directors.

The distinction between employees and shareholder-employees is important although it is one that is not always understood. This is especially the case in very small companies where both employees and shareholders may be one and the same. As we have emphasized in law the company is regarded as being a separate entity. Even if there are just two shareholders who both work full-time for the company, the company is still treated as distinct from that of the two individuals who happen to own it. They may take decisions that appear to affect no one else except themselves but because they operate the company under the protection of limited liability, they have certain obligations as well as rights. So, they are not as free to operate the company as they might otherwise be if they ran it as a partnership.

Dividends

Profits are usually distributed to shareholders in the form of a dividend. A dividend is calculated on the basis of so many pence per share. The actual dividend will be recommended by the directors to the shareholders. It will depend upon the amount of net profit earned during the year and how much profit the directors want to retain in the business.

A dividend may have been paid during the year as an *interim dividend*, i.e. a payment on account. In preparing the annual accounts, the directors recommend a *proposed* dividend (sometimes referred to as the *final dividend*). The proposed dividend has to be approved by the shareholders at a general meeting.

Taxation

Taxation is another feature which clearly distinguishes a limited liability company from that of a sole trader entity.

Sole trader entities do not have tax levied on them as entities. Instead, tax is levied on the amount of profit the owner has made during the year. The tax payable is a private matter and in accordance with the entity rule, it lies outside the boundary of the entity. Any tax that appears to have been paid by the entity on the owner's behalf is treated as part of the owner's drawings (i.e. an amount paid as part of the share of the profits).

Companies are treated quite differently. They are taxed in their own right like individuals. They have their own form of taxation, known as *corporation tax*. Corporation tax was introduced in 1965 and all companies are eligible to pay it. It is based on the company's accounting profits for a particular financial year. The accounting profit has to be adjusted, however, because some items are treated differently for tax purposes, such as the depreciation of fixed assets. Any corporation tax due at the year end is treated as a current liability.

Activity 6.2

Assume that you would like to start a small business of your own. You have heard that a limited liability company will make sure that you will not be made bankrupt if the business is unsuccessful. You decide, therefore, to form a company to run the business.

List three advantages and three disadvantages in the table below of running your business as a limited liability company.

Advantages	Disadvantages
(1)	(1)
(2)	(2)
(3)	(3)

Now that the basic structure and operation of limited liability companies have been outlined, we can begin to examine company accounts in some detail. We start with the profit and loss account.

The profit and loss account

As was suggested earlier, the preparation of a company's trading and profit and loss account is basically no different from that of sole trader entities. Almost an identical format may be adopted, and it is only after the net profit stage that some differences become apparent. Company accounts usually include, for example, a profit and loss appropriation account. The profit and loss appropriation account follows on after the profit and loss account, although no clear dividing line is usually drawn between where the profit and loss account ends and the appropriation account begins. An example of a company's profit and loss appropriation account is shown in Example 6.1.

Example 6.1

A company's profit and loss appropriation account

	£000
Net profit for the year before taxation	1 000
Taxation	(300)
Net profit for the year after taxation	700
Dividends	(500)
Retained profit for the year	200

As can be seen from Example 6.1, the company's net profit for the year is used (or appropriated) in three ways:

1 to pay tax;
2 to pay dividends;
3 for retention within the business.

Activity 6.3

Complete the following equations.

(a) _____ – taxation = net profit for the year after taxation.

(b) Net profit for the year after taxation – _____ = retained profit for the year.

The balance sheet

The structure of a limited liability company's balance sheet is also very similar to that of a sole trader. The main differences arise because of the company's share capital structure. There are, however, some other features that are not usually found in non-company balance sheets.

We illustrate the main features of a company's balance sheet in Example 6.2. Study this example carefully, note that the information has been kept to a minimum; we have not given the full details where there are insignificant differences between a company's balance sheet and those of other entities.

Example 6.2

A company's balance sheet

Exhibitor Ltd
Balance sheet at 31 March 2006

	£000	£000	£000
Fixed assets			600
Investments (1)			100
Current assets		6 000	
Less: Current liabilities			
Trade creditors	2 950		
Accruals	50		
Corporation tax (2)	300		
Proposed dividend (3)	500	3 800	2 200
			2 900

Example 6.2
continued

Financed by:

Capital and reserves (4):	Authorized	Issued and fully paid
	£000	£000
Ordinary shares of £1 each (5)	2 000	1 500
Preference shares of £0.50 each (5)	500	500
	2 500	2 000
Capital reserves (6)		200
Revenue reserves (7)		600
Shareholders' funds (8)		2 800
Loans (9)		100
		2 900

Note: The number shown after each narration refers to the tutorial notes below.

Tutorial notes

1 *Investments*. This item usually represents long-term investments in the shares of other companies. Short-term investments (such as money invested in bank deposit accounts) would be included in current assets. The shares may be either in public limited liability companies or in private limited companies. It is obviously more difficult to buy shares in private companies and to obtain current market prices for them. The market price of the investments should be stated or, where this is not available, a directors' valuation should be obtained.

2 *Corporation tax*. Corporation tax represents the outstanding tax due on the company's profits for the year.

3 *Proposed dividend*. A proposed dividend will probably be due for payment very shortly after the year end, and so it will usually be shown as a current liability.

4 *Capital and reserves*. Details of the authorized, issued and fully paid-up share capital should be shown.

5 *Ordinary shares and preference shares*. Details about the different types of shares that the company has issued should be disclosed.

6 *Capital reserves*. This section may include several different reserve accounts of a capital nature, that is, amounts that are not available for distribution to the shareholders as dividend. It might include, for example, a share premium account, i.e. the extra amount paid by shareholders in excess of the nominal value of the shares. This extra amount does not rank for dividend but shareholders are sometimes willing to pay a premium if they think that the shares are particularly attractive. Another example is that of an asset that has been revalued. The difference between the original cost and the revalued amount will be credited to a *revaluation* reserve account.

7 *Revenue reserves*. Revenue reserve accounts are amounts that are available for distribution to the shareholders. At one time profits that could be distributed to shareholders were put into a *general* reserve account, although no real purpose was served in classifying them in this way. Any profits retained in the business and not paid out to shareholders may be included under this heading. Normally, however, retained profits will be shown separately under the heading 'profit and loss account'.

8 *Shareholders' funds*. The total amount available to shareholders at the balance sheet date is equal to the share capital originally subscribed, plus all the capital and revenue reserve account balances.

Tutorial notes
continued

9 *Loans.* The loans section of the balance sheet will include all the long-term loans obtained by the company, i.e. those loans that do not have to be repaid for at least twelve months, such as debentures and long-term bank loans.

Activity 6.4

State in which section of the balance sheet you are likely to find the following items.

(a) Amount owing for corporation tax.

(b) Debenture stock.

(c) Plant and machinery.

(d) Preference shares.

(e) Trade debtors.

A comprehensive example

In this section, the structure of a company's accounts is examined in a little more detail. Example 6.3 used to show how they are prepared for internal management purposes (accounts for external purposes are dealt with later in the book). Work through the answer to Example 6.3 making sure that you understand each step in its construction.

Example 6.3

Preparation of a company's accounts

The following information has been extracted from the books of Handy Ltd as at 31 March 2005:

	Dr £	Cr £
Bank	2 000	
Capital: 100 000 issued and fully paid ordinary shares of £1 each		100 000
50 000 issued and fully paid 8% preference shares of £1 each		50 000
Debenture loan stock (10%: repayable 2020)		30 000
Debenture loan stock interest	3 000	
Dividends received		700
Dividends paid: Ordinary interim	5 000	
Preference	4 000	
Freehold land at cost	200 000	
Investments (listed: market value at 31 March 2005 was £11 000)	10 000	
Office expenses	47 000	
Motor van at cost	15 000	
Motor van: accumulated depreciation at 1 April 2004		6 000
c/f	286 000	186 700

Example 6.3
continued

		Dr	Cr
		£	£
	b/f	286 000	186 700
Motor van expenses		2 700	
Purchases		220 000	
Retained profits at 1 April 2004			9 000
Sales			300 000
Share premium account			10 000
Stocks at cost (at 1 April 2004)		20 000	
Trade creditors			50 000
Trade debtors		27 000	
		555 700	555 700

Additional information:
1 The stocks at 31 March 2005 were valued at their historical cost of £40 000.
2 Depreciation is to be charged on the motor van at a rate of 20 per cent per annum on cost. No depreciation is to be charged on the freehold land.
3 The corporation tax for the year has been estimated to be £10 000.
4 The directors propose a final ordinary dividend of 10p per share.
5 The authorized share capital of the company is as follows:
    (a) 150 000 ordinary shares of £1 each; and
    (b) 75 000 preference shares of £1 each.

Required:
Prepare (a) Handy Ltd's trading and profit and loss account for the year to 31 March 2005; and
         (b) a balance sheet as at that date.

Answer to
Example 6.3(a)

Handy Ltd
Trading and profit and loss account for the year to 31 March 2005

	£	£	£
Sales			300 000
Less: Cost of goods sold:			
Opening stocks		20 000	
Purchases		220 000	
		240 000	
Less: Closing stocks		40 000	200 000
Gross profit			100 000
Add: Incomes:			
Dividends received			700
Less: Expenditure:			100 700
Debenture loan stock interest		3 000	
Motor van depreciation (1)	3 000		
Motor van expenses	2 700	5 700	
c/f		8 700	100 700

Answer to Example 6.3(a) continued

	£	£	£
c/f		8 700	100 700
Office expenses		47 000	
			55 700
Net profit for the year future taxation			45 000
Less: Corporation tax (2)			10 000
Net profit future year after taxation			35 000
Less: Dividends (3):			
Preference dividend paid (8%)		4 000	
Interim ordinary paid (5p per share)		5 000	
Proposed final ordinary dividend			
(10p per share)		10 000	19 000
Retained profit for the year			16 000
Retained profits brought forward			9 000
Retained profits carried forward (4)			25 000

Answer to Example 6.3(b)

Handy Ltd Balance sheet at 31 March 2005

	Cost	Accumulated depreciation	Net book value
Fixed assets	£	£	£
Freehold land (5)	200 000	–	200 000
Motor van (6)	15 000	9 000	6 000
	215 000	9 000	206 000
Investments			
At cost (market value at 31 March 2005: £11 000) (7)			10 000
Current assets			
Stocks at cost		40 000	
Trade debtors		27 000	
Bank		2 000	
		69 000	
Less: Current liabilities			
Trade creditors	50 000		
Corporation tax (8)	10 000		
Proposed ordinary dividend (9)	10 000	70 000	
Net current assets			(1 000)
			215 000

		Authorized	Issued and fully paid
Financed by:			
Capital and reserves			
Ordinary shares of £1 each (10)		150 000	100 000
Preference shares of £1 each (10)		75 000	50 000
		225 000	150 000
c/f			150 000

Capital and reserves		Authorized	Issued and fully paid
	b/f		150 000
Share premium account (11)			10 000
Retained profits (12)			25 000
Shareholders' funds (13)			185 000
Loans (14)			
10% debenture stock (repayable 2009)			30 000
			215 000

Answer to Example 6.3(b) continued

Note: The number shown after each narration refers to the following tutorial notes.

Tutorial notes

1 Depreciation has been charged on the motor van at a rate of 20 per cent per annum on cost (as instructed in question note 2).

2 Question note 3 requires £10 000 to be charged as corporation tax. Remember that the corporation tax rate is applied to the *taxable* profit and not to the *accounting* profit. The taxable profit has not been given in the question.

3 A proposed ordinary dividend of 10p has been included as instructed in question note 4.

4 The total retained profit of £25 000 is carried forward to the balance sheet (see tutorial note 12 below).

5 Question note 2 states that no depreciation is to be charged on the freehold land.

6 The accumulated depreciation for the motor van of £9000 is the total of the accumulated depreciation brought forward at 1 April 2004 of £6000, plus the £3000 written off to the profit and loss account for the current year (see tutorial note 1 above).

7 Note that the market value of the investments has been disclosed on the face of the balance sheet.

8 The corporation tax charged against profit (question note 3) will be due for payment in 2006. The amount due is treated as a current liability.

9 The proposed ordinary dividend will be due for payment shortly after the year end and so it is also a current liability. As the interim dividend and the preference dividend have already been paid, they are not current liabilities.

10 Details of the authorized, issued and fully paid share capital should be disclosed.

11 The share premium is a capital account: it cannot be used for the payment of dividends. This account will normally remain unchanged in successive balance sheets, although there are a few highly restricted purposes for which it may be used.

12 The retained profits become part of a revenue account balance that the company could use for the payment of dividends. The total retained profits of £25 000 is the amount brought in to the balance sheet from the profit and loss account.

13 The total amount of shareholders' funds should always be shown.

14 The loans are long-term loans. Loans are not part of shareholders' funds, and they should be shown in the balance sheet as a separate item.

Attempt Example 6.3 without looking at the answer.

Activity 6.5

! Questions non-accountants should ask

Many of the questions that we have suggested in previous chapters that non-accountants should ask are of relevance in this chapter. For example, the various accounting rules adopted by the accountants in preparing the company's profit and loss and balance sheet, especially those have a significant impact on revenue recognition, stock valuation, depreciation and provisions for bad and doubtful debts.

The following questions relate particularly to this chapter.

● Can our accounting records disclose with reasonable accuracy (as the 1985 Companies Act requires) our financial position at any time?

● Do the accounting records contain entries for all money received and spent?

● Do they also contain a record of all assets and all liabilities?

● Is there included in the accounting records a statement of the stock held at the financial year end?*

● And are there details of stocktaking from which the statement of stock has been compiled?*

● Is a record kept of all goods sold and purchased as well as all the buyers and sellers so that they can all be identified?*

● Have both the profit and loss account and the balance sheet been prepared in accordance with the requirements of the Companies Act 1985?

● Have you dealt with anything in the accounts or missed anything out that may be in conflict with the Act or with recommended practice?

● If so, can you justify it as being 'true and fair'?

* These questions are only relevant if the company deals in goods.

Conclusion

This chapter has briefly examined the background to the legislation affecting limited liability companies. This was followed by some examples of how company accounts are prepared for *internal* purposes.

Although a great deal of information can be obtained from studying the annual accounts of a company, it is difficult to extract the most relevant and significant features. Some further guidance is needed, therefore, in how to make the best use of the financial accounting information presented to you. That guidance will be provided in Chapters 8 and 12, but in the meantime we need to examine some other types of account. We do so in the next chapter.

1 Company accounts have to be adapted in order to meet certain legal requirements. Basically, the structure of the annual accounts is similar to those of sole traders.

2 The profits of a company are taxed separately (like an individual). The tax is based on the accounting profit for the year. Any tax due at the year end will be shown in the balance sheet as a current liability.

3 The net profit after tax may be paid to shareholders in the form of a dividend (although some profit may still be retained within the business). Any proposed dividend (i.e. one recommended but not yet paid) should be shown in the balance sheet as a creditor.

Check your learning

The answers to these questions may be found within the text.

1 What is meant by 'limited liability'?

2 When was it first incorporated into company law?

3 Why was it found necessary to do so?

4 Distinguish between the authorized, issued, and fully paid share capital of a company.

5 Name two main types of shares.

6 What is the basic difference between them?

7 What are the two main types of limited liability companies?

8 What is a debenture loan?

9 What is meant by 'disclosure of information'?

10 Why do companies have to let the Registrar of Companies have certain types of information?

11 What is a director?

12 What is a dividend?

13 Name two types of dividend.

14 What name is given to the tax that a company pays on its profits?

15 Name three ways in which a company's profits are appropriated.

16 List three types of assets.

17 Name three items that may be included under the heading of 'current liabilities'.

18 Distinguish between a capital reserve and a revenue reserve.

19 What is a share premium account?

20 What are 'shareholders' funds'?

21 What is the difference between a short-term loan and a long-term one?

News story quiz

Remember the new story at the beginning of this chapter? Go back to that story and reread it before answering the following questions.

This article once again illustrates the difficulty that companies may have in dealing with complex accounting problems and the various ways that they can be dealt with. The article describes MyTravel's problems as 'accounting irregularities'.

Questions

1 What do you think is meant by the comment that 'accounting errors resulted in a £54.9m hit to the company's bottom line'?

2 How might MyTravel have changed its revenue recognition policy on to a more conservative basis?

3 What do you think is meant by the assertion that serious control failures resulted in the 'misallocations of costs between seasons and years and differences in intercompany accounts'?

4 To what extent do you think that the term 'serious control failures' is a euphemism for 'imprudent accounting policies'?

Tutorial questions

The answers to question marked with an asterisk may be found in Appendix 4.

6.1 'The concept of limited liability is an out-of-date nineteenth-century concept.' Discuss.

6.2 Appleton used to operate her business as a sole trader entity. She has recently converted it into a limited liability company. Appleton owns 80 per cent of the ordinary (voting) shares, the remaining 20 per cent being held by various relatives and friends. Explain to Appleton why it is now inaccurate for her to describe the company as 'her' business.

6.3 How far do you think that the information presented in a limited liability company's profit and loss account and balance sheet is useful to the owners of a small business?

6.4* The following balances have been extracted from the books of Margo Ltd for the year to 31 January 2006:

	Dr £000	Cr £000
Cash at bank and in hand	5	
Plant and equipment:		
At cost	70	
Accumulated depreciation (at 31.1.06)		25
c/f	75	25

		Dr	Cr
		£000	£000
	b/f	75	25
Profit and loss account (at 1.2.05)			15
Profit for the financial year (to 31.1.06)			10
Share capital (issued and fully paid)			50
Stocks (at 31.1.06)		17	
Trade creditors			12
Trade debtors		20	
		112	112

Additional information:
1   Corporation tax owing at 31 January 2006 is estimated to be £3000.
2   Margo Ltd's authorized share capital is £75 000 of £1 ordinary shares.
3   A dividend of 10p per share is proposed.

Required:
Prepare Margo Ltd's profit and loss account for the year to 31 January 2006 and a balance sheet as at that date.

6.5*   Harry Ltd was formed in 2000. The following balances as at 28 February 2007 have been extracted from the books of account after the trading account has been compiled:

	Dr	Cr
	£000	£000
Administration expenses	65	
Cash at bank and in hand	10	
Distribution costs	15	
Dividend paid (on preference shares)	6	
Furniture and equipment:		
At cost	60	
Accumulated depreciation at 1.3.06		36
Gross profit for the year		150
Ordinary share capital (shares of £1 each)		100
Preference shares (cumulative 15% of £1 shares)		40
Profit and loss account (at 1.3.06)		50
Share premium account		20
Stocks (at 28.2.07)	130	
Trade creditors		25
Trade debtors	135	
	421	421

Additional information:
1   Corporation tax owing at 28 February 2007 is estimated to be £24 000.
2   Furniture and equipment is depreciated at an annual rate of 10 per cent of cost and it is all charged against administrative expenses.
3   A dividend of 20p per ordinary share is proposed.
4   All of the authorized share capital has been issued and is fully paid.

Required:
Prepare Harry Ltd's profit and loss account for the year to 28 February 2009 and a balance sheet as at that date.

6.6* The following balances have been extracted from the books of Jim Ltd as at 31 March 2008:

	Dr £000	Cr £000
Advertising	3	
Bank	11	
Creditors		12
Debtors	118	
Furniture and fittings:		
At cost	20	
Accumulated depreciation (at 1.4.07)		9
Directors' fees	6	
Profit and loss account (at 1.4.07)		8
Purchases	124	
Rent and rates	10	
Sales		270
Share capital (issued and fully paid)		70
Stock (at 1.4.07)	16	
Telephone and stationery	5	
Travelling expenses	2	
Vehicles:		
At cost	40	
Accumulated depreciation (at 1.4.07)		10
Wages and salaries	24	
	379	379

Additional information:
1 Stock at 31 March 2008 was valued at £14000.
2 Furniture and fittings and the vehicles are depreciated at a rate of 15 per cent and 25 per cent, respectively on cost.
3 Corporation tax owing at 31 March 2008 is estimated to be £25000.
4 A dividend of 40p per share is proposed.
5 The company's authorized share capital is £100000 of £1 ordinary shares.

Required:
(a) Prepare Jim Ltd's trading and profit and loss account for the year to 31 March 2008 and a balance sheet as at that date.
(b) Why would the business not necessarily be worth its balance sheet value as at 31 March 2008?

6.7   The following trial balance has been extracted from Carol Ltd as at 30 April 2004:

	Dr	Cr
	£000	£000
Advertising	2	
Bank overdraft		20
Bank interest paid	4	
Creditors		80
Debtors	143	
Directors' remuneration	30	
Freehold land and buildings:		
At cost	800	
Accumulated depreciation at 1.5.03		102
General expenses	15	
Investments at cost	30	
Investment income		5
Motor vehicles:		
At cost	36	
Accumulated depreciation (at 1.5.03)		18
Preference dividend paid	15	
Preference shares (cumulative 10% shares		
of £1 each)		150
Profit and loss account (at 1.5.03)		100
Purchases	480	
Repairs and renewals	4	
Sales		900
Share capital (authorized, issued and fully paid		
ordinary shares of £1 each)		500
Share premium account		25
Stock (at 1.5.03)	120	
Wages and salaries	221	
	1 900	1 900

Additional information:
1   Stock at 30 April 2004 was valued at £140 000.
2   Depreciation for the year of £28 000 is to be provided on buildings and £9000 for motor vehicles.
3   A provision of £6000 is required for the auditors' remuneration.
4   £2000 had been paid in advance for renewals.
5   Corporation tax owing at 30 April 2004 is estimated to be £60 000
6   The directors propose an ordinary dividend of 10p per share.
7   The market value of the investments at 30 April 2004 was £35 000.

Required:
Prepare Carol Ltd's trading and profit and loss account for the year to 30 April 2004 and a balance sheet as at that date.

6.8 Nelson Ltd was incorporated in 2000 with an authorized share capital of 500 000 £1 ordinary shares, and 200 000 5% cumulative preference shares of £1 each. The following trial balance was extracted as at 31 May 2005:

	Dr £000	Cr £000
Administrative expenses	257	
Auditor's fees	10	
Cash at bank and in hand	5	
Creditors		85
Debentures (12%)		100
Debenture interest paid	6	
Debtors	225	
Directors' remuneration	60	
Dividends paid:		
Ordinary interim	20	
Preference	5	
Furniture, fittings and equipment:		
At cost	200	
Accumulated depreciation at 1.6.04		48
Investments at cost (market value at 31.5.05:		
£340 000)	335	
Investment income		22
Ordinary share capital (issued and fully paid)		400
Preference share capital		200
Profit and loss account (at 1.6.04)		17
Purchases	400	
Sales		800
Share premium account		50
Stock at 1.6.04	155	
Wages and salaries	44	
	1 722	1 722

Additional information:
1 Stock at 31 May 2005 was valued at £195 000.
2 Administrative expenses owing at 31 May 2005 amounted to £13 000.
3 Depreciation is to be charged on the furniture and fittings at a rate of 12½% on cost.
4 Salaries paid in advance amounted to £4000.
5 Corporation tax owing at 1.6.05 is estimated to be £8000.
6 Provision is to be made for a final ordinary dividend of 1.25p per share.

Required:
Prepare Nelson Ltd's trading and profit and loss account for the year to 31 May 2005 and a balance sheet as at that date.

6.9 The following trial balance has been extracted from the books of Keith Ltd as at 30 June 2006:

	Dr £000	Cr £000
Advertising	30	
Bank	7	
Creditors		69
Debentures (10%)		70
Debtors (all trade)	300	
Directors' remuneration	55	
Electricity	28	
Insurance	17	
Investments (quoted)	28	
Investment income		4
Machinery:		
At cost	420	
Accumulated depreciation at 1.7.05		152
Office expenses	49	
Ordinary share capital (issued and fully paid)		200
Preference shares		50
Preference share dividend	4	
Profit and loss account (at 1.7.05)		132
Provision for bad and doubtful debts		8
Purchases	1 240	
Rent and rates	75	
Sales		2 100
Stock (at 1.7.05)	134	
Vehicles:		
At cost	80	
Accumulated depreciation (at 1.7.05)		40
Wages and salaries	358	
	2 825	2 825

Additional information:
1 Stock at 30 June 2006 valued at cost amounted to £155 000.
2 Depreciation is to be provided on machinery and vehicles at a rate of 20 per cent and 25 per cent respectively on cost.
3 Provision is to be made for auditors' remuneration of £12 000.
4 Insurance paid in advance at 30 June 2006 amounted to £3000.
5 The provision for bad and doubtful debts is to be made equal to 5 per cent of outstanding trade debtors as at 30 June 2006.
6 Corporation tax owing at 30 June 2006 is estimated to be £60 000.
7 An ordinary dividend of 10p per share is proposed.
8 The investments had a market value of £30 000 at 30 June 2006.
9 The company has an authorized share capital of 600 000 ordinary shares of £0.50 each and of 50 000 8% cumulative preference shares of £1 each.

Required:
(a) Prepare Keith Ltd's trading and profit and loss account for the year to 30 June 2006 and a balance sheet as at that date.
(b) Explain why shareholders of Keith Ltd would not necessarily have been able to sell the business for its balance sheet value as at 30 June 2006.

Further practice questions, study material and links to relevant sites on the World Wide Web can be found on the website that accompanies this book. The site can be found at **www.booksites.net/dyson**

Campaigning for accruals accounting in the public sector . . .

Pushing for accruals

● **The Public Audit Forum** has criticised many public bodies for not making the most of the advantages that accruals accounting can offer. The forum has released a paper that it hopes will highlight the benefits that can be achieved through accruals accounting. Titled '*The Whole Truth: Or Why Accruals Accounting* *Means Better Management*', the paper says that improved performance and financial information available to public sector managers from accruals accounting can contribute to better management and delivery of services.

Accountancy Age, 21 November 2002.

Questions relating to this news story may be found on page 160 ▸▸

About this chapter

In previous chapters we have concentrated on sole trader and company entities operating in the private sector. However, we would be presenting an unbalanced view of accounting if we concentrated almost entirely on such entities. There are also many other types of entities operating in both the private and the public sectors. In some cases their accounting requirements are somewhat different from those entities that we have looked at so far. We cannot deal with them all but at least we can give you an indication of varying accounting practices you will find in some other types of entities. That is the main aim of this chapter.

The data collected, stored, extract and summarized does not vary all that much, irrespective of the nature of the entity and the economic sector in which it operates. What may be different is the way that it is presented. This means that the basic accounting knowledge covered in this book can be fairly easily adapted to suit different circumstances.

The chapter is divided into six main sections. In the next section we explain why this chapter is important for non-accountants. The following section deals with manufacturing accounts. Manufacturing accounts are to be found mainly in the private profit-making sector. We switch the emphasis of our studies after that, and in the next three sections we cover service sector entity accounts, not-for profit entity accounts, and Government accounts respectively. The last main section frames some questions that non-accountants should ask about the issues raised in the chapter.

By the end of this chapter you should be able to:

- outline the contents of a manufacturing account;
- prepare a simple manufacturing account;
- describe the type of account required by service sector entities;
- compare and contrast accounts in the profit-making sector with those in the not-for-profit sector;
- state why accounting in the public sector may be different from that in the private sector.

! Why this chapter is important for non-accountants

This chapter is important for non-accountants because it helps to present a more balanced and well-rounded appreciation of accounting and the presentation of accounting information in different types of entities.

Many accounting textbooks, for example, concentrate on looking at accounting practices in the private profit-making sector, especially those relating to manufacturing and trading entities. However, the service sector now forms a significant element in the private sector, so it would be misleading to ignore its accounting procedures. Similarly, in the not-for-profit sector there are many types of entities (such as charities and voluntary bodies) that play an important part in the life of many people. In addition, the Government has a major impact on economic life and it too has its own form of accounting (although this is changing).

In a book of this nature we cannot deal with every conceivable entity. In this chapter we cover just a few of them. This then gives you an indication of how basic accounting practices are used (with some modification) in other kinds of entities. You will also find that if you are involved in such entities you can adapt your accounting knowledge to suit the requirements of different entities. For example, many non-accountants will be members of various social and sporting clubs. The accounting knowledge that they have gained by working their way through this book will enable them to assess the financial position and future prospects of such entities with relative ease. Indeed, many non-accountants will have come across misleading statements prepared by club treasurers such as presenting a summary of cash received and cash paid as a 'balance sheet'! Such mistakes may not be very serious but they will certainly confuse the club members and give them a false impression of the club's assets and liabilities.

It is to be hoped that after reading this book in general and this chapter in particular, you will not make similar mistakes.

Manufacturing accounts

A manufacturing entity is an entity that purchases or obtains raw materials and converts them to a finished goods state. The finished goods are then sold to customers. Manufacturing entities are normally to be found in the private sector and they may be organized as sole traders, partnerships or companies.

Unlike the examples we have used in the previous chapters, manufacturing entities are not likely to use a *purchases account*. This is because they normally buy raw materials and then process them before they are sold in a *finished goods state*. Hence before the trading account can be compiled it is necessary to calculate the cost of converting the raw materials into a finished goods state. The conversion cost is called the *manufacturing cost* and it is the equivalent of a trading entity's purchases.

In order to calculate an entity's manufacturing cost, we need to open a *manufacturing account*. A manufacturing account forms part of the double-entry system and it is included in the periodic financial accounts. It normally only contains manufacturing *costs* since it is rare to have any manufacturing *incomes*.

Manufacturing costs are debited to the manufacturing account. They are usually classified into *direct* and *indirect* costs. Direct costs are those costs that can be easily and economically identified with a particular segment. A segment may be a department, a section, a product or a unit. Indirect costs are those costs that cannot be easily and economically identified with a particular segment. Indirect costs are sometimes referred to as 'overhead' or 'overheads'.

The format of the manufacturing account is straightforward. Normally, it contains two main sections comprising the direct and the indirect costs. Each section is then analyzed into what are called the *elements of cost*. The elements of cost include materials, labour, and other expenses.

Example 7.1 illustrates the format of a typical manufacturing account. A detailed explanation of its contents then follows.

Format of a basic manufacturing account

Example 7.1

	£000	£000
Direct costs (1)		
Direct materials (2)	20	
Direct labour (3)	70	
Other direct expenses (4)	5	
Prime cost (5)		95
Manufacturing overhead (6)		
Indirect material cost (7)	3	
Indirect labour cost (7)	7	
Other indirect expenses (7)	10	
c/f	20	95

Example 7.1
continued

		£000	£000
	b/f	20	95
Total manufacturing overhead incurred (8)			20
Total manufacturing costs incurred (9)			115
Work-in-progress (10)			
Opening work-in-progress		10	
Closing work-in-progress		(15)	(5)
Manufacturing cost of goods produced (11)			110
Manufacturing profit (12)			11
Market value of goods produced transferred to the trading account (13)			121

Notes:
(a) The number shown after each item refers to the tutorial notes immediately below. The amounts have been inserted purely for illustrative purposes.
(b) The term 'factory' or 'work' is sometimes substituted for the term *manufacturing*.

Tutorial notes

1 *Direct costs.* The exhibit relates to a *company's* manufacturing account. It is assumed that the direct costs listed for materials, labour and other expenses relate to those expenses that have been easy to identify with the specific products manufactured by the company.

2 *Direct materials.* The charge for direct materials will be calculated as follows:

Direct material cost = (opening stock of raw materials + purchases of raw materials) – closing stock of raw materials

The total of direct material cost is sometimes referred to as *materials consumed*. Direct materials will include all the raw material costs and component parts that have been easy to identify with particular products.

3 *Direct labour.* Direct labour will include all those employment costs that have been easy to identify with particular products.

4 *Other direct expenses.* Besides direct materials and direct labour costs, there are sometimes other direct expenses that are easy to identify with particular products, for example, the cost of hiring a specific machine. Such expenses are relatively rare.

5 *Prime cost.* The total of direct material costs, direct labour costs and other direct expenses is known as prime cost.

6 *Manufacturing overhead.* Overhead refers to the total of all indirect costs, and so any manufacturing costs that are not easy to identify with specific products will be classified separately under this heading.

7 *Indirect material cost, indirect labour cost* and *other indirect expenses.* Manufacturing overhead will probably be shown separately under these three headings.

8 *Total manufacturing overhead incurred.* This item represents the total of indirect material cost, indirect labour cost and other indirect expenses.

9 *Total manufacturing costs incurred.* The total of prime cost and total manufacturing overhead incurred equals the total manufacturing costs incurred.

10 *Work-in-progress.* Work-in-progress represents the estimated cost of incomplete work that is not yet ready to be transferred to finished stock. There will usually be some opening and closing work-in-progress.

11 *Manufacturing cost of goods produced.* The manufacturing cost of goods produced equals the total manufacturing costs incurred plus (or minus) the difference between the opening and closing work-in-progress.

Tutorial notes continued

12 *Manufacturing profit.* The manufacturing cost of goods produced is sometimes transferred to the finished goods stock account without any addition for manufacturing profit. If this is the case, the double-entry effect is as follows:

> DEBIT   Finished goods stock account.
> CREDIT   Manufacturing account with the
>   manufacturing cost of goods produced.

The finished goods stock account is the equivalent of the purchases account in a trading organization.

Sometimes, however, a manufacturing profit is added to the manufacturing cost of goods produced before it is transferred to the trading account. The main purpose of this adjustment is to enable management to compare more fairly the company's total manufacturing cost – inclusive of profit – with outside prices (since such prices will also be normally inclusive of profit). The profit added to the manufacturing cost of goods produced may simply be an appropriate percentage, or it may represent the level of profit that the industry generally expects to earn. Any profit element added to the manufacturing cost (irrespective of how it is calculated) is an internal book-keeping arrangement, because the profit has not been earned or *realized* outside the business. The double-entry is affected as follows:

> DEBIT   Manufacturing account.
> CREDIT   Profit and loss account with the
>   manufacturing profit.

13 *Market value of goods produced.* As explained in note 12 above, the market value of goods produced is the amount that will be transferred (that is, debited) to the trading account.

Go through Example 7.1 again. Do you think that the structure of a manufacturing account makes it easy to follow? Are you clear about the meaning of each individual item? What does the information tell you about the cost of manufacturing during the period in question?

Write down your responses to these questions in your notebook.

Activity 7.1

Construction of the account

In this section, we are going to explain how to construct a manufacturing account. We will do so by using Example 7.2.

Example 7.2	Constructing a manufacturing account

The following balances, *inter alia*, have been extracted from the Wren Manufacturing Company as at 31 March 2005:

	Dr £
Carriage inwards (on raw materials)	6 000
Direct expenses	3 000
Direct wages	25 000
Factory administration	6 000
Factory heat and light	500
Factory power	1 500
Factory rent and rates	2 000
Factory supervisory costs	5 000
Purchase of raw materials	56 000
Raw materials stock (at 1 April 2004)	4 000
Work-in-progress (at 1 April 2004)	5 000

Additional information:
1 The stock of raw materials at 31 March 2005 was valued at £6000.
2 The work-in-progress at 31 March 2005 was valued at £8000.
3 A profit loading of 50 per cent is added to the total cost of manufacture.

Required:
Prepare Wren's manufacturing account for the year to 31 March 2005.

Answer to Example 7.2	Wren Manufacturing Company Manufacturing account for the year to 31 March 2005

	£	£	£
Direct materials			
Raw material stock at 1 April 2004		4 000	
Purchases	56 000		
Carriage inwards (1)	6 000	62 000	
		66 000	
Less: Raw material stock at 31 March 2005		6 000	
Cost of materials consumed			60 000
Direct wages			25 000
Direct expenses			3 000
Prime cost			88 000
Other manufacturing costs (2)			
Administration		6 000	
Heat and light		500	
Power		1 500	
Rent and rates		2 000	
Supervisory		5 000	
Total manufacturing overhead expenses			15 000
Total manufacturing costs incurred		c/f	103 000

	£	£	£
		b/f	103 000

	£	£
Work-in-progress		
Add: Work-in-progress at 1 April 2004	5 000	
Less: Work-in-progress at 31 March 2005	(8 000)	(3 000)
Manufacturing cost of goods produced		100 000
Manufacturing profit (50%) (3)		50 000
Market value of goods produced (4)		150 000

1 Carriage inwards (i.e. the cost of transporting goods to the factory) is normally regarded as being part of the cost of purchases.

2 Other manufacturing costs include production overhead expenses. In practice, there would be a considerable number of other manufacturing costs.

3 A profit loading of 50 per cent has been added to the manufacturing cost (see note 3 of the question). The manufacturing profit is a debit entry in the manufacturing account. The corresponding credit entry will eventually be made in the profit and loss account.

4 The market value of goods produced will be transferred to the finished goods stock account.

Attempt Example 7.2 without looking at the answer.

Links with the other accounts

Example 7.2 deals with the manufacturing account in isolation. However, once the manufacturing account has been prepared, it will then be linked with the trading account and the profit and loss account by transferring either the manufacturing cost of the goods produced or the market value of the goods produced to the trading

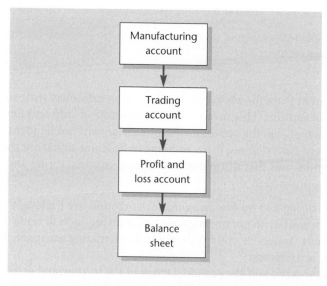

Figure 7.1 **The relationship between the main accounts**

account. Thus the manufacturing cost or the market value of the goods produced is the equivalent of the entry for 'purchases' which may be found in the trading account of a non-manufacturing entity. Apart from this slight amendment, the preparation of a trading account for a manufacturing entity is exactly the same as it is for a trading entity. This relationship is shown in outline in Figure 7.1.

Service entity accounts

The profit-making sector is made up of a great many other types of entities beside those that may be classified as manufacturing or trading. For convenience, we will describe them as *service entities*. Service entities do not normally deal in physical or tangible goods, unlike manufacturing or trading entities. Instead they offer advice and provide assistance to their customers, clients, patients or passengers. In recent years the manufacturing sector in the United Kingdom has declined and the service sector has become much more important.

The service sector is extremely diverse, but there are a number of recognizable categories. These are as follows:

1 *Hotels and catering.* Such entities are generally regarded as being part of the service sector although the service they offer includes a physical or tangible element, e.g. the supply of food and drink.
2 *Leisure and recreational activities.* Services included in this category include cinema, concerts and theatre productions, leisure and sports centres, and travel agencies.
3 *Personal.* Examples of personal services include beauticians, hairdressing, and manicuring.
4 *Professional.* The more common professional services include accounting, legal, and medical (including chiropody and optical).
5 *Transportation.* Transportation services include the movement of goods and passengers by air, land and sea.

Activity 7.3	Think of the main street in your own town or city. List in your notebook six different types of service entities.

It will be apparent from the above list that there is an extremely wide variety of different types of service entities. This means that the accounts of different entities will also be somewhat different, e.g. the accounts of a beautician will not be identical to those of a railway company. Nevertheless, there are some basic features that are common to all service sector entities and that distinguish them from manufacturing and trading entities. These may be summarized as follows:

1 *No manufacturing and trading accounts.* Such accounts are irrelevant in service entities because such entities do not normally manufacture products or trade in tangible goods.
2 *No gross profit.* As service entities do not prepare trading accounts, the calculation of gross profit is irrelevant.
3 *Primacy of the profit and loss account.* Details of the income and expenditure for a particular accounting period are shown in the profit and loss account.

4 *Format.* The format of a service-sector profit and loss account is very similar to that of trading entities. However, specific expenditure is sometimes deducted from specific income, the net amount then being highlighted in the profit and loss account. For example, suppose an entity sells some food for £1000 and the cost of providing it was £600. The £1000 income could be shown in the income section of the profit and loss account, with the £600 being shown separately as an expenditure item. However, as there is a close relationship between the income and the expenditure, it is helpful to users if the net amount earned on selling the food is disclosed. It would then be presented as shown in Example 7.3.

5 *Segmentation.* Similar categories of income or expenditure are usually grouped together in the same part of the profit and loss account with the subtotal of each category being shown separately.

Extract from the profit and loss account

Example 7.3

	£	£
Income from sale of food	1 000	
Less: cost of provision	600	400

We illustrate the presentation of a set of financial statements for a service entity in Example 7.4. As you will see, the presentation of the profit and loss account and the balance sheet is very similar to the examples used in previous chapters.

A service entity account

Example 7.4

Mei Loon: Educational training consultant
Profit and loss account for the year to 31 March 2007

	£	£
INCOME (1)		
Article fees	5 000	
Author's licensing and collecting payments	2 000	
Consultation fees	90 000	
Lecture fees	30 000	
Public lending right payment	1 000	
Royalties	20 000	148 000
EXPENDITURE (2)		
Computing	5 000	
Depreciation : equipment (3)	2 000	
: furniture (3)	500	
Heat and light	1 000	
Insurances	600	
Photocopying	200	
Postage	100	
c/f	9 400	148 000

Example 7.4
continued

	£	£
	b/f 9 400	148 000
Rates	1 500	
Secretarial	30 000	
Stationery (4)	700	
Subscriptions	400	
Travelling	6 000	48 000
Net profit for the year (5)		100 000

Balance sheet at 31 March 2007

	£	£
FIXED ASSETS (6)		
Office equipment	10 000	
Less: accumulated depreciation	4 000	6 000
Office furniture	5 000	
Less: accumulated depreciation	1 500	3 500
		9 500
CURRENT ASSETS		
Stock of stationery (7)	200	
Debtors (8)	15 000	
Prepayments (9)	3 000	
Cash at bank and in hand	52 300	
	70 500	
CURRENT LIABILITIES		
Creditors (10)	2 000	
Accruals (11)	1 000	
	3 000	67 500
		77 000
CAPITAL		
At 1 April 2001 (12)		17 000
Net profit for the year (13)	100 000	
Less: drawings (14)	40 000	60 000
Balance at 31 March 2002		77 000

Tutorial notes

1 All six of the listed income items will have been compiled on an accruals and prepayments basis, i.e. the cash received during the period will have been adjusted for any opening and closing debtors.

2 Apart from depreciation, the expenditure items will have been adjusted for any opening or closing accruals and prepayments.

3 Mei Loon appears to be depreciating her office furniture by 10 per cent per annum on cost [(£500 ÷ £5000) × 100%], and her office equipment by 20 per cent per annum on cost [(£2000 ÷ £10 000) × 100%].

4 The stationery costs for the year have been reduced by the stock at 31 March 2007 (see note 7).

Example 7.4
continued

5 The net profit for the year has been added to Mei Loon's capital at 1 April 2006 (see note 12).

6 The fixed assets are shown at their gross book value less the accumulated depreciation. Sometimes additional information would be provided by inserting separate columns for (a) the gross book value; (b) the accumulated depreciation; and (c) the net book value.

7 Mei Loon appears to have valued the stock of stationery that she held at 31 March 2007 at £200.

8 The debtors entry probably represents what is owed to Mei Loon for various fees as at 31 March 2007.

9 The prepayments represent what she has paid in advance at the end of the year for various services, such as insurances or heat and light, from which she would expect to benefit in the year to 31 March 2003.

10 The creditors represent what she owes at the end of the year for various goods and services supplied during the year.

11 The accruals are similar to the creditors, but they probably relate to services such as insurances or heat and light (see note 9).

12 Mei Loon's opening capital balance is shown as £17 000. This would be composed of her original capital contribution plus previous years' profits that she had not drawn out of the business.

13 The net profit for the year is the balance on the profit and loss account.

14 Mei Loon has drawn £40 000 out of the business during the year for her own private use. Some of the £40 000 probably relates to previous years' profits that she has drawn out during the current year, along with various amounts drawn out in advance of this year's profits.

Referring to Example 7.4, examine Mei Loon's profit and loss account and balance sheet. What does the information tell you? How well has her consultancy done during the year to 31 March 2007? Is she likely to go bankrupt in the near future?

Write down your responses to these questions in your notebook.

Activity 7.4

Not-for-profit entity accounts

As the term suggests, not-for-profit entities are those entities whose primary objective is non-profit-making, for example, voluntary associations, charities, clubs, pressure groups and societies. The main objective of such entities may be to provide leisure, social or welfare facilities for their members. It is possible that they may be involved in some trading (or even manufacturing) activities, but the profit motive would not be their main consideration.

If not-for-profit entities have some manufacturing or trading activities, they will prepare manufacturing and trading accounts. The balance on the manufacturing account would be transferred to the trading account, and the balance on the trading account (i.e. the gross profit) would then be transferred to an *income and expenditure account*. An income and expenditure account is almost identical to a profit and loss account except that the title is different and the balance on the account is described as the *excess of income over expenditure* (or expenditure over income) instead of *profit* (or loss).

An example of an income and expenditure account and a balance sheet for a social club is shown in Example 7.5. The preparation of such accounts is very similar to that used in compiling accounts for trading entities.

Example 7.5

A social club's accounts

Balli Social Club
Income and expenditure account for the year to 31 March 2008

	£	£
INCOME (1)		
Bar sales (2)	60 000	
Less: purchases	40 000	20 000
Building society interest		200
Dances (2)	1 600	
Less expenses	900	700
Food sales (2)	8 000	
Less: purchases	4 500	3 500
Members' subscriptions		36 200
		60 600
EXPENDITURE (3)		
Accountants' fees	250	
Depreciation: furniture and fittings	3 900	
Insurances	600	
Electricity	1 400	
Office expenses	22 000	
Rates	2 000	
Salaries and wages	14 000	
Telephone	3 100	
Travelling expenses	13 000	60 250
Excess of income over expenditure for the year (4)		350

Balance sheet at 31 March 2008

	Cost	Accumulated depreciation	Net book value
	£	£	£
FIXED ASSETS (5)			
Club premises	18 000	–	18 000
Furniture and equipment	39 000	17 900	21 100
	57 000	17 900	39 100
CURRENT ASSETS (5)			
Stocks	1 500		
Prepayments	200		
Members' subscriptions (in arrears)	7 000		
Building society account	2 700		
Cash	5 500	c/f 16 900	39 100

Example 7.5
continued

Balance sheet at 31 March 2008

	Cost	Accumulated depreciation	Net book value
	£	£	£
		b/f 16 900	39 100
CURRENT LIABILITIES (5)			
Trade creditors	2 000		
Members' subscriptions (paid in advance)	800		
Accruals	1 250	4 050	12 850
			51 950
ACCUMULATED FUND (6)			
Balance at 1 April 2007 (7)			51 600
Excess of income over expenditure for the year (8)			350
Balance at 31 March 2008 (9)			51 950

Tutorial notes

1   The income items will have been calculated on an accruals and prepayments basis.

2   Details relating to the bar, dances, and food sales (and other similar activities) may require separate disclosure. If so, individual accounts would be prepared for these activities, the balance on such accounts then being transferred to the income and expenditure account.

3   Expenditure items would be calculated on an accruals and prepayments basis.

4   The balance on the account (the excess of income over expenditure for the year) is transferred to the Accumulated Fund account (see note 6).

5   Fixed assets, current assets, and current liabilities are calculated and presented in exactly the same way that they are for profit-making entities.

6   The Accumulated Fund is the equivalent of the Capital element in the accounting equation. The total amount of £51 950 represents what the members have invested in the club as at the 31 March 2008 and what could have been paid back to them (in theory) if the club had been closed down at that date. In practice, of course, the various items on the balance sheet would not necessarily have been realized at their balance sheet values.

7   This was the balance in the Accumulated Fund at the beginning of the club's financial year.

8   This balance has been transferred from the income and expenditure account.

9   This is the balance in the Accumulated Fund as at the end of the club's financial year.

Referring to Example 7.5, how satisfactory do you think the Balli Social Club's financial performance has been during the year to 31 March 2008?

Write down your thoughts in your notebook.

Activity 7.5

Government accounts

Another important set of entity accounts relate to the Government sector of the economy. Such accounts may generally be regarded as part of the not-for-profit service sector. There are three broad categories: (1) central Government accounts; (2) local Government accounts; and (3) quasi-Governmental accounts.

Central Government accounts incorporate the results of major departments such as defence, the environment, social security, and trade and industry. Until fairly recently, they were prepared on a cash flow basis, i.e. cash received for the year less cash paid during that year. The Government has now adopted what it calls *resource accounting*. This is just another term for accounts prepared on an accruals and prepayments basis.

The switch to resource accounting has been made because Government services need to become more efficient, i.e. to offer a better service to the public for every pound spent. Cash accounting resulted in a lack of control of operations and projects. For example, if a project was costing more than had been budgeted for it, payments to suppliers could be delayed because departments only had to account for their operations on a cash received/cash paid basis.

Resource accounting has required Government departments to adopt a different approach to the way that they manage their affairs. It involves setting objectives, laying down long-term and short-term plans, the tight management of funds and resources, and statutory reporting similar to that required of the private sector.

Resource accounting will involve producing sets of accounts that include operating cost statements. These are similar to profit and loss accounts and balance sheets. It is claimed that it will have the following advantages:

1 Costs will be charged to departments when they are incurred and not when they are paid for.
2 Distortions will be removed between when goods and services are received, when they are paid for, and when they are consumed.
3 Departmental budgets will be more realistic.
4 It will be much more difficult to disguise the overall cost of departmental activities.

The **Ministry of Defence's** accounts have been qualified for the fifth year running after the National Audit Office was unable to confirm some figures in the operating cost statement in respect of consumption charges for certain stocks and fixed assets. The MoD issued a statement pointing out that 2001/2002 was the first year it had managed resources under the resource accounting model and said the transition had been 'a large and demanding exercise'. The MoD was also hauled over the coals for failing to seek parliamentary approval for overspending in terms of resources accounting while implementing what amounted to cuts.

Figure 7.2 MoD accounts qualified

Source: Accountancy Age, 28 November 2002.

5 There will be greater control over the safeguarding of fixed and current assets, e.g. stocks, and the monitoring of current liabilities such as creditors.

These are substantial claims. Bearing in mind that the difficulties that the commercial world has in dealing with 'accruals and prepayment' accounting, it is doubtful whether resource accounting will operate quite as smoothly as the Government hopes. The problems that it has caused one Government department are vividly illustrated in Figure 7.2.

> Consider the benefits listed above that the switch to resource accounting is expected to bring to Government activities. How far do you think that they are likely to be met? Is the absence of the profit motive in the not-for-profit sector likely to be a major difficulty?
>
> Write down your views in response to these questions.

Activity 7.6

Local government accounts include income and expenditure details relating to major services such as education, housing, police and social services. The annual budget (running from 1 April to 31 March) determines the amount of cash that the local authority needs to raise from its council tax payers in order to finance its projected expenditure for the forthcoming year. This is a highly political consideration and councillors are usually more concerned about the impact that a forthcoming budget may have on the electorate than about expenditure that has already been incurred.

Quasi-government entities include those bodies that are owned by the government but operated at arm's length (i.e. indirectly) through specially appointed authorities and councils. Examples, include the British Broadcasting Corporation (the BBC), secondary or tertiary education colleges, the Post Office, and universities. Such bodies are often heavily dependent on the Government for providing them with a great deal of their operational income.

Government accounting generally is a highly specialist activity, although the basics are similar to the procedures used in the private sector. As it is so specialized, we will not consider it any further in this book.

❗ Questions non-accountants should ask

This chapter covers a number of different types of entity so the following questions may not be relevant in all instances.

● How has a distinction been made between 'direct cost' and 'indirect' ones?

● Why bother with a book entry for manufacturing profit?

● How has the amount added for manufacturing profit been determined?

● Are there any problems in determining when income should be taken to the income and expenditure account?

● How have the depreciation rates for the fixed assets been determined?

● Should we allow for any bad debts or any doubtful ones? [*A very important question in the case of social clubs.*]

● What method is used to assess or calculate them?

● How have any accruals and prepayments been determined?

Conclusion

In describing and illustrating the nature and purpose of accounting, there is a danger that too much emphasis is placed on manufacturing industry in the profit-making sector of the economy. There are three main reasons for this tendency: (1) modern accounting practice grew out of the requirements of nineteenth-century manufacturing industry; (2) twenty or so years ago manufacturing formed a major part of the economy; and (3) a complete range of accounting techniques may be applied in manufacturing industries.

The position has changed rapidly in recent years. Manufacturing industries have declined in importance and service sector industries have taken their place. Government activities have become much more important and greater attention has been given to them. Such activities are largely financed by taxpayers in one form or another. Taxpayers appear increasingly reluctant to contribute more and more of their income in taxes, and the Government has had to search for economies and efficiencies in the way that it operates.

The profession of accountancy has not been immune from the changes taking place in the economic and political sectors, and it has had to adapt in recent years to a rapidly changing environment. This has meant moving away from traditional accounting practices that relate largely to profit-making manufacturing industries and adapting them to a service economy monitored very closely by an anxious Government.

We began the chapter by describing the nature and purpose of manufacturing accounts and demonstrating how they may be compiled. We then moved the focus away from manufacturing and trading accounts toward other types of accounts used in the service sector, the non-for-profit sector, and in Government.

You will have noticed that there is a great deal of similarity between manufacturing and trading accounts and the accounts of service sector entities. Manufacturing, trading and service sector entities all usually adopt an accruals and prepayments basis for preparing their financial statements, and they are presented in the form of a profit and loss account (or equivalent) and a balance sheet.

The main differences are in the detail. Non-manufacturing and trading entities have few (if any) raw material stocks, work-in-progress or finished goods, and product costing is largely irrelevant. There are also a few differences in the way that information is presented in the profit and loss account (alternatively the income and expenditure account) and the balance sheet. Thus if you can work your way through a manufacturing entity's accounts, you should not have too much difficulty with non-manufacturing, non-trading and service sector accounts.

In the next chapter we move on to examine another type of financial statement called a *cash flow statement*. Cash flow statements are now used widely in all sectors of the economy and in all types of entities, and they are regarded as one of the main financial statements.

Key points

1 Entities that convert raw materials and component parts into finished goods may need to prepare a manufacturing account.

2 A manufacturing account is part of the double-entry system. Normally, it will be prepared annually along with the other main financial accounts. It usually comes before the trading account.

3 The main elements of a manufacturing account include: direct materials, direct labour, direct expenses, and various indirect manufacturing costs.

4 A direct cost is a cost that can be easily and economically identified with a particular department, section, product, process or unit. An indirect cost is a cost that cannot be so easily and economically identified.

5 The type of manufacturing account described in this chapter would not be necessary if an entity operated a management accounting system. Management accounting is covered in Part 4 of this book.

6 Service-sector entities do not normally deal in physical or tangible goods or services. Hence they do not need to prepare a manufacturing or a trading account, their basic accounts consisting of a profit and loss account and a balance sheet. The preparation of such financial statements is similar to that required for compiling manufacturing and trading entity accounts.

7 The accounts of not-for-profit entities are very similar to those of service entities, except that the profit and loss account is referred to as an income and expenditure account.

8 Government accounts are highly specialized although, in essence, their basic structure is similar to that adopted in the private sector.

Check your learning

The answers to these questions may be found within the text.

1 What is a manufacturing account?

2 What is (a) a direct cost; and (b) an indirect cost?

3 What is meant by the term 'prime cost'?

4 How does an allowance for profit in the manufacturing account affect the cash position of the entity?

5 To which account is the *market value of goods produced* transferred?

6 What is the service sector?

7 List five different groups of service sector entities.

8 Name four different types of businesses operating in the service sector.

9 What is meant by a 'not-for-profit' entity?

10 What terms are applied to its main financial statement?

11 Can a not-for-profit entity make profits?

12 What is the balance called that is transferred to the accumulated fund at the end of a financial period?

13 What is an 'accumulated fund'?

14 What term does the Government now use to describe its method of accounting?

15 Name two types of local government activities.

16 Name two quasi-governmental entities.

News story quiz

Remember the news story at the beginning of this chapter? Go back to that story and reread it before answering the following question.

Much of this book concentrates on the private manufacturing and trading sectors of the economy. The Government not-for profit sector is also very important, although its accounting procedures have been different from those in the private sector. This article shows that the public sector is now being urged to adopt a private sector approach.

Questions

1 What is 'accruals accounting'?

2 What system of accounting has been common in the public sector until recently?

3 How might accruals accounting lead to 'better management and delivery of services'?

4 How far do you agree with the assertion made in the article that accruals accounting leads to improved performance and more meaningful financial information?

Tutorial questions

The answers to questions marked with an asterisk may be found in Appendix 4.

7.1 A direct cost has been defined as 'a cost that that can be easily and economically identified with a particular department, section, product or unit'. Critically examine this definition from a non-accounting manager's perspective.

7.2 Although a manufacturing account may contain a great deal of information, how far do you think that it helps managers who are in charge of production cost-centres?

7.3 It has been asserted that the main objective of a profit-making entity is to make a profit while that of not-for-profit entity is to provide a service. Discuss this assertion in the context of the accounting requirements of different types of entities.

7.4* The following information relates to Megg for the year to 31 January 2007:

	£000
Stocks at 1 February 2006:	
Raw material	10
Work-in-progress	17
Direct wages	65
Factory: Administration	27
Heat and light	9
Indirect wages	13
Purchases of raw materials	34
Stocks at 31 January 2007:	
Raw material	12
Work-in-progress	14

Required:
Prepare Megg's manufacturing account for the year to 31 January 2007.

7.5* The following balances have been extracted from the books of account of Moor for the year to 28 February 2008:

	£
Direct wages	50 000
Factory indirect wages	27 700
Purchases of raw materials	127 500
Stocks at 1 March 2007:	
Raw material	13 000
Work-in-progress	8 400
Stocks at 28 February 2008:	
Raw material	15 500
Work-in-progress	6 300

Required:
Prepare Moor's manufacturing account for the year to 28 February 2008.

7.6 The following balances have been extracted from the books of Stuart for the year to 31 March 2009:

	£000
Administration: Factory	230
Direct wages	330
Purchases of raw materials	1 123
Stocks at 1 April 2008:	
Raw material	38
Work-in-progress	29

Additional information:　　　　　　　　　　　　　　　　£000
Stocks at 31 March 2009:
　　Raw material　　　　　　　　　　　　　　　　　　　44
　　Work-in-progress　　　　　　　　　　　　　　　　42

Required:
Prepare Stuart's manufacturing account for the year to 31 March 2009.

7.7　The following balances have been extracted from the books of the David and Peter Manufacturing Company as at 30 April 2004:

	£000
Direct wages	70
Factory equipment: at cost	360
General factory expenses	13
Heat and light (factory $\frac{3}{4}$; general $\frac{1}{4}$)	52
Purchases of raw materials	100
Stocks at 1 May 2003:	
Raw material	12
Work-in-progress	18
Rent and rates (factory $\frac{2}{3}$; general $\frac{1}{3}$)	42

Additional information:
1　Stocks at 30 April 2004:　　£000
　　Raw material　　　　　　　14
　　Work-in-progress　　　　　16
2　The factory equipment is to be depreciated at a rate of 15 per cent per annum on cost.

Required:
Prepare the David and Peter Manufacturing Company's manufacturing account for the year to 30 April 2004.

Further practice questions, study material and links to relevant sites on the World Wide Web can be found on the website that accompanies this book. The site can be found at **www.booksites.net/dyson**

Cash flow – the key to survival . . .

Can't get to sleep? It's probably because of your cashflow, says Mark Sim

It's no surprise that cash flow is the biggest cause for concern for the majority of Scottish bosses – what is surprising is that nearly a third of company owners worry so much about their business finances that they actually lose sleep.

Research carried out by Abbey National business found that 32 per cent of bosses in the region said their cash flow worries were bad enough to keep them awake at night. Nationally, 30 per cent of all owner managers said their finances caused them to lose sleep, rising to 45 per cent amongst the owners of plcs.

The biggest cause for jamming up a company's cash flow is slow payers, although there is legislation in place designed to reduce late payments. The legislation was originally created for SMEs, allowing them to charge statutory interest on overdue debts plus compensation of up to £100 to cover the cost of chasing late payers. Yet when the legislation was launched in 1998, many small companies did not adopt the rules for fear of upsetting their bigger customers by demanding payment on time.

In August this year the late payment legislation was extended to all UK businesses and now many small firms are worried this will squeeze their cash flow even further. They fear their bigger suppliers will demand prompt payment for their invoices, while they have to chase their bigger customers to settle overdue invoices.

The key to a well-managed cash flow is to structure finances properly. Planning ahead and knowing what options are available to the small business is the best way to avoid problems. All too often a company automatically turns to its bank for an overdraft to help it through a funding shortfall. But an overdraft can be withdrawn at any time and payment demanded immediately.

Alternative funding options such as factoring, invoice discounting and asset finance can help free up cash flow. Factoring actually uses a company's invoices as an asset, providing them with cash up to 90 per cent of the value of the invoice. According to The Factors & Discounters Association, factoring is set to overtake the overdraft in the next few years as the first choice of lending for businesses.

Another option is asset finance that allows companies to buy items for their business over a set period of time for a fixed monthly cost. Asset finance can be used for items as small as a photocopier costing a few hundreds pounds, or machinery worth millions. Asset finance is tax efficient and does not tie up a company's valuable cash reserves. If a business does find itself with a cash shortfall it should consult its accountant first because the number of finance options available can be confusing and companies need professional help to find the product best suited to their circumstances.

CA Magazine, December 2002.

Questions relating to this news story may be found on page 178 ▶▶

About this chapter

This chapter deals with *cash flow statements.* A cash flow statement (CFS) is now considered to be one of the main financial statements along with the profit and loss accounting and the balance sheet. It lists all the cash receipts and all the cash payments during a particular accounting period. A Financial Reporting Standard (FRS 1) covers the preparation of a CFS and most entities are either required or are recommended to adopt it.

CASH FLOW STATEMENT FOR THE YEAR ENDED 31 OCTOBER 2002

	2002 £'000	2002 £'000	2001 £'000	2001 £'000
NET CASH INFLOW/(OUTFLOW) FROM OPERATING ACTIVITIES		168		(199)
RETURN ON INVESTMENTS AND SERVICING OF FINANCE				
Interest receivable	58		108	
Interest payable	(34)		(79)	
		24		29
TAXATION				
UK Corporation tax		(15)		(11)
CAPITAL EXPENDITURE AND FINANCIAL INVESTMENT				
Purchase of fixed assets	(494)		(700)	
Proceeds from sale of fixed assets	21		12	
Acquisition of investment	(210)		–	
		(683)		(688)
FINANCING ACTIVITIES				
Increase in share capital	63		119	
Withdrawal of share capital	(42)		(27)	
		21		92
DECREASE IN CASH		(485)		(777)

Note: Two notes accompanied the above statement. One gave more information about the item 'net cash inflow/(outflow) for operating activities, and the other note analyzed the changes in the cash during the year.

Figure 8.1 **An example of a cash flow statement from HF Holidays Ltd**

In order to give you an idea at this early stage in the chapter what a CFS looks like, Figure 8.1 shows you one for a for a holiday company.

You will see from Figure 8.1 that HF Holidays Limited had a *decrease in cash* at the end of Year 2002 of £485 000 and of £777 000 at the end of Year 2001. The statement itemizes where the cash came from and where it went to both years. In 2002 the main sources of cash were operating activities, interest received, sales of fixed assets, and increases in the share capital. It used the cash to pay interest, UK Corporation Tax, fixed assets, for a new investment, and the repayment of some of the share capital. Clearly, HF cannot go on losing cash and some urgent managerial action would have been needed to stop it happening.

Our main aims in this chapter are (1) to indicate the usefulness of a CFS; and (2) to show you how one is compiled

The chapter is divided into six main sections. In the next section we explain why the chapter is an important one for non-accountants. The following section explains why we cannot rely on the profit and loss account and the balance sheet to control the cash position. We then show you how to prepare a simple CFS. A further section deals with the preparation of a CFS using FRS 1's recommended format. All the material covered up to that point so far is then brought together in a comprehensive example. The last main section frames some questions on CFSs that non-accountants might like to put to their accountants.

> **By the end of this chapter you should be able to:**
>
> ● distinguish between profitability and liquidity;
>
> ● outline the importance of cash in ensuring the long-term viability of an entity;
>
> ● prepare a basic cash flow statement;
>
> ● specify the main requirements of FRS 1 (*Cash Flow Statement*);
>
> ● assess the relevance of cash flow statements for non-accounting managers.

Learning objectives

! Why this chapter is important for non-accountants

We cannot stress strongly enough just how important this chapter is for those non-accountants who are hoping to become senior managers.

The monitoring of cash flow is a vital task for managers. They must ensure that it is done on a regular and frequent basis. When cash is tight it may be necessary to do it weekly or even daily. If the cash position is less critical then once every four weeks may be sufficient. It is also a good idea to prepare *forecasted* CFSs. The actual CFSs should be compared with them and updated regularly.

Your accountants should be instructed to prepare a CFS in accordance with the timetable that you lay down. They will help to spot times when the entity might be short of cash and that enables something to be done about it before the situation becomes critical. You might, for example, expect your debtors to pay their debts more promptly or you might ask the bank for an overdraft.

The CFS will not mean much to you, of course, if you do not understand where the information comes from, what it means, how it has been prepared, and what you are supposed to do with it.

This chapter will provide you with the means to control an entity's cash position so that it remains a going concern.

Accounting profit and cash

In Chapters 3 to 7, we explained how accountants go about preparing a profit and loss account and a balance sheet for different types of entities. We have suggested that in order to get a fair comparison between one financial accounting period and another, it is necessary to adopt the following procedure:

● Distinguish between capital and revenue transactions.
● Allow for sales and purchases made on credit.
● Estimate the value of the closing stock.

- Calculate how much depreciation to write off for the period.
- Adjust for any accruals and prepayments.

This procedure enables us to calculate the profit made during a particular accounting period. You might think that such a profit will be reflected by an equivalent increase in the entity's cash and balances. This is not so for three main reasons.

1 Purchases and sales are often made on credit terms, there may be delays in paying for services provided, and some services may be paid for in advance. These factors cause a time-lag between when cash is paid and when cash is received.
2 A number of items included in the profit and loss account do not affect the cash position, e.g. depreciation, bad debts, and provisions for bad debts.
3 Some transactions, such as the issue of shares and the purchase of fixed assets, are not recorded in the profit and loss account.

All of these factors mean that it is dangerous to assume that if an entity is making a profit it will not have any cash worries. It needs to monitor its cash position to ensure that there is a balance between what cash it is receiving and what cash it is paying out.

The profit and loss account and balance sheet are inadequate for monitoring purposes. The profit and loss account is not prepared on a cash basis, and the balance sheet only shows the cash position at the balance sheet date. No information is given that enables users to trace the sources of cash and how it has been spent. This makes it difficult to monitor the entity's cash position and to take immediate action if the entity appears to be running short of cash. Hence the need for an additional financial statement that supports the profit and loss account and the balance sheet.

A cash flow statement fulfils such a purpose. Although it is sometimes regarded as a traditional financial statement it is rather a fairly recent one. It was introduced in 1991 to replace a similar statement called *source and application of funds*. This statement did not clearly show the changes in the cash position so it was replaced by *CFS 1*.

We will now explain how to prepare a simple CFS. Although we will be dealing mainly with historical CFSs, we should perhaps stress that it is desirable to prepare *forecasted* ones as well. They should be compared constantly with actual events and updated on a regular basis. Such a procedure enables swift and almost immediate action to be taken if the entity appears to be facing a cash flow crisis.

Activity 8.1	In your notebook list as many items as you can think of that are normally included in a profit and loss account that have neither been debited nor credited to the cash/bank account. Prepare a similar list for all the cash/bank items that have not been included in the profit and loss account.

Construction

A cash flow statement is simply a summary of cash received for the period and cash paid. Such information could be obtained from the cash book but it is much more helpful to a general understanding of the financial accounts if it is integrated with the profit and loss account and the balance sheet. This means that we have to take the information in the financial accounts and convert it into cash terms. We do this by examining each item in the accounts and then adjusting each one for any opening and closing creditors and debtors, accruals and prepayments, and for any non-cash and capital items. Of course, not all items will require to be adjusted and so the procedure is not quite as complicated as it might appear. The relationship between the profit and loss account, the balance sheet and the cash flow statement is clearly very close. It is shown in diagrammatic format in Figure 8.2.

In order to demonstrate how to construct a cash flow statement, we will use a simple example. The details are contained in Example 8.1.

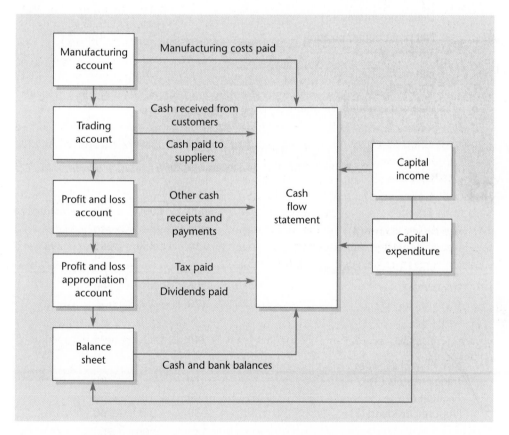

Figure 8.2 **The interrelationship between the main financial statements**

Example 8.1

Preparation of a cash flow statement

You are presented with the following information:

Durton Ltd
Trading and profit and loss account for the year to 31 December 2006

	£000	£000
Sales (1)		1 000
Less: Cost of goods sold:		
Opening stock (NA)	200	
Purchases (3)	700	
	900	
Less: Closing stock	300	600
Gross profit		400
Operating expenses (4)		(240)
Operating profit		160
Debenture interest (5)		(10)
Net profit before taxation		150
Taxation (6)		(50)
Net profit after taxation		100
Dividends (7)		(60)
Retained profit for the year		40

Durton Ltd
Balance sheet at 31 December 2006

	2005		2006	
	£000	£000	£000	£000
Fixed assets at cost (8)	900		1 050	
Less: Accumulated depreciation (4)	150	750	255	795
Current assets				
Stocks (NA)	200		300	
Trade debtors (1)	120		150	
Cash (NA)	20		45	
	340		495	
Less: Current liabilities				
Trade creditors (3)	70		90	
Taxation (4)	40		50	
Proposed dividend (7)	30		60	
	140	200	200	295
		950		1 090

Example 8.1
continued

	2005		2006	
	£000	£000	£000	£000
Capital and reserves				
Ordinary shares of £1 each (NA)		750		750
Profit and loss account (NA)		200		240
		950		990
Loans				
Debenture stock (10%: issued 1 January 2006 (2)		–		100
		950		1 090

Required:
Prepare a cash flow statement for the year to 31 December 2002.

Answer to
Example 8.1

Durton Ltd
Cash flow statement for the year to 31 December 2006

	£000
Cash receipts	
Sale of goods (£1000 + £120 – £150) (1)	970
Issue of debenture stock (£100 – £0) (2)	100
	1 070
Cash payments	
Purchases of goods (£700 + £70 – £90) (3)	(680)
Operating expenses (£240 – (£255 – £150)) (4)	(135)
Debenture interest paid (5)	(10)
Taxation (6)	(40)
Dividends (7)	(30)
Purchases of fixed assets (£1050 – £900) (8)	(150)
	(1 045)
Increase in cash during the year (9)	25
Cash at 1 January 2006 (9)	20
Cash at 31 December 2006 (9)	45

Notes: The number shown after each narration refers to the tutorial notes below.
NA = no adjustment necessary.

Tutorial notes

1 The cash received from the sale of goods has been calculated by taking the sales figure of £1 000 000, adding the opening trade debtors of £120 000, and then deducting the closing trade debtors of £150 000.

2 The issue of debenture stock equals the closing balance of £100 000 as at 31 December 2006. As there was no opening balance, all of the debenture stock must have been issued during the year.

3 The cash payments to suppliers has been calculated as follows:

Purchases + Opening trade creditors – Closing trade creditors, i.e £700 000 + £70 000 – £90 000.

Answer to Example 8.1 continued

4 The other cash payments relate to the operating expenses of £240 000 less the depreciation on the fixed assets of £105 000 (i.e. the closing accumulated balance of £255 000 less the opening accumulated depreciation balance of £150 000). As there were no opening or closing debtors or creditors for operating expenses, the whole of the £135 000 must have been paid during the year.

5 This is the total amount of debenture interest paid during the year.

6 The tax paid of £40 000 represents the taxation due for payment at 1 January 2006, since the amount outstanding at 31 December 2006 of £50 000 is the same as the figure for tax shown in the profit and loss account.

7 The dividend paid is the same as the proposed dividend at 1 January 2006, because the dividends shown in the profit and loss account as £60 000 had not been paid at 31 December 2006.

8 Purchase of fixed assets equals the closing balance of £1 050 000 less the opening balance of £900 000.

9 The increase in cash during the year of £25 000 plus the opening balance of £20 000 equals the closing balance of £45 000.

Activity 8.2   Work through Example 8.1 again but this time without looking at the answer.

Referring to Durton Limited's balance sheet in Example 8.1, we can see that at 31 December 2005 it had a cash balance of £20 000. By 31 December 2006, the cash balance was £45 000, an increase of £25 000. Note that the retained profit for the year of £40 000 does not reflect the £25 000 increase in cash during the year. We do not, of course need to prepare a CFS to find out such information but we do need some help in determining why the retained profit for the year was £40 000 while the cash only increased by £25 000. A CFS provides us with that guidance. In Durton's case, most of the cash received for the year came from sales and much of it was spent on buying goods.

If you look at the CFS a little more closely, you will also see that £100 000 was raised by issuing some debenture stock and that £150 000 was incurred on purchasing some fixed assets. These items do not appear in the profit and loss account. There is probably a connection between them, i.e. the debentures might have been issued to finance the purchase of the fixed assets. Certainly, without the debentures the cash position at the end of the year would have been very different, e.g. an overdrawn amount of £55 000 (45 000 – 100 000) instead of a favourable balance of £45 000. Similarly, if the taxation balance of £50 000 and the dividend balance of £60 000 as at 31 December 2006 had had to be paid early in 2007, the cash position would have been extremely vulnerable. Durton Ltd would then have to depend on its trade debtors (£150 000 at 31 December 2006) settling their debts before it needed to pay its trade creditors of £90 000.

Durton's CFS is a simplified example of a company's cash flow statement. Nevertheless, it does enable the major cash items to be highlighted and to bring them to the attention of the managers and the owners of the entity. Although it is to be hoped that the cash position of Durton was being closely monitored during the year (a CFS would probably be prepared on a frequent basis), an annual CFS enables the year's results to be measured in cash terms and put into perspective. A CFS is now considered as a very important financial statement. Indeed, you may regard it as being just as important as the profit and loss account and the balance sheet.

The format that we have adopted in preparing the solution to Example 8.1 demonstrates the close relationship between the profit and loss account, the balance sheet and the CFS. The various changes that have been made are, however, somewhat difficult to trace. It would be useful, therefore, to present the CFS in such a way that its close relationship with the profit and loss account and the balance sheet is more apparent. The ASB has devised such a format and we can now examine it.

FRS 1 format

The very first financial reporting standard that the ASB issued dealt with cash flow statements. This was FRS 1 – *Cash Flow Statement* issued in 1991 and revised in 1996.

In this chapter we are only going to be concerned with cash flow statements that relate to a single entity. In Chapter 11 we will deal with CFSs for groups, i.e. companies that own a substantial number of shares in other companies.

FRS 1 requires the CFS to be set out under eight main headings. These headings are summarized in Table 8.1. The table also contains some examples of what may be included under each heading.

Table 8.1 **Structure of a cash flow statement according to FRS 1**

Heading[a]	Contents[b]
1 Net cash inflow from operating activities	Operating or trading activities[c]
2 Returns on investments and servicing of finance	Investment income. Interest payments on loans. Dividends paid to preference shareholders
3 Taxation	Tax paid on profits
4 Capital expenditure and financial investment[d]	Purchases and sales of fixed assets. Loans to other entities received and paid
5 Acquisitions and disposals	Sales and purchases of other entities or of investments in them
6 Equity dividends paid	Dividends paid to ordinary shareholders
7 Management of liquid resources[e]	Purchases and sales of current asset investments
8 Financing[e]	Receipts and payments relating to share issues and redemptions, debentures, loans, and other long-term borrowings

Notes:
(a) Headings may be omitted if no cash transaction has taken place either in the current period or in the previous period. They must be in the order listed. A subtotal should be included for each heading.
(b) The contents only reflect the *cash* flow for each transaction. Cash includes cash in hand, deposits repayable on demand, and overdrafts. *Cash flow* is an increase or decrease in cash during the period.
(c) FRS 1 requires a reconciliation to be made between the operating profit and the net cash flows from operating activities.
(d) The heading 'capital expenditure' may be used if there are no cash flows relating to financial investment (such as loans).
(e) Headings 7 and 8 may be combined under one heading provided that each of their respective cash flows are shown separately and that separate subtotals are given for each heading.

FRS 1 requires the cash flow statement to be accompanied by a number of notes. These are as follows:

- a reconciliation between the operating profit and the net cash flow arising from operating activities;
- a reconciliation of net cash flow to movements in net debt;
- an analysis of the changes in net debt.

We deal with each of these notes below.

Reconciliation of operating profit to operating cash flows

This note to the CFS shows how the operating profit for the period has been converted into the respective cash flows, so that we measure the operating profit for the period in cash terms. There are two ways that this can be done. One way is to use what is called the *direct* method. If we adopt this method, all that we have to do is list for the period in question the cash received from customers and any other operating cash receipts, and the cash paid to suppliers together with any other operating cash payments. The information may be obtained from the cash book.

The other method is called the *indirect* method. As most entities have now adopted this method we will do so in this book.

The indirect method requires us to convert the operating activities for a period into the operating cash flows for the same period. We do so by comparing the current and previous period's profit and loss accounts and balance sheets. The following steps are necessary.

1 Extract the operating (or trading) profit from the profit and loss account for the current year.
2 Referring to the two balance sheets periods, calculate the movement between the following *operating* working capital balances:
   (a) stocks;
   (b) trade debtors;
   (c) other debtors;
   (d) prepayments;
   (e) trade creditors;
   (f) other creditors;
   (g) accruals.
3 Now comes the tricky bit. Determine whether in respect of each movement there has been either an increase or a decrease in cash during the period. In order to make it a little easier for you, we have summarized the various possibilities in Table 8.2.
4 If the cash movement has had the effect of *increasing* the cash for the period, add the difference to the operating profit for the year. If it has had the effect of *decreasing* the cash, then deduct it from the operating profit (deductions are usually shown in brackets).
5 Inspect the profit and loss account for any non-cash items. These should then either be added to, or deducted from, the operating profit. Additions will include losses on disposals of fixed assets, depreciation, increases in provisions for bad and doubtful debts, and bad debts written off. Deductions (shown in brackets) will include profits on sales of fixed assets and reductions in provisions for bad and doubtful debts.

Table 8.2 **The effect of working capital movements on cash flow**

Item	Movement (Closing balance less opening balance)	Effect on cash
Stocks	Increase	Down (more cash has been spent on stocks). Insert the movement in brackets
	Decrease	Up (less cash has been spent on stocks)
Trade debtors, other debtors, and prepayments	Increase	Down (less cash has been received). Insert the movement in brackets
	Decrease	Up (more cash has been received)
Trade creditors, other creditors, and accruals (excluding taxation payable and proposed dividends)	Increase	Up (less cash has been spent)
	Decrease	Down (more cash has been paid). Insert the movement in brackets

6 Total the items included in the reconciliation. The balance should now represent the net cash inflow (or outflow) from operating activities. The balance is then inserted as the first item in the CFS.

The above steps may appear somewhat confusing, but do not worry at this stage. We will put them into context in an illustrative example later in the chapter.

Activity 8.3

State whether each of the following statements is true or false.

(a) Operating activities reflect total cash inflows.   *True/False*

(b) Depreciation decreases the cash position.   *True/False*

(c) Tax paid decreases the tax position.   *True/False*

(d) A proposed dividend increases the cash position.   *True/False*

(e) A decrease in debtors increases the cash position.   *True/False*

(f) An increase in creditors decreases the cash position.   *True/False*

We can now move on to examine the second note required by FRS1. This note reconciles the net cash flow to movement in net debt.

Reconciliation of net cash flow to movement in net debt

In order to help users assess the solvency and liquidity position of a company, FRS 1 requires two other notes to accompany the CFS. One note should show a reconciliation between the net debt at the beginning of the period and the net debt at the end of it. Basically, net debt is the difference between any long-term loans and cash and bank balances. If the cash and bank balances exceed the long-term funds, the balance would be referred to as *net funds*. We will be dealing with this note in Example 8.2 later in the chapter.

An analysis of changes in net debt

The other additional note requires a detailed analysis of the changes that have taken place in the net debt position during the year. We will show you how to compile this note shortly.

We can now illustrate how to prepare a cash flow statement as required by FRS 1. We do so in Example 8.2.

An illustrative example

In order to demonstrate how a CFS is compiled in accordance with FRS 1 and how it should be presented, we are going to use the data from Example 8.1. As explained earlier, FRS 1 gives a choice between the direct and indirect methods. We will be using the indirect method.

Example 8.2

Preparation of a cash flow statement in accordance with FRS 1

Durton Ltd
Cash flow statement for the year to 31 December 2006

	£000
Net cash inflow from operating activities (1)	155
Returns on investments and servicing of finance	
Interest paid (7)	(10)
Taxation (8)	(40)
Capital expenditure	
Payments to acquire tangible fixed assets (9)	(150)
Equity dividends paid (10)	(30)
	(75)
Management of liquid resources and financing	
Issue of debenture stock (11)	100
Increase in cash (12)	25

Note 1 Reconciliation of operating profit to net cash inflow from operating activities

	£000
Operating profit (2)	160
Depreciation (3)	105
(Increase) in stocks (4)	(100)
(Increase) in trade debtors (5)	(30)
Increase in trade creditors (6)	20
Net cash inflow from operating activities (1)	155

Example 8.2
continued

Note 2 Reconciliation of net cash flow to movement in debt

	£000
Increase in cash during the period (12)	25
Cash from issuing debentures (13)	(100)
Change in net debt (14)	(75)
Net funds at 1 January 2006 (15)	20
Net debt at 31 December 2006 (16)	55

Note 3 Analysis of change in net debt

	At 1.1.06	Cash flows	At 31.12.06
	£000	£000	£000
Cash	20 (15)	25 (12)	45 (17)
Debt due after one year	– (15	(100) (13)	(100)(13)
Total	20 (15)	(75) (14)	(55)(16)

[*Note*: the number in brackets after each amount refers to the tutorial notes.]

Tutorial notes

1 The calculation of the net cash inflow from operating activities totalling £155 000 is shown in Note 1 to the CFS (as required by FRS 1).

2 The operating profit of £160 000 has been obtained from the profit and loss account.

3 The depreciation charge has been obtained from the balance sheet. It is the difference between the accumulated depreciation of £255 000 as at 31 December 2006 and £150 000 as at 31 December 2005. Note that, in more advanced examples, the depreciation charge may require some detailed calculations.

4 The increase in stocks has been obtained from the two balance sheets. It is the movement between the two balances of £300 000 and £200 000. Note that an increase in stocks is the equivalent of a *reduction* in cash because more cash will have been paid out.

5 The increase in trade debtors of £30 000 represents the movement between the opening and closing trade debtors as obtained from the two balance sheets. An increase in trade debtors represents a *reduction* in cash because less cash has been received by the entity.

6 The increase in trade creditors of £20 000 is again obtained from the balance sheets. The £20 000 represents an *increase* in cash because less cash has been paid out of the business.

7 The interest paid of £10 000 has been obtained from the profit and loss account.

8 The taxation amount of £40 000 is the balance shown on the previous year's balance sheet. As £50 000 was charged to this year's profit and loss account for taxation and this amount features on this year's balance sheet, only £40 000 must have been paid during the year. In more advanced questions, more detailed adjustments would probably be required.

9 The capital expenditure amount of £150 000 is the difference between the two balance sheet amounts for fixed assets, of £1 050 000 and £900 000 respectively. No further details are given. In practice, the calculation of this amount would normally be more complex.

10 The equity dividends of £30 000 represent the dividends paid out to ordinary shareholders during the year (there are no other groups of shareholders in this example). The amount has been obtained from the 2005 balance sheet. The 2006 balance sheet shows an amount of £60 000, which is the same amount as disclosed in the profit and loss account. This means that only last year's dividend has been paid during the current year. Normally, there would also be other payments during the year.

Tutorial notes continued

11 The debenture stock balance has been obtained from the 2006 balance sheet. There was no such balance at the end of 2005, and so all the debenture must have been issued during 2006, as indeed is stated in the example.

12 After making all the above adjustments to the financial accounts, the net increase in cash during 2006 is found to be £25 000.

13 See Tutorial note 11, above.

14 Without the issue of the debentures, there would have been a £75 000 net outflow of cash during the year.

15 The company only had cash at 1 January 2006; it did not have any debt.

16 The entity's net debt at 31 December 2006 was £55 000, i.e. the debenture stock of £100 000 less the cash in hand of £45 000.

17 This was the cash balance at 31 December 2006, as shown in the balance sheet at that date.

Note that FRS 1 permits the detailed items included under each of the main headings on the cash flow statement to be shown in notes.

Activity 8.4

Using the data contained in Example 8.1 prepare a cash flow statement in accordance with the requirements of FRS 1 without looking at the answer.

! Questions non-accountants should ask

It is unlikely that as a non-accountant you will have to prepare cash flow statements. Your accountants will do that for you and present you with them from time to time. Unlike the profit and loss account and the balance sheet, a cash flow statement should be accurate. There are no assumptions or estimates to make. It can be considered to be entirely an unbiased factual statement. You do not need, therefore, to ask questions about the way that it has been compiled. You can take it at its face value.

We will assume that after studying this chapter you know where the information comes from and what it means. So what should you do with it? What questions should you ask? We suggest that the following ones may be appropriate.

- Why has there been an increase or a decrease in cash during the period?
- What are the main items that have caused it?
- Did we anticipate them happening?
- What caused them?
- What did we do about any likely problems?
- Are we going to be short of cash in the immediate period?
- Will the bank support an extension of our overdraft?
- Can we borrow some funds from elsewhere?
- Might we need to borrow some on a long-term basis?
- How will that affect our future profitability bearing in mind interest and repayment requirements?

Conclusion

A cash flow statement using the indirect method links directly with the profit and loss account and the balance sheet. It contains some extremely useful information because it gives a lot more detail about the movement in the cash position. This is vital as it is possible for an entity to be profitable without necessarily having the cash resources to keep it going. Strict control over cash resources is absolutely essential, and a cash flow statement can help in this respect.

Key points

1 Entities may have a long-term profitable future, but in the short term they may be short of cash. This may curb their activities, and in extreme cases they may be forced out of business.

2 To avoid this happening, owners and managers should be supplied with information about the cash movement and resources of the entity, i.e. about its liquidity. This can be done by preparing a cash flow statement.

3 A cash flow statement can be presented in any format, but most companies are required to adopt the recommendations contained in FRS 1.

4 FRSs can be presented using either the direct method or the indirect one. The indirect method is to be preferred because it can be linked more obviously to the profit and loss account and the balance sheet.

Check your learning

The answers to these questions may be found within the text.

1 List five reasons why the accounting profit for a period will not necessarily result in an improvement in an entity's cash position.

2 Identify two balance sheet items that may change an entity's cash position.

3 How does depreciation affect the cash and bank balances?

4 What two methods may be used for preparing a CFS?

5 What Financial Reporting Standard covers the preparation of CFSs, and when was it issued?

6 How many headings does the standard suggest for a CFS?

7 What are they?

8 Does an *increase* in (a) stocks; (b) debtors; and (c) creditors increase or decrease the cash position?

9 Does a *decrease* in (a) stocks; (b) debtors; and (c) creditors increase or decrease the cash position?

10 What is (a) 'net debt', and (b) 'net funds'?

11 List the assumptions and estimates that have to be made when compiling a CFS.

12 How reliable is a CFS?

13 What action would you expect a manager to take on receiving a CFS based on (a) historical data; and (b) forecasted data?

News story quiz

Remember the news story at the beginning of this question? Go back to that story and reread it before answering the following questions.

This article demonstrates that cash flow is a real worry for managers. While a healthy accounting profit is necessary over the medium to long term, an entity cannot survive in the short term unless it has sufficient cash to be able to survive on a day-to-day basis.

Questions

1 Why should cash flow be a problem if an entity is making a reasonable accounting profit?

2 Why are some customers slow to settle their accounts while at the same time insisting upon almost instant settlement from their customers?

3 What do you think is meant by the statement that 'the key to a well-managed cash flow is to structure finances properly'?

4 What can small entities do to encourage larger ones to settle their debts more promptly?

Tutorial questions

The answers to questions marked with an asterisk may be found in Appendix 4.

8.1 'Proprietors are more interested in cash than profit.' Discuss.

8.2 Unlike traditional financial accounting, cash flow accounting does not require the accountant to make a series of arbitrary assumptions, apportionments and estimates. How far, therefore, do you think that there is a case for abandoning traditional financial accounting?

8.3 Does a cash flow statement serve any useful purpose?

8.4* You are presented with the following information:

Dennis Limited
Balance sheet at 31 January 2007

	31 January 2006		31 January 2007	
	£000	£000	£000	£000
Fixed assets				
Land at cost		600		700
Current assets				
Stock	100		120	
Debtors	200		250	
Cash	6		10	
	306		380	
Less: Current liabilities				
Creditors	180	126	220	160
		726		860
Capital and reserves				
Ordinary share capital		700		800
Profit and loss account		26		60
		726		860

Required:
(a) Prepare Dennis Limited's cash flow statement for the year ended 31 January 2007.
(b) Outline what it tells the managers of Dennis Limited.

8.5* The following balance sheets have been prepared for Frank Limited:

Balance sheets at:	28.2.08		28.2.09	
	£000	£000	£000	£000
Fixed assets				
Plant and machinery at cost		300		300
Less: Depreciation		80		100
		220		200
Investments at cost		–		100
Current assets				
Stocks	160		190	
Debtors	220		110	
Bank	–		10	
	380		310	
Less: Current liabilities	200		160	
Creditors	20		–	
Bank overdraft	220	160	160	150
		380		450

Balance sheets at:	28.2.08		28.2.09	
	£000	£000	£000	£000
Capital and reserves				
Ordinary share capital		300		300
Share premium account		50		50
Profit and loss account		30		40
		380		390
Shareholders' funds				
Loans				
Debentures		–		60
		380		450

Additional information:

There were no purchases or sales of plant and machinery during the year.

Required:

(a) Prepare Frank Limited's cash flow statement for the year ended 28 February 2009.

(b) What does it tell the managers of Frank Limited?

8.6   You are presented with the following information:

Starter

Profit and loss account for the year to 31 March 2009

	£	£
Sales		10 000
Purchases	5 000	
Less: Closing stock	1 000	4 000
Gross profit		6 000
Less: Depreciation		2 000
Net profit for the year		4 000

Balance sheet at 31 March 2009

	£	£
Van		10 000
Less: Depreciation		2 000
		8 000
Stock	1 000	
Trade debtors	5 000	
Bank	12 500	
	18 500	
Less: Trade creditors	2 500	16 000
		24 000
Capital		20 000
Add: Net profit for the year		4 000
		24 000

Note: Starter commenced business on 1 April 2008.

Required:
(a) Compile Starter's cash flow statement for the year ended 31 March 2009.
(b) What does it tell the owners of Starter?

8.7   The following is a summary of Gregory Limited's accounts for the year ended 30 April 2004.

Profit and loss account for the year ended 30 April 2004

	£000
Net profit before tax	75
Taxation	25
	50
Dividend (proposed)	40
Retained profit for the year	10

Balance sheet at 30 April 2004

	30.4.03		30.4.04	
	£000	£000	£000	£000
Fixed assets				
Plant at cost		400		550
Less: Depreciation		100		180
		300		370
Current assets				
Stocks	50		90	
Debtors	70		50	
Bank	10		2	
	130		142	
Less: Current liabilities				
Creditors	45		55	
Taxation	18		25	
Proposed dividend	35		40	
	98	32	120	22
		332		392
Capital and reserves				
Ordinary share capital		200		200
Profit and loss account		132		142
		332		342
Loans		–		50
		332		392

Additional information:
There were no sales of fixed assets during the year ended 30 April 2004.

Required:
(a) Prepare Gregory Limited's cash flow statement for the year ended 30 April 2004.
(b) Outline what it tells the managers of Gregory Limited.

8.8   The following summarized accounts have been prepared for Pill Limited:

Profit and loss account for the year ended 31 May 2005

	2004	2005
	£000	£000
Sales	2 400	3 000
Less: Cost of goods sold	1 600	2 000
Gross profit	800	1 000
Less: Expenses:		
Administrative expenses	310	320
Depreciation: vehicles	55	60
furniture	35	40
	400	420
Net profit	400	580
Taxation	120	150
	280	430
Dividends	200	250
Retained profits for the year	80	180

Balance sheet at 31 May 2005

	31.5.04		31.5.05	
	£000	£000	£000	£000
Fixed assets				
Vehicles at cost	600		800	
Less: Depreciation	200	400	260	540
Furniture	200		250	
Less: Depreciation	100	100	140	110
Current assets				
Stocks	400		540	
Debtors	180		200	
Cash	320		120	
	900		860	
Less: Current liabilities				
Creditors	270		300	
Corporation tax	170		220	
Proposed dividends	150		100	
	590	310	620	240
		810		890
Capital and reserves				
Ordinary share capital		500		550
Profit and loss account		120		300
Shareholders' funds		620		850
Loans				
Debentures (10%)		190		40
		810		890

Preparation of financial statements

Learning objectives

By the end of this case study you should be able to:

- identify the accounting rules adopted in preparing a set of accounts;
- evaluate the format and presentation of such accounts;
- suggest a more meaningful way of presenting them.

Background

Location	Glasgow
Personnel	Alan Marshall: a member of the All Weather Rambling Club
	Wendy Hargreaves: Treasurer, All Weather Rambling Club

Synopsis

Alan Marshall has recently joined the All Weather Rambling (AWR) Club (not its real name) based in Glasgow. A few months after joining the AWR he attended the Annual General Meeting (AGM).

Among the items on the agenda was the Treasurer's report. Alan did not know a great deal about accounting and so he was somewhat mystified by the 'accounts' presented by the Treasurer, Wendy Hargreaves. He took the opportunity to ask her a few questions but he did not understand the explanations. A copy of the accounts as presented at the meeting is shown in the Appendix. They were described as a 'balance sheet' and all the information was contained on one page.

After the meeting had ended Alan learnt that Wendy had been in post for nearly 20 years and the accounts had always been presented in that way. As long as the Club had some money at the bank nobody else seemed concerned about them.

When he got home, Alan decided to write to her, asking for clarification about certain items contained in the 'balance sheet'. Wendy was very helpful and she provided him with more information. He was still not satisfied that the accounts presented a clear picture of the Club's financial position for the year 2001/02. He also suspected that this was probably true for the preceding year as well.

The following are the questions Alan asked Wendy and the answers that she gave him.

Q What is 'Mr Smith's bequest'?

A A legacy left by ex Chairman, Arthur Smith, to the Club some years ago.

Q On the left had side, what does the item 'cheques through the bank' mean?

A Cheques that had not gone through the bank at the end of the year.

Q On the right hand side what do the 'deposits' mean?

A The New Year deposit relates to a booking made at a Youth Hostel for the forthcoming New Year. The Slide Show deposit is a payment to the hotel for the room booking for the Slide Show in December.

Q On the right hand side, what does the item 'through bank' mean?

A Cheques that had not gone through the bank at the beginning of the year.

Q Were any amounts paid in 2000/01 for 2001/02?

A Yes. A deposit of £88 paid to the Rugby Club for the Christmas party held in December 2001.

Q Did we receive any money in 2000/01 that related to 2001/02?

A Yes – subscriptions of £50 in total from five members.

Required:

1 Identify those accounting rules that the Treasurer appears to have adopted in preparing All Weather Rambling Club's accounts and explain what each of them means.

2 Giving your reasons, indicate what other accounting rules it might be appropriate for the Treasurer to adopt.

3 Prepare the Club's accounts in a format that you believe would more clearly present its financial performance and position during and at the end of the year.

Appendix

All Weather Rambling Club
Balance sheet of accounts for year 2001/2002

	£		£
Bank balance at 13/9/01	4365	Affiliation fees	20
Subscriptions	1920	Rights of Way membership	150
Donations	5	Mountain Hut membership	30
Profits from:		Youth Hostel membership	6
Bus cancellation fees	406	Youth Hostel donation	100
Private buses	144	National Trust donation	50
Christmas party	173		
Cheese and wine	17	**Expenses:**	
		Printing & stationery	330
Mr Smith's bequest	96	Leaders' expenses	16
Bank interest (2001/02)	83	Recce expenses	1072
Subscriptions (2002/03)	30	Postage/telephones	6
		Secretary	131
		Treasurer	36
		Sundry items:	
		Hire of halls	285
		Insurance	88
		General	42
		Deposits:	
		New Year 2002/03	128
		Slide Show 16/12/02	50
		Losses:	
		High tea	5
		Lecture	17
		Through bank	297
Cheques not through bank	841	**Balance in bank 23/8/02**	5221
TOTAL	**£8080**	TOTAL	**£8080**

Accounting policies

By the end of this case study you should be able to:

- outline the meaning of various conventional accounting policies used in preparing financial statements;
- explain the effect each policy has on the profit or loss for a particular period.

Learning objectives

Location	Birmingham
Personnel	Clare Cheng: Potential investor
	Kate Feng: Chartered accountant

Background

Synopsis

Brambles Industries is a public limited company (plc). It was created in 2001 by the merger of Brambles Industries Limited in Australia with part of its joint-venture partner, GKN plc in the UK. Clare Cheng had read something about the formation of the company in the newspapers and she thought that it might be suitable for her as a long-term investment. She obtained a copy of the Annual Review for the Year 2002. It was not an easy read.

The first page gave some details about the company. It appeared to be a 'global support services provider' but Clare was not sure what that meant. Turning over the pages she came across a section called 'Business Reviews'. It appeared that Brambles was a combination of a number of other companies. CHEP supplied pallet and plastic containers, Cleanaway was involved in waste management, while Recall was an information management company. Other companies appeared to be offering services to the coal and steel industries but Clare was not clear what they did.

She continued to flick through the pages. It was all very puzzling. On page 59 she got to that part of the Review dealing with the financial statements. The financial statements went on for the next 42 pages. It was all very daunting. The pages from page 42 to 64 were full of figures that frightened Clare. Page 65, however, was headed 'Notes To The Combined Financial Information' and these continued until page 95.

Clare tried to read these notes but they appeared to require both a knowledge of Brambles' various activities and a considerable knowledge of accounting. In desperation Clare had a word with her friend Kate Feng. Kate had recently qualified as a chartered accountant.

Kate was in her element. She took Clare through the Combined Financial Statements. Kate made two points: (1) the preparation of accounting statements required a great deal of individual judgement; and (2) the format and content of Brambles accounts was no different from most other companies. Clare was reassured about the second point but concerned about accounts requiring individual judgement.

'OK,' said Kate. 'Let's look at the accounting policies on pages 66 and 67. Apart from a few things that are specific to Brambles, they are pretty standard.'

Clare was beginning to feel a little less concerned.

Kate continued, 'If we go through a few of the policies, I can explain why some individual judgement is required and what impact that may have on the company's profit.'

'You mean that the profit can be fiddled?' queried Clare.

'Not in the fraud sense,' replied Kate, 'but yes. Depending upon what accounting policies are adopted and what assumptions are made, it is possible to arrive at almost any figure for profit that you want.'

Kate may have been overstating the point and Clare's face once more began to register her alarm. She was not sure any more that she wanted to buy some shares in Brambles or indeed in any other company.

Nevertheless, Kate began to explain the company's accounting policies while Clare listened very carefully.

Note: Brambles' accounting policies relating to debtors, provisions, stock, and tangible fixed assets and depreciation are shown in the Appendix below.

Required:

1 Explain what each of the accounting policies means.

2 Demonstrate how the application of each of these policies can affect the level of accounting profit (or loss) for a particular period.

Appendix

Debtors

Debtors are shown at amounts receivable less provision for doubtful debts. Trade debtors are recognized when services are provided and settlement is expected within normal credit terms.

Known bad debts are written off. In addition, a provision for doubtful debts is made in respect of the closing balance of trade debtors based on an assessment of specific exposures combined with historical experience.

Provisions

Provisions for liabilities are made on the basis that the business has a constructive or legal obligation to transfer economic benefit due to a past event that is of uncertain timing or amount.

Provision is made for the unavoidable future costs in relation to restoration and aftercare of landfill sites. The provisions are calculated based on the net present value of estimated future costs. The unwinding of the discount is reflected within the financial statements as a finance charge.

Stocks

Stocks are valued at the lower of cost and net realizable value and, where appropriate, provision is made for possible obsolescence. Work-in-progress, which represents partly completed work undertaken at pre-arranged rates but not invoiced at balance date, is recorded at the lower of cost and net realizable value.

Cost is determined on a first-in, first-out basis and, where relevant, includes an appropriate portion of overhead expenditure.

Tangible fixed assets and depreciation

Tangible fixed assets are generally included at historical cost, net of depreciation and any provision for impairment. Cost includes directly attributable finance costs in relation to major projects. Prior to the adoption of *FRS 15: Tangible fixed assets*, certain fixed assets had been included in the financial statements at revalued amounts. With effect from 1 July 1998, such valuations were frozen and effectively treated as the cost of the fixed asset and no further revaluations made.

The carrying values of tangible fixed assets are subject to review and any impairment charged to the profit and loss account.

Depreciation is charged in the financial statements so as to write off the cost less estimated residual value of all property, plant and equipment, including landfill sites but excluding other freehold land, during their expected useful lives. Predominantly, the straight-line method of calculation has been used except for landfills where the depreciation is based on capacity used of the total capacity available.

The expected useful lives of property, plant and equipment are generally:

Buildings	50 years
Leasehold improvements	5–10 years
Plant and equipment (owned and leased)	5–20 years

Cash flow statements

**Learning
objectives**

By the end of this case study you should be able to:

● **identify the main features of a cash flow statement;**

● **evaluate the main reasons for changes in the cash position of an entity.**

Background

Location	Sidmouth
Personnel	Edgar Glennie: a retired aircraft engineer

Synopsis

Edgar Glennie recently retired from his job as an aircraft engineer. He is now living in Sidmouth and he spends most of his time reading the financial press and reviewing his investments. Over recent months the company news was not good: profits were down, dividends were cut, and the accountancy profession was up to its neck in various types of scandals. One of Edgar's investments was in Aggreko plc and he had read something in his local paper about the company that had made him a little concerned.

Aggreko had 40 years' experience of providing portable power, temperature control and compressed air systems in countries around the world. The company had a very successful year to 31 December 2001. Group turnover increased by 16.6% and pre-tax profit by 10.4%.

Nevertheless, Edgar was still concerned. From his reading of the newspapers he was well aware of the importance of cash flow. He appreciated that, in order to survive in the long run, companies must make profits but in the short-run they needed enough cash to survive on a day-to-day basis. What was Aggreko's cash position?

When he received his copy of Aggreko's Annual Review for 2001 he turned to the 'Consolidated Cash Flow Statement' on pages 32 and 33 with great interest. Edgar was aware that 'consolidated' meant that the results for all Aggreko's major investments in other companies were shown in one statement. The cash flow statement showed that the company's cash had decreased by £0.5m in 2001 and by £6.2m in 2000. Edgar was very annoyed with himself for not spotting the negative cash flow the previous year, but it was too late to do anything about that now. At least the decrease in 2001 was less than the decrease in 2000.

When he checked the 'Consolidated Profit and Loss Account' on page 30, he noted that the company had made a profit on ordinary activities after taxation of £42.3m in 2001 compared with £38.6m in 2000. The 'Consolidated Balance Sheet' on page 31 showed that at 31 December 2001 the company had a cash and bank balance of £9.9m compared with £15.2m at 31 December 2000.

All of this seemed very odd to Edgar. What had happened? Could the company last for very much longer?

Note: Aggreko's Consolidated Cash Flow Statement is shown in the Appendix below.

Required:
Explain how a figure for retained profit for the financial year of £28.1 million for the year to 31 December 2001 can still result in a decrease in cash of £0.5 million by the end of the year.

Appendix

Aggreko plc
Consolidated Cash Flow Statement for the year ended 31 December 2001

	2001 £m	2000 £m
Net cash inflow from continuing operating activities	123.3	101.3
Returns on investments and servicing of finance		
Interest received	0.6	0.5
Interest paid on bank loans and overdrafts	(9.7)	(8.2)
Net cash outflow for returns on investments and servicing of finance	(9.1)	(7.7)
Taxation		
UK Corporation tax paid	(5.2)	(5.5)
Overseas tax paid	(18.5)	(17.4)
Tax paid	(23.7)	(22.9)
Capital expenditure and financial investment		
Purchase of tangible fixed assets	(99.6)	(75.5)
Proceeds from disposal of tangible fixed assets	5.2	3.6
Net cash outflow for capital expenditure and financial investment	(94.4)	(71.9)
Acquisitions		
Purchase of rental businesses and assets	0.5	(8.6)
Equity dividends paid	(13.5)	(12.3)
Cash inflow before use of liquid resources and financing	(16.9)	(22.1)
Management of liquid resources	(0.6)	3.2
Financing		
Issue of shares	1.4	4.4
Increase/(decrease) in debt due within one year	3.0	(33.5)
Increase in debt due beyond one year	12.6	41.8
Net cash inflow from financing	17.0	12.7
Decrease in cash in the period	(0.5)	(6.2)

	2001 £m	2000 £m
Reconciliation of net cash flow to movement in net debt		
Decrease in cash in the period	(0.5)	(6.2)
Cash inflow from increase in debt	(15.6)	(8.3)
Cash outflow/(inflow) from movement in liquid resources	0.6	(3.2)
Changes in net debt arising from cash flows	(15.5)	(17.7)
Exchange	(1.5)	(3.7)
Movement in net debt in period	(17.0)	(21.4)
Net debt at beginning of period	(116.2)	(94.8)
Net debt at end of period	(133.2)	(116.2)

(i) Reconciliation of operating profit to net cash inflow from operating activities

	2001 £m	2000 £m
Operating profit	76.2	68.8
Depreciation and amortization	52.4	44.1
Increase in stocks	(5.4)	(4.0)
Increase in debtors	(1.7)	(6.0)
Increase in creditors	4.7	1.3
Other items not involving the movement of cash	(2.9)	(2.9)
Net cash inflow from continuing operating activities	123.3	101.3
Included in other items not involving the movement of cash:		
Gain on sale of tangible fixed assets	(2.7)	(2.0)

(ii) Analysis of movement in net debt

	Net debt at 31 Dec 2000 £m	Cash flow £m	Translation £m	Net debt at 31 Dec 2001 £m
Cash				
Cash at bank and in hand	14.0	(5.9)	–	8.1
Overdrafts	(5.4)	5.4	–	–
	8.6	(0.5)	–	8.1
Liquid resources				
Deposits maturing within one year	1.2	0.6	–	1.8
Financing				
Debt due within one year	–	(3.0)	–	(3.0)
Debt due after one year	(126.0)	(12.6)	(1.5)	(140.1)
	(116.2)	(15.5)	(1.5)	(133.2)

In Part 3 we deal with the subject of *financial reporting*. The distinction between financial accounting (as covered in Part 2) and financial reporting is blurred. Indeed, at one time no such distinction would be made. However, financial accounting is now regarded as a rather mechanical and technical process that ends with the preparation of the profit and loss account, balance sheet, and a cash flow statement. Financial reporting is more concerned with how accounting data can best be communicated to users of financial statements in accordance with legal and professional requirements.

Part 1 INTRODUCTION TO ACCOUNTING
1 The accounting world
2 Accounting rules

Part 2 FINANCIAL ACCOUNTING	Part 3 FINANCIAL REPORTING	Part 4 MANAGEMENT ACCOUNTING
3 Recording data	9 Information disclosure	14 Foundations
4 Sole trader accounts	10 The annual report	15 Direct costs
5 Last minute adjustments	11 The annual accounts	16 Indirect costs
6 Company accounts	12 Interpretation of accounts	17 Budgeting
7 Other entity accounts	13 Contemporary issues	18 Standard costing
8 Cash flow statements		19 Contribution analysis
		20 Specific decisions
		21 Capital investment
		22 Emerging issues

Support for the accountancy profession . . .

Hewitt unveils new rules for UK accountancy

WILLIAM LYONS

Patricia Hewitt's long-awaited shake-up of the accountancy profession was unveiled yesterday, generally delighting accountants but enraging many who said the proposals did not go far enough.

The new proposals include creating a single regulator to govern accounting standards, and setting time limits on how long auditors can work on the accounts of one company.

The Trade and Industry Secretary said: "The collapse of Enron and WorldCom – and the accountancy malpractice they revealed – appalled investors all over the world.

"We owe it to savers, investors and employees, as well as honest business people, to ensure that our defences are as robust as they sensibly can be."

A ban on auditors doing non-audit work was one option considered during her year-long deliberation, but Hewitt said it would be left up to clients to decide what services they bought from accountants.

"I think it's a better way to do that, by looking at the particular position of each company, rather than trying to do a one-size-fits-all set of regulations."

Hewitt denied the measures were too weak, and said the main accountancy firms would have to "sit up and take notice".

Bob Dallas, a senior partner at Campbell Dallas in Glasgow, said: "At the end of the day, we have to restore confidence in the auditing system. Obviously I would prefer for us to continue regulating ourselves but if the only way to restore confidence is to introduce a new regulatory body than so be it."

But Stuart Riddell, head of ACCA Scotland, said his organisation had concerns.

"These proposals risk leaving the UK lagging well behind the US in corporate governance."

Hewitt was also attacked for not banning accountancy firms from doing other work, such as giving taxation advice, for clients whose accounts they also audit.

Prem Sikka, a professor of accountancy at the University of Essex, called the measures "a big fudge".

Cahal Dowds, president of the Institute of Chartered Accountants of Scotland, added: "I particularly welcome the proposed creation of a single authoritative regulator; and it will be important in the public interest for it to enjoy independent funding to achieve its tasks."

Mathew Farrow, head of policy for CBI Scotland applauded Hewitt for taking "effective and proportionate" action, adding: "These measures will boost confidence in UK boardrooms."

The Scotsman, 31 January 2003.

Questions relating to this news story may be found on page 207 ▸▸

About this chapter

In this part of the book we are dealing with financial reporting. Our discussion in this part is mainly concerned with limited liability companies in the United Kingdom. By law such companies must make available some information about the company's affairs to their shareholders and to the public. In addition, there are some professional requirements that most companies are required to follow. For listed companies there are also some Stock Exchange requirements.

This chapter gives you the background to these requirements and regulations. It provides a foundation for Chapters 10 and 11. Chapter 10 deals with the various types of non-statutory reports that companies normally publish and Chapter 11 with the statutory and professional requirements.

The chapter is a relatively short and simple one. It is divided into five main sections. After the learning objectives we explain why the chapter is important non-accountants. The following section examines the nature and purpose of information disclosure. We then outline the groups that are interested in the reports and accounts that companies publish. The following section covers the main sources of authority covering the disclosure of information in the UK, viz. statutory, professional, and the Stock Exchange. The last main section of the chapter then lists some questions that non-accountants may like to ask about the application of the various disclosure requirements.

> **Learning objectives**
>
> **By the end of this chapter you should be able to:**
> - **explain what is meant by disclosure of information;**
> - **list seven groups that use financial information;**
> - **outline the main sources of authority for the disclosure of company information in the United Kingdom.**

❗ Why this chapter is important for non-accountants

This chapter is of considerable importance for non-accountants. As a manager in a limited liability company you should know what basic legal requirements cover the disclosure of information to your shareholders and to parties external to the company. Similarly, you must be aware of other requirements both of a professional and a Stock Exchange nature that you are expected to follow. If you do not do so, there could be serious legal consequences for the future of your company.

The chapter is also important because it provides a background and a framework for the following two chapters. These chapters deal with the contents of a company's annual report and accounts.

Disclosure

You might be surprised to find that there are laws requiring companies to disclose certain types of information to parties that have an interest in the company. By 'disclosure' we mean making known or letting those parties know something about the company's affairs. Why is this necessary? What right have those parties (whoever they are) to be given some information about the company? And what information do they want?

It is perhaps even more surprising to learn that the main party that the law has in mind are *shareholders*. This seems odd. Shareholders are *owners* of the company. Surely there is no need for the law to lay down what they are entitled to? As owners are they not entitled to anything they want? As far as the last question is concerned, the answer is 'no'.

Until the second half of the twentieth century shareholders had few rights about a company in which they had invested and they were given very little information about it. They also had no right of access to the company's premises; this is still the position today.

Why are companies only required to supply a *minimum* amount of information to their owners? Why is there no right of access? There are two possible reasons why shareholders' rights are restricted. They are as follows.

1 *Fairness.* Large shareholders might believe that they are entitled to more information and more freedom to deal with the company than small shareholders. By treating them all alike there is no question of one shareholder being given some favourable treatment. In practice, of course, important shareholders who visit the company's premises are likely to receive some highly deferential treatment.

2 *Practical.* Some companies are very large and they may have thousands of shareholders. It would not be practical to expect every minor piece of information to be given to shareholders. Similarly, it would be inconvenient (to say the least) if all shareholders could wander around the company' premises just when they felt like it and give instructions to the employees.

| Activity 9.1 | Do you think that shareholders in limited liability companies should be entitled to be told anything that they wish to know or to receive any information that they would like to have about a company's affairs? Why should directors be allowed to keep information away from the owners of the company? Are the reasons outlined above for restricting access and information plausible?

Write down in your notebook the responses that you would make to these questions. |

Given that shareholders are only entitled to receive certain specified information, what should they receive, how and in what format? In the next two chapters we will be dealing with what currently is required. In recent years, the information supplied has increased substantially and it is also very hard to understand. There is little evidence to suggest, however, that more information has necessarily led to a greater understanding among shareholders of company accounts.

So far we have perhaps indicated that shareholders are the main parties requiring company information. Indeed, the law hardly recognizes other parties that may be interested. Creditors and employees are recognized to a limited extent if a company goes into liquidation but that is about all the acknowledgement that other users get.

Nevertheless, there is an increasing recognition that other parties are interested in how companies are doing. Who are they? And what information do they want? We consider the various user groups (as they are called) in the next section.

User groups

As indicated in Chapter 1, the Accounting Standards Board (ASB) has identified seven main user groups. We discuss each of them below and they are also represented pictorially in Figure 9.1

1 *Investors*. The investors' group includes both present and potential investors. Investors provide the risk capital and as shareholders they are, of course, also the owners of the company. Nevertheless, the law has always regarded it as being impractical for every shareholder (in some large companies, there could be hundreds of thousands of individual shareholders) to have an automatic right of access to the company's premises to inspect the books of account, and to demand an unrestricted amount of information. Thus, since shareholders' rights are legally defined, they may be regarded as one of the main *external* user groups.

2 *Lenders*. Lenders are groups of people who have loaned funds to the business under some formal agreement, e.g. by buying debentures in the company. It is considered that they need to be supplied with some information about the company's affairs in order to be reassured that the company will be able to continue paying interest on their debt, and that their loans will eventually be repaid.

3 *Suppliers and other trade creditors*. This group is similar to the lenders group. Suppliers and trade creditors need some information about the company in order to decide whether to sell to it. Thereafter, they need some reassurance that they will be paid what they are owed.

4 *Employees*. Without an appropriate amount of *financial* capital, a company could not be formed, but it would soon go out of business without the input of some *human* capital, i.e. someone to manage and operate it. It follows that employees must be an

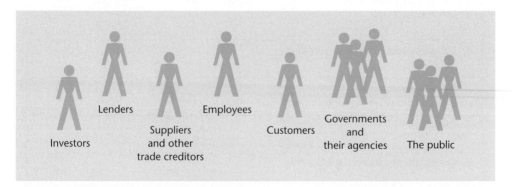

Figure 9.1 **The main users of financial reports**

Source: ASB (1999) *Statement of Principles for Financial Reporting*

important user group of financial information, because they need some assurance about the stability and profitability of the company. It could be argued, of course, that employees are hardly an *external* group since they work within the company. However, this does not necessarily mean that they have ready access to the type of information about the company that is of interest to them; e.g. its stability and profitability.

5 *Customers.* Customers often have a long-term involvement with a company, and like many of the other groupings they too need some reassurance about its long-term future. They may, for example, have long-term warranties and might require parts of machinery to be replaced.

6 *Governments and their agencies.* Governments and their agencies (as the ASB puts it) are another important user group interested in a company's progress, whether this is in respect of employment prospects, the collection of taxes (such as value added tax or corporation tax), or the compilation of statistics.

7 *The public.* A company does not work in isolation, and its success or otherwise does have an indirect impact on many other people with whom it comes into contact. A company that happens to be a major employer in a small town, for example, helps to generate employment outside the company itself, since other entities provide services to the company's employees and their families. Hence the public, in the form of the local community, has an interest in a company's performance and future prospects.

It should be noted that not all observers accept the above classification. It could be argued, for example, that the public's interest is too remote for a company to be required to inform the local community about its affairs (although it may be good public relations to do so). Similarly, the government can obtain all the information it wants about a company by other means, without necessarily having to establish a separate reporting system.

Activity 9.2	The table below shows the ASB's seven user groups. Insert the most important piece of information that you think each user group needs about a company. We have inserted one for shareholders but try to think of another important one.

User group	Information required
1 Investors	1 Dividend to be paid 2
2 Lenders	
3 Suppliers and other trade creditors	
4 Employees	
5 Customers	
6 Governments and other agencies	
7 The public	

We now move on to a discussion of what information *has* to be disclosed publicly by a company. We do so in the next three sections.

Sources of authority

As we suggested earlier in the chapter, the law only requires companies to supply their shareholders with a *minimum* amount of information about their financial affairs. However, there are now some 'professional' requirements formulated by the accountancy profession in conjunction with the business community that add to what the law requires. These requirements have some semi-statutory status. The capital markets have also some additional ones. We will refer to these as 'Stock Exchange' requirements.

These three sources of authority (statutory, professional, and Stock Exchange requirements) are discussed in some detail below.

Statutory requirements

For well over 150 years the United Kingdom has adopted what might be called a *permissive* system of financial reporting. This means that Parliament lays down a body of general accounting law but the detailed implementation of it is left mainly to those parties who have a direct interest in the legislation. Until recently, this meant mainly the accountancy profession, but nowadays the wider business and professional community has also become involved. The permissive system is in marked contrast to the *prescriptive* system of financial reporting, which is found in most Continental European countries (such as France and Germany). In a prescriptive system, some very detailed accounting rules and regulations are laid down in law. Hence there is not the same opportunity for individual interpretation of the law as there is in a permissive system.

The present British statutory requirements are contained in an Act of Parliament known as the Companies Act 1985. This Act is a consolidating measure. It includes the earlier Companies Acts of 1948, 1967, 1976, 1980 and 1981 respectively, although some provisions have been amended by the Companies Act 1989.

Companies Act legislation since 1981 has been brought about mainly by the UK's membership of the European Union. Strictly speaking, therefore, it is no longer UK law but *European* law that has set the pace and direction for change.

The Companies Act 1985 (as amended by the Companies Act 1989) lays down the *minimum* disclosure requirements that companies must disclose to their shareholders. Although the Act lays down the minimum requirements, the inclusion of additional professional and stock exchange requirements means that shareholders are now supplied with a considerable amount of detailed information about a company's affairs.

In effect, the statutory disclosure of information to external parties takes two forms:

1 *The Annual Report and Accounts.* Shareholders are automatically supplied with a copy of the company's annual report and accounts. They can opt for a summary version although this is still quite detailed and technical.
2 *Filing.* The annual report and accounts has to be 'filed' with the Registrar of Companies. The reports are left in Companies House (there is one in Edinburgh and one in Cardiff) and anyone can go along to have a look at them. 'Large' companies

must file the full annual report, but 'medium' and 'small' companies may file a modified version. The terms 'large', 'medium' and 'small' are defined in the Act, but they can be amended from time-to-time by means of a 'statutory instrument'. The definitions are based on a combination of size criteria, viz. turnover, gross assets and number of employees.

Professional requirements

Until 1970 there were no 'professional' requirements covering the disclosure of information to shareholders. The law laid down what was required. The details were contained in a major Act of Parliament (the 1948 Companies Act) and a minor one (the 1967 Companies Act). There were also certain Stock Exchange requirements for listed companies. The accountancy profession were only involved in making recommendations but professionally qualified accountants did not have to follow them.

That all changed at the end of the 1960s. A number of major mergers and takeovers took place that made the public realize that accounting practices were not mechanical and that different results could be obtained by making different assumptions. There was a danger that the accountancy profession's reputation would be damaged and so the Institute of Chartered Accountants in England and Wales (ICAEW) decided to act. It formed the *Accounting Standards Steering Committee* (ASSC) [later to become the Accounting Standards Committee (ASC)]. By 1976 all of the six major professional accountancy boards had become members of the ASC.

The objectives of the ASC were as follows:

> *To define accounting concepts, to narrow difference of financial accounting and reporting treatment, and to codify generally accepted best practice in the public interest.*

In order to help achieve these objectives the ASC issued *Statements of Standard Accounting Practice* (SSAPs). SSAPs laid down the procedures for dealing with various contentious accounting issues, such as depreciation and stock valuation. Professionally qualified accountants were obliged to follow the requirements contained in SSAPs and they could be disciplined by their respective professional bodies if they did not do so.

The ASB was disbanded in 1990. It had failed to achieve its objectives, partly because it was slow to act as all six accountancy bodies had to approve a draft standard, and partly because the standards generally allowed a great deal of flexibility. During its 20-year life, the ASB had issued 25 SSAPs although by the time it was disbanded, three had been withdrawn.

It was replaced by a new regime under the umbrella of the 'Financial Reporting Council'. For convenience the FRC and its related bodies is shown in diagrammatic format in Figure 9.2.

The details are summarized below.

1 The Financial Reporting Council (FRC)

The FRC is a company limited by guarantee (i.e. it does not issues shares). It is financed by the accountancy profession, the City of London (through the London Stock Exchange and the banking and insurance communities), and the Government. Its objectives are:

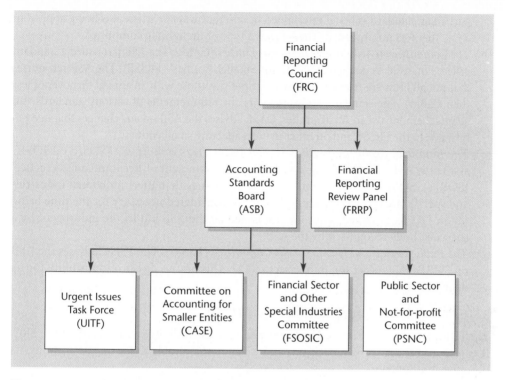

Figure 9.2 **Standard setting in the United Kingdom**

(a) to provide support for the Accounting Standards Board and the Financial Reporting Review Panel (see below); and (b) to encourage good financial reporting generally.

2 The Accounting Standards Board (ASB)

The ASB is also a company limited by guarantee. It is a subsidiary of the FRC. Its role is to formulate accounting standards. This involves making, amending, and withdrawing them. An accounting standard is defined as follows:

> *An authoritative statement of how particular types of transactions and other events should be reflected in financial statements.*

The ASB was formed on 1 August 1990. Unlike the old ASC it is autonomous and it does not need any outside approval for its actions. It does not even need approval from the FRC.

The ASB took over the then current 22 SSAPs from the ASC. As of March 2003 twelve of them were still in existence, the other ten having been withdrawn. The ASB also issues its own accounting standards. These are called Financial Reporting Standards (FRSs). By March 2003 19 FRSs had been issued. They cover such topics as acquisitions and mergers, goodwill and intangible assets, pensions, and deferred tax. As you can appreciate, these are highly technical subjects and they go way beyond the context of this book.

The ASB's work is undertaken through four main committees. These are as follows:

(a) *The Urgent Issues Task Force (UITF)*. The UITF deals with issues that relate to existing standards. The committee has the task of responding to cases where the application of a particular standard is being interpreted in different ways or where it is being applied in a way that was not intended. The UITF is a type of firefighting committee.

(b) *The Committee on Accounting for Smaller Entities (CASE).* The ASB has issued a standard called 'Financial Reporting Standard for Smaller Entities' (FRSSE). The ASB recognizes that not all FRSs are relevant for small entities (i.e. those with an annual turnover of less than £2.8m). The standard brings together the requirements of various standards and adapts them for use in small entities. CASE advises the ASB on any changes that need to be made to the FRSSE and on other matters affecting small entities.

(c) *The Financial Sector and Other Special Industries Committee (FSOSIC).* FSOSIC assists the ASB in supervising and developing 'Statement of Recommended Practice' (SORPs). SORPs are statements that relate to issues that affect individual industries and specific areas of accounting when it not considered necessary for the time being for an FRS to be issued. They are not issued by the ASB but by the industry or by a specialist body recognized by the ASB.

(d) *The Public Sector and Not-for profit Committee (PSNC).* The PSNC advises the ASB on SORPs that affect the public sector. The ASB has no direct responsibility for its deliberations.

3 The Financial Reporting Review Panel (FRRP)

The FRRP is a company limited by guarantee. Like the ASB, it is a subsidiary of the FRC. It is responsible for its own decisions and it is not answerable to anyone or anybody. Its objective is as follows:

> *To examine departures from the accounting requirements of the Companies Act 1985 and applicable accounting standards.*

The FRRP has investigated a number of cases of apparent defective accounts but it only does so when matters are drawn to its attention. Those companies that have been investigated usually agree to amend their accounts in accordance with the FRRP's wishes. However, it is possible for the FRRP to insist on the reissuing of accounts and, if need be, it can seek a court order so as to force the company to comply with its wishes.

Activity 9.3

Do you think that it is sufficient for the FRRP to wait until apparent disregard for accounting standards is drawn to its attention? Should it be more pro-active and go about actually looking for cases where accounting standards might have been ignored?

Write down your ideas in your notebook.

The last point enables us to review the legal position of accounting standards. The details are contained in the Companies Act 1989 (the Act is subsumed into the Companies Act 1985). A summary of the 1989 Act's requirements is as follows:

1 *Definition.* Accounting standards are statements of standard accounting practice issued by such body or bodies as may be prescribed by regulations.

2 *References.* Reference in the Act to accounting standards relate to those that are relevant for a company's circumstances and to the accounts.

3 *Compliance.* It must be stated whether the accounts have been prepared in accordance with applicable accounting standards. Reasons must be given if there are any material departures from such standards.

It follows from the above that it is not a direct requirement of the Companies Act 1985 that accounts *must* by prepared in accordance with appropriate accounting standards. However, if they are not followed, reasons must be given. Furthermore, the Secretary of State has the power to seek revision of what are called 'defective accounts and reports'. Hence it can be argued that the ASB's accounting standards now have a *semi-statutory* status.

This means that if directors do not comply with the Act, they may be 'guilty of an offence and liable to a fine'.

It is unlikely that any director would be put in that position. The Companies Act 1985 has a very important clause that gives directors a great deal of room for individual judgement. We reproduce the clause below.

> *The balance sheet shall give <u>a true and fair view</u> of the state of affairs of the company as at the end of the financial year; and the profit and loss account shall give <u>a true and fair view</u> of the profit and loss of the company for the financial year.*

The 'a true and fair view' (twice mentioned) has been underlined. The phrase was first introduced in the Companies Act 1947 and it has been a feature of UK company law ever since. Indeed, it has now been incorporated into European law so it is now a statutory requirement throughout the European Union. But what does it mean?

The 1985 Companies Act requires companies to publish details of their financial performance. The Act lays down certain formats for the presentation of the accounts and what should be included in them and the various accounting standards all add to the amount of information required. This information has to be presented in such a way that it is 'true and fair'.

However, the Act recognizes that in some specific cases accounts may not represent a true and fair view if they follow the provisions laid down either in the Act or in accounting standards. In such an event, directors may ignore the respective statutory or professional requirement. This provision has become known as 'the true and fair view override' rule.

Thus directors have to decide whether by following the Act or the accounting standards their accounts would then *not* present a true and fair view. So what have they got to go on? Not much. Although the clause has been around for over 50 years it has never been tested in court. No company has ever been challenged when they have fallen back on this rule. It is relatively easy for them to argue that their accounts would not be true and fair if they followed the requirements of a particular standard.

In effect this means that directors can decide for themselves what 'true and fair' means. They can always argue that '*Yes, we have ignored the 1985 Companies Act (or a certain standard) because in our view our accounts would not represent a true and fair view if we followed the Act (or the standard)*'. It would be very difficult for any external party to challenge their judgement because no one from the outside would have the detailed information to be able to question the directors' view. Of course the directors would have to convince the company's auditors but once the auditors had agreed with them, it is almost inconceivable that the company's decision could then be disputed.

Even so, it is rare for it to get to this stage as no company likes to appear before the UITF.

In the vast majority of cases it is accepted that accounts do represent a true and fair view if they have been prepared in accordance with the 1985 Companies Act and applicable accounting standards. Accounting standards, in particular, are regarded as the most authoritative and definitive view of how certain accounting matters should be treated. So they have considerable weight behind them. No company, therefore, would ignore their requirements without much discussion, not least because it might generate a great deal of unwelcome publicity. Such publicity could affect the company's share price and ultimately cause problems with the capital markets, e.g. over borrowing requirements.

Stock Exchange requirements

Those companies who want to sell their shares to the public have to obtain what is called a Stock Exchange listing, i.e. they need a means of marketing their shares and this can only be done through the Stock Exchange. In order to get a listing, a company has to provide a great deal of information about its history, constitution, management, financial conditions, continuing obligations, and it future prospects.

Once a company is listed it has also to disclose some additional financial reporting information besides that required by statute and by the accountancy and business community. The additional information required does not now amount to very much. Most of what used to be required has been incorporated into statutory and professional requirements. Some examples of the extra information still required is as follows:

1 *Issue of reports.* Annual reports and accounts must be issued within six months of the end of the relevant financial period.
2 *Directors' report.* Some additional information must be included in the directors' report (see Chapter 10). This includes reasons for departing from accounting standards, an explanation of why (if material) actual trading results differ from forecasted results, a geographic analysis of turnover, the principal country of each subsidiary, and details of other companies in which the equity share is 20% or more.
3 *Interim reports.* Half-yearly accounts are required although in much less detail than the annual accounts.

The above extra requirements are not particularly significant. The 1985 Companies Act and professional requirements are (as you will see when we reach Chapter 11) much more onerous.

Activity 9.4

Do you think that the requirement to produce interim accounts on a sixth monthly basis is unnecessary? There is currently (April 2003) an EU proposal to require interim accounts to be produced on a quarterly basis. Would this be of benefit to current and prospective shareholders? How far would it be of any help to other users of accounts?

What is your answer to these questions? Write down what you think in your notebook.

Questions non-accountants should ask

The Companies Act 1985 requires directors to 'lay before the company in a general meeting copies of the company's annual accounts, the directors' report and the auditors' report on those accounts'.

We will assume that you will want to make sure that your company obeys the law and that it abides by the professional and Stock Exchange reporting requirements. We imagine that few directors would want to appear before the FRRP and have to agree to amend their company's accounts. So what questions should you ask of your accountants? We suggest the following.

● Can you assure us that these accounts have been prepared fully in accordance with the Companies Act 1985?

● Have all applicable accounting standards been followed?

● Are there any relevant Stock Exchange requirements that we need to follow?

● Are there any requirements that cause a difficulty for our company?

● Do we have to follow the accounting standards on those issues?

● What effect would it have on our results if we followed them?

● Can we invoke the true and fair view override rule?

● What do the auditors think?

● If we ignore the requirements are we likely to be investigated by the FRRP?

Conclusion

In this chapter, we have provided you with some background information about the external disclosure requirements relating to limited liability companies. Seven user groups of published financial information can be recognized but the Companies Act 1985 almost exclusively concentrates on the investor group. Indeed, it is only in the event of liquidation of the company that two other groups (creditors and employees) are given some recognition.

In addition to statutory requirements, SSAPs and FRSs add to the amount of information to be disclosed. Listed companies are also bound by a few extra Stock Exchange requirements. As will be seen in the next two chapters, all these requirements mean that the amount of information supplied to shareholders in the form of an annual report and accounts results in a document of daunting proportions.

Key points

1 The Companies Act 1985 lays down the minimum amount of information that must be given to company shareholders.

2 This is supplemented by professional requirements issued by the ASB in the form of SSAPs and FRSs.

3 Such accounting and financial reporting standards have semi-statutory status.

4 Listed companies are also bound by a number of additional Stock Exchange requirements.

5 Accounts should be prepared in such a way that they represent a 'true and fair view' of the company's affairs. This is an overriding rule of the Companies Act 1985. It takes precedence over other legislative, professional and Stock Exchange requirements.

Check your learning

The answers to these questions may be found within the text.

1 What is meant by 'disclosure'?

2 Why do shareholders not have an automatic right to information?

3 Why do they not have a right to visit the company's premises as and when they wish?

4 List seven user groups of accounting information

5 Name three sources of authority for the disclosure of information required by companies.

6 What is the main piece of legislation covering such disclosure?

7 What was the ASC?

8 What did it try to do?

9 When was it abandoned?

10 What took its place?

11 What do the following initials stand for: (a) FRC; (b) ASB; (c) UITF; (d) CASE; (e) FSOSIC; (f) PSNC; (g) FRRP?

12 What is the role of (a) the ASB; and (b) the FRRP?

13 What is meant by the 'true and fair view override rule?

14 Name three items required by the Stock Exchange that listed companies have to do or disclose.

News story quiz

Remember the new story at the beginning of this chapter? Go back to that story and reread it before answering the following questions.

Throughout its history the UK accountancy profession has been relatively free of direct government involvement in its affairs. Now, as a result of various alleged accounting scandals in the USA and the UK, the Government could become more and more involved in the operation of the profession.

Questions

1 Do you think that Parliament should lay down detailed legislative rules and regulations for the preparation of accounting statements?

2 Should Parliament determine how the UK accountancy profession should be organized and how it should operate?

3 Do you agree with the idea of 'a single regulator to govern accounting standards'?

4 Should a time limit be set on how long auditors can work on the accounts of one company?

5 Should accountancy firms be banned from doing other work for clients whose accounts they audit?

6 Do you think that partners and senior employees of accountancy firms should be barred from taking up employment with an audit client within two years (or some other period) of leaving the firm?

Tutorial questions

9.1 What type of information do you think a company should disclose to its shareholders?

9.2 Should the disclosure of accounting information for companies be prescribed in detail in an Act of Parliament?

9.3 'Accounting standards should become enshrined in company law.' Discuss.

9.4 Do you think that the 'true and fair view' rule should be abandoned?

Further practice questions, study material and links to relevant sites on the World Wide Web can be found on the website that accompanies this book. The site can be found at **www.booksites.net/dyson**

A plea for narrative reporting . . .

Company annual reports need to consider user's needs, report says

A lack of focus on the user in the process of setting reporting standards is undermining quality in business reporting, according to a research report published by ICAS. "Voluntary Annual Report Disclosures: What Users Want", aims to seek out users' views in relation to a comprehensive set of disclosure items.

During the last decade, the importance of narrative reporting in corporate annual reports has increased significantly. This is due to the rapid pace of change in business, which has meant that past performance has become a less useful guide to future prospects. It is also due to the growth of intangible assets, including those generated from intellectual capital, that are not recognised in the traditional financial statements.

This growth in importance of narrative reporting is currently being recognised in the UK in the Company Law Review proposal for a statutory Operating and Financial Review (OFR), which has been endorsed by the draft Companies Bill, and in the revision to the OFR Statement being developed by the Accounting Standards Board.

ICAS Director of Research and co-author of the report, Professor Vivien Beattie says: "The findings of this report should be of value both to preparers seeking to improve the usefulness of their disclosures and to regulators whose decisions are influenced by the preferences of their constituencies."

To assist in the research, a questionnaire was sent to 1,645 interested parties representing finance directors, audit partners, private shareholders and expert users.

CA Magazine, January 2003.

Questions relating to this news story may be found on page 222 ▸▸

About this chapter

We explained in the previous chapter that a limited liability company usually publishes an annual report and accounts. Some of the contents are statutory, i.e. required by law, some are professional and some are Stock Exchange requirements, while others are voluntary, i.e. companies can decide for themselves what to put in.

The annual report and accounts of a large international company can be extremely long and highly technical. In order to make your studies a little easier we are going to cover the subject in two chapters. This chapter deals largely with the non-statutory information normally found in an annual report. The next chapter, Chapter 11, covers the annual accounts. These include main the statutory items, especially those relating to financial matters.

This chapter is divided into nine main sections. After listing the learning objectives, the first section explains why the chapter is an important one for non-accountants. The following seven sections cover the contents of a typical annual report, viz. introductory material, a chairman's statement, an operating and financial review statement, a directors' report, a corporate governance statement, a remuneration report, and finally some general information for shareholders. The last main section in the chapter lists some questions that non-accountants should ask about the contents of the chapter.

The outline of the chapter is shown in Figure 10.1. The Figure should make it easier for you to see how the chapter fits together.

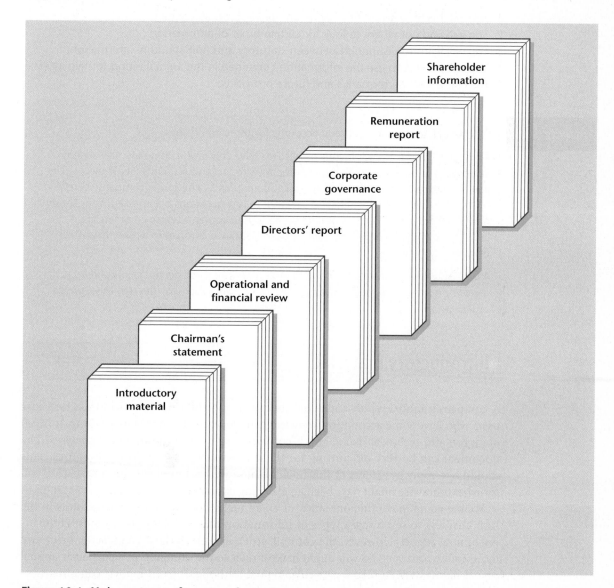

Figure 10.1 **Main contents of an annual report**

Learning objectives

By the end of this chapter you should be able to:

● identify the main sections of an annual report;

● outline the main contents of a chairman's statement;

● list a number of other non-statutory reports and summarize their contents.

! Why this chapter is important for non-accountants

This chapter is important for non-accountants for the following reasons:

1 You will become aware of what an annual report may contain.
2 You will find out where to look for certain types of information.
3 You will learn to distinguish between statutory and non-statutory information.
4 You will be able to use the information contained in the annual report to help assess the company's performance and future prospects.

Activity 10.1

Get hold of an annual report and accounts for three companies.

Guidance: If some of your friends or relatives have shares in a company they should automatically receive a copy of that company's report and accounts. See if they will let you have them. Otherwise select three companies and write to the company secretary. Most companies will let you have a set without any questions being asked. Your library may also hold copies but it is best if you have your copies. Choose commercial or industrial companies and avoid banking and insurance companies as they have their own requirements.

Note: It is important that you do this activity and have some annual report and accounts available otherwise you will find it more difficult to work your way through this chapter.

Introductory material

A company's annual report and accounts can be a formidable document even for those users who have some accounting knowledge. It can easily be over 50 pages long. It is full of jargon and technical detail, and it contains a great deal of numerical analyses. The document can be very off-putting for those users who are frightened of figures. This should not apply to readers of this book because we have gradually been preparing you for what otherwise might have been an alarming experience.

We are going to confine our study of an annual report (we cover the accounts in the next chapter) to seven main types of information that will be found in most companies' annual report. However, the content order, as well as the format, style, print and terminology, can vary. So you might have to refer to the 'contents' of a particular annual report if you want to read a particular report (although not all reports contain a contents list).

Nevertheless, it is likely that the first few pages include what we have called 'introductory material'. Such material probably tells you something about the company along with a brief summary of the financial results for the year. For example, Devro plc makes the following statement on the inside cover of the front page (in a large font):

> Devro is one of the world's leading producers of manufactured casings for the food industry, supplying a wide range of products and technical support to manufacturers of sausages, salami, hams and other cooked meats. The group's main focus is edible collagen-based products, which are a key component of our customers' product offerings to the end consumer, and have been steadily replacing gut casings in markets around the world.

Unless you had heard about Devro, you might be mystified by this statement. 'Collagen' appears to be a technical term (it is explained later) and you might be put off by some of the jargon, e.g. 'key component', 'product offerings', and 'end consumer'. Nevertheless, the statement is very eye-catching.

The bottom of that page also includes a list of the contents of the report. Opposite (on page 1) is a summary of the key financial statistics. This is a very clear, simple summary of the results for the year, so we have reproduced it for you (see Figure 10.2).

Some of the information shown in Figure 10.2 will not mean anything to you yet, so you can appreciate how difficult it must be for those users who have not had any training

Key financials		
	2001*	2000*
Earnings per share	**5.1p**	9.0p
Dividends per ordinary share	**2.0p**	5.0p
Turnover	**£208.3m**	£229.5m
Gross profit	**£62.2m**	£70.9m
−margin	**29.9%**	30.9%
Operating profit	**£18.6m**	£24.0m
−margin	**8.9%**	10.5%
Profit before taxation	**£15.2m**	£21.3m
Net cash from operating activities	**£31.1m**	£29.7m
Capital expenditure	**£7.9m**	£13.2m
Net debt	**£24.7m**	£29.0m
Net gearing	**30.2%**	30.9%
Net interest cover	**5.4**	8.8

*Before exceptional charges of £52.1 million (2000: £1.5 million)

Figure 10.2 **An example of introductory material**

Source: Devro plc, *Annual Report and Accounts 2001*.

in accounting. Pages 2 and 3 of Devro's report provide a summary of the company (headed '*Group at a glance*') and entitled '*A focused business*'. The information presented is in several colours and it is accompanied by various types of pictures. On pages 4 and 5 we are then presented with a '*Market report*' on '*The collagen market*'. A collagen, by the way, is 'the main structural protein found in animal connective tissue'. Such tissue is now being used as a new type of sausage casing.

Devro's introductory material ends after page 5 and we move on to the chairman's statement. In many other companies, especially those that are consumer orientated, you will also find pages of publicity material promoting the company's products.

Activity 10.2	Consult your copies of the three sets of annual report and accounts that you obtained when you completed Activity 10.1. Read through the introductory material and summarize the contents in your notebook.

Chairman's statement

Most company chairmen like to include a report or statement of their own in the annual report. There are no statutory, professional or Stock Exchange specifications requiring chairmen to publish a report, so the format and content will vary from company to company.

You will probably find the chairman's statement in the first few pages of the annual report. You can expect it to be anything from one page to four pages in length. It will be largely narrative in style although it will not be entirely devoid of some quantitative information. Research evidence suggests that chairmen's statements are the most widely read section of an annual report, perhaps because they are usually fairly easy to read.

Chairmen tend to adopt an up-beat approach about the recent performance and are extremely optimistic about the future. You must, therefore, read their reports with a great deal of scepticism, and you should check their comments against the detailed results contained elsewhere within the overall annual report and accounts. Nevertheless, chairmen have to be careful that they do not become too optimistic. Their remarks can have a significant impact on the company's share price and they might have to answer to the Stock Exchange authorities if they publish misleading statements.

The contents of a typical chairman's statement include the following:

- *Results.* A summary of the company's results for the year covering such items as turnover, pre- and post-tax profits, earnings per share, and cash flow.
- *Dividend.* Details about any interim dividend paid for the year and any proposed final dividend.
- *Prospects.* A summary of how the chairman sees the general economic and political outlook and the future prospects for his own company.
- *Employees.* A comment about the company's employees including any notable successes, concluding with the Board's thanks to all employees for their efforts.
- *Directors.* A similar note may be included about the Board of Directors including tributes to retiring directors.

A relatively brief chairman's statement is reproduced in Figure 10.3.

J. Smart & Co. (Contractors) PLC

CHAIRMAN'S REVIEW

ACCOUNTS

As forecast in the interim report, profits for the second half of the year exceeded first half profits resulting in a Group profit for the full year of £4,613,000.

The Board is recommending a Final Dividend of 8.50p nett making a total for the year of 11.40p nett, which compares with 11.00p nett for the previous year. After waivers by members holding approximately 50% of the shares the Dividends will cost the Company £574,000.

Unappropriated profits for the year amounted to £2,879,000 which, when added to the retained profits brought forward and the surplus on the revaluation reserve, bring the consolidated capital and reserves of the Group to £60,964,000.

TRADING ACTIVITIES

Group turnover decreased by 6%, own work capitalised increased by 193% and other operating income increased by 8%. Improvements across all sectors of your Company's activities fuelled an increase in Group profit by 27%.

The amount of contracting work carried out decreased compared with the previous year although margins improved slightly. Sales in precast concrete manufacture improved and losses were substantially reduced. A healthy increase in private house sales boosted profitability.

Commercial and industrial activity increased considerably compared with the previous year. Office developments completed at Carnegie Campus, Dunfermline and Glenbervie Business Park, Larbert and shortly due to complete at East London Street, Edinburgh are attracting varying degrees of interest. Industrial units completed at Arran Road, Perth and Swanfield, Edinburgh were pre-let.

Following on the letting of the second phase of the joint venture development with EDI (Industrial) Ltd at A1 Industrial Estate, Edinburgh the third phase of 31,000 square feet was commenced during the year under review.

FUTURE PROSPECTS

While there is a certain amount of interest expressed in our industrial and commercial floorspace available for let, the sector could not be described as buoyant and development activity in the current year will be substantially less than last year.

The value of the work in hand in contracting is more than at this time last year. Approximately two thirds of this work is on a design and construct basis, the balance having been obtained by traditional competitive tender. Private housing developments are continuing in Edinburgh and Dunfermline and sales are still brisk.

It is not possible at this stage to forecast whether or not the profit for the current year will match the profit for last year.

J. M. SMART
Chairman

19th November 2002

Figure 10.3 **A Chairman's Statement**

Activity 10.3

Referring to your three sets of annual reports and accounts, find the chairmen's statement and read through each of them carefully. Are there any items not included in the summary shown above?

List the main contents of each chairman's statement in your notebook.

Operating and financial review

An operating and financial review (OFR) may be defined as follows:

> *An OFR is an exposition of a company's performance and prospects supported by both narrative and quantitative information.*

The Cadbury Committee was set up in 1991 by the accountancy profession and the financial community to examine what has come to be called 'corporate governance' (we will be returning to this topic later in the chapter). One of its suggestions was that companies should issue an OFR. The idea was taken up by the business and financial community and in 1993 the ASB issued a statement supporting the suggestion.

An OFR is not covered by any statute or by any accounting standard. The recommendation to publish one is persuasive and not mandatory. The ASB's recommendation is of relevance mainly to listed companies although other entities are encouraged to publish one.

The form and content will vary from company to company but it will normally contain an operating section and a financial section. An OFR can easily be up to ten pages in length so it is not possible to reproduce one here. However, in order to give you an idea of what might be included we summarize below some of the possible contents.

The operating review

- *Review.* A review of the business environment in which the company operates, any developments in the business, and the impact they have had on the company's results.
- *Prospects.* The main factors affecting the company's future prospects.
- *Expansion.* Details of investments aimed at increasing future income and profits.
- *Returns.* The dividends paid to shareholders and the changes in shareholders' funds.

The financial review

- *Capital.* Details of the capital funding of the company and of its capital structure.
- *Taxation.* Additional information about the tax items included in the accounts.
- *Cash.* Details of cash inflows and outflows.
- *Liquidity.* An assessment of the company's liquidity at the end of the period.
- *Going concern.* A statement of the company's ability to remain a going concern.

> Consult your three annual reports and accounts. Find the pages containing the operating and financial review. Read through them carefully, taking your time over the exercise. Then summarize the contents of each OFR in your notebook.

Activity 10.4

Directors' report

The directors of the company are required to publish a report of their activities and responsibilities. This is a statutory requirement of the 1985 Companies Act [s234(1)]:

> *The directors of a company shall for each financial year prepare a report –*
>
> (a) *containing a fair review of the development of the business and its subsidiary undertakings during the financial year and of their position at the end of it, and*
> (b) *stating the amount (if any) which they recommend should be paid as dividend and the amount (if any) which they propose to carry to reserves.*

The Act also requires some other matters to be disclosed. For example:

● *Business review.* A fair review of the development of the business, the principal activities of the company, important events, future developments, research and development activities, dividend payments, and transfers to reserves.
● *Fixed assets.* Changes to fixed assets and details of differences between book values and market values.
● *Directors.* The names of the directors and their holdings in the company's shares and debentures.
● *Political and charitable donations.* Details of amounts given for (a) political; and (b) charitable purposes.
● *Shares.* Details concerning the purchase of the company's owns shares.
● *Disabled persons.* Information about the employment of disabled persons.
● *Employee involvement.* Details about keeping employees informed and involved in the company's activities.
● *Employees' health, safety and welfare.* This includes what steps the company has taken to protect the employees while they are at work.

In accordance with 'corporate governance' principles (as issued by the London Stock Exchange in a document called the *Combined Code on Corporate Governance*), you may also find other items in a directors' report. The following are examples of items that you might find:

● A statement about the application of the principles in the Combined Code.
● A statement of directors' responsibilities.
● Details of internal financial control procedures.
● A short section explaining how the company deals with its shareholders.
● A statement confirming that the company is a going concern.

● Results and dividends	● Close company status
● Statement of directors' responsibilities	● Corporate governance
● Review of the business and principal activities	● The Board
● Fixed assets	● Directors' remuneration
● Future developments	● Relation with shareholders
● Employee involvement	● Going concern
● Disabled employees	● Accountability and audit
● Political and charitable donations	● Internal control
● Creditor statement policy	● Internal audit
● Directors and their interests	● Audit committee and auditors
● Substantial shareholders	● Auditors

Figure 10.4 Contents of J. Smart & Co. (Contractors) PLC 2002 directors' report

The statutory and corporate governance items required in a directors' report is quite formidable. This part of the annual report can take up many pages, perhaps between six and twelve. The directors' report for even a relatively small company like J. Smart & Co. (Contractors) PLC stretches over five pages and contains 22 separate items (see Figure 10.4).

Activity 10.5	Referring to your three companies' annual reports and accounts, read through each directors' report. Then, in your notebook, list in three adjacent columns the headings used in each report. Try to list them so that similar headings are opposite each other. Are there any items that are only included by one company? Do the other two companies include such items elsewhere within the annual report? If so, make a note of the differences.

Corporate governance

We have already referred to the Cadbury Committee. The idea of 'corporate governance' was taken up by both the business and the financial communities, and the London Stock Exchange has issued some guidance on the subject in its *Combined Code on Corporate Governance*. You will find, therefore, that many annual reports and accounts (especially those of large companies) contain frequent references to corporate governance. These may be scattered through the report and accounts and they may be in the OFR, the directors' report or in separate statement.

Cairn Energy plc (2001)	Devro plc (2001)
● The Board	● The Board and its committees
● Board committees	● Chairman and chief executive
● Relations with shareholders	● Board balance
● Annual General Meeting	● Supply of information
● Directors' responsibility statement	● Appointments to the Board
● Going concern	● Re-election of directors
● Internal control	● Directors' remuneration
● Compliance with combined code	● Dialogue with shareholders
	● The Annual General Meeting
	● Financial reporting
	● Internal control
	● Audit committee and auditors
	● Compliance
	● Going concern

Figure 10.5 **Contents of corporate governance statements**

In order to give you some idea of what a separate corporate governance statement may include, in Figure 10.5 we have listed the headings used in two such statements, one for Cairn Energy plc and one for Devro plc.

As you can see from Figure 10.5 the contents of both Cairn's and Devro's corporate governance statements include some items that some companies might have included in the directors' report. There may be little disagreement about what should be disclosed but there is obviously an argument about where it should go. This is a good illustration of the difficulties that users of financial statements face when there is some inconsistency about the presentation of annual reports and accounts. Indeed, there is a strong case for the professional bodies to make the requirements prescriptive.

Once again turn to your collection of annual reports and accounts. Check whether they include a corporate governance statement. Read through them. Then copy the headings into adjacent columns, listing similar items on the same line opposite each other.

Activity 10.6

Remuneration report

As part of the corporate governance requirements, companies are expected to set up a remuneration committee. The purpose of this committee is to determine the remuneration (i.e. what they are paid) of the company's directors. The committee members should only include non-executive directors and they should not have a personal or financial interest in the outcome of the committee's deliberations.

The remuneration committee is then expected to submit an annual report to the shareholders, either attached to or included within the annual report and accounts. Their report should set out the remuneration policies and criteria for determining the pay of directors. It should also include the pay of each director by name along with any information about pension entitlements and share options. This information has to be audited.

Remuneration policies are expected to be such that directors are paid a fair rate for the job, the notice attached to service contracts should be for no longer than one year, and compensation schemes should not appear to reward failure. The remuneration report has to state that recognition has been given to these principles. Any departure from them has to be explained.

The contents of Cairn and Devro's remuneration reports are shown in Figure 10.6. Cairn's remuneration report is five pages long, and Devro's three.

Cairn Energy plc (2001)	Devro plc (2001)
• Remuneration policy and procedure	• Composition of the executive directors' remuneration committee
• Share option schemes	• Compliance
• Executive share option scheme ('the 1988 scheme')	• Policy on remuneration of executive directors
• 1996 second share option scheme ('the 1996 scheme')	• Other incentive schemes
• Directors' interests in share options	• Company policy on contracts of service
• Long-term incentive plan	• Company pensions policy regarding executive directors
• Tier one [a share scheme]	• Pension benefits earned by the directors
• Tier two [another share scheme]	• Directors' emoluments
• Save as you earn scheme	• Directors' interests
• Annual cash bonus scheme	
• Pension scheme	
• Service contract	
• Directors' remuneration	

Figure 10.6 **Contents of remuneration reports**

As you can see from Figure 10.6 a remuneration report contains a great deal of information about the directors' pay (in all sorts of forms) and the arrangements that they may have to buy shares in the company. Some of it is highly technical and probably most users of accounts are only interested in the directors' basic pay. The range of pay for Cairn's executive directors was from £253,467 to £431,288, and for Devro's executive directors, from £165,000 to £288,000.

> **Activity 10.7**
>
> Consult your set of three annual reports and accounts. Check whether a remuneration report is included. Work your way through each one and then list the headings in columnar form as in Figure 10.6. Try to put similar items on the same line. Note the ones that are specific to one company. List in your notebook the reasons you think the company has decided to disclose them.

Shareholder information

The order and type of the various reports and statements in an annual report and accounts will vary. However, when you are about halfway through you should come across the financial accounts sections. We will deal with these in the next chapter. Following the 'notes to the accounts' you will probably come cross some miscellaneous information. For convenience we have called this 'shareholder information'.

This part of the annual report contains mainly administrative matters. Its likely content includes the following:

- Notice of Annual General Meeting (AGM).
- Company information (names of senior staff and advisers and company addresses).
- Proxy form (to be used if a shareholder cannot attend the AGM).
- Shareholder information (the financial calendar, details about dividend payments and shareholder enquiries).
- List of principal companies of the group.

> **Activity 10.8**
>
> List in your notebook the shareholder information contained in each of your three sets of annual reports and accounts.
>
> *Note*: Such additional information may not necessarily be towards the end of the annual report and accounts.

❗ Questions non-accountants should ask

In previous chapters we have stressed that the detailed accounting information presented to you will have been prepared by your accountants and that you are unlikely to be involved in that process. This chapter is different. The matters with which we have been dealing will be the responsibility of a large team of non-accountants with the assistance of the accountants. So what do you need to ask if you are involved in preparing your company's annual report? We suggest the following.

● What information is legally required and where should it be shown?

● What information is a professional requirement and where should that go?

● What corporate governance information and other matters are we duty-bound to disclose and where is the best place to put it?

● Are we sure that any statements made are in line with the financial data presented in the annual accounts?

● Do we have some evidence to justify any predictions we make about our future prospects?

● Are we presenting too much information to our shareholders and, if so, can we cut it back?

● Is the design, format and general content of the material likely to encourage recipients to read it?

● Do the various reports contain any jargon and, if so, can we either cut it out or reduce it?

● Are the publicity pages likely to annoy our shareholders?

Conclusion

A company usually publishes an annual report and accounts, supplies a copy to each shareholder, and files one with the Registrar of Companies for public inspection. In this chapter we have examined the contents of the annual *report*. The next chapter examines the contents of the annual *accounts*.

In order to make our study of an annual report a little easier, we have suggested that it can be broken down into seven main sections. The first few pages usually contain some introductory material about the company, such as its objectives and a summary of the financial results for the year. In consumer orientated companies there may also be many pages advertising the company's products. Thereafter contents and order will vary from company to company.

Most companies include a short chairman's report summarizing the company's progress during the year and its prospects for the future. This will probably be followed by a fairly lengthy and detailed operating and financial review (OFR). This is a non-mandatory section recommended by the ASB. It is likely that the directors then present their report. A directors' report is a statutory requirement and the 1985 Companies Act lays down what must be included. These days it may also include a number of 'corporate governance' items. Thus a modern directors' report probably includes much more than the information required by statute.

The annual report and accounts will almost certainly include a separate 'corporate governance' statement even if some such matters are covered elsewhere in the document. In effect, a corporate governance statement informs readers how the company is operated and how it is managed. Again, as part of corporate governance proposals, there will also be a separate report about the remuneration paid and the terms and conditions of employment of the directors.

The annual reports are usually followed by the annual accounts (discussed in the next chapter), and the annual accounts by various items of 'shareholder information' such as company names and addresses and details of the AGM.

Key points

1 An annual report and accounts contains a great many reports and statements. The annual accounts are covered mainly by legislative and professional requirements. These are dealt with in the next chapter. The various annual reports are mainly voluntary.

2 It is possible to identify seven main sections of an annual report. The detailed content and structure varies from company to company. The size of such reports also varies depending partly upon the size of the company and partly on its type, e.g. consumer orientated companies usually include a great deal of publicity material.

3 The introductory section contains some details about the company, a summary of its financial results for the year and possibly some publicity material.

4 The specific reports that follow include a chairman's statement (not mandatory), an operating and financial review statement (recommended by the ASB), a directors' report (statutory), and a corporate governance statement and a remuneration report (both required by listed companies).

5 The annual accounts will normally then be presented followed by the last few pages of the overall document containing some administrative information for shareholders.

Check your learning

The answers to these questions may be found within the text.

1 List three items that may be included in the introductory section of a company's annual report.

2 What mandatory requirement covers the contents of a chairman's statement?

3 Name three items that will normally be included in a chairman's statement.

4   What is an operating and financial review?

5   What statutory and mandatory professional pronouncements require a review to be published?

6   List two items that may be found in the operating section and two items that may be found in the financial review section of an OFR.

7   What statutory and mandatory professional requirements require directors to submit a report to shareholders?

8   Name four items that should be included in a directors' report.

9   What is 'corporate governance'?

10   What is a remuneration report?

11   How has it come about?

12   List four items that it should include.

13   What type of information will normally be included in the last few pages of an annual report?

News story quiz

Remember the news story at the beginning of this chapter? Go back to that story and re-read it before answering the following questions.

Annual reports, especially those for large companies, have become extremely lengthy and complicated in recent years. And yet there are constant demands by various external parties for more and more information to be put in them. This article argues that the changing nature of business calls for more narrative reporting in annual reports.

Questions

1   Does more information supplied to shareholders necessarily make them better informed?

2   Do you think that narrative reports would be more useful to non-accountant users of annual reports than quantitative ones?

3   In terms of format and structure what type of annual report does a small shareholder need?

Tutorial questions

10.1 'A limited liability company's annual report should be made easier to understand for the average shareholder'. Discuss.

10.2 Examine the argument that annual reports are a costly irrelevance because hardly anyone refers to them.

10.3 Should companies be banned from including non-financial data in their annual reports?

Further practice questions, study material and links to relevant sites on the World Wide Web can be found on the website that accompanies this book. The site can be found at **www.booksites.net/dyson**

A rare example of non-compliance with accounting standards . . .

Results posted for holding company only

On the grounds of cost, the directors of Gameplay (distribution of online games) have taken the unusual step of producing results for the year ended 31 July 2001 for the plc only, contrary to current accounting standards.

This has obliged auditors BDO Stoy Hayward to qualify their opinion on the financial statements. The qualification arises from the company's failure to produce consolidated financial statements and a presentation of a cash flow statement for the year ended 31 July 2001 without comparative information for the year ended 31 July 2000.

In addition, the auditors note that the financial statements for the year ended 31 July 2001 have been provided on a going concern basis, the validity of which is contingent on the directors continuing to take steps to maximise the value of the remaining assets.

Gameplay's directors believe that the costs incurred in auditing the many subsidiaries around Europe – which, following their sale to the local managements, the company no longer controls – would be substantial. These costs would reduce the remaining shareholder funds (£556,000 at 31 July 2001 compared with £134,566 in the group balance sheet at 31 July 2000) and would be of little benefit or interest to shareholders.

The directors therefore concluded that issuing qualified financial statements as noted above was in the shareholders' best interests. This decision was taken after consultation with the company's financial advisers.

The effect of not consolidating the results of the trading subsidiaries into the results of the plc holding company is to exclude the sales and operating losses of the subsidiary businesses up to their dates of disposal and to include the paper losses on disposal of those businesses.

The Gameplay plc p&l account has revenues of only £79,000 compared with the group's consolidated revenues for the half year ended 31 January 2001 of £44.5m; losses before tax amount to £197.6m, a significant proportion of which related to the capital losses on sale of the subsidiaries.

The cash position has deteriorated. At 31 July, the company had £1.3m cash in hand; at 31 January 2001 the group had £12.7m, of which £8.7m was held by the company – in addition there was a further £8.3m of supplier bonds and deposits.

Gameplay's directors explain that while the p&l account is distorted by the non-consolidation of the trading subsidiaries, they believe that the balance sheet does accurately reflect the net asset position of the company at 31 July 2001.

All seemed very different when Gameplay was first floated in July 1999. Indeed, in November 2000, Gameplay was voted Alternative Investment Market Newcomer of the Year.

Accountancy, January 2003.

Questions relating to this news story may be found on page 244 ▸▸

About this chapter

This chapter is a continuation of Chapter 10. In Chapter 10 we studied the largely non-statutory report sections of a company's annual report and accounts. In this chapter we cover the mainly statutory information contained in the accounts sections.

The chapter is divided into ten main sections. After we have listed the learning objectives the first main section explains why the chapter is important for non-accountants. We then set the scene for our study of a set of annual accounts. The next six sections

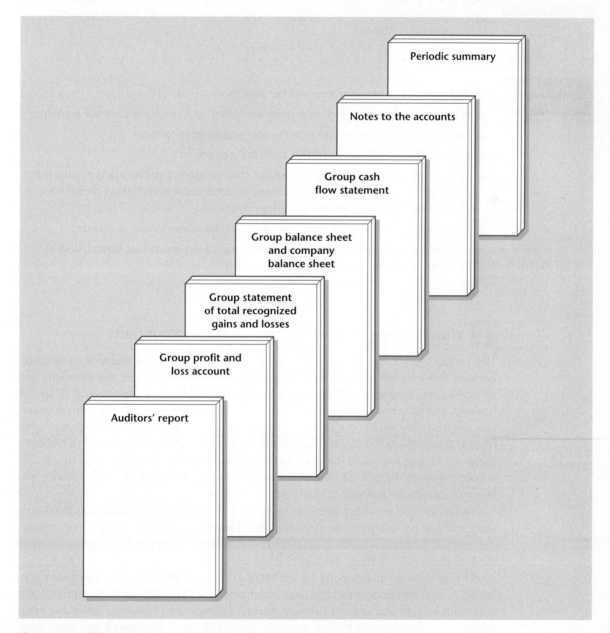

Figure 11.1 **The accounts section of an annual report**

each deal with the main financial reports, viz. the auditors' report, the profit and loss account, the statement of total recognized gains and losses, the balance sheet, the cash flow statement, notes to the accounts, and a periodic summary of the company's financial results. These reports and statements are depicted in diagrammatic format in Figure 11.1. The last main section of the chapter outlines some questions that non-accountants might like to ask about the issues raised in the chapter.

Activity 11.1	Refer to the three sets of annual reports and accounts you used in the last chapter. Find out what financial accounts are included in each set. List their titles in three adjacent columns in your notebook.

Learning objectives	**By the end of this chapter you will be able to:**
	● list the various reports and statements contained in a company's annual accounts;
	● outline what each of those reports and statements contain;
	● evaluate the significance of the auditors' report;
	● extract meaningful information about the company's performance from the profit and loss account, the statement of total recognized gains and losses, the balance sheets, and the cash flow statement;
	● locate additional information contained in the notes to the accounts;
	● compare the company's financial performance on an annual basis using a periodic summary statement.

❗ Why this chapter is important for non-accountants

The various *reports* included in a company's *annual report and accounts* are important because they provide a great deal of background information about the company and its operations. Furthermore some of the information is required by statute or by the business and financial community. The annual *accounts* are probably even more important because they inform the user about the company's profit or loss for the year, what its cash flow is like, what assets it owns, and what it owes to parties external to the company. It is vital to review all the data and information provided in the annual report and accounts in order to gain a fundamental knowledge of the company's performance and financial stability for the year in question.

The information provided becomes even more revealing when it is used to build up a story that may not altogether be apparent when the report and accounts are first examined. The exercise involved in building up this story is sometimes described as 'reading between the lines of the balance sheet' although it is not just confined to the balance sheet itself.

We shall explain how to build up this story in the next chapter. The information contained in this chapter provides the basic information for that exercise. This chapter is also important for non-accountants because you will probably be involved in providing information for inclusion in the annual accounts. It will make your job easier if you know what information is needed, why it is needed, and how it is used in the annual accounts.

Even if you are not involved in helping to prepare a company's annual accounts, you might have an interest in how companies are doing, e.g. you might want to buy some shares. A company's annual report and accounts provide the most comprehensive information that you are likely to obtain for this purpose (although you will need to use other sources as well). However, they are not easy to understand so you need to be trained in their use. This chapter provides you with that training.

Setting the scene

Disclosure in practice

The law requires companies to publish details of their annual financial performance. This is supplemented by a considerable amount of additional information required by the business and financial community. Such requirements cover the minimum amount of information that has to be disclosed and in what format. This means that there is now very little basic difference between companies in what and how they publish the required information. Much depends upon whether they are in the financial, manufacturing or financial sectors, how big they are, and whether they operate internationally.

Although the basic structure and content of most companies' accounts will be similar, you might find that the order of the numerous accounts and reports will be different, they will vary in detail and some will be very technical. There should always be five reports that you can always expect to find. These are the auditors' report, the profit and loss account, a statement of total recognized gains and losses, a balance sheet, and a cash flow statement. You may also find a summary of the company's financial results over a five- or ten-year period. We are going to study these reports and some others in this chapter.

Sources of authority

We have already discussed the sources of authority for the disclosure of a company's financial performance. A brief summary of what is required is itemized below.

1 The 1985 Companies Act

The Act requires companies to publish profit and loss accounts and a balance sheet. Various formats are laid down so there is some choice. The Act lays down the precise headings and wordings for the presentation of the information. It also requires the current year's result and the previous year's figures to be disclosed. It is permissible to miss out a prescribed line if there is no numerical data for both the current year and the previous year. Additional lines and descriptions may be added if required.

Most published sets of accounts you will come across are for a *group* of companies. A group of companies is like a family. One company (say Company A) may buy shares in another company (say Company B). When Company A owns more than 50 per cent of the voting shares in Company B, B becomes a *subsidiary* of A. If A were to own more than 20 per cent but less than 50 per cent of the voting shares in B, B would be known as an *associated company* of A. In effect, B is considered to be the offspring of A. Of course

B might have children of its own, say Company C and Company D. Thus C and D become part of the family, i.e. part of the A group of companies.

It is also the case that sometimes one company is in a position to *control* the affairs of another company, even if it does not necessarily own a substantial number of shares in the other company. If this is the case then companies that are controlled by other companies will be included as part of the group. An example of a typical group structure is shown in Figure 11.2.

The Companies Act 1985 uses the term *group undertaking* to describe a subsidiary company. Associate companies are defined as *undertakings in which the company has a participating interest*. This is because the 1989 Companies Act brought in a requirement to include other types of entities (and not just companies) in the group accounts.

The main significance of these relationships is that the Companies Act 1985 requires the accounts to be published for the *group*, i.e., in effect, as though it were one entire entity, thereby ignoring any inter-group activities (such as sales made or transfers of funds between group companies). When inspecting a set of accounts for a listed company, you can expect to see a *group* profit and loss account and a *group* balance sheet.

The Act permits group accounts to be presented in various ways. The most common method of satisfying the statutory requirements is to prepare a group profit and loss account and a group balance sheet plus a balance sheet for the *holding* company, i.e. the parent company. Cash flow statements are not required by law but you can also expect to see a *group* cash flow statement as required by FRS1.

Group accounts are prepared by adding together (i.e. consolidating) all of the company accounts within the group. This means that the subsidiary companies' results are absorbed in the holding company's accounts. The treatment is slightly different for associated companies. All of this might appear to be very complicated. It is. Fortunately, as a non-accountant you are unlikely to be involved in the detailed consolidation of the group accounts.

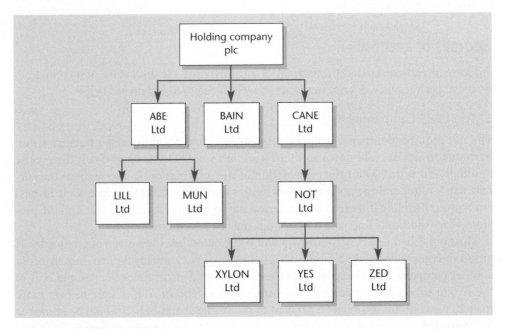

Figure 11.2 **A group of companies**

2 Professional requirements

At March 2003, there were 12 SSAPs still in force and 19 FRSs. It is not necessary for us to go through each one of them in detail with you but it would be useful to comment upon a few of them.

FRS 1 – Cash flow statement. This standard was originally issued in September 1991 and revised in 1996. We dealt with it in Chapter 8 and we shall be returning to it later in this chapter.

FRS 3 – Reporting financial performance. This standard was issued in October 1992 and amended in June 1993. It introduced a number of important changes. The format of the profit and loss account was amended so that a distinction was drawn between continuing operations, acquisitions and discontinued operations. Thus more information is now disclosed of items such as turnover and the operating profit. Exceptional items (i.e. ordinary activities that have a significant impact on the results) require disclosure either in the profit and loss account or as a note in the accounts as do extraordinary items (i.e. significant activities that are not ordinary). A statement of total recognized gains and losses was introduced (we deal with this later), as well as a reconciliation of movement in shareholders' funds.

FRS 18 – Accounting policies. This standard was issued in December 2000. It replaces SSAP 2 – Disclosure of accounting policies, issued by the ASC in November 1971. FRS 18 requires entities to disclose their accounting policies and any changes made to them. Many companies include a separate statement of their accounting policies in their annual accounts but it is also quite common to disclose them in a note to the accounts

3 Other requirements

There are no additional Stock Exchange or corporate governance requirements that we need to draw to your attention to at this stage.

Procedure

In order to outline the contents of the six types of accounts that we have chosen to study in this chapter we are going to use a set of accounts published by A.G. Barr plc for the year ended 26 January 2002. As and when required, we will also use examples from other sets of published accounts. Barr is a Glasgow based company 'engaged in the manufacture, distribution and marketing of branded soft drinks'. It is best known for its Irn-Bru brand of soft drink.

We will not reproduce everything included in Barr's accounts. In particular, we will not include the comparative figures for 2001. Similarly, we will not produce the 'Notes to the Accounts' or the references to them.

We start with the auditors' report.

Auditors' report

The auditors' report will be fairly short and most of them that you may come across are likely to be very similar. Barr's auditors' report is shown in Figure 11.3. Read through it very carefully.

Referring to Barr's auditors' report, notice the following features:

1   The accounts have been prepared on a historical cost basis.
2   Attention is drawn both to the directors' and the auditors' responsibilities.
3   The auditors state the matters on which they are reporting.
4   They state how they have gone about forming their opinion.
5   The auditors state that the accounts give 'a true and fair view'. There are no qualifications of any kind.

Activity 11.2   Find the auditors' report in each of your three sets of accounts. Read through them. Do the auditors state that the accounts represent a true and fair view? Or have they any reservations or qualifications about the accounts? If so, summarize in your notebook the nature of such reservations or qualifications.

Group profit and loss account

The Companies Act 1985 allows a choice to be made between two formats for the presentation of the profit and loss account:

1   *Horizontal.* In this format, expenditures are listed on the left-hand side of the page and incomes on the right-hand side.
2   *Vertical.* This format presents the income and expenditure on a line-by-line basis.

The vertical format should be familiar to you as it has been used exclusively throughout this book. Most UK companies have adopted it and it is the format that you are most likely to meet in practice. We shall continue to adopt it throughout this chapter and the rest of the book.

The Companies Act 1985 also permits expenditure to be disclosed using either an 'operational' format or a 'type of expenditure' format. These formats are shown in Example 11.1 using, respectively, Barr's accounts and J. Smart & Co. (Contractors) PLC's accounts. Smart is an Edinburgh based construction company.

A.G.BARR p.l.c.

Independent Auditors' Report

To the Shareholders of A.G.BARR p.l.c.

We have audited the accounts on pages 22 to 36 of A.G.BARR p.l.c. for the year ended 26th January, 2002. These accounts have been prepared under the historical cost convention and the accounting policies set out therein.

Respective responsibilities of directors and auditors

The directors' responsibilities for preparing the annual report and the accounts in accordance with applicable law and United Kingdom Accounting Standards are set out in the Statement of Directors' Responsibilities.

Our responsibility is to audit the accounts in accordance with relevant legal and regulatory requirements, United Kingdom Auditing Standards and the Listing Rules of the Financial Services Authority.

We report to you our opinion as to whether the accounts give a true and fair view and are properly prepared in accordance with the Companies Act 1985. We also report to you if, in our opinion, the Directors' Report is not consistent with the accounts, if the company has not kept proper accounting records, if we have not received all the information and explanations we require for our audit, or if the information specified by law or the Listing Rules regarding directors' remuneration and transactions with the company and other members of the group is not disclosed.

We review whether the corporate governance statement reflects the company's compliance with the seven provisions of the Combined Code specified for our review by the Listing Rules, and we report if it does not. We are not required to consider whether the board's statements on internal control cover all the risks and controls, or form an opinion on the effectiveness of the company's corporate governance procedures or its risk and control procedures.

We read other information contained in the annual report and consider whether it is consistent with the audited accounts. This other information comprises only the Chairman's Statement, the Review of Activities, the Directors' Report, the Statement on Corporate Governance and the Remuneration Committee report. We consider the implications for our report if we become aware of any apparent mis-statements or material inconsistencies with the accounts. Our responsibilities do not extend to any other information.

Basis of opinion

We conducted our audit in accordance with United Kingdom Auditing Standards issued by Auditing Practices Board. An audit includes examination, on a test basis, of evidence relevant to the amounts and disclosures in the accounts. It also includes an assessment of the significant estimates and judgements made by the directors in the preparation of the accounts, and of whether the accounting policies are appropriate to the company's circumstances, consistently applied and adequately disclosed.

We planned and performed our audit so as to obtain all the information and explanations which we considered necessary in order to provide us with sufficient evidence to give reasonable assurance that the accounts are free from material mis-statement, whether caused by fraud or other irregularity or error. In forming our opinion we also evaluated the overall presentation of information in the accounts.

Opinion

In our opinion the accounts give a true and fair view of the state of the company's and the group's affairs as at 26th January, 2002 and of the profit of the group for the year then ended and have been properly prepared in accordance with the Companies Act 1985.

Baker Tilly

Baker Tilly,
Registered Auditors,
Chartered Accountants.
Glasgow.
5th April, 2002.

Figure 11.3 **An independent auditors' report**

<table>
<tr><td>Example
11.1</td><td colspan="2">Examples of the vertical profit and loss account expenditure formats</td></tr>
</table>

(a) Operational format	(b) Type of expenditure format
A.G. Barr and its Subsidiary Companies	**J. Smart & Co. (Contractors) and Subsidiary Companies**
Consolidated profit and loss account for the year ended 26 January 2002 (extract)	*Consolidated profit and loss account for the year ended 31 July 2002 (extract)*

	£000		£000	£000
Turnover	116,261	Turnover		17,368
		Own work capitalized		3,625
				20,993
Cost of sales	63,032	Other operating income		4,948
Gross profit	53,229			25,941
		Raw materials and consumables	6,068	
Distribution costs	27,834	Other external charges	5,056	11,124
				14,817
Administrative expenses	14,908	Staff costs	8,279	
		Depreciation	486	
		Other operating charges	1,493	10,258
Operating profit	**10,487**	**Operating profit**		**4,559**

Notes:

1 The above information has been extracted from the annual report and accounts of the two companies.
2 There are no differences between the two formats in the presentation of the statutory profit and loss account information after the operating profit stage.

As can be seen from Example 11.1, the type of expenditure format is very much more detailed than the operational format. Both types are used in the UK. The operational format is more common, probably because it is a little easier to follow. It is basically the same format that we have used throughout this book. It is also easier to adapt it to suit the requirements of FRS 3 (Reporting Financial Performance), which deals with the presentation of financial statements.

Following this introduction, we can now examine Barr's profit and loss account in some detail. We do this in Example 11.2.

A published group profit and loss account

Example
11.2

A.G. Barr plc
Consolidated Profit and Loss Account for the year
ended 26 January, 2002

	Tutorial notes	2002 £000
Turnover	(1)	116,261
Cost of sales	(2)	63,032
Gross profit	(3)	53,229
Net operating expenses	(4)	42,742
Operating profit	(5)	10,487
Interest received	(6)	253
Profit on ordinary activities before tax	(7)	10,740
Tax on profit on ordinary activities	(8)	3,254
Profit on ordinary activities after tax	(9)	7,486
Dividends	(10)	4,202
Retained profit for the year	(11)	3,284
Earnings per share on issued share capital	(12)	38.47p

Notes:
1 References to the formal notes and the notes themselves are not shown.
2 Comparative figures have been ignored.

Tutorial notes

1 *Turnover.* Turnover is defined as the net sales value exclusive of value added tax of goods and services supplied to customers outside the group during the period. In this example turnover has not been analyzed between continuing operations, acquisitions and discontinued operations, i.e. sales from entities taken over or sold during the year and sales arising from activities before they were sold. FRS 3 (Reporting Financial Performance) required this breakdown of turnover. Barr had no such activities in either 2001 or 2002.

2 *Cost of sales.* The detailed calculation for the cost of sales does not have to be disclosed. The term is not defined in the Companies Act 1985.

3 *Gross profit.* The gross profit may not be identical to that shown in the internal accounts because of the definition of the cost of sales.

4 *Net operating expenses.* This item includes both distribution costs and administrative expenses. The Companies Act 1985 does not define these terms. Barr discloses them separately in a note to the accounts.

5 *Operating profit.* This is the point at which the operational and type of expenditure formats become identical. Note that FRS 3 requires the operating profit to be broken down into operating profit from continuing operations, acquisitions and discontinued operations (not applicable in Barr's case).

6 *Interest received.* Interest received includes interest received on loans made less interest paid on bank loans and other short-term borrowings. Barr's figure is shown net with the details given in the notes to the accounts.

7 *Profit on ordinary activities before tax.* This is a sub-total.

Tutorial notes
continued

8 *Tax on profit on ordinary activities.* The tax on the profit on ordinary activities consists largely of the company's corporation tax but it may also include a number of technical accounting adjustments affecting taxation.

9 *Profit on ordinary activities after tax.* This is another sub-total.

10 *Dividends.* This the amount of dividend paid and proposed to be paid to shareholders.

11 *Retained profit for the year.* The retained profit for the year is transferred to the revenue reserves. The balance is shown in the balance sheet as 'profit and loss account'.

12 *Earnings per share on issued share capital.* Earnings per share (EPS) has been calculated by dividing the profit attributable to shareholders by the weighted average number of ordinary shares in issue during the period.

Activity 11.3

Refer to your copies of the three annual accounts and turn to the page that includes the profit and loss account. Read down the statement on a line-by-line basis. If you do not understand a particular item look it up in the formal 'note to the accounts'. Compare your three accounts with Example 11.2 and write down in your notebook any significant differences between them.

Group statement of total recognized gains and losses

FRS 3 requires companies to prepare a *statement of total recognized gains and losses.* This statement will normally be presented immediately after the profit and loss account. It should include *all* the gains and losses that the company has made during the year, and not just those that are debited or credited to the profit and loss account. It is possible for some gains or losses (such as deficits or surpluses arising from the revaluation of fixed assets, and foreign currency exchange gains or losses) to be taken straight to a balance sheet reserve account. Hence they may never appear in the profit and loss account. Barr's statement of total recognized gains and losses is shown in Example 11.3.

Example 11.3

A statement of total recognized gains and losses

A.G. Barr plc and its Subsidiary Companies
Consolidated statement of total recognized gains and losses

	Tutorial notes	£000
Profit as above	(1)	7,486
Adjustment for prior periods	(2)	(3,293)
Total gains and losses recognized since last annual report	(3)	4,193

Tutorial notes

1 This figure is the profit on ordinary activities after tax. It has been extracted from the consolidated profit and loss account (see Example 11.2, tutorial note 9).

2 This item is a taxation adjustment that relates to 2001 (the previous year).

3 This figure shows the total gain from all sources that the company has made during the year.

4 Other items that you might find in a statement of total recognized gains and losses include unrealized surpluses on revaluation of properties, unrealized gains/losses on trade investments, and currency translation differences on foreign currency net investments.

Activity 11.4

Look up the statements of total recognised gains and losses in your set of three accounts. Enter all of the various items included in the statements in table format in your notebook with a separate column for each company.

Group balance sheet

As with the profit and loss account, the Companies Act 1985 allows a choice to be made between adopting a horizontal or a vertical format for the balance sheet. The horizontal format requires the assets to be laid out on the left-hand side of the page and the capital on the right-hand side. The vertical format lists the assets and then the liabilities on a line-by-line basis. The vertical format will be most familiar to you as it has been adopted almost exclusively throughout this book. It is also common among many UK companies, although some companies do use the horizontal type.

Published balance sheets do not look very different from those prepared for internal purposes. The main differences are that: (1) they will normally be prepared for a group of companies; (2) they will be far more detailed than a sole trader's balance sheets; (3) they will include comparative figures; and (4) a great many pages of formal notes will be attached to them.

Barr's group balance sheet is shown in Example 11.4. We have not included the Company's balance sheet.

Example 11.4

Example of a published group balance sheet

A.G. Barr plc and its Subsidiary Companies
Balance sheet as at 26 January 2002

	Tutorial notes	Group £000
Fixed assets	(1)	
Tangible assets	(2)	42,580
Current assets	(3)	
Stocks	(4)	11,536
Debtors	(5)	21,078
Investment	(6)	2,623
Cash at bank	(7)	8,265
	(8)	43,502

▶

Example 11.4
continued

Balance sheet as at 26 January 2002

	Tutorial notes	Group £000
Creditors: Due within one year	(9)	24,113
Net current assets	(10)	19,389
Total assets less current liabilities	(11)	61,969
Provisions for liabilities and chargers	(12)	5,576
	(13)	56,393
Capital and reserves	(14)	
Called up share capital	(15)	4,865
Share premium reserve	(16)	905
Profit and loss account	(17)	50,623
	(18)	56,393

Notes:
1 Reference to the formal notes and the notes themselves are not included.
2 Comparative figures are not shown.

Tutorial notes

1 *Fixed assets.* The net book value of the fixed assets must be shown under three headings: (a) intangible assets; (b) tangible assets; and (c) investments. Intangible assets are those assets that are not of a physical nature, such as goodwill, patents and development costs. Fixed asset investments are those investments that are intended to be held for the long term, i.e. in excess of 12 months.

2 *Tangible assets.* Tangible assets include freehold and leasehold land and buildings, plant, equipment and vehicles.

3 *Current assets.* Current assets have to be analyzed into a number of categories (see notes 4 to 7 below). These are shown on the face of the balance sheet.

4 *Stocks.* Stocks must be put into various categories, e.g. raw materials and consumables, work-in-progress, finished goods, and payments on account. The details are normally shown in the 'notes to the accounts'.

5 *Debtors.* Debtors must be analyzed into trade debtors, other debtors, prepayments, and accrued income. The details will be shown in 'notes to the accounts'.

6 *Investment.* Current asset investments are those investments held for the short term, i.e. normally for less than 12 months.

7 *Cash at bank.* Cash at bank and in hand includes physical cash and short-term accounts kept at the bank.

8 *Sub-total.* This line represents the total of all the current assets.

9 *Creditors: due within one year.* Creditors: amounts falling due within one year must be analyzed between short-term creditors (those that have to be paid within 12 months) and long-term creditors (those that do not have to be paid for over 12 months). These would be described as 'Creditors: amounts falling due after more than one year' and shown after line (11) (Total assets less current liabilities). Barr does not have any long-term creditors. Both short-term and long-term creditors are analyzed into various categories such as trade creditors, other creditors, and accruals and deferred income. The details will be shown in 'notes to the accounts'.

10 *Net current assets.* The net current assets line is a sub-total of current assets (line (8)) less creditors: amounts due within one year (line (9)).

11 *Total assets less current liabilities.* This is another sub-total: fixed assets (line (2)) plus net current assets (line (10)).

12 *Provisions for liabilities and charges.* This item will include provisions for pensions and similar obligations, and taxation. In Barr's case the balance represents various taxation adjustments (not shown).

13 *Total.* This figures represents the total net assets of the company as at 26 January 2002. This does not mean, of course, that the company was necessarily worth this amount as the assets, for example, may not be sold at their balance sheet value.

14 *Capital and reserves.* The capital and reserves section is the other main part of the balance sheet. It explains how the net assets have been financed.

15 *Called up share capital.* The called up share capital represents all of the shares that have been issued, details of which will be shown in 'notes to the accounts'.

16 *Share premium account.* The share premium account records the extra amount on top of the nominal value of the shares that shareholders were willing to pay when they bought their shares. It does not attract a dividend and the Companies Act 1985 permits only a few ways in which it can be used.

17 *Profit and loss account.* This is the balance of all the retained profit for the year that has not been paid to shareholders. The balance has probably been built up over many years. By not paying out the profits, the company has been able to use the funds for further investment within the business.

18 *Total.* This amount represents the total of the funds invested in the business at 26 January 2002. It should balance with line (13).

The balance sheet should be signed by at least one director. Two directors signed Barr's balance sheet.

Tutorial notes continued

Referring to your set of three accounts, work your way down each of the three group balance sheets. As you do so read through the various balance sheet notes. Then compare the main section headings in the three balance sheets along with Barr's (see above). Write down any headings that are not common across the four sets. Check the balance sheet notes if you are not sure what they mean.

Activity 11.5

Group cash flow statement

The construction of a cash flow statement (CFS) has already been examined in some detail in Chapter 8. Apart from reflecting the activities of a group of companies and the inclusion of comparative figures, published CFSs differ little from the format that was adopted in that chapter.

Unlike the profit and loss account and the balance sheet, CFSs do not have any statutory backing. They are, however, now considered so important that they are usually regarded as being one of the main financial statements. Indeed, FRS 1 requires most companies (small companies are the notable exception) to prepare a CFS. It is highly unlikely that you will come across a set of published accounts that does not include a CFS.

Barr's CFS is shown in Example 11.5.

Example 11.5	A group cash flow statement

A.G. BARR plc and its Subsidiary Companies
Cash flow statement for the year ended 26 January 2002

	(2002)	
	£000	£000
Net cash inflow from operating activities		12,989
Returns on investments and servicing of finance		
Interest received	268	
Interest paid	(11)	
Interest element of hire purchase paid	(4)	
Net cash outflow from returns on investments and servicing of finance		253
Tax		
Corporation tax paid		(4,181)
Capital expenditure and financial investment		
Purchase of tangible fixed assets	(7,750)	
Sales of tangible fixed assets	258	
		(7,492)
Acquisitions and disposals		
Investment in subsidiary	(105)	
Net overdraft acquired with subsidiary	(90)	
		(195)
		1,374
Dividends paid		(4,200)
		(2,826)
Financing		
Issue of share capital	50	
Capital element of hire purchase paid	(304)	
Loans repaid	(30)	
		(284)
(Decrease)/Increase in cash		(3,110)

Tutorial notes

1 The formal notes that would normally be attached to the statement have not been included. Such notes (along with various reconciliations) give details about the make-up of each heading.

2 The above format is only a guide: it is not mandatory.

3 Apart from some items that relate only to a group, e.g. dividend received from associated undertakings, and purchase of subsidiary undertakings, the statement is very similar to the example used in Chapter 8.

4 Comparative figures have not been included.

Example 11.5 is a typical example of a CFS but it is likely that you will come across other formats. Some can be a little confusing, especially when some figures are shown in brackets. It might help to remember that the basic idea of a CFS is to show where the cash has come from and where it has gone to, i.e. cash received and cash, paid. Just to remind you, a non-group CFS should contain seven main sections and a group CFS eight, namely:

1 operating activities;
2 returns on investments and servicing of finance;
3 taxation;
4 capital expenditure and financial investment;
5 acquisitions and disposals (group CFS only);
6 equity dividends paid;
7 management of liquid resources;
8 financing.

Heading 7 (management of liquid resources) and heading 8 (financing) may be combined provided that a subtotal is given for each heading.

Most of the above sections will contain both cash received and cash paid. Items representing cash paid are normally inserted in brackets. But this is not always the case, so be careful.

Turn to the cash flow statement in each of your set of three accounts. Compare them on a line-by-line basis with Barr's CFS. Examine the presentation and the layout. Are they all similar? Do all four sets have the eight main headings indicated by FRS 1? Check with the 'notes to the accounts' if there are any detailed items that are not clear to you (Barr's notes have not been reproduced). Make sure that in your three sets of accounts you can follow the notes dealing with (a) the reconciliation of net cash flow items to movements in net funds; and (b) the analysis of changes in net funds.

Activity 11.6

Notes to the accounts

The profit and loss account, the statement of total recognized gains and losses, the balance sheets and the cash flow statement are usually supported by a great deal of additional information in 'Notes to the accounts'. Such notes serve two main purposes:

1 they avoid too much detail being shown on the face of the accounts; and
2 they make it easier to provide supplementary information.

One important point to remember is that the notes form an integral part of the accounts and that they are an essential element in the total amount of information that has to be disclosed. However, it is only fair to warn you that it is sometimes difficult to understand how some of the information fits into the overall accounts (such as the movement of the various reserve accounts). By contrast, some information is straightforward. For example, a note giving details about the company's profit before taxation will include such items as the depreciation charged to the profit and loss account for the year, the auditors' remuneration, and the amount of research and development expenditure.

Barr's 'notes to the accounts' are 12 pages in length and they include 29 separate headings. Barr is a relatively small company and its operations are not complex. The notes are clear and well laid out. Nevertheless, some of the information is not easy to follow and it is difficult to imagine anyone who has no knowledge of accounting being able to sort it out. For example, Note 21 deals with deferred tax. The note begins 'Deferred tax is provided on all timing differences'.

Do you know what 'deferred tax' is? And are you clear about 'timing differences'? Just in case you did not know, the answers are as follows:

1 For tax purposes, accounting profit is adjusted for items that are and are not allowable or chargeable for tax purposes. This mean that if corporation tax is 30%, you cannot multiply the accounting profit by 30% and say that that is the tax due for the year. Hence if you look at the tax charge in the accounts the tax due in (say) Year 1 may look small and large in Year 2. In other words, the tax due to be paid on Year 1's profits is delayed or *deferred* to Year 2. In order to bring the accounts for Year 1 and Year 2 into line, an extra amount for tax will be set aside (or provided) in Year 1. The provision is kept in an account called the 'deferred tax account'. It will then be used in Year 2 to reduce the actual tax charge for that year. This means that the tax shown in the profit and loss account for Year 1 and Year 2 is smoothed out. In turn, this also smooths out the profit after tax.

2 This procedure does not affect the amount or the date when tax has to be paid. A small amount will be paid for Year 1 and a larger amount for Year 2 on the due dates. If the tax payable was calculated on an accounting basis, a different amount would be paid at a different time than it would be on a tax basis. This is known as a *timing* difference.

Periodic summary

Many companies include as part of their accounts a periodic summary. It is usually for a five-year period but some companies may produce a ten-year one. There is no statutory or professional requirement to produce such a summary.

The summary will normally be found after the 'notes to the accounts'. It will contain a few selected items such as turnover, profit and dividends for each of the five or so years. This enables users of the account to trace the company's results over a much longer period than can be done with the two years' results shown in the main accounts. Five years is probably about the right length to plot a meaningful trend. Beyond that circumstances and conditions may have changed so much that the information becomes outdated and misleading.

Barr's 'Review of the Trading Results' is shown in Example 11.6 (it is not called a 'Five-Year Summary').

A periodic summary

Example
11.6

A.G. BARR p.l.c. and it Subsidiary Companies
Review of the Trading Results

	2002 £000	2001 £000 *As restated	2000 £000	1999 £000	15 mths 1998 £000
Turnover	116,261	111,878	109,995	106,892	136,729
Operating profit	10,487	13,697	12,210	12,303	15,528
Interest	253	225	(114)	(312)	(1,118)
Profit on ordinary activities before tax	10,740	13,922	12,096	11,991	14,410
Tax profit on ordinary activities	3,254	4,159	3,451	3,415	4,339
Profit on ordinary activities before tax	7,486	9,763	8,645	8,576	10,071
Dividends	4,202	4,200	3,813	3,545	4,074
Retained profit for the year	3,284	5,563	4,832	5,031	5,997

*Restated as required for FRS 19, Deferred Tax.

Earnings per share on issued share capital	38.47p	50.17p	44.42p	44.07p	51.75p
Dividend per share	21.60p	21.60p	19.60p	18.25p	21.00p

The Earnings per share on issued share capital for each period have been calculated to reflect the shares in issue at 26th January, 2002.

> ### ❗ Questions non-accountants should ask
>
> You have been faced with a considerable amount of detailed and technical matter in this chapter. And yet you must remember that in the main, it represents the *minimum* amount of information that companies must disclose to their shareholders and to the public. It is also aimed largely at an audience untrained in accounting, so you can imagine what difficulties most users will have in understanding it. So what questions, as a non-accountant, should you ask about it? We suggest that as a senior manager (say) in a company preparing the accounts, the following questions might be appropriate.
>
> - Is this the absolute minimum information that we have to publish as perhaps more would be difficult to cope with?
> - Can the format and presentation be made clearer so that it is easier to follow?
> - Have we cut out all the jargon?
> - Can technical terms be avoided or at least explained – perhaps in a glossary?
>
> It should be noted that it is possible for shareholders to receive a simplified version of the accounts called a *summary financial statement* (SFS). The requirements are contained in the 1989 Companies Act, and they include a summarized directors' report, a summarized profit and loss account, a summarized balance sheet, and an auditors' report.
>
> A summarized version of the 'full' accounts is to be welcomed but even the simplified version is not easy to understand. The format, the contents, and the language still requires a considerable knowledge of accounting.

Conclusion

In this chapter we have looked at the accounts section of an annual report and accounts. We have suggested that the contents can be classified into seven broad groupings. These are as follows:

1 Auditors' report.
2 Group profit and loss account.
3 Group statement of total recognized gains and losses.
4 Group balance sheet and the company balance sheet.
5 Group cash flow statement.
6 Notes to the accounts.
7 Five-year summary

Most published accounts will be for a group of companies. The information presented in the accounts is complicated, detailed and technical. It requires a great deal of study to be able to assess what it all means. Much of the information is required by statute and by the professional bodies. Only the periodic summary is entirely at the discretion of the company.

1 An annual report and accounts contains a great many statements and reports. Those relating to the accounts may take up to about half of the entire contents.

2 The accounts section will include an auditors' report, a profit and loss account, a statement of total recognized gains and losses, two balance sheets (if a group), a cash flow statement, notes to the accounts and a periodic summary.

3 The information required is laid down in the Companies Act 1985, statements of standard accounting practice, and financial reporting standards. Only the periodic summary is a voluntary statement

4 The Companies Act 1985 specifies the format of the profit and loss account and the balance sheet and the description of the various headings. Some accounting standards (especially FRS 3) add to the requirements. The cash flow statement is covered by FRS 1.

5 The minimum amount of information is usually shown on the face of the various reports and statements, the remaining amount being included in 'notes to the accounts'.

Check your learning

The answers to these questions may be found within the text.

1 What is 'disclosure'?

2 List three sources of authority that cover the publication of company accounts.

3 What is a group of companies?

4 What is a group undertaking?

5 What are consolidated accounts?

6 What subject does FRS 1 deal with?

7 List three items required by FRS 3.

8 What is the subject of FRS 18?

9 What opinion does a firm of external auditors usually express about a company's accounts?

10 Explain the difference between the vertical format and the horizontal format for the presentation of accounts.

11 What is meant by the 'operational' and 'type of expenditure' formats for the presentation of a profit and loss account?

12 What is meant by 'cost of sales', 'distribution costs', and 'administrative expenses'?

13 Name two items that will be included in a statement of total recognized gains and losses.

14 What is meant by the term 'current' used in the context of 'current assets' and 'current liabilities'?

15 What is a share premium account?

16 How many directors have to sign a company's balance sheet?

17 How many headings are there in a group cash flow statement?

18 Why are 'notes to the accounts' used?

19 What statutory and professional requirements cover the publication of a periodic summary statement?

News story quiz

Remember the news story at the beginning of this chapter? Go back to that story and re-read it before answering the following questions.

According to UK company law, the overriding accounting rule is that accounts should show a 'true and fair view'. Hence in individual circumstances it is possible for a company to prepare its accounts in a way that reflects its own circumstances. This article shows that Gameplay has decided to ignore current accounting standards by producing accounts without the comparative information for the preceding year.

Questions

1 Do you think that the directors' reason for not showing comparative information is justified?

2 What effect is the qualification of the auditors' opinion likely to have?

3 What is meant by taking steps 'to maximise the value of the remaining assets'?

4 How does this affect the company's position as a 'going concern'?

5 Can Gameplay's balance sheet (or indeed any balance sheet) ever be said to 'reflect the net asset position of the company'?

Tutorial questions

11.1 Describe what is meant by a 'qualified audit report', illustrating your answer with appropriate examples.

11.2 In your view, what items could be taken out of a company's profit and loss account and its balance sheet without affecting the usefulness of such statements?

11.3 Suggest ten items that you think should be shown on a company's periodic summary statement.

Further practice questions, study material and links to relevant sites on the World Wide Web can be found on the website that accompanies this book. The site can be found at **www.booksites.net/dyson**

Slow payment of creditors helps cash flow . . .

BAE tops blue-chip list of slowest payers

BY MICHAEL HARRISON, Business Editor

BRITAIN'S BIGGEST aerospace and defence company, BAE Systems, has the dubious distinction of being the worst payer of bills in the FTSE 100. The second slowest is another aerospace giant, Rolls-Royce.

BAE's Royal Ordnance division takes an average of 102 days to settle bills from its suppliers while Rolls-Royce Power Engineering takes an average of 59 days, according to the latest late-payment league table published by the Federation of Small Businesses (FSB).

Other blue-chip companies with poor records for paying their bills promptly include the telecoms operator Cable & Wireless, which takes 58 days, and Smiths Group and Rentokil Initial, both of which take 55 days.

Among foreign companies with the poorest record on prompt payment are the French-owned CarnaudMetalbox, which takes 75 days on average to settle a bill; Peugeot Motor, which takes 59 days and the French-owned London Electricity, which takes 50 days.

According to the FSB there has been no improvement in the number of companies settling their bills on time despite the introduction of laws four years ago entitling suppliers to start charging interest after 30 days.

The FSB table, based on analysis carried out by the credit management research centre at Leeds University, showed that only one-third of public limited companies complied with best practice by settling their bills within 30 days. A fifth took more than 60 days to pay. The average time it takes PLCs to pay bills is 46 days – the same as it has been for the last three years.

The FSB said it was also concerned about the apparent decline in the number of companies setting out in their annual reports the average time it took for bills to be paid, as is now required by law. There has been a 21 per cent fall in the number of companies providing payment information, from 4,100 in 2001 to 3,243 in 2002. The federation has raised the issue of no-compliance with company law with the Small Business minister, Nigel Griffiths.

John Emmins, the chairman of the FSB, said: "A quarter of business failures continue to be the result of payment delays and I am disappointed that there has been no improvement in the average payment times."

Independent, 21 January 2003.

Questions relating to this news story may be found on page 277 ▶▶

About this chapter

This chapter covers what accountants call the 'interpretation of accounts'. In essence, this involves extracting more information from the accounts than might at first appear possible.

It is very often useful and necessary to do this because the absolute figures in the accounts are not particularly meaningful and they need to be put into context. For example, a profit of £3 million might seem a huge amount. But how does it compare with the forecasted and budgeted profit levels? How does it compare with last year's actual profit? How does it compare with similar companies?

These questions cannot always be answered from the accounts themselves. The figures have to be reworked and put into context, i.e. before we can *interpret* them. The interpretation of accounts is a type of detective work. We take the evidence disclosed in the accounts, rearrange it, and then compare and contrast it with other relevant information. We then draw all the evidence together and use it to form a conclusion about the company's financial performance and its prospects for the future.

This chapter explains how you do the detective work. There are various ways of doing so but we are going to concentrate on *ratio analysis*. Ratio analysis is one of the most common and popular approaches to interpreting accounts and we shall be spending a lot of time on it.

The chapter is divided into 12 main sections. After specifying the learning objectives, the first main section explains why this chapter is important for non-accountants. We then outline the nature and purpose of interpretation. This is followed by a section summarizing the basic procedures involved in interpreting a set of accounts. We then move on to ratio analysis. We deal with it in five separate sections (ratio analysis itself, profitability ratios, liquidity ratios, efficiency ratios and investment ratios). We then put the ratios into context using a detailed example based on a set of actual accounts. We follow this with a step-by-step guidance section on how to conduct an investigation into an entity's financial performance. The penultimate section indicates how it is possible to draw conclusions from the various techniques adopted in the chapter. The last main section outlines some questions that non-accountants should have in mind when they are presented with a report involving the interpretation of accounts.

By the end of this chapter you should be able to:

● **define what is meant by the 'interpretation of accounts';**

● **outline why it is needed;**

● **summarize the procedure involved in interpreting a set of accounts;**

● **explain the usefulness and importance of ratio analysis;**

● **calculate 15 main accounting ratios;**

● **explore the relationship between those ratios.**

! Why this chapter is important for non-accountants

This chapter is one of the most important in the book for non-accountants. In your professional life you might get by without knowing much about the source and meaning of accounting information. You might even be able to make sense of various financial statements put before you. The danger is that you might take them at their face value and you might not be able to put that information into context. This chapter explains how to do just that.

Accounts may be interpreted by subjecting them to a whole series of arithmetical and statistical analyses. Such analyses are usually very simple. They are often expressed in the form of ratios. For example, figure x might be expressed as a percentage of figure y. While your accountant may do this for you there may be some occasions when you have to do it for yourself, such as if you were at a meeting and you wanted to put some figures into context or you were considering buying some shares in a company for yourself.

After working your way through this chapter you will be able to cope with such situations on your own. And even if to do not have to calculate the figures for yourself, the ratios will mean much more to you if you are familiar with the way that they have been compiled.

All of this means that any decision that you take based on ratio analysis is likely to be much sounder and more effective. What is more, you will be able to 'read between the lines of a balance sheet' (as it is sometimes put), and that is a very important and necessary skill for a manager.

Nature and purpose of interpretation

In this section we explain what is meant by interpreting a set of accounts, why it is necessary, and who might have need of it.

Definition

The term 'to interpret' has several meanings. We often use it as an alternative to 'translation', for example, interpreting what someone says in French into English. In another context it means 'to give the meaning of' or 'to explain'. We will use the latter definition. Our definition, therefore, of what is meant by the term 'interpretation of accounts' is as follows:

> *Interpretation of accounts is a detailed explanation of the financial performance of an entity incorporating the information contained within a set of financial accounts.*

But why is it necessary to interpret accounts? Surely the accounts contain enough information to satisfy anyone? We explain below why this is not necessarily the case.

Accounting data problems

The amount of information contained in a set of internal accounts is considerable and, as you have discovered, even published accounts can be extremely detailed. Nevertheless, such information is not adequate or sufficient to be able to get a realistic assessment of an entity's past or future performance. There are three main reasons why this is so. We summarize them below.

1 *Absolute.* The information contained in financial accounts is limited to quantitative matters that can be easily translated into financial terms. The data are presented in absolute amounts such as thousands or millions of pounds. The numbers are difficult to comprehend if they are very large.

2 *Contextual.* The absolute amounts presented in financial accounts do not mean very much in isolation. Although comparative figures for the preceding year may be of some help, greater and wider comparisons need to be made before the figures begin to mean anything.

3 *Structural.* Financial accounts are prepared on the basis of a series of accounting rules (see Chapter 2). They contain a restricted amount of information and some arbitrary assessments have to be made about the treatment of certain matters, e.g. bad debts, depreciation and stock valuation. They are usually prepared for a past period of time, limited to two accounting periods (at best), and they do not take into account the impact of inflation (in some countries this can be significant, even over a one-year period).

But who wants more useful information?

Users and their requirements

Company law concentrates almost exclusively on one user group (shareholders) but, as we identified in Chapters 1 and 9, there are other user groups. We will use the ones listed in Chapter 1 to indicate what information they might need about a company's performance. Our suggestions are shown in Table 12.1.

If you examine the questions posed in Table 12.1 you will see that some information could be obtained from either the profit and loss account, the balance sheet, or the cash flow statement, e.g. the profit the company has made or the cash that it had at the end of the year. But such sources do no give any indication of its future prospects and whether the profit or liquidity position was reasonable. Without further analysis or information how would you know, for example, that GKN plc's earnings for the year to

Table 12.1 **User requirement of accounts**

User group	Main requirement
Customers	How competitive and efficient is the company at selling me its goods and services?
Employees	Has the company got enough cash to survive in the short-run and has it a profitable future?
Governments and their agencies	Is the company making enough money to pay tax? Will this continue?
Investors	Has the company enough cash to survive in the short-run? Is it likely to be a profitable in the long-run? What dividends will shareholders get and how will the share price be affected?
Lenders	Has the company enough cash to pay the interest due on any loans? Is it likely to have enough cash to pay the capital back?
Public	Is the company likely to stay in business?
Suppliers and other trade creditors	Has the company enough cash to pay what it owes?

31 December 2002 of £100m were good, bad or indifferent? Similarly, GKN had £105m of cash in hand and at the bank. Is this an adequate amount of cash to have had? Is it enough for the future?

We cannot answer the above questions without further work on the accounts. That is what is involved in interpreting a set of accounts. How do you go about it? We explain the basic procedure in the next section.

Activity 12.1

> Taking the seven user groups listed in Figure 12.1, what *specific* information do you think each user would require? List each user group and each requirement in your notebook and then insert (a) where the information could be found in the main financial accounts; and (b) what adjustment(s) it would need (if any) to meet each user group's requirements.

Basic procedure

In this section we outline the basic procedure involved in interpreting a set of accounts. Then in later sections we will go into greater detail about some of the points mentioned in the chapter. The basic procedure involves three main stages: the collection of data, the analysis of them, and the interpretation of the results.

Data collection

An exercise involving a comprehensive interpretation of accounts may be extremely wide ranging, requiring the collection of as much data and information as possible from a wide range of internal and external sources. We would need to do so, for example, if we considering a takeover bid for a large international company. The historical data would probably need to be collected for a three- to five-year period. Anything less than three years means that it is difficult to plot a meaningful trend. Beyond five years, the data may be too out of date to be reliable.

The exercise would involve examining and forecasting the economic, financial, political, and social national and international environment in which the company operates. A similar examination would be necessary of the specific economic sector and industry of which the company forms a part. And then a great deal of documentary information investigation would have to be collected, and contact made with personnel who know something about the company, e.g. analysts, customers, local business people and suppliers.

The compilation and distillation of all such information collected would enable a comprehensive picture to be built up of the company's history, its past performance and its future prospects.

Many investigations would not be as comprehensive as the one described above. Some users may only need a limited amount of information, e.g. if a small local trader is wondering how promptly a local company settles its debts. Such an investigation would be much more limited and confined than it would be in the case of a takeover bid. Thus the local trader might be able to obtain all the information that she needs from inspecting the company's annual accounts. It might be necessary to do a few calculations to put the information into context, e.g. by looking at the trade creditors in relation to its purchases, but no major arithmetical exercises would be contemplated.

Analysis

Both the qualitative and quantitative data collected in an interpretation exercise need to be analyzed, i.e. we have to explore the relationship between all of the information that we have available. With qualitative data it is much more difficult but by reading it carefully and comparing each part with another, we can usually spot any connection between them.

Quantitative data are easiest to analyze because we can use a number of statistical techniques. With financial data four main techniques may be used. These are *horizontal analysis, trend analysis, vertical analysis* and *ratio analysis*. Figure 12.1 contains a diagrammatic representation of these different types of analyses and we provide a brief summary of each technique below.

1 *Horizontal analysis.* This technique involves making a line-by-line comparison of the company's accounts for each accounting period chosen for investigation. You may observe, for example, that the sales were £100m in 2004, £110m in 2005, and £137.5m in 2006. In percentage terms the sales have increased by 10% in 2005, and by 25% in 2006. This type of comparison is something that we tend to do naturally when we look at a set of accounts. If you are going to calculate percentage changes, however, you will probably need to use a calculator.

2 *Trend analysis.* Trend analysis it similar to horizontal analysis, except that the first set of accounts in the series is given a base of 100. Subsequent accounts are then related to that base. Thus in the above example the 2004 sales would be expressed as 100, the 2005 sales as 110, and the 2006 sales as 137.5. This method enables us to see what changes have taken place much more easily than by comparing the absolute amounts. It is much easier, for example, to grasp the significance of 159 than it is £323 739 392.

3 *Vertical analysis.* This technique requires all of the profit and loss account items and all of the balance sheet items to be expressed as a percentage of their respective totals. For example, if trade debtors in 2006 were £20m and the balance sheet total was £50m, trade debtors would be expressed as 40% compared with (say) 35% in 2005, and 30% in 2004. The figures are much easier to grasp if they are expressed this way. Similarly, any change that takes place in the relationship between various items over a period of time can be quickly spotted. However, this method is now difficult to use. The vertical format now commonly adopted for presenting financial accounts and the use of sub-totals means that neither the profit and loss account nor the balance sheet shows a 'grand total'.

4 *Ratio analysis.* A ratio is a convenient way of comparing one figure with another figure, e.g. 20 with 40 and then expressing it as a factor or as percentage (e.g. to 2 or 50%). It is possible to calculate hundreds of accounting ratios but for the purposes of this book we will limit ourselves to just a small number of key ones. This is because our aim is largely to demonstrate the *principles* of ratio analysis. Furthermore, a large number of ratios is difficult to handle and it is better to concentrate on calculating just a few select ones. We will be dealing with ratio analysis in some detail in the next and subsequent sections.

Once sufficient data have been collected it is possible to plot various trends and to calculate some ratios. The exact number and type will depend upon the purpose of your

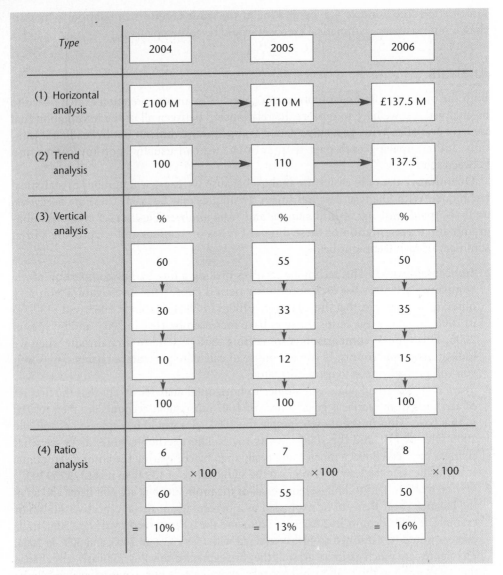

Figure 12.1 **Main analytical techniques used in interpreting accounts**

investigation and some of them may be specific to the industry and to the entity. For example, for a retailing organization you might want to calculate the sales personnel salaries as a proportion of sales revenue, and a hotel might want the restaurant turnover to be calculated as a proportion of the hotel's total turnover (i.e. sales).

Activity 12.2	State whether the following assertions are true or false:

(a) Ratio analysis is only one form of analysis that can be used in interpreting accounts.   *True/False*

(b) Ratio analysis aims to put the financial results of an entity into perspective. *True/False*

(c) Ratio analysis helps establish whether or not an entity is a going concern. *True/False*

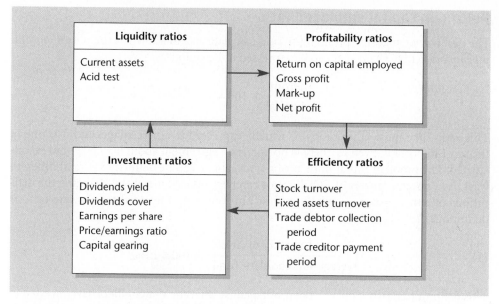

Figure 12.2 Classification of accounting ratios

Ratio analysis

We now begin our detailed study of accounting ratios. We will group them under four headings. The headings are: (a) profitability ratios; (b) liquidity ratios; (c) efficiency ratios; and (d) investment ratios. A diagrammatic representation of this classification and the names of the main ratios that we are going to consider is shown in Figure 12.2.

The classification that we have adopted is somewhat arbitrary and we have done so largely for convenience. Other accountants might use a different classification system and some of the ratios could be put in a different category. For example, we have included *earnings per share* as an investment ratio (a common practice) but it could equally be regarded as a profitability ratio.

Some of the ratios shown in Figure 12.2 would not be relevant for non-manufacturing, non-trading or not-for-profit entities, e.g. gross profit and mark-up ratios. Other ratios might need to be adapted to suit the particular circumstances of specialized types of entities. On the whole, however, most of the 15 ratios that we are going to consider will form the basis of any investigation regardless of the type of entity involved.

Profitability ratios

Users of accounts will want to know how much profit a business has made, and then to compare it with previous periods or with other entities. The absolute level of accounting profit will not be of much help, because it needs to be related to the size of the entity and how much capital it has got invested in it. There are four main profitability ratios. We examine them below.

Return on capital employed ratio

The best way of assessing profitability is to calculate a ratio known as the *return on capital employed* (ROCE) ratio. It can be expressed quite simply as:

$$\frac{\text{Profit}}{\text{Capital}} \times 100 = x \, \%$$

This ratio (like most other ratios) is usually expressed as a percentage, and it is one of the most important. Even so, there is no common agreement about how it should be calculated. The problem is that both 'profit' and 'capital' can be defined in several different ways. As a result, a variety of ROCE ratios can be produced merely by changing the definitions of either profit or capital. For our purposes you only need to be aware of four definitions of ROCE. They are as follows:

(1)
$$\frac{\text{Net profit before taxation}}{\text{Average shareholders' funds}} \times 100 = x \, \%$$

This definition measure the pre-tax profit against what the shareholders have invested in the entity. Use it if you want to know how profitable the entity has been as a whole.

(2)
$$\frac{\text{Net profit after taxation}}{\text{Average shareholders' funds}} \times 100 = x \, \%$$

This definition is similar to the previous one except that it measures post-tax profit against the shareholders' investment in the entity. Taxation is normally regarded as an *appropriation* of profit and not as an expense. The tax payable will be based on the profit for the year and an entity has no option other than to pay it. The distinction between tax as an appropriation and tax as a profit is blurred, and some accountants prefer to use this definition as a measure of overall profitability. However, bear in mind that the taxation charge in the accounts can be subject to various accounting adjustments, so you would have to be careful using this definition in comparing one entity with another entity.

(3)
$$\frac{\text{Net profit after taxation and preference dividends}}{\text{Average shareholders' funds less preference dividends}} \times 100 = x \, \%$$

This definition should be used if you want assess how profitable the entity has been from an *ordinary* shareholder's point of view. It measures how much profit could be distributed to ordinary shareholders as a proportion of what they have invested in the business.

(4)
$$\frac{\text{Profit before taxation and interest}}{\text{Average shareholders' funds plus long-terms loans}} \times 100 = x \, \%$$

This definition measures what profit has been earned in relation to what has been used to *finance* the entity in total. Interest is a cost of borrowing money, so it is added back to the profit made. Similarly, long-term loans are added to the shareholders' funds because that gives us the *total* financial investment in the entity. Use this definition if you want to know how profitable the entity has been in relation to what it has taken to finance it.

The above definitions use an *average* for shareholders' funds (usually a simple average, i.e. 2/(opening shareholders' funds plus closing shareholders' funds). The closing balance, however, is often used, especially if ROCE is being calculated over a three- to a five-year time period. This point also applies to a number of other accounting ratios.

Activity 12.3

There are many other ways of calculating ROCE other than the four listed above. In your notebook divide a page into two broad columns. In the left-hand column list all the various levels of profit that you would find in a published profit and loss account (e.g. operating profit). In the right-hand column list all the various levels or types of capital shown in a published balance sheet (e.g. total assets). Then try to relate each definition of profit to a compatible definition of capital.

Remember that what you are trying to do is to find how much profit (however defined) has been earned for the particular level or type of capital invested. So the numerator (profit) has got to be compatible with the denominator (the capital employed).

Gross profit ratio

The *gross profit ratio* enables us to judge how successful the entity has been at trading. It is calculated as follows:

$$\frac{\text{Gross profit}}{\text{Total sales revenue}} \times 100 = x\,\%$$

The gross profit ratio measures how much profit the entity has earned in relation to the amount of sales that it has made. The definition of gross profit does not usually cause any problems. Most entities adopt the definition which we have used in this book, namely sales less the cost of goods sold, and so meaningful comparisons can usually be made between different entities.

There are two points to note if you are using a company's set of *published* accounts:

1 The 'sales' figure may be described as 'turnover'.
2 The term 'cost of sales' is used in the 1985 Companies Act. It is, however, not defined and some companies may use a wider definition than the traditional one, i.e. [(opening stock + purchases) – closing stock]. Be wary, therefore, if you are making comparisons between different companies. This point also applies to the mark-up and the stock turnover ratios (see below).

Mark-up ratio

The gross profit ratio complements another main trading ratio: for convenience, we will refer to it as the *mark-up ratio*. The mark-up ratio is calculated as follows:

$$\frac{\text{Gross profit}}{\text{Cost of goods sold}} \times 100 = x\,\%$$

Mark-up ratios measure the amount of profit added to the cost of goods sold. The cost of goods sold plus profit equals the sales revenue. The mark-up may be reduced to stimulate extra sales activity, but this will have the effect of reducing the gross profit. However, if extra goods are sold, there may be a greater volume of sales and this will help to compensate for the reduction in the mark up on each unit.

Net profit ratio

Owners sometimes like to compare their net profit with the sales revenue. This can be expressed in the form of the *net profit ratio*, which is calculated as follows:

$$\frac{\text{Net profit before taxation}}{\text{Total sales revenue}} \times 100 = x \%$$

It is difficult to compare fairly the net profit ratio for different entities. Individual operating and financing arrangements vary so much that entities are bound to have different levels of expenditure, no matter how efficient one entity is compared with another. Thus it may only be realistic to use the net profit ratio in making *internal* comparisons. Over a period of time, a pattern may emerge, and it might then be possible to establish a trend. If you use the net profit ratio to make inter-company comparisons, make sure you allow for different circumstances.

In published accounts you might also want to substitute 'operating profit' or 'profit on ordinary activities before tax' for net profit.

We can now turn to our second main category of accounting ratios: liquidity ratios.

Liquidity ratios

Liquidity ratios measure the extent to which assets can be quickly turned into cash. In other words, they try to assess how much cash the entity has available in the short term (this usually means within the next twelve months). For example, it is easy to extract the total amount of trade debtors and trade creditors from the balance sheet, but are they too high? We cannot really tell until we put them into context. We can do this by calculating two liquidity ratios known as the *current assets ratio* and the *acid test ratio*.

Current assets ratio

The *current assets ratio* is calculated as follows:

$$\frac{\text{Current assets}}{\text{Current liabilities}}$$

It is usually expressed as a factor, e.g. 3 to 1, or 3 : 1, although you will sometimes see it expressed as a percentage (300% in our example, i.e. $\frac{3}{1} \times 100$).

In most circumstances we can expect that current assets will be in excess of current liabilities. The current assets ratio will then be at least 1 : 1. If this is not the case, the entity may not have sufficient liquid resources (i.e. current assets that can be quickly turned into cash) available to meet its immediate financial commitments. Some textbooks argue that the current assets ratio must be at least 2 : 1, but there is no evidence to suggest that this is a necessary relationship. Use it, therefore, only as a guide.

The term 'current' means receivable or payable within the next twelve months. The entity may not always have to settle all of its current debts within the next week or even the next month. Be careful before you assume that a factor of (say) 1 : 2 suggests that the company will be going into immediate liquidation. For example, tax and dividends may not have to be paid for some months after the year end. In the meantime, the company may receive regular receipts of cash from its debtors and it may be able to balance these against what it has to pay to its creditors. In other instances, some entities (such as supermarkets), do not do a great deal of trade on credit terms, and so it is not uncommon for them to have a current assets ratio of less than 2 : 1. This is not likely to be a problem for them, because they are probably collecting sufficient amounts of cash daily through the checkouts. In some cases, however, a current assets ratio of less than 2 : 1 may signify a serious financial position, especially if the current assets consist of a very high proportion of stocks. This leads us on to the second liquidity ratio: the acid test ratio.

Acid test ratio

It may not be easy to dispose of stocks in the short term as they cannot always be quickly turned into cash. In any case, the entity would then be depriving itself of those very assets that enable it to make a trading profit. It seems sensible, therefore, to see what would happen to the current ratio if stocks were not included in the definition of current assets. This ratio is called the acid test (or quick) ratio. It is calculated as follows:

$$\frac{\text{Current assets} - \text{stocks}}{\text{Current liabilities}}$$

Like the current ratio, the acid test ratio is usually expressed as a factor (or occasionally as a percentage). It is probably a better measure of the entity's immediate liquidity position than the current assets ratio because it may be difficult to dispose of the stocks in the short term. Do not assume, however, that if current assets less stocks are less than current liabilities, the entity's cash position is vulnerable. As we explained above, some of the current liabilities may not be due for payment for some months. Some textbooks suggest that the acid test ratio must be at least 1 : 1, but again there is no evidence to support this assertion, so once more use it only as a guide.

Activity 12.4

Fill in the blanks in the following equations.

(a) $\dfrac{\text{Current assets}}{\text{Current liabilities}} = \dfrac{£65\,500}{\underline{\hspace{3em}}} = 1.60$

(b) $\dfrac{\text{Current assets} - \underline{\hspace{4em}}}{\text{Current liabilities}}$

Efficiency ratios

Traditional accounting statements do not tell us how *efficiently* an entity has been managed, that is, how well its resources have been looked after. Profit may, to some extent, be used as a measure of efficiency but, as we have explained in earlier chapters, accounting profit is subject to a great many arbitrary adjustments, and it is not entirely reliable. What we need to do is to put whatever evidence we have into context, compare it with earlier accounting periods and, if possible, with other similar entities.

There are very many different types of ratios that we can use to measure the efficiency of an entity, but in this book we will cover only the more common ones.

Stock turnover ratio

The stock turnover ratio may be calculated as follows:

$$\frac{\textbf{Cost of goods sold}}{\textbf{Average stock}} = x \textbf{ times}$$

A simple average is usually used to calculate the average stock, i.e.

$$\frac{1}{2} \textbf{ (Opening stock + closing stock)}$$

The stock turnover ratio is normally expressed as a number (e.g. 5 or 10 times) and not as a percentage. Note that there are also various other ways in which this ratio can be calculated.

Sometimes the sales revenue is substituted for the cost of goods sold. It should not be used if it can be avoided because the sales contain a profit loading and this can cause the ratio to become distorted. Many accountants also prefer to substitute a more accurate average stock level than the simple average shown above (particularly if goods are purchased at irregular intervals). It is also quite common to compare the *closing* stock with the cost of sales in order to gain a clearer idea of the stock position at the end of the year. This may be misleading if the company's trade is seasonal, and the year end falls during a quiet period.

The greater the turnover of stock, the more efficient the entity would appear to be in purchasing and selling goods. A stock turnover of 2 times, for example, would suggest that the entity has about six months of sales in stock. In most circumstances, this would appear to be a high relative volume, whereas a stock turnover of (say) 12 would mean that the entity had only a month's normal sales in stock.

Fixed assets turnover ratio

Another important area to examine, from the point of view of efficiency, relates to fixed assets. Fixed assets (such as plant and machinery) enable the business to function more efficiently, and so a high level of fixed assets ought to generate more sales. We can check this by calculating a ratio known as the fixed asset turnover ratio. This may be done as follows:

$$\frac{\textbf{Total sales revenue}}{\textbf{Fixed assets at net book value}} = x$$

The fixed assets turnover ratio may also be expressed as a percentage. The more times that the fixed assets are covered by the sales revenue, the greater the recovery of the investment in fixed assets.

This ratio is really only useful if it is compared with previous periods or with other entities. In isolation, it does not mean very much. For example, is a turnover of 5 good and 4 poor? All we can suggest is that if the trend is upwards, then the investment in fixed assets is beginning to pay off, at least in terms of increased sales. Note also that the ratio can be strongly affected by the entity's depreciation policies. There is a strong argument, therefore, for taking the *gross* book value of the fixed assets, and not the *net* book value.

Activity 12.5

A company has a turnover of £4 000 000 for the year to 31 December 2004. At that date the gross book value of its fixed assets was £22 000 and the net book value £12 000. When measuring the efficiency with which its uses its fixed assets, is it more meaningful to use the gross book value in relation to turnover or the net book value? Give your reasons.

Gross book value ☐   Net book value ☐

Reason: _____

Trade debtor collection period ratio

Investing in fixed assets is all very well, but there is not much point in generating extra sales if the customers do not pay for them. Customers might be encouraged to buy more by a combination of lower selling prices and generous credit terms. If the debtors are slow at paying, the entity might find that it has run into cash flow problems. Thus it is important for it to watch the trade debtor position very carefully. We can check how successful it has been by calculating the *trade debtor collection period*. The ratio may be calculated as follows:

$$\frac{\text{Average trade debtors}}{\text{Total credit sales}} \times 365 \text{ days} = x \text{ days}$$

The average trade debtors are usually calculated by using a simple average [i.e ½ (opening trade debtors + closing trade debtors)]. The closing trade debtors figure is sometimes substituted for average trade debtors. This is acceptable, provided that the figure is representative of the overall period.

It is important to relate trade debtors to *credit* sales if possible, and so cash sales should be excluded from the calculation. The method shown above for calculating the ratio would relate the average trade debtors to x days' sales, but it would be possible to substitute weeks or months for days. It is not customary to express the ratio as a percentage.

An acceptable debtor collection period cannot be suggested, as much depends upon the type of trade in which the entity is engaged. Some entities expect settlement within 28 days of delivery of the goods or on immediate receipt of the invoice. Other entities might expect settlement within 28 days following the end of the month in which the goods were delivered. On average, this adds another 14 days (half a month) to the overall period of 28 days. If this is the case, a company would appear to be highly efficient in collecting its debts if the average debtor collection period was about 42 days (the United Kingdom experience is that the *median* debtor collection period is about 50 days).

Like most of the other ratios it is important to establish a trend. If the trend is upwards, then it might suggest that the company's credit control procedures have begun to weaken.

Activity 12.6	A company's sales for 2005 was £4452 million and its trade debtors for that year was £394 million. Assuming that all the sales were made on credit terms, do you think that its debtor collection was efficient?

Yes ☐   No ☐

Reason: _____

Trade creditor payment period

A similar ratio can be calculated for the trade creditor payment period. The formula is as follows:

$$\frac{\text{Average trade creditors}}{\text{Total credit purchases}} \times 365 \text{ days} = x \text{ days}$$

The average trade creditors amount would again be a simple average of the opening and closing balances, although it is quite common to use the closing trade creditors. The trade creditors must be related to credit purchases, and weeks or months may be substituted for the number of days. Like the trade debtor collection period, it is not usual to express it as a percentage. In published accounts you might have to calculate the purchases figure for yourself. The accounts should disclose the opening and closing stock figures and the cost of sales. By substituting them in the equation: [opening (stock + purchases) – less closing stock = cost of sales], you can calculate the purchases. Other expenses may have been included in cost of sales but unless these have been disclosed, you will just have to accept the cost of sales figure shown in the accounts.

An upward trend in the average level of trade creditors would suggest that the entity is having some difficulty in finding the cash to pay its creditors. Indeed, it might be a sign that it is running into financial difficulties.

Investment ratios

The various ratios examined in the previous sections are probably of interest to all users of accounts, such as creditors, employees and managers, as well as to shareholders. There are some other ratios that are primarily (although not exclusively) of interest to prospective investors. These ratios are known as *investment ratios*.

Dividend yield

The first investment ratio that you might find useful is the *dividend yield*. It usually applies to ordinary shareholders, and it may be calculated as follows:

$$\frac{\text{Dividend per share}}{\text{Market price per share}} \times 100 = x\,\%$$

The dividend yield measures the rate of return than an investor gets by comparing the cost of his shares with the dividend receivable (or paid). For example, if an investor buys 100 £1 ordinary shares at a market rate of 200p per share, and the dividend was 10p, his yield would be 5 per cent ($10/200 \times 100$). As far as the company is concerned, while he may have invested £200 ($100 \times £2$ per share), he will be registered as holding 100 shares at a nominal value of £1 each (100 shares $\times £1$). He would be entitled to a dividend of £10 ($10p \times 100$ shares), but from the shareholder's individual point of view, he will only be getting a return of 5 per cent, i.e. £10 for his £200 invested.

Dividend cover

Another useful investment ratio is called *dividend cover*. It is calculated as follows:

$$\text{Divided cover} = \frac{\text{Net profit after taxation and preference dividend}}{\text{Paid and proposed ordinary dividends}} = x\,\text{times}$$

This ratio shows the number of times that the ordinary dividend could be paid out of current earnings. The dividend is usually described as being *x* times covered by the earnings. Thus, if the dividend is covered twice, the company would be paying out half of its earnings as an ordinary dividend.

Earnings per share

Another important investment ratio is that known as *earnings per share* (EPS). This ratio enables us to put the profit into context, and to avoid looking at it in simple absolute terms. It is usually looked at from the ordinary shareholder's point of view. You may use the following formula to calculate what is called the *basic* earnings per share.

$$\frac{\text{Net profit (or loss) for the period less dividends and other appropriations in respect of non-equity shares}}{\text{Weighted average number of ordinary shares outstanding during the period}}$$

The above definition uses the term 'non-equity shares'. Preference shares are an example of such shares.

In published accounts you will sometimes see other definitions of EPS. The calculations involved in obtaining them are often highly complex. We recommend you to stick to the above definition.

EPS enables a fair comparison to be made between one year's earnings and another by relating the earnings to something tangible, i.e. the number of shares in issue.

Price/earnings ratio

Another common investment ratio is the *price/earnings ratio* (or P/E ratio). It is calculated as follows:

$$\frac{\text{Market price per share}}{\text{Earnings per share}} = x$$

The P/E ratio enables a comparison to be made between the earnings per share (as defined above) and the market price. It tells us that the market price is x times the earnings. It means that it would take x years before we recovered the market price paid for the shares out of the earnings (assuming that they remained at that level, and that they were all distributed). Thus the P/E ratio is a multiple of earnings. A high or low ratio can only be judged in relation to other companies in the same sector of the market.

A high P/E ratio means that the market thinks that the company's future is a good one. The shares are in demand and hence the price of the shares will be high. Of course, it would take you a long time to get your 'earnings' back (even if the company paid them all out as dividends) so the shares are not a good prospect from that point of view. The P/E is a signal that the company is likely to do well, and it will probably increase its earning and future dividends. Hence the shares are a good buy.

Activity 12.7	At 8 April 2003, Carphone Warehouse's P/E ratio was 37.7 while Homestyle's was 3.0. Both are grouped in the 'General retailer' sector of the economy. What do these P/E ratios tell you about the market's perception of these two companies? Write down a brief explanation in your notebook.

Capital gearing ratio

The last ratio that we are going to consider is the *capital gearing ratio*.

As we outlined in Chapter 6, companies are financed out of a mixture of share capital, retained profits and loans. Loans may be long-term (such as debentures), or short-term (such as credit given by trade creditors). In addition, the company may have set aside all sorts of provisions (e.g. for taxation) which it expects to meet sometime in the future. These may also be regarded as a type of loan. From an ordinary shareholder's point of view, even preference share capital can be classed as a loan, because the preference shareholders may have priority over ordinary shareholders both in respect of dividends and upon liquidation.

Therefore, if a company finances itself from a high level of loans, there is obviously a higher risk in investing in it. This arises for two main reasons:

1 The higher the loans, the more interest that the company will have to pay, and that may affect the company's ability to pay an ordinary dividend.
2 If the company cannot find the cash to repay its loans, the ordinary shareholders may not get any money back if the company goes into liquidation.

As far as item 1 is concerned, there will be no particular problem arising if profits are increasing, because the interest on its loans will become a smaller and smaller proportion of the total profit. But it could become a problem if profits are falling and the interest is having to be paid out of a continuing decline in profit. It might then be difficult to pay out any ordinary dividend.

There are many different ways of calculating capital gearing. The two most common methods are as follows:

(1)
$$\frac{\text{Loans}}{\text{Shareholders' funds} + \text{loans}} \times 100 = x\,\%$$

(2)
$$\frac{\text{Loans}}{\text{Shareholders' funds}} \times 100 = x\,\%$$

We prefer the first method because it is easier to understand if someone tells you that 'x% of the company has been financed by loans'. The second method tells us that the loans represent a certain proportion of the shareholders' funds (including preference shares). There is no reason why you should not use it if you wish.

We now have to decide what we mean by 'shareholders' funds' and 'loans'. It is not too difficult to define shareholders' funds. They include the following items:

- Ordinary share capital
- Preference share capital (see Note 1 below)
- Share premium account
- Capital reserves
- Revenue reserves
- Other reserves
- Profit and loss account.

Loans may (but will not necessarily) include the following items:

- Preference share capital (see Note 1 below)
- Debentures
- Loans
- Overdrafts
- Provisions
- Accruals
- Current liabilities
- Other amounts due for payment.

Notes:

1 Some accountants exclude preference share capital from shareholders' funds because they regard it as a type of loan.

2 In a complex group structure, you might also come across other items that could be classed as loans.

Company A has a capital gearing of 10%, Company B 40%, and Company C 60%. What effect will such gearing ratios have on each company's reported profits when they are either rising steeply or falling sharply?

Activity 12.8

Company	Effect on profits
A	
B	
C	

As we do not want to complicate the calculation of the ratio by getting involved in too much technical detail, we recommend that you go for a fairly straightforward approach and adopt the following definition of capital gearing:

$$\frac{\text{Preference shares} + \text{long-term loans}}{\text{Shareholders' funds} + \text{long-term loans}} \times 100\% = x\%$$

A company that has financed itself out of a high proportion of loans (e.g. in the form of a combination of preference shares and long-term loans) is known as a highly geared company. Conversely, a company with a low level of loans is regarded as being low-geared. Note that high and low in this context are relative terms. As we indicated above, a highly-geared company is potentially a higher risk investment, as it has to earn sufficient profit to cover the interest payments and the preference dividend before it can pay out any ordinary dividend. This should not be a problem when profits are rising, but if they are falling, then they may not be sufficient to cover even the preference dividend.

We have now defined 15 common accounting ratios. There are many others that could also have been included. However, the 15 selected are enough for you to be able to interpret a set of accounts. If the ratios are used in isolation, many of them are not particularly helpful. You will find that as part of a detailed analysis they are invaluable.

For your convenience a summary of the above ratios is included in an Appendix at the end of this chapter.

An illustrative example

In this section, we use the ratios outlined above to interpret a set of accounts. As we suggested earlier, in order to establish a reasonable trend, we need to adopt a three- to a five-year period. It would also be useful to compare our results with the ratios obtained from similar entities (there are some commercial organizations that provide such comparative data). However, for our purposes, such a long period would obscure the basic procedures that we want to illustrate and it would also be impractical.

We will use A.G. Barr plc's accounts for the year ended 27 January 2002. The details are shown in Example 12.1

Example 12.1	**Interpreting company accounts**

You are provided with the following set of amended published accounts relating to A.G. Barr plc, the makers of the well known soft drink Irn-Bru.

A.G. Barr plc. and its Subsidiary Companies
Consolidated Profit and Loss Accounts
for the year ended 27 January 2001 and 26 January 2002

		2001	2002
		£000	£000
Turnover		111,878	116,261
Cost of goods sold:			
Opening stock	c/f	9,027	10,800

Example 12.1
continued

		2001	2002
		£000	£000
	b/f	9,027	10,800
Purchases [see Additional information (1)]		59,772	63,768
		68,799	74,568
Closing stock		(10,800)	(11,536)
Cost of sales		(57,999)	(63,032)
Gross profit		53,879	53,229
Net operating expenses		(40,182)	(42,742)
Operating profit		13,697	10,487
Interest received		311	268
Interest paid		(86)	(15)
Profit on ordinary activities before tax		13,922	10,740
Tax on profit on ordinary activities		(4,159)	(3,254)
Profit on ordinary activities after tax		9,763	7,486
Dividends		(4,200)	(4,202)
Retained profit for the year		5,563	3,284
Basic earnings per share		51.86p	39.90p

Balance sheets as at 27 January 2001 and 26 January 2002

	2001		2002	
	£000	£000	£000	£000
Fixed assets				
Tangible assets	89,957		96,617	
Depreciation	(50,855)	39,102	(54,037)	42,580
Investments in subsidiaries and associated undertaking		100		–
		39,202		42,580
Current assets				
Stocks	10,800		11,536	
Debtors	19,834		21,078	
Investment	2,499		2,623	
Cash at bank	11,199	44,332	8,265	43,502
Creditors: Amounts falling due within one year				
Unpresented cheques	(5,193)		(4,827)	
Trade creditors	(2,823)		(2,735)	
Current corporation tax	(2,830)		(1,716)	
Other taxes and social security costs	(1,646)		(1,784)	
Accruals	(9,496)		(10,101)	
Proposed dividend	(2,771)		(2,773)	
Amounts due to subsidiary companies	–		–	
Bank overdraft	(1)		(177)	
Hire purchase creditor	(304)	(25,064)	–	(24,113)
Net current assets		19,268		19,389
Total assets less current liabilities	c/f	58,470		61,969

Example 12.1
continued

	b/f	2001 £000	2001 £000	2002 £000	2002 £000
Provision for liabilities and charges			58,470		61,969
Deferred credit	(667)			(645)	
Deferred tax	(4,744)		(5,411)	(4,931)	(5,576)
			53,059		56,393
Capital and reserves					
Called-up share capital			4,861		4,865
Share premium account			859		905
Profit and loss account			47,339		50,623
			53,059		56,393

Cash Flow Statement for the year ended 27 January 2001 and 26 January 2002

	2001 £000	2001 £000	2002 £000	2002 £000
Net cash inflow from operating activities		16,932		12,989
Returns on investment and servicing of finance				
Interest received	311		268	
Interest paid	(9)		(11)	
Interest element on hire purchase paid	(77)		(4)	
Net cash inflow from returns on investments and servicing of finance		225		253
Tax				
Corporation tax paid		(3,821)		(4,181)
Capital expenditure and financial investment				
Purchase of tangible fixed assets	(7,115)		(7,750)	
Sale of tangible fixed assets	188	(6,927)	258	
				(7,492)
Acquisitions and disposals				
Investment in subsidiary	–		(105)	
Net overdraft acquired with subsidiary	–		(90)	
		–		(195)
		6,409		1,374
Dividends paid		(3,811)		(4,200)
	c/f	2,598		(2,826)

Example 12.1
continued

	b/f	2001		2002	
		£000	£000	£000	£000
Financing			2,598		(2,826)
Issue of share capital		–		50	
Capital element of hire purchase repaid		(1,152)		(304)	
Loans repaid		–		(30)	
			(1,152)		(284)
(Decrease)/Increase in cash			1,446		(3,110)

Additional information:

1 The purchases were not disclosed in the accounts so they have had to be calculated. We have used the formula (opening stock plus purchases) less closing stock equals cost of goods sold. However, the purchases are probably overstated because they almost certainly include production costs. No information about production costs is disclosed in the accounts.

2 Some changes have been made to the presentation of the accounts in order to make the question easier to answer. Such changes are not significant.

3 Balances at 30 January 2000:
   Shareholders' funds £50,701,000.
   Trade debtors £13,014,000 (2001: £15,147,000; 2002: £17,344)
   Trade creditors £3,512,000.

4 The company's capital consists of ordinary shares of 25p each.

5 The market value of the shares at the respective year end was 411.00p (January 2001) and 461.00p (January 2002).

Required:

Calculate appropriate profitability, liquidity, efficiency and investment ratios for the two financial years 2001 and 2002.

Significant accounting ratios

Answer to
Example 12.1

A.G. Barr plc

Profitability ratios   2001   2002

Return on capital employed (ROCE):

$$\frac{\text{Profit on ordinary activities before taxation}}{\text{Average shareholders' funds}} \times 100$$

$$\frac{13\,922}{\frac{1}{2}(50\,701 + 53\,059)} \times 100$$

$$= 26.8\%$$

$$\frac{10\,740}{\frac{1}{2}(53\,059 + 56\,393)} \times 100$$

$$= 19.6\%$$

Return on capital employed:

$$\frac{\text{Profit on ordinary activities after taxation}}{\text{Average shareholders' funds}} \times 100$$

$$\frac{9763}{\frac{1}{2}(50\,701 + 53\,059)} \times 100$$

$$= 18.8\%$$

$$\frac{7486}{\frac{1}{2}(53\,059 + 56\,393)} \times 100$$

$$= 13.7\%$$

Note: Other ROCE ratios not relevant

Answer to Example 12.1 continued

Profitability ratios continued	*2001*	*2002*
Gross profit:		

Gross profit:

$$\frac{\text{Gross profit}}{\text{Turnover}} \times 100 \qquad \frac{53879}{111878} \times 100 \qquad \frac{53229}{116261} \times 100$$

$$= 48.2\% \qquad\qquad = 45.8\%$$

Mark-up:

$$\frac{\text{Gross profit}}{\text{Cost of sales}} \times 100 \qquad \frac{53879}{57999} \times 100 \qquad \frac{53229}{63032} \times 100$$

$$= 92.9\% \qquad\qquad = 84.4\%$$

Operating profit:

$$\frac{\text{Operating profit}}{\text{Turnover}} \times 100 \qquad \frac{13697}{111878} \times 100 \qquad \frac{10487}{116261} \times 100$$

$$= 12.2\% \qquad\qquad = 9.0\%$$

Liquidity ratios	*2001*	*2002*

Current assets:

$$\frac{\text{Current assets}}{\text{Current liabilities}} \qquad \frac{44332}{25064} \qquad \frac{43502}{24113}$$

$$= 1.8 \text{ to } 1 \qquad\qquad = 1.8 \text{ to } 1$$

Acid test:

$$\frac{\text{Current assets} - \text{stocks}}{\text{Current liabilities}} \qquad \frac{44332 - 10800}{25064} \qquad \frac{43502 - 11536}{24113}$$

$$= 1.3 \text{ to } 1 \qquad\qquad = 1.3 \text{ to } 1$$

Efficiency ratios	*2001*	*2002*

Stock turnover:

$$\frac{\text{Cost of sales}}{\text{Average stock}} \qquad \frac{57999}{\tfrac{1}{2}(9027 + 10800)} \qquad \frac{63032}{\tfrac{1}{2}(10800 + 11536)}$$

$$= 5.9 \text{ times} \qquad\qquad = 5.6 \text{ times}$$

Fixed assets turnover:

$$\frac{\text{Turnover}}{\text{Tangible fixed assets at net book value}} \qquad \frac{111878}{39102} \qquad \frac{116261}{42580}$$

$$= 2.9 \text{ times} \qquad\qquad = 2.7 \text{ times}$$

Efficiency ratios continued   *2001*   *2002*

Trade debtor collection period:

$$\frac{\text{Average trade debtors}}{\text{Turnover}} \times 365 \qquad \frac{\frac{1}{2}(13\,014 + 15\,147)}{111\,878} \times 365 \qquad \frac{\frac{1}{2}(15\,147 + 17\,344)}{116\,261} \times 365$$

$$= 46 \text{ days} \qquad\qquad = 51 \text{ days}$$

Trade creditor payment period:

$$\frac{\text{Average trade creditors}}{\text{Purchases}} \times 365 \qquad \frac{\frac{1}{2}(3\,512 + 2\,823)}{59\,772} \times 365 \qquad \frac{\frac{1}{2}(2\,823 + 2\,735)}{63\,768} \times 365$$

$$= 20 \text{ days} \qquad\qquad = 16 \text{ days}$$

Investment ratios   *2001*   *2002*

Dividend per share:

$$\frac{\text{Dividend}}{\text{Ordinary share capital}} \qquad \frac{4\,200 \times 100}{4\,861 \times 4} \qquad \frac{4\,202 \times 100}{4\,865 \times 4}$$

$$= 21.6p \qquad\qquad = 21.6p$$

Dividend yield:

$$\frac{\text{Dividend per share}}{\text{Market price per share}} \times 100 \qquad \frac{21.6}{411.00} \times 100 \qquad \frac{21.6}{461.00} \times 100$$

$$= 5.3\% \qquad\qquad = 4.7\%$$

Dividend cover:
Not relevant

Basic earnings per share:
(EPS) Given $= 51.86p$ $= 39.90p$

Price/earnings ratio:

$$\frac{\text{Market price per share}}{\text{Earnings per share}} \qquad \frac{411.00}{51.86} \qquad \frac{461.00}{39.90}$$

$$= 7.9 \qquad\qquad = 11.6$$

Capital gearing:
Not relevant

Note: The company has no preference shares or long-term borrowings.

Have a go at doing Example 12.1 without looking at the answer.   *Activity 12.9*

Interpretation guide

We have now reached the stage where we have explained *what* is meant by the 'interpretation of accounts'. Earlier in the chapter we outlined the basic procedure in undertaking such an analysis and then we introduced you briefly to three common techniques used in such an exercise, viz. horizontal analysis, trend analysis and vertical analysis. We also dealt with, in some depth, a fourth technique – ratio analysis. This was followed by an example of how to calculate some accounting ratios using an actual set of accounts.

It is now time for us to explain in a little more detail *how* to use all the data and information that you have obtained and the indicators that you have calculated in *interpreting* a set of accounts. We will do so using a series of steps. This will involve going over some of the procedures that we have already outlined. For convenience we will assume that we are going to interpret a *company's* financial performance.

Step 1: undertake a survey of the general business environment

The company cannot prosper (or otherwise) in isolation. It will be affected by the general economic, financial, political and social environment in which it operates both nationally and internationally. What are the prospects for the *countries* in which it operates? What are the prospects for the *industry* it is involved in? Summarize any information that has a bearing on the company's future.

Step 2: obtain as much information as you can about the company

You should obtain information produced by the company itself (e.g. its annual report and accounts, trade circulars, press releases) as well as anything available externally such as analysts' reports, newspaper reports and trade circulars. Extract and summarize that information that gives you an indication of the company's general performance and future prospects.

Step 3: conduct a detailed analysis of the company's financial results

The main source of information that you will use for this step is the company's annual report and accounts. As indicated earlier we recommend that you look at a three- to a five-year period. This step involves a number of sub-steps:

(a) *Read through the reports section of the annual report and accounts.* Make a note of any significant events that have affected the company's financial results.
(b) *Go through the financial accounts.* Work your way through the profit and loss account, the balance sheet and the cash flow on a line-by-line basis in each set of accounts Consult the 'notes to the accounts' if you are not sure what some of the items mean. Compare the current year's results with the previous year's results. In effect you are undertaking a horizontal analysis. Make a note of any significant changes, e.g. if turnover has gone up and operating profit has gone down.
(c) *Index the financial data.* This sub-step is difficult if you are working across four or five sets of accounts. It will not be easy to compare one year with the previous year. The best way to get over this problem is to index all the period information using the first year as base 100. You can the use trend analysis to assess the results. This will make it easier to spot significant changes or movements. You might also attempt a

vertical analysis but remember that you will probably have to establish a 'grand total' for both the profit and loss account and the balance sheet. A 'grand total' is either a total of all the debit or credit entries in the profit and loss account, and a total of either all the assets or liabilities plus the capital in the balance sheet.

(d) *Calculate some accounting ratios.* This may appear to be a major undertaking. However, if you restrict the number of ratios (20 is probably enough) it should not take too long even if you are using a five-year period. Use a prepared sheet with the ratios and the formulas in the left-hand column with additional columns for each year of the study for your workings. Remember that some of the ratios covered in this chapter will not necessarily be relevant for all types of entities. For example, stock turnover and trade creditor payment periods will probably not need to be calculated for non-manufacturing, not-trading and not-for-profit entities.

Step 4: work out what has happened

This is the most difficult step. Steps 1 to 3 will already have given you some indication of the main changes that have taken place over the period. Step 4 will help you to put that information into context. For example, the trade debtors may have increased substantially in absolute terms in one year but this could be proportionate to the increase in sales. But do the ratios throw up any unusual or inconsistent trends? What is the relationship between (say) the profitability and the efficiency ratios? Do they move in the same direction? Paradoxically, is the company becoming either more efficient and less profitable or less efficient and more profitable. What could be causing such a relationship?

It is vitally important that you observe very closely the liquidity indicators. The cash flow statements will already give you a clear indication of the company's liquidity position and this can be confirmed by examining the liquidity ratios. However, do not assume that a company is about to go into liquidation if its current assets are less than its current liabilities. You need to be aware of the *timing* when cash will be received and when it will be paid out. In any case, you are probably doing your investigation on a historical basis and if the company was about to go into liquidation at the time that the accounts were prepared, it will probably already have done so.

Finally, have a look at the investment ratios. Some of these incorporate data external to the firm. Thus the P/E ratio will tell you what the market thinks of the company's future.

Step 5: write up your results

This step will be necessary if you have to report to someone else. But it is a good idea to do so even if it is not necessary. You will find that by having to justify your analysis of a company's performance in writing, your ideas will become sharper and more focused.

You will need to incorporate all the information that you have obtained. Besides its overall financial performance, you will need to assess the general business and industrial environment, the company's potential markets, its products, its capital investment programme, the ability and experience of its management, the skill of its employees, and the industrial relations record. By conducting such a detailed analysis you will have produced some verifiable evidence to support your conclusions but you will also have developed an innate 'feel' for what its future may be like. Only time will tell whether you were right.

Drawing conclusions

Space does not permit us to conduct a detailed investigation of a company's performance using the step-by-step approach as described above. What we can do is to use Example 12.1 to draw together some conclusions from the ratios that we calculated in answering that example. We do so in Example 12.2.

Example 12.2

Using Barr's accounts as reproduced earlier in the chapter, comment on the financial results of the company in 2002 compared with 2001.

Answer to Example 12.2

A. G. Barr plc
Comparison of the 2001 and 2002 financial results

In order to explore the relationship between the various ratios we will adopt the headings we have used throughout the chapter, viz. profitability, liquidity, efficiency and investment.

Profitability
The company's return on capital employed before taxation is taken into account has dropped from 26.8% in 2001 to 19.6% in 2002. There has been a similar fall when ROCE is calculated on an after-tax basis (from 18.8% to 13.7%). Although the turnover has increased (from £111,878,000 to £116,261,000, or by 3.9%) the gross profit ratio has fallen from 48.2% to 45.8%. This was probably caused by a reduction in the mark-up (from 92.9% to 84.4%). The reduction in ROCE would appear, therefore, to have been caused by a reduction in the mark-up added to the cost of goods sold.

The net operating expenses also increased from £40,182,000 to just under £42,742,000, an increase of 6.4%. This again helped to reduce the pre-tax operating profit from £13,697,000 in 2001 to £10,487,000 in 2002 , a reduction of 23.4%.

It is clear, therefore, that Barr suffered a fairly large reduction in its operating profit for 2002 compared with the previous year. It would appear that this was largely due to a reduction in its margins. The mark-up was probably cut in order to maintain its turnover. If this were the case, the move was successful because turnover did increase by over £4 million. Unfortunately, the increase in turnover was not sufficient to cover the reduction in the mark-up.

Liquidity
Barr's current assets were more than sufficient to cover its current liabilities by a factor of 1.8 to 1 in both years. Even when stock are excluded from current assets, the factor only dropped to 1.3 to 1, again for both years. An inspection of the creditors falling due within one year shows that the largest item is for accruals (£9,496,000 at the end of 2001 and £10,101,000 for 2002).

After allowing for the small overdraft Barr had £11,198,000 of cash at the bank at the end of 2001 and £8,088,000 at the end of 2002, a reduction of £3,110,000 (or 27.8%), so it would appear to have had enough cash at the year end to pay for the accruals. However, there is an item for 'unpresented cheques' for both years in 'creditors: amounts falling due within one year' (£5,193,000 for 2001 and £4,827,000 for 2002). It is unusual to show unpresented cheques in this way. They are normally deducted from the bank balance. If this were done the cash at bank at the end of 2001 and 2002 would be £6,005,000 and £3,261,000 respectively, a fall of 45.7%. This was not sufficient to cover the accruals in either 2001 or 2002. In addition, the tax and the proposed dividend would probably also be due for payment shortly after each year end. Nevertheless, it may well be that Barr does a considerable amount of business on cash terms because there does not appear to be any evidence that it has had any major cash flow problems.

Barr does appear to have invested heavily in fixed assets. The cash flow statement shows that £7,750,000 was spent on the purchase of tangible fixed assets in 2002 and £7,115,000 in 2001. This clearly had a marked effect on cash flow in both years.

Efficiency
The efficiency ratios for stock turnover, fixed asset turnover and the trade debtor collection period are all slightly down on the 2001 results. On average, the company takes about seven weeks to collect its trade debtors. The average trade creditor payment period appears to have dropped from 20 days to 16 days. This is a very short period. However, as noted in the additional information, the purchases probably include production costs. If these costs were taken out of purchases we would have a more realistic result for the trade creditor payment period.

Investment
The dividend has been held steady in both years (21.6p per share) and the yield is reasonable at about 5%. The fall in profitability in 2002 has affected the earnings per share (down from 51.86p to 39.90p). The P/E ratio has increased (from 8.2 to 12.0). Despite Barr's drop in profitability, therefore, the market must sense that the company's prospects are good.

The company is largely financed out of retained profits: £47,339,000 out of £53,339,000 (89.2%) in 2001 and £50,623,000 out of £56,393,000 (89.8%) in 2002. Clearly, the company has had a policy for some time of retaining most of its earnings and of only paying a small proportion of them in dividends. There could, therefore, be pressure from the shareholders to increase the level of dividends paid out but obviously the impact on cash flow would have to be considered very seriously.

Summary
Barr was not as profitable in 2002 as it had been in 2001. Its turnover increased but its gross profit and its operating profit were lower. Nevertheless, it continued to make a healthy gross profit and a reasonable operating one. Its return on capital employed dropped but it was still at a fairly high level.

The indicators suggest that its liquidity position could be a cause for concern although the position in 2002 was little different from that of 2001. Clearly, the company has to balance the timing of its cash receipts carefully against its cash payments.

In terms of efficiency there was a slight downward trend for most of the indicators for 2002 compared with 2001. The exception was for the trade creditors payment period. This indicator is not reliable as the purchases probably include production costs.

From an investment point of view, the investment indicators reflect a weaker performance during the year but the market appears to have given it a vote of confidence.

Answer to Example 12.2

| Activity 12.10 | Write up your own conclusions about Barr's performance in 2002 compared with 2001. Insofar as you can, use the step-by-step approach described above, but do not refer to the outline answer. |

❗ Questions non-accountants should ask

As far as this chapter is concerned, there are two situations in which you might find yourself: (1) a set of financial accounts will have been interpreted for you; and (2) you might have to do it for yourself. In the first situation you might like to ask the person who has prepared the report the following questions. In the second situation you could ask yourself. The idea is to give you confidence about the information that you have used and the results that you have obtained in interpreting a set of financial accounts.

● How reliable is the basic accounting information underpinning this report?

● Have consistent accounting policies been adopted throughout the period covered?

● If not, has each year's results been adjusted on to the same accounting basis?

● Were there any unusual items in any year that may have distorted a comparative analysis?

● Was the rate of inflation significant in any year covered by the report?

● If so, should the basic accounting data be adjusted to allow for it?

● What are the three of four most significant changes in these accounts during the period they cover?

● Are there any apparent causal links between them, such as greater efficiency resulting in a higher level of profitability or higher profits causing cash flow problems?

● What are the most important factors that this report tells me about the entity's progress during the period in question and its prospects for the future?

Conclusion

This chapter has explained how you can examine the financial performance of an entity over a designated period of time (preferably over a three- to five-year period). If a detailed examination is required it may be necessary to examine the general business environment and the economic sector in which the entity operates. Much information will also be collected about the entity itself. One of the main sources will be its annual report and accounts (especially if it is a company).

While a great deal of information is disclosed in the annual accounts, it has to be put into context. The absolute numbers used in the accounts are difficult to absorb because they only relate to other similar items. Hence the accounts need to be subjected to a series of analyses. There are four main such types: (1) horizontal analysis, which involves a line-by-line inspection across the various time periods; (2) trend analysis, which involves indexing the basic accounting data to a base of 100; (3) vertical analysis, which involves converting each year's data into percentages; and (4) ratio analysis, which involves comparing one item with another and expressing it as a percentage or as some other factor.

These four types of analyses are based on accounting data which itself is subject to a number of reservations and these have to be taken into account in assessing the signals given by the analyses.

Ratio analysis is the most important type of analysis and this chapter has concentrated on it. It has been suggested that accounting ratios can be broken down into four categories: (1) profitability ratios, which measure how profitable an entity has been; (2) liquidity ratios, which measure the cash position of the entity; (3) efficiency ratios, which show how well the entity has used its resources during the period; and (4) investment ratios, which are used when considering the investment potential of an entity.

However, all of the four types of ratios are interconnected. It is likely, for example, that a highly efficient company is also a profitable one but it is possible that its success has caused it to run into cash flow problems. The market will assess its future performance and hence its investment potential. Hence the investment ratios should reflect satisfactory profitability indicators and/or any possible liquidity problems. Even though all the indicators are satisfactory, the investment indicators may be weak – possibly because the market thinks that the company has passed its peak.

The ratios should only be regarded as signposts. Calculating any number of them is not the same as *interpreting* a set of accounts. Rather, the ratios are used to understand and to explain what *has* happened, and to predict what *will* happen. Think of going on a journey. You see a number of signposts. They give you the direction and the mileage to certain places but you still have to get there. Ratios do the same. They point you in a certain direction. It is up to you to make the journey.

Key points

1   The interpretation of accounts involves examining financial accounts in some detail so as to be able to explain what has happened and to predict what is likely to happen.

2   The examination can be undertaken by using a number of techniques, such as horizontal analysis, trend analysis, vertical analysis and ratio analysis.

3   Ratio analysis is a common method of interpreting accounts. It involves comparing one item in the accounts with another closely related item. Ratios are normally expressed in the form of a percentage or a factor. There are literally hundreds of recognized accounting ratios (the main ones are included in an Appendix at the end of the chapter), as well as those that relate only to specific industries.

4   Not all of the ratios covered in this chapter will be relevant for non-manufacturing, non-trading or not-for-profit entities. It is necessary to be selective in your choice of ratios.

5   When one item is related to another item in the form of a ratio, be careful to make sure that there is a close and logical correlation between the two items.

6   In the case of some ratios, different definitions can be adopted. This applies particularly to ROCE and capital gearing. In other cases, sometimes only year-end

*Key points
continued*

balances are used and not an annual average. This applies especially to ratios relating to stocks, debtors and creditors.

7 Assessing trends and calculating ratios is not the same as interpreting a set of financial accounts. Interpretation involves using a wide range of information sources as well as the incorporation of various types of analyses into a cohesive appraisal of an entity's past performance and its future prospects.

Check your learning

The answers to these questions may be found within the text.

1 What is meant by the term 'interpretation of accounts'?

2 Give three reasons why the absolute data shown in financial accounts may need to be interpreted.

3 List the users of accounts and suggest one piece of information that each user group may require from a set of financial accounts.

4 What is the difference between (a) horizontal analysis; and (b) trend analysis?

5 What is vertical analysis?

6 What is (a) a ratio; and (b) ratio analysis?

7 What four main categories may be used for classifying accounting ratios?

8 What does ROCE mean and how may it be calculated?

9 What is the difference between the gross profit ratio and the mark-up ratio?

10 Why might it be misleading to compare the net profit ratio of one entity with that of another entity?

11 Why is liquidity important, and what two ratios may be used for assessing it?

12 How would you assess whether stock turnover and fixed asset turnover ratios were good or bad?

13 What is meant by the 'trade debtor collection period' and is a 60-day period worrying?

14 What is meant by the 'trade creditor payment period' and is a 100-day period worrying?

15 Which two investment ratios take into account market prices?

16 Explain why there may be a difference between the dividend payable and its yield.

17 What is meant by the abbreviation 'EPS' and where might you find it in a set of published accounts?

18 What is the P/E ratio, and what is its importance?

19 What is capital gearing and how might it be calculated?

20 What is a possible link between the following ratios: (a) profitability and efficiency; (b) profitability and liquidity; (c) profitability and investment; and (d) efficiency and liquidity?

21 Outline the main steps you would take if you were asked to appraise the financial performance of a company using its annual report and accounts.

News story quiz

Remember the news story at the beginning of this chapter? Go back to that story and re-read it before answering the following questions.

An important efficiency ratio is that known as the *trade debtor collection period*. This article shows that some companies are very slow at paying their bills. According to the Chairman of the Federation of Small Businesses, the delay in settling bills is a significant factor in business failures.

Questions

1 Given that published accounts do not normally show the amount of credit sales, in what way are the figures disclosed in the article likely to be distorted?

2 Is 46 days a reasonable period of time for a company to settle its debts?

3 What factors may be involved in a company being one of the 'worst payers'?
The answers to questions marked with an asterisk may be found in Appendix 4.

Tutorial questions

12.1 'Accounting ratios are only as good as the data on which they are based.' Discuss.

12.2 How far do you accept the argument that the return on capital employed ratio can give a misleading impression of an entity's profitability?

12.3 Is ratio analysis useful in understanding how an entity has performed?

12.4* The following information has been extracted from the books of account of Betty for the year to 31 January 2008:

Trading and profit and loss account for the year to 31 January 2008

	£000	£000
Sales (all credit)		100
Less: Cost of goods sold:		
Opening stock	15	
Purchases	65	
	80	
Less: Closing stock	10	70
Gross profit		30
Administrative expenses		16
Net profit		14

Balance sheet at 31 January 2008

	£000	£000
Fixed assets (net book value)		29
Current assets		
Stock	10	
Trade debtors	12	
Cash	3	
Less: Current liabilities	25	
Trade creditors	6	19
		48
Financed by:		
Capital at 1 February 2007		40
Add: Net profit	14	
Less: Drawings	6	8
		48

Required:
Calculate the following accounting ratios:
1 gross profit;
2 net profit;
3 return on capital employed;
4 current ratio;
5 acid test;
6 stock turnover; and
7 debtor collection period.

12.5*   You are presented with the following summarized accounts:

James Ltd
Profit and loss account for the year to 28 February 2009

	£000
Sales (all credit)	1 200
Cost of sales	600
Gross profit	600
Administrative expenses	(500)
Debenture interest payable	(10)
Profit on ordinary activities	90
Taxation	(30)
	60
Dividends	(40)
Retained profit for the year	20

James Ltd
Balance sheet at 28 February 2009

	£000	£000	£000
Fixed assets (net book value)			685
Current assets			
Stock		75	
Trade debtors		200	
		275	
Less: Current liabilities			
Trade creditors	160		
Bank overdraft	10		
Taxation	30		
Proposed dividend	40	240	35
			720
Capital and reserves			
Ordinary share capital			600
Profit and loss account			20
Shareholders' funds			620
Loans:			
10% debentures			100
			720

Required:

Calculate the following accounting ratios:

1 return on capital employed;
2 gross profit;
3 mark up;
4 net profit;
5 acid test;
6 fixed assets turnover;
7 debtor collection period; and
8 capital gearing.

12.6   You are presented with the following information relating to three companies:

Profit and loss accounts for the year to 31 March 2006

	Mark Limited £000	Luke Limited £000	John Limited £000
Profit before tax	64	22	55

Balance sheet (extracts) at 31 March 2006

	Mark Limited £000	Luke Limited £000	John Limited £000
Capital and reserves			
Ordinary share capital of £1 each	100	177	60
Cumulative 15% preference shares of £1 each	–	20	10
Share premium account	–	70	20
Profit and loss account	150	60	200
Shareholders' funds	250	327	290
Loans			
10% debentures	–	–	100
	250	327	390

Required:
Calculate the following accounting ratios:
1   return on capital employed; and
2   capital gearing.

12.7   The following information relates to Helena Limited:

Trading account year to 30 April

	2004 £000	2005 £000	2006 £000	2007 £000	2008 £000	2009 £000
Sales (all credit)	–	130	150	190	210	320
Less: Cost of goods sold:						
Opening stock	–	20	30	30	35	40
Purchases (all in credit terms)	–	110	110	135	145	305
	–	130	140	165	180	345
Less: Closing stock	–	30	30	35	40	100
	–	100	110	130	140	245
Gross profit	–	30	40	60	70	75
Trade debtors at 30 April	40	45	40	70	100	150
Trade creditors at 30 April	20	20	25	25	30	60

Required:
Calculate the following accounting ratios for each of the five years from 30 April 2005 to 2009 inclusive:
1 gross profit;
2 mark-up;
3 stock turnover;
4 trade debtor collection period; and
5 trade creditor payment period.

12.8 You are presented with the following information relating to Hedge public limited company for the year to 31 May 2005:
(a) The company has an issued and fully paid share capital of £500 000 ordinary shares of £1 each. There are no preference shares.
(b) The market price of the shares at 31 May 2005 was £3.50.
(c) The net profit after taxation for the year to 31 May 2005 was £70 000.
(d) The directors are proposing a dividend of 7p per share for the year to 31 May 2005.

Required:
Calculate the following accounting ratios:
1 dividend yield;
2 dividend cover;
3 earnings per share; and
4 price/earnings ratio.

12.9 The following information relates to Style Limited for the two years to 30 June 2005 and 2006 respectively:

Trading and profit and loss accounts for the years

	2005		2006	
	£000	£000	£000	£000
Sales (all credit)		1 500		1 900
Less: Cost of goods sold:				
Opening stock	80		100	
Purchases (all on credit terms)	995		1 400	
	1 075		1 500	
	100	975	200	1 300
Gross profit		525		600
Less: Expenses		250		350
Net profit		275		250

Balance sheet at 30 June

	2005		2006	
	£000	£000	£000	£000
Fixed assets (net book value)		580		460
Current assets				
Stock	100		200	
Trade debtors	375		800	
Bank	25		–	
	500		1 000	
Less: Current liabilities				
Bank overdraft	–		10	
Trade creditors	80		200	
	80	420	210	790
		1 000		1 250
Capital and reserves				
Ordinary share capital		900		900
Profit and loss account		100		350
Shareholders' funds		1 000		1 250

Required:
(a) Calculate the following accounting ratios for the two years 2005 and 2006
   respectively:
   1 gross profit;
   2 mark-up;
   3 net profit;
   4 return on capital employed;
   5 stock turnover;
   6 current ratio;
   7 acid test;
   8 trade debtor collection period; and
   9 trade creditor payment period.
(b) Comment upon the company's performance for the year to 30 June 2006.

*Further practice questions, study material and links to relevant sites on the World Wide
Web can be found on the website that accompanies this book. The site can be found at*
www.booksites.net/dyson

Appendix Summary of the main ratios

Profitability ratios

$$\text{ROCE} = \frac{\text{Net profit before taxation}}{\text{Average shareholders' funds}} \times 100$$

$$\text{ROCE} = \frac{\text{Net profit after taxation}}{\text{Average shareholders' funds}} \times 100$$

$$\text{ROCE} = \frac{\text{Net profit after taxation and preference dividends}}{\text{Average shareholders' funds less preference shares}} \times 100$$

$$\text{ROCE} = \frac{\text{Profit before taxation and interest}}{\text{Average shareholders' funds + long-term loans}} \times 100$$

$$\text{Gross profit ratio} = \frac{\text{Gross profit}}{\text{Total sales revenue}} \times 100$$

$$\text{Mark-up ratio} = \frac{\text{Gross profit}}{\text{Cost of goods sold}} \times 100$$

$$\text{Net profit ratio} = \frac{\text{Net profit before taxation}}{\text{Total sales revenue}} \times 100$$

Liquidity ratios

$$\text{Current assets ratio} = \frac{\text{Current assets}}{\text{Current liabilities}}$$

$$\text{Acid test ratio} = \frac{\text{Current assets} - \text{stocks}}{\text{Current liabilities}}$$

Efficiency ratios

$$\text{Stock turnover} = \frac{\text{Cost of goods sold}}{\text{Average stock}}$$

$$\text{Fixed assets turnover} = \frac{\text{Total sales revenue}}{\text{Fixed assets at net book value}}$$

$$\text{Trade debtor collection period} = \frac{\text{Average trade debtors}}{\text{Total credit sales}} \times 365 \text{ days}$$

$$\text{Trade creditor payment period} = \frac{\text{Average trade creditors}}{\text{Total credit purchases}} \times 365 \text{ days}$$

Investment ratios

$$\text{Dividend yield} = \frac{\text{Dividend per share}}{\text{Market price per share}} \times 100$$

$$\text{Dividend cover} = \frac{\text{Net profit after taxation and preference dividend}}{\text{Paid and proposed ordinary dividends}}$$

$$\text{Earnings per share} = \frac{\text{Net profit (or loss) for the period less dividends and other appropriations in respect of non-equity shares}}{\text{Weighted average number of shares in issue during the period}}$$

$$\text{Price/earnings ratio} = \frac{\text{Market price per share}}{\text{Earnings per share}}$$

$$\text{Capital gearing} = \frac{\text{Preference shares} + \text{long-term loans}}{\text{Shareholders' funds} + \text{long-term loans}} \times 100$$

The growing importance of international accounting standards . . .

Ministers plan to extend IAS

Private firms should prepare for international standards, writes Anita Howarth

Options set out by the government to extend international accounting standards (IAS) to all companies could cost business up to £1.4 billion, according to official figures.

An EU regulation adopted earlier this year requires listed companies in Europe to use IAS when preparing their consolidated accounts from 2005. Now the DTI is consulting on extending the regulation to unquoted companies and standalone accounts of listed companies. The potential cost implications to business of extending the regulation are contained in an appendix to the green paper outlining the options. These include whether to require or allow the regulation to be extended to the individual accounts of listed companies, unlisted companies or specific industries such as banking and insurance.

IAS could mean a big change for hundreds of private UK firms, which will have to alter the way they account for areas of their business, warned Andrew Vials, IAS partner at KPMG. "While the switch may be relatively straightforward for smaller companies, the resources required to effect the transition and the cost will depend on the complexity of the business," he said. "Those with treasury operations dealing in financial instruments may have a lot to change in terms of systems. Those with overseas subsidiaries will require more planning and time to prepare."

The government has warned that businesses need to think ahead about what IAS will mean for them. Melanie Johnson, the minister for competition, consumers and markets, launched the paper. "It is vital that com-

panies covered by the regulation and their accountants and auditors should be planning ahead for the change;' she said.

The IASB has also published an exposure draft on first-time application, which requires at least a year of comparative information under IAS. "Companies will have to use IAS to report on the financial year ending in 2005, but they will also need to include the figures for the year before, which, in turn, will require the opening balance sheet in 2003 to be set out under IAS," explained Richard Mallett, technical director at CIMA "Finance directors need to think about the move to IAS now and ensure their finance teams are up to speed with developments. The clock is ticking."

Financial Management, November 2002.

Questions relating to this news story may be found on page 306 ▸▸

About this chapter

This chapter examines four contemporary financial accounting and reporting issues that are currently the subject of debate in accounting, business and government circles.

The chapter is divided into seven main sections. The next section explains why this chapter is important for non-accountants. We then give you an overview of the subject matter of this chapter. This is followed by four sections that examine the four main topics: (1) the impact of a number of accounting scandals on accountants and the accountancy profession; (2) company law reform; (3) the move towards the international harmonization of accounting practice; and (4) the problem of revenue recognition. The last main section in the chapter outlines some questions that non-accountants might like to ask about these various financial accounting and reporting issues that are of relevance at the time of writing (spring 2003).

Learning objectives

By the end of this chapter you should be able to:

● identify four current financial accounting and reporting topics;

● explain how they are interlinked;

● outline the problems that have arisen in accounting practice in recent years;

● summarize the proposed changes to British company law;

● describe the worldwide movement towards the harmonization of accounting practice;

● assess the problems that arise in recognizing revenue in preparing accounts on a periodic basis.

❗ Why this chapter is important for non-accountants

Accounting, and especially that element of it known as financial reporting, is a dynamic discipline. It has to be in order to deal with a rapidly changing world. New problems and issues arise and some way has to be devised to cope with them. Need they be reported to interested parties? If so, how and in what form should they be reported?

Their expertise means that accountants are expected to take a lead on the reporting issues but non-accountants are also heavily involved. Many such issues are far too important to be left just to accountants to deal with. For example, a decision to write off an intangible asset such as goodwill to the profit and loss account instead of capitalizing it will have a significant effect on a company's reported results.

It is as a result of issues like this that non-accountants need to know what new accounting and reporting issues are currently under discussion and what proposals are being put forward for dealing with them. In this chapter we deal with four such issues.

We suggest that the chapter is particularly important for non-accountants for the following reasons.

1 To be briefed about the general business environment in which accounting operates both nationally and internationally.

2 To be informed about some contemporary issues in financial accounting and reporting.

3 To be able to advise your own entity of some impending changes.

4 To be able to take an active part in any debate on any proposed changes.

Overview

There are a great many other contemporary issues in financial accounting and reporting than the four topics covered in this chapter. The ASB, for example, continues to replace redundant SSAPs with new FRSs, revise existing FRSs, and issue new ones. Many of the issues dealt with are extremely technical and they are far too advanced for a book of this nature. Nevertheless, they may be a cause of some recent accounting scandals and hence they have a loose connection with the next section.

The business world is changing fast and new developments are constantly taking place. Company law and existing accounting practices were not designed to deal with such changes. As a result, preparers of accounts have found ways of presenting information that shows a company in the very best possible light. In many cases highly satisfactory turnover and profit levels in one year has soon turned to poor results in a subsequent year. And that means that yet another accounting scandal hits the headlines.

It is probably a coincidence that during the recent period of accounting scandals (2001–2002), the Government has announced that it intends to reform company law. It has been suggested that the reform will be the most significant for 150 years. In framing its proposals the Government has looked at accounting practice in the UK and the organization of the accountancy profession. It is of considerable consolation to learn that it is broadly satisfied with what is done. You may be surprised at this conclusion in the light of all these recent scandals. We will explore why the Government appears to have confidence in the accountancy profession later in the chapter.

Changes in accounting practice and a struggle to cope with a new business environment are not confined to the UK. What is happening is worldwide. So we felt it necessary to deal with various international matters. In particular, we shall be examining the work of what is called the International Accounting Standards Board (IASB).

Finally, we felt it appropriate to deal with one very important accounting issue: the recognition of revenue. This problem arises because of the periodic rule used in accounting. For the moment we will assume that 'revenue' means income arising from the sale of goods and services. Often, revenue is earned when a series of stages have been completed by the seller in providing goods and services to a buyer. So in which period do you include the income from each stage? And how do you measure it? You will be surprised to find that, in practice, the answers to these questions are very difficult to determine. Indeed, this is probably one of the main reasons why so many accounting scandals have arisen in recent years.

There is, therefore, a central theme to this chapter. We deal with some recent problems in accounting, we look at how the Government and the international accounting community are aiming to tackle them, and finally we examine one of the major causes of such problems. The relationship between these various issues is shown in diagrammatic format in Figure 13.1.

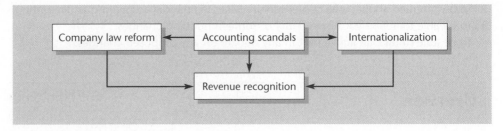

Figure 13.1 Interrelationship of chapter contents

Accounting scandals

In this section we are going consider the perceptions that there may be about accountants and the accountancy profession and how they may have been influenced by a whole series of well-reported accounting scandals.

Perceptions

You are now more than halfway through this book. What were your perceptions about accountants when you first started to study accounting? Did you think that accountants generally were honest, reliable and trustworthy? Or did you think that they were ruthless and out to make as much money as possible?

Similarly, what were your perceptions about the accountancy profession? Did you think that it was highly reputable, reliable and safe? Or did you think that it was just an exclusive organization for crooks, fraudsters and gangsters?

Have your perceptions about accountants and the accountancy profession changed in recent months? Have you perhaps been influenced by what you have read about accountants in the newspapers and seen on television? More specifically, have your perceptions changed as you have worked your way through the book? Do you now see accountants and their profession in a better or a worse light?

If your views have changed, this could be for two reasons, neither of them connected to any external influences: (1) we have emphasized throughout the book the problems that accountants have in preparing financial information; and (2) many of the news stories presented at the head of each chapter give a poor impression of how accountants behave.

If the first point is valid we would want to apologize. Our approach, however, has been quite deliberate. In the fairly recent past, non-accountants tended to have a fairly simplistic impression of what accountants were and what they did. Generally, they were perceived in a similar light to that of an old-fashioned bank manager: safe, slow and totally lacking in personality. When an accountant gave you a statement telling you that you had made a profit of £25 000 you could be certain that that was what you had made. The statement would have been carefully prepared and it would certainly be arithmetically correct.

Unfortunately it was not generally realized that accounting statements were (and are) prepared on the basis of a series of assumptions and personal judgements. Hence it is perfectly easy to change the £25 000 if you want to. All you need do is to change some of the assumptions on which the accounts are based. There is nothing ethically or inherently wrong in such a situation, although professionally qualified accountants would be expected to have a sound reason for changing their assumptions.

This flexibility inherent in traditional accounting practice was much less well known 20 years ago than it is today. Nevertheless, there is still a long way to go before most users of accounting statements are not misled by the apparent arithmetical precision of accounting statements. Irrespective of the discipline, many university courses do now include a course in accounting. In the future, therefore, we can perhaps expect managers (like yourself) to be well briefed in the deficiencies of accounting statements. But does this make such statements virtually valueless?

The short answer is 'no'. This again has been part of the message that we have been signalling in this book. In short: *accounting statements can be extremely useful provided that the assumptions upon which they are based can be justified and that the arithmetical results are only taken as a guide.*

If you had begun to lose confidence in what accounting can do for you, we hope that this message will have enhanced your faith in the accounting practice. If so, we can now address the issue of so-called accounting scandals.

Activity 13.1

What were and are your perceptions about accountants? Complete the following table using a scale of 1 to 5 (1 = very low; 5 = very high).

Quality	Before starting Chapter 1	At this stage in the book
Honest	☐	☐
Meticulous	☐	☐
Pedantic	☐	☐
Reliable	☐	☐
Selfless	☐	☐
Trustworthy	☐	☐

Definition

It would be helpful if we first defined what is meant by a 'scandal'. It is a highly emotive word and it may stir up strong emotions in people who hear about one having taken place. The *Penguin Pocket English Dictionary* (3rd edition, 1988) defines a scandal as follows:

> *A circumstance or action that causes general offence or indignation or that disgraces those associated with it (p. 742).*

This definition will do for our purposes. If we apply it to accounting, there appears to have been some circumstances that have caused a great deal of public indignation and those people who have been involved in them have been disgraced. Is this true and, if so, what is the scale of the problem?

Examples

In the sense described above there have always been accounting scandals but the ones that have occurred in the last few years have received a great deal more publicity. For example, on 26 July 2002 (p. 28) *The Guardian* newspaper published a montage of eleven American scandals that readers could cut out and keep. The details are summarized in Table 13.1.

Table 13.1 **Some recent American accounting scandals**

Company	Business	Alleged scandal
Adelphia	Cable operator	'Looting on a massive scale'
AOL Time Warner	Internet and media	Creative accounting
Bristol-Myers Squib	Pharmaceuticals	Blocking rivals to a top-selling drug*
Enron	Power and energy trading	Private equity operation
Global Crossing	Telecoms	Creative accounting to inflate earnings
Halliburton	Engineering	Overstating company revenues
Johnson & Johnson	Drugs and household products	Errors in drug manufacturing
Qwest	Telecoms	'Swaps' and inflation of sales
Tyco	Industrial conglomerate	Tax evasion and tampering with evidence
WorldCom	Telecoms	Disguising expenses
Xerox	Office machines	Booking long-term leases as revenues

* To avoid any misinterpretation, a case has been brought but there has been no finding as yet. The lawsuit, filed by 29 states and led by Ohio, is an allegation that the company profited unfairly from its monopoly.

Source: 'Uncle Sams's Scandal', *The Guardian,* 26 July 2002.

There are a number of points to note about the information summarized in Table 13.1.

1 The information relates to American companies.
2 Some of the alleged scandals refer to apparent criminal or unlawful activities.
3 The accountants do not appear to have been directly involved in the action taken by the companies concerned, although they must have had something to do with those that are accounting related.
4 Eight out of the eleven cases do appear to be accounting related (AOL Time Warner, Enron, Global Crossing, Halliburton, Quest, Tyco, Worldcom, and Xerox). As at spring 2003 we do not know whether their respective problems were genuine differences of accounting treatment or whether they were deliberate attempts to present misleading information.

The UK has also not been free from its own scandals. As *Accountancy* (the journal of the Institute of Chartered Accountants in England and Wales) reminded us (August 2002, p. 19), people in glasshouses should not throw stones. It then quotes five failures in British corporate life since 1999. These were as follows.

1   Equitable Life: cutting bonuses to customers who had bought guaranteed annuities.
2   Independent Insurance: claims not entered into the accounting system.
3   Schroders: incorrect recording of fee income.
4   SSL International: an alleged 'massive fraud'.
5   TransTec: non-disclosure of a compensation claim.

Again, some of these 'failures' in corporate life may have been caused by errors of judgement by senior management. They were not necessarily the fault of accountants because we do not know to what extent they were involved in the decision making. Nevertheless, in this context it is the public perception that is important and, as a result of such episodes, the esteem and prestige of accountants has undoubtedly fallen.

Causes

At this stage, we cannot be certain that more accounting scandals have taken place in recent years than used to be the case or whether more publicity is now given to them. Certainly, the catalyst for more publicity was the Enron case in the United States.

Enron was a large American company that was originally a natural gas supplier. It converted itself into one of the largest energy trade companies in the world, so much so that its turnover rose from \$40 billion in 1999 to \$101 billion in 2000. Before the end of 2001 it had collapsed, partly as a result of alleged fraud and partly because of questionable accounting practices. It is the latter cause that is of particular interest to us in this chapter.

US accounting principles allowed the company to keep certain items from being disclosed in the balance sheet. These are known as 'special purpose entities' (SPEs) and, according to Singleton-Green (*Accountancy*, May 2002, pp. 20–21), such entities were allegedly being used 'to conceal from the market' very large losses being made by the company and to provide large fees for Enron executives. It would appear that the auditors were in some doubt about Enron's treatment of SPEs but they went along with it. In the end, the auditors' firm collapsed along with the company.

The demise of such a high-profile company such as Enron, the sheer amount of money that it appeared to generate, its contacts in the business, financial and political world, and the fall of an international firm of accountants all helped to generate a huge amount of adverse publicity. Such publicity still continues. It has also meant that any other company that gets into financial trouble is immediately subject to a similar amount of intense scrutiny. It is then easy to gain an impression that 20 or so companies are representative of the thousands of other companies that try to operate fairly and honourably.

But what causes business executives (and perhaps accountants) to act in the way that they appear to have done? There are several reasons. We explore some of them below.

Until recently the financial markets had been booming and share prices looked as though they would go on rising for evermore. That era has now come to an end but it enabled some people to make a fortune by intervening in the financial markets.

The new industries that had been created and the innovative technologies that had been developed over the last few years (especially those relating to information technology) were not understood by either analysts or shareholders. But they looked as though they would replace the old industries such as car manufacturing, iron and steel, and ship building. Hence, for a time, anyone promoting an IT-type company could not fail. The share price would rise irrespective of whether it was doing much trading. The promoters would do very well out of buying the shares when they were low and selling them almost immediately as the price rose higher and higher.

At some time or other, of course, the promoters had to justify what they were doing. So an increase in turnover became an important performance measure and a way of assessing the bonuses to be paid to the company's executives. As competition became fiercer in such industries and as the IT revolution began to falter, such executives were less able to cash in on rising share prices and claim large bonuses. It was understandable, therefore, if they began to examine carefully what was meant by 'turnover' and, no doubt much to their delight, they found that the accountant's definition was somewhat flexible. Thus it was relatively easy to transfer to the profit and loss account certain incomes that would have been more prudent to have kept in the balance sheet. They were also helped because the type of contractual arrangements issued by the new industries were unusual and no one had ever decided how they should be accounted for.

Just to give you one simple example. Suppose an IT sells some software to a customer costing (say) £1000. The customer also takes out a service agreement costing £600 for a three-year period. The total cost is, therefore, £1600. How much revenue should be claimed in Year 1, Year 2 and Year 3 respectively? Much would depend upon the wording of the contract but prudence would suggest £1200 in Year 1, and £200 each in Year 2 and Year 3. This was not always the way it worked and some companies might claim £1440 (or 90% of the £1600) as income in Year 1. It is not clear why 90% was an appropriate amount to take as income in the first year.

Year 1's profits would, therefore, look very healthy, but the company would have to work very hard in Year 2 and Year 3 to maintain its profitability. If trading conditions become worse, it will be almost impossible. Hence a need perhaps to adjust its accounting policies so that its profitability does not appear to be in decline.

This scenario now takes us into the world of fraud. As we have indicated at various times, accounting practices can be very flexible, but if they have been stretched as far as they can, the company is in a dilemma. It is understandable, therefore, although thoroughly reprehensible, if executives faced with a ruin of their careers decide to act unlawfully. In other words, they present the financial results knowing full well that they are false. If nobody spots what they are doing, the company's share price holds up, and the executives can continue to buy and sell their share options, pay themselves high salaries and claim large bonuses.

However, there is just one major snag. They have to get the auditors to sign the accounts. We will now consider the position of the auditors.

Auditors

Auditors are usually trained accountants who specialize in auditing work. They are usually employed by firms of accountants. Some of these are very small and they do not have either the staff or the experience to audit large companies. Indeed, in the UK there are probably only about four firms of accountants that can operate on a global scale.

There is little evidence to indicate that auditors in the UK collude in committing fraud. This may not always be true elsewhere. In the Enron case, for example, there is an indication that the auditors did not act *totally* professionally. In the UK the position of auditors is different from their counterparts in the USA.

The USA uses a *rule-book* system of preparing accounts. This means that companies have to follow a huge number of rules when preparing their accounts. Generally, if a particular action is not covered by a rule then it is permissible. Thus it is very easy to engage in questionable practices simply because there does not appear to be any rule prohibiting it.

The UK uses a *principles* approach to accounting whereby Parliament lays down some general laws applying to accounting and these are supplemented by various semi-mandatory professional requirements. The Companies Act 1985 also has an overriding requirement that, notwithstanding the various requirements contained in the Act, the accounts should 'represent a true and fair view'. Hence accounts are prepared and audited on the basis of what is right for that particular company and not according to a detailed rule book.

This is what gives British (and increasingly European) financial reporting its flexibility but there is a danger that reports prepared in this way may hide what should be disclosed. It is the responsibility of the auditors to ensure that this does not happen. Does the system work? We consider this question below.

Auditor reliability

The law states that shareholders appoint the auditors of a company. In practice they cannot do so because it is impossible for them to get together and have a vote on the various merits of different firms of auditors. Thus it is usually left to the company's directors to appoint the auditors, although the appointment has to be confirmed by the shareholders at a general meeting.

It is rare for the shareholders to vote against the directors' recommendation. Hence, in effect, the directors appoint the auditors and the auditors know that they are dependent upon the directors for doing the job and being paid for it. Auditors are not, therefore, as independent as perhaps the law would like.

It is also often alleged that their independence is further compromised for a number of other reasons. These as as follows:

1 If they have been doing the job for a long time, their firm becomes dependent upon their reappointment.
2 The staff (especially the audit partner) become too close to the directors.
3 Audit staff often leave the audit firm to take up a full-time appointment with a client company.
4 Audit firms often do lucrative non-audit work for their clients, i.e. management consultancy and tax advice.

All of these factors are of very real concern, especially in view of the various accounting scandals that have occurred recently. Naturally, the question is often put, 'Should the auditors have stopped this happening?' And the follow-up, 'Were the auditors too much in with the directors to do anything about it?'

There is a strong critical undercurrent in the first question. Perhaps the auditors should have done something about it, but it depends on the problem. The public sometimes have a false impression of the role of auditors. This is known as the *expectations gap*. In other words, the public think that the auditors are there to do one job whereas they are due to do another one. The main misconception is the detection of fraud. Auditors are not appointed to detect or even to deter fraud, although they may do so in the course of their duties. Their job is to confirm that the accounts represent a true and fair view. If they do not find anything to convince them otherwise, they can sign the accounts – even if unbeknown to them a fraud has occurred.

All of the above means that it is a difficult task to explain to the public what the role of auditors is in British company law and what the true and fair view rule means.

Activity 13.2

Respond to the following questions.

1 Should an independent body appoint company auditors?

Yes ☐   No ☐

If so, which or what type of independent body?

2 Should auditors be allowed to do other work (i.e. in addition to auditing) for their clients?

Yes ☐   No ☐

3 Should auditors be allowed to take up full-time employment with former clients?

Yes ☐   No ☐

4 Should auditors be allowed to do an audit for a limited period?

Yes ☐   No ☐

If so, what?

Three years: ☐   Five years: ☐   Other: ☐

Action

What can be done to stop or at least to reduce the number of accounting scandals?

The first point is that no matter what sanctions there are, there is nothing that can be done to deter someone who is prepared to break the law. Such behaviour cannot be condoned. It is totally unacceptable anywhere in society but it is particularly so if an accountant is involved in it. Like a doctor, the public should be able to regard an accountant as absolutely upright and utterly trustworthy.

Even if the above point is accepted, we are dealing with a situation where there is considerable room for individual discretion and judgement. We can prescribe more laws but experience suggests that a more prescriptive system simply encourages people to find their way around the rules. Hence in the UK we should continue to do what we have been doing so far, but try to do it a bit better. As we shall see shortly, this is the Government's view.

If this approach is to be effective and if it is to enhance the integrity of accountants and auditors, users of accounts need to be better informed about what the accounts do and do not do. In addition, the public needs to be made more aware of the role of auditors. If these ideas are acceptable then there is still a massive educational programme to undertake. It will take time to get anywhere but considerable progress has already been made in this direction in the last 20 years. There is no reason why it should not continue.

We now turn to what is intended to be done in the next few years.

Company law reform

We explained in earlier chapters that British company law is based on the 1985 Companies Act (as amended by the Companies Act 1989). The 1985 Act consolidates the Companies Acts of 1948, 1967, 1976, 1980 and 1981. The 1967 and 1976 Acts were relatively slim, so you can see that only infrequently and at long intervals is Parliament presented with some major company reforms.

Another major Companies Act is now on its way. The Government issued a White Paper in July 2002 and it expects to have a new Companies Act on the statute book by the time of the next General Election, i.e. no later than the summer of 2006. It is thought that the new Act will be the most significant piece of legislation affecting companies for 150 years.

The new Act will range far wider than just accounting matters so, as they are our main concern in this book, we will concentrate on what changes are proposed in that direction. In summary they are as follows. The list is fairly lengthy but to make it easier for you to read we have divided it into three sections.

Organization

1 The Act will only contain primary legislation and as many matters as possible will be left to secondary legislation. For example, the Secretary of State would have the right to amend the size criteria for small and medium-sized companies without having to go back to Parliament.
2 Detailed legislation will be based on the existing professional framework, i.e. the Financial Reporting Council (FRC), the Accounting Standards Board (ASB), and the Financial Reporting Review Panel (FRRP). The existing regime will be replaced with the following:
    (a) A Company Law and Reporting Commission (CLRC) which will be an advisory statutory body responsible for keeping company law under review.
    (b) A Standards Board (SB) responsible for making detailed reporting and disclosure rules, accounting standards and non-financial matters, all of which will have a direct legal effect.
    (c) A Reporting Review Panel (RRP) which will be similar to the FRRP but with a broader remit covering financial and non-financial disclosure matters.
    (d) A Private Companies Committee responsible for advising the CLRC and the SB on company law and reporting matters affecting private companies.
3 The funding to support the above structure will come from the Government, the accountancy bodies and the City.
4 The Act will lay down the basic requirements of financial reports and statements but the details will be left to the Standards Board to determine.
5 Criminal penalties will apply to anyone who intends to deceive or mislead by making false statements or who engages in false accounting. Otherwise, the RRP will deal with companies that appear to transgress the true and fair view rule.

The annual report

1 The narrative directors' report will be abolished and replaced with a brief supplementary statement for small companies and an Operating and Financial Review (OFR) statement for larger ones.
2 The OFR will be qualitative and forward looking, and it might include environmental matters, although it will be up to directors to decide what to include.
3 The Standards Board will draw up the detailed rules for the compilation of the OFR.
4 The auditors will be required to report on the OFR.
5 Quoted companies will be required to prepare a directors' remuneration report.

The annual accounts

1 The 'principles' approach to financial reporting will be adopted whereby the spirit and reason behind the requirements is accepted rather than following rigid prescriptive pronouncements. Hence the 'cook book' approach to financial reporting, as embraced in the USA, will not be adopted in the UK.
2 The profit and loss account will become a wider performance statement so that it includes all gains and losses, such as those arising from the revaluation of fixed assets.
3 A cash flow statement will be required.
4 Small private companies (about 95% of the total) will be subject to a much simpler reporting regime.
5 Private companies will have to deliver their accounts to the Registrar of Companies within seven months (instead of ten months) of the year end. Similarly, if they lay their accounts and statements at a meeting they must do so again within ten months. Quoted public companies must lay their annual reporting documents before a general meeting and also deliver them to the Registrar of Companies within six months of the year end. They must also publish these on the Internet as soon as practical and in any event within four months of the year end. Preliminary announcements must also be made on the Internet.
6 All companies will have to file their full statutory accounts.
7 Shareholders in all companies will be able to opt for a summary statement of all the annual reporting documents, although they would still retain the right to receive the full annual reporting documents.
8 No major changes are expected to audit practice as well as to the role and responsibilities of auditors. Auditors will, however, have a statutory responsibility for the OFR and the cash flow statement. The right to receive information from the company will also be strengthened.

Activity 13.3	Read the above summary of the possible contents of the forthcoming Companies Bill once again. How far do you think that it will limit some of the accounting scandals described earlier in the chapter? Jot down in your notebook those proposals that are likely to help minimize them.

The White Paper proposals are remarkable when you consider the adverse publicity given to the accounting and auditing profession over the last two years as a result of various accounting scandals. The Government clearly has not been panicked into doing something for the sake of doing something. Just consider in outline what it has accepted:

1   A loose legislative framework.
2   A principles approach to the preparation of accounting reports and statements.
3   Minor changes to the content and format of an annual report and accounts.
4   The delegation of detailed accounting and reporting matters to an independent private sector body.
5   Criminal sanctions only in the case of false accounting or deliberate attempts to mislead or deceive.

The White Paper, therefore, does not accept that there is a crisis in the accountancy profession and that legalistic and radical measures need to be taken to control and curtail accounting practices. Thus the Government does not appear to support the negative perception that the public may have as a result of recent accounting scandals occurring either in the UK or in the USA.

As a non-accounting student you may have had some doubts about the importance of accounting and the probity of its practitioners. We hope now that you will be able to set those doubts aside, confident in the knowledge that the Government has given the accountancy profession a surprising, but welcome, vote of confidence.

Internationalization

The Government does not work in a vacuum when framing legislation. Indeed, current company legislation is no longer purely British based, but European. Thus the same company legislation applies to all of the 15 member states of the European Union (EU). It is expected that by the end of 2004 another 10 countries will have joined the EU. This will mean that the same company law will apply across most of Continental Europe.

Similarly, the ASB does not work in isolation when working on a proposed accounting standard. It consults widely, both at home and overseas. In particular, it observes very closely what is happening in the USA.

However, there is also a formal organization that deals with international accounting matters. It is called the International Accounting Standards Board (IASB) and the time is now opportune to examine what it does.

International Accounting Standards

In March 2001 an International Accounting Standards Committee Foundation was formed. It is incorporated in Delaware in the USA. The Foundation is the parent body of the IASB. The IASB was formed on 1 April 2001 and it is based in London. The IASB is the successor body to the International Accounting Standards Committee (IASC). The IASC was created in 1973 and its objective was to make financial statements more comparable on a worldwide basis. It was a private body financed largely by its members.

The IASB has a similar remit. It is solely responsible for setting and publishing International Financial Reporting Standards (IFRSs). It has also adopted the standards formerly issued by the IASC. These continue to be called International Accounting Standards (IASs). At the time of writing (April 2003) 34 such IASs were still in existence. The IASB is actively working on a number of projects at the moment, for example 'reporting performance' and 'revenue – definition and recognition – and related aspects of liabilities'. It has also identified various other topics that it wishes to pursue, such as 'impairment of assets' and 'intangible assets'.

Many countries are are either too poor or too small to have their own accounting standards. So they usually use the international standards and adapt them for their own particular requirements.

The topics covered by IASs are similar but not identical to those covered in British SSAPs and FRSs. As economic, financial, legal and political considerations differ so markedly in member countries, IASC requirements tended to be much more general than British ones. This meant that where the ASB's requirements covered the same topic as that of an international accounting standard, observance of the British one meant automatic compliance with the international requirement.

A British accounting standard usually contains a note explaining how it fits in with its sister IAS. For example, FRS 3 (Reporting financial performance) states in paragraph 34:

> *The requirements of the FRS are consistent with International Accounting Standard 5 'Information to be Disclosed in Financial Statements' [since replaced with 'Presentation of Financial Statements'] and International Accounting Standard 8 'Unusual and Prior Period Items and Changes in Accounting Policies'.*

By contrast, the revised FRS 1 (Cash flow statements) has to explain what the differences are between the standard and IAS 7 (Cash Flow Statements). The main one is the definition of cash flows. FRS 1 defines cash flows as 'increases or decreases in cash'. Cash includes cash in hand, deposits repayable on demand and overdrafts. IAS 7 defines cash flows as 'cash and cash equivalents'. Thus the FRS definition is narrower than the IAS version.

The old IASC struggled to ensure that its programme became more widespread, partly because it is enormously difficult to encourage up to 200 nations to work together, partly because of language problems (English was the working language), and partly because the USA was not a willing partner in the enterprise. Under the new IASB regime there are encouraging signs that wider cooperation may now be possible and it is to that that we now turn.

The European Union

At one time the European Union (EU) did consider issuing its own accounting standards but that proposal did not get very far. In the meantime the EU has decided to adopt International Accounting Standards. From 2005 all EU listed companies will have to prepare their consolidated accounts in accordance with IFRSs. It is hoped that other types of companies will adopt IASs.

In effect, this requirement means that, because of the need to disclose the previous year's result (and in some cases, the two previous years), from 2003 onwards IASB requirements will take precedence over national standards.

The EU requirement is a significant step in the history of financial reporting. It will mean that across a large continent of 25 countries and 400 million people, quoted companies will be complying with the same company law and the same accounting standards. As a result, the comparison of financial performance among companies in different countries will become much more realistic and reliable.

What are the implications for the UK? As we have indicated above, generally compliance with UK standards automatically means compliance with international standards. Some compromise will be necessary, e.g. in the case of cash flow statements, what is meant by 'cash'. Otherwise, in terms of accounting treatment, major changes to British financial statements should not be necessary.

The change is more likely to be organizational. The work of the current ASB and the new SB in preparing standards will be much reduced as it will no longer be necessary to issue separate ones of its own. There may be some topics not covered by IASs that the SB wishes to see covered by a British accounting standard but there should be not many of them. The SB, however, will be much busier working through the IASB to ensure that the international proposals will meet British requirements. In that context it is envisaged that a great deal of compromise will be necessary.

What about the world outside the EU and especially the United States? There the prospects for closer cooperation are not as encouraging.

The United States of America

It is a difficult task to persuade the Americans to adopt IFRSs. This is for two main reasons:

1 *Behavioural.* The USA is an extremely large and powerful country. Its citizens are very proud of being Americans and they are intensely patriotic. They are an enterprising and independent-minded people and they have a general view that '*what is American is the best*'. However, although many Americans travel abroad they are not known for their knowledge and understanding of life outside their own country. All of these factors make it difficult for them to accept proposals that are not American based and orientated.

2 *Technical.* As we have indicated earlier, the American system of financial reporting is 'rule based' as opposed to the British/European/IAS 'principles' approach. This means that a fundamental change to American accounting practice would be needed if it were to adopt IFRSs.

As far as financial reporting is concerned, the USA is something of a paradox. Few states have detailed law provisions, whereas at the federal level, a relatively small number of listed companies are bound by some very severe restrictions.

The federal system reflects the Securities Act 1933 and the 1934 Securities Exchange Act. A Securities and Exchange Commission (SEC) was established to administer the securities regulations. The SEC operates a standard-setting process through a private sector board called the Financial Accounting Standards Board (FASB). The FASB issues accounting standards similar to those of the ASB. Indeed, the ASB's proposals are strongly influenced by American ideas and requirements. The USA, however, has many more standards (well over 100) and they are much more detailed than British ones.

The stringent financial regulations for companies that have a stock exchange listing in the USA have important repercussions for overseas companies. If they wish to list on the New York Stock Exchange, for example, their accounts must comply with US GAAP (generally accepted accounting principles). This is regardless of the requirements of their own country's GAAP. As a New York Stock Exchange listing is a necessity for many international companies, US GAAP is highly influential and it can take precedence over GAAP in a company's own country. Otherwise, the company has to prepare two sets of financial reports: one in accordance with US GAAP and one in accordance with its own country's GAAP. Clearly, to have to prepare two sets of reports is time-consuming, costly and confusing.

Nevertheless, the EU has fought vigorously to ensure that US GAAP does not become the norm for world financial reports. This may be partly to ensure that the USA does not dictate to the rest of the world what should be done, and partly because US GAAP is not suitable for most European countries. Therefore, the adoption, across Europe of international standards, and elsewhere (Australia has agreed to do the same and no doubt other countries will follow), means that for the first time the USA has some powerful opposition.

The USA still holds a trump card, of course, because it can limit access to its capital markets. So what is likely to happen?

At a meeting of the FASB and IASB in September 2002 the two Boards agreed to the following:

1 To undertake a joint short-term project to eliminate a number of existing differences between IASB and FASB standards.
2 To seek convergence of current projects.
3 To enhance coordination of future agenda items on a long-term basis.

Source: IAS Briefing, KPMG, October 2002, p. 1.

Harvey Pitt (then Chairman of the FASB) backed this up in an article published in *Accountancy*. In that article the confirmed that the FASB was committed to working with the IASB 'to produce high-quality accounting standards across major international capital markets' (*Accountancy*, November 2002, p. 86).

More recently, Linda A. MacDonald, a project manager with the FASB, reported that it had issued a proposal for 'a principles-based approach to US standard-setting' (*Accountancy*, January 2003, p. 89). She concludes her article as follows:

> The Board believes that an approach focusing more clearly on the principles in accounting standards is necessary to improve the quality and transparency of US financial accounting and reporting.

This is quite a remarkable admission. No doubt it reflects the recent American experience following the fall of Enron and other corporate scandals. Ms MacDonald then continues:

> Also, because a principles-based approach is similar to the approach used by the IASB in developing IFRS, adopting such an approach could facilitate convergence as FASB works with the IASB and other national standard-setters in developing common high-quality accounting standards.

This is most encouraging, but her final sentence is even more so:

> The Board believes that if all participants in the US financial accounting and reporting process are willing to make the changes required under a principles-based approach, the benefits of adopting that approach would outweigh its costs.

So the FASB accepts that a principles-based approach is best for US financial accounting and reporting and it hopes that other participants will agree. As an extremely powerful body, the FASB is best placed to influence the debate. We await subsequent developments with great interest.

On a score of 1 to 5 (1 = highly unlikely; 5 = very likely), how likely do you think that (a) the USA will adopt a principles approach to financial accounting and reporting within the next five years; and (b) within the next ten years it will move to abandon its own accounting standards and use IFRSs? Mark your scores on the following scales.

Activity 13.4

(a) principles approach

| 1 | 2 | 3 | 4 | 5 |

(b) adoption of IFRSs

| 1 | 2 | 3 | 4 | 5 |

Revenue recognition

We now return to a topic that we touched upon at the beginning of this chapter. The IASB believes that the definition of revenue and its recognition are among the most difficult and contentious issues in practice today. The issues are currently undergoing intensive investigation, partly because of the crucial role revenue plays in the calculation of accounting profit, and partly because it appears to be at the centre of so many accounting scandals. We will illustrate the point by providing you with three examples. They are as follows.

Example 1: Orchestream

Orchestream is a provider of telecommunications software. On 15 July 2002 it reported that a sale had inappropriately been recognized as revenue. This meant that profits had been overstated by £2.7m for 2001 and £0.9m for the first quarter of 2002. It would appear that the contract relating to this sale meant that it was premature to treat the income as revenue in the accounts for those years.

Source: Accountancy, September 2002, p. 85.

Example 2: AIT

AIT is a software company operating in the financial services sector. Its turnover for the year to 31 March 2002 should have been lower by £7.3m. Apparently income sales to Channel Partners for licences had not been sold to 'end user customers'.

Source: Accountancy, October 2002, p. 92.

Example 3: Ingenta

Ingenta manages and distributes published scientific, professional and academic research using the Internet. £2.6 million of turnover for the year to 30 September 2002 should not have been included as revenue for that year. Some sales revenue and library deposit administration charges should have been recognized in future years. In other words, too much income was being taken to the profit and loss account too soon.

Source: Accountancy, February 2003, p. 198.

The detail behind these cases is sparse. We do not know how and why they incurred revenue discrepancies but the initial decisions to deal with them all had the effect of inflating turnover (i.e. sales) which in turn would have increased profits. They may all have been genuine errors of judgement.

In other cases this may not have been so. As turnover became an important performance indicator company executives would naturally want to make it as big as possible. That way their salaries, bonuses, share options and careers would all be enhanced. But in fairness it is not always easy to determine when certain incomes should be taken to the profit and loss account and when others should be carried forward on the balance sheet. This has always been the case but it has become more difficult as business activity has become more complex, especially in the new IT and telecommunications industries.

It would now be helpful if we defined what is meant by 'revenue'.

Definition

The International Accounting Standards Committee Foundation (IASCF) equates 'revenue' with 'income' and it has adopted the following definition:

> *Income is increases in economic benefits during the accounting period in the form of inflows or enhancements of assets or decreases of liabilities that result in increases in equity, other than those relating to contributions from equity participants.'*
>
> IASCF, *Revenue recognition*, 2003.

The Accounting Principles Board in the USA has a similar, albeit more convoluted, definition:

> *Gross increases in assets or gross decreases in liabilities recognized and measured in conformity with generally accepted accounting principles that result from those types of profit-directed activities of an enterprise that can change owners' equity.*
>
> APB Statement No. 4, *Basic Concepts and Accounting Principles Underlying Financial Statements of Business Enterprises*, American Institute of Certified Public Accountants, October 1970, para. 134; quoted in Davies, M., Paterson, R. and Wilson, A. (1999) *UK GAAP*, 6th edition, Croydon: Butterworths.

In effect, these definitions indicate that revenue is basically an increase in net assets during a particular period after allowing for any new capital contributed by the owners and the withdrawal of any old capital.

What problem, then, arises in 'recognizing' it?

Recognition

Traditional historical accounting is transaction based, i.e we enter activities in the books of accounts as and when they have occurred. Periodically we want to know how a business has done and so we ascertain by how much the owners' capital has increased during a particular accounting period (after allowing for new capital and withdrawals of capital).

The problem is that some transactions do not relate entirely to the accounting period that we are dealing with and that they have an impact over several periods So we have to distinguish between so-called 'capital' and 'revenue' items and we have to match 'revenue income' with 'revenue expenditure'. This exercise is often quite difficult and we have to use our judgement. If we are in doubt, we use the prudence rule and treat a transaction in such a way that it will understate profits and overstate any losses.

Those transactions that relate to more than one accounting period can cause particular difficulty. For example, in determining how much of the cost of fixed assets should be written off during each year that they are in use. There is a similar problem with those sales that generate income over several time periods. In which period and how much is it fair to take this to the profit and loss account as 'turnover'?

This question raises what is called the 'timing problem'. There are three possible approaches. We summarize them below.

1 *The critical events approach.* By adopting this approach we would take the revenue when the most critical event in the operating cycle has occurred. There are several points when this can be done: (a) when production has been completed; (b) when a sale has been made; (c) on delivery of the goods or services; and (d) when the cash is collected.
2 *The accretion approach.* This approach recognizes revenue during the production process. The most common example of this approach is long-term contract work when some profit is taken as the contract nears completion.
3 *The revenue allocation approach.* This approach is a combination of the critical events approach and the accretion approach. It involves taking some of the sale price, for example, at the point of sale and the rest in stages, perhaps upon completion and during the warranty period.

The future

You will be able to see from the above outline that revenue recognition in some cases requires considerable judgement and expertise. It has always done so, but even more is involved in dealing with complex developments and arrangements in the new industries. So what is the accountancy profession doing to help?

There is no UK accounting standard that deals specifically with revenue recognition. FRS 5 (Substance of transactions) deals indirectly with the issue and more guidance has been given in an ASB Exposure Draft issued in February 2003 called 'Amendment to FRS 5 "Reporting the Substance of Transactions": Revenue Recognition ED'. The ASB also issued a Discussion Paper in 2001 but this is not being taken any further as the ASB waits for a new international standard on the subject.

The current international standard is IAS 18: Revenue. The IASB is currently working on the subject in conjunction with the FASB. The project is intended to develop a comprehensive set of principles for revenue recognition. It is hoped that this will eliminate the inconsistencies in current practice. Details of the project are contained in the International Accounting Standards Committee Foundation's project update called *Revenue recognition*, published in 2003. The IASB expect to publish an Exposure Draft in 2004, so it will obviously be some time before an up-to-date standard becomes available.

Activity 13.5

A building has now been under construction for three years. It is expected to be completed in two years' time. The agreed contract price is £500,000. The costs to date are £300 000 and it is expected that another £100 000 will be spent on the building before it is completed.

What profit would you include in the profit and loss account for Year 3?

❗ Questions non-accountants should ask

By its very nature this chapter may soon become out of date. You might have to adapt the following questions, therefore, to accommodate new issues.

● Have we renewed all our accounting practice to ensure that we will not be accused of any accounting irregularity?

● If we are in doubt about how to treat a certain accounting issue, do we adopt a highly prudent approach?

● Are we certain that our accounting methods are not driven largely by the need to improve our financial performance indicators?

● Have we considered the implications of the Government's reform of company law on our company?

● Have we allowed for the incorporation of International Accounting Standards into our financial reports at the earliest possible opportunity?

● Are we sure that our policies on the recognition of revenue in respect of all our sales and contracts are robust enough to respond to any critical examination of them?

Conclusion

This chapter has concentrated on some contemporary issues in financial accounting and reporting at the time of writing in the spring of 2003. In two or three years they may be no longer an issue or quite as contemporary.

The last two to three years has seen an explosion in the number of articles published on 'accounting scandals'. It is not clear whether there are now more scandals than there used to be or whether more publicity is now given to those that do occur. It is possible that the sheer scale and impact of the Enron scandal in the USA has triggered a spate of newspaper articles that would otherwise have gone unreported. While many of these cases relate to the USA, the UK has also experienced a number of high-profile accounting irregularities.

Notwithstanding such occurrences, according to the White Paper on company law reform published in 2002, the British Government is not proposing to change the legislative framework underpinning financial reporting practices in the UK. It proposes that Parliament lay down some legislative guidelines but the detailed application of them will be left to some private sector bodies. Thus the present system will largely remain intact.

There are changes on the international front. By 2005 quoted companies in the EU will have had to incorporate IASB International Financial Reporting Standards into their financial reports. It is hoped that, in the meantime, other companies will adopt them on a voluntary basis Thus there will be no need for British accounting standards except on issues that are of relevance only to the UK. The IASB is also working with the FASB in the USA, so it is possible that IFRSs will become acceptable in America, thereby enabling overseas companies to seek a stock exchange listing much more easily in that country.

One specific accounting topic of major importance is that relating to revenue recognition. No clear authoritative professional guidance is currently available about this issue. It is an urgent matter because old accounting guidelines cannot cope with the new industries that have been created in recent years and the complex financial arrangements that have been devised. The IASB is working to produce an IFRS but one is not expected before 2005.

Key points

1 Accounting scandals are not necessarily all fraud related. Reported accounting irregularities may be caused by genuine alternative methods of dealing with particular issues.

2 The Government is proposing to reform company law. It does not propose to interfere directly in accounting practice. The new Act will lay down a broad framework. A number of private sector bodies will be responsible for dealing with the detail. The system will be very similar to the present one.

3 By 2005 all EU quoted companies will have to ensure that their financial accounts and reports comply with International Accounting Standards.

4 The IASB and the FASB are working towards making IFRSs acceptable in the USA.

5 Revenue recognition is a complex major issue in financial reporting. The IASB is currently working on a proposal that could lead to an IFRS within the next few years.

Check your learning

The answers to these questions may be found within the text.

1 What is meant by an 'accounting scandal'?

2 Why is meant by 'an accounting irregularity'?

3 Is this the same as doing something unlawful?

4 What appears to be the main driving force that has apparently caused more 'accounting irregularities' to occur in recent years?

5 What responsibility have auditors had for such irregularities?

6 List three reasons why company audits may not be completely independent.

7 What is the 'expectations gap'?

8 How might it be bridged?

9 How many Companies Acts have there been since the Second World War?

10 What accounting approach is the Government proposing in the new Companies Act?

11 What do the following initials mean: (a) FRC; (b) ASB; (c) FRRP; (d) CLRC; (e) SB; (f) RRP?

12 Name two additional financial statements that may become compulsory for quoted companies in the new Act.

13 For what actions will criminal proceedings be brought?

14 How many members of the EU are there expected to be by 2004?

15 What was the IASC and what is the IASB?

16 Where is the IASB based?

17 What are the two names for accounting standards associated with the IASB?

18 What type of company in the EU will be required to adopt International Accounting Standards by 2005?

19 Suggest two reason why the USA is reluctant to adopt the IASB's accounting standards.

20 What is the SEC?

21 What is revenue?

22 What is meant by the term 'revenue recognition'?

23 What are the two accounting rules that cause a problem over recognizing revenue?

24 What are the three approaches that may be adopted in dealing with the timing problem associated with revenue recognition?

25 What is the IASB doing to deal with the problem?

News story quiz

Remember the news story at the beginning of this chapter? Go back to that story and re-read it before answering the following questions.

This article indicates that as far as the UK is concerned it is likely that the requirement to adopt IASs will apply to more than just quoted companies. Clearly, the EU's proposal and the British Government's ideas are a major step towards the eventual harmonization on a world-wide basis of accounting practice.

Questions

1 What reasons might the EU have for requiring quoted companies to adopt IASs?

2 Do you think that all companies should also be required to adopt IASs?

3 What are the specific cost implications for non-quoted companies using IASs?

4 Are there any benefits for them?

5 What do you think is meant by the statement 'IAS could mean a big change for hundreds of private UK firms, which will have *to alter the way they account for areas of their business...*'? [emphasis added]

Tutorial questions

13.1 Examine the respective role and responsibilities of the various parties that may have been implicated in a number of recent accounting scandals.

13.2 Comment on the Government's proposals for company law reform.

13.3 Should accounting policies be harmonized (i.e. brought closer together) or standardized (i.e. made the same)?

13.4 Explain why revenue recognition is a major problem in accounting practice.

Further practice questions, study material and links to relevant sites on the World Wide Web can be found on the website that accompanies this book. The site can be found at **www.booksites.net/dyson**

The communication of financial information

Learning objectives

After preparing this case study you should be able to:

- identify significant features contained in a company's profit and loss account, balance sheet and cash flow statement;
- describe the financial performance of a company using the above statements;
- prepare a chairman's report based on the information extracted from the profit and loss account, balance sheet and cash flow statement and from other sources.

Background

Location	Dundee, Scotland
Company	Bett Brothers plc

Synopis

Bett Brothers plc is a housebuilding and property company based in Dundee, Scotland. The company has two divisions: Bett Homes and Bett Properties. Bett Homes is divided into three geographical divisions (Scotland, the Northwest, and the Northeast). It also includes Bett Partnerships. It works with local authorities and housing associations to provide what the company calls 'affordable homes'. Bett Properties operates throughout the UK mainly with joint venture partners on various projects.

The Appendix includes Bett Brothers plc consolidated profit and loss account for the year ended 31 August 2002, a consolidated balance sheet as at that date, and a consolidated cash flow statement for the year. In order to minimize the amount of data presented in this case study, a statement of total recognized gains and losses, a note of the historical cost profits and losses, the company's balance sheet, a note reconciling the net cash flow to the movement in net debt, and the notes to the accounts are all excluded from the Appendix.

The average monthly number of persons employed by the Group during the year was as follows:

	2002	*2001*
Housebuilding and related activities	226	194
Pubs and hotels	–	223
Property investment and development	4	4
	230	421

Discontinued activities during the year included Pitkerro Plumbing and Inns. These activities were sold on 1 September 2000 and 3 September 2001 respectively.

Interest rates were low during the year and demand for housing was strong. The commercial property market, however, was much less buoyant. Interest rates were expected to remain low in 2002 and the housing market for 2002 (especially in the southeast of England) was likely to be strong. The outlook for the commercial property market was not as optimistic.

Required:
Based on the above information and that contained in the Appendix, draft a chairman's statement covering the year to 31 August 2002.

Appendix

Bett Brothers plc
Consolidated profit and loss account for the year ended 31 August 2002

	2002 £000	2001 £000
Group turnover from continuing operations		
including share of joint venture	116 280	83 182
Share of joint ventures' turnover	(2 205)	(4 161)
Group turnover from continuing operations	114 075	79 021
Group turnover from discontinued operations	–	8 049
Group turnover	114 075	87 070
Cost of sales	(90 318)	(70 963)
Gross profit	23 757	16 107
Other operating expenses (net)	(5 856)	(6 109)
Operating profit	17 901	9 998
Operating profit from continuing operations	17 901	8 282
Operating profit from discontinued operations	–	1 716
Operating profit	17 901	9 998
Share of operating profit in joint ventures	984	2 191
Profit on sale of discontinued operations	515	–
Profit on ordinary activities before interest	19 400	12 189
Interest payable (net)	(2 246)	(2 129)
Profit on ordinary activities before taxation	17 154	10 060
Tax on profit on ordinary activities	(3 472)	(1 650)
Profit for the financial year	13 682	8 410
Dividends paid and proposed (see note below)	(2 423)	(2 009)
Retained profit for the year	11 259	6 401
Earnings per ordinary share	87.00p	53.27p
Ordinary:		
Interim paid per share	4.20p	3.65p
Final proposed per share	11.00p	9.10p

Note:

Dividends paid and proposed

	2002 £000	2001 £000
Ordinary:		
Interim paid 4.20p per share [2001 – 3.65p per share]	668	571
Final proposed 11.00p per share [2001 – 9.10p per share]	1 755	1 438
	2 423	2 009

Consolidated balance sheet at 31 August 2002

	2002 £000	2001 £000
Fixed assets		
Tangible assets	3581	13023
Investments		
Own shares	416	–
Joint ventures – share of gross assets	16643	20649
– share of gross liabilities	(14091)	(17167)
	2968	3482
	6549	16505
Current assets		
Stocks	104806	73353
Debtors	14272	7619
Cash at bank and in hand	1791	35
	120869	81007
Creditors		
Amounts falling due within one year	(45199)	(36783)
Net current assets	75670	44224
Total assets less current liabilities	82219	60729
Creditors		
Amounts falling due after more than one year	(20000)	(10000)
Net assets	62219	50729
Called-up equity share capital	3192	3161
Share premium	607	407
Revaluation reserve	125	2314
Profit and loss account	58295	44847
Equity shareholders' funds	62219	50729

Consolidated cash flow statement
Year ended 31 August 2002

	2002 £000	2001 £000
Net cash outflow from operating activities	(13199)	(4785)
Dividends received from joint ventures	1014	157
Interest paid	(1457)	(1035)
UK corporation tax paid	(2537)	(1440)
Capital expenditure and financial investment	(564)	(483)
Disposals	12791	–
Equity dividends paid	(2106)	(1871)
Cash outflow before financing	(6058)	(9457)
Financing (see note below)	10231	10054
Increase in cash in the year	4173	597

Consolidated cash flow statement
Year ended 31 August 2002

Note:

	2002	2001
	£000	£000
Issue of ordinary share capital	231	54
New borrowings	10 000	10 000
	10 231	10 054

Interpretation of accounts

After preparing this case study you should be able to:

● evaluate a set of financial statements for a public limited company;

● identify the main changes in the company's financial position over a period of time;

● summarize the information contained within such statements.

Background

Location   Scotland

Company   Robert Wiseman Dairies plc

Synopsis

Robert Wiseman Dairies is a public limited company. Its head office is in East Kilbride, near Glasgow. The Group's turnover and profits arise wholly from the supply and distribution of fresh processed milk and cream. It operates entirely in the UK with dairies at Aberdeen, Glasgow and Manchester. The average number of persons employed by the Group during 2002 was 2692 (2302 on production and distribution, and 390 on administration).

The company was originally a small family business. In recent years it has expanded rapidly. It has done this partly by natural growth and partly through acquiring other companies. It became a public company in 1994.

Appendix 1 shows the Group's consolidated profit and loss account, balance sheet and consolidated cash flow statement for each of the five years March/April 1998, 1999, 2000, 2001 and 2002 respectively. Appendix 2 contains some accounting ratios based on those financial statements.

Required:
Analyze the company's financial performance for the five years 1998 to 2002 inclusive.

Appendix 1	Robert Wiseman Dairies PLC Consolidated profit and loss accounts				

For the year ended	4.4.98 £000	3.4.99 £000	1.4.00 £000	31.3.01 £000	30.3.02 £000
Turnover					
Existing operations			286322	300182	355953
Acquired operations			376		15103
	252721	257168	286698	300182	371056
Cost of sales	(195061)	(193634)	(218842)	(226505)	(287267)
Gross profit	57660	63534	67856	73677	83789
Other operating expenses (net)	(39687)	(43780)	(48751)	(53359)	(64072)
Costs of re-organization of acquired business			(243)		(875)
Total other operating expenses	(39687)	(43780)	(48994)	(53359)	(64947)
Operating profit					
Existing operations			19255	20318	20201
Acquired operations			(393)		(1359)
	17973	19754	18862	20318	18842
Interest receivable	90	87	82	43	19
Interest payable	(383)	(398)	(1060)	(1879)	(2327)
Profit on ordinary activities before taxation	17680	19443	17884	18482	16534
Tax on profit on ordinary activities	(5310)	(5505)	(4980)	(5546)	(4960)
Profit for the financial year	12370	13938	12904	12936	11574
Dividends paid and proposed on ordinary shares	(3379)	(3679)	(3820)	(3760)	(3822)
Retained profit for the period	8991	10259	9084	9176	7752
Earnings per ordinary share					
Earnings per ordinary share before costs of re-organization of acquired business					15.33p
Costs of re-organization of acquired business					(0.77p)
Basic earnings per share	14.87p	16.58p	15.26p	15.69p	14.56p
Fully diluted earnings per share		16.42p	15.20p	15.69p	14.55p

Balance sheets

As at	4.4.98 £000	3.4.99 £000	1.4.00 £000	31.3.01 £000	30.3.02 £000
Fixed assets					
Goodwill		3617	3730	3589	3688
Tangible assets	66481	82285	104606	128776	136690
Investments		363			
	66481	86265	108336	132365	140378
Current assets					
Stocks	4283	4306	4078	3614	5114
Debtors	20532	21242	21869	22172	29799
Cash at bank and in hand	4715	6175	8273	2653	3286
	29530	31723	34220	28439	38199
Creditors: Amounts falling due within one year	(40323)	(50759)	(49101)	(60304)	(63330)
Net current (liabilities)	(10793)	(19036)	(14881)	(31865)	(25131)
Total assets less current liabilities	55688	67229	93445	100500	115247
Creditors: Amounts falling due after more than one year	(5176)	(4922)	(20043)	(20812)	(28158)
Provision for liabilities and charges	(4080)	(4636)	(6192)	(8086)	(9429)
Net assets	46432	57671	67220	71602	77660
Capital and reserves					
Called-up share capital	8379	8463	8488	7995	7811
Share premium account	13420	14833	15239	15697	16209
Special reserve	4062	4062	4062	4062	4062
Profit and loss account	24443	34185	43303	47178	52680
Merger reserve arising on consolidation	(3872)	(3872)	(3872)	(3872)	(3872)
Capital redemption reserve				542	770
Equity shareholders' funds	46432	57671	67220	71602	77660

Consolidated cash flow statements

For the year ended	4.4.98 £000	3.4.99 £000	1.4.00 £000	31.3.01 £000	30.3.02 £000
Net cash inflow from operating activities	29 831	31 144	28 360	35 085	30 626
Returns on investments and servicing of finance					
Interest received	87	87	82	38	27
Interest element of finance lease payments	(12)	(6)	(13)	(60)	(69)
Other interest paid	(371)	(392)	(902)	(1 653)	(2 391)
Net cash outflow from returns on investments and servicing of finance	(296)	(311)	(833)	(1 675)	(2 433)
UK corporation tax paid	(2 634)	(4 273)	(6 274)	(3 251)	(2 914)
Capital expenditure and financial investment					
Purchase of goodwill	(123)		(25)	(54)	(47)
Purchase of tangible fixed assets	(25 650)	(22 927)	(31 613)	(31 755)	(25 476)
Sales of tangible fixed assets	472	645	2 380	383	1 827
Sales of goodwill previously written off to reserves	279	31	34	15	25
Sales of fixed assets investments			363		
Net cash outflow for capital expenditure and financial investment	(25 022)	(22 251)	(28 861)	(31 411)	(23 671)
Acquisitions and disposals					
Acquisition of business		(1 087)	(2 138)		(2 105)
Net overdraft acquired with subsidiary undertaking		(59)	(88)		
Cash at bank and in hand acquired with subsidiary undertakings			547		
Net cash outflow for acquisitions and disposals		(1 146)	(1 679)		(2 105)
Equity dividends paid	(3 061)	(3 458)	(3 770)	(3 747)	(3 766)
Cash outflow before management of liquid resources and financing	(1 182)	(295)	(13 057)	(4 999)	(4 263)
Financing					
Issue of ordinary share capital	14 044	573	431	507	556
Share issue expenses	(586)				
Purchase of shares				(5 316)	(2 275)
New loans	4 000	4 000	21 776	15 290	21 802
Repayment of loans	(9 019)	(4 197)	(4 939)	(15 131)	(12 307)
Capital element of finance lease payments	(182)	(57)	(304)	(747)	(771)
Net cash inflow from financing	8 257	319	16 964	(5 397)	7 005
Increase/(decrease) in cash for the year	7 075	24	3 907	(10 396)	2 742

Appendix 2			Selected accounting ratios		
For the year ended	4.4.98	3.4.99	1.4.00	31.3.01	30.3.02
Return on capital employed (profit before taxation/ average shareholders' funds)	49.6%	37.4%	28.6%	26.6%	22.2%
Return on capital employed (profit after taxation/ average shareholders' funds)	34.7%	26.8%	20.7%	18.6%	15.5%
Return on capital employed (profit before taxation and interest/average shareholders' funds + long-term loans)	44.0%	34.7%	22.9%	22.5%	18.3%
Gross profit	22.8%	24.7%	23.7%	24.5%	22.6%
Mark-up	29.6%	32.8%	31.0%	32.5%	29.2%
Operating profit/turnover	7.1%	7.7%	6.6%	6.8%	5.1%
Current assets	0.7: 1	0.6: 1	0.7: 1	0.5: 1	0.6: 1
Acid test	0.6: 1	0.5: 1	0.6: 1	0.4: 1	0.5: 1
Stock turnover	45.4	45.1	52.2	58.9	65.8
Fixed assets turnover	3.8	3.1	2.7	2.3	2.7
Trade debtor collection period	27 days	26 days	24 days	23 days	24 days
Trade creditor payment period	38 days	45 days	47 days	51 days	44 days
Dividend yield	1.9%	2.3%	5.3%	4.6%	4.1%
Dividend cover	3.7	3.8	3.4	3.4	3.0
Earnings per share	14.87p	16.58p	15.26p	15.69p	14.56p*
Price/earnings	14.6	11.3	5.5	6.6	8.0 *
Capital gearing	10.0%	7.9%	23.0%	22.5%	26.7%

* 15.33p and 7.6p respectively before costs of re-organization of acquired business.

Notes:
1 Some ratios have been calculated using a simple average for the year.
2 Details of the cost of sales are not disclosed in the accounts.
3 Details of trade debtors and trade creditors are shown in a note to the accounts.
4 The item in the balance sheet 'provision for liabilities and charges' has not been included as a long-term loan. The provision relates mainly to a provision for deferred taxation.
5 Additional information may be obtained by logging on to the web (search: Robert Wiseman Dairies plc).

MANAGEMENT ACCOUNTING

Part 4 deals with management accounting. Chapter 14 provides a foundation for a study of management. Chapters 15 and 16 deal with some basic costing accounting matters, Chapters 17 and 18 with planning and control procedures, and Chapters 19, 20 and 21 with some decision-making issues. Finally, Chapter 22 reviews some emerging issues in management accounting.

Part 1
INTRODUCTION TO ACCOUNTING

1 The accounting world
2 Accounting rules

Part 2
FINANCIAL ACCOUNTING

3 Recording data
4 Sole trader accounts
5 Last minute adjustments
6 Company accounts
7 Other entity accounts
8 Cash flow statements

Part 3
FINANCIAL REPORTING

9 Information disclosure
10 The annual report
11 The annual accounts
12 Interpretation of accounts
13 Contemporary issues

Part 4
MANAGEMENT ACCOUNTING

14 Foundations
15 Direct costs
16 Indirect costs
17 Budgeting
18 Standard costing
19 Contribution analysis
20 Specific decisions
21 Capital investment
22 Emerging issues

Control of costs: an important function of management accounting . . .

Tomkins boosted by cost-cutting campaign

By Angela Jameson, Industrial Correspondent

SHARES in Tomkins rose 5 per cent yesterday as the engineering group put up a strong performance in the face of the tough US economy.

Tomkins, which supplies the US car and construction industries, reported a 5 per cent rise in interim pre-tax profits to £143 million, largely on the back of cost-cutting initiatives.

The group said that it had highlighted ten initiatives to cut costs including transferring some production facilities to cheaper locations such as Poland and Mexico.

The closures resulted in an estimated 800 to 900 job cuts, mostly in the US. But sales were also aided by one major car manufacturer adopting Tomkins's "start/stop" technology, which saves fuel and cuts down on vehicle emissions by switching off engines at the touch of the brake at traffic lights.

Tomkins will pay an unchanged first dividend of 4.6p. A change in the year end will result in a second dividend, to be announced with the preliminary results in March. The shares added 10p to $207\frac{1}{4}$p.

The Times, 15 January 2003.

Questions relating to this news story may be found on page 329 ▸▸

About this chapter

The first 13 chapters of this book have concentrated on financial accounting and financial reporting. In Part 4 we turn to management accounting. Management accounting is one of the most important branches of accounting. In this chapter we outline the nature and purpose of management accounting, trace its historical development, describe its main functions, and examine the impact it has on the behaviour of those coming into contact with it.

Thus the chapter provides you with a foundation of the subject and it should make it easier for you to deal with the chapters that go into management accounting in some depth.

The chapter is divided into six main sections. The first main section explains why the chapter is important for non-accounting students. The following section outlines the nature and purpose of management accounting. The next three sections then cover the historical development of the discipline, its main functions, and the effect that it has on human behaviour. The last main section suggests some questions that non-accountants might like to ask about the various issues discussed in the chapter.

Learning objectives

By the end of this chapter you should be able to:

- **describe the nature and purpose of management accounting;**
- **trace its historical development;**
- **outline the six main functions of management accounting;**
- **assess the impact of management accounting on human behaviour.**

! Why the chapter is important for non-accountants

Before we explain why this chapter is important for non-accountants, we need to explain why management accounting itself is important.

The previous chapters in this book covered mainly financial accounting and financial reporting. It is logical to start a study of accounting in this way because financial accounting practices have strongly influenced the development of management accounting.

Nevertheless, until you become a senior manager it is unlikely that you will be involved to any extent in the financial accounting and reporting requirements of an entity. This is not the case with management accounting. Even as a junior manager you are likely to have to provide information for management accounting purposes and to receive reports of your departmental or sectional performance.

At the very least, therefore, it is helpful to know what that information is for and what the various reports mean, especially when you are asked to act on them. It also suggests that almost all employees in an entity should know something about management accounting if they want to be good at their jobs.

Given that these points are valid, it follows that this chapter is very important for non-accountants. It tells you a great deal about management accounting: what it is, how it developed, what it involves, and its impact on human behaviour. It is also important in a more specific sense because it provides you with a basic understanding of management accounting sufficient for you to cope with the remaining chapters in this part of the book.

Nature and purpose

Accounting is a specialized service function involving the collection, recording, storage and summary of data (primarily of a financial nature), and the communication of information to interested parties. It has five main branches, the two main ones being financial accounting and management accounting. *Financial accounting* deals mainly with information normally required by parties that are *external* to an entity, e.g. shareholders or government departments. *Management accounting* has a similar role, except that the information supplied is normally for parties *within* an entity, e.g. management. In summary, therefore, we put forward the following definition of management accounting:

> Management accounting is a functional activity involving the collection, recording, storage and summary of both financial and non-financial data and the communication of information to interested parties working mainly with an entity.

It should be noted that financial accounting is also not necessarily concerned exclusively with financial information, and it is also of interest to various internal managerial parties such as the board of directors and divisional directors. Similarly, management accounting is not restricted solely to the supply of management information and it may be of relevance to some external parties (e.g. the government). The essential differences between management accounting and financial accounting, may be summarized as follows:

1 *Non-mandatory*: there are no statutory or mandatory professional requirements covering management accounting.
2 *Data*: more data are normally incorporated into a management accounting system.
3 *Qualitative data*: management accounting information increasingly includes both quantitative and qualitative data.
4 *Non-monetary*: data that cannot be translated into monetary terms is incorporated into management accounting reports.
5 *Forecasted and planned*: data of both a historic and a forecasted or planned nature is of considerable importance and relevance in management accounting.
6 *Users*: management accounting is primarily concerned with providing information for use *within* an entity.

Unlike financial accountants, therefore, management accountants have considerably more freedom in providing information that meets the specific requirements of interested parties. The main party will normally be the entity's managers.

Activity 14.1	The above section has provided you with some idea of what management accountants do. But how can they help you do a better job? Jot down in your notebook what help you think that they could give you.

Historical review

Until the eighteenth century, Britain was primarily an agrarian society and there were comparatively few recognizable industrial entities. Furthermore, most entities (of whatever type) were relatively small, and they were largely financed and managed by individuals or their families. As a result, it was largely unnecessary to have formal documentary systems for planning, control and reporting purposes because the entities were small enough for the owners to assess these considerations for themselves on a day-to-day basis.

During the eighteenth century, Britain became the first country in the world to undergo an Industrial Revolution. In just a short period of time it changed from a predominantly agricultural society to an industrial one, and by the late nineteenth century it had become a major industrial power in the world. There were two specific consequences of this development. They were as follows: (1) The new industrial enterprises needed large amounts of capital. This could not be provided by just a few individuals. Capital had to be sought from 'investors' whose interest in the enterprise was largely financial. Such investments were extremely risky and there was the strong possibility of personal bankruptcy. Hence Parliament intervened and introduced the concept of *limited liability* into company law. (2) The new enterprises needed specialist staff to operate and manage them. Such staff had often to be recruited from outside the immediate family circle.

The above two factors resulted in the ownership of the enterprise being divorced from its management. In a number of Company Acts passed in the nineteenth and twentieth centuries, Parliament decided that shareholders in limited liability companies should have a right to receive a minimum amount of information annually and that auditors should be appointed to report to shareholders on the information presented to them by the company's management.

The complexity, scale and size of the new industrial enterprises meant that it was difficult for professional managers to exercise control on the basis of personal knowledge and casual observation. It became necessary to supply them with information that was written down. At first this revolved round the statutory annual accounts, but it soon became clear that such accounts were produced too late, too infrequently, and in too little detail for effective day-to-day managerial control. As a consequence, during the period 1850 to about 1900, a more detailed recording and reporting system evolved. We now refer to this as a *cost accounting system*. Its main purposes were to provide sufficient information for the valuation of closing stock, work-in-progress and finished goods, and for calculating the costs of individual products. In the early days, it was common for financial accounting systems and cost accounting systems to run side by side. As they incorporated much common data, they gradually became merged into just one system.

The main developments in management accounting occurred in the United States at the beginning of the twentieth century. By 1925 most of the practices and techniques used today were established. Indeed, between 1925 and 1980 few new developments in management accounting took place. The position has changed somewhat during the last 25 years or so, and many new ideas have been put forward. Some of them have been incorporated into practice, albeit mainly by large companies.

The new management accounting techniques were rapidly developed and practised fairly widely in the United States from the beginning of the twentieth century. Progress was much slower in Britain. Apart from the largest industrial companies, the application of management accounting did not become common until about 1970. Even now, there is evidence that many smaller entities still depend on what is sometimes called 'back of the envelope' exercises for managerial planning and control purposes. It should also be noted that over the same period, manufacturing industry in many industrial nations has given way to service industries. This means that many of the traditional management accounting issues, such as stock control and pricing, standard costing and product costing are of much less significance than they once were. Nevertheless, they are still of some considerable relevance and we will be covering them in subsequent chapters.

Activity 14.2   Write down in your notebook two reasons why in the nineteenth century it became apparent that accounting, as it had been previously practised, was not useful in working out the cost of individual products.

Main functions

The overall role of a management accountant is to collect data and to provide information to management. Six specific functions can be readily identified. We describe them in further detail in the rest of this section. They are: (1) planning; (2) control; (3) cost accounting; (4) decision making; (5) financial management; and (6) auditing.

The interrelationship of these functions is shown in Figure 14.1.

Planning

Planning can be classified into two broad groupings: long-term planning and short-term planning.

Long-term planning

Long-term planning is commonly called *strategic planning* or *corporate planning*. We will refer to it as 'strategic planning' because this appears to be the most widely used term. *Strategy* is a military term meaning the ability to plan and organize manoeuvres in such a way that the enemy is put at a disadvantage. Over the last 20 years, strategic planning has become an important managerial function in both profit-making and not-for-profit

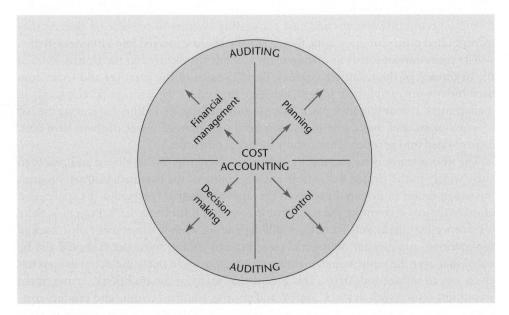

Figure 14.1   Main functions of management accounting

entities. In essence, it involves working out what the entity wants to achieve in the long term (i.e. beyond a calendar year) and how it intends to achieve it.

Six basic steps are involved in preparing a strategic plan. The details are shown in Table 14.1 below.

Table 14.1 **Steps in preparing a strategic plan**

Step	Action	Question to be asked
1	Establish the entity's objective (for example, to earn a minimum of 20% on capital employed)	*'Where do we want to be in x years' time?'*
2	Assess the entity's current position.	*'Where are we now?'*
3	Evaluate the external factors (economic, financial, political and social) that will apply during the period of the plan	*'What is the outside world likely to be like?'*
4	Specify the differences that there are between the current position and the required future one	*'What gaps are there between where we are now and where we want to be?'*
5	Conduct a SWOT analysis	*'What are our strengths, weaknesses, opportunities and threats?'*
6	Put the strategic plan together	*'What do we have to do to get towards where we want to go?'*

Strategic planning is not specifically a management accounting function. The senior management of the entity will probably set up a multidisciplined strategic planning team that may include a management accountant. The management accountant's major role will be to collect data and provide information required by the team. In particular, the strategic plan itself will normally include various financial statements, such as profit and loss accounts (or similar income statements), balance sheets, and cash flow statements.

Short-term planning

Accountants normally refer to short-term planning as *budgeting*, the short-term being regarded as being a period of up to a calendar year. Budgeting is covered in Chapter 17.

Control

A clear plan of what an entity wants to do and how it intends to get there is clearly preferable to having no plan at all. Otherwise the entity will just drift. However, an additional benefit of planning is that it can also form part of the control mechanism of the entity. What management accountants do is to measure what has actually happened over a certain period of time and then compare it with what was planned to happen. Any apparent significant differences (or *variances* as they are called) are investigated and if they are not acceptable, action is taken to ensure that future actual events will meet the agreed plan. It may be found, for example, that the actual price paid for some raw materials was £5 per kilo when the plan allowed for a payment of only £4.50 per kilo. Why was there a variance? Was it poor planning? Was it impossible to estimate the actual price more accurately? Was it inefficient purchasing? Were higher-quality materials purchased and if so, was there less wastage?

Not all variances are unwelcome. For instance, 1000 units might have been sold when the plan only allowed for sales of 950 units. The reasons for this variance should still be investigated, and if this *favourable* trend were deemed likely to continue, it would be necessary to ensure that additional resources (e.g. production, administration, distribution, and finance) were made available to meet higher expected levels of sales.

Note that it would be the responsibility of the management accounting to co-ordinate the investigation of any variances and report back to the senior management of the entity. *It would not be the responsibility of the management accountant to take any disciplinary action if a variance had been caused by inefficient management.* This is a point that is not always understood by those employees who come into contact with management accountants!

Further aspects of control are covered in Chapters 17 and 18.

Activity 14.3	Planning involves working out want you want to happen. Control involves (a) looking at what has happened and then (b) taking action if the actual events are different from the planned events. But the control element happens after the events. So how can they be controlled?
	Write down in you notebook the reasons why trying to control events after they have happened may be of some benefit.

Cost accounting

Historically, cost accounting has been the main function of management accounting. It is now much less significant and other functions, such as the provision of information for decision making, have become much more important. The cost accounting function involves the collection of the entity's ongoing costs and revenues, the recording of them in a double-entry book-keeping system (a task that these days is normally done by computer), the balancing of the 'books', and the extraction of information as and when required by management. Cost accounting also involves the calculation of *actual costs* of products and services for stock valuation, control and decision-making purposes.

We deal with cost accounting in Chapter 14 and Chapter 15.

Decision making

The provision of information for decision making is now one of the major functions of management accountants. Although actual costs collected in the cost accounting records may provide some guidance, decision-making information usually requires dealing with anticipated or expected future costs and revenues and it may include data that would not normally be incorporated in a traditional ledger system.

Most decisions are of a special or 'one-off' nature, and they may involve much ingenuity in obtaining information that is of assistance to managers in determining a particular decision. Note that it is the managers themselves who will (and should) take the decision, not the management accountants.

Various aspects of decision making are covered in Chapters 19, 20 and 21.

Financial management

The financial management function associated with management accounting generally is again one that has become much more significant in recent years. Indeed, financial management has almost become a discipline in its own right. Its main purpose is to seek out the funds necessary to meet the planning requirements of the entity, to make sure that they are available when required, and to that they are used efficiently and effectively.

Financial management is not covered in any depth in this book, although we do return briefly to it in Chapter 21.

Auditing

Auditing involves the checking and verification of accounting information and accounting reports. There are two main types of audit: external and internal.

External auditing may be regarded as part of the financial accounting function, while internal auditing is more of management accounting responsibility. External auditors are not employed by an entity. By contrast internal auditors are employed by the entity's management and answer to it. Thus there is an essential difference between the two types. In practice they may work closely together. Furthermore, internal auditors may be involved in assessing the effectiveness and efficiency of management systems generally, rather than concentrating on the cost and financial records.

The management accountant's involvement in auditing is not considered any further in this book.

Behavioural considerations

The collection of data and the supply of information are not neutral activities. They have an impact on those who are involved in supplying and receiving such material. The impact can be strongly negative and it can adversely affect the quality of the data or information. In turn, this may cause management to take some erroneous decisions because of unreliable data and biased information. This is a feature of the job that accountants are now trained to recognize, so that they are aware of the *behavioural impact* that they have on other employees. What relevance is this for non-accountants?

A great deal of the data required for financial accounting and external auditing purposes is supported by legislation. Thus the requirements cannot be ignored, irrespective of whether the entity as a whole or individuals within it regard them as being irrelevant. Data will be required to meet any statutory requirements and, if necessary, the financial accountants and auditors can *demand* whatever information they need.

Management accountants do not have statutory backing, but their position is still an extremely powerful one because they usually receive strong support from the entity's senior management. This can cause a great deal of hostility because management accountants can make demands knowing that they will be backed by the senior managers. Furthermore, they often earn salaries and enjoy working conditions that are the envy of other employees. It is not surprising, therefore, that there is often an assumption that the accountant 'runs things'.

There are three general points to make about such a view:

- financial considerations should form only a part of an overall decision;
- accountants should only make recommendations to senior managers; and
- the ultimate decision should be taken by the senior management.

Management accountants are employed to *provide a service to managers*. This means that, as nearly all employees have some managerial responsibilities, management accountants may be in direct contact with practically all employees. Thus irrespective of your own role within an entity, you can expect to have some contact with management accountants. This should not be regarded as an 'us and them' situation (neither by you nor by them); you are all part of a team and it can be mutually beneficial if you can work together in reasonable harmony.

Activity 14.4

Suppose as a departmental manager you received an email from the chief management accountant that included the following statement:

> *I wish to inform you that you over-ran your budget by £10 000 for March 2005. Please inform me immediately what you intend to do about this overspend. Furthermore, I will need to know why you allowed this gross piece of mismanagement to happen.*

Jot down what your feelings would be if you had received such an email. Then rewrite the above email using a more tactful tone.

What approaches, therefore, should you expect a management accountant to adopt when working with you? We would suggest that at the very least, you are entitled to expect the following:

1 *Equality.* Management accountants should treat you as an equal and they should make it obvious that your contribution is just as valuable as their own.
2 *Non-autocracy.* Management accountants should not adopt an autocratic, condescending and superior attitude when dealing with other employees.
3 *Diplomacy.* Management accountants should be courteous, patient, polite, and tactful when dealing with you.
4 *Information.* You are entitled to a detailed explanation of why, what and when some information is required and in what form it should be presented.
5 *Assistance.* Management accountants should be prepared to give you a great deal of help in providing the information that they need.
6 *Timing.* You should be given a realistic amount of time to provide any information that is required, taking into account your other responsibilities.
7 *Non-disciplinarian.* Management accountants should not imply that you may be subject to disciplinary action if you do not comply with their requests.
8 *Training.* You should receive some formal training in the operation of the various management accounting systems that reflects your particular responsibilities.

In practice, the above requirements may be somewhat idealistic. Sometimes, for example, senior managers do not encourage a participative approach and they may not always be willing to provide appropriate training courses. The management accountants in the entity then have a responsibility to point out that the planning and control systems that operate in such an environment are not likely to be particularly successful.

It must also not be forgotten that the relationship between management accountants and non-accountants is not one-sided and that non-accountants have an equal responsibility to be co-operative. Clearly, management accountants will find it difficult to work with staff who adopt a resentful or surly manner and who try to make life difficult for them.

❗ Questions non-accountants should ask

Some entities do not involve their employees in providing information for management. A system is imposed on them and they are expected to do just as they are told. However, experience suggests that such an approach does not work. It is much better to involve the staff in the detailed implementation and operation of information systems. What approach does your own organization take? We suggest that you ask the following questions (but remember to be tactful!).

● Who wants this information?

● What is it for?

● What's going to happen to it?

● Will I get some feedback?

● What will I be expected to do about it?

● May I suggest some changes?

● How can I help to improve what is done?

Conclusion

This chapter has provided a foundation for a more detailed study of management accounting. Management accounting is one of the five main branches of accounting. Its main purpose is to supply information to management for use in planning and controlling an entity, and in decision making. It evolved out of financial accounting towards the end of the nineteenth century when basic financial accounting systems could not provide managers with sufficient timely information for use in stock control and product costing. In the early part of the twentieth century, management accounting came to be recognized as a useful planning and control mechanism. More recently, it has become an integral part of overall managerial decision making. The discipline now has six main recognizable functions: planning, control, cost accounting, decision making, financial management and auditing.

There are no statutory or mandatory professional requirements that govern the practice of management accounting. Nevertheless, management accounting techniques are now regarded as being of considerable benefit in assisting an entity to achieve its longer-term objectives. As a result, management accountants tend to hold senior positions in most entities and they may wield considerable power and influence. However, their work can be largely ineffective and the quality of the information that they provide poor if they do not receive the wholehearted support of their fellow employees. Unless this is forthcoming, the eventual decisions taken by management, based on the information provided by the management accountants, may possibly lead to errors in the way that the entity is run.

Key points	1 Management accounting is one of the five main branches of accounting.
	2 Its main purpose is to collect data and provide information for use in planning and control, and for decision making.
	3 Management accounting evolved in the second half of the nineteenth century out of the financial accounting because more detailed and more timely information was needed for stock control and for production costing.
	4 It began to be used as a planning and control technique in the early part of the twentieth century.
	5 In more recent years, management accounting techniques have become incorporated into managerial decision making.
	6 Six main functions of modern management accounting can now be recognized: planning, control, cost accounting, decision making, financial management and auditing.
	7 Management accounting practices can have a negative impact on both the providers and the users of information if management accountants adopt an autocratic and non-participative attitude.
	8 A negative approach to management accounting requirements may result in poor-quality information and erroneous decision making.

Check your learning

The answers to these questions may be found within the text.

1 What is management accounting?

2 List six ways in which it is different from financial accounting.

3 Suggest two reasons why in pre-industrial times there was no need for entities to have a management accounting system.

4 For what purposes did nineteenth century managers need a more detailed costing system?

5 What is strategic planning?

6 How does it differ from budgeting?

7 What are the six steps involved in preparing a strategic plan?

8 What is meant by 'control'?

9 Describe briefly the nature of cost accounting.

10 What is decision making?

11 What is the main purpose of financial management?

12 To what extent are management accountants involved in auditing?

13 Why should management accountants be aware of the behavioural impact of information supply?

News story quiz

Remember the news story at the beginning of this chapter? Go back to that story and re-read it before answering the following questions.

In order for an entity to continue in business, managers need to keep a tight control over costs. Management accountants provide managers with information to help them do so. This article emphasizes the importance of cutting costs whenever and wherever possible.

Questions

1 The article mentions ten cost-cutting measures but only one is indicated: what could they be?

2 What quantitative information do you think that the management accountants would have supplied to managers so that a decision could be taken about switching production facilities to Poland and Mexico?

3 What qualitative factors would also have to be taken into account?

4 What impact would there have been on the workforce in the UK about a decision to switch production to cheaper locations overseas?

Tutorial questions

The answers to questions marked with an asterisk may be found in Appendix 4.

14.1 Examine the usefulness of management accounting in a service based economy.

14.2 The first step in preparing a strategic plan is to specify the entity's goals. Formulate three possible objectives for (a) a manufacturing entity; and (b) a national charity involved in animal welfare.

14.3   Assess the importance of taking into acount behavioural considerations when operating a management accounting system from the point of view of (a) the management accountant; and (b) a senior departmental manager.

14.4*   Distinguish between financial accounting and management accounting.

14.5*   Describe the role of a management accountant in a large manufacturing entity.

14.6   Outline the main steps involved in preparing a strategic plan.

14.7   What is the difference between 'planning' and 'control'?

14.8   'Management accountants hold an extremely powerful position in an entity, and this enables them to influence most of the decisions.' How far do you think that this assertion is likely to be true in practice?

Further practice questions, study material and links to relevant sites on the World Wide Web can be found on the website that accompanies this book. The site can be found at **www.booksites.net/dyson**

Inflation of stock and work-in-progress – part of the problem . . .

Charter dives after hole appears in US accounts

BY MALCOLM MOORE

Charter, the debt-laden industrial conglomerate, saw its share price more than halve yesterday after revealing a hole in the accounts of one of its US divisions.

David Gawler, chairman and chief executive, was battling the flu as well as analysts as Charter dropped 44 to close at 36p. The group said "certain accounting irregularities" would take about £6m off operating profits for the year, and that reported results from previous years may have been overstated by £4m. Analysts expected Charter to turn in pre-tax profits of £45m for 2002.

The hole is in the books of Howden, the company's air and gas handling division. Howden had previously been seen to be turning the corner after a painful restructuring.

Charter believes that some employees had overstated revenues, possibly for years. Mr Gawler said: "The value attributed to work in progress has been inflated and one or two smaller things, such as stock, were inflated.

"There is no justification for this and it looks like those concerned had amended them. It was discovered when someone became ill and someone else came in to do the accounts."

Charter has suspended three employees pending the outcome of an investigation. Mr Gawler said he could not see any reason why the revenues had been overstated, since the department did not pay bonuses and there was no element of personal gain. He added that it might have been prompted by a desire to safeguard jobs.

"I became aware of the problem on Thursday," said Mr Gawler. "All I can say is that when you make an announcement about something that comes out of the side-field, your share price tends to get punished." Mr Gawler said Howden would still be a profitable unit, despite the restatement.

Analysts said Charter had had a difficult year, and is struggling under the current climate, its £200m of debt and a painful restructuring.

Michael Blogg, at Old Mutual, said: "It is not good for the company's credibility. The balance sheet has very small reserves and people usually do this kind of thing when they are trying to hide something. Perhaps it was people not making their budgets or maybe even something more sinister."

Charter is audited by Price Waterhouse Coopers.

The Daily Telegraph, 29 January 2003.

Questions relating to this news story may be found on page 346 ▸▸

About this chapter

In the last chapter we explained something about the nature and purpose of management accounting, why and how it developed as a separate branch of accounting, and what its main functions are today. One such function is *cost accounting*.

Cost accounting involves collecting detailed financial data about products and services, and the recording of that data. The data may then be extracted from the books of account, summarized, and presented to the management of an entity. The managers will use the information presented to them for planning and control purposes. The information may take various forms depending upon what it is to be used for. At the very least, managers are usually interested in knowing the profit or loss made by individual products or services. For convenience, we will call this process *product costing*.

As we indicated in the last chapter, nineteenth-century financial accounting procedures were inadequate for product costing purposes. Managers needed this information so that they could base their selling prices on what products had cost to make. Hence *cost accounting* (as it came to be called) slowly began to develop as a separate branch of accounting. Similarly, during the twentieth century, cost accounting has been subsumed into a much broader branch that we now call *management accounting*.

Accountants still cost products using a technique that has hardly changed in over 100 years. This technique is generally known as *absorption costing*. In broad terms, absorption costing involves the following procedure:

1 Isolate those costs that can be easily identified with a particular product.
2 Share out on some equitable basis those other costs that cannot be easily identified with a particular product.

Accountants describe the first stage as *allocating* the direct costs, and the second stage as *absorbing* the indirect costs. In this chapter we cover the first stage and in the next chapter, the second stage.

The chapter is divided into seven main sections. The first main sections explains why it is important that non-accountants should study this chapter. The following section outlines what is meant by a responsibility accounting system. We then examine the traditional format for classifying costs. The next three sections go into some detail about the way that direct material costs, direct labour costs, and other direct costs are charged to individual products. The last main section formulates some questions that non-accountants should ask about the contents of this chapter.

Learning objectives	By the end of this chapter you should be able to: ● identify direct material, direct labour and other direct costs; ● describe three important methods of charging direct material costs to production; ● calculate prime costs.

❗ Why this chapter is important for non-accountants

This chapter is the first of two covering the subject of cost accounting.

As a non-accountant you may by puzzled why you need to know anything about cost accounting. It might seem reasonable to assume that you can safely leave that subject to your accountants. We do not think so.

We assume that as a non-accounting student your aim is to hold a senior position in some entity. When you do so, you will be responsible for all that goes on in that company. That does not mean that you will be expected to have the technical expertise and knowledge to do every job in the company (including the job of the accountants). Indeed, because there will be so much to do, you will have to be good at delegating a great deal of the work, especially if some of it is extremely specialized.

Accounting is an example of a highly specialized function. In a large company you will almost certainly employ a large team of accountants (a) to ensure that the company complies with all legal requirements involving the keeping of records and the preparation of the company's accounts; and (b) to provide you and your fellow managers with the necessary information to help you make and take effective decisions.

You might need, for example, information about what level of stock the company holds and what it is worth. Similarly, you might want to know what your products cost to manufacture so that you can determine their selling prices. Such information will be supplied by your accountants. So why should you want to know the details of how they have arrived at their calculations?

There are two main reasons.

1   To achieve greater control over the company's affairs

As a senior manager you are ultimately responsible for all that goes on in that company. You would be taking a huge risk if you accepted without question all that you were told by your junior managers. A basic grasp of cost accounting will give you the confidence to question your accountants with more conviction and to understand what they are telling you. This will help you to exercise more control over the accounting function. This is important because its decisions have repercussions for the entire company.

2   To make better decisions

As we have emphasized throughout this book, there are few right and wrong answers in accounting. Accounting information is usually compiled on the basis of a series of assumptions and estimates. In financial accounting, for example, we can adjust profit levels by increasing or decreasing the provision made for bad debts. Similarly, in cost accounting, we can do the same by changing the method used to value raw material stocks. If you are not aware, therefore, of how your accountants have arrived at any figures they put before you, you will not be in a position to question the advice that they are giving you.

Your accountants' recommendations are largely based on what they think and there is no reason why you should not challenge what they are telling you. This would be difficult if you have no idea what they are talking about.

You can then safely leave the detailed calculations to them. But as a general manager, your views on valuation methods and charging procedures are very important as they are likely to be much more broad-based than those of your accountants. It follows that any decisions that you then take based on the input you have had in preparing the cost accounting information are likely to be much more realistic.

We think that as a non-accountant you will gain by working your way through the detailed calculations shown in this chapter (and the next). By doing so you will know where the accountants have got their figures from and what they have done to arrive at them. You will then be in a much stronger position to challenge their findings and recommendations.

Responsibility accounting

A cost accounting system will normally be based on a system of 'responsibility accounting'. *Responsibility accounting* contains the following features:

1 *Segments.* The entity is broken down into separate identifiable segments. Such segments are known as 'responsibility centres'. There are three main types:
   (a) *Cost centre.* A cost centre manager would only be responsible for the costs for that centre, e.g. the personnel department. An income-earning centre (such as a sales region) is also known as a cost centre. There are two types of cost centres: *production cost centres*, where products are manufactured or processed (e.g. a machining department); and *service cost centres*, where a service is provided for other cost centres (including other service cost centres, such as the personnel department recruiting staff for the canteen or wages office).
   (b) *Profit centre.* Profit centre managers would be responsible for both costs and revenues related to their area of responsibility, e.g. a large operational unit of a national company (such as the oil products division of a chemicals company).
   (c) *Investment centre.* Investment centre managers would be responsible for costs, revenues, and investment decisions associated with their specific area of activity. Divisions of large multinational companies are usually treated as investment centres.
2 *Boundaries.* The boundaries of each segment will be clearly established.
3 *Control.* A manager will be put in charge of each separate segment.
4 *Authorization.* Segmental managers will be given the authority to operate their segments as autonomously as possible.

By establishing distinct boundaries between different segments, it is possible to identify clearly their respective costs and revenues. This means that each manager can then be expected to take charge of his costs or revenues, answer for them, and be expected to plan and control them. Furthermore, the breakdown of costs and revenues on a responsibility centre basis enables product costs and services to be readily established. You will recall that this is one of the primary purposes of a cost accounting system. We explain how costs are determined in the following sections.

Activity 15.1

What are your first thoughts about responsibility accounting? Do you think that it is possible to divide a complex organization into neat little segments? Is it realistic to say to someone *'you're in complete charge of that segment'*? Write your answers to these questions in your notebook.

How much autonomy do you think a cost centre manager can be given? Mark your answer on the following scale.

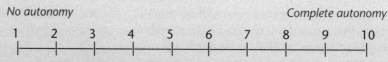

No autonomy   *Complete autonomy*

1   2   3   4   5   6   7   8   9   10

Classification of costs

We mentioned above that the establishment of a responsibility accounting system enables costs and revenues to be easily identified with various types of centres. In order to avoid tedious repetition, we will now refer to them all as 'cost centres'.

If a cost centre structure is in place, we should be able to identify each cost with a particular cost centre. In practice, this is not always easy because there are some costs that are so general and so basic that no one manager has control over them. One example is that relating to business rates. Business rates are a form of local property tax. They are levied on the property as a whole and a manager whose cost centre occupies part of the property has no control over the rates paid in respect of his own cost centre.

> In practice it is not easy to identity some costs with a specific cost centre, e.g. business rates paid by a company as a contribution towards local authority services. The amount payable is based on the property occupied and not any one department within it.
>
> Suggest which cost centre should be charged with the cost of the company's business rates.

Activity 15.2

Costs that are easily and economically identifiable with a particular segment are known as *direct costs*. Hence if it is possible to identify all the costs of the entity with particular cost centres, then all costs must be direct costs at the cost centre level. This will not be the case at a *product* level. In costing a particular unit, some costs will be easy to identity with that unit. These will be classed as *direct unit costs*. Some costs, however, will not be easy to identity with a particular unit, e.g. the canteen or the wages department expenses. Such costs will be classed as *indirect costs* as far as any particular unit is concerned. In costing a product or service, therefore, it is necessary to devise a method for dealing with indirect costs. We return to this problem in the next chapter.

Irrespective of whether costs are classified into the direct or indirect categories, we also need to have some idea of their nature. Hence management accountants usually break costs down into their elements, i.e. whether they are material costs, labour costs or other types of costs. The *elements of cost* are shown in diagrammatic form in Figure 15.1. This breakdown of costs into their elements is similar to that adopted in Chapter 7 when we were dealing with manufacturing accounts.

There are two particular points to note about Figure 15.1.

(1) In a competitive market, selling price can rarely be determined on a 'cost-plus' basis, i.e. total cost of sales plus a profit loading. If the entity's prices are more than its competitors, then it is not likely to sell very many units; however, if its selling price is less than its competitors, then it might sell many units but the profit on each sale may be low. The chances are, then, that if its selling prices are low its competitors will soon bring down their prices. Thus when the market largely determines selling prices, it is vital that the entity's total costs are strictly controlled and monitored so that the gap between its total sales revenue and its total cost of sales (i.e. its profit) is as wide as possible.

(2) The classification shown will not necessarily be relevant for all entities. For example, an entity in the service sector (such as insurance broker) is not likely to have any direct or indirect production costs.

Figure 15.1 is based on what is called *total absorption costing*. Total absorption costing is a method of costing whereby *all* costs of the entity are charged to (or absorbed into) particular products irrespective of their nature. If only production costs are absorbed into product costs, the system is referred to as *absorption costing*.

Indirect costs, however, may include some costs that do not change no matter how many units of the product are produced, i.e. they do not change with the activity level achieved during any particular period. Such costs are known as *fixed costs*. Costs that change with the activity level are known as *variable costs*. Sometimes costs are recorded

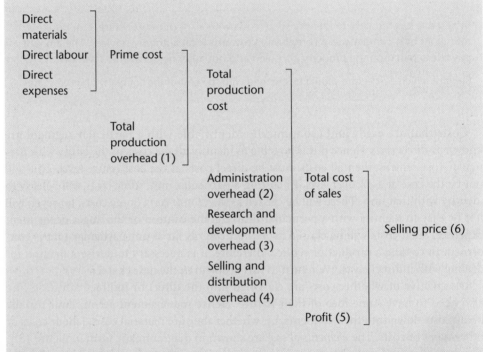

Notes

1 Total production overhead includes those indirect production costs that cannot be easily identified with specific units or processes.
2 Administration overhead includes the non-production costs of operating the entity.
3 Research expenditure includes the cost of working on new products and processes. Development expenditure will include those costs associated with trying to improve existing products, processes and production techniques.
4 Selling and distribution overhead includes the cost of promoting the entity's products and services and the cost of delivering them to its customers or clients.
5 A profit loading may be added to the total cost of sales in order to arrive at the unit's selling price.
6 In this chapter we only go as far as the prime cost level.

Figure 15.1 **The elements of cost**

on the basis of a fixed/variable classification instead of a direct/indirect one, although this is relatively uncommon. A fixed/variable classification gives rise to a form of costing known as *marginal costing*. We shall be dealing with marginal costing in Chapter 19.

We are now in a position to explain how to deal with direct costs. We start with direct materials.

Direct materials

Materials consist of raw materials and component parts. Raw materials are those basic ingredients that are incorporated into the production of a product, such as flour, sugar, and raisins used in baking a cake. Component parts include miscellaneous ready-made goods or parts that are purchased (or manufactured specially) for insertion into a main product, e.g. a car radiator.

As we discussed earlier, a direct cost is one that can be easily and economically identified with a particular segment, such as a cost centre or a particular product. However, there is a problem when relating this definition to materials. It might be easy and economic to identify them *physically* with a particular segment, but it does not necessarily follow that it is then easy to attach a cost to them. There are two main problems. They are as follows.

(1) *Size.* We might be able to identify a few screws used in assembling a chair, for example, but it would not be worthwhile costing them separately because their relative value is so small. Such costs would, therefore, be classified as *indirect* material costs.

(2) *Timing.* Materials may have been purchased at different times and at different prices. Thus it might not be possible to know whether 1000 kg of material held in stock had been purchased at £1, £2, or £3 per kilo. This problem particularly applies when materials that are purchased in separate batches are stored in the same containers, e.g. grains and liquids.

In such circumstances, it is necessary to determine an appropriate pricing method. Many such methods are available. However, as the price of materials charged to production also affects any closing stock values, regard has to be had to the financial reporting requirements of the entity. In management accounting we are not bound by any statutory or mandatory professional requirements, and so we are perfectly free to adopt any stock valuation method we wish. Unfortunately, if the chosen method is not acceptable for financial reporting purposes, we would have to revalue the closing stock for the annual accounts. This may be costly both in terms of time and of effort.

Hence even in management accounting we would normally adopt a pricing method for issuing materials to production and for valuing closing stocks that is also suitable for the annual accounts. This means following the requirements contained in SSAP 9 (Stocks and long-term contracts). There are four preferred methods. We summarize each of them below. They are also shown in diagrammatic format in Figure 15.2.

1 *Unit cost.* The unit cost is the cost of purchasing identifiable units of stocks. If it is possible to identify the specific cost of materials issued to production, then no particular pricing problem arises and we would obviously opt for this method.

2 *First-in, first-out (FIFO).* This method adopts the first price at which materials have been purchased. We consider it in more detail below.

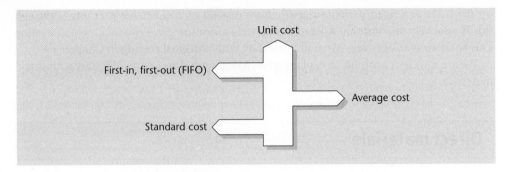

Figure 15.2 **Direct material costing methods**

3 *Average cost.* An average cost may be calculated by dividing the total value of materials in stock by the total quantity. There are a number of acceptable averaging methods, but for illustration purposes we will examine the *continuous weighted average* (CWA) cost method. More details are provided below.

4 *Standard cost.* This method involves estimating what materials are likely to cost in the future. Instead of the actual price, the *estimated* or *planned* cost is then used to charge out the cost of materials to production. The standard cost method is usually adopted as part of a standard costing system. We shall not be considering it any further in this chapter because we will be dealing with standard costing in Chapter 18.

We will now examine the FIFO method in a little more detail.

Activity 15.3

Assuming that you do not know the specific unit price of some materials, which method would you use to price them? Tick the appropriate box below and insert the main reason for your choice.

FIFO ☐   Average cost ☐   Standard cost ☐

Main reason:

_____

_____

First-in, first-out (FIFO)

It is sensible to issue the oldest stock to production first, followed by the next oldest, and so on, and this should be done wherever possible. This method of storekeeping means that old stock is not kept in store for very long, thus avoiding the possibility of deterioration or obsolescence. However, as indicated above, some materials (such as grains and liquids) may be stored in such a way that they become a mixture of old and new stock, and it is then not possible to identify each separate purchase. Nevertheless, in pricing the issue of stock to production it would still seem logical to follow the first-in, first-out procedure, and charge production with the oldest price first, followed by the next oldest price, and so on.

FIFO is a very common method used in charging out materials to production. The procedure is as follows:

1 Start with the price paid for the oldest material in stock, and charge any issues to production at that price.

2 Once all of the goods originally purchased at that price have been issued, use the next-oldest price until all of that stock has been issued.

3 The third-oldest price will be used next, then the fourth, and so on.

The prices attached to the issue of goods to production are not, of course, necessarily the same as those that were paid for the actual purchases of those goods. Indeed, they cannot be, for if it had been possible to identify specific receipts with *specific* issues, the unit cost method would have been used.

The use of the FIFO pricing method is illustrated in Example 15.1.

The FIFO pricing method of charging direct materials to production

Example 15.1

The following information relates to the receipts and issue of a certain material into stock during January 2006:

Date	Receipts into stores			Issue to production
	Quantity units	Price £	Value £	Quantity units
1.1.06	100	10	1 000	
10.1.06	150	11	1 650	
15.1.06				125
20.1.06	50	12	600	
31.1.06				150

Required:
Using the FIFO (first-in, first-out) method of pricing the issue of goods to production, calculate the following:

(a) the issue prices at which goods will be charged to production; and
(b) the closing stock value at 31 January 2006.

(a) The issue price of goods to production:

Answer to Example 15.1

Date of issue	Tutorial note	Units	Calculation	£
5.1.06	(1)	100	units × £10 =	1 000
	(2)	25	units × £11 =	275
		125		1 275
31.1.06	(3)	125	units × £11 =	1 375
	(4)	25	units × £12 =	300
		150		1 675

(b) Closing stock:

	£
25 units × £12 =	300
Check:	
Total receipts (£1000 + £1650 + £600)	3 250
Total issues (£1275 + £1675)	2 950
Closing stock	300

Tutorial notes

1   The goods received on 1 January 2006 are now assumed to have all been issued.

2   This leaves 125 units in stock out of the goods received on 10 January 2006.

3   All the goods purchased on 10 January 2006 are assumed to have been issued.

4   There are now 25 units left in stock out of the goods purchased on 20 January 2006.

Although Example 15.1 is a simple one, it can be seen that if the amount of material issued to production includes a number of batches purchased at different prices, the FIFO method involves using a considerable number of different prices.

Activity 15.4   Attempt Example 15.1 without looking at the solution.

The advantages and disadvantages of the FIFO method may be summarized as follows.

Advantages
- The FIFO method is logical.
- It appears to match the physical issue of materials to production.
- The closing stock value is closer to the current economic value.
- The stores ledger account is arithmetically self-balancing and there are no adjustments that have to be written off to the profit and loss account.
- It meets the requirements of SSAP 9 (Stocks and long-term contracts).
- It is acceptable for UK tax purposes.

Disadvantages
- It is arithmetically cumbersome.
- The cost of production relates to out-of-date prices.

Continuous weighted average (CWA)

In order to avoid the detailed arithmetical calculations that are involved in using the FIFO method, it is possible to substitute an *average* pricing method. There are a number of different types, but we are going to concentrate on one called the continuous weighted average (CWA) method.

This method necessitates frequent changes to be made in calculating issue prices. Although it appears a very complicated method, it is the easiest one to use *provided* that the receipts and issues of goods are recorded in a stores ledger account. An example of a stores ledger account in shown in Figure 15.3.

You will note from Figure 15.3 that the stores ledger account shows both the quantity and the value of the stock in store at any one time. The continuous weighted average price is obtained by dividing the total value of the stock by the total quantity. A new price will be struck each time new purchases are taken into stock.

The method is illustrated in Example 15.2. We use the same data that we have used in Example 15.1, but we have taken the opportunity to present a little more information, so that we can explain more clearly how it is calculated.

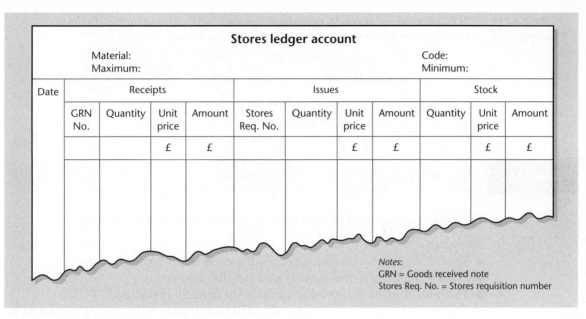

Figure 15.3 **Example of a stores ledger account**

The continuous weighted average pricing method of charging direct materials to production

You are presented with the following information relating to the receipt and issue of a certain material into stock during January 2006:

Date	Receipts into stores			Issues to production			Stock balance	
	Quantity units	Price £	Value £	Quantity units	Price £	Value £	Quantity units	Value £
1.1.06	100	10	1 000				100	1 000
10.1.06	150	11	1 650				250	2 650
15.1.06				125	10.60	1 325	125	1 325
20.1.06	50	12	600				175	1 925
31.1.06				150	11.00	1 650	25	275

Note:
The company uses the continuous weighted average method of pricing the issue of goods to production.

Required:
Check that the prices of goods issued to production during January 2006 have been calculated correctly.

Answer to Example 15.2	The issue prices of goods to production during January 2006 using the continuous weighted average method have been calculated as follows:

$$15.1.06 \quad \frac{\text{Total stock value at 10.1.06}}{\text{Total quantity in stock at 10.1.06}} = \frac{2\,650}{250} = \underline{\underline{£10.60}}$$

$$25.1.06 \quad \frac{\text{Total stock value at 20.1.06}}{\text{Total quantity in stock at 20.1.06}} = \frac{1\,925}{175} = \underline{\underline{£11.00}}$$

Activity 15.5	Attempt Example 15.2 without looking at the solution.

The main advantages and disadvantages of the CWA method are as follows.

Advantages
- The CWA is easy to calculate, especially if a stores ledger account is used.
- Prices relating to previous periods are taken into account.
- The price of goods purchased is related to the quantities purchased.
- The method results in a price that is not distorted either by low or high prices, or by small or large quantity purchases.
- A new price is calculated as recent purchases are taken into stock, and so the price is regularly being updated.

Disadvantages
- A CWA price tends to lag behind current economic prices.
- The CWA price may not relate to any actual price paid.
- It is sometimes necessary to write off any arithmetical adjustments in the stock ledger account to the profit and loss account.

We can now move on to have a look at the other main type of direct cost: labour.

Direct labour

Labour costs include the cost of employees' salaries, wages, bonuses, and the employer's national insurance and pension fund contributions. Wherever it is economically viable to do so, we will want to charge labour costs to each specific unit; otherwise they will have to be treated as part of indirect costs.

The identification and pricing of direct labour is much easier than is the case with direct materials. Basically, the procedure is as follows:

1 Employees working on specific units will be required to keep a record of how many hours they spend on each unit.
2 The total hours worked on each unit will then be multiplied by their hourly rate.
3 A percentage amount will be added to the total to allow for the employer's other labour costs (e.g. national insurance, pension fund contributions, and holiday pay).
4 The total amount is then charged directly to that unit.

The procedure is illustrated in Example 15.3.

Example
15.3

The charging of direct labour cost to production

Alex and Will are the two employees working on Unit X. Alex is paid £10 an hour, and Will £5. Both men are required to keep an accurate record of how much time they have spent on Unit X. Alex spends 10 hours and Will 20. The employer has estimated that it costs him an extra 20 per cent on top of what he pays them to meet his contributions towards national insurance, pension contributions and holiday pay.

Required:
Calculate the direct labour cost of producing Unit X.

Calculation of the direct labour cost:

Answer to
Example 15.3

	Hours	Rate per hour	Total
		£	£
Alex	10	10	100
Will	20	5	100
			200
Employer's costs (20%)			40
Total direct labour cost			240

It should be made clear that, in practice, it is by no means easy to obtain an accurate estimate of the direct labour cost of one unit. We start from an assumption that, if it is very difficult to do so, then probably it will be costly and therefore not worthwhile. But even in those cases where there is no doubt that employees are working on one unit (as in Example 15.3), we are dependent upon them keeping an accurate record. If you have ever had to do this in your own job, you will know that this is not easy, especially if you are frequently being switched from one job to another. It is also difficult to account for all those five minutes spent chatting in the corridor!

Notwithstanding the difficulties, however, it is important that management should emphasize to the employees just how important it is that they keep an accurate record of their time. Labour costs may form a high proportion of total cost (especially in service industries), and so tight control is important. This is particularly so, of course, if tender prices are based on total unit cost. A high cost could mean that the company fails to get a contract, whereas too low a cost diminishes profit.

Other direct costs

Apart from material and labour costs, there may be other types of costs that can be economically identified with specific units. These are, however, relatively rare because, unlike materials and labour, it is usually difficult to trace a physical link to specific units. It only occurs, therefore, in some very special cases. For example, the company may hire specialist plant for work on a specific unit. It is then easy to identify the physical link between the unit and the plant, and to identify the hire charge with the unit.

Notwithstanding the difficulties of identifying other expenses with production, it is important to do so wherever possible. Otherwise, the indirect charge becomes bigger and bigger, and that causes even more problems in building up the cost of a specific unit.

❗ Questions non-accountants should ask

We suggest that you ask the following questions about the contents of this chapter.

- What is included in material costs?
- What criteria do you use for determining whether the costs are direct or indirect?
- What method do you use for charging them out to production?
- How do you determine whether labour costs are direct or indirect?
- What system is used to ensure that time spent on specific jobs is recorded accurately?
- Are there any other costs that could be classified as direct?
- What are they?
- What criteria can we use for classifying them as such?

Conclusion

Responsibility accounting is a system that involves placing all costs and revenues under the control of a designated manager. The entity is divided into segments. Three main types of segments may be identified: cost centres (responsible for costs only), profit centres (responsible for costs and revenues), and investment centres (responsible for costs, revenues and investment decisions). All costs and revenues should be identified with a specific responsibility centre.

A direct cost is a cost that can be easily and economically identified with a specific cost centre. Some direct costs can then be identified with specific units or products. Those that cannot be so identified are known as *indirect* costs.

Costs are usually classified into elements of cost. By building the costs up in layers it is possible to determine a selling price (although market conditions have also to be taken into account).

Direct material costs include raw materials and component parts. They are priced out to products. If the cost of materials used in a particular product is known then there is no problem. The unit cost will be used. Otherwise, a pricing method has to be devised. The three recommended methods are first-in, first-out, an average method, or the standard cost.

Direct labour costs are those costs that can be easily and economically identified with specific products. They are charged out on the basis of hours worked and the hourly rate paid plus an allowance for employer's employment costs, such as national insurance and pension contributions.

There may be other direct costs but these are relatively rare.

Key points

1 Product costing has three main purposes: (a) stock valuation; (b) the planning and controlling of costs; and (c) the determination of selling prices.

2 The procedure involves isolating those costs that are easy and economic to identify with specific units. Such costs are described as *direct costs*. Those costs that are not easy or economic to identify with specific costs are known as *indirect costs*. The total of indirect costs is known as *overhead* (or *overheads*).

3 Some material costs can be physically identified with specific units and their cost easily ascertained. In cases where it is difficult to isolate the cost of material charged to production e.g. where batches of materials are purchased at different prices and where they are stored collectively, an estimated price has to be determined. There are four acceptable methods for pricing materials: (a) unit cost; (b) first in, first out; (c) average cost; and (d) standard cost. The average cost method recommended in this book is known as the *continuous weighted average* (CWA) cost method.

4 Wherever possible, labour costs should be charged directly to specific units. Employees will need to keep time sheets that record the hours that they have spent working on specific jobs. The amount charged to a particular unit will then be the time spent working on that unit multiplied by the respective hourly wage rate.

5 Some other services may also be identifiable with specific units, e.g. the hire of a machine for a particular contract. The cost of such services should be charged directly to production if it can be easily and economically determined.

Check your learning

The answers to these questions may be found within the text.

1 What is responsibility accounting?

2 What is (a) a cost centre; (b) a profit centre; and (c) an investment centre?

3 What is (a) a direct cost; and (b) an indirect cost?

4 What is meant by the elements of cost?

5 What is prime cost?

6 What are direct materials?

7 What four main methods may be used for charging them out to production?

8 What is direct labour?

9 How is it collected and charged out to production?

10 Give an example of a direct cost other than materials or labour.

News story quiz

Remember the new story at the beginning of the chapter? Go back to that story and re-read it before answering the following questions.

The theme of this news story has become a familiar one. Charter's share price fell more than half when it reported 'certain accounting irregularities'. A number of causes appear to have been identified: an overstatement of revenues, and an inflation of both stock and work-in-progress.

Questions

1 How does inflating the value of work-in-progress and stock increase profits?

2 What effect would this have on the following year's profits?

3 In what ways might it be possible to inflate work-in-progress and stock values?

4 Might someone have made some genuine errors or could 'something more sinister' have happened?

Tutorial questions

The answers to questions marked with an asterisk may be found in Appendix 4.

15.1   Examine the argument that an arbitrary pricing system used to charge direct materials to production leads to erroneous product costing.

15.2* The following stocks were taken into stores as follows:

    1.1.06   1000 units @ £20 per unit.
    15.1.06   500 units @ £25 per unit.

There were no opening stocks.
On 31.1.06 1250 units were issued to production.

Required:
Calculate the amount that would be charged to production on 31 January 2006 for the issue of material on that date using each of the following methods of material pricing:

1 FIFO (first-in, first-out); and
2 continuous weighted average.

15.3* The following information relates to material ST 2:

		Units	Unit price £	Value £
1.2.07	Opening stock	500	1.00	500
10.2.07	Receipts	200	1.10	220
12.2.07	Receipts	100	1.12	112
17.2.07	Issues	400	–	–
25.2.07	Receipts	300	1.15	345
27.2.07	Issues	250	–	–

Required:
Calculate the value of closing stock at 28 February 2007 assuming that the continuous weighted average method of pricing materials to production has been adopted.

15.4 You are presented with the following information for Trusty Limited:

2008	Purchases (units)	Unit cost £	Issues to production (units)
1 January	2 000	10	
31 January			1 600
1 February	2 400	11	
28 February			2 600
1 March	1 600	12	
31 March			1 000

Note: There was no opening stock.

Required:
Calculate the value of closing stock at 31 March 2008 using each of the following methods of pricing the issue of materials to production:

1 FIFO (first-in, first-out); and
2 continuous weighted average.

15.5 The following information relates to Steed Limited for the year to 31 May 2005:

	£
Sales	500 000
Purchases	440 000
Opening stock	40 000

Closing stock value using the following pricing methods:

1 FIFO (first-in, first-out)	90 000
2 Continuous weighted average	79 950

Required:
Calculate Steed Limited's gross profit for the year to 31 May 2005 using each of the above closing stock values.

15.6 Iron Limited is a small manufacturing company. During the year to 31 December 2009 it has taken into stock and issued to production the following items of raw material, known as XY1:

Date 2009	Receipts into stock			Issues to production
	Quantity (litres)	Price per unit £	Total value £	Quantity (litres)
January	200	2.00	400	
February				100
April	500	3.00	1 500	
May				300
June	800	4.00	3 200	
July				400
October	900	5.00	4 500	
December				1 400

Notes:

1 There were no opening stocks of raw materials XY1.
2 The other costs involved in converting raw material XY1 into the finished product (marketed as Carcleen) amounted to £7000.
3 Sales of Carcleen for the year to 31 December 2009 amounted to £20 000.

Required:

(a) Illustrate the following methods of pricing the issue of materials to production:
    1 first-in, first-out (FIFO); and
    2 continuous weighted average.
(b) Calculate the gross profit for the year using each of the above methods of pricing the issue of materials to production.

Further practice questions, study material and links to relevant sites on the World Wide Web can be found on the website that accompanies this book. The site can be found at **www.booksites.net/dyson**

Control over overheads is vital . . .

Murgitroyd warns rising costs are taking their toll

SHARES in Murgitroyd, the Glasgow-based intellectual property consultant, are likely to fall sharply today following a profits warning issued last night after the stock market had closed.

The AIM-listed company said costs had increased faster than anticipated during the six months to November 30 as new staff were taken on and overseas offices were opened in Ireland, France and Germany.

"This increase in overheads will have an impact on the profit gen-erated for the interim period," it warned in a trading statement.

The company said it was imple-menting cost savings of £300,000 a year, but these would not affect recruitment for its fast-growing offices in Nice and Munich.

Murgitroyd, which helps other businesses to register patents and actively manage their intellectual property rights, said turnover and gross margin were "broadly in line with analyst expectations."

The Herald, 21 January 2003.

Questions relating to this news story may be found on page 370 ▸▸

About this chapter

This is the second of two chapters in Part 4 that deal with *cost accounting*. We have split our study of cost accounting into two chapters because the subject is too big to deal with in one chapter. Chapter 15 dealt with direct costs and this chapters covers indirect costs. By then end of the chapter we will have been able to show you how accountants have traditionally gone about calculating product costs. In recent years the traditional method has been severely criticized, so before we finish the chapter we will outline a relatively new technique for dealing with indirect costs (or overheads). This technique is called *activity based costing* (ABC) and its proponents make great claims for it.

The chapter is divided into seven main sections. The first main section explains why the chapter is an important one for non-accountants. We then cover in some detail how indirect costs are charged to product costs. This is followed by a section containing a comprehensive example of the overhead absorption technique. A fairly brief section follows, discussing the problem of non-production overhead. We then consider whether indirect costs should be built into product costs on a historical or on a predetermined basis. Up to this point we will have covered the traditional approach to overhead absorption, so we then turn our attention to *activity based costing*. Finally, in the last main section, we frame some questions that non-accountants might like to ask about the material discussed in the chapter.

<table>
<tr><td>

Learning objectives

</td><td>

By then end of this chapter, you should be able to:

- **outline the nature of indirect production and non-production costs;**
- **calculate unit costs using absorption costing;**
- **assess its usefulness;**
- **explain what is meant by activity based costing;**
- **summarize its advantages and disadvantages.**

</td></tr>
</table>

! Why this chapter is important for non-accountants

In the last chapter we gave some reasons why a study of cost accounting is of importance for non-accountants.

In essence we argued that non-accountants need to know something about cost accounting so that (1) they can exercise a close managerial control over the information being presented to them by their accountants; and (2) they can challenge the assertions and assumptions that underpin such information. Those reasons hold good for this chapter as well.

In addition, this chapter is particularly important because it explains how accountants have traditionally gone about calculating the cost of making and selling products or providing services. This information is still required even though the business and technical environment is very different to what it was 100 years ago.

Product costing is still of some importance in controlling costs and in fixing the selling prices of products. This means that senior managers need to get involved in some vital decisions affecting costs and prices. Unless they do so they run the risk of delegating the running of the entity almost entirely to the accountants. This would, of course, be an extremely unwise thing for the managers to do. It is the company's directors who are responsible to the shareholders for the running of the company and not the accountants. Furthermore, it is the directors who are answerable in law for any apparent mismanagement of the company's affairs.

It follows that it would be a derogation of duty for non-accountants to argue that product costing matters were left to the accountants 'and we had nothing to do with it'. A non-accountant cannot escape quite as easily as that.

Production overhead

In the previous chapter we suggested that if management accounting is going to be used as part of a control system, it is necessary for all costs within an entity to become the direct responsibility of a designated cost centre manager. In this section we will examine how the *production* overhead gets charged to specific units. It is quite a complicated procedure, and so we will take you through it in stages. The procedure is as follows.

- *Stage 1*: Allocate all costs to specific cost centres.
- *Stage 2*: Share out the production service cost-centre costs.
- *Stage 3*: Absorb the production overhead.

The overall flow of costs in an absorption costing system is shown in Figure 16.1. The figure shows the terms associated with the technique and also how costs are absorbed into one of the units (Unit 3).

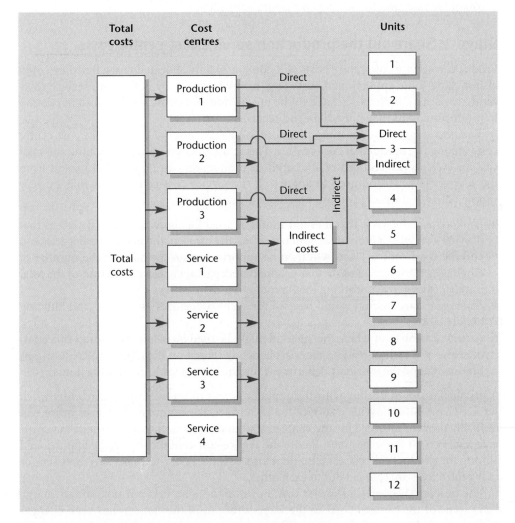

Figure 16.1 **Flow of costs in an absorption costing system**

Stage 1: Allocate all costs to specific cost centres

We cannot emphasize too strongly the importance of allocating all costs to specific cost centres. *Allocation* is the process of charging *whole* items of cost either to a cost centre or to an individual unit of production (known as a cost unit). As the entire cost can be easily identified with a cost centre or cost unit, there is no need to apportion the cost. It is not always easy to allocate *every* type of cost to a identifiable cost centre, and sometimes it is necessary to select a particular cost centre even though its manager may only be remotely responsible for the expenditure.

For control purposes, however, it is necessary to charge such costs to a particular cost centre and then, at some later stage, to *apportion* (i.e. share) them among those cost centres that have benefited from the service provided. For example, most cost centres could be expected to be charged with their share of factory rates, and so they would probably be apportioned on the basis of floor space. Thus, if the rates for the factory amounted to £5000 and it had just two cost centres, one occupying 60 per cent of the total floor space and the other the remaining 40 per cent, the first cost centre would be charged with £3000 of the rates and the second cost centre with £2000.

Stage 2: Share out the production service cost-centre costs

Production service cost-centre costs will contain mainly allocated costs, but they could also include some apportioned costs (e.g. business rates). By definition, service cost-centre costs are not directly related to the production of specific units, and so in relation to production units they must all be indirect costs.

The next stage in unit costing, therefore, is to share out the total service cost-centre costs among the production cost centres. This is usually done by apportioning the total cost for each service cost centre among those production cost centres that benefit from the service. The method used to apportion the service cost-centre costs may be very simple. A few of the more common methods are as follows:

- *Numbers of employees.* This method would be used for those service cost centres that provide a service to individual employees, e.g. the canteen, the personnel department, and the wages office. Costs will then be apportioned on the basis of the number of employees working in a particular production department as a proportion of the total number of employees working in all production cost centres.
- *Floor area.* This method would be used for such cost centres as cleaning and building maintenance.
- *Activity.* Examples of where this method might be used include the drawings office (on the basis of drawings made), materials handling (based on the number of requisitions processed), and the transport department (on the basis of vehicle operating hours).

A problem arises in dealing with the apportionment of service cost-centre costs when service cost centres provide a service for each other. For example, the wages office will probably provide a service for the canteen staff and, in turn, the canteen staff may provide a service for the wages staff. Before the service cost-centre costs can be apportioned among the production cost centres, therefore, it is necessary to make sure that service cost-centre costs are charged out to each other.

The problem becomes a circular one, however, because it is not possible to charge (say) some of the canteen costs to the wages office until the canteen has been charged with some of the costs of the wages office. Similarly, it is not possible to charge out the wages office costs until part of the canteen costs have been charged to the wages office. The problem is shown in diagramatic form in Figure 16.2. The treatment of *reciprocal service costs* (as they are called) can become an involved and time-consuming process unless a clear policy decision is taken about their treatment. There are three main ways of dealing with this problem:

1 *Ignore interdepartmental service costs.* If this method is adopted, the respective service cost-centre costs are only apportioned among the production cost centres. Any servicing that the service cost centres provide for each other is ignored.
2 *Specified order of closure.* This method requires the service cost centre costs to be closed off in some specified order and apportioned among the production cost centres and the remaining service cost centres. As the service cost centres are gradually closed off, there will eventually be only one service cost centre left. Its costs will then be apportioned among the production cost centres. Some order of closure has to be specified, and this may be quite arbitrary. It may be based, for example, on those centres that provide a service for the largest number of other service cost centres, or it could be based on the cost centres with the highest or the lowest cost in them prior to any interdepartmental servicing. It could also be based on an estimate of the benefit received by other centres.
3 *Mathematical apportionment.* Each service cost centre's total cost is apportioned among production cost centres and other service cost centres on the basis of the estimated benefit provided. The effect is that additional amounts keep being charged back to a particular service cost centre as further apportionment takes place. It can take a very long time before there is no more cost to charge out to any of the service cost centres. But when that point is reached, all the service cost centre costs will then have been charged to the production cost centres. This method involves a great deal of exhaustive arithmetical apportionment. It is also very time-consuming, especially where there are a great many service cost centres. Although it is possible to carry out the calculations manually, it is more easily done by computer program.

In choosing one of the above methods, it should be remembered that they all depend upon an *estimate* of how much benefit one department receives from another. Such an estimate amounts to no more than an informed guess. It seems unnecessary, therefore, to build an involved arithmetical exercise on the basis of some highly questionable assumptions. We would suggest that in most circumstances interdepartmental servicing charging may be ignored.

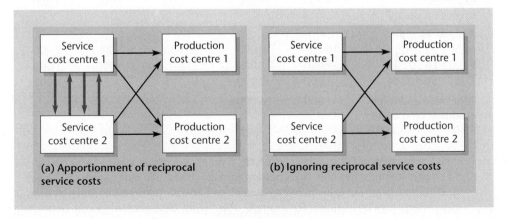

Figure 16.2 Service cost-centre costs: reciprocal costs

We have covered some fairly complicated procedures in dealing with Stages 1 and 2. So, before moving on to Stage 3, we use Example 16.1 to illustrate the procedure.

Example 16.1

Charging overhead to cost centres

You are provided with the following indirect cost information relating to the New Manufacturing Company Limited for the year to 31 March 2005:

	£
Cost centre:	
Production 1: indirect expenses (to units)	24 000
Production 2: indirect expenses (to units)	15 000
Service cost centre A: allocated expenses	20 000
Service cost centre B: allocated expenses	8 000
Service cost centre C: allocated expenses	3 000

Additional information:
The estimated benefit provided by the three service cost centres to the other cost centres is as follows:

Service cost centre A: Production 1 50%; Production 2 30%; Service cost centre B 10%; Service cost centre C 10%.
Service cost centre B: Production 1 70%; Production 2 20%; Service cost centre C 10%.
Service cost centre C: Production 1 50%; Production 2 50%.

Required:
Calculate the total amount of overhead to be charged to cost centre units for both Production cost centre 1 and Production cost centre 2 for the year to 31 March 2005.

Answer to Example 16.1

New Manufacturing Co. Ltd
Overhead distribution schedule for the year to 31 March 2005

Cost centre	Production		Service		
	1	2	A	B	C
	£	£	£	£	£
Allocated indirect expenses	24 000	15 000	20 000	8 000	3 000
Apportion service cost-centre costs:					
A (50 : 30 : 10 : 10)	10 000	6 000	(20 000)	2 000	2 000
B (70 : 20 : 0 : 10)	7 000	2 000	–	(10 000)	1 000
C (50 : 50 : 0 : 0)	3 000	3 000	–	–	(6 000)
Total overhead to be absorbed by specific units	44 000	26 000	–	–	–

Tutorial notes

1 Units passing through Production cost centre 1 will have to share total overhead expenditure amounting to £44 000. Units passing through Production cost centre 2 will have to share total overhead expenditure amounting to £26 000. Units passing through both departments may be identical. For example, they might be assembled in cost centre 1 and packed in cost centre 2.

2 The total amount of overhead to be shared amongst the units is £70 000 (44 000 + 26 000) or (£24 000 + 15 000 + 20 000 + 8000 + 3000). The total amount of overhead originally collected in each of the five cost centres does not change.

3 This exhibit involves some interdepartmental reapportionment of service cost-centre costs. However, no problem arises because of the way in which the question requires the respective service cost-centre costs to be apportioned.

4 The objective of apportioning service cost-centre costs is to share them out among the production cost centres so that they can be included in the cost of specific units.

Answer to Example 16.1 continued

Attempt Example 16.1 without looking at the answer.

Activity 16.1

Stage 3: Absorb the production overhead

Once all the indirect costs have been collected in the production cost centres, the next step is to charge the total amount to specific units. This procedure is known as *absorption*.

The method of absorbing overhead into units is normally a simple one. Accountants recommend a single factor, preferably one that is related as closely as possible to the movement of overhead. In other words, an attempt is made to choose a factor that directly correlates with the amount of overhead expenditure incurred. Needless to say, like so much else in accounting, there is no obvious factor to choose! Indeed, if there was an obvious close relationship, it is doubtful whether it would be necessary to distinguish between direct and indirect costs.

There are six main methods that can be used for absorbing production overhead. All six methods adopt the same basic equation:

$$\text{Cost-centre overhead absorption rate} = \frac{\text{Total cost-centre overhead}}{\text{Total cost-centre activity}}$$

A different absorption rate will be calculated for each production cost centre, and so by the time that a unit has passed through various production cost centres, it may have been charged with a share of overhead from a number of production cost centres.

The six main absorption methods are as follows.

Specific units

$$\text{Absorption rate} = \frac{\text{Total cost-centre overhead}}{\text{Number of units processed in the cost centre}}$$

This method is the simplest to operate. The same rate is applied to each unit, and thus it is only a suitable method if the units are identical.

Direct materials cost

$$\text{Absorption rate} = \frac{\text{Total cost-centre overhead}}{\text{Cost-centre total direct materials cost}} \times 100\%$$

The direct material cost of each unit is then multiplied by the absorption rate.

It is unlikely that there will normally be a strong relationship between the direct material cost and the level of overheads. There might be some special cases, but they are probably quite unusual, e.g. where a company uses a high level of precious metals and its overheads strongly reflect the cost of protecting those materials.

Direct labour cost

$$\text{Absorption rate} = \frac{\text{Total cost-centre overhead}}{\text{Cost-centre total direct labour cost}} \times 100\%$$

The direct labour cost of each unit is then multiplied by the absorption rate.

Overheads tend to relate to the amount of time that a unit spends in production, and so this method may be particularly suitable since the direct labour cost is a combination of hours worked and rates paid. It may not be appropriate, however, where the total direct labour cost consists of a relatively low level of hours worked and of a high labour rate per hour, because the cost will not then relate very closely to time spent in production.

Prime cost

$$\text{Absorption rate} = \frac{\text{Total cost-centre overhead}}{\text{Prime cost}} \times 100\%$$

The prime cost of each unit is then multiplied by the absorption rate. This method assumes that there is a close relationship between prime cost and overheads.

As there is probably no close relationship between either direct materials or direct labour and overheads, then it is unlikely that there will be much of a correlation between prime cost and overheads. Hence, the prime cost method tends to combine the disadvantages of both the direct materials cost and the direct labour cost methods without having any real advantages of its own.

Direct labour hours

$$\text{Absorption rate} = \frac{\text{Total cost-centre overhead}}{\text{Cost-centre total direct labour hours}}$$

The direct labour hours of each unit are then multiplied by the absorption rate.

This method is highly acceptable, especially in those cost centres that are labour-intensive, because time spent in production is related to the cost of overhead incurred.

Machine hours

$$\text{Absorption rate} = \frac{\text{Total cost-centre overhead}}{\text{Cost-centre total machine hours}}$$

The total machine hours used by each unit is then multiplied by the absorption rate.

This is a most appropriate method to use in those departments that are machine-intensive. There is probably quite a strong correlation between the amount of machine time that a unit takes to produce and the amount of overhead incurred.

The various absorption methods outlined above are illustrated in Example 16.2.

Activity 16.2   Think of all the costs of running a factory. Apart from direct material and direct labour costs, what other costs are likely to be involved? List three of them in your notebook. Then attach to each one the main factor that is likely to cause them either to increase or to decrease.

Calculation of overhead absorption rates

Example
16.2

Old Limited is a manufacturing company. The following information relates to the assembling department for the year to 30 June 2004:

	Assembling department Total £000
Direct material cost incurred	400
Direct labour incurred	200
Total factory overhead incurred	100
Number of units produced	10 000
Direct labour hours worked	50 000
Machine hours used	80 000

Required:

Calculate the overhead absorption rates for the assembling department using each of the following methods:
(a) specific units;
(b) direct material cost;
(c) direct labour cost;
(d) prime cost;
(e) direct labour hours; and
(f) machine hours.

(a) Specific units:

$$OAR = \frac{TCCO}{\text{Number of units}} = \frac{£100\,000}{10\,000} = £10.00 \text{ per unit}$$

(b) Direct material cost:

$$OAR = \frac{TCCO}{\text{Direct material cost}} \times 100 = \frac{£100\,000}{400\,000} \times 100 = 25\%$$

(c) Direct labour cost:

$$OAR = \frac{TCCO}{\text{Direct labour cost}} \times 100 = \frac{£100\,000}{200\,000} \times 100 = 50\%$$

(d) Prime cost:

$$OAR = \frac{TCCO}{\text{Prime cost}} \times 100 = \frac{£100\,000}{400\,000 + 200\,000} \times 100 = 16.67\%$$

(e) Direct labour hours:

$$OAR = \frac{TCCO}{\text{Direct labour hours}} = \frac{£100\,000}{50\,000} = £2.00 \text{ per direct labour hour}$$

(f) Machine hours:

$$OAR = \frac{TCCO}{\text{Machine hours}} = \frac{£100\,000}{80\,000} = £1.25 \text{ per machine hour}$$

Activity 16.3	Attempt Example 16.2 without looking at the answer.

Example 16.2 illustrates the six absorption methods outlined in the text. You will appreciate, of course, that, in practice, only one absorption method would be chosen for each production cost centre, although different production cost centres may adopt different methods, e.g. one may choose a direct labour hour rate, and another may adopt a machine hour rate.

The most appropriate absorption rate method will depend upon individual circumstances. A careful study would have to be made of the correlation between (a) direct materials, direct labour, other direct expenses, direct labour hours, and machine hours; and (b) total overhead expenditure. However, it is generally accepted that overhead tends to move with time, so the longer a unit spends in production, the more overhead that that particular unit will generate. Thus, each individual unit ought to be charged with its share of overhead based on the *time* that it spends in production.

This argument suggests that labour-intensive cost centres should use the direct labour hour method, while machine-intensive departments should use the machine hour method.

A comprehensive example

At this stage it will be useful to illustrate overhead absorption in the form of a comprehensive example, although it will clearly be impracticable to use one that involves hundreds of cost centres. In any case, we are trying to demonstrate the principles of absorption costing, and too much data would obscure those principles. Thus, the example, given in Example 16.3, contains only the most basic information.

Example 16.3	Overhead absorption

Oldham Limited is a small manufacturing company producing a variety of pumps for the oil industry. It operates from one factory that is geographically separated from its head office. The components for the pumps are assembled in the assembling department; they are then passed to the finishing department, where they are painted and packed. There are three service cost centres: administration, stores and work study.

The following costs were collected for the year to 30 June 2006:

Allocated cost-centre overhead costs:	£000
Administration	70
Assembling	25
Finishing	9
Stores	8
Work study	18

Example 16.3
continued

Additional information:

1 The allocated cost-centre overhead costs are all considered to be indirect costs as far as specific units are concerned.

2 During the year to 30 June 2006, 35 000 machine hours were worked in the assembling department, and 60 000 direct labour hours in the finishing department.

3 The average number of employees working in each department during the year to 30 June 2006 was as follows:

Administration	15
Assembling	25
Finishing	40
Stores	2
Work study	3
	85

4 During the year to 30 June 2006, the stores received 15 000 requisitions from the assembling department, and 10 000 requisitions from the finishing department. The stores department did not provide a service for any other department.

5 The work study department carried out 2000 chargeable hours for the assembling department, and 1000 chargeable hours for the finishing department.

6 One special pump (code named MEA 6) was produced during the year to 30 June 2006. It took 10 machine hours of assembling time, and 15 direct labour hours were worked on it in the finishing department. Its total direct costs (materials and labour) amounted to £100.

Required:

(a) Calculate an appropriate absorption rate for:
   (i)   the assembling department; and
   (ii) the finishing department.

(b) Calculate the total factory cost of the special MEA 6 pump.

Answer to
Example 16.3(a)

Oldham Ltd

Overhead distribution schedule for the year to 30 June 2006

	Production			Service	
Cost centre	Assembling	Finishing	Administration	Stores	Work study
	£000	£000	£000	£000	£000
Allocated overhead costs (1)	25	9	70	8	18
Production					
Apportion administration (2):					
25 : 40 : 2 : 3	25	40	(70)	2	3
Apportion stores (3): 3 : 2	6	4	–	(10)	–
Apportion work study: 2 : 1	14	7	–	–	(21)
Total overhead to be absorbed	70	60	–	–	–

Tutorial notes

1 The allocated overhead costs were given in the question.

2 Administration costs have been apportioned on the basis of employees. Details were given in the question. There were 85 employees in the factory, but 15 of them were employed in the administration department. Administration costs have, therefore, been apportioned on a total of 70 employees, or £1000 per employee. The administration department is the only service department to provide a service for the other service departments, so no problem of interdepartmental servicing arises.

3 The stores costs have been apportioned on the number of requisitions made by the two production cost centres, that is 15 000 + 10 000 = 25 000, or 3 to 2.

4 The work study costs have been apportioned on the basis of chargeable hours, i.e. 2000 + 1000 = 3000, or 2 to 1.

Calculation of chargeable rates:

1 Assembling department:

$$\frac{\text{TCCO}}{\text{Total machine hours}} = \frac{£70\,000}{35\,000} = \underline{\underline{£2.00 \text{ per machine hour}}}$$

2 Finishing department:

$$\frac{\text{TCCO}}{\text{Total direct labour hours}} = \frac{£60\,000}{60\,000} = \underline{\underline{£1.00 \text{ per direct labour hour}}}$$

It would seem appropriate to absorb the assembling department's overhead on the basis of machine hours because it appears to be a machine-intensive department. The finishing department appears more labour-intensive, and so its overhead will be absorbed on that basis.

Answer to Example 16.3(b)

MEA 6: Calculation of total factory cost

	£	£
Direct costs (as given in note 6)		100
Add: factory overhead:		
Assembling department (10 machine hours × £2.00 per MH)	20	
Finishing department (15 direct labour hours × £1.00 per DLH)	15	35
Total factory cost		135

Activity 16.4

Try to do Example 16.3 without looking at the answer.

Non-production overhead

In the previous section we concentrated on the apportionment and absorption of *production* overheads. Most companies will, however, incur expenditure on activities that are not directly connected with production activities. For example, there could be selling and distribution costs, research and development costs, and head office administrative expenses. How should these types of costs be absorbed into unit cost?

Before this question can be answered, it is necessary to find out why we should want to apportion them. There are three possible reasons:

1 *Control.* The more that an entity's costs are broken down, the easier it is to monitor them. It follows that just as there is an argument for having a detailed system of

responsibility accounting at cost-centre level, so there is an argument for having a similar system at unit-cost level. However, in the case of non-production expenses this argument is not a very strong one.

The relationship between units produced and non-production overhead is usually so remote that no meaningful estimate of the benefit received can be made. So the apportionment of non-production overhead is merely an arithmetical exercise, and no manager could be expected to take responsibility for such costs. From a control point of view, therefore, the exercise is not very helpful.

2 *Selling price.* In some cases, it might be necessary to add to the production cost of a specific unit a proportion of non-production overhead in order to determine a selling price that covers all costs and allows a margin for profit. This system of fixing selling prices may apply in some industries, e.g. in tendering for long-term contracts or in estimating decorating costs. In most cases, however, selling prices are determined by the market, and companies are not usually in a position to fix their selling prices based on cost with a percentage added on for profit (known as cost-plus pricing).

Nevertheless, when selling prices cannot be based on total cost it may still be useful to have an idea of the company's total unit costs in relation to its selling prices. But it must be clearly recognized that the calculation of such total units costs can only provide a general guide.

3 *Stock valuation.* You might think that we need to know the total cost of each unit for stock valuation purposes, since it will be necessary to include the cost of closing stocks in the annual financial accounts. However, SSAP 9 does not permit the inclusion of non-production overhead in stock valuation. Thus, a company is unlikely to apportion non-production overhead for internal stock-valuation purposes if a different method has to be adopted when preparing the financial accounts.

It is obvious from the above summary that there are few benefits to be gained by charging a proportion of non-production overhead to specific cost units. In theory, the exercise is attractive because it would be both interesting and useful to know the *actual* (or true) cost of each unit produced. In practice, however, it is impossible to arrive at any such cost, and so it seems pointless to become engaged in spurious arithmetical exercises just for the sake of neatness.

The only real case for apportioning non-production overhead applies where selling prices can be based on cost. What can be done in those situations? There is still no magic formula, and an arbitrary estimate has still to be made. The easiest method is simply to add a percentage to the total production cost. This is bound to be a somewhat questionable method, since there can be no close relationship between production and non-production activities. It follows that the company's tendering or selling-price policy should not be too rigid if it is based on this type of cost-plus pricing.

Activity 16.5

You are a manager in a company manufacturing consumer products. Market prices are competitive and you need to keep down your costs. Do you think that charging non-production overhead to unit costs serves any purpose in this context? Tick the box below as appropriate and then give your reasons.

Yes ☐   No ☐

Why? _____

Predetermined absorption rates

An absorption rate can, of course, be calculated on a historical basis (i.e. after the event), or it can be predetermined (i.e. calculated in advance).

As we have tried to emphasize, there is no close correlation between fixed overhead and any particular measure of activity: it can only be apportioned on what seems to be a reasonable basis. However, if we know the total actual overhead incurred, we can make sure that it is all charged to specific units, even if we are not sure of the relationship it has with any particular unit.

To do so, of course, we cannot calculate an absorption rate until we know: (a) the *actual cost of overheads*, and (b) the *actual activity level* (whether this is measured in machine hours, direct labour hours, or on some other basis). In other words, we can only make the calculation when we know what has happened.

The adoption of historical absorption rates is not usually very practicable. We have to wait until the actual period is over before an absorption rate can be calculated, the products costed and the customers invoiced. We would, therefore, normally wish to calculate an absorption rate in advance. This is known as a *predetermined absorption rate*.

In order to calculate a predetermined absorption rate, we have to estimate the overhead likely to be incurred and the direct labour hours or machine hours that are expected to be worked. If one or other of these estimates turns out to be inaccurate, then we would have either undercharged our customers (if the rate was too low), or overcharged them (if the rate was too high).

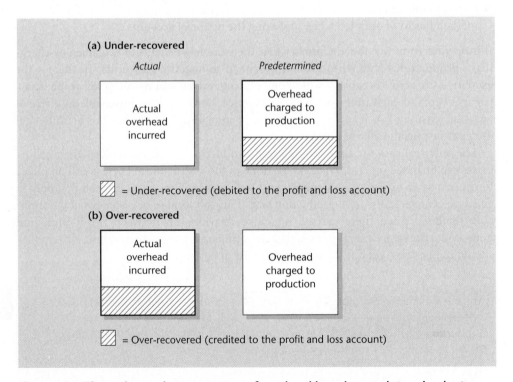

Figure 16.3 **The under- and over-recovery of overhead by using predetermined rates**

This situation could be very serious for a company. Low selling prices caused by using a low absorption rate could have made the company's products very competitive, but there is not much point in selling a lot of units if they are being sold at a loss. Similarly, a high absorption rate may result in a high selling price. Thus each unit may make a large profit, but not enough units may be sold to enable the company to make an overall profit.

The use of predetermined absorption rates may, therefore, result in an under- or an over-recovery of overhead if the company has underestimated or overestimated the actual cost of the overhead or the actual level of activity. The difference between the actual overhead incurred and the total overhead charged to production (calculated on a predetermined basis) gives rise to what is known as a *variance*. If the actual overhead incurred is in excess of the amount charged out, the variance will be *adverse*, i.e. the profit will be less than expected. However, if the total overhead charged to production was less than was estimated, then the variance will be *favourable*. (The effect of this procedure is shown in diagrammatic form in Figure 16.3.) Other things being equal, a favourable variance gives rise to a higher profit, and an adverse variance results to a lower profit.

It is a cardinal rule in costing that variances should be written off to the profit and loss account at the end of the costing period in which they were incurred. It is not considered fair to burden the next period's accounts with the previous period's mistakes. In other words, it is as well to start off the new accounting period with a clean sheet.

Throughout the preceding sections we have clearly expressed many reservations about the way in which accountants have traditionally dealt with overheads. In recent years, dissatisfaction about overhead absorption has become widespread, and now a different technique called *activity based costing* (ABC) is being advocated. We review the techinque briefly in the next section.

Activity based costing

As we have seen, the calculation of product costs involves identifying the *direct costs* of a product and then adding (or absorbing) a proportion of the *indirect costs* (i.e. the overheads) to the total of the direct costs.

This has been the method for most of the twentieth century. It was only in the 1980s that it began to be apparent that the traditional method of absorbing overhead was inappropriate in an advanced manufacturing environment. As the traditional method involves calculating the total cost of overheads in a particular cost centre and charging them out to particular units on a time basis, the total cost is *averaged* among those units that flow through that particular cost centre. The assumption behind this procedure is that the more time that a unit spends in production, the more overhead it will incur. Such an assumption means, of course, that no distinction is made between fixed and variable overhead; it also means that irrespective of whether a particular unit causes a certain cost to arise in a cost centre, it is still charged with a proportion of that cost.

We will use an example to illustrate this point. The details are contained in Example 16.4.

Example 16.4	**Overhead absorption: the unfairness of the traditional approach**

In Jasmine Ltd's Production Cost Centre 1, two units are produced: Unit A and Unit B, the total overhead cost being £1000. This is made up of two costs: (1) machine set-up costs of £800; and (2) inspection costs of £200. Overhead is absorbed on the basis of direct labour hours. The total direct labour hours (DLH) amount to 200. Unit A requires 150 DLH and Unit B 50 DLH.

The machinery for Unit A only needs to be set up once, whereas Unit B requires nine set-ups. Unit A and Unit B both require two inspections each.

Required:
Calculate the total overhead to be charged to Unit A and to Unit B using: (a) the traditional method of absorbing overhead; (b) a fairer method based on set-up and inspection costs; and (c) prepare a table comparing the two methods.

Answer to Example 16.4

(a) The traditional method
The absorption rate is £5 (£1000 total overhead ÷ 200 direct labour hours). As Unit A has 150 direct labour hours spent on it, it will absorb £750 (150 DLH × £5) of overhead. Unit B has 50 direct labour hours spent on it; it will, therefore, absorb £250 of overhead (50 DLH × £5).

(b) A fairer method
Each set-up costs £80 [£800 ÷ 10 (1 set-up for A + 9 set-ups for B)] and each inspection costs £50 [£200 ÷ 4 (2 inspections for A + 2 inspections for B)]. The total overhead charged to Unit A, therefore, would be £180: £80 for set-up costs (one set-up × £80) plus £100 inspection costs (2 inspections × £50). Unit B would be charged a total of £820: £720 of set-up costs (9 set-ups × £80) and £100 inspection costs (2 inspections × £50). The fairer method illustrated here is known as *activity based costing* (ABC).

(c) Comparing the two methods
The table below compares the two approaches to overhead absorption:

Jasmine Limited

Product	Overhead absorbed on a traditional basis £	Overhead absorbed on an activity basis £
A	750	180
B	250	820
Total	1 000	1 000

Activity 16.6	Attempt Example 16.4 without looking at the answer.

Example 16.4 illustrates the potential unfairness of the traditional method of absorbing overhead. As the method *averages* the total cost among particular units, those units

that do not benefit from a particular activity bear a disproportionate amount of the total cost. In the above example, Unit A should only be charged £180 of overhead (compared with £750 under the traditional method), whereas Unit B should be charged £820 (compared with £250 under the traditional method).

It follows that if the eventual selling price is based on cost, the traditional method would grossly inflate Unit A's selling price and deflate Unit B's selling price. Unit A's selling price would probably be highly uncompetitive and only a few units might be sold. Unit B's selling price would probably be highly competitive. Thus a great many units of Unit B might be sold, but the total sales revenue may not be sufficient to recover all of the overhead costs.

In order to illustrate the principles behind ABC, we have made reference to just one cost centre. However, in practice, overheads for the whole of the entity (including both manufacturing and non-manufacturing overheads) would be dealt with collectively. They would then be allocated to *cost pools*, i.e. similar areas of activity. It is estimated that even in the largest entities, a total of about 30 cost pools is the maximum number that it is practicable to handle. This means that some costs may be allocated to a cost pool where there is only a distance relationship between some of the costs. In other words, like the traditional method of absorbing overheads, ABC also involves some averaging of costs.

Once the overheads have all been allocated to an appropriate cost pool, a *cost driver* for each pool is selected. A cost driver is the main cause of the costs attached to that pool. Once again, some approximation is necessary because some costs collected in that pool may only have a loose connection with the selected driver. By dividing the total cost in a particular cost pool by the cost driver, an overhead cost per driver can be calculated. For example, suppose the total overhead cost collected in a particular cost pool totalled £1000 and the costs in that pool were driven by the number of material requisitions (say 200), the cost driver rate would be £5 per material requisition (£1000 cost ÷ 200 material requisitions).

The final stage is to charge an appropriate amount of overhead to each unit benefiting from the service provided by the various cost pools. Thus if a particular unit required 10 material requisitions and the cost driver rate was £5 per material requisition, it would be charged £50 (£5 per material requisition × 10 requisitions). Of course, it may benefit from the services provided by a number of other cost pools, in which case it would collect a share of overhead from each of them as well.

The above procedures may be a little difficult to follow, so read it again before working your way through Example 16.5. The exhibit illustrates the main steps involved in ABC.

Activity based costing (ABC)

Example 16.5

Shish Limited has recently introduced an activity based costing (ABC) system. The following details relate to the month of March 2006.

1 Four cost pools have been identified: (1) Parts; (2) Maintenance; (3) Stores; and (4) Administration.
2 The cost drivers that were identified with each cost pool are: (1) total number of parts; (2) maintenance hours; (3) number of material requisitions; and (4) number of employees.
3 Costs and activities during March 2006 were:

**Example 16.5
continued**

Cost pool	Total overhead	Activity	Quantity
	£000		
Parts	10 000	Number of parts	500
Maintenance	18 000	Number of maintenance hours	600
Stores	10 000	Number of material requisitions	20
Administration	2 000	Number of employees	40

4   500 units of Product X3 were produced. Each unit of X3 required 100 parts and 2000 maintenance hours; 6 material requisitions were made and 10 employees worked on the units.

Required:
Using activity based costing, calculate the total amount of overhead absorbed by each unit of Product X3.

**Answer to
Example 16.5**

Shish Ltd

Cost pool	Overhead	Cost driver	Cost driver rate	Usage by Product X3	Overhead cost charged to Product X3
(1)	(2)	(3)	(4)	(5)	(6)
	£000		£		£
Parts	10 000	500 parts	20	100 parts	2 000
Maintenance	18 000	600 hours	30	200 hours	6 000
Stores	10 000	20 requisitions	500	6 requisitions	3 000
Administration	2 000	40 employees	50	10 employees	500
Total					11 500

Tutorial notes

1   Column (4) has been obtained by dividing the data in Column (2) by the data in Column (3).

2   The data in Column (6) has been obtained by multiplying the data in Column (4) by the data in Column (5).

3   The total amount of £11 500 shown in Column (6) is the total amount of overhead to be absorbed by Product X3.

Solution
The total amount of overhead to be absorbed by each unit of Product X3 will be £23 (£11 500 ÷ 500 units).

Activity 16.7   Have a go at doing Example 16.5 without looking at the answer.

ABC is an attempt to absorb overhead into product costs on a basis that relates more closely to the overhead generated by particular activities. Its proponents claim that it is particularly suited to modern manufacturing circumstances because the more that a particular unit causes an increase in activity, the more overhead that particular unit is charged. By contrast, in traditional overhead absorption, total production overhead in any production cost centre is charged by using just one activity rate, which may not be closely related to the overhead generated by particular units.

In principle, there is no significant difference between ABC and traditional overhead absorption. ABC looks for a closer relationship between individual overhead costs and the cause of such costs, while the traditional method adopts a more general approach. However, ABC has another advantage: no distinction is made between manufacturing overhead and non-manufacturing overhead. Thus it avoids the problem inherent in total overhead absorption of finding a meaningful relationship between non-manufacturing overheads and manufacturing activity.

! Questions non-accountants should ask

The topic covered in this chapter is one that should encourage non-accountants to ask some very searching questions. We suggest that you use the following ones as a starting point.

- Have you had any problems in identifying any cost with a particular cost centre?
- If so, which costs?
- How did you decide which cost centre to charge them to?
- What methods have you used to charge service cost centre costs to production cost centres?
- Have you ignored any inter-service cost centre charging?
- If not, how have you dealt with the problem?
- What activity bases have you used to absorb overheads into product costs?
- Have you worked out absorption rates on a historical or a pre-determined basis?
- What have you done about non-production overheads?
- Is there a case for switching to activity based costing?

Conclusion

This chapter has continued our study of cost accounting that we began in Chapter 15.

We have explained how production overheads are absorbed into product costs. In summary, the procedure is as follows.

1 Allocate all costs to appropriate cost centre.
2 Distinguish between production and service cost centres.

3 Examine the individual costs in each cost centre and, where possible, apportion them on some equitable basis to other cost centres.

4 Apportion the total of any remaining service cost centre costs either to production cost centres or to production cost centres and other service cost centres. If the latter, continue to re-apportion the service cost centre costs until they have all been charged to production cost centres.

5 Select an absorption method for each production department based on the main cause of the use of overheads in that department, e.g. direct labour cost, direct labour hours, machine hours, and units.

6 Divide the total overhead in each production cost centre by the selected absorption factor.

7 Charge each unit with its share of overhead (e.g. direct labour hours or machine hours × the absorption rate).

8 Add the amount calculated to the total of the direct costs for that unit.

It is also necessary to determine whether the above procedure should be done on a historical or a predetermined basis, and whether non-production overhead should also be absorbed into product cost.

The above method has been in use for well over 100 years. Some academics and practitioners do not believe that it is suitable for modern manufacturing methods. In recent years a new method called *activity based costing* (ABC) has been adopted by some large companies. ABC is similar to traditional overhead absorption costing except that both production and non-production overheads are assigned to one of a number of identifiable cost pools. The main factor that causes those overheads to be incurred (known as a *cost driver*) is identified and a cost drive rate calculated (the pool overhead divided by the cost driver). Products are then charged with their share of each of the cost pool overheads. For example, if the purchase order cost driver rate is £10 per order and Product X places 5 orders, it will be charged £50 of overhead (5 × £10) for using the purchase order facility provided by the company.

Key points

1 In order to charge unit costs with a share of production overheads, *all* costs should first be identified with a specific cost centre.

2 Some cost centres provide a service to other cost centres. These are known as *service cost centres*. The various costs collected in the service costs centres should be shared out on an apportionment basis among the other cost centres. Some costs collected in the service cost centres may be apportioned separately; otherwise, the *total service-cost centre cost* will be apportioned. An element of cross-charging arises when the service centres provide services for each other. This can be resolved either by ignoring any cross-charging, apportioning the total of the service centre costs in some specified order, or by mathematical apportionment.

3 Once the production cost centres have received their share of the service centre costs, an absorption rate for each production cost centre should be calculated. The traditional method is to take the total of each production cost centre's indirect cost (i.e. its overhead) and divide it either by the actual (or planned)

*Key points
continued*

direct labour hours, or by the machine hours actually worked (or planned to be worked) in that particular cost centre.

4 The absorption rate calculated for each production cost centre is used to charge each unit passing through that cost centre with a share of the production overhead. For example, if the absorption rate in Department A is £10 per direct labour hour and Unit X has five direct labour hours worked on in that department, Unit X will be charged £50 (5 × £10) of production overhead.

5 The total production cost of a particular unit can then be calculated as follows:

direct materials cost + direct labour cost + direct expenses
+ share of production overhead = total production cost.

6 The absorption of non-production overhead is not recommended, except when it may be used for pricing purposes.

7 Absorption rates will normally be predetermined, i.e. they will be based on planned costs and anticipated activity levels.

8 The underabsorption or overabsorption of overhead should be written off to the profit and loss account in the period when it was incurred.

9 In recent years a new way of dealing with the absorption of overheads called *activity based costing* (ABC) has been suggested. ABC involves charging overheads to common cost pools, identifying what drives the costs in each of the respective pools, and then calculating a cost driver rate. Units are then charged with their share of each of the pool costs.

Check your learning

The answers to these questions may be found within the text.

1 What is (a) a production cost centre; and (b) a service cost centre?

2 What do the terms allocate, apportion and absorb mean?

3 Suggest three ways that service cost centre costs may be charged to other cost centres.

4 What are reciprocal service costs?

5 Indicate three ways to deal with them.

6 What is the basic formula for absorbing production overheads into product costs?

7 List six methods of how this may be done.

8 What is non-production overhead?

9 How should it be absorbed into product costs?

10 What is a predetermined absorption rate?

11   What is meant by under- and over-recovery of overhead?

12   What do the initials 'ABC' mean?

13   What is a cost pool and a cost driver?

14   How does ABC differ from traditional absorption costing?

News story quiz

Remember the news story at the beginning of this chapter? Go back to that story and re-read it before answering the following questions.

This news story emphasizes the importance of controlling overheads. Murgitroyd has opened up new offices overseas and taken on new staff. This is expected to reduce its profits so it is tackling this by attempting to reduce its costs. This company is an intellectual property consultant so it will not have the problems of dealing with production overheads. However, it presumably has to charge its clients with a share of its overheads.

Questions

1   How could Murgitroyd's costs have increased faster than anticipated when it was planning to expand overseas?

2   What is meant by the statement '*This increase in overheads will have an impact on the profit generated for the interim period*'?

3   What cost savings do you think that the company might be considering?

4   How do you think that an intellectual property consultant company might deal with the absorption of overheads into the fees that it charges?

Tutorial questions

The answers to questions marked with an asterisk may be found in Appendix 4.

16.1   'Arithmetical precision for precision's sake.' How far is this statement true of the traditional methods used in absorbing overheads into product costs?

16.2   Has total absorption costing any relevance in a service industry?

16.3   Some non-accountants believe that the technique of overhead absorption was devised simply to provide jobs for accountants. How far do you agree?

16.4   How should reciprocal service costs be dealt with when calculating product costs?

16.5   Assess the usefulness of activity based costing (ABC) in managerial decision making.

16.6* Scar Limited has two production departments and one service department. The following information relates to January 2006:

Allocated expenses:	£
Production department: A	65 000
B	35 000
Service department	50 000

The allocated expenses shown above are all indirect expenses as far as individual units are concerned.

The benefit provided by the service department is shared amongst the production departments A and B in the proportion 60 : 40.

Required:
Calculate the amount of overhead to be charged to specific units for both production department A and production department B.

16.7* Bank Limited has several production departments. In the assembly department it has been estimated that £250 000 of overhead should be charged to that particular department. It now wants to charge a customer for a specific order. The data relevant are:

	Assembly department	Specific unit
Number of units	50 000	–
Direct material cost (£)	500 000	8.00
Direct labour cost (£)	1 000 000	30.00
Prime cost (£)	1 530 000	40.00
Direct labour hours	100 000	3.5
Machine hours	25 000	0.75

The accountant is not sure which overhead absorption rate to adopt.

Required:
Calculate the overhead to be absorbed by a specific unit passing through the assembly department using each of the following overhead absorption rate methods:
1 specific units;
2 percentage of direct material cost;
3 percentage of direct labour cost;
4 percentage of prime cost;
5 direct labour hours; and
6 machine hours.

16.8   The following information relates to the activities of the production department of Clough Limited for the month of March 2007:

	Production department	Order number 123
Direct materials consumed (£)	120 000	20
Direct wages (£)	180 000	25
Overhead chargeable (£)	150 000	
Direct labour hours worked	30 000	5
Machine hours operated	10 000	2

The company adds a margin of 50 per cent to the total production cost of specific units in order to cover administration expenses and to provide a profit.

Required:
(a) Calculate the total selling price of order number 123 if overhead is absorbed using the following methods of overhead absorption:
　　1 direct labour hours;
　　2 machine hours.
(b) State which of the two methods you would recommend for the production department.

16.9　Burns Limited has three production departments (processing, assembly and finishing) and two service departments (administration and work study). The following information relates to April 2004:

	£
Direct material	
Processing	100 000
Assembling	30 000
Finishing	20 000
Direct labour	
Processing (£4 × 100 000 hours)	400 000
Assembling (£5 × 30 000 hours)	150 000
Finishing (£7 × 10 000 hours) + (£5 × 10 000 hours)	120 000
Administration	65 000
Work study	33 000
Other allocated costs	
Processing	15 000
Assembling	20 000
Finishing	10 000
Administration	35 000
Work study	12 000

Apportionment of costs:

	Process %	Assembling %	Finishing %	Work study %
Administration	50	30	15	5
Work study	70	20	10	–

Total machine hours: Processing 25 000

All units produced in the factory pass through the three production departments before they are put into stock. Overhead is absorbed in the processing department on the basis of machine hours, on the basis of direct labour hours in the assembling department, and on the basis of the direct labour cost in the finishing department.

The following details relate to unit XP6:

	£	£
Direct materials		
Processing	15	
Assembling	6	
Finishing	1	22
Direct labour		
Processing (2 hours)	8	
Assembling (1 hour)	5	
Finishing [(1 hour × £7) + (1 hour × £5)]	12	25
Prime cost		47

XP6: Number of machine hours in the processing department = 6

Required:
Calculate the total cost of producing unit XP6.

16.10 Outlane Limited's overhead budget for a certain period is as follows:

	£000
Administration	100
Depreciation of machinery	80
Employer's national insurance	10
Heating and lighting	15
Holiday pay	20
Indirect labour cost	10
Insurance: machinery	40
property	11
Machine maintenance	42
Power	230
Rent and rates	55
Supervision	50
	663

The company has four production departments: L, M, N and O. The following information relates to each department.

Department	L	M	N	O
Total number of employees	400	300	200	100
Number of indirect workers	20	15	10	5
Floor space (square metres)	2 000	1 500	1 000	1 000
Kilowatt hours' power consumption	30 000	50 000	90 000	60 000
Machine maintenance hours	500	400	300	200
Machine running hours	92 000	38 000	165 000	27 000
Capital cost of machines (£)	110 000	40 000	50 000	200 000
Depreciation rate of machines (on cost)	20%	20%	20%	20%
Cubic capacity	60 000	30 000	10 000	50 000

Previously, the company has absorbed overhead on the basis of 100 per cent of the direct labour cost. It has now decided to change to a separate machine-hour rate for each department.

The company has been involved in two main contracts during the period, the details of which are as follows:

Department	Contract 1: Direct labour hours and machine hours	Contract 2: Direct labour hours and machine hours
L	60	20
M	30	10
N	10	10
O	–	60
	100	100

Direct labour cost per hour in both departments was £3.00.

Required:
(a) Calculate the overhead to be absorbed by both contract 1 and contract 2 using the direct labour cost method.
(b) Calculate the overhead to be absorbed using a machine hour rate for each department.

Further practice questions, study material and links to relevant sites on the World Wide Web can be found on the website that accompanies this book. The site can be found at **www.booksites.net/dyson**

Optimistic budgeting can lead to problems . . .

Slug and Lettuce accounts holed

Ian Griffiths

SFI, the Slug and Lettuce and Litten Tree bars group, is facing investigation by the financial services authority and a showdown with auditors after suspending its shares over the discovery of an accounting black hole.

SFI asked for the suspension yesterday after it uncovered accounting problems including a £20m mis-statement of assets, a breakdown in internal cash flow controls and overly optimistic budgeting. The company said Tony Hill, its chairman and former chief executive, had resigned.

Last month SFI axed its final dividend, warned on profits and admitted breaching some banking covenants. Yesterday the shares were suspended at 31p, against a 12-month high of 237p. The company said that the review of the financial position being carried out with the assistance of Pricewaterhouse Coopers by Tim Andrews, who took up his post as finance director in July, had already reached some material conclusions.

In particular the financial model used at the time of the acquisition of Parisa Café Bars last year assumed operating cash flows approximately £10m in excess of those actually reported in the financial year ending May 31.

The review has also found that in the past the group has focused too much on the profit and loss account. Less attention was paid to its cash flow statements and balance sheet.

"The inadequacy of cash flow controls and procedures of the group, particularly with regard to cut-off of accounting periods, was a contributory factor in the continuation of the group's capital expenditure programme following the Parisa Café Bars acquisition," the company said.

Finally, the review has uncovered a significant overstatement of current assets and understatement of liabilities which, in aggregate, is likely to exceed £20m.

That financial review is continuing and the group's fixed assets are still being examined. At the same time chief executive Andrew Latham is conducting a full strategic review of the group, again assisted by Pricewaterhouse Coopers.

The directors now believe it is in the best interests of the company and its shareholders that dealings in its shares are suspended, pending the conclusion of the strategic and financial reviews and clarification of its financial position.

The FSA is now investigating events at SFI to assess whether it or the financial reporting review panel should handle a broader inquiry into the company's affairs.

SFI's auditor, Horwarth Clark Whitehill, is seeking a meeting to examine the situation. The auditors were not consulted about yesterday's announcement. SFI has continued to work closely with its bankers and has kept them informed of developments.

The Guardian, 13 November 2002.

Questions relating to this news story may be found on page 393 ▸▸

About this chapter

This chapter tells you something about the nature and purpose of a budget, it outlines the various types of budgets, how they all fit together, and how they may be used to keep a tight control of an entity's operations. It also explains that budgets and budgetary control are not neutral techniques. They have an impact on human behaviour and this has to be taken into account when using them.

The chapter is divided into eight main sections. The first main section explains why this is an important chapter for non-accountants. The following section examines the nature and purpose of a budget and what is meant by budgetary control. The procedure involved in using budgets is then explained. A short section on functional budgets follows. We then illustrate the overall budgetary procedure in a comprehensive example. Fixed and flexible budgets are discussed in a further section. This leads on to an important section dealing with the behavioural consequences of budgeting. The last main section of the chapter lists some questions that non-accountants might like to ask about the contents of the chapter.

Learning objectives	**By the end of this chapter you should be able to:**
	● **describe the nature and purpose of budgeting and budgetary control;**
	● **list the steps involved in operating a budgetary control system;**
	● **describe the difference between fixed and flexible budgets;**
	● **outline the behavioural consequences of a budgetary control system.**

❗ Why this chapter is important for non-accountants

Basically, the more knowledge that you have as a manager, the more influence that you will be able to exert – and that certainly applies to budgeting. It follows that this chapter is especially important for non-accountants for the following reasons:

1 Your job will probably involve you in supplying information for budgetary purposes. It is easier to supply what is needed if you know what it is for and how it will be used.
2 You are likely to have to prepare a budget for your section or department. Obviously, it is easier to do so if you have had some training in how to do it.
3 You may be supplied with various reports that show your budgeted results against actual results. It is possible that you may then be asked what you are going to do to correct any 'variance'. The impact that the 'request' will have on you will depend upon a number of factors. For example, how familiar you are with the way that the information has been compiled, what inherent deficiencies it may have, and what reliability you can place on it.

Budgeting is not a process that should be regarded as an exercise that is of interest only to accountants. If it is to mean anything at all, the entire entity ought to be involved in it. As a manager you may feel annoyed that you have to spend a lot of time preparing your budget. But if the system works, it should enable you to manage your department more efficiently and effectively. This is the reason why you should throw yourself whole-heartedly into the process and why this chapter is of particular importance to you.

Budgeting and budgetary control

We start our analysis by establishing what we mean by a 'budget' and 'budgetary control'.

Budget

The term *budget* is usually well understood by the layman. Many people, for example, often prepare a quite sophisticated budget for their own household expenses. In fact, albeit in a very informal sense, everyone does some budgeting at some time or other, even if it is only by making a rough comparison between the next month's salary and the next month's expenditure. Such a budget may not be very precise, and it may not be formally written down. Nevertheless, it contains all the ingredients of what accountants mean by a budget. The essential features of a formal budget may be summarized as follows:

1 *Policies.* A budget is based on the policies needed to fulfil the objectives of the entity.
2 *Data.* Quantitative data contained in a budget are usually translated into monetary terms.
3 *Documentation.* Details of a budget are normally contained within a formal written document.
4 *Period.* Budget details will refer to a defined future period of time.

In practice, a considerable number of budgets would be prepared. In a manufacturing entity, for example, these will include sales, production and administration budgets. These budgets would then be combined into an overall budget known as a *master budget*, comprising (a) a budgeted profit and loss account; (b) a budgeted balance sheet; and (c) a budgeted cash flow statement.

Once a master budget had been prepared, it would be closely examined to see whether the overall plan could be accommodated. It might be the case, for example, that the sales budget indicated a large increase in sales. This may have required the production budgets to be prepared on the basis of this extra sales demand. However, the cash budget might have suggested that the entity could not meet the extra sales and production activity that would be required. In these circumstances, additional financing arrangements may have had to be made, because obviously no organization would normally turn down the opportunity of increasing its sales.

In practice, the preparation of individual budgets can be a useful exercise even if nothing further is then done about them, since the exercise forces management to look ahead. It is a natural human tendency to be always looking back, but past experience is not always a guide for the future. If managers are asked to produce a budget, it encourages them to examine what they have done in relation to what they *could* do. However, the full benefits of a budgeting system are only realized when it is also used for control purposes, i.e. by the constant comparison of actual results with budgeted results, and then taking any necessary corrective action. This leads us on to consider in a little more detail what we mean by 'budgetary control'.

| Activity 17.1 | Write down in the space below three reasons why we prepare budgets. |

Reasons:

1 _____

2 _____

3 _____

Budgetary control

In simple terms, *budgetary control* involves comparing the actual results for a period with the budget for that period. If there are any differences (known as *variances*) that need attention, then corrective action will be taken to ensure that future results will conform to the budget. Budgetary control has several important features. These are as follows:

1 *Responsibilities.* Managerial responsibilities are clearly defined.
2 *Action plan.* Individual budgets lay down a detailed plan of action for a particular sphere of responsibility.
3 *Adherence.* Managers have a responsibility to adhere to their budgets once the budgets have been approved.
4 *Monitoring.* The actual performance is constantly monitored and compared with the budgeted results.
5 *Correction.* Corrective action is taken if the actual results differ significantly from the budget.
6 *Approval.* Departures from budget are only permitted if they have been approved by senior management.
7 *Variances.* Variances that are unaccounted for are subject to individual investigation.

Any variance that occurs should be carefully investigated. The current actual performance will be immediately brought back into line with the budget if it is considered necessary. Sometimes the budget itself will be changed, e.g. if there is an unexpected increase in sales. Such changes may, of course, have an effect on the other budgets, and so it cannot be done in isolation.

Now that we have outlined the nature and purpose of budgeting and budgetary control, we are in a position to investigate how the system works.

Procedure

The budget *procedure* starts with an examination of the entity's objectives. These may be very simple. They may include, for example, an overall wish to maximize profits, to foster better relations with customers, or to improve the working conditions of employees. Once an entity has decided upon its overall objectives, it is in a position to formulate some detailed plans.

These will probably start with a *forecast*. Note that there is a technical difference between a forecast and a budget. A forecast is a prediction of what is *likely* to happen, whereas a budget is a carefully prepared plan of what *should* happen.

In order to make it easier for us to guide you through the budgeting process, we will examine each stage individually. We do so below and the procedure is also depicted in Figure 17.1. We will be dealing with a manufacturing entity in the private sector. The budgeting procedures for service sector entities are similar but not as complicated. Budgets in the public sector (such as in local government) involve a different procedure.

The budget period

The main budget period is usually based on a calendar year. It could be shorter or longer depending upon the nature of the product cycle; for example, the fashion industry may adopt a short budget period of less than a year, while the construction industry may choose (say) a five-year period. Irrespective of the industry, however, a calendar year is usually a convenient period to choose as the base period, because it fits in with the financial accounting period.

Besides determining the main budget period, it is also necessary to prepare sub-period budgets. Sub-period budgets are required for budgetary control purposes, since the actual results have to be frequently compared with the budgeted results. The sub-budget periods for some activities may need to be very short if tight control is to be exercised over them. The cash budget, for example, may need to be compiled on a weekly basis, whereas the administration budget may only need to be prepared quarterly.

Administration

The budget procedure may be administered by a special budget committee, or it may be supervised by the accounting function. It will be necessary for the budget committee to lay down general guidelines in accordance with the entity's objectives, and to ensure that individual departments do not operate completely independently. The production department, for example, will need to know what the entity is budgeting to sell so that it can prepare its own budget on the basis of those sales. However, the detailed production budget must still remain the entire responsibility of the production manager.

This procedure is in line with the concept of responsibility accounting, which we out-lined in Chapter 15. If the control procedure is to work properly, managers must be

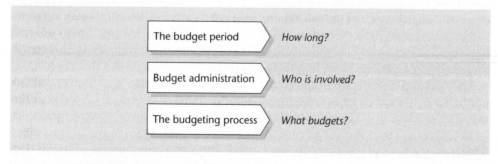

Figure 17.1 **The budgeting procedure**

given responsibility for a clearly defined area of activity, such as a cost centre. Thereafter, they are fully answerable for all that goes on there. Unless managers are given complete authority to act within clearly defined guidelines, they cannot be expected to account for something that is outside their control. This means that, as far as budgets are concerned, managers must help prepare, amend and approve their own responsibility centre's budget; otherwise, the budgetary control system will not work.

Activity 17.2	A budget can act as a measure against which actual performance can be matched. However, some experts argue that when a measure becomes a *target* ('you must meet your budget') it becomes meaningless. To what extent do you think that budgeting is a waste of time? Mark your response on the scale below.

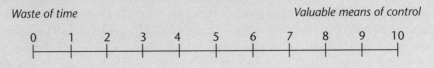

The budgeting process

The budgeting process is illustrated in Figure 17.2. Study the figure very carefully, noting how the various budgets fit together.

Later on in this chapter we shall be using a quantitative example to illustrate the budgeting process. For the moment, however, it will be sufficient to give a brief description.

In commercial organizations, the first budget to be prepared is usually the sales budget. Once the sales for the budget period (and for each sub-budget period) have been determined, the next stage is to calculate the effect on production. This will then enable an agreed level of activity to be determined. The *level of activity* may be expressed in so many units, or as a percentage of the theoretical productive capacity of the entity. Once it has been established, departmental managers can be instructed to prepare their budgets on the basis of the required level of activity.

Let us assume, for example, that 1000 units can be sold for a particular budget period. The production department manager will need this information in order to prepare his budget. This does not necessarily mean that he will budget for a production level of 1000 units, because he will also have to allow for the budgeted level of opening and closing stocks.

The budgeted production level will then be translated into how much material and labour will be required to meet that particular level. Similarly, it will be necessary to prepare overhead budgets. Much of the general overhead expenditure of the entity (such as factory administrative costs, head office costs, and research and development expenditure) will tend to be fixed, as such overheads will not be directly affected by production levels. However, in some instances a marked change in activity may lead to a change in fixed costs.

The sales and distribution overhead budget may be the one overhead budget that will not be entirely fixed in nature. An increase in the number of units sold, for example, may involve additional delivery costs.

Not all entities start the budget process with sales. A local authority usually prepares a budget on the basis of what it is likely to spend. The total budgeted expenditure is then compared with the total amount of council tax (after allowing for other income) needed

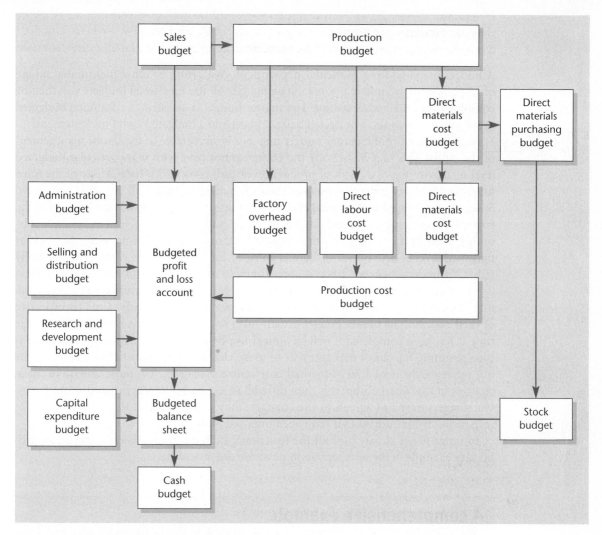

Figure 17.2 **The interrelationship of budgets**

to cover it. If the political cost of an increase in council tax appears too high, then the council will require a reduction in the budgeted expenditure. Once the budget has been set, and the tax has been levied on that basis, departments have to work within the budgets laid down. However, since the budget will have been prepared on an estimate of the actual expenditure for the last two or three months of the old financial year, account has to be taken of any a surplus or shortfall expected in the current year. If the estimate eventually proves excessive, the local authority will have overtaxed. This means that it has got some additional funds available to cushion the current year's expenditure. Of course, if it has undertaxed for any balance brought forward, departments might have to start cutting back on what they thought they could spend.

This process is quite different from the private sector, in which the budgeted sales effectively determine all the other budgets. In a local authority, it is the expenditure budgets that determine what the council tax should be, and it is only the control exercised by central government and by the local authority itself that places a ceiling on what is spent.

Functional budgets

A budget prepared for a particular department, cost centre or other identifiable sphere of responsibility is known as a *functional budget*. All the functional budgets will then be combined into the *master budget*. The master budget is, in effect, a combined budgeted profit and loss account, a budgeted balance sheet and a budgeted cash flow statement.

An initial draft of the master budget may not be acceptable to the senior management of the entity. This may be because the entity cannot cope with that particular budgeted level of activity, e.g. as a result of production or cash constraints. Indeed, one of the most important budgets is the *cash budget*. The cash budget translates all the other functional budgets (including that for capital expenditure) into cash terms. It will show in detail the pattern of cash inputs and outputs for the main budget period, as well as for each sub-budget period. If it shows that the entity will have difficulty in financing a particular budgeted level of activity (or if there is going to be a period when cash is exceptionally tight), the management will have an opportunity to seek out alternative sources of finance.

This latter point illustrates the importance of being aware of future commitments, so that something can be done in advance if there are likely to be constraints (irrespective of their nature). The master budget usually takes so long to prepare, however, that by the time it has been completed it will be almost impossible to make major alterations. It is then tempting for senior management to make changes to the functional budgets without referring them back to individual cost-centre managers. It is most unwise to make changes in this way, because it is then difficult to use such budgets for control purposes. If managers have not agreed to the changes, they will argue that they can hardly take responsibility for budgets that have been imposed on them.

In order to see clearly how all the functional budgets fit together, we use a comprehensive example in the next section to illustrate the procedure.

A comprehensive example

It would clearly be very difficult to observe the basic procedures involved in the preparation of functional budgets if we used an extremely detailed example, and so Example 17.1 cuts out all the incidental information. As a result, it only illustrates the main procedures, but this will enable you to see how all the budgets fit together.

| Example 17.1 | **Preparation of functional budgets** |

Sefton Limited manufactures one product known as EC2. The following information relates to the preparation of the budget for the year to 31 March 2005:

Example 17.1
continued

1 Sales budget details for product EC2:
   Expected selling price per unit: £100.
   Expected sales in units: 10 000.
   All sales are on credit terms.

2 EC2 requires 5 units of raw material E and 10 units of raw material C. E is expected to cost £3 per unit, and C £4 per unit. All goods are purchased on credit terms.

3 Two departments are involved in producing EC2: machining and assembly. The following information is relevant:

	Direct labour per unit of product (hours)	Direct labour rate per hour £
Machining	1.00	6
Assembling	0.50	8

4 The finished production overhead costs are expected to amount to £100 000.

5 At 1 April 2004, 800 units of EC2 are expected to be in stock at a value of £52 000, 4500 units of raw material E at a value of £13 500, and 12 000 units of raw materials at a value of £48 000. Stocks of both finished goods and raw materials are planned to be 10 per cent above the expected opening stock levels as at 1 April 2004.

6 Administration, selling and distribution overhead is expected to amount to £150 000.

7 Other relevant information:
   (a) Opening trade debtors are expected to be £80 000. Closing trade debtors are expected to amount to 15 per cent of the total sales for the year.
   (b) Opening trade creditors are expected to be £28 000. Closing trade creditors are expected to amount to 10 per cent of the purchases for the year.
   (c) All other expenses will be paid in cash during the year.
   (d) Other balances at 1 April 2004 are expected to be as follows:

	£	£
(i) Share capital: ordinary shares		225 000
(ii) Retained profits		17 500
(iii) Proposed dividend		75 000
(iv) Fixed assets at cost	250 000	
Less: Accumulated depreciation	100 000	
		150 000
(v) Cash at bank and in hand		2 000

8 Capital expenditure will amount to £50 000, payable in cash on 1 April 2004.

9 Fixed assets are depreciated on a straight-line basis at a rate of 20 per cent per annum on cost.

Required:
As far as the information permits, prepare all the relevant budgets for Sefton Limited for the year to 31 March 2005.

Answer to
Example 17.1

Even with a much simplified budgeting exercise, there is clearly a great deal of work involved in preparing the budgets. To make it easier for you to understand what is happening, the procedure will be outlined step by step

Step 1: Prepare the sales budget

Units of EC2	Selling price per unit £	Total sales value £
10 000	100	1 000 000

Step 2: Prepare the production budget

	Units
Sales of EC2	10 000
Less: Opening stock	800
	9 200
Add: Desired closing stock (opening stock +10%)	880
Production required	10 080

Step 3: Prepare the direct materials usage budget

Direct material:

E: 5 units × 10 080	50 400 units
C: 10 units × 10 080	100 800 units

Step 4: Prepare the direct materials purchases budget

Direct materials: =	E (units)	C (units)
Usage (as per Step 3)	50 400	100 800
Less: Opening stock	4 500	12 000
	45 900	88 800
Add: Desired closing stock (opening stock+10%)	4 950	13 200
	50 850	102 000
	× £3	× £4
Direct material purchases	£152 550	£408 000

Step 5: Prepare the direct labour budget

	Machining	Assembling
Production units (as per Step 2)	10 080	10 080
× direct labour hours required	× 1 DLH	× 0.50 DLH
	10 080 DLH	5 040 DLH
× direct labour rate per hour	× £6	× £8
Direct labour cost =	£60 480	£40 320

Step 6: Prepare the fixed production overhead budget

Given:	£100 000

Answer to
Example 17.1
continued

Step 7: Calculate the value of the closing raw material stock

Raw material	Closing stock* (units)	Cost per unit £	Total value £
E	4 950	3	14 850
C	13 200	4	52 800
			67 650

*Derived from Step 4.

Step 8: Calculate the value of the closing finished stock

	£	£
Unit cost:		
Direct material E: 5 units × £3 per unit	15	
Direct material C: 10 units × £4 per unit	40	55
Direct labour for machining: 1 hour × £6 per DLH	6	
Direct labour for assembling: 0.50 hours × £8 per DLH	4	10
Total direct cost		65
× units in stock		× 880
Closing stock value =		57 200

Step 9: Prepare the administration, selling and distribution budget

Given: £150 000

Step 10: Prepare the capital expenditure budget

Given: £50 000

Step 11: Calculate the cost of goods sold

	£
Opening stock (given)	52 000
Manufacturing cost:	
Production units (Step 2) × total direct cost (Step 3) = 10 080 × £65	655 200
	707 200
Less: Closing stock (Step 8: 880 units × £65)	57 200
Cost of goods sold (10 000 units)	650 000

(or 10 000 units × total direct costs of £65 per unit)

Step 12: Prepare the cash budget

	£	£
Receipts		
Cash from debtors:		
Opening debtors	80 000	
Sales	1 000 000	
	1 080 000	
Less: Closing debtors (15% × £1 000 000)	150 000	930 000

Answer to
Example 17.1
continued

Payments		£
Cash payments to creditors:		
Opening creditors	28 000	
Purchases [Step 4: (£152 550 + 408 000)]	560 550	
	588 550	
Less: Closing creditors (£560 550 × 10%)	56 055	532 495
Wages (Step 5: £60 480 + 40 320)		100 800
Fixed production overhead		100 000
Administration, selling and distribution overhead		150 000
Capital expenditure		50 000
Dividend paid for 2004		75 000
		1 008 295

	£
Net receipts	(78 295)
Add: Opening cash	2 000
Budgeted closing cash balance (overdrawn)	(76 295)

Step 13: Prepare the budgeted profit and loss account

	£	£
Sales (Step 1)		1 000 000
Less: Variable cost of sales (Step 8: 10 000 × £65)		650 000
Gross margin		350 000
Less: Fixed production overhead (Step 6)	100 000	
Depreciation [(£250 000 + 50 000) × 20%]	60 000	160 000
Production margin		190 000
Less: Administration, selling and distribution overhead (Step 9)		150 000
Budgeted net profit		40 000

Step 14: Prepare the budgeted balance sheet

	£	£	£
Fixed assets (at cost)			300 000
Less: Accumulated depreciation			160 000
			140 000
Current assets			
Raw materials (Step 7)		67 650	
Finished stock (Step 8)		57 200	
Trade debtors (15% × £1 000 000)		150 000	
		274 850	
Less: Current liabilities			
Trade creditors			
[Step 4: 10% × (£152 550 + 408 000)]	56 055		
Bank overdraft (Step 12)	76 295	132 350	142 500
			282 500

Answer to
Example 17.1
continued

Financed by:	
Share capital	
Ordinary shares	225 000
Retained profits (£17 500 + 40 000)	57 500
	282 500

Example 17.1 is a complicated example, although unnecessary detail has been avoided, e.g. it has been assumed that the company produces only one product and that the value of the opening stocks at 1 April 2004 will be the same as the budgeted costs for the year to 31 March 2005.

> Now have a go at doing Example 17.1 again but this time without looking at the answer.   **Activity 17.3**

Fixed and flexible budgets

The master budget becomes the detailed plan for future action that everyone is expected to work towards. However, some entities only use the budgeting process as a *planning* exercise. Once the master budget has been agreed, there may be no attempt to use it as a control technique. Thus the budget may be virtually ignored, and it may not be compared with the actual results. If this is the case, then the entity is not getting the best out of the budgeting system.

As was suggested earlier, budgets are particularly useful if they are also used as a means of control. The control is achieved if the actual performance is compared with the budgeted performance. Significant variances should then be investigated and any necessary corrective action taken.

The constant comparison of the actual results with the budgeted results may be done either on a *fixed budget basis* or a *flexible budget basis*. A fixed budget basis means that the actual results for a particular period are compared with the original budgets. This is as you would expect, because the budget is a measure – you would get some very misleading results, for example, if you used an elastic ruler to measure distances. Similarly, an elastic-type budget might also give some highly unreliable results. In some cases, however, a variable measure is used in budgeting in order to allow for certain circumstances that might have taken place since the budgets were prepared. Accountants call this *flexing* the budget. A flexible budget is an original budget that has been amended to take account of the *actual* level of activity.

This procedure might appear somewhat strange and a little contradictory. How can a budget be changed once it has been agreed? Surely that is like using an elastic ruler to measure distances? In practice, however, a fixed budget can be misleading.

It was explained earlier that, in order to prepare their budgets, managers (especially production managers) will need to be given the budgeted level of activity. Such budgets, therefore, will be based on that level of activity. If, however, the *actual* level of activity is greater (or less) than the budgeted level, managers will have to allow for more (or less) expenditure on materials, labour and other expenses.

Suppose, for example, that a manager has prepared his budget on the basis of an anticipated level of activity of 70 per cent of the plant capacity. The company turns out to be much busier than it expected, and it achieves an actual level of activity of 80 per cent. The production manager is likely to have spent more on materials, labour and other expenses than he had originally budgeted. If the actual performance is then compared with the budget (i.e. on a fixed budget basis), it will appear as though he had greatly exceeded what he thought he would spend. No doubt he would then argue that the differences had arisen as a result of a greatly increased level of activity (which may be outside his control). While this may be true, there is no certainty that all of the variances are as a result of the increased activity.

Hence, the need to flex the budget, i.e. it needs to be revised on the basis of what it would have been if the manager had budgeted for an activity of 80 per cent instead of 70 per cent. The other assumptions and calculations made at the time the budget was prepared (such as material prices and wage rates) should not be amended.

If the entity operates a flexible budget system, the original budgets may be prepared on the basis of a wide range of possible activity levels. This method, however, is very time-consuming, and managers will be very lucky if they prepare one that is identical to the actual level of activity. The best method is to wait until the actual level of activity is known, and then amend the budget on that basis.

This procedure might appear fairly complicated, and so it is best if it is illustrated with an example. This is done in Example 17.2.

Example 17.2	Flexible budget procedure

The following information had been prepared for Carp Limited for the year to 30 June 2005.

	Budget	Actual
Level of activity	50%	60%
	£	£
Costs:		
Direct materials	50 000	61 000
Direct labour	100 000	118 000
Variable overhead	10 000	14 000
Total variable cost	160 000	193 000
Fixed overhead	40 000	42 000
Total costs	200 000	235 000

Required:
Prepare a flexed budget operating statement for Carp Limited for the year to 30 June 2005.

Carp Ltd
Flexed budget operating statement for the year 30 June 2005

Activity level	Fixed budget 50% Note 1 £	Flexed budget 60% Note 2 £	Actual costs 60% Note 3 £	Variance (col. 2 less col. 3) favourable/ (adverse) Note 4 £
Direct materials (1)	50 000	60 000	61 000	(1 000)
Direct labour (1)	100 000	120 000	118 000	2 000
Variable overhead (1)	10 000	12 000	14 000	(2 000)
Total variable costs	160 000	192 000	193 000	(1 000)
Fixed overhead (2)	40 000	40 000	42 000	(2 000)
Total costs (3)	200 000	232 000	235 000	(3 000)

1 All the budgeted *variable* costs have been flexed by 20% because the actual activity was 60% compared with a budgeted level of 50%, i.e. a 20% increase

$$\left(\frac{60\% - 50\%}{50\%} \times 100 \right).$$

2 The budgeted fixed costs are not flexed because by definition they should not change with activity.

3 Instead of using the total fixed budget cost of £200 000, the total flexed budget costs of £232 000 can be compared more fairly with the total actual cost of £235 000.

4 Note that the terms 'favourable' and 'adverse' (as applied to variances) mean favourable or adverse to profit. In other words, profit will be either greater (if a variance is favourable) or less (if it is adverse) than the budgeted profit.

5 The reasons for the variances between the actual costs and the flexed budget will need to be investigated. The flexed budget shows that even allowing for the increased activity, the actual costs were in excess of the budget allowance.

6 Similarly, it will be necessary to investigate why the actual activity was higher than the budgeted activity. It could have been caused by inefficient budgeting, or by quite an unexpected increase in sales activity. While this would normally be welcome, it might place a strain on the productive and financial resources of the entity. If the increase is likely to be permanent, management will need to make immediate arrangements to accommodate the new level of activity.

Attempt Example 17.2 without looking at the answer.   **Activity 17.4**

The primary purpose of a budgetary control system is to control as closely as possible the activities of the entity. There will invariably be differences between the actual and the budgeted results, no matter how carefully the budgets are prepared. This does not matter unduly, as long as it is possible to find out why there were differences, and to take action before it is too late to do anything about them.

Behavioural consequences

Budgeting and budgetary control systems are not neutral. They have an impact on people so that they react favourably, unfavourably or with indifference.

If managers react favourably, then the data that they supply are likely to be accurate and relevant. Similarly, any information supplied to them will be received with interest and it will be taken seriously. As a result, any necessary corrective action that is required will be pursued with some vigour.

Managers who react unfavourably or with indifference may supply data that are inaccurate or irrelevant, and they may do so only under protest. Obviously, such managers are not likely to take seriously any subsequent information they receive that is based on data that they know to be suspect. Furthermore they will be unlikely to take any apparent necessary 'corrective action' unless they are forced to do so.

All of this means that for budgeting and budgetary control systems to work effectively and efficiently, a number of important elements must be present. These are as follows:

1 *Consultation.* Managers must be consulted about any proposal to install a budgeting or a budgetary control system.
2 *Education and training.* Managers must undergo some education and training so that they are fully conversant with the relevance and importance of budgeting and budgetary control systems and the part that the managers are expected to play in them.
3 *Involvement.* Managers must be directly involved in the installation of the systems, at least in so far as their own sphere of responsibility is concerned.
4 *Participative.* Ideally, managers should prepare their own budgets (subject to some general guidelines) rather than having budgets imposed on them. Imposed budgets (as they are called) usually mean that managers do not take them seriously and they will then disclaim responsibility for any variances that may have occurred.
5 *Disciplinary action.* Managers should not be disciplined for any variances (especially if a budget has been imposed) unless they are obviously guilty of gross mismanagement. Budgetary control is a means of finding out *why* a variance occurred. It is not supposed to be a means of catching managers out so that they can be disciplined.

As far as the last point is concerned, if managers believe that the budgeting or budgetary control system operates against them rather than for them, they are likely to undermine it. This may take the form of *dysfunctional behaviour*, i.e. behaviour that may be in their own interest but not in the best interests of the company. They may, for example, act aggressively, become unco-operative, blame other managers, build a great deal of slack (i.e. tolerance) into their budgets, take decisions on a short-term basis or avoid taking them altogether, and spend money unnecessarily up to the budget level that they have been given.

All of these points emphasize the importance of consulting managers and involving them fully both in the installation and operation of budgeting and budgetary control systems. If this is not the case, experience suggests that such systems will not work.

Activity 17.5

As a departmental manager you budgeted to spend £10 000 in 2003. You spent £9000. You budgeted to spend £12 000 in 2004 but you were told you could only spend £11 000 as you had 'over-budgeted in 2003'. What is likely to happen when you come to prepare your budget for 2005? Write down your likely reactions in your notebook.

Questions non-accountants should ask

This is a most important chapter for non-accountants because you are likely to be involved in the budgetary process no matter what junior or senior position you hold. If your entity uses an imposed budgetary control system you may not have as much freedom to ask questions but you might want to point out as discreetly as you can that there are problems with such systems. Otherwise, try the following questions.

● How far is the time spent on preparing the budgeting system cost effective?
● Do you think that budgets prepared for a calendar year is too long a period?
● Should those costs and revenues that relate to a longer time-scale be apportioned to sub-budget periods?
● Is it appropriate to compare actual events with fixed budgets?
● Why can't I be responsible for preparing my own department's budget?
● Why do you alter my budget after I have prepared it?
● How can you expect me to be responsible for any variances that are outside my control?
● Is it fair to punish me and my staff when we were not responsible either for the budget or for what went wrong with it?

Conclusion

It has been suggested in this chapter that the full benefits of budgeting can only be gained if it is combined with a budgetary control system. The preparation of budgets is a valuable exercise in itself because it forces management to look ahead to what *might* happen, rather than to look back to what *did* happen. However, it is even more valuable if it is also used as a form of control.

Budgetary control enables actual results to be measured frequently against an agreed budget (or plan). Departures from that budget can then be quickly spotted, and steps can be taken to correct any unwelcome trends. However, the comparison of actual results with a fixed budget may not be particularly helpful if the actual level of activity is different from that budgeted. It is advisable, therefore, to compare actual results with a flexed budget.

As so many of the functional budgets are based upon the budgeted level of activity, it is vital that it is calculated as accurately as possible, since an error in estimating the level of activity could affect all of the company's financial and operational activities. Thus it is important that any difference between the actual and the budgeted level of activity is carefully investigated.

Budgeting and budgetary control systems may be resented by managers. Thus the managers might react to the systems in such a way that their own position is protected. This may not be of benefit to the entity as a whole.

Key points

1 A budget is a plan.

2 Budgetary control is a cost control method that enables actual results to be compared with the budget, thereby enabling any necessary corrective action to be taken.

3 The preparation of budgets will be undertaken by a budget team.

4 Managers must be responsible for producing their own functional budgets.

5 Functional budgets are combined to form a master budget.

6 A fixed budget system compares actual results with the original budgets.

7 In a flexed budget system, the budget may be flexed (or amended) to bring it into line with the actual level of activity.

8 A budgeting and budgetary control system is not neutral. It may cause managers to act in a way that is not in the best interests of the entity.

Check your learning

1 What is a budget?

2 List its essential features.

3 What is budgetary control?

4 List its essential features.

5 What is a variance?

6 What is a forecast?

7 How long is a normal budgeting period?

8 What is a sub-budget period?

9 What administration procedures does a budgeting system require?

10 In a commercial organization which budget is normally the first to be prepared?

11 What initial criterion is given to production managers before they begin to prepare their budgets?

12 What is a functional budget?

13 List six common functional budgets.

14 What is a fixed budget?

15 What is a flexible budget?

16 Why is it desirable to prepare one?

17 List five desirable behavioural elements necessary to ensure a budgeting system is effective.

News story quiz

Remember the news story at the beginning of this chapter? Go back to that story and re-read it before answering the following questions.

This article illustrates a catalogue of problems for Slug and Lettuce: misstatement of assets, a breakdown in internal cash flows, questionable cut-off accounting periods *and* 'overly optimistic budgeting'.

Questions

1   What do you think SFI meant when it reported that it had uncovered 'optimistic budgeting'?

2   What effect will it have had on the company's control procedures?

3   What impact will it have had on its cash flow?

4   What difficulties arise in the budgeting process if a company uses 'cut-off accounting periods'?

Tutorial questions

The answers to questions marked with an asterisk may be found in Appendix 4.

17.1   The Head of Department of Business and Management at Birch College has been told by the Vice Principal (Resources) that his departmental budget for the next academic year is £150 000. What comment would you make about the system of budgeting used at Birch College?

17.2   Suppose that when all the individual budgets at Sparks plc are put together there is a shortfall of resources needed to support them. The Board suggests that all departmental budgets should be reduced by 15 per cent. As the company's Chief Accountant, how would you respond to the Board's suggestion?

17.3   Does a fixed budget serve any useful purpose?

17.4   'It is impossible to introduce a budgetary control system into a hospital because, if someone's life needs saving, it has to be saved irrespective of the cost.' How far do you agree with this statement?

17.5* The following information has been prepared for Tom Limited for the six months to 30 September 2004:

Budgeted production levels for product X

	Units
April	140
May	280
June	700
July	380
August	300
September	240

Product X uses two units of component A6 and three units of component B9. At 1 April 2004 there were expected to be 100 units of A6 in stock, and 200 units of B9. The desired closing stock levels of each component were as follows:

Month end 2004	A6 (units)	B9 (units)
30 April	110	250
31 May	220	630
30 June	560	340
31 July	300	300
31 August	240	200
30 September	200	180

During the six months to 30 September 2004, component A6 was expected to be purchased at a cost of £5 per unit, and component B9 at a cost of £10 per unit.

Required:
Prepare the following budgets for each of the six months to 30 September 2004:
1 direct materials usage budget; and
2 direct materials purchase budget.

17.6* Don Limited has one major product that requires two types of direct labour to produce it. The following data refer to certain budget proposals for the three months to 31 August 2005:

Month	Production units
30.6.05	600
31.7.05	700
31.8.05	650

Direct labour hours required per unit:

	Hours	Budgeted rate per hour £
Production	3	4
Finishing	2	8

Required:
Prepare the direct labour cost budget for each of the three months to 31 August 2005.

17.7 Gorse Limited manufactures one product. The budgeted sales for period 6 are for 10 000 units at a selling price of £100 per unit. Other details are as follows:

1 Two components are used in the manufacture of each unit:

Component	Number	Unit cost of each component £
XY	5	1
WZ	3	0.50

2 Stocks at the beginning of the period are expected to be as follows:
  (a) 4000 units of finished goods at a unit cost of £52.50.
  (b) Component XY: 16 000 units at a unit cost of £1.
      Component WZ: 9600 units at a unit cost of £0.50.
3 Two grades of employees are used in the manufacture of each unit:

Employee	Hours per unit	Labour rate per hour £
Production	4	5
Finishing	2	7

4 Factory overhead is absorbed into unit costs on the basis of direct labour hours. The budgeted factory overhead for the period is estimated to be £96 000.
5 The administration, selling and distribution overhead for the period has been budgeted at £275 000.
6 The company plans a reduction of 50 per cent in the quantity of finished stock at the end of period 6, and an increase of 25 per cent in the quantity of each component.

Required:
Prepare the following budgets for period 6:
1 sales;
2 production quantity;
3 materials usage;
4 materials purchase;
5 direct labour;
6 the budgeted profit and loss account.

17.8 Avsar Limited has extracted the following budgeting details for the year to 30 September 2009:

1 Sales: 4000 units of V at £500 per unit
　　　　　7000 units of R at £300 per unit

2 Materials usage (units):

	Raw material		
	O1	I2	L3
V	11	9	12
R	15	1	10

3 Raw material costs (per unit):

	£
O1	8
I2	6
L3	3

4 Raw material stocks:

	Units		
	O1	I2	L3
At 1 October 2008	1300	1400	400
At 30 September 2009	1400	1000	200

5 Finished stocks:

	Units	
	V	R
At 1 October 2008	110	90
At 30 September 2009	120	150

6 Direct labour:

	Product	
	V	R
Budgeted hours per unit	10	8
Budgeted hourly rate (£)	12	6

7 Variable overhead:

	Product	
	V	R
Budgeted hourly rate (£)	10	5

8 Fixed overhead: £193 160 (to be absorbed on the basis of direct labour hours).

Required:
(a) Prepare the following budgets:
 (i) sales;
 (ii) production units;
 (iii) materials usage;
 (iv) materials purchase; and
 (v) production cost.
(b) Calculate the total budgeted profit for the year to 30 September 2009.

17.9 The following budget information relates to Flossy Limited for the three months to
31 March 2007:

1   **Budgeted profit and loss accounts:**

Month	31.1.06	28.2.07	31.3.07
	£000	£000	£000
Sales (all on credit)	2 000	3 000	2 500
Cost of sales	1 200	1 800	1 500
Gross profit	800	1 200	1 000
Depreciation	(100)	(100)	(100)
Other expenses	(450)	(500)	(600)
	(550)	(600)	(700)
Net profit	250	600	300

2   **Budgeted balance sheets:**

Budgeted balances	31.12.06	31.1.07	28.2.07	31.3.07
	£000	£000	£000	£000
Current assets:				
Stocks	100	120	150	150
Debtors	200	300	350	400
Short-term investments	60	–	40	30
Current liabilities:				
Trade creditors	110	180	160	150
Other creditors	50	50	50	50
Taxation	150	–	–	–
Dividends	200	–	–	–

3 Capital expenditure to be incurred on 20 February 2007 is expected to amount to
£470 000.
4 Sales of plant and equipment on 15 March 2007 is expected to raise £30 000 in
cash.
5 The cash at bank and in hand on 1 January 2007 is expected to be £15 000.

Required:
Prepare Flossy Limited's cash budget for each of the three months during the quarter
ending 31 March 2007.

17.10 Chimes Limited has prepared a flexible budget for one of its factories for the year to 30 June 2008. The details are as follows:

% of production capacity	30%	40%	50%	60%
	£000	£000	£000	£000
Direct materials	42	56	70	84
Direct labour	18	24	30	36
Factory overhead	22	26	30	34
Administration overhead	17	20	23	26
Selling and distribution overhead	12	14	16	18
	111	140	169	198

Additional information:

1 The company only expects to operate at a capacity of 45%. At that capacity, the sales revenue has been budgeted at a level of £135 500.
2 Variable costs per unit are not expected to change, irrespective of the level of activity.
3 Fixed costs are also not likely to change, irrespective of the level of activity.

Required:

Prepare a flexible budget for the year to 30 June 2008 based on an activity level of 45%.

Further practice questions, study material and links to relevant sites on the World Wide Web can be found on the website that accompanies this book. The site can be found at **www.booksites.net/dyson**

The speed of reporting as well as the method is also important . . .

Accountants make reporting improvements a priority

Improving the efficiency and speed of financial reporting tops the agenda for more than 85 per cent of financial managers, according to research by the organiser of the Softworld accounting and finance exhibition.

Changes to the accountancy profession's regulation, the Higgs and Smith reports and the imminent introduction of international accounting standards have put the spotlight on the reliability and efficiency of information – and technology plays a key role. Over 80 per cent of firms use IT to help reporting and planning

processes. Improving management information systems across the organisation is also important for meeting regulatory obligations.

"Firms can no longer wait for the close of their books before they review financial performance," said Scott Parker, managing director of financial management consultancy Parson Consulting. "Increased regulation and the greater responsibilities of audit committees mean that the finance team must provide a trail to justify every number quickly – at anytime."

Financial Management, March 2003.

Questions relating to this news story may be found on page 420 ▶▶

About this chapter

This chapter examines *standard costing*, another planning and control technique used in management accounting. Like budgeting and budgetary control, standard costing involves estimating future sales revenue and product costs. However, standard costing goes into a great more detail than is the case with budgeting. In standard costing, for example, the total *budgeted* cost is broken down into the elements of cost (direct materials, direct labour, variable overhead and fixed overhead) and these costs are then compared with the *actual* cost of those elements. The differences between the standard cost and the actual cost are known as variances. The total variances can then be analyzed into volume and price variances and, in some cases, even into various sub-variances. Significant variances are then investigated and immediate action is taken to correct any unexpected or unwelcome ones. The difference between budgeted sales and actual sales can also be analyzed into various variances (such as volume and price), and again sub-variance analysis may also be possible.

Standard costing is of particular relevance in manufacturing industry where specific products or processes are produced and where all three elements of cost (materials, labour and overheads) are relevant. It is of less relevance in non-manufacturing entities and few such entities use the technique.

The chapter is broken down into seven main sections. The first main section explains why this chapter is important for non-accountants. The following one describes how a standard costing system is organized and how it operates. We then examine in some detail the main cost variances and these are then illustrated in a comprehensive example. At that point we turn to have a look at sales variances before we put all the variances together in the form of a typical standard cost operating statement. The last main section in the chapter then poses some questions for non-accountants to ask about standard costing and variance analysis.

Learning objectives

By the end of this chapter you should be able to:

- describe the nature and purpose of standard costing;
- identify the main steps involved in implementing and operating a standard costing system;
- calculate three standard costing performance measures;
- calculate sales, direct materials, direct labour, variable overhead and fixed overhead variances;
- prepare a standard cost operating statement;
- outline the importance of standard costing and variance analysis.

❗ Why this chapter is important for non-accountants

Standard costing is a major management accounting planning and control technique of benefit mainly in manufacturing entities. As a non-accountant, therefore, unless you already work in a manufacturing industry or you may do at some time in the future, it is unlikely that you will come across the technique in your day-to-day work.

However, for those non-accountant managers for whom it is of immediate relevance now or in the near future, it is important that they know something about the technique for the following reasons:

1 You will be required to provide information for standard costing purposes.
2 You will be presented with standard costing operating statements.
3 You will be asked what action you propose to take in order to control those areas that show significant variances. In order to provide an answer, you need to know where the figures come from, how reliable they are and what they mean.

For those non-accountants who do not think that standard costing is likely to be of relevance for them, this chapter may be just one of general interest. Nevertheless, no one can be absolutely sure where their career is likely to take them. It would be as well, therefore, if you work your way through the chapter in case you do move into the manufacturing industry at some time in the future.

Operation

Standard costing is a sophisticated means of planning an entity's operations. It is expensive and time-consuming both to implement and to operate. If it is to work effectively it has to be accepted by all of the entity's employees. If they do not, it is unlikely to work. Employees will be required to produce the basic information for it and they will be expected to act on what it then tells them.

Definitions

It would be helpful if we first define four terms that will be occurring throughout this chapter. These are as follows:

> **Standard:** *the amount or level set for the performance of a particular activity.*
> **Standard cost:** *the planned cost for a particular level of activity.*
> **Variance:** *the difference between the standard (or planned) cost and the actual cost.*
> **Variance analysis:** *an investigation into and an explanation of why variances occurred.*

Uses

Standard costing has four main uses. They are as follows.

1 *Stock valuation.* We indicated in Chapter 15 that there were four methods of pricing direct materials to production: unit cost, first-in, first-out, an average price, and the standard cost. The standard cost is the expected or planned price that the entity expects to pay for its materials. The standard cost method is simple to use and it can remain stable for some time. The main difficulties are in establishing a standard cost and in coping with significant differences between it and actual costs.
2 *Control.* By comparing frequently and in detail actual costs against the standard costs fairly swift action can be taken to correct any departures from what was planned.
3 *Performance measurement.* Standard costing provides information that enables an entity to determine whether it is meeting its objectives.
4 *Pricing.* The information provided by a standard costing system assists entities in setting their selling prices.

Types of entities

Standard costing is only appropriate for certain types of entities. Its main features are particularly suitable for incorporation into those manufacturing entities where it is possible to analyze the cost of particular units or processes into materials, labour and overheads. Standard costing is probably only cost-effective in larger entities because of the vast amount of data that it generates.

The standard costing period

The standard costing period will usually be the same as that for the main budget and sub-budget periods. Short periods are preferable so that the actual results can be compared frequently with the standard results. Corrective action can then be taken quickly before it is too late to do anything about any unexpected trends. Short standard costing periods may also be necessary where market or production conditions are subject to frequent changes or where it is particularly difficult to prepare long-term plans, e.g. in the fashion industry.

Types of standard

The preparation of standard costs requires great care and attention. As each element of cost is subject to detailed arithmetical analysis, it is important that the initial information is accurate. Indeed, the information produced by a standard costing system will be virtually worthless if subsequent analyses reveal that variances were caused by inefficient budgeting or standard setting.

In preparing standard costs, management will need to be informed of the level of activity to be used in preparing the standard costs, i.e. whether the entity will need to operate at say 80 per cent or 90 per cent of its theoretical capacity. An activity level should be chosen that is capable of being achieved. It would be possible to choose a standard that was *ideal*, i.e. one that represented a performance that could be achieved only under the most favourable of conditions. Such a standard would, however, be unrealistic, because it is rare for ideal conditions to prevail. An ideal standard is a standard that is attainable under the most favourable conditions and where no allowance is made for normal losses, waste and machine downtime.

A much more realistic standard is called an *attainable standard*. An attainable standard is one that the entity can expect to achieve in reasonably efficient working conditions. In other words, it is accepted that some delays and inefficiencies (such as normal losses (e.g. caused by evaporation), waste and machine downtime) will occur, but it is also assumed that management will attempt to minimize them.

You may also come across the term *basic* cost standards. These are standards that are left unchanged over long periods of time. This enables some consistency to be achieved in comparing actual results with the same standards over a substantial period of time, but the standards may become so out of date that meaningful comparisons are not possible.

| Activity 18.1 | Your company bases its standard costs on an ideal level, i.e. no allowance is made for losses and the standard costs can only be achieved in entirely favourable conditions. As a cost centre manager, what would your reaction be when you received a report showing that your centre had a number of large unwelcome variances?

Write down in your notebook what your reaction would be and what you would do about such variances. |

Information required

The basic information needed to operate a standard costing system is considerable. The main requirements are as follows:

1 *Direct materials*: types, quantities and price.
2 *Direct labour*: grades, numbers and rates of pay.
3 *Variable overhead*: the total variable overhead cost analyzed into various categories, such as employee and general support costs.
4 *Fixed overhead*: the total fixed overhead, also analyzed into various categories such as employee costs, building costs and general administration expenses.

The above summary shows that the standard cost of a particular unit comprises four main elements: (a) direct materials; (b) direct labour; (c) variable overhead; and (d) fixed overhead. In turn, each element comprises two factors, namely quantity and price. The total standard cost of a specific unit may be built up as shown in Example 18.1. The example is based on some fictitious data.

Calculation of the total standard cost of a specific unit using absorption costing

Example 18.1

	£
1 Direct materials	
Quantity × price (2 units × £5)	10
2 Direct labour	
Hours × hourly rate (5 hours × £10)	50
3 Variable overhead	
Hours × variable overhead absorption rate per hour (5 hours × £6)	30
4 Fixed overhead	
Hours × fixed overhead absorption rate per hour (5 hours × £3)	15
Total standard cost per unit	105

Note: The example assumes that the unit cost is calculated on the basis of standard absorption costing. This is the most common method of standard costing. It is possible, however, to adopt a system of standard *marginal* costing (see Chapter 19).

Standard hours and the absorption of overhead

Standard absorption costing requires overhead to be absorbed on the basis of *standard* hours. You will recall that in a non-standard costing system overhead is absorbed on the basis of *actual* hours. A standard hour represents the amount of work that should be performed in an hour, given that it is produced in standard conditions, i.e. in *planned* conditions. Each unit is given a standard time of so many hours in which the work should be produced. It is against that standard that the actual hours will be compared.

In order to calculate the standard overhead cost of a unit, the standard overhead absorption rate for the period is multiplied by the number of *standard* (not actual) hours that the unit should have taken to produce. The absorption of overhead by multiplying the standard absorption rate by the standard hours is a significant departure from that approach adopted in a non-standard costing system. This is a most important point and we will return to it a little later on in the chapter.

Sales variances

Some companies also use sales variances although they are not as common as cost variances. If sales variances are required, the difference between the actual sales revenue and the standard revenue is analyzed into a number of sub-variances, such as price and quantity. A detailed analysis of the budgeted sales will be needed in order to obtain the following information:

1 the range and number of each product to be sold;
2 the selling price of each product;
3 the respective periods in which sales are to take place.

Performance measures

Management may find it useful if some performance measures are extracted from the standard costing data. There are three particularly important ones. They assist in informing managers about the level of efficiency of the entity, help them to spot unfavourable trends and enable them to take immediate corrective action.

Before these performance measures are examined, we must emphasize once again that, in *standard* costing, *actual* costs are compared with the standard cost for the actual level of activity. It is tempting to compare the actual cost with the *budgeted* cost, but it is not customary to do so in standard costing. By comparing the actual cost with the standard cost for the actual production, the budget is, in effect, being *flexed*. This means that any variances that do then arise can be more realistically assessed, as the same level of activity is being used to measure the actual costs against the budgeted costs. We can now examine the three performance measures. Referring to Figure 18.1, the actual hours are those direct labour hours actually worked. The budgeted direct labour hours are those

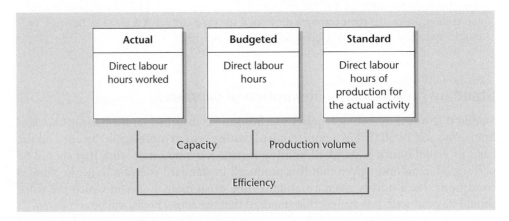

Figure 18.1 **Three performance measures**

that were expected or planned to be worked. The standard direct labour hours of production for the actual activity measure the output produced in standard direct labour hours. For example, if each unit produced *should have* taken five hours each and 100 units were produced, the total standard direct labour hours for the actual activity would be 500 (5 DLH × 100). The budget might have been planned on the basis of 120 units, in which case the total budgeted labour hours would have been 600 (5 DLH × 120).

The three performance measures may be expressed as ratios. The details are given as follows.

The efficiency ratio

This ratio compares the total standard (or allowed) hours of units produced with the total actual hours taken to produce those units. It is calculated as follows:

$$\frac{\text{Standard hours produced}}{\text{Actual direct labour hours worked}} \times 100$$

With respect to this formula, the standard hours produced = the standard direct labour hours of production for the actual activity.

The efficiency ratio enables management to check whether the company has produced the units in more or less time than had been allowed.

The capacity ratio

The capacity ratio compares the total actual hours worked with the total budgeted hours. It is calculated as follows:

$$\frac{\text{Actual direct labour hours worked}}{\text{Budgeted direct labour hours}} \times 100$$

This ratio enables management to ascertain whether all of the budgeted hours were used to produce the actual units.

The production volume ratio

This ratio compares the total allowed hours for the work actually produced with the total budgeted hours. It is calculated as follows:

$$\frac{\text{Standard hours produced}}{\text{Budgeted direct labour hours}} \times 100$$

With respect to this formula, the standard hours produced = the standard direct labour hours of production for the actual activity.

The production volume ratio enables management to compare the work produced (measured in terms of standard hours) with the budgeted hours of work. This ratio gives management some information about how effective the company has been in using the budgeted hours.

Note that machine hours may be substituted for direct labour hours.

The calculation of efficiency, capacity and production volume ratios is illustrated in Example 18.2.

Example
18.2

Calculation of efficiency, capacity and production volume ratios

The following information relates to the Frost Production Company Limited for the year to 31 March 2004:

1 Budgeted direct labour hours: 1000.
2 Budgeted units: 100.
3 Actual direct labour hours worked: 800.
4 Actual units produced: 90.

Required:
Calculate the following performance ratios:
(a) the efficiency ratio;
(b) the capacity ratio; and
(c) the production volume ratio.

Answer to
Example 18.2

(a) The efficiency ratio:

$$\frac{\text{Standard hours produced}}{\text{Actual direct labour hours worked}} \times 100\% = \frac{900^*}{800} \times 100\% = \underline{\underline{112.5\%}}$$

* Each unit is allowed 10 standard hours (1000 hours/100 units). Since 90 units were produced, the total standard hours of production must equal 900.

It would appear that the company has been more efficient in producing the goods than was expected. It was allowed 900 hours to do so, but it produced them in only 800 hours.

(b) The capacity ratio:

$$\frac{\text{Actual direct labour hours worked}}{\text{Budgeted hours}} \times 100\% = \frac{800}{1000} \times 100\% = \underline{\underline{80\%}}$$

All of the time planned to be available (the capacity) was not utilized, either because it was not possible to work 1000 direct labour hours, or because the company did not undertake as much work as it could have done.

(c) The production volume ratio:

$$\frac{\text{Standard hours produced}}{\text{Budgeted hours}} \times 100\% = \frac{900^*}{1000} \times 100\% = \underline{\underline{90\%}}$$

* As calculated for the efficiency ratio.

It appears that if 90 units had been produced in standard conditions, another 100 hours would have been available (10 units × 10 hours). In fact, since the 90 units only took 800 hours to produce, at least another 20 units could have been produced in standard conditions.

$$\left(\frac{1000 - 800}{10} = \underline{\underline{20 \text{ units}}} \right)$$

The budget allowed for 100 units to be produced and each unit was expected to take 10 direct labour hours to complete, a total budgeted activity of 1000 direct labour hours. However, only 90 units were actually produced. If these units had been produced in standard time, they should have taken 900 hours (90 units × 10 direct labour hours). These are the standard hours produced. The 90 units were completed in 800 actual hours. It appears, therefore, that the units were produced more efficiently than had been expected. The management will still need, of course, to investigate why only 90 units were produced and not the 100 expected in the budget.

Comments on the results

Attempt Example 18.2 without looking at the answer.

Activity 18.2

We have now covered the operation of a standard costing system. In the next section we will examine how standard cost variances may be calculated and whether they may be viewed as being either favourable or unfavourable.

Cost variances

Structure

The difference between actual costs and standard costs consists of two main variances: price and quantity. These variances may either be favourable (F) to profit, or adverse (A). This means that the actual prices paid or costs incurred can be more than was anticipated (adverse to profit), or less than anticipated (favourable to profit). Similarly, the quantities used in production can result in more being used (adverse to profit) or less than expected (favourable to profit).

The main standard production cost variances are shown in diagrammatic form in Figure 18.2 and as equations as shown below. Sales variances will be dealt with later in the chapter. The cost variances are as follows:

1 *Direct material:* Total = price + usage.
2 *Direct labour:* Total = rate + efficiency.
3 *Variable production overhead:* Total = expenditure + efficiency.
4 *Fixed production overhead:* Total = expenditure + volume. *

* The fixed production overhead volume variance may be subanalyzed into a capacity variance and an efficiency variance.

Variance analysis formulae

Before we explain how to calculate cost variances, it would be useful if we were first to summarize the basic formulae. You will then find it convenient to refer back to this summary when dealing with later exhibits.

The formulae used in calculating the main standard cost variances are as follows:

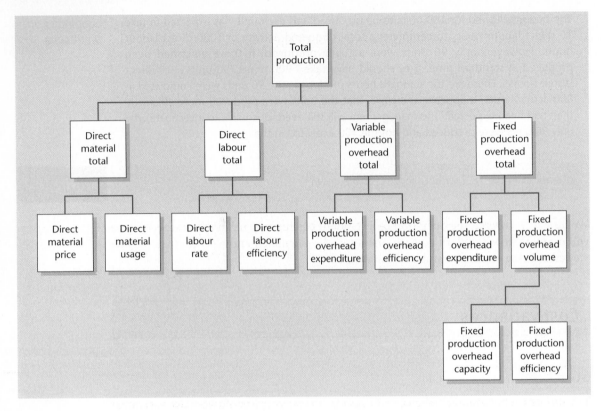

Figure 18.2 **Main standard production cost variances**

Direct materials

1 **Total** = (actual cost per unit × actual quantity used) − (standard cost per unit × standard quantity for actual production)
2 **Price** = (actual cost per unit − standard cost per unit) × total actual quantity used
3 **Usage** = (total actual quantity used − standard quantity for actual production) × standard cost

These relationships are shown in Figure 18.3.

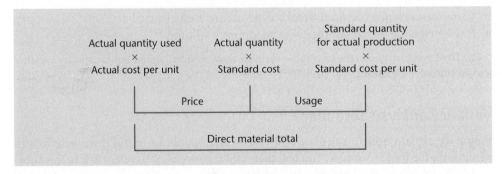

Figure 18.3 **Calculation of direct material variances**

Direct labour

1 **Total** = (actual hourly rate × actual hours) – (standard hourly rate × standard hours for actual production).
2 **Rate** = (actual hourly rate – standard hourly rate) × actual hours worked.
3 **Efficiency** = (actual hours worked – standard hours for actual production) × standard hourly rate.

These relationships are shown in Figure 18.4.

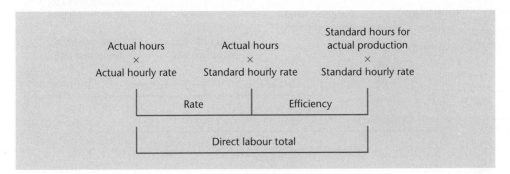

Figure 18.4 **Calculation of direct labour variances**

Variable production overhead

1 **Total** = actual variable overhead – [standard hours for actual production × variable production overhead absorption rate (V.OAR)]
2 **Expenditure** = actual variable overhead – (actual hours worked × V.OAR)
3 **Efficiency** = (standard hours for actual production – actual hours worked) × V.OAR

These relationships are shown in Figure 18.5.

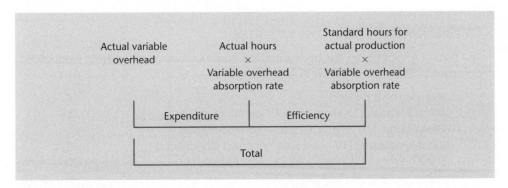

Figure 18.5 **Calculation of variable production overhead variances**

Fixed production overhead

1 **Total** = actual fixed overhead – [standard hours of production × fixed overhead absorption rate (FOAR)]
2 **Expenditure** = actual fixed overhead – budgeted fixed expenditure
3 **Capacity** = budgeted fixed overhead – (actual hours worked × FOAR)

4 **Efficiency** = (actual hours worked – standard hours for actual production) × FOAR
5 **Volume** = budgeted fixed overhead expenditure – (standard hours for actual production × FOAR)

Note: Volume = capacity + efficiency

These variances are shown in Figure 18.6.

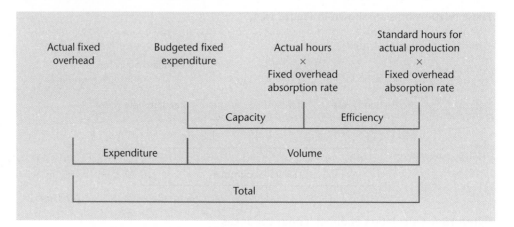

Figure 18.6 **Calculation of fixed production overhead variances**

A comprehensive example

We will now use a comprehensive example to illustrate the main cost variances. The details are contained in Example 18.3.

| Example 18.3 | ### Calculation of the main cost variances |

The following information has been extracted from the records of the Frost Production Company Limited for the year to 31 March 2004:

Budgeted costs per unit:	£
Direct materials (15 kilograms × £2 per kilogram)	30
Direct labour (10 hours × £4 per direct labour hour)	40
Variable overhead (10 hours × £1 per direct labour hour)	10
Fixed overhead (10 hours × £2 per direct labour hour)	20
Total budgeted cost per unit	100

The following budgeted data are also relevant:

1 The budgeted production level was 100 units.
2 The total standard direct labour hours amounted to 1000.
3 The total budgeted variable overhead was estimated to be £1000.
4 The total budgeted fixed overhead was £2000.
5 The company absorbs both fixed and variable overhead on the basis of direct labour hours.

Actual costs:	£
Direct materials	2 100
Direct labour	4 000
Variable overhead	1 000
Fixed overhead	1 600
Total actual costs	8 700

Note: 90 units were produced in 800 actual hours, and the total actual quantity of direct materials consumed was 1400 kilograms.

Required:
(a) Calculate the direct materials, direct labour, variable production overhead and fixed production overhead total cost variances.
(b) Calculate the detailed variances for each element of cost.

In answering part (a) of this question we need to summarize the total variance for each element of cost for the Frost Production Company Ltd for the actual 90 units produced:

Answer to Example 18.3(a)

	Actual costs	Total standard cost for actual production	Variance
	£	£	£
Direct materials	2 100	2 700 (1)	600 (F)
Direct labour	4 000	3 600 (2)	400 (A)
Variable production overhead	1 000	900 (3)	100 (A)
Fixed production overhead	1 600	1 800 (4)	200 (F)
Total	8 700	9 000	300 (F)

Notes:
(a) F = favourable to profit; A = adverse to profit.
(b) The numbers in brackets refer to the tutorial notes below.

1 The standard cost of direct material for actual production = the actual units produced × the standard direct material cost per unit, i.e. 90 × £30 = £2700.

Tutorial notes

2 The standard cost of direct labour for actual production = the actual units produced × standard direct labour cost per unit, i.e. 90 × £40 = £3600.

3 The standard variable cost for actual performance = the actual units produced × variable overhead absorption rate per unit, i.e. 90 × £10 = £900.

4 The fixed overhead cost for the actual performance = the actual units produced × fixed overhead absorption rate, i.e. 90 × £20 = £1800.

(a) As can be seen from the answer to Example 18.3(a) comments on the answer to Example 18.3(a), the total actual cost of producing the 90 units was £300 less than the budget allowance. An investigation would need to be made in order to find out why only 90 units were produced when the company had budgeted for 100. Furthermore, although the 90 units have cost £300 less than might have been expected, a number of other variances have contributed to the total variance. Assuming that these variances are considered significant, they would need to be carefully investigated in order to find out what caused them. Both the direct materials

Comments on the answers to Example 18.3(a)

▶

Example 18.3(a) continued

and the fixed production overhead, for example, cost respectively £600 and £200 less than the budget allowance, while the direct labour cost £400 and the variable production overhead £100 more than might have been expected.

As a result of calculating variances for each element of cost, it would now be much easier for management to investigate why the actual production cost was £300 less than might have been expected. However, by analyzing the variances into their major causes, the accountant can provide even greater guidance. This is illustrated in part (b) of the answer to the question.

Activity 18.3

Have a go at doing Example 18.3(a) without looking at the answer.

Answer to Example 18.3(b)

In answering part (b) of Example 18.3, we deal with each element of cost in turn. As we do so we will take the opportunity to comment on the results.

Direct materials

1 **Price** = (actual cost per unit – standard cost per unit)
            × total actual quantity used
   Thus:
$$\text{Price variance} = (£1.50 - 2.00) \times 1400 \text{ (kg)} = \underline{£700 \text{ (F)}}$$

The actual price per unit was £1.50 (£2100/1400) and the standard price was £2.00 per unit. There was, therefore, a total saving (as far as the price of the materials was concerned) of £700 (£0.50 × 1400). This was favourable (F) to profit.

2 **Usage** = (total actual quantity used – standard quantity for actual production)
            × standard cost
   Thus:
$$\text{Usage variance} = (1400 - 1350) \times £2.00 = \underline{£100 \text{ (A)}}$$

In producing 90 units, Frost should have used 1350 kilograms (90 × 15 kg), instead of the 1400 kilograms actually used. If this extra usage is valued at the standard cost (the difference between the actual price and the standard cost has already been allowed for), there is an adverse usage variance of £100 (50 (kg) × £2.00).

3 **Total** = price + usage:
$$= £700 \text{ (F)} + £100 \text{ (A)} = \underline{£600 \text{ (F)}}$$

The £600 favourable total variance was calculated earlier in answering part (a) of the question. This variance might have arisen because Frost purchased cheaper materials. If this were the case, then it probably resulted in a greater wastage of materials, perhaps because the materials were of an inferior quality.

Direct labour

1 **Rate** = (actual hourly rate – standard hourly rate) × actual hours worked
   Thus:
$$\text{Rate variance} = (£5.00 - £4.00) \times 800 \text{ DLH} = \underline{£800 \text{ (A)}}$$

The actual hourly rate is £5.00 per direct labour hour (£4000/800) compared with the standard rate per hour of £4. Every extra actual hour worked, therefore, resulted in an adverse variance of £1, or £800 in total (£1 × 800).

2 Efficiency = (actual hours worked − standard hours for actual production) × standard hourly rate.

Thus:

$$\text{Efficiency variance} = (800 - 900) \times £4.00 = \underline{\underline{£400 \text{ (F)}}}$$

Answer to Example 18.3(b) continued

The actual hours worked were 800. However, 900 hours would be the allowance for the 90 units actually produced (90 ¥ 10 DLH). If these hours were valued at the standard hourly rate (differences between the actual rate and the standard rate having already been allowed for when calculating the rate variance), a favourable variance of £400 arises. The favourable efficiency variance has arisen because the 90 units took less time to produce than the budget allowed for.

3 Total = rate + efficiency

$$£800 \text{ (A)} + £400 \text{ (F)} = \underline{\underline{£400 \text{ (A)}}}$$

The £400 adverse total variance was calculated earlier in answering part (a) of the question. It arises because the company paid more per direct labour hour than had been budgeted, although this was offset to some extent by the units being produced in less time than the budgeted allowance. This variance could have been caused by using a higher grade of labour than had been intended. Unfortunately, the higher labour rate per hour was not completely offset by greater efficiency.

Variable production overhead

1 Expenditure = actual variable overhead − (actual hours worked × variable production overhead absorption rate)

Thus:

$$\text{Expenditure variance} = £1000 - (800 \times £1.00) = \underline{\underline{£200 \text{ (A)}}}$$

2 Efficiency = (standard hours for actual production − actual hours worked) × variable production overhead absorption rate

Thus:

$$\text{Efficiency variance} = (900 - 800) \times £1.00 = \underline{\underline{£100 \text{ (F)}}}$$

3 Total = expenditure + efficiency

$$= £200 \text{ (A)} + £100 \text{ (F)} = \underline{\underline{£100 \text{ (A)}}}$$

The adverse variance of £100 (A) arises because the variable overhead absorption rate was calculated on the basis of a budgeted cost of £10 per unit. In fact the absorption rate ought to have been £11.11 per unit (£1000/90), because the total actual variable cost was £1000. There would, of course, be no variable production overhead cost for the ten units that were not produced. The £100 adverse total variance was calculated earlier in answering part (a) of the question.

Fixed production overhead

1 Expenditure = actual fixed overhead − budgeted fixed expenditure

Thus:

$$\text{Expenditure variance} = £1600 - £2000 = \underline{\underline{£400 \text{ (F)}}}$$

The actual expenditure was £400 less than the budgeted expenditure. This means that the fixed production overhead absorption rate was £400 higher than it needed to have been if there had not been any other fixed overhead variances.

2 Volume = budgeted fixed overhead − (standard hours of production × fixed production overhead absorption rate)

Thus:

$$\text{Volume variance} = £2000 − (900 × £2.00) = \underline{\underline{£200 \text{ (A)}}}$$

As a result of producing fewer units than expected, £200 less overhead has been absorbed into production.

3 Capacity = budgeted fixed overhead − (actual hours worked × fixed production overhead absorption rate)

Thus:

$$\text{Capacity variance} = £2000 − (800 × £2.00) = \underline{\underline{£400 \text{ (A)}}}$$

The capacity variance shows that the actual hours worked were less than the budgeted hours. Other things being equal, therefore, not enough overhead would have been absorbed into production. It should be noted that the capacity variance will be favourable when the actual hours are in excess of the budgeted hours. This might seem odd, but it means that the company has been able to use more hours than it had originally budgeted. As a result, it should have been able to produce more units, thereby absorbing more overhead into production. This variance links with the capacity ratio calculated earlier in the chapter in Example 18.2. The capacity ratio showed that only 80 per cent of the budgeted capacity had been utilized, and so probably not as much overhead was absorbed into production as had been originally expected.

4 Efficiency = (actual hours worked − standard hours for actual production) × fixed production overhead absorption rate.

Thus:

$$\text{Efficiency variance} = (800 − 900) × £2.00 = \underline{\underline{£200 \text{ (F)}}}$$

This variance shows the difference between the 900 standard hours that the work is worth ($90 × 10 = 900$ hours), compared with the amount of time that it took to produce those units (i.e. 800 hours). Thus the factory has been more efficient in producing the goods than might have been expected. This variance complements the efficiency ratio of 112.5 per cent that was illustrated earlier in the chapter in Example 18.2.

Remember: Volume variance = capacity variance + efficiency variance

Thus:

$$\text{Volume variance} = £400 \text{ (A)} + £200 \text{ (F)} = \underline{\underline{£200 \text{ (A)}}}$$

(See also 2 above.)

5 The fixed production overhead total variance was calculated earlier in answering part (a) of the question. The simplified formula is as follows:

$$\text{Total} = \text{expenditure} + \text{volume}$$

$$= £400 \text{ (F)} + £200 \text{ (A)} = \underline{\underline{£200 \text{ (F)}}}$$

As the actual activity was less than the budgeted activity, only £1800 of fixed overhead was absorbed into production instead of the £2000 expected in the budget. However, the actual expenditure was only £1600. The overestimate of expenditure, therefore, compensated for the overestimate of activity.

Activity 18.4

Using the data in Example 18.3 calculate the detailed variances for direct materials, direct labour, variable production overhead, and fixed production overhead. Do not look at the answers but you may refer to the variance analysis formulae on pages 408 to 410.

Sales variances

As well as calculating cost variances, it is also possible to do the same for sales. In an absorption costing system, a total sales variance would be classified into a selling price variance and a sales volume profit variance (see Figure 18.7).

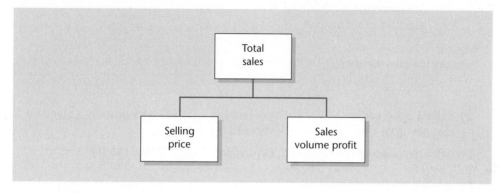

Figure 18.7 **Main sales variances**

The sales variance formulae are as follows:

1 **Total sales variance** = [actual sales revenue – (actual sales quantity × standard cost per unit)] – (budgeted quantity × standard profit per unit).

2 **Selling price variance** = [actual sales revenue – (actual sales quantity × standard cost per unit)] – (actual quantity × standard profit per unit). An alternative formula for the calculation of the selling price variance is as follows: (actual selling price per unit – standard selling price per unit) × actual sales quantity.

3 **Sales volume profit variance** = (actual quantity – budgeted quantity) × standard profit per unit.

The above integrated formulae are shown diagrammatically in Figure 18.8.

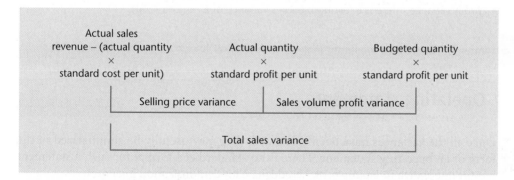

Figure 18.8 **Calculation of sales variances based on profit**

We illustrate the use of the above sales variance formula in Example 18.4.

Example 18.4

Calculating sales variances

The following data relate to Frozen Limited for the year to 31 July 2004:

	Budget/standard	Actual
Sales (units)	100	90
Selling price per unit	£10	£10.50
Standard cost per unit	£7	–
Standard profit per unit	£3	

Required:
Calculate the sales variances.

Answer to Example 18.4

(a) **Selling price variance** = [actual sales revenue − (actual sales quantity × standard cost per unit)] − (actual quantity × standard profit per unit)

= [£945 − (90 units × £7) − (90 units × £3) = (£945 − 630) − 270 = <u>£45 (F)</u>

The actual selling price per unit was £0.50 more than the standard selling price (£10.50–10.00), and so the variance is favourable. Other things being equal, the profit would be £45 higher than budgeted *for the actual number of units sold*.

(b) **Sales volume profit variance** = (actual quantity − budgeted quantity) × standard profit per unit.
The standard profit is £3 per unit. Thus:

$$(90 \text{ units} - 100 \text{ units}) = 10 \times £3 = \underline{£30 \text{ (A)}}$$

The sales volume profit variance is £30 adverse because only 90 units were sold instead of the budgeted amount of 100 units. As a result, £30 less profit was made.

(c) **Total sales variance** = [actual sales revenue − (actual sales quantity × standard cost per unit)] − (budgeted quantity × standard profit per unit).
The actual sales revenue = £945 (90 units × £10.50). Thus:

$$[£945 - (90 \text{ units} \times £7)] - (100 \text{ units} \times £3) = (£945 - 630) - 300 = \underline{£15 \text{ (F)}}$$

When the £45 favourable selling price is set off against the £30 adverse sales volume profit variance, there is a favourable sales variance of £15 (£45 − 30).

Activity 18.5

Attempt Example 18.4 without looking at the answer.

Operating statements

Once all the variances have been calculated, they may usefully be summarized in the form of an operating statement. There is no standardized format for such a statement but the one shown in Example 18.5 is adequate for demonstration purposes.

**Example
18.5**

Preparation of a standard cost operating statement

Example 18.3 gave some information relating to the Frost Production Company Limited for the year to 31 March 2004. The cost data used in that example will now be used in this Exhibit, but some additional information is required.

Additional information:
1 Assume that the budgeted sales were 100 units at a selling price of £150 per unit.
2 90 units were sold at £160 per unit.

Required:
Prepare a standard cost operating statement for the year to 31 March 2004.

Frost Production Company Limited. Standard cost operating statement for the year to 31 March 2004:

	£
Budgeted sales (100 × £150)	15 000
Budgeted cost of sales (100 × £100)	10 000
Budgeted profit	5 000
Sales volume profit variance (1)	(500)
Budgeted profit from actual sales	4 500

Variances: (2)	(F)	(A)	
	£	£	
Sales price (3)	900		
Direct materials usage		100	
Direct materials price	700		
Direct labour efficiency	400		
Direct labour rates		800	
Variable overhead efficiency	100		
Variable overhead expenditure		200	
Fixed overhead			
Fixed overhead capacity		400	
Fixed overhead efficiency	200		
Fixed overhead expenditure	400		
	2 700	1 500	1 200
Actual profit			5 700

1 **Sales volume profit variance** = (actual quantity – budgeted quantity) × standard profit per unit

    = (90 – 100) × £50 = £500 (A)

Tutorial notes

2 Details of the cost variances were shown in the answer to Example 18.3.

3 **Selling price variance** = (actual selling price per unit – standard selling price per unit) × actual sales quantity

    = (£160 – £150) × 90 = £900 (F)

The format used in Example 18.5 is particularly helpful because it shows the link between the budgeted profit and the actual profit. Thus, management can trace the main causes of sales and cost variances. In practice, the statement would also show the details for each product.

The operating profit statement will help management decide where to begin an investigation into the causes of the respective variances. It is unlikely that they will all need to be investigated. It may be company policy, for example, to investigate only those variances that are particularly significant, irrespective of whether they are favourable or adverse. In other words, only *exceptional* variances would be investigated. A policy decision would then have to be taken on what was meant by 'exceptional'.

Activity 18.6	Attempt Example 18.5 without looking at the answer.
	You will need to refer back to Example 18.3 and the answers you obtained when you did Activities 18.3 and 18.4.

! Questions non-accountants should ask

The calculation of standard cost variances is a complex arithmetical exercise. The process can become even more complicated if some of the variances are broken down into sub-variances. For example, the sales volume profit variance can be analysed into sales mix profit and sales quantity profit variances, and the direct material quantity variance into direct material mix and direct material yield variances.

It is unlikely that as a non-accountant you will have to calculate variances for yourself. However, it is important for you to have some idea of how the variances are calculated so that you are in a stronger position to start investigating them and to determine how they may have occurred. Indeed, your main task will probably be to carry out a detailed investigation of the cause of any significant variance and then to take any necessary corrective action.

So what questions should you ask? We suggest that you can use the following ones as a basis for any subsequent investigation.

- Was the given level of activity accurate?
- Was the standard set realistic?
- Is there anything unusual about the actual events?
- Is the measure (i.e. the standard) reliable?
- Are there any particular variances that stand out?
- Are there any that are the main cause of any total variance?
- Is there a linkage between variances, e.g. between a favourable price variance and an unfavourable quantity/volume variance?
- Are there any factors that could not possibly have been seen at the time that the standards were prepared?

Conclusion

We have now come to the end of a long and complex chapter. You may have found that it has been extremely difficult to understand just how standard cost variances are calculated. Fortunately, it is unlikely that, as a non-accountant, you will ever have to calculate variances for yourself. It is sufficient for your purposes to understand their meaning and to have some idea of the arithmetical foundation on which they are based.

Your job will largely be to investigate the causes of the variances, and to take necessary action. A standard costing system is supposed to help management plan and control the entity much more tightly than can be achieved in the absence of such a system. However, it can only be of real benefit if it is welcomed by those managers whom it is supposed to help. It can hardly be of help if it just produces a great deal of incomprehensible data. After reading this chapter, it is hoped that the data will now mean something to you.

Key points

1 A standard cost is the planned cost of a particular unit or process.

2 Standard costs are usually based on what is reasonably attainable.

3 Actual costs are compared with standard costs.

4 Corrective action is taken if there are any unplanned trends.

5 Three performance measures used in standard costing are: the efficiency ratio, the capacity ratio, and the production volume ratio.

6 Variance analysis is an arithmetical exercise that enables differences between actual and standard costs to be broken down into the elements of cost.

7 The degree of analysis will vary, but usually a total cost variance will be analyzed into direct material, direct labour, variable overhead and fixed overhead variances. In turn, these will be analyzed into quantity and expenditure variances. An even more detailed analysis is possible.

8 Sales variances may also be calculated. Like cost variances, sales variances may also be analyzed in greater detail, e.g. into a selling price variance and a sales volume profit variance.

9 The variances help in tracing the main causes of differences between actual and budgeted results, but they do not explain what has actually happened.

Check your learning

1 Explain what is meant by the following terms: (a) a standard; (b) a standard cost; (c) a variance; and (d) variance analysis.

2 List four uses of standard costing.

3 What type of entities might benefit from a standard costing system?

4 How long should a standard costing period be?

5 What is (a) a basic standard; (b) an attainable standard; and (c) an ideal standard?

6 Name four types of information required for a standard costing system.

7 What is a standard hour?

8 Name three standard cost performance measures.

9 What are their respective formulae?

10 Complete the following equations:
   (a) direct materials total = _____ + _____;
   (b) direct labour total = _____ + _____;
   (c) variable production overhead total = _____ + _____; and
   (d) fixed production overhead total = _____ + _____ + _____.

11 What is (a) an adverse variance; and (b) a favourable variance.

12 Complete the following equation: total sales variance = _____ + _____.

13 Complete the following statement: a standard cost operating statement links the budgeted profit to the _____ _____ for the period.

News story quiz

Remember the news story at the beginning of this chapter? Go back to that story and re-read it before answering the following questions.

This article does not deal specifically with standard costing but it does emphasize that managers need better information and to receive it more quickly.

Questions

1 How far do you think that standard costing is a reliable measure of performance?

2 How can information technology help produce more accurate standard costing information?

3 To what extent would the more speedy supply of standard cost information improve managers' control of resources?

4 Is it realistic to expect that the standard costs can be changed '*quickly – at any time*' and is this desirable?

Tutorial questions

The answers to questions marked with an asterix may be found in Appendix 4.

18.1 Is it likely that a standard costing system is of any relevance in a service industry?

18.2 'Standard costing is all about number crunching, and for someone on the shop floor it has absolutely no relevance.' Do you agree with this statement?

18.3 'Sales variance calculations are just another example of accountants playing around with numbers.' Discuss.

18.4* You are presented with the following information for X Limited:

Standard price per unit: £10.
Standard quantity for actual production: 5 units.
Actual price per unit: £12.
Actual quantity: 6 units.

Required:
Calculate the following variances:

1 direct material total variance;
2 direct material price variance; and
3 direct material usage variance.

18.5 The following information relates to Malcolm Limited:

Budgeted production: 100 units.
Unit specification (direct materials): 50 kilograms × £5 per kilogram = £250.
Actual production: 120 units.
Direct materials used: 5400 kilograms at a total cost of £32 400.

Required:
Calculate the following variances:

1 direct material total;
2 direct material price; and
3 direct material usage.

18.6* The following information relates to Bruce Limited:

> Actual hours: 1000.
> Actual wage rate per hour: £6.50.
> Standard hours for actual production: 900.
> Standard wage rate per hour: £6.00.

Required:
Calculate the following variances:

1 direct labour total;
2 direct labour rate; and
3 direct labour efficiency.

18.7 You are presented with the following information for Duncan Limited:

> Budgeted production: 1000 units.
> Actual production: 1200 units.
> Standard specification for one unit: 10 hours at £8 per direct labour hour.
> Actual direct labour cost: £97 200 in 10 800 actual hours.

Required:
Calculate the following variances:

1 direct labour total;
2 direct labour rate; and
3 direct labour efficiency.

18.8* The following overhead budget has been prepared for Anthea Limited:

> Actual fixed overhead: £150 000.
> Budgeted fixed overhead: £135 000.
> Fixed overhead absorption rate per hour: £15.
> Actual hours worked: 10 000.
> Standard hours of production: 8000.

Required:
Calculate the following fixed production overhead variances:
1 total;
2 expenditure;
3 volume;
4 capacity; and
5 efficiency.

18.9* Using the data contained in the previous question, calculate the following performance measures:

1 efficiency ratio;
2 capacity ratio; and
3 production volume ratio.

18.10 The following information relates to Osprey Limited:

>Budgeted production: 500 units.
>Standard hours per unit: 10.
>Actual production: 600 units.
>Budgeted fixed overhead: £125 000.
>Actual fixed overhead: £120 000.
>Actual hours worked: 4900.

Required:
Calculate the following fixed production overhead variances:

1 total;
2 expenditure;
3 volume;
4 capacity; and
5 efficiency.

18.11 Using the data from the previous question, calculate the following performance measures:

1 efficiency ratio;
2 capacity ratio; and
3 production volume ratio.

18.12* Milton Limited has produced the following information:

>Total actual sales: £99 000.
>Actual quantity sold: 9000 units.
>Budgeted selling price per unit: £10.
>Standard cost per unit: £7.
>Total budgeted units: 10 000 units.

Required:
Calculate the selling price variance, the sales volume profit variance, and the sales variance in total.

18.13 You are presented with the following budgeted information for Doe Limited:

Sales units	*100*
Per unit:	*£*
Selling price	30
Cost	(20)
Profit	10
Actual sales	120 units
Actual selling price per unit	£28

Required:
Calculate the sales variances.

18.14 The budgeted selling price and standard cost of a unit manufactured by Smillie Limited is as follows:

	£
Selling price	30
Direct materials (2.5 kilos)	5
Direct labour (2 hours)	12
Fixed production overhead	8
	25
Budgeted profit	5

Total budgeted sales: 400 units

During the period to 31 December 2007, the actual sales and production details for Smillie were as follows:

	£
Sales (420 units)	13 440
Direct materials (1260 kilos)	2 268
Direct labour (800 hours)	5 200
Fixed production overhead	3 300
	10 768
Profit	2 672

Required:
(a) Prepare a standard cost operating statement for the period to 31 December 2007 incorporating as many variances as the data permit.
(b) Explain what the statement tells the managers of Smillie Limited

18.15 Mean Limited manufactures a single product, and the following information relates to the actual selling price and actual cost of the product for the four weeks to 31 March 2007:

	£000
Sales (50 000 units)	2 250
Direct materials (240 000 litres)	528
Direct labour (250 000 hours)	1 375
Variable production overhead	245
Fixed production overhead	650
	2 798
Loss	(548)

The budgeted selling price and standard cost of each unit was as follows:

		£
Selling price		55
Direct materials (5 litres)		10
Direct labour (4 hours)		20
Variable production overhead		5
Fixed production overhead		15
		50
Budgeted profit		5

Total budgeted production: 40 000 units.

Required:

(a) Prepare a standard cost operating statement for the four weeks to 31 March 2007 incorporating as many variances as the data permit.

(b) Explain how the statement may help the managers of Mean Limited to control the business more effectively.

Further practice questions, study material and links to relevant sites on the World Wide Web can be found on the website that accompanies this book. The site can be found at **www.booksites.net/dyson**

Another way of breaking even . . .

Eurotunnel breaks even in cash

Andrew Clark

Eurotunnel yesterday announced it had reached a "cash breakeven" point for the first time since the Queen opened the Channel tunnel in 1994, although the company insisted it needed more rail traffic to achieve long-term growth in profits.

The Anglo-French firm generated enough cash during 2001 to pay the interest on its £6.5bn debt but, taking into account tax and depreciation, it remained in the red, with underlying losses off 29% at £105m.

Chief executive Richard Shirrefs said it was "never enough" for a business merely to break even. But he added: "This is a significant milestone. We've met a target we set ourselves three years ago, when the world was a much easier place than it is today."

Eurotunnel's shuttle services contributed a 6% increase in revenue to £333m, as a strategy of concentrating on holidaymakers, rather than daytrippers, paid off.

However, income from other rail operators – principally Eurostar and freight firm EWS – edged up by just 1% to £217m, following disruption to freight services due to incursions by asylum seekers last year, which added £4m to the company's security costs.

Over the past year, Mr Shirrefs has complained that the tunnel is an "under-utilised piece of kit", with capacity for many more freight and passenger trains. He called yesterday for more help from the strategic rail authority and the French and British governments in increasing traffic.

"There needs to be more involvement in a broader dialogue on the whole issue of railways," he said. "There's a common interest in looking at the conditions under which traffic can be stimulated."

Mr Shirrefs wants to establish a new freight container service running non-stop between terminals in northern France and the home counties. He has held talks with French firm SNCF about running the engines to pull freight containers.

In the year ahead, he said Eurotunnel intends to keep "chipping away" at its balance sheet to minimise debt repayments. A refinancing last year cut its annual interest payments by more than £30m by putting loans on a longer term footing.

The Guardian, 11 February 2003.

Questions relating to this news story may be found on page 449 ▶▶

About this chapter

In the previous two chapters we have been concerned with the planning and control functions of management accounting. We now turn our attention to another important function of management accounting: *decision making*. In this chapter we explore a basic technique of decision making known as *contribution analysis*.

Contribution analysis is based on the premise that in almost any decision situation some costs are irrelevant, that is, they are not affected by the decision. They can, therefore, be ignored. In such circumstances management should concentrate on the *contribution* that a project may make. Contribution (C) is the difference between the sales revenue (S) of a project and the variable or extra costs (V) incurred by investing in that project. Other things being equal, as long as S – V results in C being positive, management should go ahead or continue with the project. A positive C means that something is left over to make a *contribution* to the fixed (or remaining) costs (F) of the entity. If the fixed costs have already been covered by other projects, then the contribution increases the entity's profit.

The chapter is divided into twelve main sections. The first main section explains why the chapter is important for non-accountants. In successive sections we then examine the background to contribution analysis, the concept of contribution, the assumptions underpinning marginal costing, and the format of a marginal cost statement. A further section demonstrates the application of the marginal cost technique, and the following one shows how charts and graphs may help to make the information more meaningful. The following two sections provide a critique of the technique and a summary of the basic formulae. The discussion is then brought together in an illustrative example. Finally, we incorporate some *limiting factors* into the analysis before the last main sections frames some questions for non-accountants to ask about the material contained in the chapter.

Learning objectives

By the end of this chapter you should be able to:
- **explain why absorption costing may be inappropriate in decision making;**
- **describe the difference between a fixed cost and a variable cost;**
- **use contribution analysis in managerial decision making;**
- **assess the usefulness of contribution analysis in problem solving.**

❗ Why this chapter is important for non-accountants

All of the chapters in this book are, of course, important for non-accountants, otherwise we would not have included them. However, some chapters are more important than others and this is one of them. Indeed, it is one of the most relevant and vital chapters in the book. Why?

Whatever job you are doing and at whatever level, you will be required to make or to take decisions. Many of those decision will be straightforward day-to-day ones such as, '*Do we order a week's or a month's supply of paper towels?*' Other decisions will be more significant and long-term. For example, '*Should we increase our selling prices?*' or '*Do we buy this other company?*'

While there is a cost implication in these sorts of decisions it is unlikely that you would have to work it out for yourself. Your accountants will do this for you and then present you with the results. However, in order to make sense of the information and to take an informed decision, you need to know where the information has come from and how it has been compiled.

This is a valid point irrespective of the particular issue but it is especially valid for specific one-off decisions. If such decisions are based on absorbed costs you might make a spectacularly wrong decision. A more reliable approach is to base your decision on the project's *relevant* costs. This means that you should only include those costs that are likely to be affected by that particular decision.

This chapter will help you appreciate more clearly the nature of relevant costs and their importance in managerial decision making. As a result, you will be able take more soundly based decisions and be more confident about their eventual outcome.

Marginal costing

Chapters 15 and 16 dealt with cost accounting. The costing method described in some detail in those chapters is known as *absorption costing*. The ultimate aim of absorption costing is to charge out all the costs of an entity to individual units of production. The method involves identifying the *direct costs* of specific units and then absorbing a share of the *indirect costs* into each unit. Indirect costs are normally absorbed on the basis of direct labour hours or machine hours. Assuming that an overhead absorption rate is predetermined, i.e. calculated in advance, this method involves estimating (a) the total amount of overhead likely to be incurred; and (b) the total amount of direct labour hours or machine hours expected to be worked. Hence the absorption rate could be affected by: (1) the total cost of the overhead; (2) the hours worked; or (3) by a combination of cost and hours.

The total of the indirect costs (overhead) is, however, likely to be made up of a combination of costs that change depending on how many units a department produces and those costs that are not affected by the number of units produced. Costs that change with activity are known as *variable costs*. It is usually assumed that variable costs vary directly with activity, e.g. if 1 kg costs £1, then 2 kg will cost £2, 3 kg will cost £3, and so on. Those costs that do not change with activity are known as *fixed costs*.

As indicated in Chapters 15 and 16, if we are attempting to work out the total cost of manufacturing particular units, or if we want to value our stocks, it is appropriate to use absorption costing. Indeed, most cost book-keeping systems are based on this method of costing. Absorption costing is not, however, normally appropriate in decision making.

Decision making is a major part of most managers' jobs. They are constantly faced with having to take many decisions, both on a day-to-day basis and for the longer term, e.g. *'Can we quote a special price for this job?' 'Are we prepared to offer a special discount for a large order?' 'Is it possible to increase the output of this machine?' 'Are there cheaper ways of making this unit?'* or *'Should we close this production line down?'* All of these questions involve taking various decisions. As part of the decision-making process, managers will have to take into account the cost and revenue implications. Decisions based on absorption costing may not always be appropriate, however, as the fixed element inherent in many costs may not be affected by that particular decision. In order to illustrate this point, let us use an example.

Suppose that a manager is costing a particular journey that a member of his staff is proposing to make to visit a client. The staff member has a car that is already taxed and insured. Thus the main cost of the journey will be for petrol, although the car may depreciate slightly more quickly and it may require a service sooner. The tax and insurance costs will not be affected by one particular journey: they are *fixed costs*, no matter how many extra journeys are undertaken. The manager is, therefore, only interested in the *extra* cost of using the car to visit the client. He can then compare the cost of using the car with the cost of the bus, the train, or going by air. Note that cost alone would not necessarily be the determining factor in practice; non-quantifiable factors such as comfort, convenience, fatigue and time would also be important considerations.

The extra cost of making the journey is sometimes described as the *marginal cost*. Hence the technique used in the above example is commonly referred to as *marginal costing*. Economists also use the term 'marginal cost' to describe the extra cost of making an additional unit (as with the extra cost of a particular journey). When dealing with production activities, however, units are more likely to be produced in batches. It is then perhaps more appropriate to substitute the term *incremental costing* and refer to the *incremental cost*, meaning the extra cost of producing a batch of units. The terms 'marginal costing' and 'marginal cost' are, however, still in frequent use.

The application of marginal (or incremental) costing revolves round the concept of what is known as *contribution*. We explore this concept in the next section.

Activity 19.1

A business college has recently considered starting some extra evening classes on basic computing. The college runs other courses during the evening. The proposed course fee has been based on the lecturer's fee and the cost of heat, light, caretaking and other expenses incurred solely as a result of running the extra classes. However, the principal has insisted that a 25% loading be added to the fee to go towards the college's day-to-day running costs. This is in accordance with the college's normal costing procedures.

Jot down in your notebook the reasons why the principal's requirement may be inappropriate when costing the proposed evening class lectures.

Contribution

In order to illustrate what is meant by 'contribution' we will use a series of equations. The first equation is straightforward:

$$\text{Sales revenue} - \text{total costs} = \text{profit (or loss)} \qquad (1)$$

The second equation is based on the assumption that total costs can be analyzed into variable costs and fixed costs:

$$\text{Total costs} = \text{variable costs} + \text{fixed costs} \qquad (2)$$

By substituting equation 2 into equation 1 we can derive equation 3:

$$\text{Sales revenue} - (\text{variable costs} + \text{fixed costs}) = \text{profit (or loss)} \qquad (3)$$

By rearranging equation 3 we can derive the following equation:

$$\text{Sales revenue} - \text{variable costs} = \text{fixed costs} + \text{profit} \qquad (4)$$

Equation 4 is known as the *marginal cost equation*. Let us simplify it and substitute symbols for words, namely Sales revenue = S, Variable costs = V, Fixed costs = F, and Profit = P (or loss = L). The equation now reads as follows:

$$S - V = F + P \qquad (5)$$

But where does contribution fit into all of this? Contribution (C) *is the difference between the sales revenue and the variable costs of that sales revenue.* Hence, in equation form:

$$S - V = C \qquad (6)$$

Contribution can also be looked at from another point of view. If we substitute C for (S − V) in Equation 5, the result will be:

$$C = F + P \qquad (7)$$

In other words, contribution can be regarded as being either the difference between the sales revenue and the variable costs of that sales revenue, or the total of fixed cost plus profit.

What do these relationships mean in practice and what is their importance? The meaning is reasonably straightforward. If an entity makes a contribution, it means that it has generated a certain amount of sales revenue and the variable cost of making those sales is less than the total sales revenue ($S - V = C$). Hence there is a balance left over that can go towards contributing towards the fixed costs ($C - F$); any remaining balance must be the profit ($C - F = P$). Alternatively, if the contribution is insufficient to cover the fixed costs, the entity will have made a loss: $C - F = L$.

The importance of the relationships described above in equation format is important for two main reasons. First, fixed costs can often be ignored when taking a particular decision because, by definition, fixed costs will not change irrespective of whatever decision is taken. This means that any cost and revenue analysis is made much simpler. Second, managers can concentrate on decisions that will maximize the contribution, since every additional £1 of contribution is an extra amount that goes toward covering the fixed costs. Once the fixed costs have been covered, every extra £1 of contribution is an extra £1 of profit.

| **Activity 19.2** | Company M's annual sales were £100 000, its variable costs £40 000, and its fixed costs £50 000. |
| | Calculate the profit for the year using the marginal cost equation. |

Assumptions

The marginal cost technique used in contribution analysis is, of course, based on a number of assumptions. At this stage it would be convenient to summarize them for you. They are as follows:

- Total costs can be split between fixed costs and variable costs.
- Fixed costs remain constant irrespective of the level of activity.

- Fixed costs do not bear any relationship to specific units.
- Variable costs vary in direct proportion to activity.

The reliability of the technique depends very heavily on being able to distinguish between fixed and variable costs. Some costs may be semivariable, i.e. they may consist of both a fixed and variable element. Electricity costs and telephone charges, for example, both contain a fixed rental element plus a variable charge; the variable charge depends upon the units consumed or the number of telephone calls made. Such costs are relatively easy to analyze into their fixed and variable elements.

In practice, it may be difficult to split other costs into their fixed and variable components. The management accountants may need the help of engineers and work study specialists in determining whether a particular cost is fixed or variable. They may also have to draw upon a number of graphical and statistical techniques. These techniques are somewhat advanced and beyond this book, and so we will assume that, for our purposes, it is relatively easy to analyze costs into their fixed and variable components.

Reread the assumptions summarized above. Do you think that these assumptions are reasonable? Rank them in the order of how far you think that they are generally valid (1 = the most valid; 2 = the next most valid, and so on).

Activity 19.3

Format

In applying the marginal cost technique, the cost data are usually arranged in a vertical format on a line-by-line basis. The order of the data reflects the marginal cost equation $(S - V = F + P)$. This format enables the attention of managers to be directed towards the contribution that may arise from any particular decision. In modern parlance, this is called *contribution analysis*. The basic procedure is illustrated in Example 19.1.

A typical marginal cost statement

Example 19.1

	Symbol	Product			Total
		A	B	C	
		£000	£000	£000	£000
Sales revenue (1)	S	100	70	20	190
Less: variable costs of sales (2)	V	30	32	18	80
Contribution (3)	C	70	38	2	110
Less: fixed costs (4)	F				60
Profit (5)	P				50

Notes:
1 The number in brackets after each item description refers to the tutorial notes below.
2 The marginal cost equation is represented in the 'symbol' column, i.e. $S - V = C$; $C = F + P$; and thereby $S - V = F + P$.

Tutorial notes

1   The total sales revenue would normally be analyzed into different product groupings. In this Example there are three products: A, B and C.

2   The variable costs include direct materials, direct labour costs, other direct costs, and variable overheads. Variable costs are assumed to vary *in direct proportion* to activity. Direct costs will normally be the same as variable costs, but in some cases, this will not be so. A machine operator's salary, for example, may be fixed under a guaranteed annual wage agreement. It is a direct cost in respect of the machine but it is also a fixed cost because it will not vary with the number of units produced.

3   As stated above, the term *contribution* is used to describe the difference between the sales revenue and the variable cost of those sales. A positive contribution helps to pay for the fixed costs.

4   The fixed costs include all the other costs that do not vary in direct proportion to the sales revenue. Fixed costs are assumed to remain constant over a period of time. They do not bear any relationship to the units produced or the sales achieved. Consequently, it is not possible to apportion them to individual products. The *total* of the fixed costs can only be deducted from the *total contribution*.

5   The total contribution less the fixed costs gives the profit (if the balance is positive) or a loss (if the balance is negative).

Managers supplied with information similar to that contained in Example 19.1 may subject the information to a series of 'What if?' possibilities. The following are some of the questions that they might pose:

● What would the profit be if we increased the selling price of Product A, B or C?
● What would be the effect if we reduced the selling price of Product A, B or C?
● What would be the effect if we eliminated one or more of the products?
● What would happen if we changed the quality of any of the products, thereby increasing (or otherwise) the variable cost of each product?
● Would any of the above decisions have an impact on fixed costs?

We will now examine the application of the marginal cost technique in a little more detail. We do so in the next section.

Activity 19.4

Rearrange the following data in a marginal cost format.

Annual rent £3000; direct labour £20 000; direct material £10 000; sales £75 000; staff salaries £47 000.

Application

As we have seen, the basic assumptions used in marginal costing are somewhat simplistic. In practice, they would probably only be regarded as appropriate when a particular decision was first considered. Thereafter, each of the various assumptions would be rigorously tested and they would be subject to a number of searching questions, such as: '*If we change the selling price of this product, will it affect the sales of the other products?*' '*Will variable costs always remain in direct proportion to activity?'* or *'Will fixed costs remain fixed irrespective of the level of activity?'*

We will now use a simple example to illustrate the application of the technique. The details are shown in Example 19.2. The Example illustrates the effect of a change in variable costs on contribution.

Changes in the variable cost

Example 19.2

	One unit £	Proportion %	100 units £	1000 units £
Sales revenue	10	100	1000	10 000
Less: variable costs	5	50	500	5 000
Contribution	5	50	500	5 000

Tutorial notes

1 The selling price per unit is £10, and the variable cost per unit is £5 (50 per cent of the selling price). The contribution, therefore, is also £5 per unit (50 per cent of the selling price).

2 These relationships are assumed to hold good no matter how many units are sold. Hence, if 100 units are sold the contribution will be £500; if 1000 units are sold there will be a contribution of £5000, i.e. the contribution is assumed to remain at 50 per cent of the sales revenue.

3 The fixed costs are ignored because it is assumed that they will *not* change as the level of activity changes.

Every extra unit sold will increase the profit by £5 per unit *once the fixed costs have been covered* – an important qualification. This point is illustrated in Example 19.3.

Changes in profit at varying levels of activity

Example 19.3

Activity (units)	1000 £	2000 £	3000 £	4000 £	5000 £
Sales	10 000	20 000	30 000	40 000	50 000
Less: variable costs	5 000	10 000	15 000	20 000	25 000
Contribution	5 000	10 000	15 000	20 000	25 000
Less: fixed costs	10 000	10 000	10 000	10 000	10 000
Profit/(Loss)	(5 000)	–	5 000	10 000	15 000

Tutorial notes

1 The exhibit illustrates five levels of activity: 1000 units, 2000 units, 3000 units, 4000 units, and 5000 units.

2 The variable costs remain directly proportional to activity at all levels, i.e. 50 per cent. The contribution is, therefore, 50 per cent (100% – 50%). The contribution per unit may be obtained by dividing the contribution at any level of activity level by the activity at that level, e.g. at an activity level of 1000 units the contribution per unit is £5 (£5000 ÷ 1000).

3 The fixed costs do not change, irrespective of the level of activity.

Tutorial notes
continued

4 The contribution needed to cover the fixed costs is £10 000. As each unit makes a contribution of £5, the total number of units needed to be sold in order to break even (i.e. to
reach a point where sales revenue equals the total of both the variable and the fixed
costs) will be 2000 (£10 000 ÷ £5).

5 When *more than* 2000 are sold, the increased contribution results in an increase in profit.
Thus, for instance when 3000 units are sold instead of 2000, the increased contribution
is £5000 (£15 000 – 10 000); the increased profit is also £5000 (£5000 – 0). Similarly,
when 4000 units are sold instead of 3000, the increased contribution is another £5000
(£20 000 – 15 000) and the increased profit is also £5000 (£10 000 – 5000). Finally, when
5000 units are sold instead of 4000 units, the increased contribution is once more £5000
(£25 000 – 20 000), as is the increased profit (£15 000 – 10 000).

6 The relationship between contribution and sales is known (rather confusingly) as the
profit/volume (or P/V) ratio. Note that it does not mean *profit* in relationship to sales but
the *contribution* in relationship to sales.

7 Assuming that the P/V ratio does not change, we can quickly calculate the profit at any
level of sales. All we need to do is to multiply the P/V ratio by the sales revenue and then
deduct the fixed costs. The balance will then equal the profit at that level of sales. It is also
easy to accommodate any possible change in fixed costs as the activity level moves above
or below a certain range.

While Example 19.2 and Example 19.3 are simple examples, we hope that they demonstrate just how useful contribution analysis can be in managerial decision making. While
the basic assumptions may be somewhat simplistic, they can readily be adapted to suit
more complex problems.

Activity 19.5

You are presented with the following data: number of units sold 5000; sales revenue
£50 000; variable costs £25 000, fixed costs £10 000.

If the company wanted to make the same amount of profit, how many units would have
to be sold if the fixed costs rose to £15 000?

Charts and graphs

Contribution analysis lends itself to the presentation of information in a pictorial
format. Indeed, the $S – V = F + P$ relationship is often easier to appreciate when it is
reported to managers in this way.

The most common format is in the form of what is called a *break-even chart*. A break-even
chart is illustrated in Example 19.4. The chart is based on the data used in Example 19.3.

Example 19.4 shows quite clearly the relationships that are assumed to exist when the
marginal costing technique is adopted. Sales revenue, total costs and fixed costs are all
assumed to be linear, so that they are all drawn as straight lines. Note also the
following points:

1 When no units are sold, the sales revenue line runs from the origin up to £50 000
when 5000 units are sold. It may then continue as a straight line beyond that point.

2 The total cost line is made up of both the fixed costs and the variable costs. When
there is no activity, the total costs will be equal to the fixed costs, so the total cost line

runs from the fixed cost point of £10 000 up to £35 000 when 5000 units are sold. It may then continue beyond that point.

3 The fixed cost line is drawn from the £10 000 point as a straight line parallel to the x axis irrespective of the number of units sold.

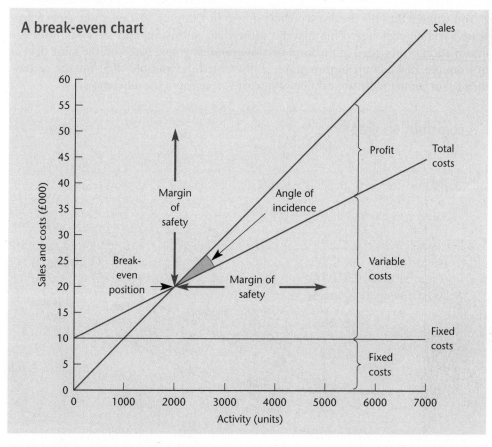

A break-even chart

Example 19.4

Tutorial notes

1 The total costs line is a combination of the fixed costs and the variable costs. It thus ranges from a total cost of £10 000 (fixed costs only) at a nil level of activity, to £35 000 when the activity level is 5000 units (fixed costs of £10 000 + variable costs of £25 000).

2 The angle of incidence is the angle formed between the sales line and the total cost line. The wider the angle, the greater the amount of profit. A wide angle of incidence and a wide margin of safety (see 3 below) indicates a highly profitable position.

3 The margin of safety is the distance between the sales achieved and the sales level needed to break even. It can be measured either in units (along the x axis of the graph) or in sales revenue terms (along the y axis).

4 Activity (measured along the x axis) may be measured either in units, or as a percentage of the theoretical maximum level of activity, or in terms of sales revenue.

In practice, the above relationships are not likely to hold good over the range of activity indicated in the example. They are usually assumed to remain valid over only a small range of activity. This is known as the *relevant range*. In this example the relevant range may be from (say) 1000 to 3000 units. Above or below these levels, the selling prices, the variable costs and the fixed costs may all change.

While this point might appear to create some difficulty, it should be appreciated that wide fluctuations in activity are not normally experienced. It is usually quite reasonable to assume that the entity will be operating in a fairly narrow range of activity and that the various relationships will be linear. It must also be remembered that the information is meant to be only a *guide* to managerial decision making and that it is impossible to be absolutely precise.

You will see that the break-even chart shown in Example 19.4 does not show a separate variable cost line. This may be somewhat confusing, and so sometimes the information is presented in the form of a *contribution graph*. Based on the same data as in Example 19.4 a contribution graph is illustrated in Example 19.5. You are recommended to compare the two exhibits and see if you can spot the differences.

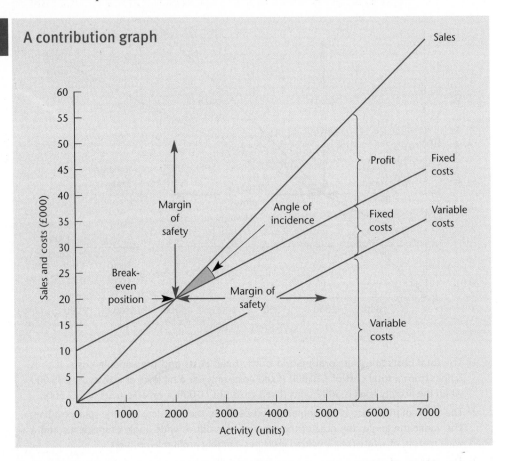

Example 19.5

A contribution graph

If you have studied the two examples closely, you will have observed that Example 19.4 (the break-even chart) is very similar to Example 19.5 (the contribution graph), although there are some differences. The main ones are as follows:

1 The contribution graph shows the variable cost line ranging from the origin when there is no activity to £25 000 when 5000 units are sold. It then continues beyond that point in a straight line.
2 The fixed cost line is drawn parallel to the variable cost line, i.e. higher up the y axis. As the fixed costs are assumed to remain fixed irrespective of the level of activity, the

fixed cost line runs from £10 000 when there is no activity to £35 000 when 5000 units are sold. It is then continued as a straight line beyond that point.

3 The fixed cost line also serves as the total cost line.

Apart from the above differences, the break-even chart and the contribution graph are identical. Which one should you adopt? There is no specific guidance that we can give you since the decision is one largely of personal preference. The break-even chart is more common, but the contribution chart is probably more helpful since the fixed and the variable cost lines are shown separately.

One problem with both the break-even chart and the contribution graph is that they do not show the *actual amount of profit or loss* at varying levels of activity. Thus, if you wanted to know what the profit was when (say) 4000 units were sold, you would have to use a ruler to measure the distance between the sales line and the total cost line. This is not very satisfactory. In order to avoid this problem, the information may be displayed in the form of a profit/volume chart (or graph).

A profit/volume chart shows the effect of a change in activity on profit. An example of such a chart is shown in Example 19.6. It is based on the data used in Example 19.3.

A profit/volume chart

Example 19.6

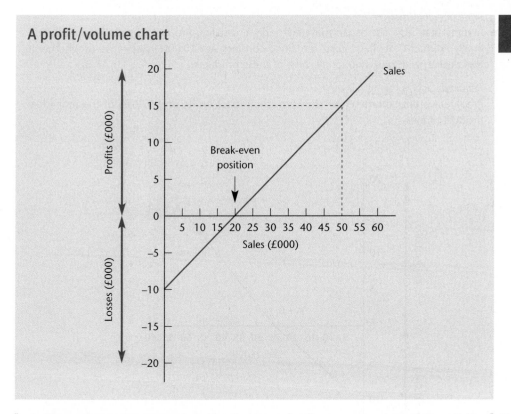

Tutorial notes

1 The *x* axis can be represented either in terms of units, as a percentage of the activity level, or in terms of sales revenue.

2 The *y* axis represents profits (positive amounts) or losses (negative amounts).

3 With sales at a level of £50 000, the profit is £15 000. The sales line cuts the *x* axis at the break-even position of £20 000 sales. If there are no sales, the loss equals the fixed costs of £10 000.

As you can see from Example 19.6 the profit/volume chart only shows the entity's *total* profit or loss. It does not show the profit or loss made on individual products.

It is possible to show the impact of individual products on profits on the chart although the result is somewhat simplistic. We do so in Example 19.7.

<table>
<tr><td>Example
19.7</td><td>

Tilsy Limited

</td></tr>
</table>

You are presented with the following information.

Product	A	B	C	Total
	£	£	£	£
Sales	5 000	20 000	25 000	50 000
Less: variable costs	3 000	10 000	12 000	25 000
Contribution	2 000	10 000	13 000	25 000
Less: fixed costs				10 000
Profit				15 000

Additional information:
Assume that Tilsy first began manufacturing and selling Product A, then Product B, and finally Product C. Its fixed costs remained constant at £10 000 irrespective of whether it was dealing with one, two, or all three of these products.

Required:
Prepare a profit/volume chart showing the impact on its profit/(loss) of the individual product ranges.

Answer to Example 19.7

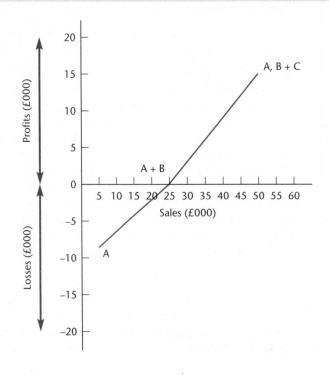

Tutorial notes

1 If the Product A is the first product, the company makes a loss of £8 000 (£2 000 – 10 000). Once Product B is introduced, a profit of £2 000 is made (£10 000 – 8 000). Then when Product C is added, the profit becomes £15 000 (£2 000 + 13 000).

2 It would be possible to plot the three product ranges in a different order, e.g. Product B, then Product C, then Product A or possibly Product C, then Product A, then Product B.

3 The disclosure of the impact of individual products on profit is useful because it can highlight the performance of a poorly performing product. Product A does make a small contribution of £2 000 (£5 000 – 3 000) but this is not sufficient to off-set the fixed costs of £10 000. It is only when Product B is introduced that the company begins to make a profit. The chart shows this fairly clearly.

On a scale of 1 to 5, how useful do you think that the following diagrams are to management (5 = very useful; 1 = not at all useful)?

(a) a break-even chart ☐

(b) a contribution graph ☐

(c) a profit/volume chart ☐

Activity 19.6

We have been at pains throughout this chapter to stress that while contribution analysis is extremely useful as an aid to managerial decision making, there are many criticisms that can be levelled at it. We summarize them in the next section.

Criticisms

The assumptions adopted in preparing marginal cost statements and their use in contribution analysis lead to a number of important reservations about the technique. The main ones are as follows:

1 *Cost classification.* Costs cannot be easily divided into fixed and variable categories.

2 *Variable costs.* Variable costs do not necessarily vary in direct proportion to sales revenue at all levels of activity. The cost of direct materials, for example, may change if supplies are limited in availability or if they are bought in bulk. It is also questionable whether direct labour should be treated as a variable cost (as is often the case) since current legislative practice makes it difficult to dismiss employees at short notice.

3 *Fixed costs.* Fixed costs are unlikely to remain constant over a wide range of activity. There is a good chance that they will change both beyond and below a fairly narrow range. They may perhaps move in 'steps', so that between an activity level of 0 and 999 units, for example, the fixed costs may be £10 000, be £12 000 between an activity level of 1000 and 2999 units, be £15 000 between an activity level of 3000 and 5000 units, and so on.

4 *Time period.* The determination of the time period over which the relationship between the fixed and variable costs may hold good is difficult to determine. In the very short term (say a day), all costs may be fixed. In the long term (say five years), all cost may be variable as the entity could go out of business.

5 *Complementary products.* A specific decision affecting one product may affect other products. For example, a garage sells both petrol and oil. A decision to stop selling oil may affect sales of petrol.

6 *Cost recovery*. It may be unwise to exclude fixed costs altogether from the analysis. In the medium-to-long term, an entity must recover all of its costs. Decisions cannot be taken purely in terms of the impact that they may have on contribution.

7 *Diagrammatic presentations*. Break-even charts, contribution graphs and profit/volume charts are somewhat simplistic. The sales of individual products are considered in total and it is assumed that any change made to one product will have a proportionate effect on all the other products.

8 *Non-cost factors*. Decisions cannot be taken purely on the basis of cost. Sometimes factors that cannot be easily quantified and costed are more important – for instance comfort, convenience, loyalty, reliability or speed.

9 *Behavioural factors*. In practice, behavioural factors also have to be considered. Individuals do not always act rationally and an actual behaviour pattern may be quite different from what was expected. A decrease in the selling price of a product, for example, may reduce the quantity of good purchased because it is *perceived* to be of poor quality.

The factors listed above are all fairly severe criticisms of the marginal costing technique and its use in contribution analysis. Nevertheless, experience suggests that it has still a useful part to play in managerial decision making, provided that: (1) the basis upon which the information is built is understood; (2) its apparent arithmetical precision is not regarded as a guarantee of absolute certainty; and (3) non-cost factors are also taken into account.

With these reservations in mind, we can now move on to look at the technique in a little more detail. Before we do so, however, it would be useful to summarize the main formulae so that it will be easier for you to refer back to them when dealing with the various examples.

Activity 19.7	Reread the criticisms outlined above. Judging them from a non-accountant's point of view, select the three most significant weaknesses of the marginal costing approach and summarize them in your notebook.

Formulae

Earlier in the chapter we explained that marginal costing revolves around the assumption that total costs can be classified into fixed and variable costs. This then led us on to an explanation of what we called the *marginal cost equation*, i.e. $S - V = F + P$. This equation can be used as the basis for a number of other simple equations that are useful in contribution analysis. The main ones are summarized below.

Abbreviation:

1 Sales – variable cost of sales = contribution $S - V = C$

2 Contribution – fixed costs = profit/(loss) $C - F = P/(L)$

3 Break-even (B/E) point = contribution – fixed costs $C - F$

4 B/E in sales value terms = $\dfrac{\text{Fixed costs} \times \text{sales}}{\text{Contribution}}$ $\dfrac{F \times S}{C}$

5 B/E in units $= \dfrac{\text{Fixed costs}}{\text{Contribution per unit}}$ $\dfrac{F}{C \text{ per unit}}$

6 Margin of safety (M/S) in sales value terms $= \dfrac{\text{Profit} \times \text{sales}}{\text{Contribution}}$ $\dfrac{P \times S}{C}$

7 M/S in units $= \dfrac{\text{Profit}}{\text{Contribution per unit}}$ $\dfrac{P}{C \text{ per unit}}$

Example 19.8 illustrates the use of some of these formulae.

| | Example 19.8 |

The use of the marginal cost formulae

The following information relates to Happy Limited for the year to 30 June 2001:

Number of units sold: 10 000

	Per unit	Total
	£	£000
Sales	30	300
Less: Variable costs	18	180
Contribution	12	120
Less: Fixed costs		24
Profit		96

Required:
In value and unit terms, calculate the following:
(a) the break-even position; and
(b) the margin of safety.

(a) Break-even position in value terms:

$$\frac{F \times S}{C} = \frac{£2400 \times 300\,000}{120\,000} = £60\,000$$

Break-even in units:

$$\frac{F}{C \text{ per unit}} = \frac{£24\,000}{12} = 2000 \text{ units}$$

(b) Margin of safety in value terms:

$$\frac{P \times S}{C} = \frac{£96\,000 \times 300\,000}{120\,000} = 240\,000$$

Margin of safety in units:

$$\frac{P}{C \text{ per unit}} = \frac{£96\,000}{12} = 8000 \text{ units}$$

Answer to Example 19.8

Note the relationship between the sales revenue and the margin of safety. The sales revenue is £300 000 and £60 000 of sales revenue is required to break even. The margin of safety is, therefore, £240 000 (£300 000 – 60 000).

Tutorial note

Activity 19.8   Attempt Example 19.8 without looking at the answer. Then prepare (a) a break-even chart; and (b) a profit/volume chart.

An illustrative example

It would now be helpful to incorporate the principles behind contribution analysis into a simple example. Example 19.9 outlines a typical problem that a board of directors might well face.

Example 19.9

Marginal costing example

Looking ahead to the financial year ending 31 March 2005, the directors of Problems Limited are faced with a budgeted loss of £10 000. This is based on the following data:

Budgeted number of units: 10 000

	£000
Sales revenue	100
Less: Variable costs	80
Contribution	20
Less: Fixed costs	30
Budgeted loss	(10)

The directors would like to aim for a profit of £20 000 for the year to 31 March 2005. Various proposals have been put forward, none of which require a change in the budgeted level of fixed costs. These proposals are as follows:

1 Reduce the selling price of each unit by 10 per cent.
2 Increase the selling price of each unit by 10 per cent.
3 Stimulate sales by improving the quality of the product, which would increase the variable cost of the unit by £1.50 per unit.

Required:
(a) For each proposal calculate:
    (i)   the break-even position in units in value terms;
    (ii) the number of units required to be sold in order to meet the profit target.
(b) State which proposal you think should be adopted.

Answer to Example 19.9

Problems Limited
(a) (i) and (ii)

Workings:	£
Profit target	20 000
Fixed costs	30 000
Total contribution required	50 000

The budgeted selling price per unit is £10 (£100 000/10 000). The budgeted variable cost per unit is £8 (£80 000/10 000).

Answer to Example 19.9 continued

The budgeted outlook compared with each proposal may be summarized as follows:

Per unit:	Budgeted position	Proposal 1	Proposal 2	Proposal 3
	£	£	£	£
Selling price	10	9	11	10.00
Less: Variable costs	8	8	8	9.50
(a) Unit contribution	2	1	3	0.50
(b) Total contribution required to break even (= fixed costs)	£30 000	£30 000	£30 000	£30 000
(c) Total contribution required to meet the profit target	£50 000	£50 000	£50 000	£50 000
Number of units to break even [(b)/(a)]	15 000	30 000	10 000	60 000
Number of units to meet the profit target [(c)/(a)]	25 000	50 000	16 667	100 000

(b) Comments:

1 By continuing with the present budget proposals, the company would need to sell 15 000 units to break even, or 25 000 units to meet the profit target. Thus in order to break even the company needs to increase its unit sales by 50%
$$\left(\frac{£15\,000 - 10\,000}{10\,000} \times 100 \right) \text{ and by 150% } \left(\frac{£25\,000 - 10\,000}{10\,000} \times 100 \right) \text{ to meet}$$
the profit target.

2 A reduction in selling price of 10% per unit would require unit sales to increase by 200% $\left(\frac{£30\,000 - 10\,000}{10\,000} \times 100 \right)$ in order to break even, and by 400%
$\left(\frac{£50\,000 - 10\,000}{10\,000} \times 100 \right)$ to meet the profit target.

3 By increasing the selling price of each unit by 10%, the company would only have to sell at the budgeted level to break even, but its unit sales would have to increase by 66.7% $\left(\frac{£16\,667 - 10\,000}{10\,000} \times 100 \right)$ to meet the profit target.

4 By improving the product at an increased variable cost of £1.50 per unit, the company would require a 500% $\left(\frac{£60\,000 - 10\,000}{10\,000} \times 100 \right)$ increase in unit sales to
break even, or a 900% $\left(\frac{£100\,000 - 10\,000}{10\,000} \times 100 \right)$ to meet the profit target.

Conclusion:

It would appear that increasing the selling price by 10% would be a more practical solution for the company to adopt. In the short run at least, it will break even, and there is the possibility that sales could be sufficient to make a small profit. In the long run this proposal has a much better chance of meeting the profit target than do the

Answer to
Example 19.9
continued

others. Some extra stimulus would be needed, however, to lift sales to this level over such a relatively short period of time. It is not clear, why an increase in price would increase sales, unless the product is one that only sells at a comparatively high price, such as cosmetics and patent medicines. It must also be questioned whether the cost relationships will remain as indicated in the exhibit over such a large increase in activity. In particular, it is unlikely that the fixed costs will remain entirely fixed if there were to be a 66.7% increase in sales.

Activity 19.9   Now have a go at doing Example 19.9 on your own without looking at the solution.

Limiting factors

When optional decisions are being considered, the aim will always be to maximize contribution, because the greater the contribution, the more chance there is of covering the fixed costs and hence of making a profit. When managers are faced with a choice, therefore, between (say) producing product A at a contribution of £10 per unit, or of producing product B at a contribution of £20 per unit, they would normally choose product B. Sometimes, however, it may not be possible to produce unlimited quantities of product B because there could be a limit on how many units could either be sold or produced. Such limits are known as *limiting factors* (or key factors).

Limiting factors may arise for a number of reasons. It may not be possible, for example, to sell more than a certain number of units; there may be production restraints (such as shortages of raw materials, skilled labour, or factory space), or the company may not be able to finance the anticipated rate of expansion.

If there is a product that cannot be produced and sold in unlimited quantities, then it is necessary to follow a simple rule in order to decide which product to concentrate on producing. The rule can be summarized as follows:

> *Choose the work that provides the maximum contribution per unit of limiting factor employed.*

This sounds very complicated, but it is easy to apply in practice. In outline, the procedure is as follows:

We will assume that direct labour hours are in short supply.

1 Calculate the contribution made by each product.
2 Divide the contribution that each product makes by the number of direct labour hours used in making each product.
3 This gives the contribution per direct labour hour employed (i.e. the limiting factor).
4 Select the project that gives the highest contribution per unit of limiting factor.

Thus, if we had to choose between two jobs, (say) A and B, we would convert A's contribution and B's contribution into the amount of contribution earned for every direct labour hour worked on A and on B respectively. We would then opt for the job that earned the most contribution per direct labour hour. The technique is illustrated in Example 19.10.

Example 19.10

Application of key factors

Quays Limited manufactures a product for which there is a shortage of the raw material known as PX. During the year to 31 March 2007, only 1000 kilograms of PX will be available. PX is used by Quays in manufacturing both product 8 and product 9. The following information is relevant:

Per unit:	Product 8	Product 9
	£	£
Selling price	300	150
Less: Variable costs	200	100
Contribution	100	50
P/V ratio $\left(\dfrac{£100}{300} \times 100\right) ; \left(\dfrac{£50}{150} \times 100\right)$	$33\frac{1}{3}$	$33\frac{1}{3}$
Kilograms of PX required	5	2

Required:
State which product Quays Limited should concentrate on producing.

Answer to Example 19.10

	Product 8	Product 9
	£	£
Contribution per unit	100	50
Limiting factor per unit (kg)	5	2
Contribution per kilogram	20	25

Decision:
Quays should concentrate on product 9 because it gives the highest contribution per unit of limiting factor.

Check:
Maximum contribution of product 8:

200 units (1000kg/5) × contribution per unit = 200 × £100 = £20 000

Maximum contribution of product 9:

500 units (1000kg/2) × contribution per unit = 500 × £50 = £25 000

In Example 19.10 it was assumed that there was only one limiting factor, but there could be many more. This situation is illustrated in Example 19.11. The basic data are the same as for Example 19.10.

Example 19.11

Marginal costing using two key factors

Information:

1 Assume now that it is not possible for Quays Limited to sell more than 400 units of product 9.

2 The company would aim to sell all of the 400 units because product 9's contribution per unit is greater than product 8's. The total contribution would then be £20 000 (400 × £50).

3 The 400 units would consume 800 units of raw materials (400 × 2 kilograms), leaving 200 (1000 – 800) kilograms for use in producing product 8.

4 Product 8 requires 5 kilograms per unit of raw materials, so 40 units (200kg ÷ 5kg) could be completed at a total contribution of £4000 (40 × £100).

Summary of the position:

	Product 8	Product 9	Total
Units sold	40	400	
Raw materials (kilograms used)	200	800	1 000
Contribution per unit (£)	100	50	
Total contribution (£)	4 000	20 000	24 000

Note: The £24 000 total contribution compares with the contribution of £25 000 that the company could have made if there were no limiting factors affecting the sales of product 9.

Activity 19.10

A few examples of limiting factors are given in the text. List them into your notebook. Now think about the concept. An entity will choose to make and sell as many units as it can of those products that make the highest contribution per unit of limiting factor. What other specific factors (think of finance, land, labour, management, materials and premises) might stop it from doing so? Add them to your list.

> **!** ## Questions non-accountants should ask
>
> When you have a specific decision to take as a manager, it is almost certain that your accountants will do the detailed calculative work for you. They are likely to present you with a summary of their results and their recommendations.
>
> We will assume that you have asked them for some guidance on a specific decision that you have to take. What should you ask them when you receive the information? The following questions are suggested, although you will, of course, need to adapt them to meet your own particular circumstances.
>
> - Where have you got the basic data from?
> - What estimates have you had to make in adapting the original data?
> - Has the information been compiled on a contribution basis?
> - If not, why not? What other method have you used? Why is the contribution approach not appropriate in this case?
> - If the contribution approach has been used, how have the variable costs been separated from the fixed costs?
> - Have you assumed that variable costs move in direct proportion to sales revenue?
> - Over what time-scale are the fixed costs fixed?
> - Over what time period will the various cost relationships last?
> - What impact will your recommendations have on other aspects of the business?
> - What non-quantifiable factors have you been able to take into account?
> - What non-quantifiable factors have been ignored
> - Generally, how reliable is the information that you have given me?
> - What confidence can I have in it?
> - Is there anything else that I should know?

Conclusion

Contribution analysis is particularly useful in short-term decision making, but it is of less value when decisions have to be viewed over the long term. The system revolves around two main assumptions:

1 some costs remain fixed, irrespective of the level of activity;
2 other costs vary in direct proportion to sales.

These assumptions are not valid over the long term but, provided that they are used with caution, they can be usefully adopted in the short term.

It should also be remembered that the technique is only a *guide* to decision making, and that other non-cost factors have to be taken into account.

In the next chapter we use contribution analysis to deal with other managerial problems.

Key points

1 Total cost can be analyzed into fixed costs and variable costs.

2 Fixed costs are assumed to be unrelated to activity. They may be ignored in making short-term managerial decisions.

3 A company will aim to maximize the *contribution* that each unit makes to profit.

4 The various relationships between costs can be expressed in the form of an equation: $S - V = F + P$, where S = sales, V = variable costs, F = fixed costs, and P = profit.

5 It may not always be possible to maximize unit contribution, because materials, labour, finance or other factors may be in short supply.

6 In the long run, fixed costs cannot be ignored.

Check your learning

The answers to these questions may be found within the text.

1 What system of costing is normally used for the costing of products and for stock valuation purposes?

2 Why is this system not suitable for specific decision making?

3 What is decision making?

4 What term is given to the extra cost of a phenomenon?

5 What is incremental costing?

6 What is (a) a fixed cost; and (b) a variable cost?

7 What is meant by the term 'contribution'?

8 What is the marginal cost equation?

9 List four main assumptions that underpin marginal costing.

10 What is a break-even chart?

11 What is meant by the terms (a) 'break-even'; (b) 'angle of incidence'; and (c) 'margin of safety'?

12 What is a contribution graph?

13 What is a profit/volume chart?

14 List six assumptions that are adopted when preparing a marginal cost statement.

15 What is the formula for calculating (a) the break-even position in sales value terms; (b) the break-even position in units; (c) the margin of safety in sales value terms; and (d) the margin of safety in units?

16 What is a limiting factor?

17 Give three examples of limiting factors.

18 State the rule that is used when activity is restricted by the presence of a limiting factor.

News story quiz

Remember that news story at the beginning of this chapter? Go back to that story and re-read it before answering the following questions.

In this chapter we have defined 'break-even' as the point where sales revenue just covers the variable cost of those sales plus the fixed costs of the entity. Eurotunnel has another definition of break-even.

Questions

1 What do you think the company meant when it announced that it had reached 'a 'cash breakeven' point'?

2 What would be the impact on its 'cash breakeven' point if it achieved 'more rail traffic'?

3 Why is the company still 'in the red' after taking into account tax and depreciation?

4 Do you think that the Chief Executive is confused by the terms 'cash breakeven' and 'breakeven' as described in this chapter?

5 What will be the effect on variable costs and fixed costs if the company manages to attract more freight and passenger trains?

Tutorial questions

The answers to questions marked with an asterisk may be found in Appendix 4.

19.1 'It has been suggested that although contribution analysis is fine in theory, fixed costs cannot be ignored in practice.' Discuss this statement.

19.2 'Contribution analysis described in textbooks is too simplistic and is of little relevance to management.' How far do you agree with this statement?

19.3 Do break-even charts and profit graphs help management to take more meaningful decisions?

19.4* The following information relates to Pole Limited for the year to 31 January 2007.

	£000
Administration expenses:	
Fixed	30
Variable	7
Semi-variable (fixed 80%, variable 20%)	20
Materials:	
Direct	60
Indirect	5
Production overhead (all fixed)	40
Research and development expenditure:	
Fixed	60
Variable	15
Semi-variable (fixed 50%, variable 50%)	10
Sales	450
Selling and distribution expenditure:	
Fixed	80
Variable	4
Semi-variable (fixed 70%, variable 30%)	30
Wages:	
Direct	26
Indirect	13

Required:
Using the above information, compile a contribution analysis statement for Pole Limited for the year to 31 January 2007.

19.5* You are presented with the following information for Giles Limited for the year to 28 February 2008:

	£000
Fixed costs	150
Variable costs	300
Sales (50 000 units)	500

Required:
(a) Calculate the following:
  (i) the break-even point in value terms and in units; and
  (ii) the margin of safety in value terms and in units.
(b) Prepare a break-even chart.

19.6 The following information applies to Ayre Limited for the two years to 31 March 2008 and 2009, respectively:

Year	Sales	Profits
	£000	£000
31.3.2008	750	100
31.3.2009	1 000	250

Required:
Assuming that the cost relationships had remained as given in the question, calculate the company's profit if the sales for the year to 31 March 2009 had reached the budgeted level of £1 200 000.

19.7 The following information relates to Carter Limited for the year to 30 April 2007:

Units sold: 50 000

Selling price per unit	£40
Net profit per unit	£9
Profit/volume ratio	40%

During 2008 the company would like to increase its sales substantially, but to do so it would have to reduce the selling price per unit by 20 per cent. The variable cost per unit will not change, but because of the increased activity, the company will have to invest in new machinery which will increase the fixed costs by £30 000 per annum.

Required:
Given the new conditions, calculate how many units the company will need to sell in 2008 in order to make the same amount of profit as it did in 2007.

19.8 Puzzled Limited would like to increase its sales during the year to 3l May 2005. To do so, it has several mutually exclusive options open to it:

1 reduce the selling price per unit by 15 per cent;
2 improve the product resulting in an increase in the variable cost per unit of £l.30;
3 spend £15 000 on an advertising campaign;
4 improve factory efficiency by purchasing more machinery at a fixed extra annual cost of £22 500.

During the year to 31 May 2004, the company sold 20 000 units. The cost details were as follows:

	£000
Sales	200
Variable costs	150
Contribution	50
Fixed costs	40
Profit	10

These cost relationships are expected to hold in 2005.

Required:
State which option you would recommend and why.

19.9 The following information relates to Mere's budget for the year to 31 December 2007:

	Product			
	K	L	M	Total
	£000	£000	£000	£000
Sales	700	400	250	1350
Direct materials	210	60	30	300
Direct labour	100	200	200	500
Variable overhead	90	60	50	200
Fixed overhead	20	40	40	100
	420	360	320	1100
Profit/(loss)	280	40	(70)	250
Budgeted sales (units)	140	20	25	

Note: Fixed overheads are apportioned on the basis of direct labour hours.

The directors are worried about the loss that product M is budgeted to make, and various suggestions have been made to counteract the loss, viz.:

1 stop selling product M;
2 increase M's selling price by 20 per cent;
3 reduce M's selling price by 10 per cent;
4 reduce its costs by purchasing a new machine costing £350 000, thereby decreasing the direct labour cost by £100 000 (the machine would have a life of five years; its residual value would be nil).

Required:
Evaluate each of these proposals.

A classic specific decision-making problem . . .

Spade maker cuts 160 jobs and closes factory

ELIZA TINSLEY, the manufacturer of shovels, spades, mowers and motorway maintenance equipment, is closing its loss-making Chesterfield factory and making 160 staff redundant. The group, which will have four plants in the UK after the closure, one in Italy and one in the US, cited the high cost of manufacturing in the UK as one reason for its decision. The closure will cost £2.8m but the group said it expected to recoup about £1.5m by selling the plant.

Independent, 29 January 2003.

Questions relating to this news story may be found on page 472 ▸▸

About this chapter

You will recall that in the previous chapter we suggested that the use of absorption costing in most decision-making situations may lead to some unwise decisions. We suggested that a contribution approach using marginal costing would normally be more appropriate. Marginal costing involves classifying costs on a fixed/variable basis instead of as in absorption costing on a direct/indirect basis. There are, however, other ways of classifying costs and we outline some of them in this chapter.

The chapter also uses our overall knowledge of management accounting to examine some specific decision-making situations. We cover four main types of decisions: (1) those that involve determining whether to close or shut down a plant or a factory; (2) those that involve deciding whether we supply or make our own materials and components; (3) those that involve determining what price we charge for our goods and services; and (4) those that involve deciding what we should charge for one-off or special orders.

The structure of the chapter follows this pattern. It is divided into eight main sections. The first main section explains why this chapter is important for non-accountants. We then outline the nature of decision-making and in the following one the various ways in which costs may be classified. The next four sections then examine various decision-making issues, viz. closure and shutdown decisions, make or buy decisions, pricing decisions, and special order decisions. The last main section frames some questions that non-accountants might like to ask about the contents of the chapter.

By the end of this chapter you should be able to:

● outline the nature of decision making;

● list six ways of classifying costs for decision-making purposes;

● incorporate cost and financial data into managerial problems involving closure and shutdown decisions, make or buy decisions, pricing decisions and special order decisions.

! Why this chapter is important for non-accountants

We stated in the last chapter that that particular chapter was one of the most important in the book. This chapter is also very important. It tells you a little more about decision making and the classification of costs. It then uses some numerical examples to illustrate the particular direction that various decisions should take.

Thus this chapter is heavily biased towards helping you make and take effective decisions. It follows that it is of considerable importance in ensuring that you become an all-round first-class manager.

Decision making

We start our examination of some specific decision-making problems by considering what is involved in decision making.

The term *decision* will be familiar to you in your everyday life. It means coming to a conclusion about a particular issue – for example, determining (i.e. deciding) when to get up in the morning, whether to have tea or coffee for breakfast, or choosing between a holiday and buying some new clothes. Similarly, in a managerial context, decisions have to be taken about whether or not to sell in particular markets, buy some new machinery or spend more money on research.

Management accountants will be involved in collecting data and supplying information for such decisions. While the information that they supply will be primarily of a financial nature, they will highlight other considerations that need to be taken into account before a decision is made. The eventual decision will rest with the cost centre manager concerned. It may well be that non-cost factors turn out to be more important than measurable financial considerations. Instead of manufacturing its own components, for example, it may be cheaper for them to be purchased from an external supplier. But that supplier could be unreliable. So it might be worth the extra cost of manufacturing the components internally in order to avoid the risk of any disruption to the entity's normal production processes.

The data required for decision-making purposes tend to be more wide-ranging and less constrained than those used in cost accounting. Their main characteristics are summarized below and they are also illustrated in diagrammatic format in Figure 20.1.

1 *Forward looking*. While historical data may be used as a guide, information for decision making is much more concerned with what *will* happen rather than with what *did* happen. So because much of the information required is concerned with the future, considerable initiative and intuitive judgement is required in being able to obtain it.

2 *One-off decisions*. Decision making often involves dealing with a problem that is unique. Thus a solution has to be geared towards dealing with that particular problem.

3 *Data availability*. While some of the data required for decision making may be extracted from the cost accounting system, much of what is required may have to be specially obtained.

4 *Net cash flow approach*. Managers will be concerned with the impact that a decision may have on the expected net cash flow of a particular project (i.e. future cash receipts less future cash expenditure). The calculation of periodic profit and loss based on accruals and prepayments will be largely irrelevant.

5 *Relevant costs*. Costs and revenues that are not affected by a decision are excluded from the analysis. Fixed costs, for example are not likely to change as a result of taking a particular decision will be ignored.

6 *Opportunity costs*. Those benefits that would be foregone or lost as a result of taking a particular decision are known as opportunity costs. They form an important part of any decision-making analysis. You may decide, for example, to look after your own garden yourself instead of doing some paid overtime. The opportunity cost would be the wages you lose by not working overtime less the amount you save by not employing a gardener. Opportunity costs are not usually stored in the cost accounting system and it is not always easy to determine them.

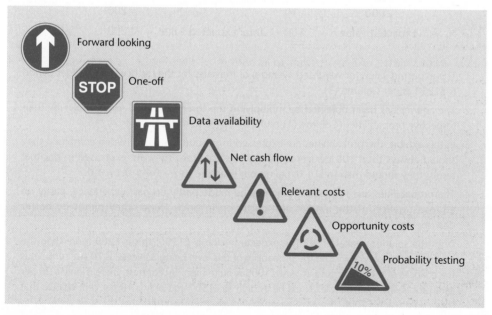

Figure 20.1 **The nature of decision making**

7 *Probability testing.* Much of the information used in problem solving is speculative because it relates to the future and so it is advisable to carry out some probability testing. This is a complex area and it goes beyond this book. Essentially, probability testing involves calculating the *expected value* of a particular project or proposal. The basic idea is exemplified in Example 20.1.

Example 20.1

Probability testing

Company X sells one product codenamed A1. The marketing department has estimated that the sales of A1 for a forthcoming budget period could be £1000, £1500, or £2000. Upon further investigation, it would appear that there is a 70 per cent chance that the sales will be £1000, a 20 per cent chance that the sales will be £1500, and a 10 per cent chance that the sales will be £2000.

Required:
Calculate the expected value of sales for product A1 during the forthcoming budget period.

Answer to Example 20.1

The question requires us to calculate the expected value of the sales of A1 for the forthcoming period. It might be easier for you to think of the expected value as the *weighted average*, which perhaps provides a clue to what is required. In order to calculate the expected values the budgeted sales figures are multiplied by their respective chances or probabilities. Thus:

Budgeted sales (1) £	Probability (2) %	Expected value (3) £
1 000	70	700
1 500	20	300
2 000	10	200
Expected value	100　Total expected value	1 200

Tutorial notes

1　The expected value (or weighted average) of the sales for the forthcoming budget period is £1200 as per Column (3).

2　The answer has been obtained by multiplying the three estimated level of sales by their respective probabilities (Column (1) multiplied by Column (2)).

3　In this exhibit, the probabilities are expressed in percentage terms. When combined they should always total 100 per cent. Note that sometimes they are expressed in decimal terms; they should then total 1.0, i.e. (in our example) 0.7 + 0.2 + 0.1 = 1.0.

4　The probabilities are estimates. They may be made partly on past experience, partly on an investigation of the market and partly on instinct. Hence they might be better described as 'guesstimates'.

5　Does the solution make sense? The expected value is £1200; this is £200 more than the lowest level of sales of £1000; the probability of this level being achieved is 70 per cent. Thus the chances of the sales being at least £1000 is quite high. By contrast, there is only a 20 per cent probability that the sales could be as high as £1500 and only a 10 per cent chance that they could reach £2000. It seems reasonable to assume, therefore, that the sales are likely to be nearer £1000 than £1500. Thus £1200 appears to be a reasonable compromise.

Attempt Example 20.1 without looking at the answer.

Activity 20.1

Before we examine some specific decision-making situations, it would be useful to examine some common cost terms used in decision making. We do so in the next section.

Cost classification

As we saw in Chapters 15 and 16, costs (and revenues) may be classified into various categories depending upon the purpose for which they are going to be used. In cost accounting, information is required mainly for product costing and stock valuation purposes, and so the most important category is the distinction between direct costs and indirect ones.

A direct/indirect cost classification is not normally appropriate in decision making. The preferred classification is that relating to fixed and variable costs, but other cost classifications are also used. We summarize the main ones used in decision making below. They are also shown in pictoral form in Figure 20.2.

Fixed and variable costs

As we saw in the last chapter, fixed costs are those costs that are likely to remain unchanged irrespective of the level of activity. Variable costs are those that move directly proportional to activity (one unit results in £1 of variable cost, two units results in £2 of variable cost, three units in £3 of variable cost, and so on).

In theory, those costs classified as 'fixed' will remain the same irrespective of whether the entity is completely inactive or if it is operating at full capacity. In practice, fixed

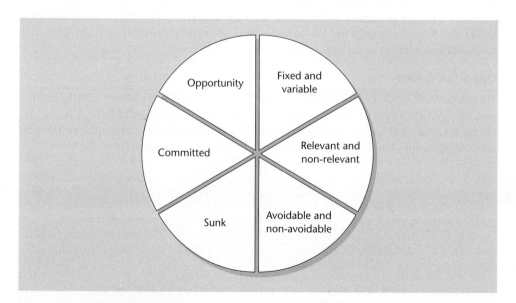

Figure 20.2 **Cost classification**

costs tend to remain fixed only over a relatively small range of activity range and only in the short term.

The assumption that some costs remain unchanged means that, in a decision-making exercise, fixed costs do not normally need to be taken into account. In other words, fixed costs can be ignored, because they will not be affected by the decision and are not therefore relevant to a consideration of the issues.

Relevant and non-relevant costs

Relevant costs are those future costs that are likely to be affected by a particular decision. It follows that non-relevant costs are those that are *not* likely to be affected by the decision. This means that non-relevant costs (e.g. those fixed costs not affected by the decision) can be excluded from any cost analysis.

Avoidable and non-avoidable costs

Avoidable costs are those costs that may be saved by not taking a particular decision. Non-avoidable costs will still be incurred if the decision is taken. Avoidable and non-avoidable costs are very similar to relevant and non-relevant costs. Indeed, sometimes the terms are used synonymously.

Sunk costs

Sunk costs are those costs that have already been incurred as a result of a previous decision. Hence they are not relevant as far as future decisions are concerned and they can be excluded from any decision-making analysis.

Committed costs

A committed cost arises out of a decision that has previously been taken, although the event has not yet taken place. For example, a proposal to increase the capacity of a factory from 1000 to 1500 units per annum will result in increased capital expenditure. A decision to accept the proposal means that certain costs are *committed*, and it only becomes a matter of timing before there is a cash outflow. Once the proposal has gone ahead and it has been paid for, the costs become *sunk* costs. Committed costs (like sunk costs) are not relevant as far as *future* decisions are concerned.

Opportunity costs

We referred to opportunity costs in the previous section of this chapter. Just to remind you, an opportunity cost is a measure of the net benefit that would be lost if one decision is taken instead of another decision. Such costs are rarely recorded in the cost accounting system and they usually require to be calculated separately.

| *Activity 20.2* | Carla Friar is a mature student at university. Her university fees and maintenance cost her £7000 a year. Carla gave up her job in a travel centre to become a full-time student. Her take-home pay was then £20 000 a year but she also lost various travel concessions worth £1000 a year. As a student she has little free time, she socializes infrequently, and so she does not spend as much. This saves her about £2000 a year but of course she misses her friends and her nights out.

What factors do you think that Carla should take into account if she tried to work out the opportunity cost of becoming a student? |
| :--- | :--- |

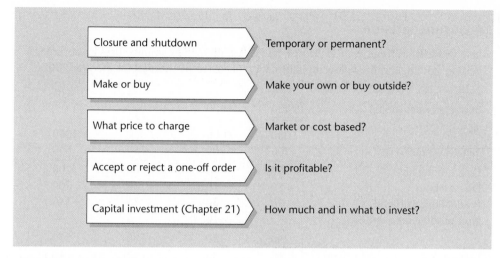

Figure 20.3 **Types of decisions**

We can now turn to some specific decisions that managers may face and the type of management accounting information that can help them arrive at an appropriate solution. Such decisions are shown in diagrammatic format in Figure 20.3. An additional important decision relates to the purchase of capital assets but we leave that to the next chapter as we need to devote more space to discussing it.

Closure and shutdown decisions

A common problem that managers may face from time to time is whether to close some segment of the enterprise, such as a product, a service, a department, or even an entire factory. This is a *closure* decision; the assumption behind it is that the closure would be permanent. A similar decision may have to be taken in respect of a temporary closure. This is known as a *shutdown* decision.

A closure decision sometimes needs to be taken because a segment within the overall entity may perhaps have become unprofitable, out of date or unfashionable, and therefore no future is seen for it. A decision to close a segment of an entity temporarily would be taken when the segment's problems are likely to be overcome in the near future. Thus a segment may be unprofitable at the moment but is expected to recover in (say) 12 months' time.

Closure and shutdown decisions are often required because a section is regarded as being 'unprofitable'. The definition of 'unprofitable' has to be looked at very closely. A product, for example, may not be making a *profit* but it may be making a *contribution* towards the fixed costs of the company. Should it be abandoned? Great care would need to be taken before such a decision was taken. The abandonment of one product may have an impact on the sales of other products in such circumstances, it may even be beneficial to sell the product below its variable cost (at least in the short term).

Closure and shutdown decisions are not easy to make. They cannot be determined purely on narrow cost grounds, as other wide-ranging factors may need to be considered. We illustrate a relatively straightforward closure decision in Example 20.2.

Example 20.2

A closure decision

Vera Limited has three main product lines: 1, 2, and 3. The company uses an absorption costing system, and the following information relates to the budget for the year 2007.

Product line	1	2	3	Total
Budgeted sales (units)	10 000	4 000	6 000	
	£000	£000	£000	£000
Sales revenue	300	200	150	650
Direct materials	100	40	60	200
Direct labour	50	70	80	200
Production overhead	75	30	35	140
Non-production overhead	15	10	5	30
	240	150	180	570
Profit (Loss)	60	50	(30)	80

Additional information:
1 Both direct materials and direct labour are considered to be variable costs.
2 The total production overhead of £140 000 consists of £40 000 variable costs and £100 000 fixed costs. Variable production overheads are absorbed on the basis of 20 per cent of the direct labour costs.
3 The non-production overhead of £30 000 is entirely fixed.
4 Assume that there will be no opening or closing stock.

Required:
Determine whether Product line 3 should be closed.

Answer to Example 20.2

Points
1 The first step in determining whether to recommend a closure of Product line 3 is to calculate the *contribution* that each product line makes.
2 To do this, it is necessary to rearrange the data given in the question in a marginal cost format, i.e. separate the fixed costs from the variable costs.
3 If Product line 3 makes a contribution, then other factors will have to be taken into account before an eventual decision can be made.

Calculations

Product line	1	2	3	Total
Budgeted sales (units)	10 000	4 000	6 000	
	£000	£000	£000	£000
Sales revenue	300	200	150	650
Less: Variable costs:				
Direct materials	100	40	60	200
Direct labour	50	70	80	200
Variable production overhead (Question Note 2: 20% of direct labour cost)	10	14	16	40
	160	124	156	440
Contribution	140	76	(6)	c/f 210

	1	2	3	Total		Answer to
			b/f	210		Example 20.2
Less: Fixed costs:						
Production overheads						
(£140 – 40)				(100)		
Non-production overheads						
(See Note 3)				(30)		
Profit				80		

Observations

It would appear that Product line 3 neither makes a profit nor contributes towards the fixed costs. Should it be closed? Before such a decision is taken a number of other factors would have to be considered. These are as follows.

1 Are the budgeted figures accurate? Have they been checked? How reliable are the budgeted data?
2 What method has been used for identifying the direct material costs that each product line uses? Is it appropriate for all three product lines?
3 The question states that direct labour is a variable cost. Is direct labour really a variable cost? Is the assessment of its cost accurate and realistic?
4 Variable production overheads are absorbed on a very broad basis related to direct labour costs. Does this method fairly reflect Product line 3's use of variable overheads?
5 Product line 3's appears to result in only a small negative contribution. Can this be made positive by perhaps a small increase in the unit selling price or by the more efficient use of direct materials and direct labour?
6 Assuming that the cost data supplied are both fair and accurate, would the closure of Product line 3 affect (a) sales for the other two product lines; or (b) the overall variable costs?
7 If closure of Product line 3 is recommended, should it be closed permanently or temporarily? More information, is needed of its prospects beyond 2007.

The decision

Clearly, without more information it is impossible to come to a firm conclusion. Assuming that the cost accounting procedures are both accurate and fair, it would appear that *on purely financial grounds*, Product line 3 should be closed. However, there are too many unknown factors to put this forward as a conclusive recommendation.

Have a go at doing Example 20.2 without looking at the answer.   *Activity 20.3*

Make or buy decisions

Make or buy decisions require management to determine whether to manufacture internally or purchase externally. For example, should a car company manufacture its own components or purchase them from a specialist supplier? Similarly, should a glass manufacturer concentrate on producing glass and purchase all its other requirements (e.g. safety equipment and containers for the glass) externally? In local government, should a housing department employ its own joiners or contract outside firms to do the necessary work?

The theory beyond make or buy decisions revolves round the argument that entities should do what they are best at doing and employ others to undertake the peripheral activities. In other words, they should concentrate on their main objective and contract out (or 'privatize', in the case of governmental activities) all other essential activities.

A decision to contract out will often be taken on a purely financial basis ('*Is it cheaper to buy in this service?*'). This may be unwise. There could be important non-financial and non-quantifiable factors that should be taken into account. If a supplier has labour relations' problems, for example, deliveries may be uncertain and production could be disrupted. This could then cause problems with the entity's own customers. It would be extremely difficult to estimate an accurate cost of such a possible outcome. Nevertheless, a make or buy decision will be based partly on cost and partly on other such factors, including an assessment of any opportunity costs.

A simple make or buy decision is illustrated in Example 20.3.

Example 20.3	**A make or buy decision**

Zam Limited uses an important component in one of its products. An estimate of the cost of making one unit of the component internally is as follows.

	£
Direct materials	5
Direct labour	4
Variable overhead	3
Total variable cost	12

Additional information:
1   Fixed costs specifically associated with manufacturing the components are estimated to be £8000 per month.
2   The number of components normally required is 1000 per month.

An outside manufacturer has offered to supply the components at a cost of £18 per component. Should the components be manufactured internally or purchased externally?

Required
Determine whether Zam Limited should purchase the components from the outside supplier.

Answer to Example 20.3	**Points**

Assuming that the cost data given in the question are accurate, the first step in answering the question is to calculate the cost of manufacturing the components internally. Although the variable cost of each unit is given, there are some fixed costs directly associated with manufacturing internally and these have to be taken into account.

The fixed costs cause us a problem because the monthly activity levels may vary. However, we can only work on the data given in the question, i.e. 1000 units per month.

Calculations
Total cost of manufacturing internally 1000 units per month of the component:

	£
Total variable cost (1000 units × £12)	12 000
Associated fixed costs	8 000
Total cost	20 000
Total unit cost (£20 000 ÷ 1000) =	£20

1 Assuming that Zam Limited requires 1000 units per month, it would be cheaper to obtain them from the external supplier (£20 compared with £18 per component).

2 The above assumption is based on purchases of 1000 units. The more units required, the cheaper they would be to manufacture internally. In order to match the external price, the fixed costs can be no more than £6 per unit (the external purchase price of £18 less the internal variable cost of £12 per unit). If the fixed costs were to be limited to £6 per unit, the company would need to manufacture 133 units (£8000 ÷ £6). The cost would then be the same as the external price, of course, but it would involve a one-third increase in the activity level.

3 The cost data should be carefully checked (especially the estimated associated fixed costs) and the monthly activity level reviewed. It might then be possible to put forward a tentative recommendation.

The decision

Given the data provided in the question, it would be cheaper to purchase the components externally. This would free some resources within Zam Limited, enabling it to concentrate on manufacturing its main product.

However, there are a number of other considerations that need to be taken into account. In particular the following questions would require some answers.

1 How accurate are the cost data?
2 How variable is the monthly activity level?
3 Is the external supplier's component exactly suited to the company's purposes?
4 How reliable is the proposed supplier?
5 Are there other suppliers who could be used in an emergency and, if so, at what cost?
6 What control could be exercised over the quality of the components received?
7 How firm is the price quoted of £18 per component, and for what period will that price be maintained?
8 How easy would it be to switch back to internal manufacturing if the supplier proved unreliable?

It follows that much more information (largely of a non-cost nature) would be required before a conclusive decision could be taken.

Attempt Example 20.3 without looking at the solution.

Activity 20.4

Pricing decisions

A very important decision that managers in both the profit-making sector and the not-for-profit sector have to take is that relating to pricing. Supermarkets, for example, have to decide what to charge their customers, while local authorities have similar decisions to take in respect of charges for various services, such as adult education fees, leisure centres and meals on wheels.

Two types of pricing decisions can be distinguished. The first type relates to the prices charged to customers or clients external to the entity. We will refer to this type as *external pricing*. The second type relates to prices charged by one part of an entity to another

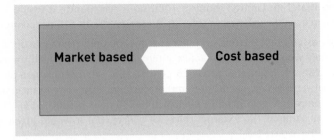

Figure 20.4 **External pricing decisions**

part, such as when components are supplied by one segment to another segment. This type of pricing is known as *transfer pricing*. We will deal with each type separately, although it should be borne in mind that pricing is a complicated subject and we have only the space to go into it very briefly.

External pricing

There are two basic ways of determining external selling prices, meaning the price to be charged for goods and services offered to parties *outside* an organization. External selling prices may be based either on market prices or on cost. The dilemma is defined in Figure 20.4. We will deal first with market-based prices.

Market-based pricing

Many goods and services are sold in highly competitive markets. This means that there may be many suppliers offering identical or near-identical products, and they will be competing fiercely in respect of price, quality, reliability and service. If the demand for a product is *elastic*, then the lower the price the more units that will be sold. The opposite also applies and higher prices will result in fewer goods being sold. The demand for most everyday items of food, for example, is elastic.

It follows that when demand is elastic it is unlikely that individual sellers can determine their own selling prices. Hence within narrow limits they will have to base their selling prices on what is being charged in the market. Otherwise, if they charge more than the market price, their sales will be reduced. If they charge less than the market, then their sales will increase but the market will quickly adjust to a lower level of selling prices.

Where market conditions largely determine a supplier's selling prices, it is particularly important to ensure that tight control is exercised over costs. Otherwise, the gap between total sales revenue and total costs (i.e. the profit) will be insufficient to ensure an adequate return on capital employed.

The demand for some goods, in contrast, is *inelastic* – i.e. price has little or no effect on the number of units sold. The demand for writing paper and stationery, for example, tends to be inelastic, probably because it is an infrequent purchase and it is not a significant element in most people's budgets. Thus when the demand for goods is inelastic, suppliers have much more freedom in determining their own selling prices. In such circumstance they may then base them on cost.

Cost-based pricing

There are a number of cost-based pricing methods. We summarize the main ones below and the circumstances in which they are most likely to be used.

1 *Below variable cost.* This price would be used (1) when an entity was trying to estab-lish a new product on the market; (2) when an attempt was being made to drive out competitors; and (3) as a loss leader (i.e. to encourage other goods to be bought). A price at this level could only be sustained for a very short period (unless it is used as a loss leader) since each unit sold would not be covering its variable cost.

2 *At variable cost.* Variable cost prices may be used (1) to launch a new product; (2) to drive out competition; (3) in difficult trading conditions; and (4) as a loss leader. Price could be held for some time but ultimately some contribution will be needed to cover the fixed costs.

3 *At total production cost.* The total production cost will include the unit's direct costs and a share of the production overheads. Prices at this level could be held for some time (perhaps when demand is low) but eventually the entity would need to cover its non-production overheads and to make a profit.

4 *At total cost.* The total cost of a unit will include the direct cost and a share of both the production and non-production overheads. Again, such prices could be held for a very long period, perhaps during a long recession. Eventually, however, some profit would need to be earned.

5 *At cost plus.* The cost-plus method would either relate to total production cost or to total cost. The 'plus' element would be an addition to the cost to allow for non-production overhead and profit (in the case of total production cost) and for profit alone (in the case of total cost). In the long run, cost-plus prices are the only option for a profit-making entity. However, if prices are based on cost, inefficiencies may be automatically built into the costing system and this could lead to uncompetitiveness.

As far as external price determination is concerned, we can generalize by arguing that prices tend to be governed by the market. Hence it is important to ensure that tight control is exercised over costs since there will normally be little opportunity to raise selling prices.

Transfer pricing

In large entities it is quite common for one segment to trade with another segment. Thus what is 'revenue' to one segment will be 'expenditure' to a fellow segment. This means that when the results of all the various segments are consolidated (meaning added together), the revenue recorded in one segment's books of account will cancel out the expenditure in the other segment's books. Does it matter, therefore, what prices are charged for internal transfers?

The answer is 'Yes it does', because some segments (particularly if they are divisions of companies) are given a great deal of autonomy. They may have the authority, for ex-ample, to purchase the goods and services that they need from outside the entity. They almost certainly will do so if the price and service offered externally appears superior to any internal offer. Thus it may cause them to suboptimize, i.e. to act in their own best interest although it may not be in the best interests of the entity as a whole.

Let us suppose that Segment A fixes its transfer price on a cost-plus basis, say at £10 per unit. Segment B finds it can purchase an identical unit externally at £8 per unit.

Segment B is very likely to accept the external offer. But Segment A's costs may be based on *absorbed costs*. The *extra cost* (i.e. the variable cost) of meeting Segment B's order may be much less the external price of £8 per unit. Thus it may not be beneficial for the *entity as a whole* for Segment B to purchase the units from an outside supplier.

Do you follow the above argument? It is somewhat complicated, so read it again if you do not follow the point. When you do, read on.

It follows from what has been said that a transfer price has to be set at a level that will encourage a supplying segment to trade internally and to discourage a receiving segment to purchase its requirements in the external market. Within this broad overall aim, a number of different transfer-pricing methods can be distinguished. The main ones are itemized below and they are also illustrated in Figure 20.5.

1 *At market prices.* If there are identical or similar goods and services offered externally, transfer prices based on market prices will neither encourage nor discourage supplying or receiving segments to trade externally.

2 *At adjusted market prices.* Transfer prices based at market levels do not encourage segments to deal with each other. Market prices may be reduced in order to act as an incentive for segments to trade internally. This approach also gives some recognition to lower costs normally attached to internal trading, e.g. advertising, administration, and financing.

3 *At total cost or total cost plus.* A transfer price based on total cost will include the direct costs plus a share of both production and non-production overhead. Total cost-plus methods allow for some profit. The main problems attached to the total cost methods is that they build inefficiencies into the transfer price (as there is no incentive to control costs) and they therefore encourage suboptimization.

4 *At variable cost or variable cost plus.* The variable cost method does not encourage a supplying segment to trade internally as no incentive is built into the transfer price. A percentage addition may provide some incentive since it enables some contribution to be made towards fixed costs. Transfer prices based on variable costs may be very attractive to receiving segments as they normally compare favourably with external prices.

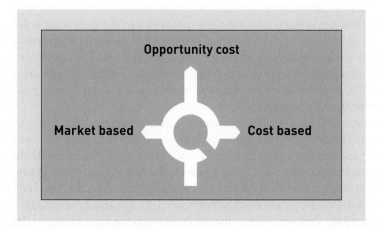

Figure 20.5 **Transfer pricing decisions**

5 *Negotiated prices.* This method involves striking a bargain between the supplying and the receiving segments based on a combination of market price and costs. As long as the discussions are mutually determined, this method can be a highly successful one.

6 *Opportunity costs.* This method may be somewhat impractical, but if it can be determined it is the ideal one to adopt. A transfer price based on the opportunity cost comprises two elements: first, the standard variable cost in the supplying segment; and second, the entity's opportunity cost resulting from the transaction. It is the second element that is the hardest to determine.

As you have no doubt gathered, pricing decisions are extremely complex. The main role of management accounting (as always) is to supply relevant data and to provide advice. The eventual decision ranges far beyond the remit of the management accountant. Besides incorporating basic cost and financial data, it also incorporates a great many other internal and external considerations, including macro-economic, environmental, financial, political and social factors.

What is the best way out of the transfer price dilemma? Should it be based on market prices or on costs? Suppose as a manager you have the freedom to negotiate your own transfer prices with other divisional managers. Summarize in your notebook the arguments that you would use in any ensuing discussions.

Activity 20.5

Special orders

On some occasions an entity may be asked to undertake an order beyond its normal trading arrangement and to quote a price for it. Such arrangements are known as *special orders*. The potential customer or client would normally expect to pay a lower price than the entity ordinarily charges and possibly to receive some favourable treatment. What pricing policy should the entity adopt when faced with such demands?

Much will depend upon whether the entity has some surplus capacity. If this is the case, it may be prepared to quote a price below variable cost if it wants to avoid a possible shutdown problem. However, the minimum price that it would normally be willing to accept would be equal to the incremental (or extra) cost of fulfilling the order.

The incremental cost involved may be the equivalent of the variable cost. Prices based at or below the variable cost would be extremely competitive, thereby helping to ensure that the customer accepted the quotation. The work gained would then absorb some of the entity's surplus capacity and help to keep its workforce occupied. There is also the possibility that the customer may place future orders at prices that would enable the entity to make a profit on them. However, there is the danger that in the meantime more profitable work has to be rejected because the entity cannot cope with both the special order and additional work.

A price in excess of the variable cost would make a contribution towards fixed costs and this would clearly be the preferred option. The quoted price would have to be judged very finely because the higher the price the greater the risk that the customer would reject the quotation. Hence the decision would involve trying to determine what other suppliers are likely to charge and the other terms that they may offer.

An indication of the difficulties associated with determining whether a special order should be accepted is demonstrated in Example 20.4. Although the exhibit is a highly simplified one, it illustrates the basic approach to decision making when faced with such an issue.

Example 20.4	**A special order**	

Amber Limited has been asked by a customer to supply a specially designed product. The customer has indicated that he would be willing to pay a maximum price of £100 per unit. The cost details are as follows.

Unit cost	£	£
Contract price		100
Less: Variable costs		
Direct materials	40	
Direct labour (2 hours)	30	
Variable overhead	10	80
Contribution		20

At a contract price of £100 per unit, each unit would make a contribution of £20. The customer is prepared to take 400 units, and so the total contribution towards fixed costs would be £8000 (400 units × £20). However, Amber has a shortage of direct labour, and some of the staff would have to be switched from other orders to work on the special order. This would mean an average loss in contribution of £8 for every direct labour hour worked on the special order.

Required:
Determine whether Amber Limited should accept the special order.

Answer to Example 20.4

In order to determine whether Amber Limited should accept the special order, the extra contribution should be compared with the loss of contribution by having to switch the workforce from other orders. The calculations are as follows.

	£
Total contribution from the special order (400 units × £20 per unit)	8 000
Less: the opportunity cost of the normal contribution foregone	
[800 direct labour hours (400 units × 2 DLH) × £8 per unit]	6 400
Extra contribution	1 600

Tutorial notes

Before coming to a decision, the following points should also be considered. You will see that they range well beyond simple cost factors.

1 The costings relating to the special order should be carefully checked.

2 The customer should be asked to confirm in writing that it would be willing to pay a selling price of £100 per unit.

3 Determine whether the customer is likely to place additional orders for the product.

4 Check that the *average* contribution of £8 per direct labour hour, obtained from other orders, applies to the workforce that would be switched to the special order, i.e. is the

contribution from the other orders that would be lost more or less than £8 per direct labour hour?

5 Is it possible that new staff could be recruited to work on the special order?

6 Is more profitable work likely to come along in the meantime? Would it mean that it could not be accepted during the progress of the order?

Answer to
Example 20.4
continued

Recommendation

Assuming that the points raised in the above notes are satisfied, then the recommendation would be to accept the special order at a price of £100 per unit. This would mean that Amber's total contribution would be increased by £1600.

The management accountant's main role in dealing with special orders would be to supply historical and projected cost data of the financial consequences of particular options. The eventual decision would be taken by senior management using a wide range of quantitative and qualitative information. The type of questions asked would be similar to some of the issues covered in the tutorial notes in the solution to Example 20.4.

Attempt Example 20.4 without looking at the answer.

Activity 20.6

 ## Questions non-accountants should ask

The questions that you should put to your accountants about any specific decision-making problem will revolve round the robustness of the data that they have used and any non-quantitative factors they have incorporated into their recommendations. You could use the following ones as a guide.

● Where have you got the data from?

● How reliable are the basic facts?

● What assumptions have you adopted?

● Have you only included relevant costs?

● Have you tested the results on a probability basis?

● What non-quantitative factors have you been able to identify?

● Is it possible to put any monetary value on them?

● On balance, do you think that we should go ahead with this proposal?

Conclusion

An important function of the modern management accountant is to assist in managerial decision making. In such a role, the primary task of the management accountant is to provide managers with financial and non-financial information in order to help them take more effective decisions. Although the information provided may include much historical data, decision making often means dealing with future events. Thus the information provided consists of a great deal of speculative material. This means that the management accountant needs to exercise considerable skill and judgement in collecting information that is both accurate and relevant for a particular purpose. Non-relevant information can be ignored as it only obscures the broader picture.

The significance of including only relevant data is seen when managers have to take special decisions, such as whether to close or shut down a segment of an entity, make or provide internally goods and services instead of obtaining them from an outside supplier, determine a selling price for the entity's goods and services, or whether to accept a special order and at what price. These are all-important and complex decisions and managers need reliable information before they can take them.

Key points

1   Decision making involves having to resolve an outcome for a specific problem.

2   The information required relates to the future, it is specific to the problem, it may have to be collected specially for the task and it is geared towards estimating the future net cash flows of particular outcomes.

3   The information provided to management should include only relevant costs and revenues, including an estimate of any opportunity costs.

4   The data used in a management accounting information report should be subject to some probability testing.

5   The terms 'fixed and variable costs', 'relevant and non-relevant costs', 'avoidable and non-avoidable costs', 'sunk costs', 'committed costs' and 'opportunity costs' are all of special significance in decision making.

6   Closure and shutdown decisions should be based on the contribution earned or likely to be earned on the segment under consideration and compared with the likely closure or shutdown costs.

7   Generally, it is more profitable to make goods or to provide services internally than to obtain them externally if their variable cost is less than or equal to external prices.

8   The pricing goods and services for selling externally will normally be determined by the market price for similar goods and services. In some cases, however, selling prices can be based on cost. Depending on market conditions, the cost could be at or below variable cost, the absorbed or the total absorbed cost, with or without an addition for profit.

9   The internal transfer of goods and services should be based on market price or adjusted market price. Where this is not possible, any price at or in excess of the variable cost should be acceptable.

Key points continued

10 The ideal transfer price is one that is based on the standard variable cost in the supplying segment plus the entity's opportunity cost resulting from the transaction.

11 Special orders should be priced so that they cover their variable cost. There may be some circumstances when it is acceptable to price them below variable cost but this can only be a short-term solution. Any price in excess of variable costs helps to cover the entity's fixed costs.

12 Cost and financial factors form only one part of decision making. There are other factors of a non-financial and non-quantifiable nature (such as behavioural factors) that must be taken into account.

Check your learning

1 Define what is meant by a 'decision'.

2 List seven main characteristics of decision-making data.

3 Identify six ways of classifying costs.

4 What is an opportunity cost?

5 What is a closure or a shutdown decision?

6 What is a make or buy decision?

7 What is a pricing decision?

8 What are the two main types of pricing decisions?

9 What is meant by a 'market' price?

10 List six cost based pricing methods.

11 What is the basic problem in determining pricing between segments within the same entity?

12 How might it be resolved?

13 What is a special order?

14 How does it differ from the general pricing problem?

News story quiz

Remember the news story at the beginning of this chapter? Go back to that story and re-read it before answering the following questions.

This short article reflects what must have been a classic decision-making situation: the cost of closing a factory against the cost of keeping it open. Although the total cost of closure is put at £2.8m, £1.5m of it reflects 'asset write-offs' (this information was given in a press release issued by the company). As a result, there is a £1.3m effect on cash flow but this is expected to be offset by selling the factory for a *book* value of £1.5m. The management obviously sees no long-term future for the Chesterfield factory because it appears that it is going to be closed permanently.

Questions

1 Is it appropriate to include asset write-off in the cost of closing the factory?

2 Should the market value of the property have been included in the calculations?

3 What costs are likely to have been included in the net cash closure cost of £1.3m?

4 What non-quantitative factors should the management consider before deciding to close the Chesterfield factory?

Tutorial questions

The answers to questions marked with an asterisk may be found in Appendix 4.

20.1 This chapter has emphasized that it is managers that take decisions and not management accountants. How far do you agree with this assertion?

20.2 Many of the solutions to the problems posed in this chapter depend upon being able to isolate the variable cost associated with a particular decision. In practice, is it realistic to expect that such costs can be readily identified and measured?

20.3 Assume that you were an IT manager in a large entity, and that the services that you provide are made available to both internal and external parties. Specify how you would go about negotiating an appropriate fee for services sought by other departments within the entity.

20.4* Micro Limited has some spare capacity. It is now considering whether it should accept a special contract to use some of the spare capacity. However, this contract will use some specialist direct labour that is in short supply. The following details relate to the proposed contract:

	£000
Contract price	50
Variable costs:	
Direct materials	10
Direct labour	30

In order to complete the contract, 4000 direct labour hours would be required. The company's budget for the year during which the contract would be undertaken is as follows:

	£000
Sales	750
Variable costs	(500)
Contribution	250
Fixed costs	(230)
Profit	20

There would be 50 000 direct labour hours available during the year.

Required:
Determine whether the special contract should be accepted.

20.5* Temple Limited has been offered two new contracts, the details of which are as follows:

Contract	(1)	(2)
	£000	£000
Contract price	1 000	2 100
Direct materials	300	600
Direct labour	300	750
Variable overhead	100	250
Fixed overhead	100	200
	800	1 800
Profit	200	300
Direct materials required (kilos)	50 000	100 000
Direct labour hours required	10 000	25 000

Note: The fixed overhead has been apportioned on the basis of direct labour cost. Temple is a one-product firm. Its budgeted cost per unit for its normal work for the year to 31 December 2007 is summarized below.

	£
Sales	6 000
Direct materials (100 kilos)	700
Direct labour (200 hours)	3 000
Variable overhead	300
Fixed overhead	1 000
	5 000
Profit	1 000

The company would only have the capacity to accept one of the new contracts. Unfortunately, materials suitable for use in all of its work are in short supply and the company has estimated that only 200 000 kilos would be available during the year to December 2007. Even more worrying is the shortage of skilled labour; only 100 000 direct labour hours are expected to be available during the year. The good news is that there may be an upturn in the market for its normal contract work.

Required:
Calculate:

(1)   the contribution per unit of each limiting factor for
    (a)   the company's normal work;
    (b)   Contract 1; and
    (c)   Contract 2.
(2)   the company's maximum contribution for the year to 31 December 2007, assuming that it accepts either Contract 1 or Contract 2.

20.6   Agra Limited has been asked to quote a price for a special contract. The details are as follows:

1   The specification required a quotation for 100 000 units.
2   The direct costs per unit for the order would be: materials £3; labour £15; distribution £12.
3   Additional production and non-production overhead would amount to £500 000, although £100 000 could be saved if the order was for less than 100 000 units.
4   Agra's normal profit margin is 20 per cent of total cost.

Required:
Recommend a minimum selling price if the order was for (a) 100 000 units; and (b) 80 000 units.

20.7   Foo Limited has been asked to quote for a special order. The details are as follows:

1 Prices are to be quoted at order levels of 50 000, 100 000 and 150 000 units respectively. Foo has some surplus capacity and it could deal with up to 160 000 units.
2 Each unit would cost £2 for direct materials, and £12 for direct labour.
3 Foo normally absorbs production and non-production overhead on the basis of 200 per cent and 100 per cent respectively of the direct labour cost.
4 Distribution costs are expected to be £10 per unit.
5 Foo's normal profit margin is 20 per cent of the total cost. However, it is prepared to reduce this margin to 15 per cent if the order is for 100 000 units, and to 10 per cent for an order of 150 000 units.
6 The additional non-production overhead associated with this contract would be £200 000, although this would be cut by £25 000 if the output dropped below 100 000 units.

Required:
Suggest (a) a selling price per unit that Foo Limited might charge if the contract was for 50 000, 100 000, and 150 000 units respectively; and (b) the profit that it could expect to make at these levels.

20.8   Bamboo Limited is a highly specialist firm of central heating suppliers operating exclusively in the textiles industry. It has recently been asked to tender for a contract for a prospective customer. The following details relate to the proposed contract.

1 Materials:
   (a) £20 000 of materials would need to be purchased.
   (b) £10 000 of materials would need to be transferred from another contract (these materials would need to be replaced).
   (c) Some obsolete stock would be used. The stock had originally cost £18 000. Its current disposable value is £4 000.
2 The contract would involve labour costs of £60 000, of which £30 000 would be incurred regardless of whether the contract was undertaken.
3 The production manager will have to work several evenings a week during the progress of the contract. He is paid a salary of £30 000 per year, and on successful completion of the contract he would receive a bonus of £5 000.
4 Additional administrative expenses incurred in undertaking the contract are estimated to be £1 000.
5 The company absorbs its fixed overheads at a rate of £10 per machine hour. The contract will require 2 000 machine hours.

Required:
Calculate the minimum contract price that would be acceptable to Bamboo Limited.

20.9 Dynasty Limited has been involved in a research project (code named DNY) for a number of months. There is some doubt as to whether the project should be completed. If it is, then it is expected that DNY will require another 12 months' work. The following information relates to the project.

1 Costs incurred to date: £500 000.
2 Sales proceeds if the project continues: £600 000.
3 Direct material costs amount to £200 000. The type of material required for DNY had already been purchased for another project, and it would cost £20 000 to dispose of it.
4 Direct labour costs have come to £150 000. The direct labour used on DNY is highly skilled and it is not easy to recruit the type of staff required. In order to undertake DNY, some staff would have to be transferred from other projects. This would mean that there was a total loss in contribution from such projects of £350 000.
5 Research staff costs amount to £200 000. The staff would be made redundant at the end of project DNY at a cost of £115 000. If they were to be made redundant now, there would be a cost of £100 000.
6 The company can invest surplus cash at a rate of return of 10% per annum.
7 Non-production overhead budgeted to be apportioned to DNY for the forthcoming 12 months amounts to £60 000.

Required:
Determine whether or not the project DNY should continue.

Further practice questions, study material and links to relevant sites on the World Wide Web can be found on the website that accompanies this book. The site can be found at **www.booksites.net/dyson**

Capital expenditure: the key to future prosperity . . .

Hilton to cut back project spend

HOTELS group Hilton yesterday said it had pegged back capital expenditure for next year after seeing little sign of an upturn in trading conditions.

The company intends to spend £130m on projects in its hotels division during 2003 compared with a figure of around £200m this year.

However, Hilton said the quality of its estate meant that the figure would still be sufficient to ensure its portfolio stayed in good shape.

The budget will also be enough to cover the £46m being spent on the redevelopment of the Hilton Sydney.

The company's budget review comes after figures for the four months to October 31 showed profits were 9 per cent lower than a year ago. That compares with a 10 per cent fall in half-year profits reported in August.

It said yesterday that "political and economic uncertainties" had resulted in widely varying performances in different parts of the world, with hotels in key European cities among those affected.

It added: "The timing of a sustained recovery in the hotels business remains difficult to predict."

The latest trading figures for September and October show Hilton's UK hotels division improved its revenues per average room figure by 4.6 per cent, although the figure benefits from weaker comparisons last year because of September 11.

In the company's five-star London hotels, the increase was 10.5 per cent after a 12.9 per cent decline in July and August, while four-star properties rose 6.5 per cent after a dip of 7.5 per cent in the previous period.

A Hilton spokesman said its London hotels had benefited from aggressive marketing to attract customers on weekend and leisure-based breaks.

In the UK provinces, Hiltons continued their resilient performance with revenues up 2.4 per cent in September and October compared with a rise of 1.4 per cent in the previous two-month period. Across the group, the hotels division revenues per average room figure rose 7.7 per cent.

Yorkshire Post, 15 December 2002.

Questions relating to this news story may be found on page 498 ▶▶

About this chapter

This is the third chapter in Part 4 of the book dealing with management accounting decision making. The chapter explains how various calculative techniques can help management select a particular investment. Accountants call this exercise *capital invest-*

ment appraisal. The chapter also explores the main sources of short-, medium-, and long-term finance available for the financing of a project once it has been selected.

The chapter is divided into seven main sections. The first main section explains the importance of the chapter for non-accountants. This is followed by an exploration of the background to capital investment appraisal. The next section then examines five calculative methods that can be used for determining which project to select. The following section provides some guidance on which method to select. The section after that considers the problem of estimating net cash flow. We then review the main sources of short-, medium-, and long-term finance available for the financing of capital projects. The last main section of the chapter frames some questions that non-accountants may like to ask about the issues discussed in the chapter.

By the end of this chapter you should be able to:

- describe what is meant by capital investment appraisal;
- identify five capital investment appraisal techniques;
- incorporate such techniques into quantitative examples;
- recognize the significance of such techniques;
- list the main sources of financing capital investment projects.

! Why this chapter is important for non-accountants

It is possible that even as a junior manager you will be involved in capital investment decisions. At that level, the amount of money involved may be very small and all you might be doing is deciding which one of two filing cabinets your section should buy. As you become senior, however, you may become involved in deciding upon competing projects that cost millions of pounds. You will have to decide upon the profitability of such projects and rank them accordingly. In addition, you may have to determine what is the best way of financing them.

These sorts of decision involve a consideration of various projects on both a quantitative and qualitative basis. Your accountants will process the numbers for you and they may use one of the techniques discussed in this chapter. They will then present the results to you. Hence it is extremely unlikely that you will be involved in the detailed number crunching. However, in order to take a decision about which project you should select, you will need to question your accountants about their recommendations.

You will not be able to do so with any confidence unless you have some knowledge of their methods. This chapter provides you with the basic material. After studying it you will be in a much better position to make and to take your own capital investment decisions and not just do what your accountants tell you to do.

Background

We explained in Chapter 4 that accountants make a distinction between capital expenditure and revenue expenditure (the same distinction also applies to income). The borderline between capital and revenue expenditure is somewhat imprecise. Generally, expenditure that is likely to be of benefit in more than one accounting period is classed as capital.

However, expenditure that is classed as capital would normally have other significant characteristics. These can be summarized as follows:

1 it will help the entity to achieve its organizational objectives;
2 it will probably involve substantial expenditure;
3 the benefits may be spread over very many years;
4 it is difficult to predict what the benefits will be;
5 it will have some impact on the entity's employees.

Indeed, if the entity is to survive and especially if it wants to grow, it will need to invest continually in capital projects. Existing fixed assets will begin to wear out, and more efficient ones will become available. Furthermore, capital expenditure may be required not just in the administration, production and stores departments but also on social and recreational facilities. In the public sector also, universities and colleges may be faced with capital expenditure decisions that go beyond providing lecture halls and tutorial rooms, e.g. student accommodation and union facilities.

Irrespective of where the demand for capital expenditure arises, however, all entities face two common problems: (a) the priority to be given to individual projects; and (b) how they can be financed. Hence, competing projects will need to be ranked according to either their importance or their potential profitability. In the next section we examine how this may be done.

Main methods

We will assume that we are dealing with a profit-making entity. There is, then, little point in investing in a project unless it is likely to make a profit. The exceptions are those projects that are necessary on health, social and welfare grounds, and these are particularly difficult to assess. There are five main techniques that accountants can use in CI appraisal. They are shown in diagrammatic form in Figure 21.1 and examined in each of the following subsections.

Payback

The payback method is an attempt to estimate how long it would take before a project begins to pay for itself. For example, if a company was going to spend £300 000 on purchasing some new plant, the accountant would calculate how many years it would take before £300 000 had been received back in cash. The recovery of an investment in a project is usually measured in terms of *net cash flow*. Net cash flow is the difference between cash received and cash paid during a defined period of time. In order to adopt this method, therefore, the following information is required:

1 the total cost of the investment;
2 the amount of cash instalments to be paid back on the investment;

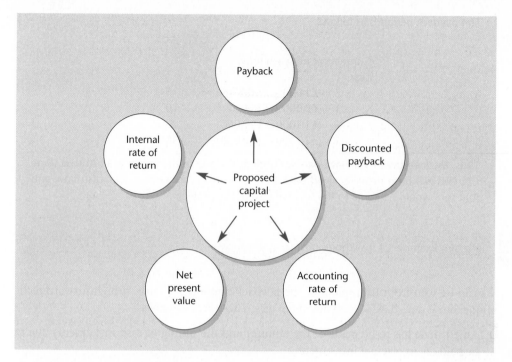

Figure 21.1 Methods of capital investment appraisal

3 the accounting periods in which the instalments will be paid;
4 the cash receipts and any other cash payments connected with the project;
5 the accounting periods in which they fall.

As the payback measures the rate of recovery of the original investment in terms of net cash flow, it follows that non-cash items (such as depreciation, and profits and losses on sales of fixed assets) are not taken into account.

The payback method is illustrated in Example 21.1.

The payback method			Example 21.1

Miln Limited is considering investing in some new machinery. The following information has been prepared to support the project:

	£000	£000
Cost of machinery		20
Expected net cash flow:		
Year 1	1	
2	4	
3	5	
4	10	
5	10	30
Net profitability		10

Required:
Calculate the prospective investment's payback period.

Answer to Example 21.1	The payback period is as follows:

		£000
Cumulative net cash flow:		
Year 1		1
2	(£1 000 + £4 000)	5
3	(£5 000 + £5 000)	10
4	(£10 000 + £10 000)	20
5	(£20 000 + £10 000)	30

Thus, the investment will have paid for itself at the end of the fourth year. At that stage £20 000 will have been received back from the project in terms of net cash flow and that sum would be equal to the original cost of the project.

Activity 21.1	Attempt Example 21.1 without looking at the answer.

As can be seen from Example 21.1 the payback method is a fairly straightforward technique, but it does have several disadvantages. These are as follows:

1 An estimate has to be made of the amount and the timing of cash instalments due to be paid on an original investment.
2 It is difficult to calculate the net cash flows and the period in which they will be received.
3 There is a danger that projects with the shortest payback periods may be chosen even if they are less profitable than projects that have a longer payback period. The method only measures cash flow; it does not measure profitability.
4 The total amount of the overall investment is ignored and comparisons made between different projects may result in a misleading conclusion. Thus a project with an initial investment of £10 000 may have a shorter payback period than one with an initial investment of £100 000, although in the long run the larger investment may prove more profitable.
5 The technique ignores any net cash flows received after the payback period.
6 The timing of the cash flows is not taken into account: £1 received now is preferable to £1 received in five years' time. Thus, a project with a short payback period may recover most of its investment towards the end of its payback period while another project with a longer payback period may recover most of the original investment in the first few years. There is clearly less risk in accepting a project that recovers most of its cost very quickly than there is in accepting one where the benefits are deferred.

Notwithstanding these disadvantages, the payback method has something to be said for it. While it may appear to be rather simplistic, it does help managers to compare projects and to think in terms of how long it takes before a project has recovered its original cost. The timing problem can also be overcome by adopting what is called the *discounted payback method*.

Discounted payback

As was explained above, the simple payback method ignores the timing of net cash receipts. This problem can be overcome by *discounting* the net cash receipts. You will probably be familiar with discounting in your everyday life. You know, for example, that if you put £91 into the building society, and the rate of interest is 10% per annum, your original investment will be worth about £100 [£91 + £9 (10% × £91)] at the end of the year. We could look at this example from another point of view. Assuming a rate of interest of 10% per annum, what amount of money do you have to invest in the building society in order to have £100 at the end of the year? The answer is, of course, £91 (ignoring the odd 10p). In other words, £91 received now is about the same as £100 received in a year's time. This is what is meant by *discounting*. The procedure is as follows:

1 Calculate the future net cash flows.
2 Estimate an appropriate rate of interest.
3 Multiply the net cash flows by a discount factor.

The discount factor will depend on the cost of borrowing money. In the case of the building society example above, the discount factor is based on a rate of interest of 10%. The factor itself is 0.9091, i.e. £100 × 0.9091 = £90.91. To check: take the £90.91 and add the year's interest, i.e. £90.91 × 10% = £9.091 + £90.91 = £100.00. You will not have to calculate discount factors: these are readily available in tables. One is included in Appendix 2 to this book.

To check that you understand the point about discounting, turn to Appendix 2. Look along the top line for the appropriate rate of interest: in our case it is 10%. Work down the 10% column until you come to the line opposite the year (shown in the left-hand column) in which the cash would be received. In our example, the cash is going to be received in one year's time, so it is not necessary to go further than the first line. The present value of £1 receivable in a year's time is, therefore, £0.9091, or £90.91 if £100 is to be received in a year's time.

Assuming a rate of interest of 15% per annum, what is the present value of £200 receivable in two years' time?	*Activity 21.2*

Do you feel reasonably confident that you now know what is meant by the net present value of future net cash flows and what is involved in discounting? If so, we can move on to examine how discounting can be applied to the payback method. We do so in Example 21.2.

Example 21.2	The discounted payback method

Newland City Council has investigated the possibility of investing in a new project, and the following information has been obtained:

	£000	£000
Total cost of project		500
Expected net cash flows:		
Year 1	20	
2	50	
3	100	
4	200	
5	300	
6	30	700
Net return		200

Required:
Assuming a rate of interest of 8%, calculate the project's overall return using the following methods:
(a) payback; and
(b) discounted payback.

Answer to Example 21.2

(a) **Payback method**

Year	Net cash flow	Cumulative net cash flow
	£000	£000
0	(500)	(500)
1	20	(480)
2	50	(430)
3	100	(330)
4	200	(130)
5	300	170
6	30	200

Calculation
By the end of the fifth year, the original investment of £500 000 will have been covered. Assuming that the net cash flows accrue evenly throughout the year, therefore, the payback period is about 4 years 5 months. After 4 years the total cash flows received = £370 000 (£20 000 + 50 000 + 100 000 + 200 000). The £130 000 still necessary to equal the original cost of the investment (£500 000 – 370 000) will be met part way through Year 5, i.e. (£130 000 ÷ 300 000) × 12 months = 5.2 months. The payback period is, therefore, about 4 years and 5 months (41 months)

(b) Discounted payback

Year	Net cash flow	Discount factors	Present value at 8% [Column (2) × Column (3)]	Cumulative present value
(1)	(2)	(3)	(4)	(5)
	£000		£000	£000
0	(500)	1.0	(500)	(500)
1	20	0.9259	19	(481)
2	50	0.8573	43	(438)
3	100	0.7938	79	(359)
4	200	0.7350	147	(212)
5	300	0.6806	204	(8)
6	30	0.6302	19	11

Calculation

Using the discounted payback method, the project would recover all of its original cost during Year 6. Assuming that the net cash flows accrue evenly, this would be about the end of the fifth month because (£8000 ÷ 19 000) × 12 months = 5.1 months. Hence the discounted payback period is about 5 years 5 months (65 months).

Attempt Example 21.2 without looking at the answer.

Activity 21.3

The discounted payback method has the following advantages:

1 It is relatively easy to understand.
2 It is not too difficult to compute.
3 It focuses on the cash recovery of an investment.
4 It allows for the fact that cash received now may be worth more than cash receivable in the future.
5 It takes into account more of the net cash flows, since the discounted payback period is always longer than under the simple payback method.
6 It enables a clear-cut decision to be taken, since a project is acceptable if the discounted net cash flow throughout its life exceeds the cost of the original investment.

However, like the simple payback method, it has some disadvantages. These are as follows:

1 It is sometimes difficult to estimate the amount and timing of instalments due to be paid on the original investment.
2 It is difficult to estimate the amount and timing of future net cash receipts and other payments.
3 It is not easy to determine an appropriate rate of interest.
4 Net cash flows received after the payback period are ignored.

Irrespective of these disadvantages, the discounted payback method can be usefully and readily adopted by those entities that do not employ staff specially trained in capital investment appraisal techniques.

Accounting rate of return

The *accounting rate of return* (ARR) method attempts to compare the *profit* of a project with the capital invested in it. It is usually expressed as a percentage. The formula is as follows:

$$ARR = \frac{Profit}{Capital\ employed} \times 100$$

Two important problems arise from this definition. These are as follows:

1 *The definition of profit.* Normally, the average annual net profit earned by a project would be used. However, as was explained in earlier chapters, accounting profit can be subject to a number of different assumptions and distortions (e.g. depreciation, taxation and inflation), and so it is relatively easy to arrive at different profit levels depending upon the accounting policies adopted. The most common definition is to take profit before interest and taxation. The profit included in the equation would then be a simple average of the profit that the project earns over its entire life.

2 *The definition of capital employed.* The capital employed could be either the initial capital employed in the project or the average capital employed over its life.

Thus, depending upon the definitions adopted, the ARR may be calculated in one of two ways, as follows:

1 Using the original capital employed:

$$ARR = \frac{Average\ annual\ net\ profit\ before\ interest\ and\ taxation}{Initial\ capital\ employed\ on\ the\ project} \times 100$$

2 Using the average capital employed:

$$ARR = \frac{Average\ annual\ net\ profit\ before\ interest\ and\ taxation}{Average\ annual\ capital\ employed\ on\ the\ project\ ^*} \times 100$$

$$^*\ \frac{Initial\ capital\ employed + residual\ value}{2}$$

The two methods are illustrated in Example 21.3.

Example 21.3	**The accounting rate of return method**

Bridge Limited is considering investing in a new project, the details of which are as follows:

Project life		5 years
	£000	£000
Project cost		50
Estimated net profit:		
Year 1		12
2		18
3		30
4		25
5		5
Total net profit		90

The estimated residual value of the project at the end of Year 5 is £10 000.

Example 21.3
continued

Required:
Calculate the accounting rate of return of the proposed new project, using the two methods described above.

The accounting rate of return would be calculated as follows:

Answer to
Example 21.3

(a) *Using the initial capital employed*:

$$\frac{\text{Average annual net profits}}{\text{Cost of the investment}} \times 100$$

Average annual net profits = £18 000 (£90 000/5)

$$\therefore \text{Accounting rate of return} = \frac{£18\,000}{50\,000} \times 100 = \underline{\underline{36\%}}$$

(b) *Using the average capital employed*:

$$\frac{\text{Average annual net profits}}{\text{Average capital employed}} \times 100$$

$$= \frac{£18\,000}{\frac{1}{2}(£50\,000 + 10\,000)} \times 100 = \underline{\underline{60\%}}$$

Attempt Example 21.3 without looking at the answer.

Activity 21.4

Like the payback and discounted payback methods, the accounting rate of return method has several advantages and disadvantages. These are as follows:

Advantages
1 The method is compatible with a similar accounting ratio used in financial accounting.
2 It is relatively easy to understand.
3 It is not difficult to compute.
4 It draws attention to the notion of overall profit.

Disadvantages
1 Net profit can be subject to different definitions, e.g. it can mean net profit before or after allowing for depreciation on the project.
2 It is not always clear whether the original cost of the investment should be used, or whether it is more appropriate to substitute an average for the amount of capital invested in the project.
3 The use of a residual value in calculating the average amount of capital employed means that the higher the residual value, the lower the ARR. For example, with no residual value, the ARR on a project costing £100 000 and an average net profit of £50 000 would be 100%, i.e.:

$$\frac{£50\,000}{\frac{1}{2} \times (100\,000 + 0)} \times 100 = 100\%$$

With a residual value of (say) £10 000, the ARR would be 90.9%, i.e.:

$$\frac{£50\,000}{\frac{1}{2} \times (100\,000 + 10\,000)} \times 100 = 90.9\%$$

The estimation of residual values is very difficult, and it can make all the difference between one project and another.

4 The method gives no guidance on what is an acceptable rate of return.

5 The benefit of earning a high proportion of the total profit in the early years of the project is not allowed for.

6 The method does not take into account the time value of money.

Notwithstanding these disadvantages, the ARR method may be suitable where very similar short-term projects are being considered.

Net present value

One of the main disadvantages of using the payback and ARR methods in CI appraisal is that both methods ignore the time value of money. This concept has already been examined when we were dealing with the discounted payback method. There are two other methods that also adopt this concept: the net present value method, and the internal rate of return method. In this subsection, the net present value (NPV) method is examined.

The NPV method recognizes that cash received today is preferable to cash receivable sometime in the future. There is more risk in having to wait for future cash receipts and, while a smaller sum may be obtained now, at least it is available for other purposes. For example, it can be invested, and the subsequent rate of return may then compensate for the smaller amount received now (or at least be equal to it).

As was seen earlier in the chapter, £91 received now (assuming a rate of interest of 10%) is just as beneficial as receiving £100 in a year's time. This is also the principle behind the NPV method of CI appraisal. Basically, it involves taking the following steps:

1 calculate the annual net cash flows expected to arise from the project;
2 select an appropriate rate of interest, or required rate of return;
3 obtain the discount factors appropriate to the chosen rate of interest or rate of return;
4 multiply the annual net cash flow by the appropriate discount factors;
5 add together the present values for each of the net cash flows;
6 compare the total net present value with the initial outlay;
7 accept the project if the total NPV is positive.

This procedure is outlined in Example 21.4.

Example 21.4	The net present value method

Rage Limited is considering two capital investment projects. The details are outlined as follows:

Project	1	2
Estimated life	3 years	5 years
Commencement date	1.1.01	1.1.01
	£000	£000
Project cost at year 1	100	100

Example 21.4
continued

Estimated net cash flows:

Year:			
	1	20	10
	2	80	40
	3	40	40
	4	–	40
	5	–	20
		140	150

The company expects a rate of return of 10% per annum on its capital employed.

Required:
Using the net present value method of project appraisal, assess which project would be more profitable.

Rage Ltd

Answer to
Example 21.4

Project appraisal:

	Project 1			Project 2		
Year	Net cash flow	Discount factor	Present value	Net cash flow	Discount factor	Present value
(1)	(2)	(3)	(4)	(5)	(6)	(7)
	£	10%	£	£	10%	£
1	20 000	0.9091	18 182	10 000	0.9091	9 091
2	80 000	0.8264	66 112	40 000	0.8264	33 056
3	40 000	0.7513	30 052	40 000	0.7513	30 052
4	–	–	–	40 000	0.6830	27 320
5	–	–	–	20 000	0.6209	12 418
Total present value			114 346			111 937
Less: Initial cost			100 000			100 000
Net present value			14 346			11 937

1 The net cash flows and the discount factor of 10% (i.e. the rate of return) were given in the question.

2 The discount factors may be obtained from the discount table shown in Appendix 2.

3 Column (4) has been calculated by multiplying column (2) by column (3).

4 Column (7) has been calculated by multiplying column (5) by column 6.

Tutorial notes

Both projects have a positive NPV, but project 1 will probably be chosen in preference to project 2 because it has a higher NPV, even though its total net cash flow of £140 000 is less than the total net cash flow of £150 000 for project 2.

Attempt Example 21.4 without looking at the answer.

Activity 21.5

The advantages and disadvantages of the NPV method are as follows:

Advantages

1 The use of net cash flows emphasizes the importance of liquidity.
2 Different accounting policies are not relevant as they do not affect the calculation of the net cash flows.
3 The time value of money is taken into account.
4 It is easy to compare the NPV of different projects and to reject projects that do not have an acceptable NPV.

Disadvantages

1 Some difficulties may be incurred in estimating the initial cost of the project and the time periods in which instalments must be paid back (although this is a common problem in CI appraisal).
2 It is difficult to estimate accurately the net cash flow for each year of the project's life (a difficulty that is again common to most other methods of project appraisal).
3 It is not easy to select an appropriate rate of interest. The rate of interest is sometimes referred to as the *cost of capital*, i.e. the cost of financing an investment. One rate that could be chosen is that rate which the company could earn if it decided to invest the funds outside the business (the external rate of interest). Alternatively, an internal rate of interest could be chosen. This rate would be based on an estimate of what return the company expects to earn on its existing investments. In the long run, if its internal rate of return is lower than the external rate, then it would appear more profitable to liquidate the company and invest the funds elsewhere. A local authority, however, may not have the same difficulty, because it would probably use a rate of interest that is set by central government.

NPV is considered to be a highly acceptable method of CI appraisal. It takes into account the timing of the net cash flows, the project's profitability, and the return of the original investment. However, an entity would not necessarily accept a project just because it had an acceptable NPV, because there are many non-financial factors that must be allowed for. Furthermore, other less profitable projects (or even projects with a negative NPV) may go ahead, perhaps because they are concerned with employee safety or welfare.

Internal rate of return

An alternative method of investment appraisal based on discounted net cash flow is known as the *internal rate of return* (IRR). This method is very similar to the NPV method. However, instead of discounting the expected net cash flows by a predetermined rate of return, the IRR method seeks to answer the following question:

> *What rate of return would be required in order to ensure that the total NPV equals the total initial cost?*

In theory, a rate of return that was lower than the entity's required rate of return would be rejected. In practice, however, the IRR would only be one factor to be taken into account in deciding whether to go ahead with the project. The method is illustrated in Example 21.5.

The internal rate of return method

Example
21.5

Bruce Limited is considering whether to invest £50 000 in a new project. The project's expected net cash flows would be as follows:

Year	£000
1	7
2	25
3	30
4	5

Required:
Calculate the internal rate of return for the proposed new project.

Bruce Ltd

Calculation of the internal rate of return:

Step 1: Select two discount factors
The first step is to select two discount factors, and then calculate the net present value of the project using both factors. The two factors usually have to be chosen quite arbitrarily, but they should preferably cover a narrow range. One of the factors should produce a *positive* net present value (NPV), and the other factor a *negative* NPV. As far as this question is concerned, factors of 10% and 15% will be chosen to illustrate the method. In practice, you may have to try various factors before you come across two that are suitable for giving a positive and a negative result.

Year	Net cash flow	Discount factors		Present value	
(1)	(2)	(3)	(4)	(5)	(6)
		10%	15%	10%	15%
	£			£	£
1	7 000	0.9091	0.8696	6 364	6 087
2	25 000	0.8264	0.7561	20 660	18 903
3	30 000	0.7513	0.6575	22 539	19 725
4	5 000	0.6830	0.5718	3 415	2 859
Total present values				52 978	47 574
Initial cost				50 000	50 000
Net present value				2 978	(2 426)

Notes

1 Column (2) has been obtained from the question.

2 Columns (3) and (4) are based on the arbitrary selection of two interest rates of 10% and 15% respectively. The discount factors may be found in Appendix 2.

3 Column (5) has been calculated by multiplying column (2) by column (3).

4 Column (6) has been calculated by multiplying column (2) by column (4).

The project is expected to cost £50 000. If the company expects a rate of return of 10%, the project will be accepted, because the NPV is positive. However, if the required rate of return is 15% it will not be accepted, because its NPV is negative. The maximum rate of return that will ensure a *positive* rate of return must, therefore, lie ▶

Answer to
Example 21.5
continued

somewhere between 10% and 15%, so the next step is to calculate the rate of return at which the project would just pay for itself.

Step 2: Calculate the specific break-even rate of return

To do this, it is necessary to interpolate between the rates used in Step 1. This can be done by using the following formula:

$$\text{IRR} = \text{Positive rate} + \left\{ \frac{\text{Positive NPV}}{\text{Positive NPV} + \text{Negative NPV*}} \times \text{Range of rates} \right\}$$

*Ignore the negative sign and add the positive NPV to the negative NPV.

Thus in our example:

$$\text{IRR} = 10\% + \left\{ \frac{2978}{(2978 + 2426)} \times (15\% - 10\%) \right\}$$
$$= 10\% + (0.5511 \times 5\%)$$
$$= 10\% + 2.76\%$$
$$= \underline{\underline{12.76\%}}$$

The project will be profitable provided that the company does not require a rate of return in excess of about 13%. Note that the method of calculation used above does not give the precise rate of return (because the formula is only an approximation), but it is adequate enough for decision-making purposes.

Activity 21.6   Attempt Example 21.5 without looking at the answer.

Example 21.5 demonstrates that the IRR method is similar to the NPV method in two respects:

1 The initial cost of the project has to be estimated, as well as the future net cash flows arising from the project.
2 The net cash flows are then discounted to their net present value using discount tables.

The main difference between the two methods is that the IRR method requires a rate of return to be estimated in order to give an NPV equal to the initial cost of the investment. The main difficulty arises in deciding which two rates of return to use so that one will give a positive NPV and the other will give a negative NPV. The range between the two rates should be as narrow as possible. You will find that if you use a trial-and-error method, you may have to try many times before you arrive at two suitable rates!

The advantages and disadvantages of the IRR method may be summarized as follows:

Advantages
1 Emphasis is placed on liquidity.
2 Attention is given to the timing of net cash flows.
3 An appropriate rate of return does not have to be calculated.
4 The method gives a clear percentage return on an investment.

Disadvantages
1 It is not easy to understand.
2 It is difficult to determine which two suitable rates to adopt unless a computer is used.

3 The method gives only an approximate rate of return.
4 In complex CI situations, the method can give some misleading results – for example, where there are negative net cash flows in subsequent years and where there are mutually exclusive projects.

As a non-accountant, you do not need to be too worried about the details of such rather technical considerations. All you need to know is that, in practice, the IRR method has to be used with some caution.

Selecting a method

We have kept our description of CI techniques deliberately simple. As a non-accountant you probably would not have to decide what appraisal technique to adopt and it is highly unlikely that you would have to do the detailed calculations for yourself; your accountant would probably present you with a summary of his calculations and you would then be expected to come to a decision. In doing so, you would probably find it easier if you knew what CI appraisal method had been adopted and what data had been included in the calculations. A knowledge of the various appraisal methods and their respective advantages and disadvantages should enable you to arrive at a particular decision with a great deal more confidence. Which CI appraisal method is the most appropriate?

We consider it important that the time value of money is taken into account in a CI appraisal since the profitability of a future project may be grossly optimistic if such a concept is ignored. The discounted payback method, the net present value method and the internal rate of return method, therefore, are all strong possibilities.

The internal rate of return method involves some complex calculations, although the overall result is relatively easy to understand. Nonetheless, it may be a little too sophisticated for most entities. The discounted payback method is simple to understand and intuitively appealing. Its main disadvantage, however, is that net cash flow received after the payback period may be ignored. Almost by default, therefore, the net present value method would appear to be the most favoured method. The main difficulty with the NPV method is the selection of a suitable rate of return for a particular project. Thus great care needs to be taken before accepting or rejecting a project based on the NPV method because it is highly dependent on the arbitrary determination of a specified rate of return.

Net cash flow

Decision making normally involves dealing with future events, and CI appraisal is no exception. Irrespective of the particular method adopted, a crucial stage in CI appraisal is the estimation and timing of *future* net cash flow.

It is not always easy to estimate how much a project will cost, how much cash it will earn over its lifetime, and the precise periods in which the cash will be received. As inflation and taxation changes cause particular difficulties, we will deal with each of them in some detail.

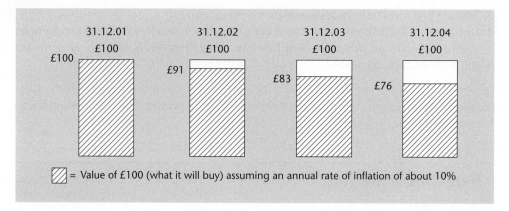

Figure 21.2 The impact of inflation

Inflation

As we have seen, NPV revolves round the concept that £1 receivable now is not the same as £1 receivable in 12 months' time. Cash that is in hand now can be invested. Assume that we have the choice between receiving (say) £0.90 now and £1 in 12 months' time. We may be prepared to accept £0.90 now if we can invest it for 12 months at a rate of interest of at least 10%. However, £1 receivable in 12 months' time may not be worth as much as £1 now because the purchasing power of the currency may fall. We need to allow for such changes in estimating future net cash flows, i.e. inflation (and *deflation*) should be taken into account.

In order to allow for changing prices, future net cash flows should be put on the same *price base* so that a fair comparison can be made between the cash received and paid in different time periods. In CI appraisal this can be done in one of two ways:

1 *Indexing.* Future net cash flows may be indexed. For example, assume that the net cash flow arising from a particular project will be £100 in Year 1, £150 in Year 2 and £200 in Year 3. The relevant current price index at the beginning of Year 1 is 100 but the index is expected to rise to an average level of 120 for Year 1, 140 for Year 2 and 175 for Year 3. In order to compare the net cash flows over the next three years more fairly, they need to be put on the same price base. If they are indexed, Year 1's net cash flow becomes £83 [(£100 × 100) ÷ 120]; Year 2's net cash flow becomes £107 [(£150 × 100) ÷ 140]; and Year 3's net cash flow becomes £114 [(£200 × 100) ÷ 175]. The adjusted future net cash flows of £83, £107 and £114 for Years 1, 2 and 3 respectively will then be incorporated into an NPV exercise and discounted at the entity's cost of capital.

2 *Adjusting the rate of return.* Instead of indexing, we could select a higher rate of return. The easiest approach would be to add the expected rate of inflation to the entity's cost of capital. Thus with inflation at a rate of 5% per annum and a required rate of return of 10%, £100 receivable in 12 months' time would be discounted at a rate of return of 15%, i.e. £86.96 [(£100 × 100) ÷ 115 or using discount tables £100 × 0.8696].

Taxation

Corporation tax is based on the *accounting profit* for the year. In order to calculate the amount of *tax payable* for the year, the accounting profit is adjusted for those items that are not allowable against tax, e.g. depreciation, as well as for some tax concessions that are not included in the calculation of accounting profit. Capital allowances, for example, are a tax allowance given when fixed assets are purchased. In essence, they are the equivalent of a depreciation allowance. Sometimes up to 100% capital allowances are given, so that the entire cost of purchase can be deducted from the profit in the year that a fixed asset was purchased. This means that in the year that a fixed asset is purchased, other things being equal, the amount of corporation tax will be low, although in subsequent years it can be expected to be higher.

Thus, in estimating future net cash flows, it is necessary to estimate what changes are likely to take place in the taxation system, what allowances will be available, what effect any changes will have on the amount of corporation tax payable, and in what periods tax will have to be paid. Needless to say, the forecasting of such events is enormously difficult!

Sources of finance

Once a decision has been taken to invest in a particular project, it is then necessary to search out a suitable method of financing it. There are a considerable number of available sources, although they vary depending upon what type of entity is involved. Central and local government, for example, are heavily dependent upon current tax receipts for financing capital investment projects, while charities rely on loans and grants. In this section, we will concentrate on the sources of finance available to limited liability companies.

The sources of finance available to companies depend upon the time period involved. For convenience, we will break our discussion down into (a) the short term; (b) the medium term; and (c) the long term. The various sources of finance are also shown in diagrammatic format in Figure 21.3.

Short-term finance

There are five major sources of short-term finance. They are as follows.

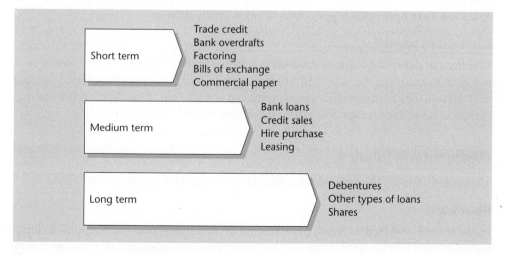

Figure 21.3 Sources of finance

Trade credit

Trade credit is a form of financing common in all companies (and all other entities). An entity purchases goods and services from suppliers and agrees to pay for them some days or weeks after they have been delivered. This method is so common that sometimes discounts are given for prompt payment. By delaying the payment of creditors, the entity's immediate cash needs are less strained and it may be able to finance projects that otherwise could not be considered. However, it is clearly only a temporary method of financing projects (particularly long-term ones). The entity is also highly vulnerable to pressure from its creditors. Note that this method often operates in tandem with a demand being made to debtors to settle their accounts promptly.

Bank overdrafts

Bank overdrafts are a form of loan where the bank's customer is allowed to draw out more from the bank than has been deposited. An entity's overdraft may have to be secured by a *floating charge*. This means that the bank has a general claim on any of the entity's assets if the entity cannot repay the overdraft. There is usually an upper limit, the amount overdrawn can usually be called in at any time, and the interest charge may be high. The main advantages of an overdraft are that it is flexible and that interest is normally only charged on the outstanding balance on a daily basis.

Factoring

Factoring relates to an entity's debtors. There are two types of factoring: recourse factoring, where an entity obtains a loan based on the amount of its debtor balances; and non-recourse factoring, where the debtor balances are sold to a factor and the factor then takes responsibility for dealing with them. Factoring is a convenient way of obtaining ready cash, but either the interest rate on the loan or the discount on the invoices may be high.

Bills of exchange

A bill of exchange is simply an invoice that has been endorsed (i.e. accepted) by a merchant bank. It can then be sold by the legal holder to obtain immediate finance. The interest charged depends upon the creditworthiness of the parties involved. Clearly, if an entity has a poor reputation, it will expect to pay more interest.

Commercial paper

Commercial paper is a form of short-term borrowing used by large listed companies. It is a bearer document, i.e. a person to whom the document is payable without naming that person. The minimum amount permitted is £100 000. This form of borrowing, therefore, is not appropriate for very many entities.

Medium-term finance

There are four types of medium-term finance that should be noted.

Bank loans

Banks may be prepared to loan a fixed amount to a customer over the medium- to long-term period. The loan may be secured on the company's assets and the interest charge may be variable. Regular repayments of both the capital and the interest will be expected. Bank loans are a common form of financing but the restrictions often placed on the borrower may be particularly demanding.

Credit sales

Credit sales are a form of borrowing in which the purchaser agrees to pay for goods (and services) provided on an instalment basis over an agreed period of time. Once the agreement has been signed, the legal ownership of the goods is passed to the purchaser and the seller cannot reclaim them. Sometimes, very generous terms can be arranged, e.g. no payment may be necessary for at least 12 months. It is possible, however, that the basic cost of the goods may be far higher than other suppliers are charging.

Hire purchase

Hire purchase (HP) is similar to credit sales except that the seller remains the legal owner of the goods until all payments due have been completed. An immediate deposit may be necessary, followed by a series of regular instalments. Once the goods have been paid for, the ownership passes to the purchaser. HP is usually an expensive method of financing the purchase of fixed assets.

Leasing

Leasing is a form of renting. A fixed asset (such as a car or a printing press) remains legally in the ownership of the lessor. In the case of some leases, the asset may never actually be returned. In effect, the lessee becomes the *de facto* owner. Leasing can be expensive, although if the lessor passes on what can sometimes be some very generous tax allowances. It can be a reasonably economic method of financing projects.

Long-term finance

Long-term finance can generally be obtained from the following three main sources.

Debentures

Debentures are formal long-term loans made to a company; they may be for a certain period or open-ended. Debentures are usually secured on all or some of an entity's assets. Interest is payable but because it is allowable against corporation tax, debentures can be an economic method of financing specific projects.

Other types of loans

Besides debentures, there are other types of loans. *Loan capital*, for example is a form of borrowing in which investors are paid a regular amount of interest and their capital is eventually repaid. The investors are creditors of the entity but they have no voting rights. *Unsecured loan stock* is similar to debenture stock except that there is no security for the loan. The interest rate tends to be higher than that on debenture stock because of the greater risk. *Convertible unsecured loan stock* gives stockholders the right to convert their stock into ordinary shares at specified dates. *Eurobond loan capital* can be obtained by borrowing overseas in the 'Euro' market. The loans are usually unsecured and they are redeemed at their face value on a certain date. Interest is normally paid annually. The rate depends partly on the size of the loan and partly on the particular issuer.

Shares

Expansion of the company could be financed by increasing the number of ordinary shares available, either on the open market or to existing shareholders in the form of a *rights issue*. An increase in an entity's ordinary share capital dilutes the holding of existing shareholders and all shareholders will expect to receive increasing amounts of dividend. Alternately, new or additional preference shares could be offered; preference shareholders would have an automatic right to a certain percentage level of dividend, and so the issue of preference shares limits the amount of dividend available to ordinary shareholders.

Activity 21.7

You are in a small business as (a) a sole trader; (b) a partnership; and (c) a limited liability company. You wish to purchase some new machinery costing £50 000.

In each case, which main form of financing the project would you prefer?

(a) ————————————————————————————————————

(b) ————————————————————————————————————

(c) ————————————————————————————————————

❗ Questions non-accountants should ask

Capital investment appraisal is a most important decision-making function. The selection of a particular project and the most appropriate means of financing it are difficult decisions to take. In both cases, as a senior manager, you will receive some expert advice. But, ultimately, the final decision will be one for you. As far as the financial data are concerned, what questions should you put before your accountants? We suggest that the following ones may provide a framework for some detailed questioning.

- What capital appraisal method have you used?
- Why did you select that one?
- What problems have you encountered in calculating the net cash flow (or estimated net profit)?
- What allowances have you made for (a) inflation; and (b) taxation?
- What rate of return have you used and why?
- What qualitative factors do you think should be taken into account?
- Are you able to put a monetary cost or value on them?

Conclusion

CI appraisal is a complex and time-consuming exercise. It is not possible to be totally accurate in determining the viability of individual projects but a reasoned comparison can be made between them.

Managers tend to be very enthusiastic about their own sphere of responsibility. Thus a marketing manager may be sure that additional sales will be possible, a production director may be certain that a new machine will pay for itself quickly, and the data processing manager may be convinced that a new high-powered computer is essential.

In helping management to choose between such competing projects, the accountant's role is to try to assess their costs and to compare them with the possible benefits. Once a choice has been made, he then has to ensure that the necessary finance will be available for them. CI appraisal should not be used as a means of blocking new projects. It is no different from all the other accounting techniques. It is meant to provide additional guidance to management and, ultimately, it is the responsibility of management to ensure that other factors are taken into account.

Key points

1 Capital investment appraisal forms part of the budgeting process.
2 There are five main methods of determining the viability of a project:
   (a) payback;
   (b) discounted payback;
   (c) accounting rate of return;
   (d) net present value;
   (e) internal rate of return.
3 All the methods listed in item 2 above have their advantages and disadvantages, but the recommended methods are discounted payback and net present value.
4 Capital expenditure may be financed by a variety of sources. Sources of short-term finance for entities include trade credit, bank overdrafts, factoring, bills of exchange and commercial paper. Medium-term sources include bank loans, credit sales, hire purchase and leasing. Long-term sources include debentures and other types of loans, and share issues.

Check your learning

The answers to these questions may be found within the text.

1   What is the distinction between capital and revenue expenditure?
2   List five characteristics associated with capital expenditure.
3   What is net cash flow?

4   What is the payback method of capital investment appraisal?

5   What information is needed to adopt it?

6   List four disadvantages of the payback method.

7   What is the discounted payback method of capital investment appraisal?

8   What is discounting?

9   Upon what does a discount factor depend?

10   List four advantages and four disadvantages of the discounted payback method.

11   What is the accounting rate of return method of capital investment appraisal?

12   What formula should be used in adopting it?

13   In that context how should (a) the numerator; and (b) the denominator be determined?

14   List three advantages and three disadvantages of the accounting rate of return method.

15   What is the net present value method of capital investment appraisal?

16   Outline seven steps needed to adopt it.

17   List three advantages and three disadvantages of the method.

18   What is the internal rate of return method of capital investment appraisal?

19   What is its basic objective?

20   What formula is used to determine the required rate of return?

21   List three advantages and three disadvantages of the method.

22   How may (a) inflation; and (b) taxation be allowed for in capital investment appraisal?

23   List three main sources of (a) short-term finance; (b) medium-term finance; and (c) long-term finance.

News story quiz

Remember the news story at the beginning of this chapter? Go back to that story and re-read it before answering the following questions.

At a particularly difficult time for the hotel industry, the Hilton Group has decided to cut back on its capital expenditure programme.

Questions

1   What impact is Hilton's decision likely to have on the company's ability to attract more customers in the future?

2 Apart from 'seeing little sign of an upturn in trading conditions' for next year, what other reasons might there be for pegging back its capital expenditure programme?

3 How might the company be proposing to finance the £130m of capital expenditure that it intends to spend?

4 In the conditions described, how difficult might it be to carry out the traditional forms of capital expenditure appraisal as described in this chapter?

Tutorial questions

The answers to questions marked with an asterisk may be found in Appendix 4.

21.1 'In capital expenditure appraisal, management cannot cope with any technique that is more advanced than payback.' How far do you think that this assertion is likely to be true?

21.2 'All capital expenditure techniques are irrelevant because (a) they cannot estimate accurately future cash flows, and (b) it is difficult to select an appropriate discount rate.' Discuss.

21.3 Do any of the traditional capital investment appraisal techniques help in determining social and welfare capital expenditure proposals?

21.4 'We can all dream up new capital expenditure proposals', asserted the Managing Director, 'but where is the money coming from?' How might the proposals be financed?

21.5* Buchan Enterprises is considering investing in a new machine. The machine will be purchased on 1 January in Year 1 at a cost of £50 000. It is estimated that it would last for 5 years, and it will then be sold at the end of the year for £2000 in cash. The respective net cash flows estimated to be received by the company as a result of purchasing the machine during each year of its life are as follows:

Year	£	
1	8 000	(excluding the initial cost)
2	16 000	
3	40 000	
4	45 000	
5	35 000	(exclusive of the project's sale proceeds)

The company's cost of capital is 12%.

Required:
Calculate (a) the payback period for the project; and (b) its discounted payback period.

21.6* Lender Limited is considering investing in a new project. It is estimated that it will cost £100 000 to implement, and that the expected net profit after tax will be as follows:

Year	£
1	18 000
2	47 000
3	65 000
4	65 000
5	30 000

No residual value is expected.

Required:
Calculate the accounting rate of return of the proposed project.

21.7* The following net cash flows relate to Lockhart Limited in connection with a certain project that has an initial cost of £2 500 000:

Year	Net cash flow £000	
1	800	(excluding the initial cost)
2	850	
3	830	
4	1 200	
5	700	

The company's required rate of return is 15%.

Required:
Calculate the net present value of the project.

21.8 Moffat District Council has calculated the following net cash flows for a proposed project costing £1 450 000:

Year	Net cash flow £000	
1	230	(excluding the initial cost)
2	370	
3	600	
4	420	
5	110	

Required:
Calculate the internal rate of return generated by the project.

21.9 Prospect Limited is considering investing in some new plant. The plant would cost £1 000 000 to implement. It would last five years and it would then be sold for £50 000. The relevant profit and loss accounts for each year during the life of the project are as follows:

Year to 31 March	1	2	3	4	5
	£000	£000	£000	£000	£000
Sales	2 000	2 400	2 800	2 900	2 000
Less: Cost of goods sold					
Opening stock	–	200	300	550	350
Purchases	1 600	1 790	2 220	1 960	1 110
	1 600	1 990	2 520	2 510	1 460
Less: Closing stock	200	300	550	350	50
	1 400	1 690	1 970	2 160	1 410
Gross profit	600	710	830	740	590
Less: Expenses	210	220	240	250	300
Depreciation	190	190	190	190	190
	400	410	430	440	490
Net profit	200	300	400	300	100
Taxation	40	70	100	100	10
Retained profits	160	230	300	200	90

Additional information:
1   All sales are made and all purchases are obtained on credit terms.
2   Outstanding trade debtors and trade creditors at the end of each year are expected to be as follows:

Year	Trade debtors	Trade creditors
	£000	£000
1	200	250
2	240	270
3	300	330
4	320	300
5	400	150

3   Expenses would all be paid in cash during each year in question.
4   Taxation would be paid on 1 January following each year end.
5   Half the plant would be paid for in cash on 1 April Year 0, and the remaining half (also in cash) on 1 January Year 1. The resale value of £50 000 will be received in cash on 31 March Year 6.

Required:
Calculate the annual net cash flow arising from the purchase of this new plant.

21.10 Nicol Limited is considering investing in a new machine. The machine would cost £500 000. It would have a life of five years and a nil residual value. The company uses the straight-line method of depreciation.

It is expected that the machine will earn the following extra profits for the company during its expected life:

Year	Profits
	£000
1	200
2	120
3	120
4	100
5	60

The above profits also represent the extra net cash flows expected to be generated by the machine (i.e. they exclude the machine's initial cost and the annual depreciation charge). The company's cost of capital is 18%.

Required:
(a) Calculate:
    (i) the machine's payback period; and
    (ii) its net present value.
(b) Advise management as to whether the new machine should be purchased.

21.11 Hewie Limited has some capital available for investment and is considering two projects, only one of which can be financed. The details are as follows:

	Project	
	(1)	*(2)*
Expected life (years)	4	3
	£000	£000
Initial cost	600	500
Expected net cash flows (excluding the initial cost)		
Year		
1	10	250
2	200	250
3	400	50
4	50	–
Residual value	Nil	Nil

Required:
Advise management on which project to accept.

21.12 Marsh Limited has investigated the possibility of investing in a new machine. The following data have been extracted from the report relating to the project:

Cost of machine on 1 January Year 6: £500 000.
Life: 4 years to 31 December Year 9.
Estimated scrap value: Nil.
Depreciation method: Straight-line.

Year	Accounting profit after tax	Net cash flows	
	£000	£000	
6	100	50	(excluding the initial cost)
7	250	200	
8	250	225	
9	200	225	
10	–	100	

The company's required rate of return is 15%.

Required:

Calculate the return the machine would make using the following investment appraisal methods:

1 payback;
2 accounting rate of return;
3 net present value; and
4 internal rate of return.

Further practice questions, study material and links to relevant sites on the World Wide Web can be found on the website that accompanies this book. The site can be found at **www.booksites.net/dyson**

A glowing tribute for management accounting . . .

Uplifting growth for on-line underwear company

Internet lingerie retailer Figleaves. com is expanding its management accounting function in recognition of the key contribution it made to the firm's first break-even result.

In December 2002 the company reported break-even at EBITDA on net sales of £1 million. This compares with Amazon.com's break-even on turnover of £550 million in September 2002.

"We are in rarefied territory for dotcoms," said Figleaves.com's finance director, Howard Bryant ACMA. "The management accounting team is crucial to that success, continually adding value to the business. The unique role of man-

agement accountants, experts in everything from investment to general management, makes them ideal for a smaller firm such as Figleaves."

Over the past year the management accounting team has been involved in projects including the introduction of a scorecard design covering key metrics and interrelationships for discussion at company meetings; the development of budget and forecast control mechanisms; and the integration of rolling sales forecasts with inventory capacity planning.

Financial Management, March 2003.

Questions relating to this news story may be found on page 527 ▶▶

About this chapter

In this chapter, the last in the book, we deal with some emerging issues in management accounting. The basic management accounting techniques have hardly changed in over 100 years and although some new ones were introduced as the twentieth century progressed, there were few changes until about 1980. Since that time management accounting practices have begun to be reviewed and reconsidered as a result of major developments in the commercial and industrial world.

This chapter explores some of the changes that have taken place in the business environment towards the end of the twentieth century and the impact that such changes are beginning to have on management accounting practice. We then review some of the ideas that have emerged for bringing management accounting up to date to meet the requirements of business in the twenty-first century.

The chapter is divided into 13 main sections. The first main section explains why the chapter is important for non-accountants. We follow this with an exploration of the changes that have taken place in the business environment in the second half of the twentieth century and the beginning of the twenty-first century. The impact of such changes on management accounting practice is then reviewed. The next nine sections introduce you to some of the newer management accounting techniques that are perhaps going to be of increasing relevance in the new business environment, viz. activity based management, better budgeting, environmental accounting and reporting, performance measurement, product life cycle costing, social accounting and reporting, strategic management accounting, target costing, and value chain analysis. The last main section suggests some questions that non-accountants might like to ask about the contents of the chapter.

Learning objectives

By the end of this chapter you should be able to:

- **review the changes in the business environment during the last 25 years;**
- **explain why changes in the commercial and industrial environment have affected traditional management accounting practice;**
- **consider the usefulness of a number of emerging developments in management accounting, such as activity based management, better budgeting, environmental accounting and reporting, performance measurement, product life cycle costing, social accounting and reporting, strategic management accounting, target costing, and value chain analysis.**

❗ Why this chapter is important for non-accountants

This chapter is important for non-accountants for the following reasons.

1 You will be able to judge the value of any management accounting information presented to you if you have some knowledge of its historical development.
2 You will be able to contribute to any debate that involves examining whether traditional management accounting practices have a place in the new business environment.
3 You will be able to question your accountants on the proposals that they may have for introducing new management accounting techniques into your own entity.
4 You will be able to determine whether the management accounting function could be reorganized in order to provide a better service to management.

The business environment

The Second World War (1939 to 1945) had a profound effect on the financial, economic, political and social life of the United Kingdom. The country had to be rebuilt. A great deal of damage had been done to the infrastructure, there had been a lack of investment in its traditional industries, and the UK found it difficult to compete with the emerging countries in overseas' markets. Many of these countries had a large labour force and the UK found that they could offer their goods much more cheaply than it could. Furthermore, as they were able to create entirely new businesses it was much easier to introduce new ways of doing things into them. By contrast, the UK had an industrial base rooted in the nineteenth century with a backward looking rather than a forward looking approach to business.

The main country that heralded the new business era was Japan. Prior to the Second World War, Japan had been a relatively unknown and somewhat backward country. The impact of the war required it to be almost completely rebuilt and modernized without having the benefit of many indigenous raw materials. Japan's leaders realized that the country could only survive if it sold high-quality low-cost products to the rest of the world. It had to start from an almost zero industrial base, but progress was helped by the close family traditions of Japanese culture and society. It took some time but eventually Japan was able to introduce the most modern practices into its industrial life.

These practices enabled the Japanese to be flexible in offering high-quality and reliable competitive products to its customers and to make sure that they were delivered on time. A detailed discussion of the managerial philosophy and various production techniques used by the Japanese is beyond this book, but you should note the following developments pioneered in Japan:

1 *Advanced manufacturing technology (AMT)*. AMT production incorporates highly automated and highly computerized methods of design and operation. It enables machines to be easily and cheaply adapted for short production runs, thereby enabling the specific requirements of individuals to be met.

2 *Just-in-time (JIT) production*. Traditional plant and machinery was often time-consuming and expensive to convert if it needed to be switched from one product to another; once the plant and machinery was set up, therefore, long production runs were the norm. This meant that goods were often manufactured for stock (resulting in heavy storage and finance costs). By contrast, AMT (see item 1) leads to an overall JIT philosophy in which an attempt is made to manufacture goods only when they have been specifically ordered by a customer. The JIT approach has implications for management accountants. As goods are only manufactured when ordered, raw materials and components are similarly purchased only when they are required for a particular order. Hence no stock pricing problem arises and stock control becomes less of an issue since stock levels will, by definition, be kept to a minimum.

3 *Total quality management (TQM)*. Another approach that the Japanese have incorporated into their production methods is TQM. The basic concept of TQM reflects two concepts:

(a) *Getting it right the first time*. Whatever task is being undertaken, it should be done correctly the first time that it is attempted. This means that there should then be savings on internal failure costs, e.g. no wastage, reworking, re-inspections, downgrading or discounted prices. There will also be savings on external costs, such as repairs, handling, legal expenses, lost sales and warranties. There could, however, be additional preventive costs – for example, planning, training and operating the system – as well as appraisal costs, such as administration, audit and inspection.

(b) *The quality of the output should reflect its specification*. In this context, the concept of 'quality' should not be confused with the feeling of 'luxury'. A small mass-produced car, for example, may be regarded as a quality product (because its performance meets its specification) in exactly the same way that we equate a luxury car (such as a Rolls-Royce) with quality.

> Do you think that a just-in-time production system avoids the type of materials pricing problem discussed in Chapter 15? List in your notebook the reasons why (a) it may do; and (b) why it may not.

Activity 22.1

The industrial changes that had taken place in Japan were observed by other countries (especially the United States) and the new developments have now been widely adopted in many countries, including the UK. They tend to be found, however, in large international companies rather than small domestic ones in a wide range of industries. TQM, for example, is an approach that can be adopted by all types of entities.

Other changes that have taken place since the end of the Second World War are more general. Among them are the following developments.

1 *Decline of manufacturing industry.* Traditional extractive and heavy manufacturing industries (such as coal mining, iron and steel, shipbuilding and indigenous car manufacturing) is now much less important, and in some cases non-existent. Those manufacturing industries that do still exist are much less labour-intensive than they used to be and labour costs themselves can no longer be regarded as a variable cost.

2 *Growth of service industries.* There has been a growth of service industries such as finance services, entertainment, information supply and tourism. Service industries do not generally employ the thousands of employees that manufacturing industries used to employ. The service sector now forms a major part of the economy of the UK.

3 *Organization change.* Another noticeable development that has taken place in recent years in both the profit-making and not-for-profit sectors is the move to *outsourcing* or *privatization*. This means that entities now concentrate to a considerable extent on developing their core activities. Everything else is bought in and supplied outside the entity. For example, firms that build bathrooms and kitchens will subcontract electricians, joiners and plumbers to do the basic work on an order-by-order basis. Similarly, an industrial company may employ an outside organization to look after its payroll.

4 *Automation and computerization.* Production processes and the administrative back-up is now intensively automated and computerized. Indeed, the impact of computerization has been phenomenal. Most employees will now have a personal computer on their desk and this means that they have ready access to a vast internal and external data bank. In turn, this means that if they need (say) a report on a particular issue they can print it out immediately. Thus they no longer need to wait for the accountants to prepare the report for them.

Changes in management accounting

The changes that have taken (and are still taking) place in business life in recent years have also begun to have an effect on management practices. However, as we commented in Chapter 14, during the period 1920 to 1980 management accounting changed very little and there were very few new developments. Since 1980 the pace has changed and some entities have incorporated new ideas into their reporting procedures. Such changes have been largely in medium- and large-scale industrial entities. The pace has been much less obvious in smaller service-based and not-for-profit entities.

We should not expect, therefore, a *revolution* to take place in management accounting. We can expect a very slow *evolution* and it might take at least 20 years before nineteenth-century management accounting practices become much less common.

What changes can we expect? Although the pace will be slow, we suggest that management accounting is likely to be affected as follows:

- The collection, recording, extraction and summary of data for information purposes will be performed electronically. This function will no longer be serviced by a large army of management accountants.
- As JIT procedures become dominant, stock control, materials pricing and stock valuation will become relatively insignificant tasks.
- Product costing involving the use of more sophisticated overhead absorption techniques will still be important. However, it will become a relatively routine task as the data will be processed by computer.
- Budgeting and budgetary control procedures will also become much more computerized. They will also be capable of being subject to a variety of different possible outcomes.
- Standard costing is likely to become less significant in a TQM environment. If it survives, it will be possible to produce different standard costs for a variety of different outcomes.
- The management accountant for an entity will become more of a general manager specializing in the financial implications of decision making, and he or she will use a wide variety of internal and external data.
- The management accountant will need to be able to develop and incorporate new techniques in order to cope with a commercial and industrial world that will be subject to rapid change.

It follows that if the above changes take place, as a non-accountant working in the future in a large organization, you are likely to meet a very different type of management accountant from the one that you are familiar with today. Tomorrow's management accountant will be much more of a team player, less bound to arithmetical recording of past events and more involved in taking highly informed decisions about future events.

Activity 22.2   By this stage of the book you should have a good knowledge of the purpose of management accounting and the techniques used. List in your notebook three changes that you would like to see incorporated into management accounting practice.

Taking into account the changing business environment and the need for management accounting to adapt to such changes, which of the newer *techniques* can we see management accountants developing over the next few years? We review some of the possibilities in the next nine sections. It is important to recognize, however, that none of them are entirely new techniques. Indeed, some of them have featured in the management accounting literature for many years. But we predict that for some of them their time has come.

Activity based management

Activity based management (ABM) is sometimes referred to as activity based cost management (ABCM).

You will recall that in Chapter 16 we introduced you to the topic of activity based costing (ABC). ABC deals with overheads. We will first review the technique before we explain how it may be adapted for widespread use.

ABC is a management accounting technique developed in the 1980s as a way of absorbing overheads into product costs. The traditional method is to collect indirect costs in appropriate costs centres, apportion those costs among the production cost centres, and then divide the total indirect costs in each production cost centre by some measure of activity. Usually, this is either on the basis of direct labour hours or machine hours. Products are then charged with a share of overheads based on how much time they spend in the respective production cost centres. This method tends either to under-cost some products or to over-cost other ones because it does not capture the impact that they have on product costs. It also does not deal adequately (if at all) with non-production overheads.

ABC is thought to charge more fairly *all* overhead costs to products that cause them to arise in the first place. A six-stage process is involved. It is as follows:

1 Identify those activities that cause costs to be incurred.
2 Attach them to common cost pools.
3 Trace the main cause of each activity, i.e. the driver that causes those costs in each pool to be incurred.
4 Calculate the cost driver rate by dividing the cost pool costs by the driver.
5 Multiply the cost driver rate by the number of times the product uses the activity.
6 Charge the cost for each activity to the product.

ABM takes the concept of ABC a little further. It is argued that all costs are caused by *activities*. By identifying the activities and the factors that drive them it is much easier to control an entity's costs. The traditional method of controlling costs is to organize the entity into cost centres, put a manager in charge of each cost centre, allocate the cost of operating that cost centre to him, and then require him to control his cost centre costs. It is argued that this method does not work because it fails to recognize what *causes* costs to be incurred.

The causes arise from *activities* and not from the cost centres themselves. Thus if you control the activities, you control the costs. This argument is very similar to that used by proponents of ABC. The major difference is that ABM deals with *all* costs whereas ABC is only concerned with overheads. How does ABM work? Basically, it is a four-stage process. In summary it is as follows:

1 Identify the various *activities* that take place throughout the entity.
2 Collect the costs in separate activity cost pools.
3 Trace the main cause of each activity's cost, i.e. identify the cost driver.
4 Divide the total cost in each cost pool by the cost driver and do the same for each element of cost.

Managers then know how much each activity costs to deliver and how much is incurred on each element of cost.

The recognition of 'activities' is obviously the key to achieving an effective ABM system. So in order to explain what is meant by an 'activity' we will use the example of *purchasing*. Traditionally, a company would have a separate purchasing department. Its main costs would be salaries and wages, IT support, telephone costs, travel and stationery. However, purchasing may involve using the services of many other departments, such as accounting, credit control, customer care, finance and the legal department. As a result, some of the purchasing function costs are hidden in other departments' costs. An ABM approach would attempt to trace the total cost of operating the purchasing function, no matter where the various activities took place. This then means that a more accurate cost for purchasing can be established.

The same procedure can be applied to other activities. If it is, then the entity becomes aware of the *real* cost of its various activities and steps can be taken to control them. Managers can ask questions such as, '*What makes up this cost?*' '*Is the activity necessary?*' '*Can it be done a different way?*' and '*Can it be obtained more cheaply by buying it in?*'

The benefits of ABM are such that by tracing costs to activities, activities can be better managed (or even eliminated), accurate product costs are established, and more realistic selling prices can be determined.

Of course, like all other techniques there are problems involved in operating an ABM system. The most obvious one is that it is difficult to isolate a manageable number of activities across a complex and large organization. The method also cuts across traditional department and management lines, and staff can become confused because they do not know to whom they are responsible.

There is no reason these days, however, for not organizing an entity on traditional functional lines and, by using information technology, to collect and to report costs on an activity basis.

Activity 22.3	What do you think the reaction of the staff would be if a company switched from being organized on departmental lines to being based on activities where staff worked in multidisciplinary teams? List in your notebook the likely reactions.

Better budgeting

We discussed the practice of budgeting in Chapter 17. A traditional budgeting system normally requires budgets to be prepared for a calendar year in order to fit in with the annual financial reporting system, although it may be broken down into sub-budget periods. This method takes a great deal of time and it tends to be backward looking. It is not now considered an effective method of controlling costs.

There have been various changes suggested that can be accommodated, largely as a result of developments in IT. We summarize the suggested changes below.

1 The budgeting process should be divorced from the annual financial reports procedure.
2 Budget periods should be shorter.

3 Budgets should be prepared on a rolling basis, i.e. drop the last month's budget and add the following one at the end of the current period.

4 There should be less emphasis on what has happened in the past and a greater concentration on what should happen in the future.

5 There should be less detail.

6 Budgets should incorporate external data about the entity's competitors and the market in general.

7 Non-financial performance measures should be incorporated into reports for managers.

8 Managers should be responsible for preparing their budgets and accountable for them (this has always supposed to be the case).

9 There should be a reward system for all staff when a department meets the objective laid down for it.

Identify one crucial factor that in your view makes the entire traditional budgeting process ineffective in controlling the costs and revenues of an entity. Enter your selection below.

Activity 22.4

Factor: _____

Reasons: _____

Environmental accounting and reporting

Environmental accounting and reporting may be defined as follows.

> *The collection, recording, classification, extraction, and summary of information relating to the natural environment, and the reporting of it to specified users of such information.*

Environmental accounting is closely connected to social accounting and reporting. We deal with social matters later in this chapter. Environment matters relate to the natural environment and social matters to society generally.

In recent years a great many people throughout the world have become increasingly worried about the replenishment of natural resources sufficient to be available to cope with the growth in the world's population. Modern society consumes vast amounts of raw materials. Some of these are irreplaceable (e.g. minerals) while other resources take a long term to grow (e.g. timber). The way we live also damages the environment: we despoil the land and pollute the air, the rivers and the sea. This use and misuse of the world's resources is likely to intensify. This is because as more countries become wealthy, they tend to make greater demands on the world's natural resources.

Such concerns have shown themselves in the growth of a number of pressure groups that advocate a halt, or at least a pause, on consumption. The issue is one that causes great concern (especially among young people) and pressure has been brought to bear on those entities and those individuals who appear to be the major perpetrators of the misuse of natural resources.

This movement has not gone unnoticed in accounting circles and a number of professional accountancy bodies have begun to take an interest in the subject. They have, for example, set up working parties and published various documents and reports. There now appears to be a strong belief among many accountants that entities ought to report on the impact that they have on the environment. For example, it is argued that they should report on the balance they achieve between the benefits that their operations provide to society and the costs of doing so. The benefits include the provision of jobs and the contribution that they make towards the growth of the economy. The costs include their consumption of finite resources, and the pollution that they may cause to the air, land, rivers and the sea.

You will appreciate that an exercise involving the compilation of environmental benefits and costs and the reporting of them is one that should suit the accountancy profession admirably. However, such benefits and costs are difficult to collect, quantify and translate into monetary terms, so they do take accountants into unfamiliar territory. Indeed, until recently accountants would not have ventured into such territory because they are bound by the traditional accounting rules that we outlined in Chapter 2.

Environmental accounting and reporting is a relatively new development and as yet there are no statutory or professional requirements. Thus there is little guidance on what data to collect, how it should be stored, extracted, summarized and reported, and in what form. Some companies, however, are beginning to include environmental matters in their annual report and accounts. For example, Devro plc (a provider of casings for the food industry) has a one-page statement about environmental matters in its 2001 Annual Report and Accounts (see Figure 22.1). It covers such items as energy, effluent, spillage control and waste.

Some companies are now publishing an environment report separate from the annual report and accounts. One such company is Cairn Energy plc. Its *Environmental and Social Review* for 2001 (with a sub-heading 'A Measure of Our Success') is 14 pages long. It reports on the following matters under the heading of 'Our environmental performance':

1 Emissions to air.
2 Energy consumption.
3 Waste generation and effluent disposal.
4 Prevention of pollution.
5 Regulatory compliance.

Much of the report is narrative, it is printed in several colours, and there are some photographs, charts and tables. There are some statistics but they are not translated into financial terms. Overall, it is a readable document even if it is somewhat self-congratulatory in tone.

As far as management accounting is concerned, we can expect to see management accountants in future giving much greater attention to environmental benefits and costs in reports that they present to management, e.g. in strategic planning and in capital investment appraisal. Potential projects will be subject to a critical examination for the impact that they may have on the environment, and they will be subject to a searching audit. However, as with Cairn Energy, it is likely that there will be more emphasis on reporting environmental matters in operational terms and less on their financial impact.

As more companies publish environmental reports, it is possible that the ASB or the IASB will need to issue an accounting standard on the subject. This will not be easy because accounting standards have to suit a general audience while environmental issues

Environmental report

The group has always recognised that environmental protection is of fundamental importance to a successful and responsible business strategy. We take pride in our business activities and are committed to minimising our environmental impact in the countries in which we operate and the communities we serve.

The diverse range of group operations around the world is subject to a variety of regulatory regimes and cultures. As a consequence, environmental issues are dealt with through a network of specialists operating within the business units. To ensure consistency of approach, all group companies operate within an agreed corporate framework which promotes exchange of information and best practice.

It is a group objective that none of its products, processes or operations shall pose any threat to the environment. Commitment to this objective is highlighted in the Safety and Environmental Policy, which complements the Company Philosophy. Recognising that teamwork and co-operation are key to success, training arrangements are in place to raise employee awareness of environmental issues and level of support for future initiatives.

Environmental update
During the course of this year, the collagen operating plants have made significant improvements to their processes with the aim of reducing the impact to the environment. Some of the key projects are summarised below:

- **Energy**
  Last year the UK government imposed a climate change levy to provide manufacturing businesses with an incentive to reduce the amount of energy consumed, through the adoption of more energy efficient practices. Companies who achieve a series of agreed energy reduction milestones receive an 80% discount on the levy. The Scottish operations are on target to meet these milestones. This year's contribution has been achieved by improving of the gas-fired boilers, the introduction of high-intensity, low-energy lighting and upgrading insulation on drier ducting.

- **Effluent**
  A new process had been introduced into our Australian facility to treat and recycle our waste water. This is reducing both the load on the effluent treatment plant and the volume of effluent discharged.

Key parts of our process require to be operated under conditions of very low pressure. The vacuum systems which are used to achieve these low pressures use considerable volumes of water as sealants. Modifications were carried out in 2001 to improve the operation of our vacuum system. These modifications now allow us to recycle a considerable proportion of this water, thus, again reducing the volume of effluent discharged.

- **Spillage control**
  In our Czech plants we have completed a number of installations to improve the storage and handling of fuel oils and chemicals. The new facilities are designed to contain and control spillages until they can be dealt with in an appropriate manner.

- **Waste**
  At several stages of our operation, filtration processes are applied to a variety of collagen streams. These filtration processes generate considerable quantities of solid collagen waste. Significant investment in new filtration systems in our Scottish and Australian manufacturing facilities has allowed us to reduce the quantity of solid matter being discharged as waste.

  The US facility has invested in training and process control which is resulting in the improved recovery of a major raw material and a reduction in the amount of waste.

- **Accreditation**
  The Scottish plants were awarded higher level accreditation to the European Food Safety Inspection Service during last year and although the principal focus is food safety, it also encompasses several areas covering environmental responsibility.

The group has demonstrated compliance with regulations, permits and consent limits in its various activities. However, with a philosophy of continuous improvement in all areas of the business, improved environmental performance is expected.

Environmental issues will continue to be a high priority within the group.

Figure 22.1 An environmental report

Source: Devro plc, *Annual Report and Accounts 2001*.

tend to be specific to individual entities. An alternative would be for a SORP (Statement of Recommended Practice) to be formulated. SORPs offer guidance on specific accounting matters that may be of particular interest to a specific industry. They do not carry any mandatory status.

| Activity 22.5 | Do you think that environmental matters should be included in an entity's management accounting systems? Complete the questionnaire below. |

(a) Environmental costs and revenues can be recognized:	*Yes/No*
(b) They can be easily quantified:	*Yes/No*
(c) It is possible to put a monetary value on them:	*Yes/No*
(d) Non-financial measures only should be used:	*Yes/No*

Performance measurement

Performance measurement may be defined as a means of assessing whether an entity is managing to achieve its objectives using both financial and non-financial indicators.

Both financial accounting and management accounting have traditionally concentrated on collecting and reporting on *financial* information. Thus data that could not be quantified and valued in monetary terms were usually ignored and hence not reported either to shareholders or managers. This meant that an exercise involving the interpretation of accounts was also largely confined to financial data.

This rather narrow approach to reporting the performance of an entity is now beginning to change. There are a number of reasons why this is happening. They may be summarized as follows:

- Users are now much more aware that financial information is narrow in scope.
- They are also aware that it is compiled on the basis of a number of arguable assumptions, assertions and estimates.
- It is largely based on past performance.
- It does not take into account other aspects of the entity's activities.
- It does not provide the information managers need for decision making and control.

As a result of the above factors there is now gradual development towards widening the type of reports submitted to managers. Their main features are as follows:

1 The incorporation of a wide range of statistics and ratios ('metrics') to cover all aspects of the organization.
2 The adoption of non-financial data.
3 The inclusion of metrics relating to the entity's market competitors.

Point 3 is a form of what is called *benchmarking*. Benchmarking is a technical term meaning the collection of data in order to establish targets so that comparisons can be made between different segments and entities.

We will illustrate the above points using the Weir Group's 'Statement of Purpose' printed in its 2001 Annual Report and Accounts (p. 1). This may not be quite the same as a 'Statement of Objectives' because it is written in very general terms, but it will do for our purposes. It reads as follows:

> We work together to create engineering solutions which help our customers deliver processes vital to society.
>
> We achieve this by
> - operating as a global family
> - exceeding our customer expectations
> - helping our people fulfil their potential
> - leading the industry
> - delivering sustainable value for shareholders.

Performance measures could be used to test whether the company has achieved what it wants to do, as set out in its 'Statement of Purpose'. Presumably if the company has sold its services, it is helping its customers. We could, therefore, use profitability ratios to see whether the company has achieved this aim. It might be more difficult to test whether its customers deliver 'processes vital to society' but, again, if its customers sell its goods, it is possible that society considers them vital.

However, the way that it sets out to achieve its purpose is more difficult to assess:

1 What is a 'global family' and how do you test it?
2 How do you test whether you have exceeded 'customer expectations'?
3 How do you test whether you have helped 'our people fulfil their potential'?
4 How do you know that you lead the industry?
5 How do you measure whether you have delivered 'sustainable value' to your shareholders?

Item 1 appears difficult to test using any form of indicator. It might be possible to use non-financial performance indicators to test items 2, 3 and 4. Item 5 possibly lends itself to a financial performance indicator because the company is probably referring to its dividend policy.

You will see from the above just how important it is to set clear, testable objectives if you then want to know whether your entity has achieved them. Furthermore, you will need to use non-financial indicators as well as financial ones.

We can be reasonably specific about what financial indicators to use. They include all the various types of accounting ratios we examined in Chapter 12, such as return on capital employed, gross and net profit ratios, stock turnover and trade debtor collection periods. Some of these may need adapting for internal purposes. For example, return on capital employed may be converted to a 'return on investment' ratio (ROI). ROI measures the profit a segment of the business has made against the investment made in the segment. Another way of assessing segmental performance is to calculate what is called the *residual income* (RI). RI involves charging a notional amount for interest to the profit and loss account based on the investment in the segment. The assumption here is that without the investment in the segment the company could have invested the money in some other project that would have made it a profit or a return on what it had invested.

By their very nature it is much more difficult to generalize about non-financial performance measures. This is because they relate more to a particular industry and especially to individual entities within it. They could be used to test the *competitiveness* of an entity (e.g. its market share and sales growth), its *flexibility* (e.g. order size and delivery), the *quality* of the goods or service provided (e.g. the appearance of the goods or the courtesy and reliability of the service), and how well it uses its manufacturing *utilization* (e.g. its efficiency and productivity).

Such determinants would require various indicators to be attached to them. For example, a metric for market share would probably be expressed as a percentage, a metric for flexibility could be the machine set-up time, a measure of quality could be the number of customer complaints received, and manufacturing utilization could be assessed by calculating the number of rejected units.

It follows that an enormous number of various types of performance measures could be calculated. It would be important not to overload managers, so they should only be supplied with those that are useful to them. However, it is equally important that a balanced view of the entity's overall performance is also presented.

Two American academics (Kaplan and Norton) have become well known for their work in this context. They have promoted the idea of a *balanced scorecard*. The idea is that an entity should set itself some objectives, work out a strategy for achieving those objectives, and then specify the tactics required to do so. Kaplan and Norton's model has four perspectives. These are as follows:

1 *Financial perspective*: how do we look to shareholders?
2 *Internal business perspective*: what must we excel at?
3 *Innovation learning perspective*: can we continue to improve value?
4 *Customer perspective*: how do customers see us?

Objectives (or goals, as they call them) would be set for each perspective and then the actual performance of the entity would be measured against how successful the entity had been at meeting them. You will find that this description is very similar to the definition of performance measurement that we gave at the beginning of this section: *a means of assessing whether an entity is managing to achieve its objectives using both financial and non-financial indicators.*

Activity 22.6	'Financial performance measures are too misleading for managerial decision making. They should be replaced with non-financial measures.' Do you agree with this statement?

Agree ☐   Disagree ☐

What approach would you support?

Financial performance measures only ☐   Non-financial performance measure only ☐

A combination of the two ☐

Reasons: _____

_____

_____

Product life cycle costing

Product *life cycle costing* is a relatively new form of management accounting. The idea is to capture the total costs and revenues of a product over its entire lifetime. Indeed, the system is sometimes referred to as *'cradle to grave' costing*, albeit strictly speaking some costs may arise even before the cradle stage! Although life cycle costing is practised by many large companies (especially vehicle manufacturers), it still needs considerable development before it becomes more commonly used.

The lifetime of some products may range from just a few week or months (e.g. designer clothes) while others may last several generations (e.g. an aircraft). Irrespective of their lifespan, however, most products go through several stages. The main ones can be summarized as follows:

1 *Design.* This stage includes the period during which an idea for a new product is conceived, worked on, planned, designed and developed.
2 *Prototype.* At this stage a trial product has been produced and it is being tested.
3 *Development.* After assessing the test results, the product is further refined and prepared for going into production.
4 *Manufacturing.* The product is now in production. Depending upon the type of product, it may well continue to be manufactured for very many years.
5 *Disposal.* Eventually, the demand for the product declines to such an extent that it is taken out of production. There may then be a cost of disposing of it and of its production facilities (such as oil rigs and nuclear power plants).

Product cycle costing was developed by the American defence industry during the early 1960s. It was realized that traditional costing methods could be somewhat misleading when the profitability of various projects were being assessed. Traditional accounting methods would require design, prototype, development and disposal costs to be written off in the period in which they were incurred. The main interest would focus on the control of costs while the product was in its manufacturing stage.

It is, therefore, unusual to give as much attention to all of the costs of a project from the time that it is first conceived until the time that it is finally abandoned. This means that the overall total cost is not always closely correlated with the overall total revenues. In other words, the lifetime profitability of a project tends to be ignored, especially if it gets beyond its development stage.

As up to 90 per cent of the costs of a project could be incurred at the design stage, merely by agreeing to consider a particular project, entities have already committed themselves to considerable expenditure. This clearly has considerable resource implications within an entity. Thus it has became apparent that managers need to pay at least as much attention to the design and disposal stages as they do to the manufacturing stage.

The consequence for management accounting is that information for management should no longer be prepared on the basis of data being neatly packaged into calendar-year compartments. Instead, attempts need to be made to cost products on a much longer-term basis. Product life cycle costing should, therefore, be of considerable benefit to non-accounting managers because it will enable them to assess more accurately the profitability of a particular project over its entire life.

| Activity 22.7 | Identify one major problem that you would face if you tried to introduce product life cycle costing into an entity. |

Problem: _____

_____

_____

Social accounting and reporting

Social accounting and reporting may be defined as follows.

> *The collection, recording, classification, extraction and summary of information relating to the social environment and the reporting of it to specified users of such information.*

Thus the aim of social accounting and reporting is to find out how an entity looks after the people with whom it does business. The people concerned may be either employed by the entity or they have some external relationship with it, such as borrowers, creditors, customers, lenders and the general public.

This is a fairly new topic for accountants and it has not received the same amount of attention as environmental accounting and reporting. There are no statutory or professional accounting requirements covering social accounting and reporting (apart from a few minor ones relating to employee matters). Thus there are no guidelines on what, how and in what form social matters might be accounted for and reported. However, we can summarize for you some matters that might be considered 'social'. These are as follows:

Matters affecting employees

- Number of people employed classified into grades.
- Average salary and wages of all employees and by grade.
- Pension contribution arrangements.
- Social security costs.
- Number of disabled people employed.
- Provisions made for disabled employees, e.g. what educational, financial and training facilities are provided and what physical assistance is given.
- Provision of education and training facilities.
- Health, leisure, safety, and welfare provisions.
- Time off for public and voluntary service.

Matters affecting the community

- Donations made to charities.
- Support for external educational, leisure, research and training activities.
- Sponsorship of community projects.
- Debtor collection and creditor payment periods.

- Contact with the public, e.g. general enquires and public relations.
- Involvement in the community, e.g. managers acting as school governors.

But why should an entity want to account and report on such matters? The answer to this question can be answered quite simply: '*It is in its own best interest*'.

Most entities of any size (especially industrial and manufacturing companies) have a major influence in their local community, and the larger ones nationally and internationally. They do not and cannot operate in isolation. They may do something or try to do something that is questionable and if it angers the public, the company's image, reputation and ultimately its future may all be irreparably damaged. In such circumstances the company will not prosper and it may even cease to exist.

There is also, of course, an ethical or moral reason why entities should care about society. They have an enormous impact on whom they employ and to a lesser extent on those with whom they deal in the outside world. Low wages, the threat of redundancy, or terrible working conditions have a significant impact on employees, their families and their friends. Entities that have no concern for the community in which they operate, such as treating suppliers unfairly or threatening to shut down a plant, can have a similar devastating impact on thousands of people indirectly affected by an unsympathetic decision taken by an uncaring management team. Common decency and humanity would suggest that since the entity cannot survive without the assistance of the community and the community cannot survive without it, the entity has a duty to offer as much protection as it can to all who depend on it.

In any case, employers can no longer behave like autocratic mill owners as they once did. The following passage illustrates the management style that was common in British industry (the incident took place during the First World War):

> Once, when Jenny was unwell and could not take me to the mill, mother ignored the factory regulations and walked out. She had the misfortune to run headlong into the time-keeper at the gate.
>
> 'Here, where t'goin'?' he demanded.
> 'Home, t'feed child, it's clemmin'.'
> 'If tha goes out now, tha stays out!'
> Mother returned to the cardroom.
>
> (Woodruff, W. (1999) *The Road To Nab End*, pp. 20–21, London: Abacus.)

Perhaps it is only in the last 20 to 30 years that entities have begun to pay much more attention to their social responsibilities. This has probably been brought about by trade union action, the fact that high employment results in difficulties in recruiting employees and retaining them, and because people are better educated, read and informed about their 'rights'.

Whatever the reasons and whether you agree or not about an entity's social responsibility, the trend towards accountability on a wider scale is likely to continue. Hence as a manager (or a potential one), it might pay you to think about which users your entity should report to, what it should report, and in what form.

Many companies already include in their annual report and accounts matters that can be considered to be 'social'. For example, we referred in an earlier section to Cairn Energy plc's *Environmental and Social Review 2001*. Its report refers specifically to the following 'Milestones and progress: 2001 highlights'. We reproduce it overleaf.

> **Social**
>
> → Introduction of Corporate Social Responsibility Policy
>
> → Provision of humanitarian aid to Gujarat earthquake relief effort
>
> → Ongoing support for medical, educational, local infrastructure, reforestation and drinking water projects in Ravva local communities
>
> → Provision of assistance to local schools in Rajasthan
>
> → Medical facilities and expertise enhanced at Ravva

We expect the trend towards more social accounting and reporting to continue. Indeed, we would expect some fairly detailed reporting requirements on social matters to be made mandatory within the next five to ten years.

Activity 22.8

The above section includes a summary of some social matters that some entities may include in a social report. Using ASB's user group specification (customers, employees, governments and their agencies, investors, lenders, the public, suppliers and other trade creditors) write down in your notebook three social responsibility matters that you think a company operating in a town of some 200 000 people and employing 25 000 workers should supply to each user group.

Strategic management accounting

Strategic management accounting (SMA) has begun to develop as a separate branch of management accounting during the last 20 years, although it is not yet well developed. SMA supports the move to a more strategic approach to managerial decisions.

The objective of SMA is to supply information to management for strategic decision-making purposes, incorporating both internal and external data of both a financial and non-financial nature. Thus in order to support a particular decision or a proposal of a long-term nature, a management accountant would not restrict the data collected either to that available within the entity or to that primarily related to costs and revenues. The external information would include financial and non-financial data relating to the entity's competitors because their long-term plans are likely to have a significant impact on what the entity itself proposes to do.

The procedures available for external data collection are extremely speculative. Indeed, they cannot be anything else because obviously the entity's competitors would wish to keep their plans as confidential as possible. However, some information should be available from such published sources as annual reports and accounts, trade circulars, press releases, and newspaper and journal articles. It has also been suggested that several rather unorthodox sources may be available, such as information that might be provided by former employees of competitor companies or from visiting suppliers' representatives. In other words, management accountants may need to undertake a certain amount of detective work in order to obtain the data that they need!

In taking on this role, the main aim of the management accountants would be to compile competitors' plans in the form of financial statements similar to those of their own entity. The strategic planning team should then be able to make comparisons between sets of internal and external financial statements (including non-financial data) and, if need be, adjust their own strategic plan.

SMA should be of considerable assistance to the strategic planning team and it has the potential to be of considerable importance and relevance to non-accountants.

Apart from obtaining external data, what main factor sets strategic management accounting apart from traditional management accounting? Write down your thoughts in your notebook.	*Activity 22.9*

Target costing

Target costing is a cost-reduction technique. A target cost is established by subtracting the difference between the perceived or expected selling price of a product and the entity's desired profit margin. Suppose, for example, that a company is launching a new product on the market and expects to be able to sell it at £10 per unit. The company's desired profit margin is given as 10 per cent (i.e. £1 per unit), and so the cost per unit must be no more than £9 (£10 – £1). The target cost is usually set very tightly so that everyone throughout the entity has to search rigorously for economies.

In order to meet the target, the design of the product, the production process and the selling and distribution arrangements may all have to be carefully determined and re-examined. Hence the implementation of a target costing system can act as a considerable incentive to search for more efficient ways of manufacturing and selling the product. It is also very much part of a TQM environment.

Target costing is not a specific management accounting technique. Management accountants may be responsible for collecting the required data and submitting information to management. However, the application of target costing is the responsibility of management generally. In particular, use will be made of scientific principles and methods such as *value engineering*, a discipline that searches for the minimization of product and service costs without sacrificing quality and reliability.

Target costing is of considerable significance to those non-accountants who work in advanced manufacturing technology companies, although there is no reason why the principles cannot be applied in all types of entities.

How realistic (on a scale of 1 to 10) do you think that it is to expect managers to achieve a target set for them when it is based on an estimated selling price and an expected profit margin?	*Activity 22.10*

Completely realistic   *Quite unrealistic*

```
    1    2    3    4    5    6    7    8    9    10
    |----|----|----|----|----|----|----|----|----|
```

How would managers behave if given such a target?

Try to meet it: Yes ☐   Ignore it ☐   Try to work to it ☐

Value chain analysis

In order to explain what is mean by value chain analysis we first have to define what is meant by 'value added' (or added value) and the 'value chain'. We will use the definitions published by the Chartered Institute of Management Accountants in its *Management Accounting Official Terminology* published in 2000. They are as follows.

> **Value added**: *Sales value less the cost of purchased materials and services. (p. 19)*

Value added, therefore, is simply the cost of making a sales item excluding the material costs

> **Value chain**: *The sequence of business activities by which, in the perspective of the end user, value is added to the product or services produced by an organization. (p. 41)*

This definition includes the term 'sequence'. In other words, a series of events that come after one another. The main sequences that a product may go through before it is finally sold to the customer are as follows:

- *Research*: work is done in devising or inventing a new product.
- *Design*: once a prototype is agreed, a specification is worked on and a design drawn up.
- *Production*: it is put into production.
- *Marketing*: the product is marketed.
- *Distribution*: it is distributed to customers.
- *Customer care*: the entity keeps in touch to ensure that its customers have no complaints.

The above sequence of activities is shown in diagrammatic form in Figure 22.2.

A similar sequence of activities could be drawn up for a service industry. Generally, the chain would not be as long or as complicated as in a manufacturing industry since there is no tangible product to manufacture.

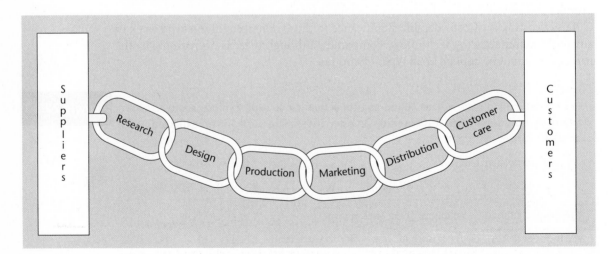

Figure 22.2 The value chain in a production company

Now that we have explained what we mean by value added and the value chain we can define what we mean by 'value chain analysis'. Our definition is as follows.

> *A thorough examination of value chain activities in order to undertake them more efficiently, effectively and economically.*

The activities that add value are usually classified into *primary* activities and *support* activities. Primary activities are those that result in the physical creation of the product including the sales, distribution and customer care. Support activities provide assistance to the primary activities, such as accounting, finance, human resource management, legal, product development and purchasing services.

The following steps are involved in undertaking a value chain analysis.

Step 1: Divide the entity into strategic business units (SBUs)

An SBU is 'a section of the entity responsible for planning, developing, producing and marketing its own products or services' (CIMA, 2000, p. 39). A large international manufacturing company, for example, will probably be organized on divisional lines. Hence within it there may be many semi-autonomous units that operate almost independently of the rest of the company.

Step 2: Identify those activities within each SBU that add value

This step involves identifying the broad value activities within the SBU similar to the ones illustrated in Figure 22.2, i.e. research and development, design, production, marketing, distribution and customer care. These activities are then disaggregated into sub-activities. Sub-activities must form a significant part of the overall activity and they must each have their own cost driver (see below).

Step 3: Allocate revenue, costs and assets to each value creating activity

This step is similar to the procedures adopted by accountants in setting up an investment cost centre structure.

Step 4: Identify a cost driver for each value activity

This step involves selecting one factor that is primarily responsible for causing or driving the value activity. By dividing the cost of a value added activity by the cost driver we can calculate the value added by that cost driver.

Step 5: Compare the result for each value added activity

This step allows us to spot those activities that appear to add little value. We would then determine whether the activity could be made more efficient, whether it could be bought-in, or even eliminated altogether.

Step 6: Compare the result with other similar entities

This is a difficult step because it involves undertaking a value chain analysis for each of the entity's competitors. Data will be very hard to obtain and it may only be possible to make some broad comparisons. Nevertheless, some information is better than no information.

A value chain analysis is a complicated exercise. It involves identifying activities and isolating the costs attached to them. It is perhaps even more difficult to select just one factor that is responsible for driving that activity (i.e. a cost driver). If it can be done the results should be worthwhile. Management will be able to spot those activities that do not add much, if any, value. It can then be decided if those activities really need to be carried out.

| Activity 22.11 | Identify the similarities between activity based management and value chain analysis and write them down in your notebook. |

! Questions non-accountants should ask

This chapter has indicated some of the changes that management accounting may undergo over the next five to ten years. You might like to check what changes your own entity is experiencing or envisaging. Try asking the following questions.

- Should we re-allocate our management accountants to operating units, involve them more in strategic decision making, and just keep a small centralized accounting unit?
- Should managers access what reports they want from their PCs instead of leaving it to the management accountants to report to them?
- How satisfied are we that absorption costing is appropriate for our business?
- Should we move over to an ABM or at least an ABC approach?
- Could both financial and non-financial indicators be incorporated into management reports?
- Is it time to revise our budgeting and budgetary control system?
- Should we incorporate environment and social costs and benefits into our internal decision-making projects and reports?
- Would it be a good idea to produce an external environmental and social report?
- Is there any place in our organization for target costing and value chain analysis?

Conclusion

Part 4 of this book has dealt with management accounting. Most of the chapters have concentrated on traditional management accounting techniques and their usefulness for managers. However, most of those techniques originated in the late nineteenth and early twentieth centuries. They were devised to cope with a growing industrial nation at a time when companies concentrated on expanding output. Apart from their shareholders, little regard was given even to their customers, still less their employees and the local community.

Great changes have taken place in economic activity since the Second World War ended in 1945. The main ones first took place in the Far East. These emerging countries were not bound by past practices. They were able to build up their industries using different organizational structures and new production methods. Increasing automation and development in information technology hastened the changes that were taking place. And, of course, labour was relatively cheap compared with the 'old world'.

All of this resulted in the decline of old industries in countries like the UK. Indeed, the UK found it impossible to compete with these emerging nations. The result was that by the end of the twentieth century the UK had very little manufacturing industry and its economy was largely serviced based.

These changes in the business environment have begun to have a significant impact on management accounting practices. Until 1980 there had been little movement but change became necessary as the 'old world' began to realize that it too had to accept some fundamental changes to business life. Orders were hard to get, customers were more demanding, prices were competitive, costs had to be controlled more rigorously, goods and services had to be of the highest quality, and an efficient aftercare service was vital.

Traditional management techniques could not cope with these requirements so they also had to change. Perhaps the most significant of these changes has been a move towards *activity based costing* (see Chapter 16) subsequently extended to *activity based management*. Even so, only large industrial companies have taken much interest in either ABC or ABM and much work still needs to be done in encouraging medium and small industrial entities and many service entities of their usefulness.

There are also some other techniques that are not necessarily new but which are beginning to receive some attention. There is a call, for example, for 'better' budgeting, and for the incorporation of financial and non-financial indicators into performance measurement. Similarly, there is a growing interest in such cost control techniques as product life cycle costing, target costing, and value chain analysis. Irrespective of the type or size of industry, most entities now recognize that they must give some attention to environmental and social matters. Indeed, some companies are now publishing their own environmental and social reports on a voluntary basis.

We should not expect major changes to take place in management accounting practice very quickly or indeed on any scale. Such developments take a great deal of time to become known and to become accepted. Progress will be slow and it will certainly be evolutionary rather than revolutionary.

Key points

1 Management accounting developed as a main branch of accounting towards the end of the nineteenth century.

2 By 1925 most management accounting techniques used today were in place and there was little further development until about 1980.

3 The decline of old industries in the Western world and the emergence of new economies in the Far East (particularly Japan), the introduction of new management philosophies (such as total quality management and just-in-time procedures), and new technologically based industries have together necessitated the development of more relevant management accounting techniques.

4 We can expect a slow movement towards incorporating relatively new management accounting techniques into practice over the next few years. Activity based management will probably become more widespread. Better budgeting procedures will be devised, and managers will be supplied with more financial and non-financial performance indicators.

5 As the world becomes even more competitive there will be a need for greater cost control techniques and methods such as product life cycle costing, target costing, and value chain analysis may gain greater prominence. Greater attention will be given to environmental and social accounting and reporting.

Check your learning

The answers to these questions may be found within the text.

1   What were the main causes of industrial change after the Second World War?

2   What do the following initials mean: AMT, JIT, TQM?

3   List four major causes of the change in the UK economic environment over the last 20 years.

4   Identify four implications for management accounting of such changes.

5   What do the initials ABM and ABCM mean?

6   What is the difference between ABC and ABM?

7   Name the four stages involved in an ABM exercise.

8   What is meant by 'better budgeting'?

9   List five ways in which the traditional budgeting process may be improved.

10   What is environment accounting and reporting?

11   What is meant by 'environmental'?

12   Identify four areas of management accounting where environmental issues might have an impact.

13   What is 'performance measurement'?

14   What two categories are used to classify them?

15   Give three examples of performance measures that may be included in each category.

16   What is a 'balanced scorecard'?

17   List the four perspectives into which it may be classified.

18   How may they be classified?

19   List four reasons why performance measurement is now gaining greater prominence.

20   What is the product life cycle?

21   List its main stages.

22   What is social accounting and reporting?

23   List eight items that may be included in a social report.

24   What is strategic management accounting?

25   What is the main factor that distinguishes it clearly from traditional management accounting?

26   What is target costing?

27   What is its main aim?

28   What is value chain analysis?

29 List six main stages involved in a manufacturing company's value chain analysis.

30 What is its main purpose?

News story quiz

Remember the news story at the beginning of this chapter? Go back to that story and re-read it before answering the following questions.

This article illustrates the management accounting changes that are taking place in one company. Some of the items mentioned in the article have been covered in this chapter, viz. adding value, scorecard design, metrics, and budget and forecast control mechanisms.

Questions

1 What do you think Figleaves meant when it reported 'break-even at EBITDA on net sales of £1 million'?

2 Does this method of calculating break-even differ from Amazon.com's 'break-even on turnover of £550 million'?

3 How do you think that the management accountants' expertise 'makes them ideal for a smaller firm such as Figleaves'?

4 And why might this be particularly so for a 'smaller' firm?

5 In what ways might the various techniques mentioned (scorecard design, budget and forecast control mechanisms, and the integration of rolling sales forecasts with inventory capacity planning) be crucial in helping the company to break-even?

Tutorial questions

22.1 'Activity based management is fine in theory but impossible in practice'.

Discuss.

22.2 How far do you think that short budget forecasts would be more useful than budgets tied in with the traditional annual financial reporting system?

22.3 Do you think that environmental and social accounting and reporting is of any benefit to a company?

22.4 'Ugh!' snorted the chairman when confronting the chief accountant. 'Strategic management accounting is another of those techniques dreamed up by you and your mates to keep you in a job.' Could the Chairman have a point?

22.5 Do you think that target costing serves any useful purpose in a service entity?

22.6 How far do you think that value chain analysis is just another version of activity based management?

Further practice questions, study material and links to relevant sites on the World Wide Web can be found on the website that accompanies this book. The site can be found at ***www.booksites.net/dyson***

Fixed and flexible budgets

After preparing this case study you should be able to:
- distinguish between fixed and flexible budgets;
- evaluate a budgetary control variance report;
- indicate what action should be taken to deal with any reported variances.

Location   Larkhill, Central Scotland

Company   Larkhill Products Limited

Personnel   Robert Jordan, Product Manager
                 Dave Ellis, Management Accountant

Robert Jordan recently joined Larkhill Products Limited as a product manager. The company manufactures, distributes, and sells a range of popular card games. At the end of his first month in post, Robert received the following statement from the management accountant (Dave Ellis).

Larkhill Products Limited
Monthly variance report: January 2004

	Original budget per unit	Units	Flexed budget Units	Actual Units	Quantity variance	Price variance	Total variance
Sales volume		20 000	18 000	18 000			2 000(A)
Production volume		20 000	18 000	18 500			1 500(A)
	£	£000	£000	£000	£000	£000	£000
Sales	40	800	720	648	–	72(A)	72(A)
Direct material	18*	360	324	360	45(F)	81(A)	36(A)
Direct labour	12†	240	216	270	90(F)	44(A)	54(A)
	30	600	540	630	135(F)	225(A)	90(A)
Contribution	10	200	180	18			162(A)
Fixed costs		150	150	140		10(F)	(10)(F)
Profit/(loss)		50	30	(122)	135(F)	287(A)	152(A)

* = 2m × £9. † 3 DLH × £4.

Robert left school at the age of 18 with a couple of GCE advanced level passes. He had started his career promoting double glazing for a local company before moving into selling central heating systems. He was good at persuading people to buy what he was selling and for the first ten years of his career he rarely stayed in one job for longer than two years. His ability and experience enabled him to gain promotion to more senior positions in sales and marketing.

Robert was never interested in going to college or university and he was far too busy to think of studying part time for a professional qualification. So when he joined Larkhill he knew a great deal about selling, but little about the other functional activities of the company, e.g. accounting, distribution, human relations and production. His interview had not been handled particularly well but Robert was good at dealing with people so he had been able to give the impression that he had a wide knowledge of business.

Robert panicked when he received the management accountant's statement. What was it? What did it mean? What was he supposed to do with it? Dare he ask anybody to help him?

After thinking about the problem overnight he decided to tackle it head on. The next morning he telephoned David Ellis, the management accountant. He was very authoritative and at the same time apologetic. 'Sorry about this, Dave,' he wheedled, 'As you know, I'm new here and my other companies had different ways of doing things. I'd appreciate it if you would do me a position paper about the monthly variance report.' He then indicated in more detail what he wanted. Dave agreed to supply him with some more information.

Robert was pretty sure that he had not convinced Dave about the reason why he wanted a 'position paper'. Nevertheless, he was confident that charm and warm words would see him through an embarrassing problem – as it always had.

Required:
Prepare an explanation for Robert Jordan explaining what the monthly variance report means and what action he should take over it.

Standard cost operating statements

After preparing this case study you should be able to:
- describe the nature and purpose of a standard cost operating statement;
- evaluate the information presented in such a statement;
- suggest ways in which that information may be enhanced.

Learning objectives

Background

Location	Burnley, Lancashire
Company	Amber Textiles Limited
Personnel	Ted Finch, Managing Director

Synopsis

Amber Textiles Limited is a small textile processing company based in Burnley in Lancashire. It is one of the few remaining such companies in the United Kingdom but it is also struggling to survive as a result of intense competition from the Far East.

The board of directors has been well aware for some time that if the company is to survive, it must retain its customer base by being extremely competitive. There is little scope to increase selling prices and so costs have to be controlled extremely tightly.

The board has done everything possible to control the company's costs. For example, it recently introduced an 'information for management' (IFM) system. The system involves using budgets for control purposes but it also produces standard costs for each of the company's main product lines. A firm of management consultants installed the system with the assistance of the company's small accounting staff.

The new IFM system seemed to involve an awful lot of paperwork and Ted Finch, the managing director, was struggling to cope with the sheer volume of reports that mysteriously appeared on his desk almost every day. By profession, Ted was a textile engineer. He had little training in numerical analysis and none related to accounting.

One morning, shortly after the new system was up and running he found the following statement on his desk.

Amber Textiles Limited
Standard Cost Operating Statement

Period: Four weeks to 31 March 2004

	£	£	£
Budgeted sales			700 000
Budgeted cost of sales			(490 000)
		c/f	210 000

	£	£	£
		b/f	210000
Sales volume profit variance			17600
Budgeted profit from actual sales			227600
Variances	Favourable	Adverse	
Sales price		20000	
Direct material price	6700		
Direct material usage	15400		
Direct labour rate		17600	
Direct labour efficiency	20800		
Variable production overhead expenditure		3140	
Variable production overhead efficiency	2600		
Fixed production overhead expenditure		30000	
Fixed production overhead volume	12000		
	57500	70740	(13240)
Actual profit			214360

Ted studied the statement carefully. What was it? How had it been produced? What did it mean? What was he supposed to do with it?

He was still somewhat puzzled after studying it for some time so he decided to telephone the management consultants responsible for installing the IFM system. They referred him to a manual that they had prepared, a copy of which lay untouched on Ted's bookshelf. Sure enough, the manual contained an example and an explanation of a 'standard costing operating statement' and what management should do to action it.

After consulting the relevant section, Ted felt a little more confident about what the statement meant and what he was supposed to do with it. Nevertheless, he thought that it might be useful to take some advice. So he contacted his chief accountant and asked him to prepare a written report dealing with the specific standard cost operating statement for the four weeks to 31 March 2004. He stressed that he wanted to know precisely what action management should take (if any) to deal with its contents.

Required:

1 Prepare the section of an 'Information for Management' manual dealing with standard cost operating statements. The section should include an outline of the nature and purpose of such a statement, an explanation of its contents, and the action management should take on receiving it.

2 With regard to the specific standard cost operating statement for the four weeks to 31 March 2004, prepare a report explaining what the data means, what interrelationship there may be among the variances, and what specific action Ted Finch might expect his line managers to take in dealing with it.

3 Outline what additional information might be useful to include in a standard cost operating statement.

After preparing this case study you should be able to:

- distinguish between an absorption approach to costing and a marginal costing approach;
- prepare a quotation for a customer using a number of different costing approaches;
- identify a number of other factors that must be considered when preparing a quotation.

Location	Dewsbury, West Yorkshire	
Company	Pennine Heating Systems Limited	
Personnel	Ali Shah, Managing Director	
	Hugh Rodgers, Production Manager	

Pennine Heating Systems Limited is a small heating and ventilation system company located in Dewsbury in West Yorkshire. It provides customer-designed systems for small businesses. The systems are designed, manufactured and installed specially for each customer. This means that each individual contract has to be priced separately.

The company has expanded rapidly in recent years but as it has done so, its overhead costs have continued to increase. The managing director, Ali Shah, has always insisted that contracts should be priced on an absorption cost basis. This was not a problem in the early days of the company. There was a considerable demand for what Pennine Systems was able to offer and customers accepted almost whatever it quoted for doing a particular job.

More recently, however, the demand for heating and ventilation systems had become less strong, competitors have come into the market, the national economy is in recession, and customers are much conscious about their costs than they used to be when the economy was expanding.

Thus, while Pennine's reputation is good, it has to be particularly sensitive about the price that it charges its orders. Indeed, Ali senses that the company is beginning to lose some business because its quotations are too high. He wonders whether he should review its pricing system in order to make sure that it attracts sufficient business.

Ali was reminded of what he intended to do when a request for a quotation landed on his desk late one Friday night. On the Monday, he asked Hugh Rodgers, his production manager, to cost and price it. He had the results on the Wednesday morning. Hugh's calculations were as follows.

	£
Direct materials	14 000
Direct labour	41 500
Prime cost	55 500
Factory overhead	11 100
Factory cost of production	66 600
Administration overhead	6 660
Selling and distribution overhead	9 990
Total operating cost	83 250
Profit	16 650
Suggested contract price	99 900*

* say £100,000

Note: Factory overhead, administration overhead, and selling and distribution overhead is added to the factory cost of production at rates of 20%, 10% and 15% respectively. A profit loading of 20% is added to the total operating cost.

Ali suspects that a contract price of £100 000 may be too high to gain the contract. He wonders whether the company can afford to accept a price lower than £100 000. He asks the production manager to conduct an intensive investigation of the cost build-up and other matters relating to the contract. Hugh does so and discovers, inter alia, the following information:

1 All of the overheads include a share of the fixed costs of the company. 75% of the factory overhead, 80% of the administration overhead, and 60% of the selling and distribution overhead are fixed costs.
2 Hugh has been informed privately that a number of other companies have been asked to quote for the contract and that three other companies are being considered at a contract price of £70 000, £75 000, and £95 000 respectively.

Required:
1 Advise Ali Shah what price Pennine Heating Systems Limited should quote for the contract.
2 Outline what factors other than price Ali should take into account before offering a firm quotation.

Further reading

This book contains sufficient material for most first-year modules in accounting for non-accounting students. Some students may require additional information, however, and it may be necessary for them to consult other books when attempting exercises set by their tutors.

There are many very good accounting books available for *accounting* students, but they usually go into considerable technical detail. *Non-accounting* students must use them with caution, otherwise they will find themselves completely lost. In any case, non-accounting students do not need to process vast amounts of highly technical data. It is sufficient for their purpose if they have an understanding of where accounting information comes from, why it is prepared in that way, what it means, and what reliance can be placed on it.

Bearing these points in mind, the following books are worth considering:

Financial accounting

Elliott, B. and Elliott, J. (2002) *Financial Accounting and Reporting*, 7th edn, Financial Times/Prentice Hall, Harlow. This is an excellent textbook that is now into its seventh edition. It should be a very useful reference book for non-accounting students.

Holmes, G. and Sugden, A. (2002) *Interpreting Company Reports and Accounts*, 8th edn, Financial Times/Prentice Hall, Harlow. A well-established text that deals with company financial reporting in some detail.

Wood, F. and Sangster, A. (2002) *Business Accounting*, Volumes 1 and 2, 9th edn, Financial Times/Prentice Hall, Harlow. Wood is the master accounting textbook writer. His books can be recommended with absolute confidence.

Management accounting

Arnold, J. and Turley, S (1996) *Accounting for Management Decisions*, 3rd edn, Prentice Hall, Hemel Hempstead. This book is aimed at first- and second-year undergraduate and professional courses. Non-accounting students should be able to follow it without too much difficulty.

Ashton, D., Hopper, T. and Scapen, R.W. (eds) (1995) *Issues in Management Accounting*, 2nd edn, Prentice-Hall Europe, Hemel Hempstead. This book will be useful for those students who are interested in current developments in management accounting. However, be warned! It is written in an academic style and some of the chapters are very hard going. It is also now becoming a little dated.

Drury, C. (2000) *Management and Cost Accounting*, 5th edn, Business Press Thomson Learning, London. This book has become the established British text on management accounting. It is a big book in every sense of the word. Non-accounting students should only use it for reference.

Horngren, C.T. (2002) *Cost Accounting: A Managerial Emphasis*. 11th edn, Prentice Hall, Harlow. Horngren is a long established American text. It will be of benefit for non-accounting students mainly for reference purposes.

Discount table

Present value of £1 received after *n* years discounted at *i* %

i / *n*	1	2	3	4	5	6	7	8	9	10
1	0.9901	0.9804	0.9709	0.9615	0.9524	0.9434	0.9346	0.9259	0.9174	0.9091
2	0.9803	0.9612	0.9426	0.9246	0.9070	0.8900	0.8734	0.8573	0.8417	0.8264
3	0.9706	0.9423	0.9151	0.8890	0.8638	0.8396	0.8163	0.7938	0.7722	0.7513
4	0.9610	0.9238	0.8885	0.8548	0.8227	0.7921	0.7629	0.7350	0.7084	0.6830
5	0.9515	0.9057	0.8626	0.8219	0.7835	0.7473	0.7130	0.6806	0.6499	0.6209
6	0.9420	0.8880	0.8375	0.7903	0.7462	0.7050	0.6663	0.6302	0.5963	0.5645

i / *n*	11	12	13	14	15	16	17	18	19	20
1	0.9009	0.8929	0.8850	0.8772	0.8696	0.8621	0.8547	0.8475	0.8403	0.8333
2	0.8116	0.7929	0.7831	0.7695	0.7561	0.7432	0.7305	0.7182	0.7062	0.6944
3	0.7312	0.7118	0.6931	0.6750	0.6575	0.6407	0.6244	0.6086	0.5934	0.5787
4	0.6587	0.6355	0.6133	0.5921	0.5718	0.5523	0.5337	0.5158	0.4987	0.4823
5	0.5935	0.5674	0.5428	0.5194	0.4972	0.4761	0.4561	0.4371	0.4190	0.4019
6	0.5346	0.5066	0.4803	0.4556	0.4323	0.4104	0.3898	0.3704	0.3521	0.3349

APPENDIX 3 Answers to activities

1.2 a) account; b) double-entry book-keeping; c) profit; d) entity; e) Industrial Revolution.

1.3 a) false; b) false; c) true; d) true; e) false.

1.4 The AAT. It is not a chartered body and it is not considered to be one of the six major professional accountancy bodies.

1.5

Type of entity	Advantage	Disadvantage
(a) Sole trader	The owner has total control of the business	It may be difficult to obtain sufficient finance
(b) Partnership	The management of the business is shared	If the business is unsuccessful the partners may go bankrupt
(c) Limited liability company	The liability of the owners is restricted	Certain financial information about the company has to be disclosed publicly

1.6   1 Broadcasting: quasi-governmental.
2 Famine relief: social organization.
3 Postal deliveries: quasi-governmental.
4 Social services: local government.
5 Work and pensions: central government.

2.2 *Advantages*
1 Easy to compare this year's events with those that happened a year ago.
2 Annual comparisons are commonly made in other spheres and therefore acceptable
3 A year reflects the normal climatic seasonal pattern.

Disadvantages
1 It is an artificial period of time.
2 It is either too short or too long for certain types of businesses.
3 Some of the information included in the annual accounts could be well over 12 months old by the time it is reported and it may by then be out of date.

2.3 Profit should only be taken on an order when there is a high possibility that the expected revenue will exceed the costs to date plus costs to be incurred. Even then only a proportion of the anticipated profit should be taken before the contract is fully complete. It would, therefore, by imprudent to apportion the profit over the three years. There might, however, be a case for taking some profit in late 2005.

2.4   It is understandable that a supermarket company would wish to take the discount to its profit and loss account as early as possible. However, it would be imprudent to do so. There is bound to be some doubt that the target set for it will be met and the discount might have to be returned. When there is a strong possibility that the target will be met it might be appropriate to take some of the discount to the profit and loss account before the agreed period has come to an end.

Chapter 3   3.1   (a) Assets = capital + liabilities.
           (b) Twice.

3.2   (a) A record or a history of a certain event.
      (b) A book in which a number of accounts are kept (a book of account).
      (c) To receive something or the value received.
      (d) To give something or the value given.

3.3   (a) Cash account; sales account.
      (b) Rent paid account; bank account.
      (c) Wages account; cash account.
      (d) Purchases account; bank account.

3.4   The entries are on the wrong side.

3.5   *Debit*   *Credit*
      (a) Suppliers   Cash
      (b) Office rent   Bank
      (c) Cash   Sales
      (d) Bank   Dividends received

3.7   A debit balance on an account means that the total on the debit side is greater than the total on the credit side. A credit balance is the opposite.

3.9   (a) no; (b) yes; (c) no.

Chapter 4   4.1   (a) false; (b) false; (c) false.

4.2   (a) cost of goods sold; (b) gross; expenditure; net.

Chapter 5   5.1   (a) £3 500 [£10 000 less (2 000 + 6 000 − 1 500)]
           (b) £4 000 [£10 000 less (2 000 + 6 000 − 2 000)]
           (c) £4 500 [£10 000 less (2 000 + 6 000 − 2 500)]

5.2   £2 250 [£50 000 − 5 000 = 45 000 ÷ 20]

5.3   £4 500 [£4 000 + 1 000 – 500]

5.4   £11 000 [£3 000 + 10 000 – 2 000]

5.5   Probably yes. Debit the profit and loss account and credit Gibson's account. £70 000 (£75 000 – 5 000).

5.6   £1 500 [£9 000 – (250 000 × 3%)]. It will increase his profit by £1 500.

5.8   (a) false; (b) true; (c) true.

Chapter 6

6.2   *Advantages*
       1 free from personal bankrupcy
       2 the business carries on in perpetuity
       3 gives some status in the community.

       Disadvantages
       1 formal accounting records to be kept
       2 the Companies Act 1985 accounting requirements apply
       3 disclosure of information to the public.

6.3   (a) net profit for the year before taxation; (b) dividends.

6.4   (a) current liabilities; (b) loans; (c) fixed assets; (d) capital; (e) current assets.

Chapter 8

8.3   (a) false; (b) false; (c) true; (d) false; (e) true; (f) false.

Chapter 12

12.2   (a) true; (b) true; (c) true.

12.4   (a) £40 938; (b) stocks.

12.8   *Company*   *Effect*
       A   Not much
       B   Considerable
       C   Highly significant

Chapter 13

13.5   The expected profit on the contract is now £100 000 [£500 000 – (300 000 + 100 000)]. Depending upon a review of the expected outcome, it might be appropriate to claim some profit on account. One way would be to apporption the expected profit on the basis of costs incurred to date as a proportion of the total cost. This would give a profit of £75 000 for Year 3 (£100 000 × 300 000/400 000). However, as the contract is only 60% through it life, some accountant might reduce this by an arbitrary factor of 2/3. The profit taken would then be £50 000 (£75 000 × 2/3). This is a normal accounting approach to the problem of revenue/profit recognition on contract work. But notice how judgemental the whole exercise appears to be.

Chapter 19   19.2 $S - V = F + P$ so £100 000 – 40 000 = 50 000 + 10 000, i.e. £10 000

19.4

	£000	£000
Sales		75
Less: variable costs		
Direct material	10	
Direct labour	20	30
		45
Less: fixed costs		
Staff salaries	47	
Rent	3	50
Loss		(5)

19.5 The contribution per unit is £5 (£50 000 – 25 000/5 000) so another 1 000 units

19.8 (a) Break-even chart

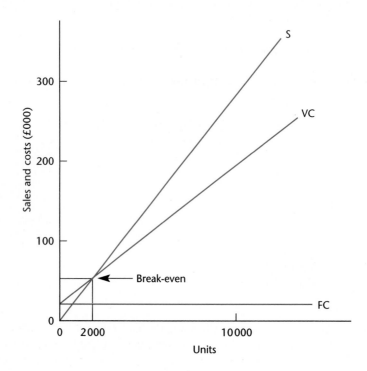

(b) Profit/volume graph

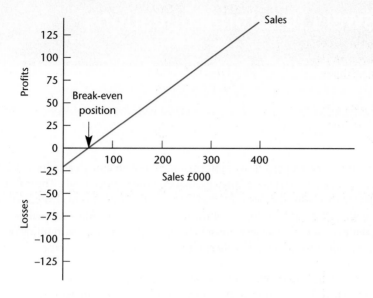

21.2 £151.22 (£200 × 0.7561).

Answers to tutorial questions

Chapter 1

1.4   Accountants collect a great deal of information about an entity's activities and then translate it into monetary terms – a language that everyone understands. The information that is collected can help non-accountants do their job more effectively because it provides them with better guidance upon which to take decisions. Any eventual decision is still theirs. Futhermore, all managers must be aware of the statutory accounting obligations to which their organization has to adhere if they are to avoid taking part in unlawful acts.

1.5   (1) To collect and store detailed information about an entity's activities. (2) To abstract and summarize information in the most effective way for the requirements of a specified user or group of users.

1.6   None. The preparation of management accounts is for the entity to decide if it believes that they serve a useful purpose.

1.8   Statutory obligations are contained in the Companies Act 1985. In addition, listed companies have to abide by certain Stock Exchange requirements, and qualified accountants are also bound by a great many mandatory professional requirements.

Chapter 2

2.4   Matching.
Historic cost.
Quantitative.
Periodicity.
Prudence.
Going-concern.

2.5   Relevance.
Entity.
Consistency.
Materiality.
Historic cost.
Realization.

2.6   Entity.
Objectivity.
Periodicity.
Prudence.
Dual aspect.
Realization.

3.4   Adam's books of account:

Account

Debit	*Credit*
Cash	Capital
Purchases	Cash
Van	Cash
Rent	Cash
Cash	Sales
Office machinery	Cash

3.5   Brown's books of account:

Account

Debit	*Credit*
Bank	Cash
Cash	Sales
Purchases	Bank
Office expenses	Cash
Bank	Sales
Motor car	Bank

3.10 Ivan's ledger accounts:

Cash Account

		£			£
1.9.06	Capital	10 000	2.9.06	Bank	8 000
12.9.06	Cash	3 000	3.9.06	Purchases	1 000

Capital Account

		£			£
			1.9.06	Cash	10 000

Bank Account

		£			£
2.9.06	Cash	8 000	20.9.06	Roy	6 000
30.9.06	Norman	2 000			

Purchases Account

		£			£
3.9.06	Cash	1 000			
10.9.06	Roy	6 000			

Roy's Account

		£			£
20.9.06	Bank	6 000	10.9.06	Purchases	6 000

Sales Account

		£			£
			12.9.06	Cash	3 000
			15.9.06	Norman	4 000

Norman

		£			£
15.9.06	Sales	4 006	30.9.06	Bank	2 000

3.11 Jones's ledger accounts:

Bank Account

		£			£
1.10.06	Capital	20 006	10.10.06	Petty cash	1 000
			25.10.06	Lang	5 000
			29.10.06	Green	10 000

Capital Account

		£			£
			1.10.06	Bank	20 000

Van Account

		£			£
2.10.06	Lang	5 000			

Lang's Account

		£			£
25.10.06	Bank	5 000	2.10.06	Van	5 000

Purchases Account

		£			£
6.10.06	Green	15 006			
20.10.06	Cash	3 000			

Green's Account

		£			£
28.10.06	Discounts received	500	6.10.06	Purchases	15 000
29.10.06	Bank	10 000			

Petty Cash Account

		£			£
10.10.06	Bank	1 000	22.10.06	Miscellaneous expenses	500

Sales

		£			£
			14.10.06	Haddock	6 000
			18.10.06	Cash	5 000

Haddock

		£			£
14.10.06	Sales	6 000	20.10.06	Discounts allowed	600
			31.10.06	Cash	5 400

Cash Account

		£			£
18.10.06	Sales	5 000	20.10.06	Purchases	3 000
31.10.06	Haddock	5 400			

Miscellaneous Expenses

		£			£
22.10.06	Petty cash	500			

Discounts Received Account

		£			£
			28.10.06	Green	500

Discounts Allowed Account

		£			£
30.10.06	Haddock	600			

3.13 (a), (b) and (c) Pat's ledger accounts:

Cash Account

		£			£
1.12.07	Capital	10 000	24.12.07	Office expenses	5 000
29.12.07	Fog	4 000	31.12.07	Grass	6 000
29.12.07	Mist	6 000	31.12.07	Seed	8 000
			31.12.07	Balance c/d	1 000
		20 000			20 000
1.1.08	Balance b/d	1 000			

Capital Account

		£			£
			1.12.07	Cash	10 000

Purchases Account

		£			£
2.12.07	Grass	6 000			
2.12.07	Seed	7 000			
15.12.07	Grass	3 000			
15.12.07	Seed	4 000	31.12.07	Balance c/d	20 000
		20 000			20 000
1.01.08	Balance b/d	20 000			

Grass's Account

		£			£
12.12.07	Purchases returned	1 000	2.12.07	Purchases	6 000
31.12.07	Cash	6 000	15.12.07	Purchases	3 000
31.12.07	Balance c/d	2 000			
		9 000			9 000
			1.1.08	Balance b/d	2 000

Seed's Account

		£			£
12.12.07	Purchases returned	2 000	2.12.07	Purchases	7 000
31.12.07	Cash	8 000	15.12.07	Purchases	4 000
31.12.07	Balance c/d	1 000			
		11 000			11 000
			1.1.08	Balance b/d	1 000

Sales Account

		£			£
			10.12.07	Fog	3 000
			10.12.07	Mist	4 000
			20.12.07	Fog	2 000
31.12.07	Balance c/d	12 000	20.12.07	Mist	3 000
		12 000			12 000
			1.1.08	Balance b/d	12 000

Fog's Account

			£				£
10.12.07	Sales		3 000	29.12.07	Cash		4 000
20.12.07	Sales		2 000	31.12.07	Balance c/d		1 000
			5 000				5 000
1.1.08	Balance b/d		1 000				

Mist's Account

			£				£
10.12.07	Sales		4 000	29.12.07	Cash		6 000
20.12.07	Sales		3 000	31.12.07	Balance c/d		1 000
			7 000				7 000
1.1.08	Balance b/d		1 000				

Purchases Returned Account

			£				£
				12.12.07	Grass		1 000
31.12.07	Balance c/d		3 000	12.12.07	Seed		2 000
			3 000				3 000
				1.1.08	Balance b/d		3 000

Office Expenses Account

			£		£
24.12.07	Cash		5 000		

Tutorial note

It is unnecessary to balance off an account and bring down the balance if there is only a single entry in it.

3.13 (d) Pat's trial balance:

Pat
Trial Balance at 31 December 2007

	£ Dr	£ Cr
Cash	1 000	
Capital		10 000
Purchases	20 000	
Grass		2 000
Seed		1 000
Sales		12 000
Fog	1 000	
Mist	1 000	
Purchases returned		3 000
Office expenses	5 000	
	28 000	28 000

3.14 (a) Vale's books of account:

Bank Account

		£			£
1.1.05	Balance b/d	5 000	31.12.05	Dodd	29 000
31.12.05	Fish	45 000	31.12.05	Delivery van	12 000
31.12.05	Cash	3 000	31.12.05	Balance c/d	12 000
		53 000			53 000
1.1.06	Balance b/d	12 000			

Capital Account

		£			£
			1.1.05	Balance b/d	20 000

Cash Account

		£			£
1.1.05	Balance b/d	1 000	31.12.05	Purchases	15 000
31.12.05	Sales	20 000	31.12.05	Office expenses	9 000
31.12.05	Fish	7 000	31.12.05	Bank	3 000
			31.12.05	Balance c/d	1 000
		28 000			28 000
1.1.06	Balance b/d	1 000			

Dodd's Account

		£			£
31.12.05	Bank	29 000	1.1.05	Balance b/d	2 000
31.12.05	Balance c/d	3 000	31.12.05	Purchases	30 000
		32 000			32 000
			1.1.06	Balance b/d	3 000

Fish's Account

		£			£
1.1.05	Balance b/d	6 000	31.12.05	Bank	45 000
31.12.05	Sales	50 000	31.12.05	Cash	7 000
			31.12.05	Balance c/d	4 000
		56 000			56 000
1.1.06	Balance b/d	4 000			

Furniture Account

		£			£
1.1.05	Balance b/d	10 000			

Purchases Account

		£			£
31.12.05	Dodd	30 000			
31.12.05	Cash	15 000	31.12.05	Balance c/d	45 000
		45 000			45 000
1.1.06	Balance b/d	45 000			

Sales Account

		£			£
			31.12.05	Cash	20 000
31.12.05	Balance c/d	70 000	31.12.05	Fish	50 000
		70 000			70 000
			1.1.06	Balance b/d	70 000

Office Expenses Account

		£		£
31.12.05	Cash	9 000		

Delivery Van Account

		£		£
31.12.05	Bank	12 000		

3.14 (b) Vale's trial balance:

Vale
Trial balance at 31 December 2005

	Dr	Cr
	£	£
Bank	12 000	
Capital		20 000
Cash	1 000	
Dodd		3 000
Fish	4 000	
Furniture	10 000	
Purchases	45 000	
Sales		70 000
Office expenses	9 000	
Delivery van	12 000	
	93 000	93 000

Chapter 4   4.4   Ethel's accounts:

Ethel
Trading, profit and loss account for the year to
31 January 2004

	£
Sales	35 000
Less: Purchases	20 000
Gross profit	15 000
Less: Expenses:	
Office expenses	11 000
Net profit	4 000

Ethel
Balance sheet at 31 January 2004

	£	£
Fixed assets		
Premises		8 000
Current assets		
Debtors	6 000	
Cash	3 000	
	9 000	
Less: Current liabilities		
Creditors	3 000	6 000
		14 000
Financed by:		
Capital		
Balance at 1 February 2000		10 000
Net profit for the year		4 000
		14 000

4.5   Marion's accounts:

Marion
Trading, profit and loss account for the year to 28 February 2005

	£000	£000
Sales		400
Less: Purchases		200
Gross profit		200
Less: Expenses:		
Heat and light	10	
Miscellaneous expenses	25	
Wages and salaries	98	133
Net profit		67

Marion
Balance sheet at 28 February 2005

	£000	£000
Fixed assets		
Buildings		50
Current assets		
Debtors	30	
Bank	4	
Cash	2	
	36	
Less: Current liabilities		
Creditors	24	12
		62

Marion
Balance sheet at 28 February 2005

	£000	£000
Financed by:		
Capital		
Balance at 1 March 2001		50
Net profit for the year	67	
Less: Drawings	55	12
		62

Chapter 5   5.4   (a)   Lathom's trading account:

Lathom
Trading account for the year to 30 April 2004

	£	£
Sales		60 000
Less: Cost of goods sold:		
Opening stock	3 000	
Purchases	45 000	
	48 000	
Less: Closing stock	4 000	44 000
Gross profit		16 000

(b)   The stock would be shown under current assets, normally as the first item.

5.6   Standish's accounts:

Standish
Trading, profit and loss account for the year
to 31 May 2006

	£	£
Sales		79 000
Less: Cost of goods sold:		
Opening stock	7 000	
Purchases	52 000	
	59 000	
Less: Closing stock	12 000	47 000
Gross profit		32 000
Less: Expenses:		
Heating and lighting	1 500	
Miscellaneous	6 700	
Wages and salaries	17 800	26 000
Net profit		6 000

Standish
Balance sheet at 31 May 2006

	£	£
Fixed assets		
Furniture and fittings		8 000
Current assets		
Stock	12 000	
Debtors	6 000	
Cash	1 200	
	19 200	
Less: Current liabilities		
Creditors	4 300	14 900
		22 900
Financed by:		
Capital		
Balance at 1 June 2005		22 400
Net profit for the year	6 000	
Less: Drawings	5 500	500
		22 900

5.9   Pine's accounts:

Pine
Trading, profit and loss account for the year to
30 September 2005

	£	£
Sales		40 000
Less: Cost of goods sold:		
Purchases	21 000	
Less: Closing stock	3 000	18 000
Gross profit		22 000
Less: Expenses:		
Depreciation: furniture		
(15% × £8 000)	1 200	
General expenses	14 000	
Insurance (£2 000 – 200)	1 800	
Telephone (£1 500 + 500)	2 000	19 000
Net profit		3 000

Pine
Balance sheet at 30 September 2005

	£	£	£
Fixed assets			
Furniture			8 000
Less: Depreciation			1 200
		c/f	6 800

Pine
Balance sheet at 30 September 2005

	£	£	£
			b/f 6 800
Current assets			
Stock		3 000	
Debtors		5 000	
Prepayments		200	
Cash		400	
		8 600	
Less: Current liabilities			
Creditors	5 900		
Accrual	500	6 400	2 200
			9 000
Financed by:			
Capital			
At 1 October 2001			6 000
Net profit for the year			3 000
			9 000

Chapter 6   6.4   Margo Ltd's accounts:

Margo Limited
Profit and loss account for the year to 31 January 2006

	£000
Profit for the financial year	10
Tax on profit	3
Profit after tax	7
Proposed dividend (10p × £50)	5
Retained profit for the year	2

Margo Limited
Balance sheet at 31 January 2006

	£000	£000	£000
Fixed assets			
Plant and equipment at cost			70
Less: Accumulated depreciation			25
			45
Current assets			
Stocks		17	
Trade debtors		20	
Cash at bank and in hand		5	
	c/f	42	45

Margo Limited
Balance sheet at 31 January 2006

	£000	£000	£000
		b/f 42	45
Less: Current liabilities			
Trade creditors	12		
Taxation	3		
Proposed dividend	5	20	22
			67

Capital and reserves	*Authorized*	*Issued and fully paid*
	£000	£000
Share capital (ordinary shares of £1 each)	75	50
Profit and loss account (£15 + 2)		17
		67

6.5   Harry Ltd's accounts:

Harry Limited
Profit and loss account for the year to 28 February 2007

	£000	£000
Gross profit for the year		150
Administration expenses		
[£65 + (10% × £60)]	71	
Distribution costs	15	86
Profit for the year		64
Taxation		24
Profit after tax		40
Dividends: Ordinary proposed	20	
Preference paid	6	26
Retained profit for the year		14

Harry Limited
Balance sheet at 28 February 2007

	£000	£000	£000
Fixed assets			
Furniture and equipment at cost			60
Less: Accumulated depreciation			42
			18
Current assets			
Stocks		130	
Trade debtors		135	
Cash at bank and in hand		10	
	c/f	275	18

Harry Limited
Balance sheet at 28 February 2007

	£000	£000	£000
	b/f	275	18
Less: Current liabilities			
Trade creditors	25		
Taxation	24		
Proposed dividend	20	69	206
			224

	Authorized, issued and fully paid £000
Capital and reserves	
Ordinary shares of £1 each	100
Cumulative 15% preference shares of £1 each	40
	140
Share premium account	20
Profit and loss account (£50 + 14)	64
	224

6.6   Jim Ltd's accounts:

(a)
Jim Limited
Trading and profit and loss account for the year to 31 March 2008

	£000	£000	£000
Sales			270
Less: Cost of goods sold:			
Opening stock		16	
Purchases		124	
		140	
Less: Closing stock		14	126
Gross profit			144
Less: Expenses:			
Advertising		3	
Depreciation: furniture			
and fittings (15% × £20)	3		
vehicles (25% × £40)	10	13	
Directors' fees		6	
Rent and rates		10	
Telephone and stationery		5	
Travelling		2	
Wages and salaries		24	63
Net profit			81
Corporation tax			25
Net profit after tax			56
Proposed dividend			28
Retained profit for the year			28

Jim Limited
Balance sheet at 31 March 2008

	Cost	Depreciation	Net book value
	£000	£000	£000
Fixed assets			
Vehicles	40	20	20
Furniture and fittings	20	12	8
	60	32	28
Current assets			
Stocks		14	
Debtors		118	
Bank		11	
		143	
Less: Current liabilities			
Creditors	12		
Taxation	25		
Proposed dividend	28	65	78
			106

	Authorized	Issued and fully paid
	£000	£000
Capital and reserves		
Ordinary shares of £1 each	100	70
Profit and loss account (£8 + 28)		36
		106

(b) According to Jim Limited's balance sheet as at 31 March 2008 the value of the business was £106 000. This is misleading. Under the historic cost convention the balance sheet is merely a statement listing all the balances left in the double-entry book-keeping system after the preparation of the profit and loss account.

It would be relatively easy, for example, to amend the balance of £106 000 by adjusting the method used for calculating depreciation and for valuing stocks. Furthermore, when a business is liquidated it does not necessarily mean that the balances shown in the balance sheet for other items (e.g. fixed assets, debtors and creditors) will be realised at their balance sheet amounts. There will also be costs associated with the liquidation of the business.

Chapter 7   7.4   Megg's accounts:

Megg
Manufacturing account for the year to 31 January 2007

	£000	£000
Direct materials:		
Stock at 1 February 2006	10	
Purchases	34	
	44	
Less: Stock at 31 January 2007	12	
Materials consumed		32
Direct wages		65
Prime cost		97
Factory overhead expenses:		
Administration	27	
Heat and light	9	
Indirect wages	13	49
		146
Work-in-progress at 1 February 2006	17	
Less: Work-in-progress at 31 January 2007	14	3
Manufacturing cost of goods produced		149

7.5   Moor's accounts:

Moor
Manufacturing account for the year to 28 February 2008

	£	£
Direct materials:		
Stock at 1 March 2007	13 000	
Purchases	127 500	
	140 500	
Less: Stock at 28 February 2008	15 500	125 000
Direct wages		50 000
Prime cost		175 000
Factory overheads		27 700
		202 700
Work-in-progress at 1 March 2007	8 400	
Less: Work-in-progress at 28 February 2008	6 300	2 100
Manufacturing cost of goods produced		204 800

8.4   Dennis Ltd's accounts:

(a)   **Dennis Limited**
              Cash flow statement for the year ended 31 January 2007

	£000	£000
Net cash inflow from operating activities		4
Capital expenditure		
Payments to acquire tangible fixed assets		(100)
		(96)
Management of liquid resource and financing		
Issue of ordinary share capital		100
Increase in cash		4

Reconciliation of operating profit to net cash inflow from operating activities

	£000
Operating profit (£60 – 26)	34
Increase in stocks	(20)
Increase in debtors	(50)
Increase in creditors	40
Net cash inflow from operating activities	4

(b) Dennis Limited generated £4 000 cash from its operating activities during the year
     to 31 January 2007. It also increased its cash position by that amount during the
     year. However, it did invest £100 000 in purchasing some tangible fixed assets
     during the year, but this appeared to be paid for out of issuing another £100 000 of
     ordinary shares.
          The cash from operating activities seems low. Its probably needs to examine its
     stock policy and its debtor collection arrangements because both stocks and debtors
     increased during the year. Its creditors also increased. Taken together, these changes
     might indicate that it is beginning to run into cash flow problems.

8.5   Frank Ltd's accounts:

                               Frank Limited
              Cash flow statement for the year ended 28 February 2009

	£000	£000
Net cash inflow from operating activities		70
Management of liquid resources and financing		
Issue of debenture loan		60
Purchase of investments		(100)
Increase in cash		30

Reconciliation of operating profit to net cash inflow from operating activities

	£000
Operating profit (£40 – 30)	10
Depreciation charges	20
Increase in stocks	(30)
Decrease in debtors	110
Decrease in creditors	(40)
Net cash inflow from operating activities	70

No details of debenture interest were given in the question.

Reconciliation of net cash flow to movement in net debt

	£000	£000
Increase in cash in the period	30	
Cash inflow from increase in debt	(60)	(30)
Net debt at 1.3.08		(20)
Net debt at 28.2.09		(50)

Analysis of changes in net debt

	At 1.3.08	Cash flows	At 28.2.09
	£000	£000	£000
Cash at bank	(20)	30	10
Debt due after 1 year	–	(60)	(60)
Total	(20)	(30)	(50)

(b) The cash flow statement for the year ended 28 February 2009 tells the managers of Frank Limited that the company increased its cash position by £30 000 during the year. Its operating activities generated £70 000 in cash. This was supplemented by issuing £60 000 of debenture stock making the total increase in cash £130 000. £100 000 of cash was used, however, to purchase some investments.

More tests would need to be done but on the limited evidence available, the company's cash position as at the end of the year looked healthy.

Chapter 12   12.4 Betty

Accounting ratios year to 31 January 2008:

1 Gross profit ratio:

$$\frac{\text{Gross profit}}{\text{Total sales revenue}} \times 100 = \frac{30}{100} \times 100 = \underline{\underline{30\%}}$$

2 Net profit ratio:

$$\frac{\text{Net profit}}{\text{Sales}} \times 100 = \frac{14}{100} \times 100 = \underline{\underline{14\%}}$$

3 Return on capital employed:

$$\frac{\text{Net profit}}{\text{Average capital}} \times 100 = \frac{14}{\frac{1}{2}(40 + 48)} \times 100 = \underline{\underline{31.8\%}}$$

$$or \ \frac{\text{Net profit}}{\text{Capital}} \times 100 = \frac{14}{48} \times 100 = \underline{\underline{29.2\%}}$$

4 Current ratio:

$$\frac{\text{Current assets}}{\text{Current liabilities}} = \frac{25}{6} = \underline{\underline{4.2 \text{ to } 1}}$$

5 Acid test:

$$\frac{\text{Current assets} - \text{stock}}{\text{Current liabilities}} = \frac{25 - 10}{6} = \underline{\underline{2.5 \text{ to } 1}}$$

6 Stock turnover:

$$\frac{\text{Cost of goods sold}}{\text{Average stock}} = \frac{70}{\frac{1}{2}(15 + 10)} = \underline{\underline{5.6 \text{ times}}}$$

7 Debtor collection period:

$$\frac{\text{Trade debtors}}{\text{Credit sales}} \times 365 = \frac{12}{100} \times 365 = \underline{\underline{44 \text{ days}}} \text{ (rounded up)}$$

12.5 James Limited
Accounting ratios year to 28 February 2009:

1 Return on capital employed:

$$\frac{\text{Net profit before taxation and dividends}}{\text{Average shareholders' funds}} \times 100 = \frac{90}{\frac{1}{2}(600 + 620)} \times 100 = \underline{\underline{14.8\%}}$$

$$or \ \frac{\text{Net profit before taxation and dividends}}{\text{Shareholders' funds}} \times 100 = \frac{90}{620} \times 100 = \underline{\underline{14.5\%}}$$

2 Gross profit:

$$\frac{\text{Gross profit}}{\text{Sales}} \times 100 = \frac{600}{1200} \times 100 = \underline{\underline{50\%}}$$

3 Mark-up:

$$\frac{\text{Gross profit}}{\text{Cost of goods sold}} \times 100 = \frac{600}{600} \times 100 = \underline{\underline{100\%}}$$

4 Net profit:

$$\frac{\text{Net profit before taxation and dividends}}{\text{Sales}} \times 100 = \frac{90}{1200} \times 100 = \underline{\underline{7.5\%}}$$

5 Acid test:

$$\frac{\text{Current assets} - \text{stock}}{\text{Current liabilities}} = \frac{275 - 75}{240} \times 100 = \underline{\underline{0.83 \text{ to } 1}}$$

6 Fixed assets turnover:

$$\frac{\text{Sales}}{\text{Fixed assets (NBV)}} = \frac{1200}{685} = \underline{\underline{1.75 \text{ times}}}$$

7 Debtor collection period:

$$\frac{\text{Trade debtors}}{\text{Credit sales}} \times 365 = \frac{200}{1200} \times 365 = \underline{\underline{61 \text{ days}}} \text{ (rounded up)}$$

8 Capital gearing:

$$\frac{\text{Long-term loans}}{\text{Shareholders' funds and long-term loans}} \times 100 = \frac{100}{720} \times 100 = \underline{\underline{13.9\%}}$$

Chapter 14   14.4 The main function of *accounting* is to collect quantifiable data, translate it into monetary terms, store the information, and extract and summarize it in a format convenient for those parties who require such information.

Financial accounting and management accounting are two important branches of accounting. The main difference between them is that financial accounting specializes in supplying information to parties *external* to an entity, such as shareholders or governmental departments. Management accounting information is mainly directed at the supply of information to parties *internal* to an entity, such as the entity's directors and managers.

14.5 A management accountant employed by a large manufacturing entity will be involved in the collecting and storing of data (largely, although not exclusively, of a financial nature) and the supply of information to management for planning, control and decision-making purposes. Increasingly, a management accountant is seen to be an integral member of an entity's management team responsible for advice on all financial matters.

Depending upon his or her seniority, the management accountant may be involved in some routine and basic duties such as the processing of data and the calculation of product costs and the valuation of stocks. At a more senior level, the role may be much more concerned with advising on the financial impact of a wide variety of managerial decisions, such as whether to close down a product line or determining the selling price of a new product.

Chapter 15   15.2 Charge to production

1 FIFO:

		£
1000 units	@ £20 =	20 000
250 units	@ £25 =	6 250
Charge to production		26 250

2 Continuous weighted average:

Date	Units		Value
		£	
1.1.06	1 000	@ £20	20 000
15.1.06	500	@ £25	12 500
	1 500		32 500

$$\text{Average} = \frac{£32\,500}{1\,500} = \underline{\underline{£21.67}}$$

Charge to production on 31.1.06 = 1 250 × £21.67 = £27 088

15.3 Value of closing stock

Material ST 2

	Stock	Units	Total stock value	Average unit price
			£	£
1.2.07	Opening	500	500	1.00
10.2.07	Receipts	200	220	
		700	720	1.03
12.2.07	Receipts	100	112	
		800	832	1.04
17.2.07	Issues	(400)	(416)	
25.2.07	Receipts	300	345	
		700	761	1.09
27.2.07	Issues	(250)	(273)	
28.0.07	Closing stock	450	488	

16.6 Scar Ltd's overhead

Chapter 16

Scar Limited
Overhead apportionment January 2006:

	Production Department		Service Department
	A	B	
	£000	£000	£000
Allocated expenses	65	35	50
Apportionment of service department's expenses in the ratio 60 : 40	30	20	(50)
Overhead to be charged	95	55	–

16.7 Bank Ltd's overhead:

Bank Limited
Assembly department – overhead absorption methods:

1 Specific units:

$$\frac{\text{Total cost centre overhead}}{\text{Number of units}} = \frac{£250\,000}{50\,000} = \underline{\underline{£5 \text{ per unit}}}$$

2 Direct materials:

$$\frac{\text{Total cost centre overhead}}{\text{Direct materials}} \times 100 = \frac{£250\,000}{500\,000} \times 100 = 50\%$$

Therefore 50% of £8 = $\underline{\underline{£4 \text{ per unit}}}$

3 Direct labour:

$$\frac{\text{Total cost centre overhead}}{\text{Direct labour}} \times 100 = \frac{£250\,000}{1\,000\,000} \times 100 = 25\%$$

Therefore 25% of £30 = $\underline{\underline{£7.50 \text{ per unit}}}$

4 Prime cost:

$$\frac{\text{Total cost centre overhead}}{\text{Prime cost}} \times 100 = \frac{£250\,000}{1\,530\,000} \times 100 = 16.34\%$$

Therefore 16.34% of £40 = $\underline{\underline{£6.54 \text{ per unit}}}$

5 Direct labour hours:

$$\frac{\text{Total cost centre overhead}}{\text{Direct labour hours}} = \frac{£250\,000}{100\,000} = £2.50 \text{ per direct labour hour}$$

Therefore £2.50 of 3.5 DLH = $\underline{\underline{£8.75 \text{ per unit}}}$

6 Machine hours:

$$\frac{\text{Total cost centre overhead}}{\text{Machine hours}} = \frac{£250\,000}{25\,000} = £10 \text{ per machine hour}$$

Therefore £10 of 0.75 = $\underline{\underline{£7.50 \text{ per unit}}}$

17.5 Direct labour cost budget for Tom Ltd.

Chapter 17

TOM LIMITED
1 Direct materials usage budget:

Month	30.4.04	31.5.04	30.6.04	31.7.04	31.8.04	30.9.04	Six months to 30.9.04
Number of units							
Component:							
A6 (2 units for X)	280	560	1 400	760	600	480	4 080
B9 (3 units for X)	420	840	2 100	1 140	900	720	6 120

2 Direct materials purchase budget:

Component A6

	30.4.04	31.5.04	30.6.04	31.7.04	31.8.04	30.9.04	Six months to 30.9.04
Material usage (as above)	280	560	1 400	760	600	480	4 080
Add: Desired closing stock	110	220	560	300	240	200	200
	390	780	1 960	1 060	840	680	4 280
Less: Opening stock	100	110	220	560	300	240	100
Purchases (units) ×	290	670	1 740	500	540	440	4 180
Price per unit =	£5	£5	£5	£5	£5	£5	£5
Total purchases	£1 450	£3 350	£8 700	£2 500	£2 700	£2 200	£20 900

Component B9

	30.4.04	31.5.04	30.6.04	31.7.04	31.8.04	30.9.04	Six months to 30.9.04
Material usage (as above)	420	840	2 100	1 140	900	720	6 120
Add: Desired closing stock	250	630	340	300	200	180	180
	670	1 470	2 440	1 440	1 100	900	6 300
Less: Opening stock	200	250	630	340	300	200	200
Purchases (units)	470	1 220	1 810	1 100	800	700	6 100
Price per unit	£10	£10	£10	£10	£10	£10	£10
Total purchases	£4 700	£12 200	£18 100	£11 000	£8 000	£7 000	£61 000

17.6 Direct labour budget for Don Ltd.

Don Limited
Direct labour cost budget:

Grade:	30.6.05	31.7.05	31.8.05	Three months to 31.8.05
		Quarter		
Production (units) ×	600	700	650	1 950
Direct labour hours per unit =	3	3	3	3
Total direct labour hours	1 800	2 100	1 950	5 850
Budgeted rate per hour (£) ×	4	4	4	4
Production cost (£) =	*c/f* 7 200	8 400	7 800	23 400

Don Limited
Direct labour cost budget:

| | | | *Quarter* | | |
		30.6.05	31.7.05	31.8.05	*Three months to 31.8.05*
Production cost (£) =	b/f	7 200	8 400	7 800	23 400
Finishing (units)		600	700	650	1 950
Direct labour hours per unit ×		2	2	2	2
Total direct labour hours =		1 200	1 400	1 300	3 900
Budgeted rate per hour (£) ×		8	8	8	8
Finishing cost (£) =		9 600	11 200	10 400	31 200
Total budgeted direct labour cost (£)		16 800	19 600	18 200	54 600

Chapter 18

18.4 Variances for X Ltd

1. Direct materials total variance:

	£
Actual price per unit × actual quantity = £12 × 6 units	72
Less: Standard price per unit × standard quantity for actual production = £10 × 5 units	50
	22 (A)

2. Direct materials price variance:
   (Actual price – standard price) × actual quantity
   = (£12 – 10) × 6 units

   £12 (A)

3. Direct materials usage variance:
   (Actual quantity – standard quantity) × standard
   price = (6 – 5 units) × £10

   £10 (A)

18.6 Variances for Bruce Ltd

1. Direct labour total variance:

	£
Actual hours × actual hourly rate = 1000 hrs × £6.50	6 500
Less: Standard hours for actual production × standard hourly rate = 900 hrs × £6.00	5 400
	£1 100 (A)

2. Direct labour rate variance:
   (Actual hourly – standard hourly rate)
   × actual hours = (£6.50 – 6.00) × 1000 hrs

   £500 (A)

3. Direct labour efficiency variance:
   (Actual hours – standard hours for actual production)
   × standard hourly rate = (1000 hrs – 900) × £6.00

   £600 (A)

18.8 Overhead variances for Anthea Ltd

1 Fixed production overhead total variance: £

Actual fixed overhead   150 000

Less: Standard hours of production × fixed
production overhead absorption rate = (8000 hrs × £15)   120 000

£30 000   (A)

2 Fixed production overhead expenditure variance:
Actual fixed overhead – budgeted fixed overhead =
(£150 000 – 135 000)   £15 000   (A)

3 Fixed production overhead volume variance:
Budgeted fixed overhead – (standard hours of
production × fixed production overhead
absorption rate) = [£135 000 – (8000 × £15)]   £15 000   (A)

4 Fixed production overhead capacity variance:
Budgeted fixed overhead – (actual hours worked
× fixed production overhead absorption rate)
= [£135 000 – (10 000 hrs × £15)]   £15 000   (F)

5 Fixed production overhead efficiency variance:
Actual hours worked – standard hours of production
× fixed production overhead absorption rate
= [(10 000 hrs – 8000) × £15]   £30 000   (A)

18.9 Performance measures for Anthea Ltd

Performance measures:

1 Efficiency ratio:

$$\frac{\text{SHP}}{\text{Actual hours}} \times 100 = \frac{8000}{10\,000} \times 100 = \underline{\underline{80\%}}$$

2 Capacity ratio:

$$\frac{\text{Actual hours}}{\text{Budgeted hours}^*} \times 100 = \frac{10\,000}{9000} \times 100 = \underline{\underline{111.1\%}}$$

3 Production volume ratio:

$$\frac{\text{SHP}}{\text{Budgeted hours}^*} \times 100 = \frac{8000}{9000} \times 100 = \underline{\underline{88.9\%}}$$

$$^*\frac{135\,000}{15}$$

18.12   **Selling price variance for Milton Ltd**

1   Selling price variance:

[Actual sales revenue – (actual quantity × standard cost per unit)]   £9000   (F)
– (actual quantity × standard profit per unit) = [£99 000 –
(9000 × £7)] – (9000 × £3*) =

* £10 – 3

2   Sales volume profit variance:

(Actual quantity – budgeted quantity) × standard
profit = (9000 units – 10 000) × £3   £3000   (A)

3   Sales variances = £9000 (F) + 3000 (A)   = £6000   (F)

Chapter 19

19.4 Contribution analysis for Pole Ltd

Pole Limited
Marginal cost statement for the year to 31 January 2007

	£000	£000
Sales		450
Less: Variable costs:		
Direct materials	60	
Direct wages	26	
Administration expenses: variable (£7 + 4)	11	
Research and development expenditure:		
variable (£15 + 5)	20	
Selling and distribution expenditure:		
variable (£4 + 9)	13	130
		320
Contribution		
Less: Fixed costs:		
Administration expenses (£30 + 16)	46	
Materials: indirect	5	
Production overhead	40	
Research and development expenditure		
(£60 + 5)	65	
Selling and distribution expenditure		
(£80 + 21)	101	
Wages: indirect	13	270
Profit		50

19.5 Break-even chart for Giles Ltd.

Giles Limited

(a) (i) *Break-even point:*

In value terms:

$$\frac{\text{Fixed costs} \times \text{sales}}{\text{Contribution}} = \frac{£150\,000 \times 500}{(500 - 300)} = \underline{\underline{£375\,000}}$$

In units:

	£
Selling price per unit (£500 ÷ 50)	10
Less: Variable cost per unit (£300 ÷ 50)	6
Contribution per unit	4

$$\frac{\text{Fixed costs}}{\text{Contribution per unit}} = \frac{£150\,000}{4} = \underline{\underline{37\,500 \text{ units}}}$$

(ii) *Margin of safety:*

In value terms:

$$\frac{\text{Profit} \times \text{sales}}{\text{Contribution}} = \frac{£50\,000 \times 500}{200} = \underline{\underline{£125\,000}}$$

In units:

$$\frac{\text{Profit}}{\text{Contribution per unit}} = \frac{£50\,000}{4} = \underline{\underline{12\,500 \text{ units}}}$$

(b) *Break-even chart:*

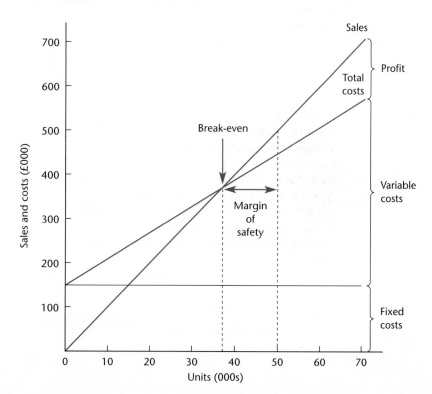

Chapter 20   20.4 **A special contract for Micro Ltd**

Budgeted contribution per unit of limiting factor for the year:

$$\frac{£250\,000}{50\,000} = \underline{\underline{£5 \text{ per direct labour hour}}}$$

Contribution per unit of limiting factor for the special contract:

	£	£
Contract price		50 000
Less: Variable costs:		
Direct materials	10 000	
Direct labour	30 000	40 000
Contribution		10 000

Therefore contribution per unit of limiting factor:

$$\frac{£10\,000}{4000 \text{ DLH}} = \underline{\underline{£2.20 \text{ per direct labour hour}}}$$

Conclusion:

The special contract earns less contribution per unit of limiting factor than does the *average* of ordinary budgeted work. It may be profitable to accept the contract if either it displaces less profitable work or surplus direct labour hours are available. A careful assessment should be undertaken to ascertain whether much more profitable work would be found than is the case with the contract if it will displace other more profitable contracts that could arise in the near future.

20.5 Contributions for Temple Ltd.

1 **Calculation of the contribution per unit of limiting factor**

(a) Normal work:

	£
Sales	6 000
Direct materials (100 kilos)	700
Direct labour (200 hours)	3 000
Variable overhead	300
	4 000
Contribution	2 000

Contribution per unit of key factor:

$$\text{Direct materials: } \frac{£2000}{100 \text{ kilos}} = \underline{\underline{£20 \text{ per kilo}}}$$

$$\text{Direct labour: } \frac{£2000}{200 \text{ direct labour hours}} = \underline{\underline{£10 \text{ per direct labour hour}}}$$

(b) and (c) Calculation of the contribution per unit of limiting factor for each of the proposed two new contracts:

	Contract 1	Contract 2
	£000	£000
Contract price	1 000	2 100
Less: variable costs		
Direct materials	300	600
Direct labour	300	750
Variable overhead	100	250
	700	1 600
Contribution	300	500

Contribution per unit of key factor:

	Contract 1	Contract 2
Direct materials	£300	£500
	50 kilos	100 kilos
=	£6 per kilo	£5 per kilo
Direct labour	£300	£500
	10 DLH	25 DLH
=	£30 per DLH	£20 per DLH

Summary of contribution per unit of limiting factor:

	Direct materials	Direct labour
	£	£
Normal work	20	10
Contract 1	6	5
Contract 2	30	20

2 Calculation of the total maximum contribution

Contract 1

If Contract 1 is accepted, it will earn a total contribution of £300 000. This will leave 150 000 kilos of direct material available for its normal work (200 000 kilos maximum available, less the 50 000 used on Contract 1). This means that 1 500 units of ordinary work could be undertaken (150 000 kilos divided by 100 kilos per unit).

However, Contract 1 will absorb 10 000 direct labour hours, leaving 90 000 DLH available (100 000 DLH less 10 000 DLH). As each unit of ordinary work uses 200 DLH, the maximum number of units that could be undertaken is 450 (90 000 DLH divided by 200 DLH). Thus the maximum number of units of ordinary work that could be undertaken if Contract 1 is accepted is 450 and NOT 1500 units if direct materials were the only limiting factor. As each unit makes a contribution of £2000, the total contribution would be £900 000 (450 units × £2000).

The total maximum contribution, if Contract 1 is accepted, is therefore, **£1 200 000** (£300 000 + 900 000).

Contract 2

If Contract 2 is accepted, only 100 000 kilos of direct materials will be available for ordinary work (200 000 kilos maximum available less 100 000 required for Contract 2). This means that only 1000 normal jobs could be undertaken (100 000 kilos divided by 100 kilos required per unit).

Contract 2 would absorb 25 000 direct labour hours, leaving 75 000 available for normal work (100 000 maximum DLH less the 25 000 DLH used by Contract 2). As each unit of normal work takes 200 hours, only 375 units could be made (75 000 DLH divided by 200 DLH per unit). Thus if this contract is accepted, 375 is the maximum number of normal jobs that could be undertaken. This would give a total contribution of £750 000 (375 units multiplied by £2000 of contribution per unit).

If Contract 2 is accepted, the total maximum contribution would be £1 250 000, i.e. Contract 2's contribution of £500 000 plus the contribution of £750 000 from the normal work.

The Decision

Accept Contract 2 because the maximum total contribution would be £1 250 000 compared with the £1 200 000 if Contract 1 was accepted.

Tutorial notes

1 The various cost relationships are assumed to remain unchanged at all levels of activity.
2 Fixed costs will not be affected irrespective of which contract is accepted.
3 The market for Temple's normal sales is assumed to be flexible.
4 Contract 2 will absorb one-half of the available direct materials and one-quarter of the available direct labour hours. Would the company want to commit such resources to work that may be uncertain and unreliable and that could have an adverse impact on its normal customers?

Chapter 21   21.5 Payback for Buchan Enterprises

(a) Payback period:

Year	Investment outlay £	Cash inflow £	Net cash flow £	Cumulative cash flow £
1	(50 000)	8 000	(42 000)	(42 000)
2	–	16 000	16 000	(26 000)
3	–	40 000	40 000	14 000
4	–	45 000	45 000	59 000
5	–	37 000	37 000	96 000

Net cash flow becomes positive in Year 3. Assuming the net cash flow accrues evenly, it becomes positive during August: $(26/40 \times 12) = 7.8$ months. The payback period, therefore, is about 2 years 8 months.

(b) Discounted payback period:

Year	Net cash flow	Discount factor @ 12%	Discounted net cash flow	Cumulative net cash flow
	£		£	£
0	(50 000)	1.0000	(50 000)	(50 000)
1	8 000	0.8929	7 143	(42 857)
2	16 000	0.7929	12 686	(30 171)
3	40 000	0.7118	28 472	(1 699)
4	45 000	0.6355	28 598	26 899
5	37 000	0.5674	20 994	47 893

Discounted net cash flow becomes positive in Year 4. Assuming the net cash flow accrues evenly throughout the year, it becomes positive in January of Year 4 (1 699/28 598 × 12 = 0.7). Discounted payback period therefore equals 3 years, 1 month. This value is in contrast with the payback method, where the net cash flow becomes positive in August of Year 3 (i.e. 2 years 8 months).

21.6 Lender Ltd's accounting rate of return

$$\text{Accounting rate of return (APR)} = \frac{\text{Average annual net profit after tax}}{\text{Cost of the investment}} \times 100\%$$

$$= \frac{\frac{1}{5}(£18\,000 + 47\,000 + 65\,000 + 65\,000 + 30\,000)}{100\,000} \times 100\%$$

$$= \frac{45\,000}{100\,000} \times 100\%$$

$$= \underline{\underline{45\%}}$$

Note: Based on the average investment, the ARR

$$= \frac{£45\,000}{\frac{1}{2}(100\,000 + 0)} \times 100\%$$

$$= \underline{\underline{90\%}}$$

21.7 Net present value for a Lockhart project

Net present value:

Year	Net cash flow £000	Discount factor @15%	Present value £000
1	800	0.8696	696
2	850	0.7561	643
3	830	0.6575	546
4	1 200	0.5718	686
5	700	0.4972	348
Total present value			2 919
Initial cost			2 500
Net present value			419

Index

ABC *see* activity based costing
ABCM *see* activity based cost management
ABM *see* activity based management
absorption costing 332, 336, 428
    definition 336
    procedure 428
absorption of production overhead 355–8
    calculation of overhead absorption rates
        357
    direct labour cost 356
    direct labour hours 356
    direct materials cost 355–6
    equation 355
    machine hours 356
    prime cost 356
    specific units 355
    and standard hours 403–4
ACCA *see* Association of Chartered Certified
        Accountants
account 52
    bank account 55
    capital account 54
    cash account 55
    company 125
    creditor account 55
    debtor account 55
    ledger account 53
accountability 519
accountancy profession 15–17
    the future 303
    Government confidence in 287
    organization of 287
    public perceptions of 288–9
accounting for bad and doubtful debts 103–4
accounting data problems 248–9
    absolute 248
    contextual 249
    structural 249
accounting equation 50–2
accounting information 9–10
accounting policies
    case study 187–9
    see also FRS 18 Accounting policies
accounting principles 36
Accounting Principles Board (US) 302
    revenue recognition 302
accounting profit 82, 108–9
    and cash 165–6
accounting rate of return 484–6
    advantages 485
    calculation of 484
    definition 484
    disadvantages 485
    example 484–5
accounting rules 26–46
    boundary rules 30–2
    conceptual framework 38–40
    ethical rules 36–7
    historical development 28–30
    measurement rules 32–5

summary 45–6
accounting scandals 288–94
    action 294
    American 290
    auditor reliability 293–4
    auditors 292–3
    causes 291–2
    definition 289–90
    examples 290–1
    perceptions 288–9
Accounting Standards Board (ASB) 28, 38,
        201–2
    committees 201–2
    company law reform 295
    construction of conceptual framework 38–9
    Financial Reporting Standards 201
    history 28
    and information disclosure 197–9
    objectives 201
Accounting Standards Steering Committee
        200
    objectives 200
accounting world 2–25
    accountancy profession 15–17
    branches of accounting 10–15
    development of accounting 7–10
    nature of accounting 3–7
    public and private entities 17–22
accretion 303
accruals 34, 100–2
    accounting for 100–1
    accruals 100–1
    definition 100
    loans 263
    opening and closing 34
    prepayments 34, 101–2
    see also prepayments
accumulated depreciation 99
acid test ratio 257
    calculation of 257, 283
acquisitions and disposals 239
action to prevent accounting scandals 294
activity based cost management (ABCM) 509
activity based costing (ABC) 363–7, 509
    example 365–6
    overhead absorption 364
    process 509
    traditional method 509
activity based management (ABM) 509–10
    definition 509
    process 509
adding value 523
adherence 378
administration of budget 379–80
administrators 15
    see also liquidation
advanced manufacturing technology (AMT)
        506, 525
adverse trend 363
A.G. Barr plc 229–37

comparison of financial results 272–3
    group balance sheet 235–6
    group cash flow statement 238
    group profit and loss account 233
    independent auditors' report 230
    interpreting company accounts 264–9
    profit and loss account expenditure 232
    review of the trading results 240–1
    statement of total recognized gains and
        losses 234–5
AIT 301
allocating revenue, costs and assets 523
    and value chain analysis 523
allocation of costs 332, 352
Amendment to FRS 5 'Reporting the
        Substance of Transactions' 303
American defence industry 517
amounts owing 4, 34
    loans 263
AMT *see* advanced manufacturing technology
analysis of changes in net debt 174
analysis of financial results 270–1
    calculate some accounting ratios 271
    financial accounts 270
    index financial data 270–1
    reports section 270
analysis of interpretation of accounts 251–2
annual accounts 224–45, 296
    auditors' report 230–1
    group balance sheet 235–7
    group cash flow statement 237–9
    group profit and loss account 231–4
    notes to the accounts 239–40
    periodic summary 240–1
    setting the scene 227–39
    statement of total recognized gains and
        losses 234–5
annual report 208–23, 296
    chairman's statement 212–14
    corporate governance 216–17
    directors' report 215–16
    introductory material 210–12
    operating and financial review 214–15
    remuneration report 218–19
    shareholder information 219
    statutory disclosure of information 199
AOL Time Warner 290
application of contribution analysis 432–4
    changes in profit 433–4
    changes in variable cost 433
apportionment 352–3
    mathematical 353
    of non-production overhead 361
approaches to management accountancy
        326–7
appropriation 85, 254
appropriation account 127
approval 378
ASB *see* Accounting Standards Board
assets 50

assistance 326
associated company 227
  definition 228
Association of Accounting Technicians
  16
Association of Chartered Certified
  Accountants (ACCA) 15
assumptions 430–1
attainable standard 402
auditing 13–14, 325
  external 325
  internal 325
auditor reliability 293–4
auditors 292–3
  and detection of fraud 293–4
  and Enron 292
  external 13
  internal 13
  reliability of 293–4
  true and fair view 294
  UK position versus US 292–3
auditors' report 230–1
authorization 334
authorized share capital 123
automation 507
autonomy 334
average cost 338
average pricing method 340
avoidable and non-avoidable costs 458

back of the envelope exercises 321
bad and doubtful debts 33, 102–5
  accounting for 103–4
  allowance for 36
  bad debts 33, 102–3
  provisions for 103–5
balance sheet 3, 80, 128–30
  and depreciation 99
  example 84–7
  group 235–7
  not part of double-entry system 83
  stage of sole trader accounts 83–4
balanced scorecard 516
balancing the accounts 61–3
  with a credit balance 62–3
  with a debit balance 62
bank account 55–6
bank loans 494–5
bank overdrafts 263, 494
bankruptcy 14, 121
basic financial accounts 84–7
  preparation of 84–5
  in vertical format 86–7
basic procedure for interpreting
  accounts 250–3
  analysis 251–2
  data collection 250–1
basic rule of double-entry book-keeping
  52
basic sole trader accounts 80–1
  example 84–7
basic standard 402
BBC see British Broadcasting
  Corporation
behavioural consequences
  of budgeting 390
  of contribution analysis 440
  dysfunction 390
  of management accounting 325–7
benchmarking 514
better budgeting 510–11
bills of exchange 494

blocking 497
book-keeping 11–12
books of account 12
boundaries 334
boundary rules 30–2, 45
  entity 30–1
  going concern 32
  periodicity 31
  quantitative 32
branches of accounting 10–15
  auditing 13–14
  financial accounting 10–12
  financial management 14
  management accounting 12–13
  others 14–15
  taxation 14
break-even chart 434–6
  relevant range 435
British Broadcasting Corporation
  (BBC) 21, 157
budget 377–8
  cash 379
  features of 377
  forecast 379
  interrelationship of types of 381
  master 377
  sub-period 379
budget committee 379
budget period 379
budget procedure 378–81
  administration 379–80
  budget period 379
  budgeting process 380–1
budgetary control 377–8
  budget 377–8
  budget committee 379
  budgetary control 378
  features of 378, 390
  primary purpose 389
  variance report 529–30
  variances 378
  see also budgeting
budgeting 323, 375–98
  behavioural consequences 390
  better 510–11
  and budgetary control 377–8
  example 382–7
  fixed and flexible budgets 387–9
  functional budgets 382–7
  procedure 378–81
  short-term planning 323
  see also budgetary control
budgeting process 380–81
building blocks of accounting 39
business environment 505–7
business rates 335, 352

Cadbury Committee 214, 216
Cairn Energy plc 217–19
  environmental accounting and
    reporting 512
  Environmental and Social Review
    2001 512, 519–20
calculation of actual costs 324
calculation of variances 408–10
capacity ratio 405
  calculation of 406
capital 50, 54–5, 129
capital account 54
capital allowances 493
capital employed 484
capital expenditure 82, 97, 239

capital gearing ratio 262–4
  calculation of 263–4, 284
capital income 82
capital investment 476–503
  background 477–8
  main methods 478–91
  net cash flow 491–3
  selecting a method 491
  sources of finance 493–6
capital reserves 129
  shareholder funds 263
CASE see Committee on Accounting
  for Smaller Entities
case studies
  accounting policies 187–9
  cash flow statements 190–2
  communication of financial
    information 308–11
  fixed and flexible budgets 529–30
  interpretation of accounts 312–16
  preparation of financial statements
    185–6
  pricing 533–4
  standard cost operating statements
    531–2
cash account 55–6
cash at bank 55, 236
cash budget 379, 382
cash flow accounting (CFA) 33
  profit and cash 165–6
cash flow statement (CFS) 163–92
  accounting profit and cash 165–6
  case study 190–2
  construction of 167–71
  contents 239
  example 174–6
  FRS 1 format 171–4
  group 237–9
  net cash flow decisions 455
cash in hand 55
cash transactions 81
cash versus profit 81–2
causes of accounting scandals 291–2
central government 20, 198, 249
  accounts 156–7
  services 156
  as users of accounts 249–50
CFA see cash flow accounting
CFS see cash flow statements
chairman's statement 212–14
changes in management accounting
  507–8
changes in profit 433–4
changes in variable cost 433
Chartered Institute of Management
  Accountants (CIMA) 10,
  12–13, 15
  Management Accounting
    Terminology 522
Chartered Institute of Public Finance
  and Accountancy (CIPFA) 15
charts and graphs 434–40
  break-even chart 435–6
  contribution graph 436–7
  and criticism of contribution analysis
    440
  profit/volume chart 437–8
choice 454
choice of accounts 54–7
  capital 54–5
  cash at bank 55
  cash in hand 55

choice of accounts (*Continued*)
  creditors 55
  debtors 55
  discounts allowed 56
  discounts received 56
  drawings 56
  petty cash 56
  purchases 56
  sales 56
  stock 57
  trade creditors 56
  trade debtors 56
  trade discounts 56
CIMA *see* Chartered Institute of
  Management Accountants
CIPFA *see* Chartered Institute of Public
  Finance and Accountancy
City 295
closing accruals and prepayments 34
closing stock 57, 95
  estimating value of 165
  and history of accounting 321
closure and shutdown decisions 459–61
  example 460–61
CLRC *see* Company Law and
  Reporting Commission
collagen 211–12
*Combined Code on Corporate
  Governance* 215–16
commercial paper 494
commission 67
committed costs 458
Committee on Accounting for Smaller
  Entities (CASE) 202
common ledger account entries 57–8
  example 60–1
communication of financial information
  case study 308–11
companies 19–20, 119–42
  limited liability 121–7
  see also company accounts
Companies Act 1948 199–200, 295
Companies Act 1967 199–200, 295
Companies Act 1976 199, 295
Companies Act 1980 199, 295
Companies Act 1981 199, 295
Companies Act 1985 20, 199, 227–9, 295
  formats 231
  and history of accounting 321
  information required by 125, 199, 204
  sources of authority 227–8
  true and fair view 203, 293
Companies Act 1989 199, 295
  summary of requirements 202–3
Companies House 199
company accounts 119–42
  balance sheet 128–30
  example 130–4, 264–9
  limited liability 121–2
  preparation of 130–3
  profit and loss account 127–8
  structure and operation 122–7
  see also companies
company information 270
company law 249, 287, 295–7
  and history of accounting 321
  reform 295–7
company law reform 295–7
  annual report 296
  organization 295
Company Law and Reporting
  Commission (CLRC) 295
comparability 39

compensating 67
competitiveness 515
complementary products 439
complete reversal of entry 67
compliance 203
comprehensibility 39
computerization 507
computerized recording systems 35, 52
conceptual framework of accounting
  rules 38–40
  basic accounting rules 29
conservatism 36
consistency 37, 45
consolidation 228
construction of cash flow statements
  167–71
  preparation of 168–70
construction industry 31
contemporary issues 285–316
  accounting scandals 288–94
  company law reform 295–7
  internationalization 297–301
  overview 287–8
  revenue recognition 301–3
Continental Europe 199, 297
continuous weighted average (CWA)
  338, 340–2
  advantages 342
  disadvantages 342
  pricing method 341–2
contribution 429–30
  equations 429–30
contribution analysis 426–52
  application 432–4
  assumptions 430–1
  charts and graphs 434–9
  contribution 429–30
  criticisms 439–40
  example 442–4
  format 431–2
  formulae 440–1
  limiting factors 444–6
  marginal costing 428–9
  see also marginal costing
contribution graph 436–7
control 5, 228, 323–4, 334
  of non-production overhead 360–1
  and standard costing 401
convertible unsecured loan stock 495
cook book approach 296
cooperation 298–9
corporate governance 214, 216–17
  *Combined Code on Corporate
   Governance* 215–16
  principles 215
  remuneration report 218–19
corporate planning 322–3
corporation tax 126, 129, 492
correction 378
cost accounting 324, 332
  calculation of actual costs 324
  and history of accounting 321, 332
cost book-keeping 12
cost centre 334
  charging costs to 354–5
  production cost centre 334
  service cost centre 334
  sharing out production service
   cost-centre costs 352–5
cost classification 335–7, 439, 457–9
  avoidable and non-avoidable costs
   458
  committed costs 458

fixed and variable costs 457–8
  opportunity costs 458
  relevant and non-relevant costs 458
  sunk costs 458
cost driver 365, 368, 523
  rate 365
  in value chain analysis 523
cost operating statement 417
cost plus 335, 465
cost pools 365, 368
cost recovery 440
cost reduction 521
cost unit 352
cost-based pricing 465
council tax 380
cradle to grave costing 517
credit 53
credit balance 62–3
credit sales 495
creditor account 55–6
creditors 55
  trade 56
criminal penalties 295
critical events 303
criticisms of contribution analysis
  439–40
cumulative preferences shares 123
current assets 236
current assets ratio 256–7
  calculation of 256, 283
customers 198, 249
  as users of accounts 249–50
CWA *see* continuous weighted average

data collection 250–1
debentures 124, 262, 495
  loans 263
debit 53
debit balance 62
debtor account 55–6
debtors 55, 236
  trade 56
debts owed 4
decision making 5, 324, 453–75
  closure and shutdown decisions
   459–61
  cost classification 457–9
  definition 454–7
  make or buy decisions 461–3
  pricing decisions 463–7
  special orders 467–9
  specific decisions 453–75
  types of decision 459
decline in manufacturing 507
defective accounts and reports 203
deferred tax 240
definition of accounting 319–20
deflation 492
depreciation 97–9
  accumulated 99
  annual charge 97
  balance sheet disclosure of fixed
   assets 99
  reducing balance method 97–8
  straight-line method 97
  writing off 166
design 517
deterioration 338
development of accounting 7–10
Devro plc 211–12, 217–19
  environmental accounting and
   reporting 512
  environmental report 513

diplomacy 326
direct costs 145–6, 331–48
  classification of costs 335–7
  direct labour 342–3
  direct materials 337–42
  direct unit costs 335
  other direct costs 343–4
  responsibility accounting 334
direct labour 146, 342–3
  calculation of variances 408,
    412–13
  charging to production 343
  cost, and absorption of production
    overhead 356
  and cost variances 407
  hours, and absorption of production
    overhead 356
  identification and pricing 342
  and standard costing 403
direct labour cost absorption 356
direct labour hours absorption 356
direct materials 146, 337–42
  calculation of variances 408, 412
  continuous weighted average
    (CWA) 340–2
  cost, and absorption of production
    overhead 355–6
  and cost variances 407
  first-in, first-out (FIFO) 338–40
  indirect costs 337
  raw materials 337
  size 337
  and standard costing 403
  timing 337
direct materials cost absorption 355–6
direct unit costs 335
directors 125–6, 214
directors' report 204, 215–16
disclosure 196–7
  minimum requirements 199
  in practice in the annual accounts
    227
  see also information disclosure
discount table 536
discounted payback 480–83
  advantages 483
  disadvantages 483
  example 482–3
discounting 481
discounts allowed 56
discounts received 56
dividend cover 261
  calculation of 261, 284
dividend yield 261
  calculation of 261, 284
dividends 126, 212, 234
double-entry book-keeping 7–8, 35,
  52–4
  and the accounting equation 50–2
  basic rule of 52
  history of 7–8
drawing conclusions from accounting
  ratios 272–3
drawings 56, 87
drawings account 56
dual aspect 35, 45
  and double-entry book-keeping 50
  rule 35
dysfunctional behaviour 390

earnings per share (EPS) 234, 253, 261
  calculation of 261, 284

efficiency ratio 258–60, 273, 283–4,
  405
  calculation of 406
  fixed assets turnover ratio 258–9
  stock turnover ratio 258
  summary 283–4
  trade creditor payment period 260
  trade debtor collection period ratio
    259–60
elastic demand 464
elements of cost 145, 335–6
emerging issues 504–28
  activity based management
    509–10
  better budgeting 510–11
  business environment 505–7
  changes in management accounting
    507–8
  environmental accounting and
    reporting 511–14
  performance measurement 514–16
  product life cycle costing 517–18
  social accounting and reporting
    518–20
  strategic management accounting
    520–1
  target costing 521
  value chain analysis 522–4
employees 197–8, 212, 249
  as users of accounts 249–50
end result 271
Enron 290–1
  auditors 292
entering transactions 57–9
entity 30–1, 44–5, 143–62
  Limited Liability Act 1855 121
  other entity accounts 143–62
  types of 401–2
environmental accounting and
    recording 511–14
  definition 511
  environmental report 513
  lack of statutory requirements 512
environmental recording *see*
    environmental accounting
    and recording
environmental report 513
EPS *see* earnings per share (EPS)
equality 326
Equitable Life 291
equity dividends paid 239
estimated cost 338
ethical rules 36–7, 45–6
  consistency 37
  objectivity 37
  prudence 36
  relevance 37
EU *see* European Union
Euro market 495
Eurobond loan capital 495
European law 199
European Union 298–9
  accounting standards 298
  company law legislation 297
  UK membership of 199
evolution in management accounting
  508
expectations gap 4, 293–4
expenditure 81
  capital 82
  revenue 82
external auditing 325

external auditors 13
external pricing 463–5
  cost-based pricing 465
  market-based pricing 464

factoring 494
fairness 196
fashion industry 31, 402
  product life cycle costing 517
favourable trend 324, 363
FIFO *see* first-in, first-out
filing 199, 220, 296
final dividend 126
financial accounting 10–12, 47–192
  book-keeping 11–12
  case studies 185–92
  cash flow statements 163–84
  company accounts 119–42
  definition 320
  last minute adjustments 93–118
  other entity accounts 143–62
  recording data 48–78
  sole trader accounts 79–92
Financial Accounting Standards Board
  (FASB) 299
financial investment 239
financial management 14, 325
financial reporting 11, 193–316
  annual accounts 224–45
  annual report 208–23
  case studies 308–16
  contemporary issues 285–307
  flexibility 293
  information disclosure 194–207
  interpretation of accounts 246–84
Financial Reporting Council (FRC)
  200–1
  company law reform 295
  objectives 201
Financial Reporting Review Panel
  (FRRP) 202
  company law reform 295
  objectives 202
Financial Reporting Standards (FRSs)
  28–9, 201
Financial Sector and Other Special
  Industries Committee
  (FSOSIC) 202
financing 239
finished goods state 145
  and history of accounting 321
First World War 519
first-in, first-out (FIFO) 337–40
  advantages 340
  disadvantages 340
  pricing method 339–40
  SSAP 9 340
fixed assets 82, 236
fixed assets turnover ratio 258–9
  calculation of 258, 283
fixed budgets 387–9
  budgetary control variance report
    529–30
  case study 529–30
  definition 387
fixed costs 336, 439, 457–8
  changes in profit 433
  definition 428
fixed production overhead 403, 409
  calculation of variances 409–10,
    413–15
  see also production overhead

flexibility 293
flexible budgets 387–9
   budgetary control variance report
      529–30
   case study 529–30
   definition 388
   procedure 388–9
flexing 387, 404
forecast 379
format of contribution analysis 431–2
forward-looking decisions 455
foundations of management accounting
      318–30
   behavioural considerations 325–7
   historical review 320–2
   main functions 322–5
   nature and purpose 319–20
France 199
fraud 290–91
   detection of by auditors 293–4
FRC see Financial Reporting Council
FRRP see Financial Reporting Review
      Panel
FRS 1 Cash flow statements 163,
      171–4, 229
   analysis of changes in net debt 174
   contents 171
   example 174–6
   reconciliation of net cash flow to
      movement in net debt 173
   reconciliation of operating profit to
      operating cash flows 172–3
   requirements 298
FRS 3 Reporting financial performance
      229, 232–3
   requirements 298
   statement of total recognized gains
      and losses 234–5
FRS 5 Substance of transactions 303
   see also tangible fixed assets
FRS 18 Accounting policies 229
   see also accounting policies
FRSs see Financial Reporting Standards
FSOSIC see Financial Sector and Other
      Special Industries Committee
fully paid share capital 123
functional budgets 382–7
   master budget 382
   preparation of 382–7
functions of management accounting
      322–5
   auditing 325
   control 323–4
   cost accounting 324
   decision making 324–5
   financial management 325
   planning 322–3

GAAP see generally accepted
      accounting principles
GBV see gross book value
generally accepted accounting
      principles (GAAP) 299–300
   contention 300
Germany 199
getting it right first time 506–7
Global Crossing 290
global family 515
going concern 32, 45
good presentation 39
government accounts 156–7
gross book value (GBV) 99

measuring efficiency 259
gross profit 83, 233
gross profit ratio 255
   calculation of 255, 283
group balance sheet 235–7
group cash flow statement 237–9
group profit and loss account 231–4
   examples 232
   published 233
group undertaking 228
growth of service industries 507
guide to interpretation of accounts
      270–1
   analysis of financial results 270–1
   obtain company information 270
   survey of general business
      environment 270
   work out what happened 271
   write up results 271

Halliburton 290
HCA see historic cost accounting
hire purchase 495
historic cost 33, 45
historic cost accounting (HCA) 33
   and inflation 108
historical development of accounting
      rules 28–30
history of accounting 320–2
holding company 228
horizontal analysis 251
hotels and catering 150
how to prevent accounting scandals
      294

IAS 7 'Cash Flow Statements' 298
IAS 8 'Revenue' 303
IASB see International Accounting
      Standards Board
IASC see International Accounting
      Standards Committee
IASCF see International Accounting
      Standards Committee
      Foundation
ICAEW see Institute of Chartered
      Accountants in England and
      Wales
ICAI see Institute of Chartered
      Accountants in Ireland
ICAS see Institute of Chartered
      Accountants of Scotland
ideal standard 402
IFRSs see International Financial
      Reporting Standards
impact 325–7
income 81
   capital 82
   revenue 82
income of a capital nature see capital
      income
income and expenditure account
      153–5
income of a revenue nature see revenue
      income
inconsistencies 303
incremental costing 429
Independent Insurance 291
indexing 492
indirect costs 145, 335, 337, 349–74
   activity based costing 363–7
   example 358–60
   non-production overhead 360–1

predetermined absorption rates
      362–3
   production overhead 351–8
indirect labour 146
indirect materials 146
Industrial Revolution 8–9, 121, 321
   and history of accounting 321
inelastic demand 464
inflation 33, 108, 492
   and historic cost accounting 108
   impact of 492
information 326
information disclosure 124–5,
      194–207, 227
   disclosure 196–7
   sources of authority 199–204
   user groups 197–9
   see also disclosure
information technology 291–2, 302
infrastructure 505
Ingenta 301
insolvency 14
Institute of Chartered Accountants in
      England and Wales (ICAEW)
      15, 200
Institute of Chartered Accountants in
      Ireland (ICAI) 15
Institute of Chartered Accountants of
      Scotland (ICAS) 15
integrity 194
interest received 233
interim dividend 126
internal auditing 325
internal auditors 13, 325
internal rate of return 488–91
   advantages 490
   disadvantages 490–1
   example 489
International Accounting Standards
      297–8
International Accounting Standards
      Board (IASB) 287, 297
International Accounting Standards
      Committee (IASC) 297
International Accounting Standards
      Committee Foundation
      (IASCF) 297
   revenue recognition 302
   Revenue recognition 303
International Financial Reporting
      Standards (IFRSs) 297–8
internationalization 297–301
   European Union 298–9
   International Accounting Standards
      297–8
   United States of America 299–301
interpretation of accounts 246–84
   basic procedure 250–3
   case study 312–16
   drawing conclusions 272–3
   efficiency ratios 258–60
   example 264–9
   interpretation 248
   interpretation guide 270–1
   investment ratios 260–4
   liquidity ratios 256–7
   nature and purpose of
      interpretation 248–50
   profitability ratios 253–6
   ratio analysis 253
   summary of main ratios 283–4
introduction to accounting 1–46

accounting rules 26–46
accounting world 2–25
introductory material to annual report
    210–12
inventory *see* stock
investment centre 334
investment ratios 260–4, 273, 284
    capital gearing ratio 262–4
    dividend cover 261
    dividend yield 261
    earnings per share 261
    price/earnings ratio 262
    summary 284
investments 129, 236
investors 197, 249
    as users of accounts 249–50
Irn-Bru 229
issued share capital 123

J. Smart & Co. PLC 213, 231–2
    chairman's review 213
    directors' report 216
    profit and loss account expenditure
        232
Japan 506–7
    management philosophies 506, 525
JIT *see* just-in-time production
Joint Stock Companies Act 1856 121
just-in-time (JIT) production 506

key factors 444–6
    application of 445
    marginal costing using two 446
    rule 444
key financials 211

language 5, 7, 298
last minute adjustments 93–118
    accounting profit 108–9
    accruals and payments 100–2
    bad and doubtful debts 102–5
    depreciation 97–9
    example 105–8
    stock 95–6
leasing 495
ledger 52
ledger account 53, 340–1
    common ledger account entries 57–8
    entries for depreciation 99
    example 60–1
    stores 340–1
legal requirements 31
legal title 108
leisure and recreational activities 150
lenders 197, 249
    as users of accounts 249–50
liabilities 50
    loans 263
limited liability 121–2
    definition 121
    and history of accounting 321
    legal restrictions 121
Limited Liability Act 1855 121
limited liability partnership 19
limiting factors 444–6
    application of key factors 445
    marginal costing using two key
        factors 446
    rule 444
liquidation 14–15, 197
    administrators 15
    and disclosure 197

receivers 15
liquidity ratios 256–7, 272–3, 283
    acid test ratio 257
    current assets ratio 256–7
    summary 283
listed company 123
    requirements 228
LLP *see* limited liability partnership
loan capital 495
loans 124, 130, 263, 495–6
    debentures 124
    definition 263
    other types of 495–6
local government 21
    accounts 156–7
    services 157
local property tax 335
long-term finance 495–6
    debentures 495
    other types of loan 495–6
    shares 496
long-term planning 322–3
loyalty 56

MacDonald, Linda A. 300
machine hours 356, 405
machine hours absorption 356
make or buy decisions 461–3
    example 462–3
management accounting 12–13,
        317–534
    budgeting 375–98
    capital investment 476–503
    case studies 529–34
    changes in 507–8
    contribution analysis 426–52
    definition 320
    direct costs 331–48
    emerging issues 504–28
    foundations 318–30
    and history of accounting 332
    indirect costs 349–74
    main functions of 322–5
    specific decisions 453–75
    standard costing 399–425
Management Accounting Terminology
        522
management of liquid resources 239
management philosophies 506, 525
manufacturing 517
manufacturing accounts 145–50
    construction of 147–9
    example 145–7
    format 145–7
    links with other accounts 149–50
manufacturing cost 145–7
manufacturing overhead 146
marginal costing 337, 428–9
    assumptions 430–4
    contribution 429–30
    criticisms 439–40
    definition 337, 429
    equation 440
    example 442–4
    format 431–2
    formulae 440–2
    limiting factors 444–6
    statement 431–2
    use of marginal cost formulae 441
    using two key factors 446
    see also contribution analysis
mark-up ratio 255–6

calculation of 255, 283
market thinking 271
market value 147
market-based pricing 464
master budget 377, 382
matching 34–5, 45
    rule 34
materiality 35, 38, 45
    rule 35
mathematical apportionment 353
matters affecting community 518–19
matters affecting employees 518
measurement rules 32–5, 45
    dual aspect 35
    historic cost 33
    matching 34–5
    materiality 35
    money measurement 32
    realization 33–4
median debt collection period 260
medium-term finance 494–5
    bank loans 494–5
    credit sales 495
    hire purchase 495
    leasing 495
methods of capital investment
        appraisal 478–91
    accounting rate of return 484–6
    discounted payback 481–3
    internal rate of return 488–91
    net present value 486–8
    payback 478–80
    selecting a method 491
minimum disclosure requirements
        199
misconceptions 293–4
money measurement 32, 45
monitoring 378
morality 36

natural resources 511
nature of accounting 3–7
    definition 3
    why accounting is important for
        non-accountants 4–6
nature and purpose of interpretation
        of accounts 248–50
    accounting data problems 248–9
    definition 248
    users and their requirements
        249–50
nature and purpose of management
        accounting 318–30
NBV *see* net book value
net balance 61
net book value (NBV) 99
    measuring efficiency 259
net cash flow 455, 478–9, 491–3
    estimation of future 491
    inflation 492
    taxation 492–3
net debt 173–4
    analysis of changes in 174
net funds 173
net operating expenses 233
net present value (NPV) 486–8
    advantages 488
    disadvantages 488
    example 486–7
net profit 83
net profit ratio 256

net profit ratio (*Continued*)
  calculation of 256, 283
  for internal comparisons 256
New York Stock Exchange 299–300
non-autocracy 326
non-cost factors 440
non-disciplinarianism 326
non-production overhead 360–1
  apportionment 361
  control 360–1
  selling price 361
  stock valuation 361
  see also overhead; production
    overhead
non-relevant costs 458
not-for-profit entity accounts 153–5
not-for-profit sector 20–2, 153–5
  central government 20
  local government 21
  quasi-government bodies 21
  social organizations 21–2
  and strategic planning 322–3
notes to the accounts 239–40
NPV *see* net present value
number crunching 6

objectivity 37, 46
obligation 33
OFR *see* operating and financial review
omission 67
one-off decisions 455
opening accruals and prepayments 34
opening stock 57, 95
operating activities 239
operating and financial review (OFR)
    214–15
  definition 214
  financial review 214–15
  operating review 214
operating profit 233
operating statements 416–17
  preparation of 417
operation of standard costing 401–7
  definitions 401
  information required 403
  performance measures 404–7
  sales variances 404
  standard costing period 402
  standard hours and absorption of
    overhead 403–4
  types of entities 401–2
  types of standard 402
  uses 401
opportunity costs 455, 458, 467
Orchestream 301
order of closure 352
ordinary shares 123, 129, 254
  shareholder funds 263
organization change 507
original entry 67
other entity accounts 143–62
  government accounts 156–7
  manufacturing accounts 145–50
  not-for-profit entity accounts 153–5
  service entity accounts 150–3
other types of direct cost 343–4
outsourcing 507
overdrafts 263, 494
overhead 345, 349, 354
  actual cost of 362
  non-production 360–1
  production 351–60

see also non-production overhead;
    production overhead
overhead absorption rates 357–60, 364
  calculation of 357
  example 358–60, 364
  fairer method 364
  traditional method 364, 367
override rule 203

P/E ratio *see* price/earnings ratio
Pacioli 8
Partnership Act 1890 19
partnerships 19
payback 478–80
  example 479–80
perceptions of accountants 288–9
performance measurement 4, 514–16
  features 514
  segmental performance 515
  and standard costing 401
performance measures 404–7
  capacity ratio 405
  efficiency ratio 405
  production value ratio 405
periodic summary 240–1
periodicity 31–3, 45
permissive system of financial
    reporting 199
personal services 150
petty cash 56
petty cash account 56
Pitt, Harvey 300
planned cost 338
planning 5, 322–3
  long-term 322–3
  short-term 323
Post Office 21, 157
practicality 196
predetermined absorption rates 362–3
preferences shares 123, 129
  cumulative 123
  loans 263
  shareholder funds 263
preparation of annual accounts 227–9
  case study 185–7
  disclosure in practice 227
  procedure 229–30
  sources of authority 227–9
preparation of sole trader accounts
    83–4
  balance sheet stage 83–4
  trading and profit and loss account
    stage 83
preparation of strategic plan 323
prepayments 100–2
  accounting for 101
  accruals 100–1
  definition 101
  prepayments 101–2
  see also accruals
prescriptive system of financial
    reporting 199
pressure groups 511
price base 492
price/earnings ratio (P/E ratio) 262
  calculation of 262, 284
  and company's future 271
pricing decisions 463–7
  case study 533–4
  external pricing 463–5
  transfer pricing 464–7
prime cost 146, 356
prime cost absorption 356

principle 67
principles approach 293, 299
Private Companies Committee 295
private company 123
privatization 462, 507
probability testing 455–6
product costing 332
product life cycle costing 517–18
  features 517
production cost centre 334
  sharing out production service
    cost-centre costs 352–5
production overhead 351–60
  absorption of 355–8
  allocation of costs 352
  calculation of variances 408–9, 413–15
  procedure 351
  sharing cost-centre costs 352–5
  see also non-production overhead;
    overhead
production volume ratio 405
  calculation of 406
professional requirements on
    disclosure 200–4
  the Accounting Standards Board
    (ASB) 201–2
  the Financial Reporting Council
    (FRC) 200–1
  the Financial Reporting Review
    Panel (FRRP) 202
professional services 150
profit centre 334
profit loading 335
profit and loss account 3, 80, 127–8
  appropriation account 127
  example 84–7
  group 231–4
  shareholder funds 263
  and trading stage of sole trader
    accounts 83
  writing off debt 102
profit-making sector 17–20
  companies 19–20
  partnerships 19
  sole traders 19
  and strategic planning 322–3
profit/volume chart 437–8
profitability ratios 253–6, 272, 283
  gross profit ratio 255
  mark-up ratio 255–6
  net profit ratio 256
  return on capital employed ratio 254–5
  summary 283
proposed dividend 126, 129
prospects 212
prototype 517
provision 103
  loans 263
proxy 219
prudence 36, 45, 303
  and revenue recognition 303
  rule 36, 303
PSNC *see* Public Sector and Not-for-
    profit Committee
public 198, 249
  as users of accounts 249–50
public company 123
public and private entities 17–22
  not-for-profit sector 20–2
  profit-making sector 17–20
Public Sector and Not-for-profit
    Committee (PSNC) 202
publicity 291
purchases 56

purchases account 56, 145

quality of output should reflect
        specification 507
quantitative rule 32, 45
    data 251
quasi-government bodies 21
    accounts 156–7
    services 157
Quest 290

rate of return adjustment 492
ratio analysis 247, 251, 253
raw materials 145, 337
realization 33–4, 45
receivers 15
recent accounting scandals 290–1
reciprocal service costs 353
    treatment of 353
recognition 302–3
    definitions 302
    problems 302–3
reconciliation 229
    of net cash flow to movement in net
        debt 173
    of operating profit to operating cash
        flows 172–3
recording data 48–78
    accounting equation 50–2
    balancing the accounts 61–3
    double-entry book-keeping 52–4
    ledger account example 60–1
    trial balance 63–6
    trial balance errors 66–8
    working with accounts 54–9
reducing balance depreciation 97–8
Registrar of Companies 120, 125, 220
    delivery of accounts 296
    statutory disclosure of information
        199
relevance 37, 39, 46, 325–7
relevant costs 428, 455, 458
relevant range 435
reliability 39
    of auditors 293–4
remuneration report 218–19
Reporting Review Panel (RRP) 295
reserves 129
residual income (RI) 515
residual value 98
resource accounting 156–7
    advantages 156–7
responsibility accounting 334
    features of 334
results 212
return on capital employed ratio
        (ROCE) 254–5
    calculation of 254, 283
return on investment ratio (RIO) 515
returns on investments and servicing
        of finance 239
revenue allocation 303
revenue expenditure 82
revenue income 82
Revenue recognition 303
revenue recognition 287, 301–3
    AIT 301
    contention 301
    definition 302
    the future 303
    Ingenta 301
    Orchestream 301
    recognition 302–3

revenue reserves 129
    shareholder funds 263
review of trading results 240–41
revolution in management accounting
        508
RI see residual income
right of access 196
rights 519
rights issue 496
RIO see return on investment ratio
risk 121
ROCE see return on capital employed
        ratio
Rolls-Royce 507
Royal Charter 15
RRP see Reporting Review Panel
rule-book system of accounting (US) 293

sales 56
sales account 56
sales variances 404, 415–16
    calculation of 416
    formulae 415
sanctions 294
SB see Standards Board
SBUs see strategic business units
scandals see accounting scandals
Schroders 291
SEC see Securities and Exchange
        Commission
Second World War 505–6
    changes since 507
secondary accounting bodies 16
Secretary of State 203, 295
Securities Act 1933 299
Securities Exchange Act 1934 299
Securities and Exchange Commission
        (SEC) 299
segmental performance 515
segments 334
    cost centre 334
    investment centre 334
    profit centre 334
selling price 361
semivariable costs 431
sequence 522
service cost centre 334
    apportionment 352
    sharing out production service cost-
        centre costs 352–5
service entities 150–53
    hotels and catering 150
    leisure and recreational activities 150
    personal 150
    professional 150
    transportation 150
service entity accounts 150–3
share capital 123
    authorized 123
    fully paid 123
    issued 123
share premium account 263
shareholder funds 129
    definition 263
shareholder information 196–7, 219
    see also disclosure
shareholders 196
shares 123, 496
    ordinary 123
    preferences 123
    rights issue 496
sharing cost-centre costs 352–5
    charging overhead to cost centre 354–5

short-term finance 493–4
    bank overdrafts 494
    bills of exchange 494
    commercial paper 494
    factoring 494
    trade credit 494
short-term planning 323
shutdown decisions see closure and
        shutdown decisions
skill 32
SMA see strategic management
        accounting
small and medium-sized companies
        295
social accounting and reporting
        518–20
    definition 518
    matters affecting the community
        518–19
    matters affecting employees 518
social organizations 21–2
social reporting see social accounting
        and reporting
social security costs 518
sole trader accounts 79–92
    basic 80–1
    cash versus profit 81–2
    illustrative example 84–7
    preparation of 83–4
sole traders 17, 19
sources of authority 199–204, 227–9
    1985 Companies Act 227–9
    professional requirements 200–4,
        229
    statutory requirements 199–200
    Stock Exchange requirements 204
sources of finance 493–6
    long-term finance 495–6
    medium-term finance 494–5
    short-term finance 493–4
special orders 467–9
    example 468
special purpose entities 291
specific decisions 453–75
    closure and shutdown decisions
        459–61
    cost classification 457–9
    decision making 454–7
    make or buy decisions 461–3
    pricing decisions 463–7
    special orders 467–9
    types of decision 459
specific units absorption 355
SSAP 9 Stocks and long-term contracts
        337, 340, 361
SSAPs see Statements of Standard
        Accounting Practice
SSL International 291
standard cost 338
    calculation of 403
    definition 401
standard costing 399–425
    case study 531–2
    example 410–15
    operating statements 416–17
    operation 401–7
    sales variances 415–16
    uses 401
    variances 407–10
standard costing period 402
standard hours 403
    and absorption of overhead 403–4
Standards Board (SB) 295

Statement of Principles for Financial Reporting 38–9
  comparability 39
  comprehensibility 39
  materiality 38
  relevance 39
  reliability 39
statement of total recognized gains and losses 234–5
Statements of Standard Accounting Practice (SSAPs) 28–9, 200
  procedures of 200
statutory requirements on disclosure 199–200
stewardship 4
stock 57, 95–6, 236
  adjustments 95–6
  closing 57, 95
  inventory 95
  opening 57, 95
  trading account with stock adjustments 96
stock adjustments 95–6
  example 96
Stock Exchange 124, 195
  Combined Code on Corporate Governance 215–16
  corporate governance principles 215
  listing 204
  requirements on disclosure 199, 204
stock turnover ratio 258
  calculation of 258, 283
stock valuation 361, 401
storekeeping 338
stores ledger account 340–1
straight-line depreciation 97
strategic business units (SBUs) 523
  and value chain analysis 523
strategic management accounting (SMA) 520–1
strategic plan 323
strategic planning 322–3
structure and operation of limited liability companies 122–7
  accounts 125
  directors 125–6
  disclosure of information 124–5
  dividends 126
  loans 124
  share capital 123
  taxation 126
  types 123–4
sub-period budget 379, 402
sub-variances 404
subsidiary 227
  group undertaking 228
sunk costs 458
suppliers 197, 249
  as users of accounts 249–50
survey of general business environment 270

tangible fixed assets 189, 236
target costing 521
tax avoidance 14
tax concessions 492–3
tax evasion 14
taxation 14, 126, 239, 492–3
  business rates 335, 352
  capital allowances 493
  corporation tax 126, 129, 492
  council tax 380
  local property tax 335

tax avoidance 14
tax concessions 492–3
tax evasion 14
techniques for management accounting 508
timing 326, 439
timing difference 240, 303
total absorption costing 336
total quality management (TQM) 506–7, 525
  getting it right first time 506–7
  quality of output should reflect specification 507
TQM *see* total quality management
trade credit 494
trade creditor 56, 197
  account 56
  payment period 260
trade creditor payment period 260
  calculation of 260, 284
trade debtor 56
trade debtor account 56
trade debtor collection period ratio 259–60
  calculation of 259, 283
trade discounts 56
trading account 80–1
  example 84–7
trading items 34
trading and profit and loss account 83
  stage of sole trader account 83
training 326
transfer pricing 464–7
transportation 150
TransTec 291
trend analysis 251
trial balance 12, 63–6
  compilation 64–6
  errors 66–8
true and fair view 203, 293
  confirmation of by auditors 294
  override rule 203
turnover 233, 255
  versus efficiency 258
Tyco 290
types of company 123
  listed 123
  private 123
  public 123
types of decision 454–7, 459
types of entities 401–2
types of standard 402
  attainable 402
  basic 402
  ideal 402

UITF *see* Urgent Issues Task Force
UK membership of European Union 199
undisclosed errors in trial balance 67
unfairness 364
unit cost 337
United States of America 299–301
  accounting principles 291
  accounting scandals 290
  adoption of IFRSs 299–300
  auditors' position versus that in UK 292–3
  Financial Accounting Standards Board (FASB) 299
  financial regulations 299–300
  and history of accounting 321
  and industrial changes in Japan 507

New York Stock Exchange 299–300
  rule-book system of accounting 293, 299
  Securities Act 1933 299
  Securities Exchange Act 1934 299
  Securities and Exchange Commission (SEC) 299
  US GAAP 299–300
unsecured loan stock 495
  convertible 495
Urgent Issues Task Force (UITF) 201–2
US GAAP 299–300
  and European opposition 300
user groups 197–9, 249–50
  objectives of 37–8
utilization 516

value chain analysis 522–4
  adding value 523
  allocating revenue, costs and assets 523
  cost drivers 523
  definition 523
  results 523
  sequence 522
  steps involved 523
  strategic business units 523
value engineering 521
variable costs 336, 439, 457–8
  changes in 433
  definition 428
variable production overhead 403, 407
  calculation of variances 409, 413
  see also production overhead
variance analysis 407–10
  definition 401
  formulae 407–10
variances 323–4, 363, 407–10
  adverse trend 363
  and budgetary control 378
  budgetary control variance report 529–30
  calculation of 410–15
  cost 407
  definition 401
  favourable trend 324, 363
  and individual investigation 378
  sales 404, 415–16
  structure 407
  sub-variances 404
  variance analysis formulae 407–10
vertical analysis 251
voluntary organizations 35

Weir Group 514–15
  Statement of Objectives 515
Western Europe 31
work-in-progress 146, 149, 321
  and history of accounting 321
working with accounts 54–9
  choice of accounts 54–7
  entering transactions in accounts 57–9
working capital movements 172–3
Worldcom 290
writing off debt 102

Xerox 290

zero industrial base 506